The
Pilgrim Migration

The Pilgrim Migration

Immigrants to Plymouth Colony 1620-1633

Robert Charles Anderson

Great Migration Study Project
New England Historic Genealogical Society
Boston 2004

Published and distributed by
New England Historic Genealogical Society
101 Newbury Street
Boston, Massachusetts 02116-3007

All rights reserved.

International Standard Book Number: 0-88082-181-7
Library of Congress Control Number: 2004114987

No part of this publication may be reproduced or transmitted
in any form or by any means, electronic or mechanical, including
photocopying, recording, or any information storage or retrieval
system, without permission in writing from the copyright holder,
except for the inclusion of brief quotations in a review.

Copyright © 2004
New England Historic Genealogical Society

Printed in the United States of America by McNaughton-Gunn, Inc., Saline, Michigan

Dedicated to the memory of

Robert S. Wakefield

Who Made

Great Contributions

to the

Great Migration

Study Project

TABLE OF CONTENTS

List of Sketches	ix
Preface and Acknowledgements	xv
SCOPE	xvii
Criteria for Inclusion	xvii
Goal	xviii
METHODS	xxi
Constructing a Sketch	xxi
Chronological Analysis	xxii
Documentation and Citation	xxv
SOURCES	xxix
Passenger Lists	xxix
Lists of Freemen	xxx
Colony and Court Records	xxxi
Town Records	xxxii
Vital Records	xxxii
Probate Records	xxxiii
Land Records	xxxiv
Church Records	xxxiv
Journals and Letters	xxxv
HOW TO USE THIS BOOK	xxxix
Key to Sketch Headings	xxxix
Key to Titles	xlvii
GENEALOGICAL SKETCHES	1
PHANTOM FILE	527
INDEXES	531
Index of Surnames	533
Index of First Names	589
Index of Places	633
Index of Ships	639

LIST OF SKETCHES

John Adams	1
Webb Adey	2
John Alden	4
Isaac Allerton	10
John Allerton	16
Anthony Annable	16
Edward Ashley	20
William Baker	21
Edward Bangs	23
Robert Barker	29
John Barnes	35
Robert Bartlett	42
William Bassett	48
William Beale	52
John Beaven	52
William Bennett	52
John Billington	56
Thomas Blossom	58
Thomas Boreman	60
John Bowman	62
William Bradford	62
William Brewster	66
Thomas Brian	70
William Bridges	70
Clement Briggs	76
Richard Britteridge	80
John Brown	80
Peter Brown	82
Mary Buckett	85
Edward Bumpas	85
Edward Burcher	88
John Bursley	89
William Button	92
John Cannon	93

Priscilla Carpenter	92
Robert Carter	95
John Carver	95
Edmund Chandler	97
Roger Chandler	101
James Chilton	103
Richard Church	105
Richard Clark	109
Thomas Clark	109
Richard Clough	115
Henry Cobb	118
James Cole	122
Job Cole	126
William Collier	128
Christopher Conant	133
Roger Conant	134
William Conner	143
Francis Cooke	144
John Cooke	148
Josias Cooke	149
John Coombs	153
Humility Cooper	156
John Crackstone	157
Robert Cushman	158
John Deacon	161
Stephen Deane	162
Philip Delano	164
Anthony Dike	169
John Doane	171
Edward Doty	177
John Dunham	182
Francis Eaton	187
John Eddy	189
Samuel Eddy	194
_____ Ely	198
Thomas English	199
John Faunce	201
Thomas Flavell	203
Moses Fletcher	204
Edmond Flood	205
Ralph Fogg	206

List of Sketches

_____ Ford	211
Edward Foster	212
George Foster	215
Edward Fuller	215
Samuel Fuller	217
Richard Gardiner	223
William Gilson	223
Godbert Godbertson	226
John Goodman	228
Robert Gorges	229
Richard Greene	230
John Hampden	231
Martha Harding	232
Walter Harris	233
Timothy Hatherly	234
William Heard	240
John Hewes	240
Robert Hicks	243
Richard Higgins	249
Thomas Higgins	253
John Hill	254
William Hilton	254
John Hocking	261
William Holbeck	262
Edward Holman	263
John Holmes	265
William Holmes	267
William Honywell	270
John Hooke	271
Stephen Hopkins	271
Henry Howland	275
John Howland	279
James Hurst	284
John Irish	287
John Jenny	291
Manasseh Kempton	297
Richard Lanckford	303
John Langmore	303
William Latham	304
Edward Leister	304
Thomas Little	305

Robert Long	309
John Lyford	309
Edmund Margesson	315
Christopher Martin	315
Richard Masterson	316
William Mendlove	318
Robert Mendum	319
Desire Minter	324
Experience Mitchell	324
Ellen More	329
Jasper More	329
Mary More	329
Richard More	330
Bennett Morgan	335
William Morrell	335
George Morton	336
Thomas Morton	338
William Mullins	339
Samuel Nash	341
John Newcomen	344
Ellen Newton	344
Austen Nicholas	344
John Oldham	345
William Palmer	349
Christian Penn	352
William Phips	352
John Pickworth	353
Abraham Pierce	356
William Pitt	359
Mary Plumer	359
William Pontus	360
Thomas Pope	362
Joshua Pratt	365
Phineas Pratt	369
Thomas Prence	374
Degory Priest	382
James Rand	385
Robert Rattlife	385
Daniel Ray	385
William Richards	388
John Rigsdale	389

Mary Ring	389
Isaac Robinson	391
_____ Rogers	395
Thomas Rogers	396
_____ Rowland	397
Henry Rowley	398
Henry Samson	401
Anthony Savory	405
Thomas Savory	405
Richard Sears	409
Edward Shaw	412
John Shaw	413
William Sherman	416
Moses Simonson	419
John Smalley	422
John Smith	424
Ralph Smith	425
Nicholas Snow	428
George Soule	432
Constant Southworth	437
Thomas Southworth	440
Richard Sparrow	443
Francis Sprague	447
Hugh Stacy	450
Miles Standish	451
James Steward	457
Elias Story	457
Thomas Symons	457
William Tench	459
Edward Thomson	459
John Thorpe	459
Thomas Tilden	461
Edward Tilley	461
John Tilley	462
Thomas Tinker	463
Stephen Tracy	463
William Trevor	466
Humphrey Turner	466
John Turner	470
Christopher Wadsworth	473
Ralph Wallen	476

Richard Warren	477
John Washburn	480
George Watson	483
Francis Weston	487
Thomas Weston	490
John Whiston	493
William White	495
Roger Wilder	497
Thomas Willett	497
Roger Williams	503
Thomas Williams	506
Edward Winslow	507
Gilbert Winslow	510
John Winslow	511
Josiah Winslow	515
Kenelm Winslow	518
Walter Woodworth	521
William Wright	524

PREFACE & ACKNOWLEDGEMENTS

This volume arose out of a discussion between Brenton Simons and myself, in which Brenton mentioned that he was looking for a project in which the New England Historic Genealogical Society and Plimoth Plantation could both participate. Since nearly a decade had passed since the publication of *The Great Migration Begins: Immigrants to New England, 1620-1633*, the idea we came up with was to select from those three volumes the sketches that pertained to Plymouth Colony, and to revise and update them.

Once the more than two hundred sketches had been selected, the first step was to review the literature of the last decade in order to identify all new discoveries relating to the early Plymouth Colony settlers. This decade has been especially fruitful, with identifications of the English origins of Stephen Hopkins, Richard Warren, Francis Eaton and Peter Brown, along with much additional information on many of these settlers.

In the process of incorporating this new material into the old sketches, the sketches were read carefully in order to correct any errors that had been made in the original volumes. Also, nearly all the sketches were revised to conform with the evolving style of the Great Migration Study Project. In particular, much effort was expended on making the section on officeholding more useful. In the early days of the Great Migration Study Project, this information was not well organized. Now, the data is organized by colony, then county, then town, and finally military offices.

Many people have given me assistance of all varieties during the preparation of this volume. I hope that I have included here all those who have helped, but if I have omitted anyone, it is only by inadvertence.

Sharon Carmack proofread the text and, as usual, Roger D. Joslyn FASG did the indexing. They both went beyond their basic duties and found many errors and inconsistencies, the correction of which has made this a better volume.

Jeremy D. Bangs gave this volume the benefit of his vast knowledge of Pilgrim and Leiden affairs and read the entire manuscript. His many pages of suggestions have saved me from numerous errors and have added much value to the book.

Peter Follansbee of Plimoth Plantation gave me a tour of his woodworking shop and increased my knowledge in his area of specialty. The sections on occupation in a number of the sketches have benefited from this assistance.

David C. Dearborn FASG, reference librarian at the New England Historic Genealogical Society, has responded cheerfully and expeditiously to my many detailed bibliographic requests. David L. Greene FASG, Coeditor of *The American Genealogist*, also provided bibliographic aid from his extensive private genealogical library.

Leslie Mahler has kindly allowed me to publish here some items which he has uncovered but has not yet published, especially the Ipswich apprenticeship record for the Allerton family.

Lynn Betlock, Martha Bustin and Jean Powers in the Publications Department at the New England Historic Genealogical Society have supported me throughout this project, attending to many details of production.

I also wish to thank those many individuals who have, over the past decade, sent me corrections to *The Great Migration Begins*. I have attempted to incorporate as many as possible here.

Even with all this help, there will still be errors here, and they are all attributable to the author. Please send any suggested corrections to Great Migration Study Project, 101 Newbury Street, Boston MA 02116.

Robert Charles Anderson
Derry, New Hampshire
13 October 2004

SCOPE

For the user of this volume to understand what is being presented, we must define carefully the scope of this phase of the Great Migration Study Project. Who were the participants in the Pilgrim Migration? What information is being collected on these people?

CRITERIA FOR INCLUSION IN
THE PILGRIM MIGRATION:
IMMIGRANTS TO PLYMOUTH COLONY, 1620-1633

The Pilgrim Migration attempts to identify and describe all those Europeans who settled in Plymouth Colony prior to the end of 1633. This ending date was chosen in part in an effort to include all those Plymouth Colony residents who had earlier resided in Leiden. This date also conforms with that used in preparing *The Great Migration Begins: Immigrants to New England, 1620-1633*. Some of the examples given in this section will be taken from that earlier work.

In the absence of a complete set of passenger lists for these years, how do we decide which persons had arrived by the end of 1633 and which came later? We have compiled our list of immigrants by employing three broad sets of criteria:

1) appearance in a record generated prior to 14 May 1634,
2) direct or indirect implication of arrival by the end of 1633 included in a record of later date, and
3) appearance as a member of the immediate family of a person known to have arrived by 1633.

Let us examine each of these categories a little more closely.

First, we have examined all available records generated in Plymouth Colony, or elsewhere about Plymouth Colony, before 14 May 1634. and have extracted the names of all persons in those records who appear as residing in Plymouth Colony by that time. These records are described in more detail in the various subheadings under SOURCES. The date in May of 1634 is chosen because of some features of the migration process. Most passenger ships did not leave England until spring, because of the bad weather in the North Atlantic earlier in the year. Anyone first appearing in New England records in the spring of 1634 almost certainly arrived in 1633 or earlier.

Second, records exist which were generated after 1633, but which clearly imply that a person named in that document was in Plymouth

Colony in 1633 or earlier. Most frequently this will be a deposition, made as late as half a century after the arrival of the immigrant, in which the immigrant would recall some event in which he or she was involved in New England before 1634. Another record of this sort might be a grant of land to a man in 1638, for example, stating that he had been a servant to a New England resident for the previous five years. (These delayed statements must be handled with care, for they are sometimes at odds with other, more reliable evidence.)

Third, although there were many single men and women in the Pilgrim Migration, the majority of the immigrants came in family groups. For the purposes of this study we will adopt the somewhat arbitrary rule that a married man arrived in New England with his wife and all his children, unless there is evidence to the contrary (and in like manner a widowed woman would be assumed to arrive with all her children). If any more distant relatives of an immigrant, such as a sibling or niece or nephew, are known to have come to New England, they will not be assumed to have arrived at the same time; independent evidence will be required for such kinsmen. As an example, Henry Woolcott is known to have left two sons behind when he came to Dorchester, but all his other children are assumed to have come with him on the *Mary & John* in 1630. On the other hand, the three children of Emanuel Downing by his first wife (James, Mary and Susan) came to New England in 1630 and 1633, but their father, with his second wife and children by that wife, did not arrive until 1637.

Having studied the available records with these criteria in mind, we have compiled a list of slightly more than two hundred families or unattached men and women who arrived in Plymouth Colony between 1620 and 1633. There exist claims for more who had also arrived by this time, but most of these claims are demonstrably false. These claims have been rejected when they are not consistent with one or more of the three tests described above. Undoubtedly some immigrants who did arrive in 1633 or earlier have been omitted because of this strict exclusion, but we deem this preferable to the arbitrary and ungrounded inclusion of persons who did not in fact come until some years later.

GOAL

The goal of the Great Migration Study Project may be stated very simply: to provide a concise, reliable summary of past research on the early immigrants to New England, which will reduce the amount of time which must be spent in discovering this past work, and will therefore serve as a foundation for future research.

The Project may be viewed, then, as an immense literature search, a scouring of the journals and books published in the last century and a half. This is not to say that the Great Migration volumes contain no new research and no new discoveries.

A researcher interested in immigration to New England in the quarter-century after the arrival of the *Mayflower* has had, until now, to look in dozens of places to learn what is known about any one immigrant. After 140 years, the first place to go is still James Savage's *Genealogical Dictionary of New England*. This set was a marvel of its time and remains the only source attempting to cover all families in New England for the seventeenth century. But there have been many genealogical advances since the days of Savage, and we must also look in thousands of other books and periodicals when researching these early immigrants.

The purpose of the present volume is to summarize and, to a limited extent, evaluate what we know about the immigrants to Plymouth Colony from 1620 to 1633. Modern researchers should not have to waste large amounts of time in searching out or, worse, redoing the research of earlier genealogists. With the current state of the genealogical literature this can be difficult. The Great Migration volumes aim to provide a solid base that researchers of the future can use as a stepping-off point for doing new research on a given immigrant.

The primary goal is to document each life as completely as possible. In some cases this is a relatively easy task, since there may be only one or two records for the person in New England, and no clues to trace him or her back to England, or forward into a later career. In the majority of cases, however, an abundance of evidence exists, and a way must be found to bring it under control. After some experimentation, a standard format was developed to organize what is known about these participants in the Great Migration.

The standard sketch consists of three formatted sections: migration, biographical detail, and genealogical detail. This is followed by a section of *COMMENTS*, which allows discussion of material not accommodated elsewhere, and also discussion of discrepancies or matters of dispute between various authorities. The contents of the standard sketch are demonstrated in more detail in the Sample Sketch below.

There are several things, though, that the standard sketch, and the Great Migration Study Project as a whole, does not attempt to accomplish.

If the parentage of the immigrant is known, that will be included. If a reasonably close relation to another immigrant is known, that will also be stated, perhaps naming other relatives who remained in England. But if the ancestry of the immigrant is known beyond his parents, it will usually not be presented or discussed, although a citation to anything published on the subject will be included.

Not every detail of the life of the immigrant will be incorporated into each sketch. If the subject of the sketch was one of the leaders of the colony, his lesser offices and day-to-day activities, as recorded in official records, will not be recorded here. If the immigrant was a land speculator, not every deed or land grant will be noted. In general, the more obscure and the more poorly recorded the immigrant in question, the greater will be the effort to find and include every known record.

The children of immigrants will not be traced until their deaths. We will attempt, of course, to identify every child, and to find the best evidence for that child's date and place of birth. After that we will look only for enough documentation to place that child beyond infancy, to distinguish him or her from others of the same name. Thus we will attempt to document the marriages of all children (although occasionally this may only be a first marriage). A death date will be sought for those who lived to adulthood and did not marry, and in these instances we may also include a probate record of the deceased, as it will frequently help in establishing the complete list of children of the immigrant. A death date may also be sought if it includes an age at death, and thus establishes an approximate year of birth.

METHODS

CONSTRUCTING A SKETCH

In most instances, the construction of a sketch begins with consultation of Savage and Pope (both *Pioneers of Massachusetts* and *Pioneers of Maine and New Hampshire*). The information from these brief accounts of the immigrants is entered into the appropriate categories in the sketches with the clear understanding that many changes and additions will be necessary before the sketch may be called complete. Sometimes problems in the presentations by Savage and Pope arise immediately, especially if the two sources are in clear contradiction. On other occasions problems appear only at a later stage in the process.

For the majority of the immigrants who were married, the next step is to consult Clarence Almon Torrey's "New England Marriages Prior to 1700." For this purpose, the complete manuscript of the index, available at the New England Historic Genealogical Society in Boston (and now on CD-ROM), is examined. This manuscript includes for each marriage one or more citations to sources in which some mention of the married couple may be found. These citations may be to contemporary source documents or to secondary sources of many varieties. Torrey ceased work on his index in 1960, shortly before his death, and for the period after 1960 his work is supplemented by a privately generated card index, mostly to the periodical literature, covering the years from 1961 to the present.

As many as possible of the sources cited by Torrey are then collected and examined. At this point additional material from these sources may be added to the growing sketch. As the sketch continues to develop in this way, a number of things may happen. Points of dispute or controversy between two or more sources may appear, and they are noted so that they may be investigated and, if possible, resolved. Ideas for additional places to search may also come to light, and these are also added to the list of additional avenues of research.

Once the basic outline of the sketch has been created in this way, and many of the outstanding problems have been defined, research in primary sources begins. The vital records and church records are examined, deeds and wills are abstracted, and court records are surveyed.

As will be explained in more detail in the next section, the best source possible is sought for each fact and for each genealogical connection.

The form of a sketch, in which a defined set of categories is filled in for each immigrant, forces research into the necessary areas, so that the same documents used to answer the genealogical questions or to complete the information on *ESTATE* are also examined for evidence of *EDUCATION*.

The last step is to review the work done on the sketch, and return to Savage, Pope and any other secondary sources of value to the immigrant under study. The *COMMENTS* section is then used to discuss the problem areas, in which two or more earlier researchers are in conflict. In many instances the conflict can be resolved, but, as this is not always possible, one can do no more than state the dispute, and perhaps suggest a path of research that might lead to a resolution.

This is also the stage at which the immigrant himself or herself may be evaluated. If the subject of the sketch was unusually contentious, or unusually innocuous, it might be reason for comment. The sketch should now be complete, with the immigrant's life outlined, using the best sources, and taking note of any remaining problems or of any unusual features of the person's life.

CHRONOLOGICAL ANALYSIS

CRITERIA FOR APPROXIMATING DATES

When we do not have an exact date for a vital event, such as a birth, baptismal, marriage or death date, we will in all instances create an approximated date for that event. We do this for a number of reasons. Sometimes this type of chronological analysis will reveal an unsuspected contradiction in previous treatments of a family, indicating perhaps that not all the children of a man could have been born to his only known wife. Even when the analysis does not reveal anything of immediate import, it may help to narrow the parameters within which future research must be conducted.

The approximation of dates may be done in a variety of ways. The most desirable manner of approximating dates is from a piece of evidence that states an age, or in some other way describes a specific span of years. If an age at death or an age at the time of a deposition is available, then a year of birth may be estimated, and in such a case the entry will read "b. about 1634," indicating a date that is reliable within a relatively narrow span of years, perhaps just two years above or below the estimated date.

More frequently the evidence for estimating an age will be less precise, and we will have to state an age in a different way: saying that someone was "b. say 1634," meaning that this is our best estimate, but that it may be some years off in either direction. We may only have a date of first marriage, from which we will state a likely birth date based on the usual age at first marriage. There are many other indicators that help us to establish these broad ranges.

Although some of the dates approximated in this study will in the future be found to be wide of the mark, we believe that it is important to provide some context for future research, and at least try to get a feel for what is chronologically possible with some of these immigrants. As will be seen, when a birthdate is estimated through a long string of other estimations, the date arrived at will generally be the latest date that the birth could have taken place, or close to it. Thus, in examining English records we will ignore candidates of that name who were born some years after the suggested birth date.

The criteria for producing "say" dates are many and varied, and only a few will be mentioned here. As noted above, a likely time for first marriage will be assumed. In a large number of cases men married for the first time in their early to mid twenties, and so an age of twenty-five will be used in this study. Women married for the first time in their late teens or early twenties, so an arbitrary age at first marriage of twenty will be assumed for women in the absence of evidence to the contrary.

"Say" dates may also be generated by reliance on other milestones in life, such as the age at which one could choose a guardian, or sell real estate, or become a freeman. The particular criterion used in a given case will generally be stated explicitly.

ORDERING FAMILIES

The next step in chronological analysis is the examination of whole families for the purpose of establishing birth-order for the children. This task poses no great problems when we have a complete set of birth or baptismal records, and when there are no internal inconsistencies among them.

When there are children without any precise date of birth, we begin, if possible, with those that do. This provides a framework around which we can attempt to place the others. We then look for those who have been assigned an "about" date of birth, based usually on age at death or age as given in a dated deposition. (If it happens that we do not have any children with known birth or baptismal dates, then we must erect our basic framework from those with "about" dates.)

We wish to fit the children with well-estimated years of birth into the framework at the most likely intervals. The first rule that we observe is that the births come about two years apart (unless we have strong evidence for multiple births, or for the employment of a wet nurse, which would allow the mother to conceive again soon after childbirth). We look, then, for gaps of three years or more into which a child might be placed (not enforcing the two-year interval rule too strictly).

At this point we will be left with children who have been assigned only "say" dates (based, perhaps, on a known date of first marriage, or on some other age-constrained life event), or for whom no clues on age are yet available. Those with "say" dates can be fitted into any remaining places. Those without any age information at all, perhaps children who died young with a known death date but no age at death, or unmarried children who died at a more advanced age, will now be placed into any plausible available slots.

Throughout this process we try to make the sequence of births as continuous as possible, for reasons that will emerge in a moment. We must be on the lookout for conflicts and contradictions, which may be indications that we have made an error in estimating or recording one of the dates. Also, by placing some of those without any age information into available gaps in the sequence, we should be able to assign "say" dates to most of the remaining children.

By making it our goal to place all the children in a single, compact sequence, we may obtain some useful information about other matters. If after all our efforts, there remains a large gap, or more than one, in the list of children, we may wish to seek for an explanation. Such a gap may indicate nothing more than a string of stillbirths or deaths in infancy, but other possible explanations may direct our research into new channels.

One explanation for the gap might be that the immigrant had more than one wife, with an early group of children by a first wife, a gap before a second marriage, and then a second wife. Even without a gap, a second wife would be indicated if the sequence of children was spread out over much more than twenty years.

Another explanation, usually more difficult to verify, would be that the couple were separated for a number of years. Sometimes the immigrant head of household came to New England alone, while his wife was still of child-bearing age, and did not send for her or return to fetch her until some years later.

This process of determining the order of birth of the children in a family, although time-consuming, frequently provides some of the best new data on that family. While some of the positions assigned to the children may turn out to be incorrect, the value of this process in pointing out conflicts and contradictions and in directing further research is worth the effort.

DOCUMENTATION AND CITATION

Although the terms documentation and citation are sometimes used interchangeably, they are employed here to describe two distinct but related steps in the process of supplying evidence to support one's conclusions.

DOCUMENTATION is the inclusion of complete or partial copies of the records in a sketch, whether as lengthy extracts or brief abstracts.
CITATION is the presentation of that information that identifies a source or a record, and allows the reader to find that source for himself or herself easily.

DOCUMENTATION

In some instances an abstract of a document or record may be sufficient. Perhaps only a small portion of the document is relevant to the matter at hand, or perhaps the document is burdened with much formulaic or legalistic language that does not in itself advance the argument. When an abstract is made, those portions of the record that have been used without change of verbiage are included in quotation marks, while the portions not in quotation marks have been abbreviated or paraphrased.
In other cases a complete document, or large uninterrupted portions of a document, may be incorporated in the sketch. This may be because the entire document is important for making a specific point, or simply because it is intrinsically interesting, and gives an insight into the life and times of the immigrants we are studying. In some cases the language of a document is so convoluted and complex that it is simply safer to produce a lengthy extract, as an attempted paraphrase might be just as long as the original, and not convey the point so well.
Whether a document is abstracted or transcribed in full, the Modernized Method of transcription is employed. In this technique,

modern spelling, punctuation and capitalization are used, and abbreviations are expanded. In the case of personal and place names, however, the spellings of the document itself are retained, and abbreviations are expanded in square brackets. The original author or scribe's choice and sequence of words are not disturbed. The edition of William Bradford's history of Plymouth Colony which we are most often using here, prepared by Samuel Eliot Morison, employs the Modernized Method. (See Frank Freidel, ed., *Harvard Guide to American History*, revised edition, two volumes in one, pp. 27-36, for a complete discussion of this subject, with examples.)

CITATION

Most citations will be given in an abbreviated form in the text, with the expansion of these short forms presented in the **Key to Titles**, to be found in the front of each volume of this set. If a source is used in only a few sketches, the full citation may be given at each occurrence, in which case no entry will appear in the **Key to Titles**. In some cases, generally a single-family genealogy, a source will be used, but the full citation will also appear in that sketch, and nowhere else.

Vital records may sometimes appear without citation. In the case of entries from English parish registers, this means that the item has been taken directly from the original or a microfilm copy of the register, which has been examined in the course of preparing the sketches. When an English parish register entry has been taken from another source, that source will be given.

When citing New England town vital records, especially from Massachusetts, no citation will appear if the entry has been taken from a volume published in alphabetic order (unless the entry appears in an unlikely part of the alphabet).

FORM OF DATES

Since England and the English colonies were still using the Julian calendar in the seventeenth century, a date that fell between 1 January and 24 March of the year could be ambiguous as to the year of the date. We employ various conventions in presenting these dates. If the double-dating is given explicitly in the record, or if the double-dated year can be deduced with confidence from the sequence of chronologically arranged records, the date will be given in the form "28 February 1636/7." If the double-dating can be deduced with reasonable but not complete confidence, the form will be "28 February 1637[/8]." If the double-dating cannot be determined with much assurance, the date will be given as "28 February 1637[/8?]." And in some cases no attempt will be made to resolve the date, and it will be presented simply as "28 February 1637."

The use of "[NS]" to indicate New Style dates will be employed only for records created in jurisdictions already using the Gregorian calendar. Most of these will be from Leiden or New Amsterdam. In no case will a date created under the Julian calendar be adjusted to the Gregorian calendar.

SOURCES

Hundreds of sources were consulted for this study, in libraries, archives and courthouses. Some were viewed in the original, some on microfilm, and some only in printed versions. We cannot describe in detail here every source consulted, but rather we will comment briefly on some of the more important documents employed in constructing these sketches. Many of these sources have been discussed in the pages of the *Great Migration Newsletter*, and where appropriate reference will be made to that publication.

We discuss here only those sources which are of broad application in the study of the inhabitants of Plymouth Colony. For information on a wider range of early New England sources (some of which are occasionally cited in this volume), consult the *SOURCES* section in other volumes published by the Great Migration Study Project.

In 1966 George D. Langdon Jr. published an excellent bibliographic essay, covering both printed and manuscript sources, as part of his history of Plymouth Colony [George D. Langdon Jr., *Pilgrim Colony: A History of New Plymouth, 1620-1691* (New Haven 1966), pp. 247-66]. (This essay appears only in the paperback edition, and not in the hardback edition.)

PASSENGER LISTS

No passenger lists have survived for any of the ships which arrived in Plymouth Colony from 1620 to 1630. From other records, however, we are able to reconstruct lists of several of these ships, and for most of the passengers.

For the first and most important of these voyages, that of the *Mayflower* in 1620, we rely upon a record made about 1651 by William Bradford, in which he first cataloged those who arrived at Plymouth in 1620, and then recounted what had been the fate and progeny of each of these passengers in the succeeding decade. The most accessible version may be found in Morison's edition of Bradford.

Additional passengers arrived at Plymouth in 1621 on the *Fortune* and in 1623 on the *Anne* and the *Little James*. Our main source for reconstructing the lists of passengers on these ships is the grant of lands made in 1623, in which each person residing in Plymouth at that time or previously was awarded one acre. In 1974 Robert S. Wakefield analyzed this list, and we follow his conclusions in the present volume [MQ 40:7-13, 55-62]. Since this list also included many of the passengers on the *Mayflower,* we have a check on the list for that ship derived from Bradford's accounting.

During these same years two attempts were made to establish settlements on the south shore of Massachusetts Bay, just outside the limits of Plymouth Colony. As these plantations collapsed and failed, some of the settlers made their way to Plymouth and were accepted as residents there. These people are also included in the 1623 grant of lands.

The final contingent of immigrants to Plymouth from Leiden took passage on two ships that were part of the large movement to Massachusetts Bay, the *Mayflower* in 1629 and the *Handmaid* in 1630. We have no way to reconstruct the full passenger lists for these ships, but we do have some clues. Most particularly, Winthrop tells us that John Eddy (and presumably also his brother Samuel Eddy) came on the *Handmaid.* More broadly, for those migrants from Leiden to Plymouth who arrived after 1624 and before 1633, we are probably safe in assuming that they came on one of these vessels of 1629 and 1630.

One surviving passenger list from 1632 is important for the settlement of Plymouth. The *William & Francis* sailed from London on 9 March 1631/2, carrying such Plymouth passengers as John Smalley, John Whiston and the returning Edward Winslow [Hotten 149; WJ 1:93-94].

LISTS OF FREEMEN

The status of freeman was primarily of political importance, for it gave one the right to vote for colony officers. In some colonies, though, freemanship was tied to church membership, and so the meaning was somewhat different. Massachusetts Bay and New Haven, the most Puritan of the Puritan colonies, made church membership a prerequisite for freemanship, while the rest of the New England colonies did not.

Lists of freemen may be used for a number of purposes beyond providing biographical information about an immigrant. Like tax lists at a later time, a list of freemen provides basic information about the presence or absence of a person on a given date.

PLYMOUTH COLONY

The Plymouth Colony court records include lists of men propounded for freemanship and of men admitted to freemanship. The records of being propounded are not found in other colonies, and must in Plymouth Colony have taken the place of prior admission to a gathered church. As can be seen from examination of the periodic compiled lists of Plymouth Colony freeman, not all the men who were made free in the colony appear in the lists of admission to freemanship found in some court records.

The freemen of Plymouth Colony were recorded also in a different form, as lists of freemen as of a given date. Six of these lists were compiled during the independent existence of Plymouth Colony. In each case, these lists were augmented and annotated between their dates of compilation and the dates of compilation of the next lists in the series. The first two lists, for 1633 and for 7 March 1636/7, covered the entire colony in one undifferentiated list [PCR 1:3-4, 52-53]. The remaining four lists, for 1639, 1658, 29 May 1670 and 1 [blank] 1683/4, each have separate sections for each of the towns [PCR 5:274-279, 8:173-187, 197-209]. As men died, moved from one town to another within Plymouth Colony, or removed from Plymouth Colony entirely, these lists were annotated appropriately. (See GMN 5:17 for a more detailed discussion of the Plymouth records of freemen.)

COLONY AND COURT RECORDS

In the early colonies the full separation of executive, legislative and judicial powers had not been attained, and the records of the General Court of the colony could encompass business of all varieties. The colonial court records for Plymouth Colony have been transcribed and published, in volumes that are cited frequently here. (Full bibliographic detail for this set may be found in the **Key to Titles** under PCR.)

The first six volumes of PCR (bound as four) include the court minutes from 1633 to 1691 in one chronological sequence.

The seventh volume of PCR contains the records of civil cases from 1633 to 1691. In addition to the summaries of the cases themselves, these records also contain many lists of the members of the petit juries which sat on these cases.

Volume eight of PCR comprises a miscellaneous group of records. The vital records and the lists of freemen are discussed in other sections of this chapter. The volume also includes the accounts of the colony treasurer.

The small quantity of loose court papers which have survived from Plymouth Colony have been published in the *Plymouth Scrapbook*. Most of these documents pertain to probate matters.

TOWN RECORDS

Most of the town records of Plymouth Colony remained unpublished. More than in other colonies, the town clerks in Plymouth Colony had the habit of consolidating "useful" material from original record volumes that were only a few decades old, and discarding the older volumes. Two sets of published town records deserve individual mention.

Three volumes of the records of the town of Plymouth were published in 1889, 1892 and 1903 [PTR]. The first of these, covering the years 1636 through 1705, has been exploited for the present volume.

More recently, Jeremy D. Bangs has prepared three volumes of transcriptions of records for the town of Scituate, these volumes having been published in 1997, 1999 and 2001 [ScitTR]. The first volume included a transcript of the earliest volume of town records, along with summaries of the records arranged by topic. The second volume covered the records of the Connihasset Partners. The third volume includes transcripts of some town record volumes from the latter part of the seventeenth century, along with some documents pertaining to Scituate but not generated by the town.

VITAL RECORDS

Like Massachusets Bay Colony and Connecticut Colony, Plymouth Colony required that the town maintain records of births, marriages and deaths, and submit copies to the central government for recording there. Also like those other colonies, compliance with this requirement was sporadic. What has survived from this process has been published in Volume Eight of the Plymouth Colony Records [PCR 8:3-89].

Many of the Plymouth Colony towns had their vital records published in the alphabetized, systematic series of volumes sponsored by the Commonwealth of Massachusetts in the early decades of the twentieth century. More recently, the laudable practice has arisen of publishing town vital records in their original order. This has been done for Plymouth, Marshfield, Swansea, Middleborough, Yarmouth, Falmouth and some other towns.

In 1978 Robert S. Wakefield published a compilation of information on marriages (not necessarily marriage records) of all couples who had married in Plymouth Colony up to 1650 [Robert S. Wakefield, *Plymouth Colony Marriages to 1650* (Warwick, Rhode Island, 1978]].

PROBATE RECORDS

Plymouth Colony began to maintain a separate set of probate records in 1633 and by the time of the establishment of counties in Plymouth Colony in 1685 this category of records had reached four volumes [PCPR]. All of this material has been microfilmed and some has been printed. George Ernest Bowman published much of this material in the *Mayflower Descendant* [MD]. He began a transcription of these documents in the order that they were recorded, but only reached into the third volume. He also published in the same periodical transcriptions or abstracts of some particular documents which pertained to specific families he was studying. In 1996 C.H. Simmons Jr. published transcriptions of the Plymouth Colony probate documents from 1633 through 1669, comprising volumes 1 and 2 of the originals [*Plymouth Colony Records, Volume 1, Wills and Inventories, 1633-1669* (Camden, Maine, 1996)].

In 1685 three counties were erected covering the territory of Plymouth Colony: Barnstable, Bristol and Plymouth. Each of these counties immediately began its own series of probate records [cited in this volume as BarnPR, BrPR and PPR].

In 1983 Ruth Wilder Sherman and Robert S. Wakefield compiled the *Plymouth Colony Probate Guide: Where to find Wills and Related Data For 800 People of Plymouth Colony, 1620-1691* (Warwick, Rhode Island, 1983). The main part of this volume is an alphabetical inventory of "information concerning more than 725 men and 75 women – everyone for whom we found probate material in the Plymouth Colony records, and also every Colony resident for whom we could find probate records elsewhere." There is also an informative introduction, and an appendix listing published probate records for individuals from Barnstable, Bristol and Plymouth counties.

LAND RECORDS

Since the town and colony of Plymouth were coextensive for more than a decade, the earliest grants of land from the government to the town may be found in the court records [PCR volumes 1 through 6 *passim*]. As the towns other than Plymouth were established, the government granted large tracts of land to the towns, and then the towns made grants to individuals, the classical proprietorial system of early New England.

Transfers of land from person to person could in the earliest years be recorded in either town or colony records. The separate series of Plymouth Colony deeds runs to six volumes (some of these volumes being in two parts) [PCLR]. The first of these volumes was transcribed and published as the twelfth volume of the Plymouth Colony Records [PCR 12]. Volume Two and most of Volume Three of the Plymouth Colony deeds have been published in the *Mayflower Descendant*.

When the three counties of Plymouth, Barnstable and Bristol were erected in 1685, they took over the recording of deeds. Unfortunately, the early Barnstable County deeds were lost in a fire in the early nineteenth century.

CHURCH RECORDS

Because religious conviction was the primary motivation for migration for most of those who came to New England during the Great Migration, establishing a church in each new settlement was one of the first matters attended to. Although the survival of records from these churches is spotty, what does survive provides some of the most important evidence we have for the immigrants to New England during this period. For some reason, the towns in Plymouth Colony had greater difficulty than did their neighbors in Massachusetts Bay in filling their pulpits, and so the church records in Plymouth Colony were not kept as diligently as those in Massachusetts Bay.

Plymouth did not have a minister for most of its early history, and lay leaders such as William Brewster carried out many of the pastoral duties. The earliest Plymouth church records include a history of the early church, written many decades later. Death records for a few of the early immigrants appear here, but it is otherwise not very helpful for the years of the Pilgrim Migration. (See PChR in **Key to Titles**.)

When Rev. John Lothrop arrived at Scituate, he organized a church, and kept records of that church during its few years at Scituate, and then for many more years after he and the church removed to Barnstable [NEHGR 9:279-87, 10:37-43; GMN 5:12]. He recorded baptisms, marriages, burials, admissions and disciplinary matters.

JOURNALS AND LETTERS

The sources discussed in the sections above are almost entirely official documents, which are generally of a formal nature and do not provide as much insight into individual character and behavior as we might like. There do exist a number of private documents, generally in the form of letters and diaries, which help to give us a more complete picture of the lives of the immigrants. The most important of these for Plymouth Colony are the writings of William Bradford and Edward Winslow. We also include here discussion of the documents created and collected by Governor John Winthrop of Massachusetts Bay, since he frequently took notice of events in Plymouth Colony.

BRADFORD'S HISTORY OF PLYMOUTH

William Bradford wrote a history of the first twenty years of the existence of Plymouth Colony, prefaced by a history of the congregations in Scrooby and Leiden. This volume was written late in his life, relying heavily on correspondence which Bradford had retained. As a consequence, the chronology of the earlier years is sometimes muddled. Nevertheless, this is an essential source, the most accessible published version of which was prepared by Samuel E. Morison. The edition published by Worthington C. Ford is also valuable.

BRADFORD LETTERBOOK

William Bradford also kept a letterbook, into which he copied both incoming and outgoing correspondence. As with so many of Bradford's manuscripts, this volume had an unusual history, and only a small portion has been preserved, covering the years 1624 through 1630, the surviving portion beginning on page 339 of the original. Even this small remnant is filled with useful information.

These letters were first published in 1794, accompanied by an account of how they were rescued [MHSC 1:3:27-76]. George Ernest Bowman reprinted them more than a century later, and in the interim the original pages had been mislaid again [MD 5:5-16, 75-81, 164-71, 198-201, 6:16-17, 141-47, 207-15, 7:5-12, 79-82]. These several installments were then gathered into a separate publication in 1906 [*Governor William Bradford's Letter Book* (Boston 1906)].

PAMPHLETS OF EDWARD WINSLOW

Edward Winslow authored or co-authored a number of detailed accounts of the earliest years of Plymouth Colony. The most important of these are *Mourt's Relation* and *Good News from New England* (for full biographical details see the **Key to Titles** under Mourt and Good News).

WINTHROP JOURNAL

The most important diary is more than a diary - John Winthrop's History of New England (also known as Winthrop's Journal, and referred to hereinafter as WJ). This lengthy record includes private items, matters relating to the development of Massachusetts Bay and all the other early New England colonies, events at court which did not make it into the official court records, and much more. Winthrop took notice of many Plymouth Colony events. (In the work of the Great Migration Study Project, we use the 1853 edition prepared by James Savage, which contains many useful annotations. The 1908 edition, part of the Original Narratives of Early American History series, was heavily bowdlerized, and should not be relied on. In 1996 Richard S. Dunn and Laetitia Yeandle published an updated version of *The Journal of John Winthrop, 1630-1649*, in which the readings are more accurate than those of Savage, but the annotations not as interesting [Cambridge 1996].)

In one brief line Winthrop could provide a morsel of biographical detail available nowhere else, as, for example, under date of 7 April 1636 when he records that "Mr. Benjamin's house burnt, and 100 pounds in goods lost" (WJ 1:220). This refers to John Benjamin of Watertown, and from this short entry we learn about his social status, the possibility that he was involved in trade, and a setback in his affairs.

Acting as magistrate, Winthrop recorded various misdemeanors in the back of his journal, such as the 20 July 1637 confession of John Hobby, apparently of Dorchester, that he had stolen some beaver skins from Samuel Cole of Boston (WJ 2:425-26). Entries of this sort are the equivalent of extracts from records of a magistrate's court, which otherwise do not exist this early.

Winthrop maintained his journal right up until his death in 1649, and so for the first two decades of Massachusetts Bay Colony this is an essential source for information about individuals and about the growth and change of New England communities and institutions.

WINTHROP LETTERS

Just as John Winthrop's journal is the most important diary for the earliest years in Massachusetts, so the vast archive of correspondence collected by the Winthrop family is the largest collection of letters for the period. The Massachusetts Historical Society has published the papers of the Winthrop family from 1498 through 1654 in six volumes, with more to come (*Winthrop Papers*, 6 volumes [Boston, 1925-1992], hereinafter WP). The Winthrop correspondence was also published much earlier in the *Massachusetts Historical Society Collections*, Fourth Series, Vol. 6 & 7, and Fifth Series, Vol. 1 & 8. In this earlier version the letters were arranged by correspondent rather than chronologically, and so for some purposes may be a more convenient source.

Many extracts from the letters appear in the sketches of individual immigrants. Frequently the Winthrop correspondence provides direct evidence of the English origin of an immigrant, especially of those who had lived in the neighborhood of Winthrop's old home in Groton. In a letter to John Winthrop of 17 January 1636/7, Robert Ryece described a dispute that had arisen in Lavenham, Suffolk, and had been carried over into New England. In support of his story Ryece stated that "the widdow Onge, now of Waterton in N:E but then of Lavenham," had witnessed one stage of the dispute in her own shop and could testify to the same (WP 3:347-48).

HOW TO USE THIS BOOK

This volume on the Pilgrim Migration consists of sketches of more than two hundred families or unattached individuals who came to Plymouth Colony between 1620 and 1633. Each sketch follows a regular format, which is described below in more detail in the section titled KEY TO SKETCH HEADINGS. Every statement in each sketch is supported by citation to a document. Most of the citations appear in an abbreviated form, the abbreviations being expanded in the section below entitled KEY TO TITLES.

Two additional conventions employed in these sketches will help the reader navigate through this book:

When a name is given all in capital letters, this means that that person came to New England during the Great Migration (1620-1643), and is, or will be, the subject of a sketch elsewhere in the Great Migration volumes. If that person is not included in this volume, the name will be followed by a year and a place, indicating the known or estimated year of migration, and the first residence in New England. If a sketch for this person has already been published in the Great Migration volumes, a volume and page citation will also be added. For example, SAMUEL COLE {1630, Boston} [GMB 1:430-35] represents a sketch published in the first Great Migration volume, while NICHOLAS BUSBY {1637, Dedham} represents a sketch to be published in a future volume. If the subject of the sketch is included in this volume, an internal cross-reference to this volume will follow the name, for example, CONSTANT SOUTHWORTH [PM 437].

A string of citations of the form [Dawes-Gates 1:74, citing Perley 1:254, citing ELR 20:12] or [MD 16:181-82, citing PCLR 2:2:73] may serve one of two purposes. It may indicate a secondary source that cites a document, when the document itself has not been examined; or it may indicate a published transcript of a document, followed by the citation of the document itself.

KEY TO SKETCH HEADINGS

Except for that minority of persons who left behind one or two records in New England, each of the persons treated in these three volumes is presented according to a fixed format, which forces research to answer a series of questions. There are three sections that are rigidly formatted, and then a more informal section.

The first section asks questions related directly to the movements of the family or individual from the date of the last known residence in England to the end of his, her or their lives. Entries in this section will generally be brief.

The second group of questions is of a biographical nature, attempting to provide answers about education, officeholding, wealth and so on.

The third formatted section presents the specifically genealogical material: birth, death, spouses and children.

These three sections are followed by a free-form space, in which a variety of matters may be discussed, and finally, in some cases, a bibliographic note for those families that have been treated in print several times.

The rest of this section proceeds through the parts of a sketch, pointing out what is likely to be found under each heading, and what is not.

PRESERVED PURITAN

ORIGIN: The origin for our purposes is the last known residence in England or Holland before migration. This will frequently be different from the place of birth, and knowledge of this difference can be important in assessing the motivation for migration, and connecting the immigrant with others who made the move about the same time. The place of birth will be given as the place of origin only when no other residence in England is known.

If any residence in England other than the place of birth is known, it will be given here even if it was many years before the date of migration. For example, Bigod Eggleston, who was born at Settrington, Yorkshire, lived at a later date in Norwich, Norfolk, but was last seen there in 1614, sixteen years before he came to New England. Presumably he lived somewhere else in England in the 1620s, but for now we give his origin as Norwich.

An origin will be given only when there is solid evidence. If someone in the past has made a plausible suggestion, or if there is a leading clue, the entry here will be "Unknown," and there will be discussion of the possibilities in the *COMMENTS* section. (Information on place and date of birth, if known, will be given in the genealogical portion of the sketch, under *BIRTH*.)

MIGRATION: In this section we attempt to determine the year in which this person or family migrated to New England. If we are fortunate enough to have an entry on a passenger list, the year will be given, along with the name of the vessel. Where there is no passenger list entry (the majority of the cases), the year of migration is estimated from the evidence available. For example, it will frequently be the case that the first evidence we have for the presence of a person in Plymouth Colony is on the tax of 25 March 1633. Since most of the passenger ships arrived in May and June in these years, we assume that anyone appearing in this tax list must have arrived no later than 1632, and that year will be given at this point. Thus, in some cases the year given here will be precise, and in other cases it will be the latest possible date of arrival; in either case, if no citation is given here, the year chosen may be deduced from information given in a later section.

FIRST RESIDENCE: The evidence on first residence in New England will usually come from the surviving town or church records, although it may also be learned from court or literary sources. In many instances the evidence on first residence will be from several years after arrival in New England, and so the possibility remains that the immigrant settled in one place for a short time without leaving a record, and then moved on to another settlement. The entry here will simply be based on the best surviving evidence.

REMOVES: If the subject of the sketch resided in more than one New England settlement, that information is given here. When the year of removal is known or can be deduced, the entry would say, for example, "Hartford 1635"; in this example, we would probably not have a record which explicitly stated that the person made the move in that year, but we would learn from the Cambridge records that the person had received land grants in 1633 and 1634, but did not appear in the land inventory taken in the fall of 1635, indicating early removal to Hartford, in advance of the main party. In many instances we will not be able to fix the date of migration so precisely, and the entry might then read "Windsor by 1648," indicating that the person was of record in Windsor in that year, but his or her last record in the prior place of residence was two or more years earlier. In some cases a family might reside in one of those towns that subdivided itself early, and so a date of "removal" might be impossible to determine. In Charlestown, for instance, many families soon established homes on the opposite side of the Mystic River from Charlestown proper. When this area was set off some years later as Malden, it cannot be said that the family moved, only that the town line had shifted around them. Similar situations arise with Beverly and

Braintree. In these instances the new town will be included in the list of *REMOVES*, but without a date attached.

RETURN TRIPS: This section encompasses movements in which the sometime New England resident returned to England temporarily or permanently, or moved on to a colony outside New England, whether on the mainland or in the Caribbean.

OCCUPATION: This heading will frequently be blank, as many of the early New Englanders left no direct evidence of occupation. In a few instances when a detailed inventory allows a deduction that the person was a subsistence farmer, the occupation will be stated as husbandman. In most instances when no evidence is available and this section is omitted, we may assume that the person could be described as yeoman or husbandman.

CHURCH MEMBERSHIP: When we have direct evidence from surviving church records of membership in a given church, that knowledge will appear here. In addition, when church membership can be deduced from other records, most commonly from admission to freemanship in Massachusetts Bay after 1 May 1631, that will be included here as well. For many settlements we have no surviving church records and no information on church membership. Most importantly, since no records exist for the early Plymouth church, and since no minister was settled there for a long period of time, we will only enter data on membership in Plymouth church for a few people who are mentioned directly in that context by Bradford or some other contemporary writer.

FREEMAN: For some Plymouth Colony men, records of admission to freemanship were entered in the court minutes. Many freemen were not so recorded, but lists of freemen were compiled periodically, at first for the colony as a whole, and then for the entire colony, but organized town by town. The court records also have some entries for men who were propounded for freemanship, but not admitted to that condition. There are also lists of men who took the oath of fidelity, and that data is also recorded in this section.

OFFICES: This section includes both civil service, whether at the town, county or colony level, and also military service. In most sketches we attempt to include all discoverable service, with the limitation that much of the evidence, especially for town offices, remains in manuscript form, not all of which has been searched. For those community leaders who held many higher offices, no attempt has been made here to collect evidence on all lesser offices.

All civil service will be presented first, usually with separate paragraphs for each colony, county or town in which service has been found. All military service will then be grouped at the end of this section. All able-bodied adult males were expected to serve in the local train band, and evidence of that service will be included here; this may amount to nothing more than an entry for a weapon or two in the probate inventory for that individual.

EDUCATION: The most direct evidence for education will be for those men, mostly ministers, who attended one of the universities in England – Cambridge or Oxford. Our source for these institutions will be Venn and Foster. Some immigrants also attended a grammar school in England (preparatory to university in some cases). Beyond evidence of this sort, we will rely principally on three other sources to get some idea of the level of education and literacy reached by a given immigrant: holding an office that required reading and writing ability, such as town clerk; ownership of books, usually found in probate inventories; and ability to sign one's name.

ESTATE: Most of the material included under this heading will be from land and probate records. At this early period much of the evidence on landholding (not limited to proprietorial grants) is to be found in town records; since much of this material remains unpublished, not all records of land transactions for the persons of interest to us have been included here.

Much of the evidence for the identities of the children of the immigrants, and the birth order, will be found here. When more detailed argumen-tation on these points is needed, it will be found under *COMMENTS*.

BIRTH: When we know the English origin of the immigrant, and have the baptismal record, that will be entered here, along with the names of the parents of the immigrant. More frequently, we will not have this information; nevertheless, in almost all cases, an attempt will be made to estimate a year of birth for the immigrant, however crudely. This will be based largely on certain assumptions about the minimum or average age at which certain life events occurred: fourteen to witness a document or choose a guardian; sixteen to become a church member; twenty-one to become a freeman; twenty-five as the approximate age of first marriage for most men.

DEATH: In the absence of a specific record of death, an estimate will be made based on the appearance of the subject in other records. This will frequently be based on probate documents, but there are many other possibilities. In such cases there may be no direct citation of the relevant documents here, as they will almost always be cited more directly under some other heading.

MARRIAGE: For each spouse data on date and place of marriage, when known, is given, as well as the parents of the spouse, any previous or later spouses of that spouse, and a date of death.

CHILDREN: Evidence that allows us to compile a list of children born to a given couple, and to deduce their birth order, will be found mostly under *ESTATE, COMMENTS*, or both.

When we do not have a specific date of birth of baptism from primary sources, we attempt to assign an approximate date, in order to bring the family into better focus. In some cases that date will be relatively precise, and will be entered as, for example, "about 1638." Such a date will generally be derived from an age at death or an age given in a deposition, but may also be imposed by our knowledge of the structure of the rest of the family. An "about" date should be considered to be accurate within a year or two on either side of the stated year. Dates that are known less precisely will be entered as, for example, "say 1638." These dates may be assigned somewhat arbitrarily, based on our knowledge of other dates in the family, on birth order, and on a number of assumptions, including the expectation of a two-year interval between births (unless the earlier child died very soon) and the exclusion of multiple births without specific evidence for such events.

We do not attempt here to outline the full career of each child. We wish only to determine whether the child died young, and if not, whether the child eventually married. Thus, although all known marriages of the child will usually be given, in some cases we may only present the first marriage, just to differentiate this child from others of the same name in other families. We do not make a special effort to determine the date of death, although this may be included if it assists in estimating the year of birth.

ASSOCIATIONS: Two different types of information may appear here. First, when the subject of the sketch is related, whether by marriage or by blood, to some other immigrant to New England prior to 1643, and when that relationship existed prior to migration, that information will be shown here. This may simply demonstrate the influence of kinship on migration, or it may provide clues for further research in England. Second, if no such tie to another participant in the Great Migration is known, this will be the place to point out persistent associations with other immigrants, which may provide clues to English origins and group or chain migrations.

COMMENTS: This section provides an opportunity for discussing any matter that does not fit neatly into one of the sections described above. It may include, but is not restricted to, the following:

Specific records that do not fall into any of the narrowly-defined categories above, but which are thought to be of interest. The most common of these will be court appearances, whether in civil or criminal proceedings.

Various activities that fall outside the categories of the biographical section, such as William Aspinwall's trading and exploratory expedition up the Delaware River, or the evidence for George Alcock as a butcher.

Discussion of errors or discrepancies, whether in primary or secondary sources. If possible the discrepancy will be corrected; if not, the arguments in favor of various positions will be presented. Errors in obscure sources may be ignored, but all problems in Savage and Pope will be discussed.

Evidence and arguments for specific genealogical conclusions. In some cases the records given under the *ESTATE* section will be sufficient, without further interpretation, to establish the list of children. But when this is not the case, further evidence and argumentation will be given here.

Suggestions for further research. This will be the case when not all available records have been searched, or when some likely line of research suggests itself.

BIBLIOGRAPHIC NOTE: For some families, there has been sufficient material published to require separate discussion. This will be the case especially when a late-nineteenth-century genealogy has been corrected by more recent articles in the periodical literature, or when there are two or more published genealogies of greatly different value. This note will attempt to point out the relative value of what is in print, in hopes of deterring the continued reliance on outdated and incorrect claims.

KEY TO TITLES

This listing includes all titles employed in more than one sketch in *The Pilgrim Migration*. If a source is used in only one sketch, the full bibliographic details are given in that sketch.

Ackley-Bosworth   Nathan Grier Parke II, *The Ancestry of Lorenzo Ackley & His Wife, Emma Arabella Bosworth*, Donald Lines Jacobus, ed. (Woodstock, Vermont, 1960)

Ancestral Roots   Frederick Lewis Weis, *Ancestral Roots of Sixty Colonists Who Came to New England between 1623 and 1650*, 6th ed. (Baltimore 1988)

Aspinwall   "A Volume Relating to the Early History of Boston Containing the Aspinwall Notarial Records from 1644 to 1651," in *Reports of the Record Commissioners of the City of Boston*, Volume 32 (Boston 1903)

Austin   John Osborne Austin, *The Genealogical Dictionary of Rhode Island ...* (Albany 1887; rpt. Baltimore 1969 [with *addenda et corrigenda* as published in TAG])

BA   "A Book of All the Lands which Planters at First or by Alienation Since Possess[ed] Within New Haven Began by R[ichard] P[erry] 1645" [GMN 13:3-7, 9-16, 19-21]

Bangs   *The Pilgrims in The Netherlands, Recent Research, Papers Presented at a Symposium held by The Leiden Pilgrim Documents Center and The Sir Thomas Browne Institute*, Jeremy D. Bangs, ed. (Leiden, The Netherlands, 1984)

BarbPR	Joanne McRee Sanders, comp., *Barbados Records, Wills and Administrations, 1639-1680*, Volume 1 (1979)
BarnChR	Barnstable, Massachusetts, Church Records
BarnPR	Barnstable County, Massachusetts, Probate Records
Bassett Gen	Buell Burdett Bassett, *One Bassett Family in America* ... (Springfield, Massachusetts, 1926)
Bassett-Preston	Belle Preston, *Bassett-Preston Ancestors* (New Haven 1930)
BChR	*The Records of the First Church in Boston, 1630-1868*, Publications of the Colonial Society of Massachusetts, Volumes 39, 40 and 41, Richard D. Pierce, ed. (Boston 1961)
Bodge	George Madison Bodge, *Soldiers in King Philip's War being A Critical Account of That War with A Concise History of the Indian Wars of New England From 1620-1677* (Leominster, Massachusetts, 1896; rpt. Baltimore 1967)
Bond	Henry Bond, *Genealogies of the Families and Descendants of the Early Settlers of Watertown, Massachusetts ...*, two volumes in one, second edition (Boston 1860)
Bradford	William Bradford, *Of Plymouth Plantation, 1620-1647*, Samuel Eliot Morison, ed. (New York 1952)

Key to Titles

Bradford LB — *Governor William Bradford's Letter Book* (Boston, 1906; rpt. *from Mayflower Descendant*, 1904-6)

Brainerd Anc — Thomas Chalmers Brainerd, *Ancestry of Thomas Chalmers Brainerd*, Donald Lines Jacobus, ed. (Montreal 1948)

BridTR — Bridgewater, Massachusetts, Town Records

Briggs Gen — L. Vernon Briggs, *History and Genealogy of the Briggs Family, 1254-1937, In Three Volumes* (Boston 1937)

BrLR — Bristol County, Massachusetts, Land Records

BrPR — Bristol County, Massachusetts, Probate Records

BrVR — *Records of the Town of Braintree, 1640 to 1793*, Samuel A. Bates, ed. (Randolph 1886), pp. 627-940

BTR — "Boston Town Records," in *Second Report of the Record Commissioners of the City of Boston; containing the Boston Records, 1634-1660, and the Book of Possessions*, 2nd ed. (Boston 1881)

Burrage — Champlin Burrage, *The Early English Dissenters, 1550-1641* (Cambridge, England, 1912)

BVR — *Boston Births, Baptisms, Marriages, and Deaths, 1630-1699*, Ninth Report of the Boston Record Commissioners (Boston 1883; rpt. Baltimore 1978)

CCCR — *The Public Records of the Colony of Connecticut, 1636-1776*, 15 volumes (Hartford 1850-1890)

CCL	Leonard H. Smith Jr., comp., *Cape Cod Library of Local History and Genealogy*, 2 vols. (Baltimore 1992)
Chapin	Howard M. Chapin, *Documentary History of Rhode Island*, 2 vols. (Providence 1916, 1919)
ChBOP	*Charlestown Land Records, 1638-1802*, Third Report of the Boston Record Commissioners, 2nd ed. (Boston 1883)
ChChR	*Records of the First Church in Charlestown, Massachusetts, 1632-1789*, James Frothingham Hunnewell, ed. (Boston 1880)
ChTR	Charlestown Town Records
ChVR	*Vital Records of Charlestown, Massachusetts, to the Year 1850*, Volume I, Roger D. Joslyn, ed. (Boston 1984)
Clap	Roger Clap, *Memoirs of Capt. Roger Clap* (Boston 1731; rpt. Boston 1844)
Coldham	Peter Wilson Coldham, *The Complete Book of Emigrants, 1607-1660* (Baltimore 1987)
Conant Gen	Frederick Odell Conant, *A History ... of the Conant Family* (Portland, Maine, 1887)
Copp's Hill [B]	Thomas Bridgman, *Epitaphs from Copp's Hill Burial Ground, Boston* (Boston 1851; rpt. Bowie, Maryland, 1989)
Copp's Hill [W]	William H. Whitmore, *The Graveyards of Boston. First Volume, Copp's Hill Epitaphs* (Albany 1878)

Council NE	"Records of the Council for New England," *Proceedings of the American Antiquarian Society*, Meeting of April 24, 1867, pp. 53-131
Dawes-Gates	Mary Walton Ferris, *Dawes-Gates Ancestral Lines*, 2 vols. (n.p., 1943, 1931)
DChR	*Records of the First Church at Dorchester in New England, 1636-1734* (Boston 1891)
DeVR	*The Record of Births, Marriages and Deaths... in the Town of Dedham*, Volumes 1 & 2..., Don Gleason Hill, ed. (Dedham 1886)
Dexter	Henry Martyn Dexter and Morton Dexter, *The England and Holland of the Pilgrims* (London, 1906; rpt. Baltimore 1978)
Doggett Gen	Samuel Bradlee Doggett, *A History of the Doggett-Daggett Family* (Boston 1894)
DSGRM	*Detroit Society for Genealogical Research Magazine*, Volume 1 to present (Detroit, Michigan, 1937+)
DTR	*Fourth Report of the Record Commissioners of the City of Boston. 1880. Dorchester Town Records* (Boston 1883)
DVR	*Dorchester Births, Marriages, and Deaths to the End of 1825, Twenty-first Report of the Boston Record Commissioners* (Boston 1890)
Early Rehoboth	Richard LeBaron Bowen, *Early Rehoboth: Documented Historical Studies of Families and Events in This Plymouth Colony Township*, 4 volumes (Rehoboth 1945-1950)

Edward Winslow	Jeremy Dupertuis Bangs, *Pilgrim Edward Winslow: New England's First International Diplomat, A Documentary Biography* (Boston 2004)
Eddy Gen	Ruth Story Devereux Eddy, comp., *The Eddy Family in America* (Boston 1930)
EIHC	*Essex Institute Historical Collections*, Volume 1 to present (1859+)
ELR	Essex County, Massachusetts, Deeds, microfilm copies
English Adventurers	Peter Wilson Coldham, *English Adventurers and Emigrants, 1609-1660* (Baltimore 1984)
English Homes	Charles Edward Banks, *The English Ancestry and Homes of the Pilgrim Fathers ...* (New York c1929)
EPR	*The Probate Records of Essex County, Massachusetts, 1635-1681*, 3 volumes (Salem 1916-1920; rpt. Newburyport, Massachusetts, 1988). Citations to the unpublished probate records are to case numbers, or to register volumes (which begin with volume 301).
EQC	*Records and Files of the Quarterly Courts of Essex County, Massachusetts, 1636-1686*, 9 volumes (Salem 1911-1975)
Essex Ant	*The Essex Antiquarian*, Volume 1 through 13, Sidney Perley, ed. (Salem 1897-1909)
Farmington LR	Farmington, Connecticut, Deeds

Farm VR Barbour	Farmington Vital Records, Barbour Collection, Connecticut State Library, Hartford, Connecticut
Ford	William Bradford, *History of Plymouth Plantation, 1620-1647*, Worthington Chauncey Ford, ed., 2 volumes (Boston 1912)
Foster	Joseph Foster, *Alumni Oxonienses: The Members of the University of Oxford, 1500-1714 ...*, 4 volumes (Oxford 1891-1892)
GDMNH	Sybil Noyes, Charles Thornton Libby and Walter Goodwin Davis, *Genealogical Dictionary of Maine and New Hampshire* (Portland, Maine, 1928-1939; rpt. Baltimore 1972)
Gen Adv	*The Genealogical Advertiser*, v. 1-4 (Cambridge, 1898-1901; rpt. Baltimore, GPC, 1974)
Gen Bull	*The Genealogical Bulletin*
Gen Mag	*The Genealogical Magazine* (Salem, Massachusetts 1810-1915)
Gillespie Anc	Paul W. Prindle, *Ancestry of Elizabeth Barrett Gillespie (Mrs. William Sperry Beinecke)* (New Orleans 1976)
GM	Robert Charles Anderson, George F. Sanborn Jr. and Melinde Lutz Sanborn, *The Great Migration: Immigrants to New England, 1634-1635*, Volume I, A-B (Boston 1999)
GMB	Robert Charles Anderson, *The Great Migration Begins: Immigrants to New*

	England, 1620-1633, 3 volumes (Boston 1995)
GMN	*Great Migration Newsletter*, Volume 1 through present (1990+)
GMNJ	*Genealogical Magazine of New Jersey*, Volume 1 through present (1925+)
Good News	"Good Newes From New England: or a true Relation of things very remarkable at the Plantation of Plimoth in New England..." by E[dward] W[inslow], in Alexander Young, *Chronicles of The Pilgrim Fathers of The Colony of Plymouth, From 1602 to 1625...*, 2nd edition (Boston 1844; rpt. Baltimore 1974); pp. 271-375
Goodwin Anc	Frank Farnsworth Starr, *Various ancestral lines of James Goodwin and Lucy (Morgan) Goodwin, Hartford, Connecticut*, 2 vols. (Hartford 1915)
Gorges Gen	Raymond Gorges, *The Story of a Family Through Eleven Centuries ... Being a History of the Family of Gorges* (Boston 1944)
Gravesend TR	Gravesend, New York, Town Records
HAHAC	Oliver Ayer Roberts, *History of... the Ancient and Honorable Artillery Company of Massachusetts, 1637-1888*, 4 volumes (Boston 1895-1901)
Hale, House	Donald Lines Jacobus and Edgar Francis Waterman, *Hale, House and Related Families, Mainly of the Connecticut River Valley* (Hartford 1952; rpt. Baltimore 1978)

Hammatt Papers	Abraham Hammatt, *The Hammatt Papers. Early Inhabitants of Ipswich, Massachusetts. 1633-1700* (Ipswich 1880-1899; rpt. Baltimore 1980)
Hingham Hist	George Lincoln, *History of the Town of Hingham, Massachusetts*, 3 volumes (Hingham 1893; rpt. Somersworth, New Hampshire, 1982)
Hotten	*The Original Lists of Persons of Quality...*, John Camden Hotten, ed. (London 1874; rpt. Baltimore 1974)
Hubbard	William Hubbard, *A General History of New England from the Discovery to MDCLXXX* (Cambridge 1815)
Hull	"Diary of John Hull" *in Transactions and Collections of the American Antiquarian Society*, Volume 3 (Worcester 1857)
Hypocrisie Unmasked	"Hypocrisie Unmasked: By a true Relation of the Proceedings of the Governour and Company of the Massachusetts against Sameul Gorton ..." by Edward Winslow, in Alexander Young, *Chronicles of The Pilgrim Fathers of The Colony of Plymouth, From 1602 to 1625...*, 2nd edition (Boston 1844; rpt. Baltimore 1974); pp. 378-408
Joseph Neal Anc	Walter Goodwin Davis, *The Ancestry of Joseph Neal, 1769-c.1835* (Portland, Maine, 1945)
Kempton Anc	Dean Crawford Smith, *The Ancestry of Eva Belle Kempton, 1878-1908, Part I: The Ancestry of Warren Francis Kempton, 1817-1879* (Boston 1996) and *Part IV:*

	The Ancestry of Linda Anna Powers, 1839-1879 (Boston 2000)
King's Chapel	Thomas Bridgman, *Memorials of The Dead In Boston, Containing Select Transcripts of Inscriptions...in the King's Chapel Burial Ground, in the City of Boston* (Boston 1853)
LCVR	James N. Arnold, *Vital Record of Rhode Island, 1636-1850*, First Series, Volume 4, Part VI, Little Compton (Providence 1893)
Lechford	*Note-book Kept by Thomas Lechford, Esq., Lawyer, in Boston, Massachusetts Bay, from June 27, 1638, to July 29, 1641*, Edward Everett Hale, Jr., ed. (Cambridge 1885; rpt. Camden, Maine, 1988). Citations herein refer to the pagination as printed (and not to the manuscript pagination) and will therefore differ from the index entries of the 1885 edition.
Leiden Pilgrims	Johanna W. Tammel, comp., *The Pilgrims and other People from the British Isles in Leiden. 1576-1640* (Isle of Man 1989)
Lyme VR	Verne M. Hall and Elizabeth B. Plimpton, comps., *Vital Records of Lyme, Connecticut to the End of the Year 1850* (Lyme 1976)
M&JCH	*Search for the Passengers of the Mary & John 1630*, Volume 1 through present (Toledo, Ohio, 1985+)
MA Arch	"Massachusetts Archives," being bound volumes of loose papers at the Commonwealth Archives of Massachusetts, Boston, Massachusetts

Macdonough-Hackstaff	Rodney MacDonough, *The MacDonough-Hackstaff Ancestry* (Boston 1901)
Magna Charta Sureties	Frederick Lewis Weis, *The Magna Charta Sureties, 1215, The Barons Named in the Magna Charta, 1215 and Some of Their Descendants Who Settled in America During the Early Colonial Years*, 4th ed. (Baltimore 1991)
Manwaring	*A Digest of the Early Connecticut Probate Records, Volume One, Hartford Probate District, 1635-1700*, Charles William Manwaring, comp. (Hartford 1904)
MarVR	*Vital Records of Marshfield, Massachusetts, to the year 1850*, Robert M. Sherman and Ruth Wilder Sherman, eds. (n.p. 1970)
Martha's Vineyard Hist	Charles Edward Banks, *The History of Martha's Vineyard, Dukes County, Massachusetts in Three Volumes* (Edgartown 1966)
MBCR	*Records of the Governor and Company of the Massachusetts Bay in New England*, 1628-1686, Nathaniel B. Shurtleff, ed., 5 volumes in 6 (Boston 1853-1854)
MD	*Mayflower Descendant*, Volume 1 through present (1899-1937, 1985+)
MF	*Mayflower Families* (the "silver" books)
MFIP	*Mayflower Families in Progress* (the "pink" books)
MHSC	*Collections of the Massachusetts Historical Society*, Volume 1 through present (1792+). This serial is divided into a number of series, so the citations will

	sometimes be in three parts, designating series, volume and page.
MHSP	*Proceedings of the Massachusetts Historical Society*, Volume 1 through present (1791+). This serial is divided into a number of series, so the citations will sometimes be in three parts, designating series, volume and page.
MiddleVR	*Middleborough, Massachusetts Vital Records*, Barbara Lambert Merrick and Alicia Crane Williams, eds., 2 vols. (Boston 1986, 1990)
MLR	Middlesex County, Massachusetts, Deeds
Monnette	Orra Eugene Monnette, *First Settlers of Ye Plantations of Piscataway and Woodbridge, Olde East New Jersey, 1664-1714*, parts 1-7 (Los Angeles 1930-1935)
Moore Anc	L. Effingham deForest and Anne Lawrence deForest, *Moore and Allied Families: The Ancestry of William Henry Moore* (New York 1938)
Morison	Samuel Eliot Morison, *The Founding of Harvard College* (Cambridge 1935) [especially for Appendix B, "English University Men Who Emigrated to New England Before 1646," pp. 359-410]
Morton	Nathaniel Morton, *The New-England's Memorial* ... (Plymouth 1826)
Mourt	*A Journal of the Pilgrims at Plymouth. Mourt's Relation. A Relation or Journal of the English Plantations Settled at Plymouth in New England, by Certain*

English Adventurers Both Merchants and Others, Dwight B. Heath, ed. (New York 1963)

MPCR	*Province and Court Records of Maine*, 6 volumes (Portland 1928-1975; volumes 1-3 rpt. Newburyport, Massachusetts, 1991)
MPR	Middlesex County, Massachusetts, Probate Records
MQ	*Mayflower Quarterly*, Volume 1 to present (1935+)
Munsey-Hopkins	D.O.S. Lowell, *A Munsey-Hopkins Genealogy*... (Boston 1920)
NEA	*New England Ancestors*, Volume 1 through present (2000+)
NEHGR	*New England Historical and Genealogical Register*, Volume 1 through present (1847+)
New English Canaan	Thomas Morton, *New English Canaan* (Amsterdam 1637; rpt. Boston 1883)
NGSQ	*National Genealogical Society Quarterly*, Volume 1 through present (1912+)
NHCR	*Records of the Colony and Plantation of New Haven*, 1638-1649, 1653-1664, 2 volumes, Charles J. Hoadly, ed. (Hartford 1857-1858)
NHLR	New Haven, Connecticut, Land Records
NHPR	New Haven, Connecticut, Probate Records
NJHSP	*New Jersey Historical Society Proceedings*, four series, 1845 to present

Norwich Hist	Frances Manwaring Caulkins, *History of Norwich, Connecticut: From Its Possession by the Indians to the Year 1866* (Hartford 1874)
NYGBR	*The New York Genealogical and Biographical Record*, Volume through present (1869+)
NYHM:D	New York Historical Manuscripts: Dutch
NYHM:E	New York Historical Manuscripts: English
OED	*Oxford English Dictionary*
Otis	Amos Otis, *Genealogical Notes of Barnstable Families...*, 2 volumes (Barnstable, Massachusetts, 1888, 1890; rpt. Baltimore 1979, in 1 volume)
Oxford DNB	*Oxford Dictionary of National Biography*, 60 volumes (Oxford 2004)
Parker-Ruggles	John William Linzee, Jr., *The History of Peter Parker and Sarah Ruggles of Roxbury, Mass., and Their Ancestors and Descendants* (Boston 1913)
PCC	Prerogative Court of Canterbury, England
PChR	*Plymouth Church Records, 1620-1859, Part 1 and Part 2* in Publications of the Colonial Society of Massachusetts, volumes 22 and 23 (Boston 1920, 1923)
PCLR	Plymouth Colony Deeds (from microfilm; Volume 1 has been published as Volume 12 of PCR)
PCPR	Plymouth Colony Probate Records (from microfilm)

Key to Titles

PCR   *Records of the Colony of New Plymouth in New England*, Nathaniel B. Shurtleff and David Pulsifer, eds., 12 volumes in 10 (Boston 1855-1861)

Perley   Sidney Perley, *The History of Salem, Massachusetts*, 3 volumes (Salem 1924-1928)

Phoebe Tilton Anc   Walter Goodwin Davis, *The Ancestry of Phoebe Tilton, 1775-1847, The Wife of Capt. Abel Lunt of Newburyport, Massachusetts* (Portland 1947)

Pillsbury Anc   Mary Lovering Holman, *Ancestry of Charles Stinson Pillsbury and John Sargent Pillsbury ...* 2 vols. (Concord, 1938)

Plooij   D. Plooij and J. Rendel Harris, *Leyden Documents Relating to the Pilgrim Fathers: Permission to Reside at Leyden and Betrothal Records; together with Parallel Documents from the Amsterdam Archives* (Leiden 1920)

PLR   Plymouth County, Massachusetts, Deeds (from microfilm)

Plymouth Wills   C.H. Simmons, Jr., *Plymouth Colony Records, Volume 1, Wills and Inventories, 1633-1669* (Camden, Maine, 1996)

PM   Robert Charles Anderson, *The Pilgrim Migration: Immigrants to Plymouth Colony, 1620-1633* (Boston 2004)

PNQ   *Pilgrim Notes and Queries*, Volume 1 through 5 (1913-1917)

Pope	Charles Henry Pope, *The Pioneers of Massachusetts...* (Boston 1900; rpt. Baltimore 1965)
PPR	Plymouth County, Massachusetts, Probate Records (from microfilm)
Prince	Thomas Prince, *A Chronological History of New England ...,* Samuel G. Drake, ed., third edition (Boston 1852)
PrTR	*The Early Records of the Town of Providence,* 21 volumes (Providence 1892-1915)
PTR	*Records of the Town of Plymouth,* Volume 1, 1636 to 1705 (Plymouth 1889)
PVR	*Vital Records of Plymouth, Massachusetts, to the Year 1850,* Lee D. van Antwerp, comp., and Ruth Wilder Sherman, ed. (Camden, Maine, 1993)
RCA	*Records of the Court of Assistants,* 3 volumes (Boston 1901-1928)
RChR	*Roxbury Land and Church Records,* Sixth Report of the Boston Record Commissioners (Boston 1884), pp. 74-191
ReVR	James N. Arnold, *Vital Record of Rehoboth, 1642-1896...* (Providence 1897)
RICR	*Records of the Colony of Rhode Island and Providence Plantations...,* 1636-1692, 10 volumes, John Russell Bartlett, ed. (Providence 1856-1865)
RICT	*Rhode Island Court Records: Records of the Court of Trials of the Colony of*

Providence Plantations, 1647-1662, Volume I (Providence 1920) [RICT 1]; *Rhode Island Court Records: Records of the Court of Trials of the Colony of Providence Plantations, 1662-1670*, Volume II (Providence 1922) [RICT 2]; Jane Fletcher Fiske, trans., *Rhode Island General Court of Trials, 1671-1704* (Boxford, Massachusetts, 1998) [RICT 3]

RIVR   James N. Arnold, *Vital Record of Rhode Island, 1636-1850*, Volumes 1 through 21 (Providence 1891-1912)

RWCorr   *The Correspondence of Roger Williams, Volume One 1629-1653, Volume Two 1654-1682*, Glenn W. LaFantasie, ed. (Providence 1988)

Saints   George F. Willison, *Saints and Strangers...* (New York 1945)

Savage   James Savage, *A Genealogical Dictionary of the First Settlers of New England*, 4 volumes (Boston 1860-1862; rpt. Baltimore 1965)

SayVR   *The Vital Records of Saybrook Colony, 1635-1860*, ed. Elizebeth Bull Plimpton (Old Saybrook, Connecticut, 1985)

SChR   *The Records of the First Church in Salem, Massachusetts, 1629-1736*, Richard D. Pierce, ed. (Salem 1974)

SCC   *Records of the Suffolk County Court, 1671-1680*, 2 vols., in *Publications of The Colonial Society of Massachusetts*, vols. 29 and 30 (Boston, 1933)

Scituate Hist	Samuel Deane, *History of Scituate, Massachusetts, From Its First Settlement to 1831* (Boston 1831; rpt. Scituate 1975)
ScitTR	Jeremy Dupertuis Bangs, *The Seventeenth-Century Town Records of Scituate, Massachusetts*, 3 volumes (Boston 1997, 1999, 2001)
Scott Gen	Mary Lovering Holman, *The Scott Genealogy....* (Boston 1919)
Scrapbook	*The Plymouth Scrap Book, The Oldest Original Documents Extant In Plymouth Archives...*, Charles Henry Pope, ed. (Boston 1918)
ScVR	*Vital Records of Scituate, Massachusetts, to the Year 1850*, 2 volumes (Boston 1909)
Sewall	*The Diary of Samuel Sewall,* Volume One 1674-1708, Volume Two 1709-1729, M. Halsey Thomas, ed. (New York 1973)
Shattuck	Lemuel Shattuck, *A History of the Town of Concord...* (Boston 1835)
Sibley	John Langdon Sibley, *Biographical Sketches of Graduates of Harvard University, 1642-1689*, 3 volumes (Cambridge 1873-1885)
SJC	Supreme Judicial Court, Massachusetts
SLR	*Suffolk Deeds*, Volumes 1 through 14 (Boston 1880-1906). Citations to later volumes are from the microfilm copies of the originals.
Small Gen	Lora Altine Woodbury Underhill, *Descendants of Edward Small of New*

	England and the Allied Families with Tracings of English Ancestry, revised edition, 3 volumes (Boston and New York, 1934)
Snow-Estes	Nora E. Snow, *The Snow-Estes Ancestry*, 2 volumes (Hillburn, New York, 1939)
SPR	Suffolk County, Massachusetts, Probate Records
Stevens-Miller Anc	Mary Lovering Holman (and Winifred Lovering Holman), *Ancestry of Colonel John Harrington Stevens and his wife Frances Helen Miller*, 2 volumes (n.p. 1948, 1951)
STR	*Town Records of Salem, Massachusetts*, 1634-1691, 3 volumes (Salem 1868, 1913, 1934)
Stratton	Eugene Aubrey Stratton, *Plymouth Colony: Its History & People, 1620-1691* (Salt Lake City 1986)
SwVR	*Vital Records of Swansea, Massachusetts To 1850*, transcribed by H.L. Peter Rounds (Boston 1992)
TAG	*The American Genealogist*, Volume 9 to present (1932+)
TG	*The Genealogist*, Volume 1 to present (1980+)
Thomas Cooke Gen	Jane Fletcher Fiske, *Thomas Cooke of Rhode Island*, 2 volumes (Boxford, Massachusetts, 1987)

Three Episodes	Charles Francis Adams, *Three Episodes of Massachusetts History*, 2 volumes (Boston and New York, 1903)
Three Visitors	Sydney V. James, Jr., *Three Visitors to Early Plymouth* (Plymouth 1963)
Tingley-Meyers	Raymon Meyers Tingley, *Some Ancestral Lines* (Rutland, Vermont, 1935)
Topo Dict	Charles Edward Banks, *Topographical Dictionary of 2885 English Emigrants to New England, 1620-1650*, Elijah Ellsworth Brownell, ed. (Philadelphia 1937; rpt. Baltimore 1957)
Torrey	Clarence Almon Torrey, *New England Marriages Prior to 1700*, 12 volumes, original manuscript, New England Historic Genealogical Society
Tracy Gen	Sherman Weld Tracy, comp., *The Tracy Genealogy, Being Some of the Descendants of Stephen Tracy of Plymouth Colony, 1623* (Rutland 1936)
Venn	John Venn and J.A. Venn, *Alumni Cantabrigienses, Part I (From the Earliest Times to 1751)*, 4 volumes (Cambridge 1922-1927)
WaBOP	"Lands, Grants, Divisions, Allotments, Possessions and Proprietors' Book," Section Two in *Watertown Records Comprising the First and Second Books of Town Proceedings* ... (Watertown 1894)
Waterhouse Anc	Walter Goodwin Davis, *The Ancestry of Joseph Waterhouse, 1754-1837, of Standish, Maine* (Portland 1949)

Waterman Gen	E.F. Waterman, *The Waterman Family*, Donald Lines Jacobus, ed., 3 volumes (New Haven 1939-1954)
Waters	Henry FitzGilbert Waters, *Genealogical Gleanings In England*, 2 volumes (Boston 1901)
WaTR	"Records of Town Proceedings - First and Second Books," Section One in *Watertown Records Comprising the First and Second Books of Town Proceedings* ... (Watertown 1894)
WaVR	"Records of Births, Deaths and Marriages - First Book and Supplement," Section Three in *Watertown Records Comprising the First and Second Books of Town Proceedings* ... (Watertown 1894)
Weymouth Hist	George Walter Chamberlain, *History of Weymouth, Massachusetts, Volumes Three and Four, Genealogy of Weymouth Families* (Weymouth 1923; rpt. Baltimore 1984, 2 volumes in 1)
Windsor Hist	Henry Reed Stiles, *The History and Genealogies of Ancient Windsor, Connecticut* ..., 2 vols. (Hartford, 1891-92)
WJ	John Winthrop, *The History of New England from 1630 to 1649*, James Savage, ed., 2 volumes (Boston 1853). Citations herein refer to the pagination of the 1853 and not the 1826 edition, even though the index to the 1853 edition continues to use the 1826 pagination.
WP	*Winthrop Papers, 1498-1654*, 6 volumes, various editors (Boston 1925-1992)

Wyman	Thomas Bellows Wyman, *The Genealogies and Estates of Charlestown, Massachusetts: 1629-1818*, 2 volumes (Boston 1879; rpt. in 1 volume Somersworth, New Hampshire, 1982)
YarVR	Robert M. Sherman and Ruth Wilder Sherman, *Vital Records of Yarmouth, Massachusetts To The Year 1850*, 2 vols. (Warwick, Rhode Island, 1975)
YLR	*York Deeds*, 18 volumes (Portland, Maine, 1887-1910)
Young's First Planters	*Chronicles of the First Planters of the Colony of Massachusetts Bay ...*, Alexander Young, ed. (Boston 1846; rpt. Baltimore 1975)
Young's Pilgrim Fathers	*Chronicles of the Pilgrim Fathers of the Colony of Plymouth ...*, Alexander Young, ed. (Boston 1844; rpt. Baltimore 1974)

JOHN ADAMS

ORIGIN: Unknown.
MIGRATION: 1621 on the *Fortune* [PCR 12:5].
FIRST RESIDENCE: Plymouth.

OFFICES: His inventory included "one piece" valued at £1 10s. [MD 1:158, citing PCPR 1:14].
FREEMAN: In 1633 Plymouth list of freemen, John Adams appears ahead of those persons admitted on 1 January 1632/3 [PCR 1:3].
ESTATE: In the 1623 Plymouth land division John Adams was granted one acre, as a passenger on the *Fortune* [PCR 12:5]. In the 1627 Plymouth cattle division John Adams, "Eliner Adams," and James Adams were the second, third and fourth persons in the sixth company [PCR 12:11].

With four others, John Adams was on 1 July 1633 assigned to mow where Mr. Gilson had mowed the year before [PCR 1:14]. John Adams was assessed 9s. in the tax list of 25 March 1633, and "Widow Adams" was assessed the same amount on 27 March 1634 [PCR 1:10, 28].

On 24 October 1633, John Winslow and John Jenny took an inventory of the goods of John Adams; the total was £71 14s., of which £37 10s. was in neat cattle [MD 1:157-58, citing PCPR 1:14]. The inventory was presented on 11 November 1633, and the widow Ellen Adams was named adminstratrix, the deceased having left no will; she was bound in the sum of £140, John Barnes surety, to provide £5 apiece to her three children by John Adams - James, John and Susan - when they came of age, if she should choose to remarry [PCR 1:19]. The payment to son James, made by Kenelm Winslow, was recorded on 26 December 1651 [PCR 2:176].

BIRTH: By about 1600 (based on estimated date of marriage).
DEATH: Between 1 July 1633 (assignment of mowing ground) and 24 October 1633 (date of inventory).

MARRIAGE: About 1625 ELLEN NEWTON [PM 344] (this identification, long in print, is based on the fact that she is the only Ellen in the 1623 land division, and there was no other known addition to the Plymouth population in the next few years). She married (2) in June 1634 KENELM WINSLOW [PCR 1:30; PM 518], and was buried at Marshfield 5 December 1681 "being 83 years old" (probably an inflated age) [MarVR 13].

CHILDREN:
- i JAMES ADAMS, b. before 22 May 1627 [PCR 12:11]; m. Scituate 15 or 16 June or 16 July 1646 Frances Vassall, daughter of WILLIAM VASSALL {1630, Boston} [ScVR 2:11; PCR 2:108, 8:19; GMB 3:1871-75].
- ii JOHN ADAMS, b. after 22 May 1627; m. (1) Marshfield 27 December 1654 Jane James [MarVR 1]; m. (2) by 10 December 1666 Elizabeth ____ [TAG 55:214].
- iii SUSAN ADAMS, b. after 22 May 1627; no further record.

COMMENTS: The best treatment in print of John Adams and his two sons is Robert S. Wakefield, "Men of the *Fortune*: John Adams" [TAG 55 (1979):212-14]. (An earlier account is in NEHGR 33:410-13.)

Banks has published some records for the name John Adams in London, but none of these can be connected with John Adams of Plymouth [English Homes 105].

WEBB ADEY

ORIGIN: Unknown.
MIGRATION: 1632.
FIRST RESIDENCE: Plymouth.

OFFICES: "Webb Addey" appears in the 1643 Plymouth list of men able to bear arms [PCR 8:188]. His inventory included "a small birding piece" valued at 10s. and "a stock lock" valued at 1s. [PCPR 1:104; MD 11:8].

ESTATE: As "Addy Web," assessed 9s. (the lowest rate) in the Plymouth tax lists of 25 March 1633 and 27 March 1634 [PCR 1:11, 28].

On 7 November 1636, he was granted three acres in Plymouth [PCR 1:46]. On 6 February 1636/7, William Paddy, having been awarded £3 12s. 9d. in a suit for debt against Webb Adey, arranged for a schedule of payments [PCR 7:4].

On 2 October 1637, "Webb Adey" was one of four men "presented for disorderly living, & therefore to be required to give an account of how they live" [PCR 1:68]. On 5 June 1638, he was presented "for working upon the Lord's day in his garden" and "for disorderly living in idleness & nastiness"; he was sentenced to sit in the stocks, to provide himself with a master before the next court, and, "for the convenient apparelling of him to be fit for service, either to let or sell his house & garden to any that will either take or purchase the same" [PCR 1:86, 87]. On 2 July 1638, he was ordered to serve Thomas Prence, his house and lands "to be set to them that will give the most for them," and his goods to be sold to cover his debts [PCR 1:91]. On 2 July 1638, he was again found guilty of working on the Sabbath, and again sentenced to sit in the stocks [PCR 1:92]. On 29 August 1638, "Web Adey" sold to Mr. John Jenny "his house and garden place adjoining scituate in Plymouth, together with three acres of lands in the New Field" [PCR 12:35]. On 1 March 1641/2, Webb Adey was presented again for disorderly living, and, on 7 June 1642, was jailed for the same [PCR 2:36, 42].

In an instrument recorded on 24 September 1645, John Harmon sold to Webb Adey "six acres of upland lying in the New Field on the west side of the lands of Andrew Ring" [PCR 12:113-14].

On 4 March 1651/2 [the day of his death], "Webb Audey" made a nuncupative will, in which he noted that he had sold a house to Thomas Sherive for £4 5s., of which only 6s. had been paid, and asked that of the remainder left due, £1 10s. go to Mr. John Reyner, teacher, and the rest be used for funeral expenses; then, "being demanded what he would do with his other house, he said there was poor enough in the town"; finally, out of the debts due him, he bequeathed one bushel of corn to Goodman Pratt, and a half-bushel of corn each to Goodman Savory and Goodman Sherive [PCPR 1:104; MD 11:8-9].

His inventory, taken 17 March 1651/2, totalled £7 7s. 10d. (against which were debts of £2 6s.), of which £2 10s. was real estate: "one small house and garden," £1 10s.; and "one parcel of land in the New Field, about 12 acres," £1. In the settlement of his estate, dated 4 May 1652, the small house and garden were given to John Reyner to satisfy the bequest of 30s., and 17s. in moveables was given to John Bower for his troubles in administering the estate [PCPR 1:104; MD 11:8-9].

BIRTH: By about 1612 (based on inclusion in 1633 tax list).
DEATH: Plymouth 4 March 1651/2 (as "Audey Webb") [PCR 8:13].
MARRIAGE: None recorded.
CHILDREN: None recorded.

COMMENTS: In the inventory of the estate of Francis Eaton, taken on 8 November 1633, there was a debt "to Web for 12 days' work about him in sickness," 12s. [MD 1:200]. On 5 March 1638/9, Ralph Gorham the elder was presented for beating Webb Adey [PCR 1:118].

Webb Adey is probably the best-recorded antisocial pauper in Plymouth Colony. Although he seems to have done his best at all times to live by his own rules and not those of the colony, he did receive grants of land, and at his death had not one house but two.

In some records his names are reversed, and he appears as Addy Webb; this version of his name is seen only at his first appearance, in the tax lists, and in his death record. At all other times he is Webb Adey, and that is the sequence used here. (Savage entered him under the surname "Webb," and in another place misrepresented him as "William Adey" [Savage 1:18].)

JOHN ALDEN

ORIGIN: Southampton.
MIGRATION: 1620 on the *Mayflower*.
FIRST RESIDENCE: Plymouth.
REMOVES: Duxbury 1632.

OCCUPATION: Cooper (his inventory included "coopers tools" valued at £1 2s. [PPR 1:10; MD 3:10]).
FREEMAN: In 1633 Plymouth list of freemen, among those admitted prior to 1 January 1632/3 [PCR 1:3] and in list of 7 March 1636/7 [PCR 1:52]. In Duxbury sections of lists of 1639 and 1658 [PCR 8:174, 198].
EDUCATION: Although there is no direct evidence for his literary and educational attainments, his extensive public service, including especially his appointments as colony treasurer and to committees on revising the laws, certainly indicates that he must have been well-educated.
OFFICES: Assistant, 6 February 1631/2 [WP 3:65], 1 January 1632/3, 1 January 1633/4, 1 January 1634/5, 5 January 1635/6, 3 January 1636/7, 6 March 1637/8, 4 March 1638/9 [PCR 1:5, 21, 32, 36, 48, 79, 116 (the assistants elected on 3 March 1639/40 were not sworn until 2 June 1640, so John Alden continued to serve as assistant at a few courts in early 1640)]. Assistant each year from 1650 to 1686 [PCR 2:153, 166, 3:7, 30, 48, 77, 99, 114, 134, 162, 187, 214, 4:13, 36, 60, 90, 122, 147, 179, 5:17,

34, 55, 90, 112, 143, 163, 194, 229, 256, 6:9, 34, 58, 83, 106, 127, 164, 185].

Acted as Deputy Governor on two occasions, in absence of Governor, 7 March 1664/5, 30 October 1677 [PCR 4:81, 5:245]. Treasurer, 3 June 1656, 3 June 1657, 1 June 1658 [PCR 3:99, 115, 135]. Council of War, 27 September 1642, 10 October 1643, 2 June 1646, 6 April 1653, 12 May 1653, 1 June 1658, 2 April 1667 [PCR 2:46, 63, 100, 3:26, 28, 138, 4:145].

Committee to revise laws, 4 June 1645, 3 June 1657 [PCR 2:85, 3:117]. Committee on Kennebec trade, 3 March 1645/6, 7 June 1648, 8 June 1649, 5 March 1655/6 [PCR 2:96, 127, 144, 3:96]. Appointed to numerous other minor posts and committees by Plymouth General Court.

Deputy for Duxbury to Plymouth General Court 1641, 1642, 1644 and 1646 to 1649, and also at courts of 20 August 1644, 28 October 1645 and 3 March 1645/6 [PCR 2:16, 40, 72, 75, 94, 95, 104, 117, 123, 144].

"Mr. John Alden Senior" is in the Duxbury section of the 1643 list of men able to bear arms [PCR 8:189]. His inventory included "2 old guns" valued at 11s. [PPR 1:10; MD 3:10].

ESTATE: In the 1623 Plymouth land division granted an unknown number of acres as a passenger on the *Mayflower* in 1620 [PCR 12:4]. In the 1627 Plymouth cattle division, included in company of John Howland, along with wife Priscilla, daughter Elizabeth and son John [PCR 12:10].

Assessed £1 4s. in Plymouth tax lists of 25 March 1633 and 27 March 1634 [PCR 1:9, 27].

Assigned mowing ground for the year, 14 March 1635/6, 20 March 1636/7 [PCR 1:40, 56].

On 6 March 1636/7, "[a] parcel of land containing a knoll, or a little hill, lying over against Mr. Alden's land at Blewfish River, is granted by the Court unto the said Mr. John Alden in lieu of a parcel of land taken from him (next unto Samuel Nash's lands) for public use" [PCR 1:51].

Granted "certain lands at Green's Harbor," 5 February 1637/8 [PCR 1:76]. Granted to Miles Standish and John Alden three hundred acres "on the north side of the South River," 2 July 1638 [PCR 1:91]. Granted "a little parcel of land ... lying at the southerly side of his lot," 3 September 1638 [PCR 1:95].

On 3 June 1657, "[l]iberty is granted unto Mr. John Alden to look out a portion of land to accommodate his sons withall, and to make report thereof unto the Court, that so it may be confirmed unto him" [PCR 3:120].

On 13 June 1660, "[i]n regard that Mr. Alden is low in his estate, and occasioned to spend much time at the courts on the country's occasions, and so hath done this many years, the Court have allowed him a small gratuity, the sum of ten pounds, to be paid by the Treasurer" [PCR 3:195].

Granted "a competency of land" at Namasskett, 7 June 1665 [PCR 4:95]. Granted one hundred acres at Teticutt, 4 March 1673/4 [PCR 5:141].

On 8 July 1674, John Alden of Duxbury "for love and natural affection and other valuable causes and considerations" deeded to "David Alden his true and natural son all that his land both meadow and upland that belongs unto him situate or being at or about a place called Rootey Brook within the Township of Middleborough ... excepting only one hundred acres," containing about three hundred acres [PLR 3:330]. On 1 April 1679, "John Alden of Duxborough ..., gentleman," deeded to "Joseph Alden my true and natural son ... all that my share of land ... within the township of Bridgewater" [PLR 3:194].

A description of a parcel of land of "Mr. John Aldin, of Duxbery," is entered under date of 4 December 1637, but with the modern annotation that this is a later entry, and with the internal statement that one of the abuttors was "Philip Delano, deceased," which means that the entry must have been made in 1687 or later; this is immediately followed by an entry for another parcel of land which Alden bought of Edward Hall in 1651 [PCR 1:71, 73].

On 1 January 1684[/5] [36 Charles II], John Alden Sr. of Duxbury for "that real love and parental affection which I bear to my beloved and dutiful son Jonathan Alden" deeded to him all my upland in Duxbury, for which "see old book of grants and bounds of land anno 1637 folio 137," and all other lands at Duxbury whether granted by court at Plymouth or town of Duxbury [PLR 6:53].

On 13 January 1686[/7] [2 James II], John Alden Sr. of Duxbury for "that natural love and affection which I bear to my firstborn and dutiful son John Alden of Boston" deeded him one hundred acres at Pekard Neck *alias* Pachague with one-eighth of the meadow belonging to that place, and one hundred acres at Rootey Brook (brother David Alden is to have first right of purchase if John should wish to sell this hundred acres), together with a sixteen shilling purchase being the fifteenth lot, all in Middleborough, and one hundred acres, the first in a division of one thousand acres in Bridgewater [PLR 5:427].

On 19 August 1687, "John Alden Senior of Duxborough ..., cooper," deeded to "my two sons Jonathan & David Alden ... five acres of salt marsh at Duxbury" and "my whole proportion in the Major's Purchase commonly so-called being the thirty-fifth part of said purchase" [MD 9:145, citing PLR 4:65].

The inventory of the estate of John Alden, taken 31 October 1687, totalled £49 17s. 6d., all moveables. On 13 June 1688, the heirs of John Alden Sr. of Duxbury signed a release in favor of Jonathan Alden, stating that they had received their portion of the estate; those signing were Alexander Standish (in the right of his wife Sarah deceased), John Bass (in the right of his wife Ruth deceased), Mary Alden, Thomas Delano, John Alden, Joseph Alden, David Alden, Priscilla Alden and William Pabodie [PPR 1:10, 16; MD 3:10-11].

BIRTH: About 1599 (deposed on 6 July 1682 "aged 83 years or thereabouts" [PCR 7:256; MD 3:120]; in his 89th year at death on 12 September 1687 [MF Alden 1:22; MD 9:129]; "about eighty-nine years of age" at death on 12 September 1687 [MF Alden 1:21; MD 34:49]).
DEATH: Duxbury 12 September 1687 [Sewall 150; MD 9:129, 34:49].
MARRIAGE: Plymouth about 1623 Priscilla Mullins, daughter of WILLIAM MULLINS [PM 339]. She died after 1651, when she is mentioned in Bradford's summary of *Mayflower* passengers.
CHILDREN:
 i ELIZABETH ALDEN, b. about 1624; m. Plymouth 26 (or 20) December 1644 William Pabodie [PCR 2:79; DuVR]; she d. Little Compton 31 May 1717 [LCVR 143], "a. 92" [*Boston News-Letter*]. (Her tombstone at Little Compton gives her age at death as "in the 94th year of her age," but as the current monument was erected in 1882, this may not have been on the original stone.)
 ii JOHN ALDEN, b. about 1626; m. Boston 1 April 1660 "Elizabeth Everill, widow, relict of Abiell Everill, deceased" (although the correct date should probably be 1659, as a child was born to John and Elizabeth Alden on 17 December 1659 [BVR 69], and in the original form of the vital records, given in the second of the following citations but not in the first, this record is imbedded among others for 1659) [BVR 76; NEHGR 18:333; but see NEHGR 52:162 and Munsey-Hopkins 55, which interpret the 1659 birth record to imply that John Alden had had an earlier wife, also named Elizabeth]; she was born before 1640, daughter of WILLIAM PHILLIPS {1639, Charlestown}, and m. Boston 6 July 1655 Abiel Everill [BVR 52], son of JAMES

EVERILL {1634, Boston} [GM 2:2:469-76]; John Alden d. 14 March 1701/2 [Sewall 463].

iii JOSEPH ALDEN, b. about 1627 (in list of men able to bear arms in 1643, and therefore at least 16 [PCR 8:189]); m. by about 1660 Mary Simonson, daughter of MOSES SIMONSON {1621, Plymouth} [MD 31:60; GMB 3:1681-83; PM 419].

iv PRISCILLA ALDEN, b. say 1630; living unm. in 1688 [PPR 1:16].

v JONATHAN ALDEN, b. about 1632; m. Duxbury 10 December 1672 Abigail Hallett, daughter of ANDREW HALLETT {1635, Dorchester} [GM 2:3:195-200]. Jonathan Alden d. Duxbury 14 February 1696/7 "in the 65 year of his age" [MD 9:159; NEHGR 52:365]. (The date on the tombstone is 14 February 1697, but the double-dating problem is resolved by the probate papers, as administration on the estate was granted on 8 March 1696/7 [MD 6:174-78].)

vi SARAH ALDEN, b. say 1634; m. by about 1660 Alexander Standish (date based on approximated birthdates of children [NEHGR 52:363-65]), son of MILES STANDISH [PM 451].

vii RUTH ALDEN, b. say 1636; m. Braintree 3 February 1657/8 John Bass [BrVR 716], son of SAMUEL BASS {1633, Roxbury} [GMB 1:122-27].

viii MARY ALDEN, b. say 1638; living unm. in 1688 [PPR 1:16].

ix REBECCA ALDEN, b. say 1640; subject of unfounded rumor that she was "with child," 1 October 1661 [PCR 4:7]; m. in 1667, before 30 October, Thomas Delano [PCR 4:168, 8:122; NEHGR 102:83, 86], son of PHILIP DELANO [PM 165].

x DAVID ALDEN, b. say 1642; m. by 1674 Mary Southworth, daughter of CONSTANT SOUTHWORTH [PM 437] (in his will, dated 27 February 1678, Constant Southworth bequeathed to daughter Mary Alden [PCPR 4:1:18-20]).

COMMENTS: According to Bradford, "John Alden was hired a cooper at Southampton where the ship victualled, and being a hopeful young man was much desired but left to his own liking to go or stay when he came here; but he stayed and married here" [Bradford 443]. In his accounting of the *Mayflower* families in 1651, Bradford stated under William

Mullins that "his daughter Priscilla survived, and married with John Alden; who are both living and have eleven [*sic*] children. And their eldest daughter is married and hath five children" [Bradford 445]. (As the marginal annotation for this entry gives the "increasing" as fifteen, and the eldest daughter already had five children, the correct number of children for John and Priscilla is more likely ten, which conforms with our overall knowledge of the family [MD 39:111].)

Many suggestions have been made as to the English origin of John Alden. Alicia Crane Williams has examined all the relevant evidence carefully and exhaustively, and comes to the conclusion that, although one or two of the suggested origins are "tempting," all are far from proved [MD 39:111-22, 40:133-36, 41:201]. By entering "Southampton" under *ORIGIN* above, we are only taking note of Bradford's statement that Alden was hired at that port; we are not implying that he was born or raised there.

The present account differs somewhat from other accounts in the birth order of the children and the approximated ages. The estimated dates of birth for the first two children (Elizabeth and John) are reasonably well-defined because they fell between the 1623 land division and the 1627 cattle division. The third child (Joseph) must have been born late in 1627 to appear on the 1643 list of men able to bear arms. The next date that we are able to fix is that of Jonathan, who was said at his death early in 1697 to be in his sixty-fifth year, and so born in 1632 (or possibly early in 1633); note that this gives us a gap of about five or six years between Joseph and Jonathan. We arbitrarily place one of the unmarried daughters, Priscilla, in this gap, although it might as well be Mary who fits here. The remainder of the children are then ranged after Jonathan at two-year intervals. This makes Ruth about twenty-two when she married John Bass, and Rebecca about twenty-one when she was the subject of the unfortunate rumor. Given the paucity of solid evidence on many of these points, other plausible arrangements may be easily constructed.

Some accounts of the family of John Alden include a son Zachariah, who had a daughter Anne Alden who married in 1699 Josiah Snell. In 1948 Hallock P. Long demonstrated that this son never existed, and that Anna Alden was almost certainly the daughter of John Alden's son Jonathan [NEHGR 102:82-86; see also MF 16:1:45, 122-23].

Attempts have been made to include Henry Alden of Billerica, Roxbury and Dedham as a descendant of John Alden, but this cannot be. Henry Alden was rated in Billerica in 1688 [NEHGR 31:303], so he must have been born no later than 1667. The wills of John Alden's sons John and Joseph make it clear that neither of them had a son Henry. John

Alden's son Jonathan did not marry until 1672, and his son David apparently even later than that. Henry Alden must have been a late immigrant to New England, with no known genealogical connection with John Alden of Plymouth and Duxbury [MD 42:21ff.].

As noted above, John Alden was frequently a member of the committee on the Kennebec trade. He had actively participated in the trade himself, and in early 1634 he became involved in an incident in which a party of Plymouth men led by himself and John Howland became embroiled with a group of men from the Piscataqua settlement which would grow into Dover. One man on each side was killed, and in the aftermath Alden was detained at Boston as security against the final resolution of the conflict. [For particulars of this incident, see WJ 1:155-56, 162-63; WP 3:167-68; MBCR 1:119; and Bradford 262-68.]

The results of a 1960 season of digging are given by Roland Wells Robbins in *Pilgrim John Alden's Progress: Archaeological Excavations in Duxbury* (Plymouth: The Pilgrim Society 1969).

BIBLIOGRAPHIC NOTE: The Five Generations Project of the General Society of Mayflower Descendants will require five volumes to cover the descendants of John Alden not already covered in other volumes in the series. These five volumes will be designated Volume Sixteen, Parts 1 through 5, the first two of which have appeared, compiled by Esther Littleford Woodworth-Barnes and edited by Alicia Crane Williams. The first volume, published in 1999, covers the first four generations of descent from John Alden. The second volume, published in 2002, was devoted to the fifth generation descendants through Elizabeth (Alden) Pabodie.

In 1998, prior to the publication of the first Alden volume of the Five Generations Project, Alicia Crane Williams prepared a brief overview of the first four generations [MD 48:107-10].

ISAAC ALLERTON

ORIGIN: Leiden, Holland.
MIGRATION: 1620 on the *Mayflower*.
FIRST RESIDENCE: Plymouth.
REMOVES: Marblehead, New Amsterdam, New Haven.
RETURN TRIPS: Frequent trips to England, especially in the 1620s and 1630s, on personal and colony business.

OCCUPATION: Merchant.

CHURCH MEMBERSHIP: "Mr. Alderton" was admitted to Salem church on 21 March 1646/7 [SChR 12]. "Mr. Allerton" and "Sister Allerton" were assigned pews in New Haven meeting house, 10 March 1646/7 [NHCR 1:302, 304]. (The Salem record may refer to a different man, as these two records come so close together, and Allerton had not lived at Marblehead for some time.)

FREEMAN: In 1633 Plymouth list of freemen, immediately after Assistants, and well before those admitted on 1 January 1632/3 [PCR 1:3]. In Plymouth list of 7 March 1636/7 [PCR 1:52].

EDUCATION: Although there is no direct evidence of Isaac Allerton's education, and nothing written in his own hand, he must have been well-educated to engage in business, political and diplomatic activities as extensively as he did. His inventory included, in a list of miscellaneous items, "1 old book."

OFFICES: In early 1621, after the death of John Carver, William Bradford was chosen Governor, and "Isaac Allerton was chosen to be an assistant unto him who, by renewed election every year, continued sundry years together" [Bradford 86]. Chosen Assistant, 1 January 1633/4 [PCR 1:21].

ESTATE: In the 1623 Plymouth land division, "Mr. Isaak Alerton" received seven acres [PCR 12:4; MQ 40:10]. In the 1627 Plymouth cattle division, Mr. Isaac Allerton, his wife Feare Allerton, Bartholomew Allerton, Remember Allerton, Mary Allerton and Sarah Allerton were the first six persons in the second company [PCR 12:9].

Assessed £3 11s. in Plymouth tax list of 25 March 1633 and £1 16s. in list of 27 March 1634 [PCR 1:9, 27].

Assigned mowing ground for year, 1 July 1633 [PCR 1:14].

On 6 May 1635, the Massachusetts Bay General Court noted that "Mr. Ollerton hath given to Moses Maveracke, his son-in-law, all his houses, buildings, & stages, that he hath at Marble Head, to enjoy to him & his heirs forever" [MBCR 1:147].

On 27 October 1646, "Isacke Allerton" of New Amsterdam in the province of New Netherlands, merchant, confirmed to son-in-law Thomas Cushman of New Plymouth a debt of one hundred pounds owed to Isaac by John Coombe [PCR 2:133].

In the New Haven Book of Alienations, in an entry from 1646, "Isaack Allerton" held four parcels of land "bought of Lawr[ence] Ward": "6 acres ½ upland in the first division"; "1 acre ¼ & 8 rods in the neck"; "2 acres ½ of meadow"; and "10 acres in the 2d division" [BA 5].

In his "will," undated and proved 19 October 1659, "Isaac Alerton, late of New Haven, deceased," devoted most of the space to a list of debts owing to him, and then ordered "my son Isaac Allerton and my wife, as trustees to receive in my debts, & to pay what I owe, as far as it will go & what is overplus I leave to my wife and my son Isaac, as far as they receive the debts to pay what I owe" [MD 2:155-56, citing NHPR 1:1:82].

The inventory, taken 12 February 1658/9, totalled £118 5s. 2d., of which £75 was real estate: "the dwelling house, orchard & barn with two acres of meadow," £75 [MD 2:156-57, citing NHPR 1:1:83].

On 4 May 1680, "[w]hereas there was agreements between Mr. Isaac Allerton sometime of New Haven in the Colony of Connecticut now deceased and Will[iam] Holt of the aforesaid New Haven respecting a small quantity of land granted to the lots that butted on the Oystershell Field which proportion of land the said Will[iam] Holt did make and pass over to the said Allerton ... and there having not yet been any written or recorded deed to declare the same now I Johanah the widow and relict of the said Allerton ... and well knowing the agreement with the said Holt and John Holt son of the said William ... do both of them ratify and confirm the said agreement" [NHLR 1:38]. On 19 May 1684, "Elizabeth Eyer, formerly Elizabeth Allerton now wife of Simon Eyre of New Haven ..., having the reversion of a house that my grandmother Mrs. Johanna Allerton now dwells in situate in New Haven aforesaid with the appurtenances thereunto belonging ... when it was in the possession of my deceased grandfather ... together with the house was bought by my father of my grandfather's creditors and given to me by my father Mr. Isaac Allerton to be possessed thereof as my propriety and right given me by my father after the death of my grandmother Mrs. Johanna Allerton which reversion ... I the said Elizabeth Eyre for good consideration me thereunto moving do give, grant and alienate ... unto my dear and loving husband Simon Eyre" [NHLR 1:265].

BIRTH: About 1586 (on 26 September 1639, "Isaacke Allerton of New Plimmouth in New England merchant" deposed that he was "aged about 53 years" [Lechford 189-90; MD 4:109-10]).

DEATH: New Haven between 1 February 1658/9 (court appearance) and 12 February 1658/9 (date of inventory).

MARRIAGE: (1) Leiden 4 November 1611 [NS] Mary Norris "single woman from Newbury in England" [Plooij IX; Leiden Pilgrims 27-28; MD 7:129-30]. She died at Plymouth on 25 February 1620/1 [Prince 289].

(2) Plymouth between 1623 and 1627 Fear Brewster, daughter of WILLIAM BREWSTER [PM 66]. She died not long before 12 December 1634, presumably at Plymouth [MD 30:97-98; WP 3:177].

(3) By 1644 Joanna Swinnerton, probably the "Mrs. Swinnerton" who received a grant of land at New Haven on 17 March 1640/1 [NHCR 1:50; NEHGR 124:133; MD 42:124]. On 17 February 1644/5, "Mr. Allerton coming from New Haven in a ketch, with his wife and diverse other persons, were taken in a great storm at northeast with much snow, and cast away at Scituate, but the persons all saved" [WJ 2:258]. She was living on 19 May 1684 [NHLR 1:265].

CHILDREN:
With first wife
- i BARTHOLOMEW ALLERTON, b. say 1613; he returned to England, became minister at "Bamfield," Suffolk (probably Bramfield); m. (1) Margaret ____; m. (2) Sarah Fairfax, dau. of Benjamin Fairfax; and had at least four children [MD 40:7-10].
- ii REMEMBER ALLERTON, b. say 1615; m. by 6 May 1635 Moses Maverick [MBCR 1:147], son of Rev. JOHN MAVERICK {1630, Dorchester} [GMB 2:1241-43; MD 5:129-41; NEHGR 96:358-61; Small Gen 669-80].
- iii MARY ALLERTON, b. say 1617; m. by about 1636 Thomas Cushman, son of ROBERT CUSHMAN [MD 4:37-42; PM 158]. A late annotation to Bradford's 1651 list indicated that "Mary Cushman the daughter of Mr. Allerton" was still alive in 1690 [Bradford 448]. She d. Plymouth 28 November 1699 [PVR 136; MD 16:63], the last of the *Mayflower* passengers to die.
- iv Child ALLERTON, bur. Pieterskerk, Leiden, 5 February 1620 [NS] [Dexter 601; NEA 3:2:48].
- v Son ALLERTON, stillborn aboard the *Mayflower* 22 December 1620 in Plymouth Harbor [Mourt 41].

With second wife
- vi SARAH ALLERTON, b. about 1626; listed with rest of family in 1627 cattle division [PCR 12:9]; no further record.
- vii ISAAC ALLERTON, b. Plymouth say 1630; Harvard 1650 [Sibley 1:253-56]; m. (1) about 1652 Elizabeth _____ [NEHGR 124:83-84 argues that she was a daughter of Joanna Swinnerton, third wife of Isaac's father]; m. (2) in Virginia about 1663 Elizabeth (Willoughby) (Overzee) Colclough, dau. of Capt. Thomas Willoughby and widow of

Simon Overzee and George Colclough [MF 7:6-7]. (All modern authorities agree that the Isaac Allerton born at New Haven in 1655, son of this Isaac Allerton with his first wife, died without issue, and some other origin must be found for the Allertons who appear in New Haven late in the seventeenth century [MQ 45:23; MD 42:117].)

ASSOCIATIONS: Brother of Sarah Allerton, wife successively of John Vincent, DEGORY PRIEST [PM 382] and GODBERT GODBERTSON [PM 226]. On 2 December 1633, as part of the settlement of the estate of Godbert Godbertson, it was noted that "the greater part of his debts are owing to Mr. Isaack Allerton, of Plym., merchant, late brother of the said Zarah" [PCR 1:20].

COMMENTS: On 12 June 1609, "Isack Allerton son of Bartholomew Allerton of Ipswich in County Suffolk tailor" was apprenticed to James Glyn of the Blacksmiths' Company of London [Blacksmiths' Company, Court Minutes, 1605-1611 (translated from the Latin; reference courtesy of Leslie Mahler)]. This cannot be the Isaac Allerton of this sketch, who would already have been in his mid-twenties at the time of this apprenticeship, and would be married within two years. The juxtaposition of the names Isaac and Bartholomew, however, indicates a close relationship. Bartholomew Allerton of Ipswich, tailor, could have been an elder brother of Isaac of the *Mayflower*.

Some records of Allerton in New Netherland describe him as "of Suffolk." This would support the conclusion that the apprenticeship record given above involves close kin of this immigrant.

In his list of *Mayflower* passengers Bradford included "Mr. Isaac Allerton and Mary his wife, with three children, Bartholomew, Remember and Mary. And a servant boy John Hooke" [Bradford 441]. In his 1651 accounting of these families, he reported that "Mr. Allerton his wife died with the first, and his servant John Hooke. His son Bartle is married in England but I know not how many children he hath. His daughter Remember is married at Salem and hath three or four children living. And his daughter Mary is married here and hath four children. Himself married again with the daughter of Mr. Brewster and hath one son living by her, but she is long since dead. And he is married again and hath left this place long ago. So I account his increase to be eight, besides his son's in England" [Bradford 444-45].

Isaac Allerton was one of the busiest and most complicated men in early New England, and no attempt is made here to cover his career comprehensively. A full-scale biography would be needed for that, and an outline of what is available is given in the next section below. Records for Allerton may be found in virtually every colony on the Atlantic seaboard and in the Caribbean, including Newfoundland, New Netherland, New Sweden, Virginia, Barbados, and Curaçao.

In noting his various residences above, we do not estimate years of removal, as he seems to have maintained residences simultaneously at more than one location. Also, the attempt made above to describe the estate of Allerton does not come close to showing the magnitude and intricacy of his business activities. No one has yet tried to survey comprehensively this, the major part of Allerton's life.

Since Moses Maverick, the husband of Remember Allerton, received Isaac Allerton's estate at Marblehead, and Isaac Jr. received his father's estate at New Haven, it is likely that Thomas and Mary (Allerton) Cushman were at some time given Allerton's property at Plymouth (assuming that there was more at Plymouth than the debt assigned by Allerton to Cushman in 1646 [PCR 2:133]).

BIBLIOGRAPHIC NOTE: The descendants of Isaac Allerton were treated extensively by Walter S. Allerton about a century ago, but this account is now obsolete [*A History of the Allerton Family in the United States, 1585 to 1885* ... (New York 1888, rev. 1900)].

More recently Lora Underhill published an extremely detailed account of Isaac Allerton and his children [Small Gen 756-851]. Although this version of the life of Isaac Allerton has been shown to have errors, and although many new discoveries have been made, it has great value because it attempts to cite every record in which Allerton ever appeared (as available in 1934), and prints many of the records in full.

Much of the modern research on Allerton has been carried out by Newman Hall, presented in a series of periodical articles [NEHGR 124:133; MQ 45:23-24, 47:14-18; *Virginia Genealogist* 32:83-92, 171-78, 287-96; MD 40:7-10]. More recently Robert S. Wakefield has prepared the Mayflower Five Generations Project volume on Isaac Allerton, as Volume 17 of the series [*Mayflower Families Through Five Generations ... Family of Isaac Allerton* (Plymouth 1998)].

For a different interpretation of the character of Isaac Allerton, see Michael McGiffert, "Religion and Profit Do Jump Together: The First American Pilgrim," *Reflections* 87:15-23 (a publication of Yale Divinity School).

JOHN ALLERTON

John Allerton was a seaman on the *Mayflower*, and upon arrival in Plymouth was "reputed as one of the company but was to go back (being a seaman) for the help of others left behind," but he "died here before the ship returned," in the general sickness (i.e., before 5 April 1621) [Bradford 443, 447]. John Allerton signed the Mayflower Compact on 11 November 1620.

COMMENTS: "Jan Alaerton" had a child buried at the Pieterskerk at Leiden on 21 May 1616 [NS] [NEA 3:2:48]. He was probably the *Mayflower* passenger and probably brother of ISAAC ALLERTON..

ANTHONY ANNABLE

ORIGIN: Cambridge, Cambridgeshire.
MIGRATION: 1623 on the *Anne*.
FIRST RESIDENCE: Plymouth.
REMOVES: Scituate 1633, Barnstable 1639.

OCCUPATION: Planter [PCR 12:82-83, 85].
CHURCH MEMBERSHIP: "Goodman Anniball and his wife" were #4 and #5 among the founding members of the Scituate church on 8 January 1634/5 [NEHGR 9:279]; they may well have been members of the Plymouth church earlier. They stayed with Lothrop and his church when it moved to Barnstable.
FREEMAN: In 1633 Plymouth list of freemen, before those admitted 1 January 1632/3 [PCR 1:3] and in list of 7 March 1636/7 [PCR 1:52]. In Scituate section of list of 1639, then erased from that section and entered in Barnstable section [PCR 8:175, 177]. In Barnstable sections of lists of 1658 and 29 May 1670 [PCR 5:277, 8:200].
EDUCATION: No direct evidence of education or literacy, but his inclusion on the 1636 and 1645 committees to reform the laws, given the nature of the task and the known educational level of the other members of the committees, speaks of a well-educated man. His inventory included "books" valued at 15s. [PCPR 3:1:102].
OFFICES: Deputy for Scituate to Plymouth General Court, 4 June 1639 [PCR 1:126]. Deputy for Barnstable to Plymouth General Court, 2 June 1640, 1 June 1641, 7 June 1642, 27 September 1642, 6 June 1643, 10 October 1643, 5 March 1643/4, 5 June 1644, 20 August 1644, 28

October 1645, 1 June 1647, 4 June 1650, 5 June 1651, 7 June 1653, 3 June 1656, 3 June 1657 [PCR 1:155, 2:16, 40, 46, 57, 63, 68, 72, 75, 94, 117, 154, 168, 3:32, 99, 115].

Plymouth petit jury 4-5 October 1636, 6 March 1637/8, 2 March 1640/1, 1 March 1641/2 [PCR 1:44, 7:8, 19, 29]. Coroner's jury 15 March 1657/8, 22 October 1668 [PCR 3:147, 5:7].

Plymouth Colony committee on "the trade," 1 October 1634 [PCR 1:31]. Committee to reform colony laws, 4-5 October 1636, 4 June 1645 [PCR 1:44, 2:85]. Committee for the defense of Barnstable, 10 October 1643 [PCR 2:65]. Committee on taxes, 2 June 1646 [PCR 2:101].

Constable for "ward of Scituate," 1 January 1633/4 and continued in same position 1 January 1634/5 [PCR 1:21, 32].

In Barnstable section of the 1643 Plymouth Colony list of men able to bear arms [PCR 8:193]. His inventory included "1 gun and sword" valued at 20s. and "powder and lead" valued at 4s. [PCPR 3:1:102].

ESTATE: In the 1623 Plymouth land division, "Anthony Anable" was granted four acres "on the other side of the town towards Eel River" [PCR 12:6]. In the 1627 division of cattle the eighth company included Anthony, Jane, Sara and Hannah Anable [PCR 12:11-12].

On 9 June 1630, Anthony Anable sold to Daniel Ray his dwelling house, garden plot, fence and "and all the privileges thereunto belonging" [PCR 12:17-18].

Assessed 18s. on the tax lsit of 25 March 1633 and 9s. on the list of 27 March 1634 [PCR 1:10, 27].

Granted five parcels of land beginning on 12 April 1633: eight acres of marsh; "sixth lot ... four acres"; twenty-two acres of upland; a portion of marsh; and eighty acres of upland [ScitTR 1:231-32]. By the end of September 1634 Anthony Annable had built a "small plain pallizadoe" house [NEHGR 10:42]. On 29 September 1639, Anthony Annable of Barnstable, planter, sold to Thomas Rawlins of Scituate "my dwelling house and out house and all my lands thereunto appertaining, viz:" twenty-two acres ..., nine acres of marsh ..., eighty acres of upland ... and thirteen acres of marsh [PCR 12:82-83, 85; ScitTR 1:252].

Anthony Annible was one of the Purchasers or Old Comers [PCR 2:177]. On 5 March 1660/1, he had permission to purchase at Saconeesett [PCR 3:216], and, on 1 June 1669, he was granted "competent accommodation of land" at Teticut [PCR 5:20, 24].

In his will, dated 24 February 1672 and probated 4 June 1674, Anthony Annible bequeathed to wife Ann Annible dwelling house and all lands "which lyeth between that land which I have formerly given to my son, Samuel Annible, and Goodman Blush's land," along with half the meadow and half the Great Meadow, for life, and all moveables to be at wife's disposal; to daughter Desire Annible household stuff left at wife's decease; to each of my daughters 12d. In a codicil of 23 April 1674, he gave his remaining lands to son Samuel Annible at his wife's decease, Samuel to pay £30 to [Anthony's] daughter Desire Annible [PCPR 3:1:102; MD 25:90-91].

His inventory, presented 18 June 1674, totalled £100 9s. 6d., with no real estate included [PCPR 3:1:101-2; MD 25:91].

BIRTH: About 1594 (based on date of marriage).
DEATH: Between 23 April 1674 (codicil to will) and 4 June 1674 (probate of will).
MARRIAGE: (1) All Saints, Cambridge, Cambridgeshire, 26 April 1619 Jane Moumford [NEHGR 65:380]. "Sister Anniball [was] buried the 13th day of the tenth month [December] 1643 in the Calves pasture" at Barnstable [NEHGR 9:285].

(2) Barnstable 3 March 1644 or 1 March 1645 Ann Elcock or Clark [MD 2:212; PCR 2:80, 8:41; see also Otis 17-18]. In his will of 25 June 1672, Thomas Shaw of Barnstable bequeathed to "Ann Annible, the wife of Anthony Annible" (without stating any relation to himself), his bed and all his bedding [PCPR 3:1:42; NEHGR 7:236]. On 30 October 1677, "Anne Annible of Barnstable, widow," was fined 20s. "for selling of beer to English and Indians without license" [PCR 5:246]. She was still living as late as 30 October 1678, when she was named in the settlement of the estate of her son Samuel Annable [PCR 5:272].
CHILDREN:
  With first wife
    i   SARAH ANNABLE, b. say 1620; m. "Greens-harbour" [Marshfield] 22 or 23 November 1638 HENRY EWELL {1634, Scituate} [PCR 1:108; NEHGR 9:286; GM 2:2:476].
    ii   HANNAH ANNABLE, b. Plymouth 1623 (so stated because she was presumably one of those accounted for in the grant of four acres to her father in 1623, and in a 3 June 1662 list of those eligible for a grant of land "as being the first born children of this government" is "Anthony Anible for his daughter, Hannah Burman" [PCR 4:19]); m. 10 March 1645[/6] Thomas Bourman [MD 3:51 (other dates recorded are 3 March 1644 and 1 March 1645 [PCR 2:80, 8:41], to be compared against the dates of marriage of her father to his second wife)]. Anthony Annible was appointed adminstrator on the estate of Thomas Burman, 1 June 1663 [PCR 4:41].

iii SUSANNA ANNABLE, b. about 1630; "Will[iam] Hatch married to Susanna Anniball daughter of Anth[ony] Anniball" at Scituate 13 May 1652 [MD 2:33], son of THOMAS HATCH {1638, Scituate} [Joseph Neal Anc 115].
iv Daughter ANNABLE, "Brother Anniball buried a maid child being born somewhat before the time" Scituate 8 April 1635 [NEHGR 9:284].
v DEBORAH ANNABLE, bp. Scituate 7 May 1637 [NEHGR 9:281]; no further record.

With second wife

vi SAMUEL ANNABLE, b. Barnstable "about 22 of January 1646 [i.e, 1645/6]" [MD 2:212], bp. Barnstable 8 February 1645/6 [NEHGR 9:283]; m. Barnstable 1 June 1667 Mehitable Allyn [MD 2:213].
vii ESEK ANNABLE, bp. Barnstable 29 April 1649 [NEHGR 9:284]; no further record.
viii DESIRE ANNABLE, b. Barnstable "about beginning of October 1653" [MD 2:212], bp. Barnstable 16 October 1653 [NEHGR 9:284]; m. Barnstable 18 January 1676[/7] John Barker [MD 3:52].

COMMENTS: In a set of Plymouth Colony vital records published in 1855 are records that indicate that Anthony Annable's second wife died in 1651, that Annable married a third time, and that this third wife also soon died [NEHGR 9:315, 317]. Since Annable names a wife Ann in his 1672 will, a fourth wife is implied. Savage apparently based his treatment of the Annable family on these records, but Otis noted that events occurring in the family of Abraham Blish (or Blush) had been applied to Anthony Annable, that Annable had only two wives, and that Savage would be correcting his account, which he did in his fourth volume [Savage 1:59, 4:674; Otis 18]. The problem arose because the records published in 1855 had been rearranged and do not correspond to the originals.

In his marriage index, Torrey identified the wife of Alexander Kennedy/Canedy as Elizabeth Annable. This does not derive from any of the sources cited by Torrey and is apparently a suggestion based on the fact that this couple named a child Annable in 1698 [MD 1:209]. The chronology, however, makes such an identification unlikely.

BIBLIOGRAPHIC NOTE: The most recent treatment of this immigrant and his descendants, *The Anable Family in America: 1623-1967*, authored by Anthony Anable and published in 1967, is inadequately documented and makes unsubstantiated claims about the English origin of the immigrant.

EDWARD ASHLEY

Edward Ashley, according to his own deposition of 11 February 1631/2, first came to New England in the spring of 1628 and stayed for sixteen months, returning to England about August of 1629 [Ford 2:108-9]. It would be during this stay that Ashley, in Bradford's words, "lived among the Indians as a savage and went naked amongst them and used their manners, in which time he got their language" [Bradford 219].

While in England Ashley arranged for the Muscongus Patent, for land around Penobscot Bay, which was issued by the Council for New England in the names of John Beauchamp and Thomas Leverett [Bradford 386]. Ashley then returned to New England in the spring of 1630 on the *Lyon* and set up a trading post near Castine. This enterprise was established in conjunction with the financiers who had also underwritten Plymouth Colony, as can be seen by the involvement of Beauchamp, and in letters to Bradford from Sherley [Bradford 386-90].

As usual, the ideas of the London merchants for economic endeavors involving the Plymouth settlers did not work out to the advantage of the latter. In addition, Ashley began to trade extensively with the natives in weapons and ammunition, at that time proscribed by England. Ashley was arrested by Walter Neal in May of 1631 and was sent back to England later that year [Ford 2:108-9].

COMMENTS: The principal sources for the story of Edward Ashley are Bradford's history, the depositions of various people associated with Ashley (given after he was arrested in 1631) and Ashley's own deposition a few months later [Bradford 219-22, 226, 232-33, 237-38, 243-44, 386-90; MHSP 45:493-98; Ford 2:108]. Bradford tells us that Ashley was offered a chance "to go into Russia because he had such good skill in the beaver trade; the which he accepted of and in his return home was cast away at sea. This was his end" [Bradford 233]. Among modern historians, Spencer tells the story well and in greater detail [pp. 367-72 *et passim*]. Savage places Ashley's second landing at Penobscot in June of 1630, arguing that the *Lyon* sailed directly to Salem, where it arrived in late May, and then went back downeast to drop off Ashley and his goods [WJ 1:34].

B

WILLIAM BAKER

16 February 1632/3: "Richard Church hired William Baker from the first of March to the last of September to do him service for & in consideration of fourteen bushels of corn & 12s. of money. Also the said Richard to give him one month's diet after the expiration of the said term, & to provide a sufficient mate to saw with the said William, & the said Richard to give him the squaring & help for pitting of so much timber as the said William can saw in the month aforesaid; the board being sawn to be equally divided between the said Richard & the said William. This they both acknowledged before the Governor" [PCR 1:8].

About 26 October 1637, Roger Williams to John Winthrop: "Sir I heard that there is now at Pequat with the Monhiganeucks one William (Baker I think his name is) who was pursued, as is said, by the English of Qunnihticut for uncleanness with an Indian squaw, who is now with child by him. He hath gotten another Squaw and lies close unknown to the English. They say he came from a trading house which Plymmouth men have at Qunnihticut, and can speak much Indian. If it be he, when I lived at Plymmouth, I heard the Plymmouth men speak much of his evil course that way with the Natives" [WP 3:500-1; RWCorr 126, 128n].

In letters of 10 January 1637/8, 28 February 1637/8, 22 May 1638 and 27 May 1638, interspersed with other matter, Williams continued to report to Winthrop on the escapades of William Baker (no longer uncertain of his name), noting that he had been captured by Connecticut authorities, escaped, captured again and whipped twice at Hartford [WP 4:7, 15, 31, 35; RWCorr 140, 145, 155, 158; surviving Connecticut Colony records do not mention this William Baker]. No more is heard of him.

COMMENTS: The several early William Bakers are very much tangled up in the secondary sources. Without always addressing each assumption made by Savage, Pope and others, we will attempt here to sort them out, and show that there were at least five in the earliest decades.

The earliest record we have is that above for William in Plymouth Colony on 16 February 1632/3. The various reports of Roger Williams make it quite clear that this is the same man who lived as an Indian, and presumably left New England by the middle of 1638, or at least the Europeanized portion thereof.

There is then a Plymouth Colony record of 5 November 1638 in which "William Baker, of Water Towne, is licensed to come to dwell within this government, provided he bring good testimony of his good conversation" [PCR 1:102]. Some secondary sources have suggested that this man is identical with the escapee to the wilderness, but there are a number of reasons this cannot be so. First, the Plymouth authorities would not welcome back the William who had been with them earlier, given his behavior in the immediate aftermath of the Pequot War; the proviso of this 1638 record for bringing "good testimony" was a standard requirement and not indicative of recent wrongdoing. Second, this William of 1638 is specifically stated to be from Watertown, and there is a William Baker attested there in land grants on 25 July 1636, 28 February 1636/7, 26 June 1637 and 9 April 1638 [WaBOP 5, 8, 9, 11]; in one of these grants he is called Nathaniel and in another John, but these grants are all for one man, and at least three of the parcels came into the hands of Joseph Bemis [WaBOP 58, 140]. This William Baker was the holder therefore of a proprietary share at Watertown and may well have been there a year or two before 1636. His grants in the Beaverbrook Plowlands and Remote Meadows were for five acres, indicating a family as large as five persons. This William Baker is very likely the man involved in the land transaction with John Barnes in 1640 and on the list of men able to bear arms in 1643, but he has not been traced further [PCR 2:13, 8:188].

Another WILLIAM BAKER first appeared in Charlestown in 1633, and was continuously of record there through the 1640s, and then moved to Billerica not long before his death [GMB 1:80-83]. Some have claimed that this was the Watertown man as well, but this is impossible. The Watertown William Baker, as we have just seen, moved on to Plymouth, and in no case would a man have been allowed to draw a full complement of proprietary grants simultaneously in Charlestown and Watertown.

There was in addition a William Baker in Portsmouth, Rhode Island, in the 1638 list of freemen and thereafter [RICR 1:59, 91, 92]. He also would not be the troublemaker of 1637 and 1638, and likewise could not be identical with the men of Charlestown and Watertown who are well attested elsewhere in 1638.

Finally, there is a William Baker who was admitted an inhabitant in Boston in 1651 [BTR 1:105], and married twice, his second wife being Pilgrim Eddy, daughter of JOHN EDDY of Watertown [PM 189]. Attempts have been made to link him to either or both of the William Bakers known to have been in Plymouth, but this would seem to be a man a generation younger than the other four men. Note, however, that the William Baker of Watertown and then Plymouth apparently had a family, and this William Baker of Boston in the 1650s did take for his second wife a Watertown woman.

Summarizing, we have

> William Baker in Plymouth as early as 1632, then to the Plymouth trading post on the Connecticut, in hiding with the remnants of the Pequots in 1637 and 1638, and not heard of again. He had at least one consort and one child among the Indians.
>
> William Baker of Charlestown in 1633, then to Billerica. His wife was named Joan.
>
> William Baker of Watertown from 1636 (or perhaps earlier) to 1638, then to Plymouth from 1638 to 1643, and perhaps beyond. He probably had a wife and children, but no names are known.
>
> William Baker of Portsmouth 1638 and after. His wife was named Mary.
>
> William Baker of Boston in 1651 and later. He had first wife Mary Eddington and second wife Pilgrim Eddy.

EDWARD BANGS

ORIGIN: Unknown (but see *COMMENTS*).
MIGRATION: 1623 on the *Anne* [PCR 12:6].
FIRST RESIDENCE: Plymouth.
REMOVES: Eastham by 1645.

OCCUPATION: Innkeeper ("Liberty is granted unto Edward Bangs to draw and sell wine and strong waters at Eastham, provided it be for the refreshment of the English, and not to be sold to the Indians," 6 October 1657 [PCR 3:123]; an account of liquor brought into Eastham dated 28 November 1664 included "Edward Bangs, six gallons of liquor" [PCR 4:100]).

FREEMAN: In 1633 Plymouth list of freemen in proximity to those admitted on 1 January 1632/3 [PCR 1:4]. In list of 7 March 1636/7 [PCR 1:52]. In Plymouth section of list of 1639, annotated as gone and added to list for Eastham [PCR 8:174, 177]. In Eastham portion of lists of 1658 and 29 May 1670 [PCR 5:278, 8:201].

EDUCATION: Signed his will and several deeds.

OFFICES: Deputy to Plymouth Court for Eastham, 7 June 1652 [PCR 3:9]. Committee to lay out land, 3 January 1627/8, 1 February 1640/1 [PCR 12:14, 2:7]. Committee to divide meadow, 1 July 1633 [PCR 1:14]. Committee to assess taxes, 5 January 1634/5, 1 March 1635/6 [PCR 1:33, 38]. Plymouth representative to committee to reunite Plymouth and Duxbury (but he did not serve), 14 March 1635/6 [PCR 1:41]. Committee to allocate hay ground, 20 March 1636/7, 2 October 1637, 1 June 1640 [PCR 1:55, 67, 153]. Committee to lay out highway, 1 February 1640/1, 24 February 1652 [PCR 2:7, 3:61].

Plymouth grand jury, 7 March 1636/7, 5 June 1638, 2 June 1640, 1 March 1641/2, 7 June 1652 [PCR 1:54, 87, 155, 2:34, 3:9]. Petit jury, 4 October 1636, 3 January 1636/7, 3 September 1639, 3 December 1639, 3 March 1639/40, 3 August 1641, 6 September 1641, 7 December 1641, 1 March 1641/2, 6 June 1643, 7 November 1643 [PCR 1:44, 7:4, 13, 14, 16, 22, 23, 25, 28, 35, 36]. Coroner's jury, 30 October 1667 [PCR 4:169].

Eastham highway surveyor, 1 June 1647, 4 June 1650, 3 June 1651 [PCR 2:115, 155, 168]. Treasurer, 1646-1665 [Bangs Gen 11].

In Plymouth section of 1643 list of men able to bear arms [PCR 8:189].

ESTATE: In the 1623 Plymouth division of land "Bangs" [no first name] received four acres as a passenger on the *Anne* in 1623 [PCR 12:6]. In the 1627 Plymouth division of cattle "Edward Banges" was the thirteenth person in the twelfth company [PCR 12:1].

In the Plymouth tax lists of 25 March 1633 and 27 March 1634 Edward Bangs was assessed 12s. [PCR 1:10, 27]. He was included in the undated list of Purchasers [PCR 2:177].

On 20 March 1636/7, "John Banges" was assigned hay ground at Saggaquash (jointly with Edward Doty) [PCR 1:56, presumably a simple scribal error]. On 2 November 1640, he was granted ten acres of meadow in the South Meadows [PCR 1:166]. On 7 September 1641, "Edward Banges is granted a parcel of fourscore acres of upland about Warren's Wells" [PCR 2:25]. On 17 October 1642, "[w]hereas fourscore acres of upland are formerly granted to Edward Banges at Warren's Wells, he now desiring to have some land near his house, it is granted that he shall look out a parcel of land, which upon view shall be laid forth for him, and to be deducted out of the 80 acres he should have at Warren's Wells" [PCR 2:48].

On 7 September 1643, Joyce Wallen, widow, sold to Edward Bangs of Plymouth "all that her house and messuage situate and being at Hobs Hole or Wellingsly with the garden place and uplands thereunto adjoining" [PCR 12:95]. On 22 June 1651, Edward Bangs of Eastham sold to Samuel Hicks of Plymouth "a parcel of marsh meadow lying at the high pines on the Salthouse Beach" [PCR 12:208-9]. On 22 June 1651, "Edward Banges of the town of Nawsett *alias* Eastham ..., yeoman," sold to "Mannasses Kemton" of Plymouth, yeoman, forty acres of upland in Plymouth near Browne's Rock, as well as "all the meadow or marsh that is on the island or spot of land commonly called and known by the name of Sagaquas"; "Rebeckah the wife of the said Edward Banges" consented to this deed [PCR 12:209].

On 12 November 1666, "Edward Banges and Daniel Cole Senior of Eastham, yeomen," sold to James Mathews of Yarmouth, yeoman, "all the purchase lands that belonged unto and were the lands of Edward Banges and Daniell Cole ... between the two brooks commonly called Bound Brook and Stony Brook ... in Yarmouth" [PCLR 3:91-92].

On 23 February 1676, Edward Bangs of Eastham for "my tender love and fatherly love unto my natural son Joshua Bangs" deeded him "all that my messuage, dwelling house and housing and lands, both upland and meadowing, lying and being in the township of Eastham," viz: five acres of upland "granted to me by the town for a houselot," with the dwelling house on it; four acres granted to Daniel Cole Sr. for a houselot; three acres granted to George Crispe for a houselot; four acres and half granted to John Jenkins for a houselot; two acres granted to Job Cole; fourteen acres granted to Ralph Smith; three acres "of meadow granted me by the town"; four acres of meadow at Great Blackfish River; one acre of meadow granted to John Jenkins; all of which parcels "appear more at length in the town book of records" [PCLR 4:134-36].

In his will, dated 19 October 1677 and proved 5 March 1677/8, "Edward Banges, aged 86 years," made son Jonathan sole executor and bequeathed to him "all my purchased land at Namskekett," two acres and a half of meadow, "all my purchase land at Pocomett[?]," an acre and a half of meadow "at a place called the acars," one acre at the harbor's mouth, "a parcel of upland and meadow lying at Rock harbour which I had in exchange of John Done," and "all those things which I have at his house"; to son John "that twenty acres of upland at Pochett that he hath built upon," five acres adjoining to the twenty acres, "that land which I have at Pochett Island," two acres of meadow at Boat Meadow, and three-quarters of an acre at the head of Boat Meadow; to son Joshua "the house that I lived in and all the housing belonging to it," twenty-eight acres of land adjoining, three acres of meadow at Boat Meadow, one acre of meadow at Boat Meadow, four acres of meadow at the head of Blackfish Creek, and fourteen acres of upland at Pochett; to son Jonathan's eldest son Edward Bangs twenty-five acres of upland at Pochett Field, one acre of meadow at Rock Harbor, and "half an acre of meadow lying at Great Namsceket which I bought of Daniell Cole"; to "my daughter Howes, my daughter Higgens, my daughter Done, my daughter Hall, my daughter Merricke, and my daughter Attwood, four pounds apiece at my decease, and I give to my grandchildren, viz: the children of my daughter Rebecka deceased four pounds at my decease" [PCPR 3:2:106].

BIRTH: About 1591 (based on his stated age of eighty-six on 19 October 1677 [PCPR 3:2:106], although this may be exaggerated).
DEATH: Eastham between 19 October 1677 (date of will) and 5 March 1677/8 (date of probate).
MARRIAGE: (1) By about 1633 Lydia Hicks, baptized St. Mary Magdalen, Bermondsey, Surrey, 6 September 1612, daughter of ROBERT HICKS [TAG 51:58; PM 243]. She apparently died within a year or two.

(2) By about 1635 Rebecca ____. She gave birth to twins on 15 October 1651 [PCR 8:15].
CHILDREN:
   With first wife
    i JOHN BANGS, b. say 1634; m. Eastham 23 January 1660[/1] Hannah Smalley [PCR 8:28; MD 7:17], daughter of JOHN SMALLEY [PM 422]. (If his deed to George Partridge, recorded in 1657, is correctly dated 21 June 1652, then he was probably born as early as 1631, which would also push back the date on which his father married Lydia Hicks [MD 12:83-84].)
   With second wife
    ii REBECCA BANGS, b. say 1636; m. Eastham 26 October 1654 Jonathan Sparrow [PCR 8:15], daughter of RICHARD SPARROW [PM 443].
    iii SARAH BANGS, b. say 1638; m. about 1657 Thomas Howes, son of THOMAS HOWES {1638, Yarmouth} [MD 6:233].

iv   JONATHAN BANGS, b. say 1640; m. (1) Eastham 16 July 1664 Mary Mayo [PCR 8:56]; m. (2) by 1719 Sarah _____; m. (3) Eastham (int.) 23 July 1720 "Mrs. Ruth Young" [MD 28:111] (daughter of Daniel Cole and widow of John Young).

v   LYDIA BANGS, b. say 1642; m. Eastham 24 December 1661 Benjamin Higgins [MD 8:12], son of RICHARD HIGGINS [PM 249].

vi   HANNAH BANGS, b. say 1644; m. Eastham 30 April 1662 John Doane [MD 8:89], son of JOHN DOANE [PM 171].

vii   JOSHUA BANGS, b. say 1646; m. Eastham 1 December 1669 Hannah Scudder [PCR 8:58], daughter of John Scudder [TAG 72:297].

viii   BETHIA BANGS, b. Eastham 28 May 1650 [PCR 8:15]; m. by 1669 Gershom Hall [Bangs Gen 27-28, reproducing original Barnstable deed of 1 April 1729 in which Samuel Hall, Jonathan Hall and Mary Chess sell land in Eastham "that descended to us by the right & title of our honorable deceased mother Bethiah Hall wife of our honored father Gershom Hall which said right descended to her our said deceased mother from her honored father Edward Bangs deceased our honored grandfather"], son of JOHN HALL {1630, Boston} [GMB 2:840-44].

ix   MERCY BANGS (twin), b. Eastham 15 October 1651 [PCR 8:15]; m. Eastham 28 December 1670 Steven Merrick [PCR 8:57].

x   APPHIA BANGS (twin), b. Eastham 15 October 1651 [PCR 8:15]; m. (1) Eastham 28 December 1670 John Knowles [PCR 8:57; NEHGR 79:293-95]; m. (2) by 6 March 1677 Stephen Wood Jr. [PCR 5:220].

COMMENTS: Mary Walton Ferris argued that the immigrant to Plymouth was the Edward Bangs baptized at Panfield, Essex, on 28 October 1591, but she does not present all the evidence, and the evidence that is printed is not sufficient to prove the origin [Dawes-Gates 2:61].

How many wives did Edward Bangs have, and when? Since he was granted four acres in the 1623 land division, some have proposed that he brought with him a wife and at least one child, and that they must have died by 1627, when they do not appear in the 1627 cattle division. However, this is not the only possible interpretation of this record: the other three persons with Edward Bangs may have been servants, or the record itself may be erroneous. Thus, pending discoveries in English records, no wife prior to Lydia Hicks is assumed here. (Although, if Edward's claimed age is close to correct, he certainly would have been old enough to have a family in 1623.)

Both ROBERT HICKS and his wife Margaret name in their wills grandson John Bangs. John, the son of Edward Bangs, married in 1660, which would be consistent with a birthdate about 1635, thus making him the eldest child of Edward. On 1 May 1660, "George Watson requested the Court in the behalf of his son, John Watson, and his nephew, John Banges," that the records be altered to reflect Robert Hicks as purchaser at Dartmouth, rather than Samuel Hicks [PCR 3:186]; George Watson had married a daughter of Robert Hicks, which explains the relationship to John Bangs.

In a deed of 22 June 1651, Edward Bangs is joined by his wife Rebecca in selling land in Plymouth. Thus, she was certainly mother of the twins born later in 1651 and almost certainly mother of all other children except John Bangs. Citing a supposed entry in the Hobart diary, Mary Walton Ferris suggested that Rebecca was daughter of Edmund Hobart of Hingham [Dawes-Gates 2:66], but this entry may not have existed, and the identity of Rebecca (_____) Bangs remains unknown [NEHGR 121:4, 56].

On 8 November 1638, "Edward Banges, of [Plymouth], yeoman," posted bond of £20 as surety for John Smith of Plymouth, laborer [PCR 1:103]. On 5 March 1643/4, he was surety for John Smith of Eel River [PCR 2:69].

BIBLIOGRAPHIC NOTE: The basic genealogy for this family is Dean Dudley's *History and Genealogy of The Bangs Family in America, with Genealogical Tables and Notes* (Montrose MA 1896, cited above as Bangs Gen). This volume is basically sound, with complete transcripts of many important documents, including some Barnstable deeds that are probably not otherwise accessible. But there are also the usual idiosyncrasies typical of this author. As an example we are told that "The court at Plymouth granted to Edward Bangs eighty acres of land on condition that he contribute one-sixteenth part toward building a barque of 40 or 50 tons. He is said to have superintended the building of the vessel, being a shipwright by trade" [p. 10]. The Plymouth records state merely that on 23 January 1641/2 Edward Bangs contributed one-sixteenth of the cost of building the bark, and say nothing about any award of land in connection with this contribution [PCR 2:31]. The grant of land was made at court on 7 September 1641, five months before the contribution [PCR 2:25]. Beyond this, there is no evidence that he had anything to do with building the bark, or that he was a shipwright. As noted above, he was at times an innkeeper, and was otherwise called yeoman.

Half a century later Mary Walton Ferris did her usual thorough job on Edward Bangs [Dawes-Gates 2:61-68].

ROBERT BARKER

ORIGIN: Unknown.
MIGRATION: 1632 [PCR 1:7].
FIRST RESIDENCE: Plymouth.
REMOVES: Marshfield by 1643, Duxbury by 1653.

OCCUPATION: Ferryman (co-partner in purchase of ferry, 12 January 1641 [PCR 12:77]; on 28 October 1645, "Rob[er]te Barker of the North River, made it appear to the Court that there was due unto him for carrying prisoners and passengers over the North River, which the country promised to pay him iiijs. ijd." [PCR 2:89]; sold his share in ferry, 20 January 1645[/6?]).

Innkeeper (licensed on 7 July 1646 "to keep an ordinary at Marshfield, and to draw wine" [PCR 2:105]; on 5 June 1666, "whereas there is a great neglect in both Will[i]am Barstow and Robert Barker in not keeping of an ordinary fit for the entertaining of strangers, the Court have ordered, that William Barstow shall make competent provision for strangers for their entertainment and refreshment this year, and that the other be required to forbear" [PCR 4:129]).

FREEMAN: Propounded for freeman of Plymouth 7 June 1653 (where he is listed between William Clarke and Stephen Bryant, both of Duxbury at the time), and admitted 6 June 1654 [PCR 3:31, 48]. In Duxbury section of Plymouth lists of freemen of 1658, 29 May 1670 and 1 [blank] 1683/4 [PCR 5:275, 12:198, 204].

EDUCATION: He signed his will and all deeds with a distinctive mark. His inventory included "a Bible and Psalm Book and spectacles" valued at 17s.

OFFICES: Plymouth grand jury, 1 June 1669, 2 June 1685 [PCR 5:18, 6:165]. Petit jury, 3 June 1668 [PCR 4:187]. Coroner's jury, 14 December 1652 [PCR 3:28].

Marshfield surveyor of highways, 4 June 1645, 7 June 1648 [PCR 2:84, 124]. Constable, 2 June 1646 [PCR 2:102].

Duxbury surveyor of highways, 6 June 1654, 8 June 1655, 5 June 1672, 5 June 1677, 3 June 1679 [PCR 3:49, 82, 5:93, 232, 6:11].

In Marshfield section of 1643 Plymouth Colony list of men able to bear arms [PCR 8:196].

ESTATE: On 12 January 1641, Jonathan Brewster sold to Robert Barker, John Barker, Thomas Howell and Ralph Chapman "his farm lying at the North River containing one hundred acres of upland with the meadow belonging unto it ... and also the ferry and ferryboats with all the things thereunto belonging" [PCR 12:77]. On 20 January 1645, whereas "Robert Barker is bound to attend and maintain the ferry at New Harbor in Marshfield the aforesaid Ralph Chapman doth take upon him and bind himself ... to attend this ferry and wholly to discharge Rob[er]te Barker and all men else of it, and in consideration hereof the aforesaid Rob[er]te Barker doth freely give him a horseboat and a skiff and the ferry house and barn and two acres of planting ground adjoining to the house," with certain conditions appended [PLR 12:126-27].

On 22 June 1648, Robert Barker gave to "my brother John Barker & his heirs forever the one half of my three acres of marsh that lyeth in the marsh between his upland & the South River which said acre & half is in consideration of part of the meadow my brother lost by the agreement with John Phillips which said agreement beareth date the nineteenth day of June 1648"; this deed was acknowledged by Robert Barker on 6 August 1686 [PLR 1:1].

On 2 August 1653, "Robert Barker desired some course might be taken for the laying out of the meadow allowed him at Namassakeesett, and was referred unto those that were first deputed by the Court to do it" [PCR 3:39].

On 19 March 1663, "Robert Barker and Luce Barker wife to the said Robert Barker of Duxborough" sold to John Magoone of Hingham "fourscore acres of upland more or less with six acres & quarter of meadow adjoining to said land which said parcels of upland & meadows were formerly granted & given by the town of Scituate to Henry Merrick inhabitant of the same town"; Luce Barker did not sign or acknowledge this deed [PCLR 5:412].

On 5 March 1666/7, in "reference unto the desire of Robert Barker, that a parcel of meadow might be recorded unto him lying at the North River at Robinson's Creek, and that he hath produced several evidences to satisfy the Court about it, the Court have ordered, that if the town of Duxburrow, or any of that town, do not produce anything to the contrary betwixt this Court and the shutting up of June Court next, that then he, upon such evidence as he shall then produce, may have the said meadow recorded unto him" [PCR 4:141]. On 5 March 1667/8, Plymouth Court noted that the town of Duxbury had not come forward with any evidence against Robert Barker, and so confirmed to him "the said parcel of meadow, being nine acres and an half" [PCR 4:174].

On 31 January 1688/9, Robert Barker Sr. of Duxbury granted to Robert Barker of Duxbury, "in consideration of the tender love and fatherly affection that I have and bear to my natural and wellbeloved son," forty acres of upland lying "between my other lands late in the tenure & occupation of my son Isaac Barker deceased and the land of John Stetson deceased," forty acres of upland near Barstow's Bridge, three acres of meadow near Palmer's Landing Place, four acres of meadow on the southwest side of Robinson's Creek, and "all that my meadow and swamp land that lyeth up a certain brook called Pudden Brook and lies to the southeast of my son Robert his house with all that tract of land whereon my said son Robert now liveth & dwelleth, all which said granted uplands & meadows are situate within the township of Duxborough aforesaid and for sometime past hath been and now are in the tenure and occupation of my said son Robert Barker" [PLR 1:310-11].

In his will, dated 18 February 1689 and proved 16 March 1691/2, "Robert Barker senior of Duxborough" ordered that he "be decently buried as near unto my wellbeloved wife and my eldest son as conveniently may be," appointed "my wellbeloved son Francis Barker" his executor, and bequeathed to son Francis Barker £20 in silver money; to son Robert Barker £10 in silver money; to daughter Rebeckah Snow £5 in silver money; to daughter Abigail Rogers £5 in silver money; to grandson Samuel Barker the land that was bounded out to him and 40s. in money; to grandson Francis Barker the land that was bounded out to him and 40s.; to grandson Robert Barker the land that was bounded out to him and 40s. when he comes to the age of twenty-one; to grandson Jabiz Barker the land that was bounded out to him and 40s. when he comes to the age of twenty-one; to grandson Isaac Barker the land that was bounded out to him and 40s. when he comes to the age of twenty-one; to "my son Isaac's six daughters Rebeckah, Mary, Lidia, Judeth, Martha and the youngest of all" £5 apiece; and to son Francis Barker the residue [MD 31:102-3, citing PPR 1:123-25].

On 14 March 1691/2, Francis Barker, James Bishop and Robert Barker drew up the division of the lands which Robert Barker had bequeathed to the five sons of his son Isaac [MD 31:103-4 (which dates the document one day late), citing PPR 1:125-26].

The inventory of the estate of Robert Barker of Duxbury, taken 15 March 1691/2, totalled £142 1s. 11d., of which "his purse and apparel" were valued at £96 1s. 8d. [PPR 1:126].

BIRTH: By about 1616 (based on terms of apprenticeship).
DEATH: Between 18 February 1689 (date of will) and 14 March 1691/2 (date of division of lands to the sons of his son Isaac).
MARRIAGE: By 1663 (and by about 1642 if she was the mother of all his children) Luce (or Lucy) _____ [PCLR 5:412]. No other record gives her name, but she was still living on 7 March 1681/2 when "Leiftenant Robert Barker, in behalf of his mother, the wife of Robert Barker, Senior, is fined £2 10s. for that his said mother sold cider to the Indians, contrary to the law of this government" [PCR 6:82]. (Most secondary sources identify her as daughter of John and Anna Williams of Scituate, but she is not named in the will of John Williams; the confusion may arise because Anna Williams, daughter of John, did marry John Barker, the brother of Robert. On 6 October 1659, "Robert Barker and Deborah Barker, the daughter of John Barker," complained against Ensign John Williams for having misused her, and the court ordered that "Deborah Barker should not be returned again unto her said uncle, Ensign Williams" [PCR 3:164, 171-72]; perhaps someone misread this as calling Deborah Barker daughter of Robert rather than of John Barker. The deed of 1663 in which "Robert Barker and Luce Barker" his wife sell land originally granted to Henry Merrick of Scituate may eventually lead to her identification [PCLR 5:412]. Note that both daughters of Robert Barker named daughters "Luceanna," which would indicate that Lucy was the mother of all his children.)
CHILDREN:
  i   ISAAC BARKER, b. say 1642; m. Plymouth 28 December 1665 Judith Prence [PCR 8:31], daughter of THOMAS PRENCE [PM 374].
  ii FRANCIS BARKER, b. say 1646; m. Duxbury 5 January 1674 Mary Lincoln, daughter of Thomas Lincoln, husbandman, of Hingham [Hingham Hist 3:16].
  iii REBECCA BARKER, b. say 1650; m. (1) by 1670 Josiah Snow (eldest known child b. Marshfield 6 December 1670; her name given incorrectly in some sources as Baker [MarVR 15, 427]); m. (2) Marshfield 23 [blank] 1694 John Sawyer [MarVR 19].
  iv ROBERT BARKER, b. about 1651 (Robert Barker Sr. d. Duxbury 25 September 1729, a. 78); m. (1) by 1682 Alice

Snow, daughter of Anthony and Abigail (Warren) Snow, and granddaughter of RICHARD WARREN [PM 477] (eldest known child b. Duxbury 24 August 1682) [MF 18:35]; m. (2) Jamestown 7 October 1705 Phebe (Cook) (Arnold) Marsh [RIVR 4:5:5], daughter of Thomas and Thomasin (____) Cook, and widow of Oliver Arnold and Jonathan Marsh [Thomas Cooke Gen 57-61].

v   ABIGAIL BARKER, b. say 1657; m. by 1677 Joseph Rogers, son of John Rogers of Marshfield [Joseph Neal Anc 45-46].

ASSOCIATIONS: Brother of John Barker of Marshfield [PLR 1:1].

COMMENTS: On 20 January 1632/3, "Rob[er]t Barker, servant of John Thorp, complained of his master for want of clothes. The complaint being found to be just, it was ordered, that Thorp should either forthwith apparel him, or else make over his time to some other that was able to provide for him" [PCR 1:7]. On 15 August 1633, whereas "Rob[er]t Barker had bound himself an apprentice to John Thorpe, in the trade of carpentry, the said Thorp being dead, Alice, his wife, hath turned over his time, which will be expired the first of April 1637, to William Palmer, nailer, of Plymouth, by the free consent of the said Robert; the said William promising to instruct & teach him his said trade of nailing, & at the end of his time to give him only two suits of apparel" [PCR 1:16]. On 4 December 1638, "Robert Barker, of Jones River, for breaking the King's peace in drawing blood upon Henry Blague," was fined 20s. [PCR 1:106].

The history of Robert Barker of Marshfield and Duxbury is clear from his appearance in the 1643 list of men able to bear arms until his death, but do the three records above apply to the same man? The Robert Barker who was apprentice first of JOHN THORPE [PM 459] and then of WILLIAM PALMER [PM 349] ended his service early in 1637, and so we would not expect to see records of him between 1633 and 1637. The record of a Robert Barker being fined for fighting occurs the year after the apprentice ended his service, and Jones River, although it was in an area that would remain part of Plymouth for some time, was on the north side of Plymouth, in the direction of Marshfield. Thus, although there may be some room for doubt that these early records apply to Robert of Marshfield and Duxbury, there are the threads of an argument in favor of there being but one Robert, and that is the position adopted here.

There is no direct evidence for the marriage of the younger Robert Barker to Alice Snow; in his will Alice's father, Anthony Snow, names his daughters without giving their married names [MD 5:1-5]. The identification is based on the following circumstances: when Anthony Snow bequeathed to his daughter Alice on 28 December 1685, the wife of the younger Robert Barker was Alice; Alice Snow's brother Josiah Snow married Robert Barker's sister Rebecca; and, most importantly, the inventory of Anthony Snow was taken on 12 November 1692 by Stephen Skeff, Michael Ford, Joseph Waterman and Robert Barker, and the first three of these men are known to have married daughters of Anthony Snow [MF 18:1:7-8, 31-36].

In Scituate records is the marriage on 1 April 1697 of Robert Barker to Hannah [blank], and this is assigned by some sources as a second wife to the younger Robert Barker. There are two reasons that this cannot be true: the last child of Robert and Alice Barker, Lydia, was born in Duxbury on 5 September 1697, several months after the marriage of Robert and Hannah [MF 18:1:35]; and the birth record for Isaac, first child of Robert and Hannah, as entered in the Pembroke Society of Friends records, calls the father "Robert Jr.," whereas in 1697 and later years the son of the immigrant would have been Robert Sr.

Since Robert and Hannah named their first child Isaac, it is likely that this Robert is the son of Isaac Barker, son of ROBERT BARKER. This Hannah is very likely the daughter of Edward Wanton of Scituate, who named a daughter Hannah Barker in his will. (There is a marriage in Scituate on 2 October 1710 of James Barker to Hannah Wanton, but this is Hannah (Allen) Wanton, widow of Stephen Wanton [MF 18:1:137].)

In 1662 Robert Barker, his wife and his son [presumably Isaac, the eldest] were fined for trading guns with the Indians [PCR 4:11-17]. Between 1638 and 1673 Robert Barker appeared occasionally as either plaintiff or defendant in minor civil suits [PCR 7:9, 72, 102, 125-26, 177, 180].

BIBLIOGRAPHIC NOTE: The 1899 article on the family of Robert Barker, by James Atkins Noyes [NEHGR 53:426ff.], and the 1927 *Barker Genealogy* by Elizabeth Frye are not fully documented and have many errors. The treatment by L. Vernon Briggs in his Briggs genealogy [*History and Genealogy of the Briggs Family, 1254-1937*, 3 vol. (Boston 1938), pp. 278-83, 297-304] improved greatly on these earlier versions, reproducing full texts of wills and abstracts of many deeds. Some errors remained in this rendition of the family, mostly regarding the marriages of the younger Robert; as noted above, many of these have been corrected more recently [Thomas Cooke Gen, MF 18:1]. None of these sources adequately covers Isaac, the eldest son of the immigrant.

JOHN BARNES

ORIGIN: Unknown.
MIGRATION: 1632 (based on appearance in 25 March 1633 tax list [PCR 1:10]).
FIRST RESIDENCE: Plymouth.

OCCUPATION: Yeoman [PCR 12:45-46; PCLR 2:2:86, 3:68].
Merchant (see *COMMENTS* below).
CHURCH MEMBERSHIP: On 11 September 1666, John Barnes was member of a Plymouth town committee ordered to arrange accommodations for a new minister [PTR 1:77].
FREEMAN: In 1633 list of freemen, among those admitted between 1 January 1633/4 and 1 January 1634/5 [PCR 1:4]. In list of freemen dated 7 March 1636/7 [PCR 1:52]. In Plymouth sections of lists of 1639 and 1658 [PCR 8:174, 200].
EDUCATION: Signed his deeds and his will by mark. His inventory included "2 bibles 1 English and another Indian" valued at £1 and "an old psalm book and 2 other old books" valued at 1s. 6d.
OFFICES: Plymouth petit jury, 2 January 1637/8, 6 March 1637/8 [PCR 7:7, 8]. Coroner's jury, 5 June 1638 [PCR 1:88].

Plymouth Colony committee to regulate wages, 5 January 1635/6 [PCR 1:36]. Committee on repair of highways, 5 March 1638/9 [PCR 1:117]. Committee on construction of the prison, 3 March 1639/40 [PCR 1:142]. Committee to survey meadows, 5 May 1640 [PCR 1:152]. Committee on bounds between land of Nathaniel Warren and Robert Bartlett, 1 June 1658 [PCR 3:142].

Plymouth surveyor of highways, 7 March 1642/3, 5 June 1644, 1 June 1647, 7 June 1648, 8 June 1664, 2 June 1667 [PCR 2:53, 72, 116, 124, 4:61, 149]. Surveyor of arms, 29 May 1643 [PTR 1:14]. Selectman, 18 February 1649/50 [PTR 1:30].

In Plymouth section of 1643 Plymouth Colony list of men able to bear arms [PCR 8:188]. His inventory included "2 guns 1 of them a broken musket and another great gun" valued at £3, "1 matchlock and another little old gun, 1 carbine" valued at £1 8s., "1 pistol" valued at 6s., "one sword and belt" valued at 8s., "2 old daggers and a pair of bandoliers" valued at 5s., and "a parcel of powder, 3 powderhorns, a cartridge, a small powder barrel, bullets and shot about a dozen pounds" valued at 6s.
ESTATE: Assessed 9s. in Plymouth tax list of 25 March 1633, and 18s. in list of 27 March 1634 [PCR 1:10, 28].

On 10 January 1633/4, Edward Holman sold to John Barnes one shallop and one dwelling house with twenty acres of land (for which Holman acknowledged payment on 6 May 1635), and Barnes shall "possess the said Edw[ard] Holman of 20 acres of land in some convenient place in Scituate" [PCR 1:24]. On 13 January 1633/4, John Barnes sold to Richard Higgins the dwelling house and twenty acres of land, which Barnes had recently bought of Edward Holman, and Higgins is to pay Barnes £10 and "shall possess the said John & his heirs of 20 acres of land at Scituate" [PCR 1:24].

On 20 October 1634, Edmund Chandler sold to John Rogers a lot "which the said Edward [*sic*] bought of John Barnes" [PCR 1:31].

On 4 December 1637, John Barnes was granted seven acres of land "lying on the north side ... to lie to his house at Plymouth & not to be sold from it" [PCR 1:71]. On 1 June 1640, he was granted "one hundred acres of upland and ten acres of meadow next beyond the Six Mile Brook in the way to Namascutte" [PCR 1:154, 7:78-79].

On 23 June 1639, John Winslow of Plymouth, yeoman, sold to John Barnes of the same town, yeoman, four acres of meadow at the High Pines, and on 20 July 1639 Barnes sold to Mr. Robert Hicks of Plymouth the same four acres [PCR 12:45-46]. On 7 November 1639, Edward Holman sold to John Barnes two acres of meadow at Turkey Point [PCR 1:167, 12:49].

On 5 August 1640, John Combe, gent., and Phineas Pratt, joiner, sold to John Barnes two acres, which they had of "Godbert Godbertson in marriage with their wives" [PCLR 1:101]. On 15 January 1640, Mr. Thomas Hill sold to John Barnes "all that his house & garden and lands thereunto belonging lying on the northside of Wellingsly Brook" [PCLR 1:119]. On 30 December 1642, John Barnes sold to Edward Edwards the above two parcels; on 30 October 1644, Edwards assigned this land to "Thomas Whitney" with further payments to be made to Barnes, and, on 27 October 1647, Barnes released "Thomas Whitten" from all debts [PCLR 1:154].

On 5 October 1640, Josias Winslow sold to John Barnes "all that his house, messuage and outhouses and garden place with the upland belonging to the said house in Plymouth aforesaid and the two acres of marsh meadow lying at the Wood Island" [PCLR 1:105].

On 27 November 1640, Mark Mendlove sold to John Barnes "all that his house and land lying at the fishing point upon the Eele River" [PCLR 1:109]. On 10 February 1640[/1], Barnes sold this land to William Baker [PCLR 1:119], but, on 5 April 1641, John Barnes leased to William

Baker the house and lands at Eel River, which he had lately bought of Mark Mendlove, the sale having fallen through [PCR 2:13].

On 24 August 1651 and on 14 October 1651, John Barnes of Plymouth made deeds of gift of livestock to his children "Jonathan, Mary, Hanna and Lidia" [PCR 12:214-15; note that the first wife of John Barnes had died on 2 June 1651].

In March 1651 John Barnes appeared in the list of "those that have interest and proprieties in the town's land at Punckateesett over against Rhode Island" [PTR 1:36]. On 22 March 1663[/4], John Barnes was paired with John Morton in a grant of land at Puncateesett Neck [PTR 1:68].

On 28 December 1653, John Jourdaine of Plymouth, tailor, sold to John Barnes "a small parcel of upland ground being about two pole and an half in length ... and I do hereby also acknowledge that I sold the said parcel of land unto John Barnes in the year one thousand six hundred and forty two, although not until now acknowledged and confirmed" [MD 5:93-94, citing PCLR 2:1:95]. On 26 February 1654, Josias Hallott of Barnstable sold to John Barnes "an hundred acres of upland and twenty acres of meadow"; Mary Hallott relinquished her right in the land on 3 March 1654 and noted that the marsh was at "Swan Pond River, the upland lying between Barnstable and Yarmouth" [MD 9:232-33, citing PCLR 2:1:153].

On 27 March 1660, Stephen Bryant of Plymouth sold to John Barnes his quarter part or share in purchase land at Dartmouth, which came to him from his father-in-law John Shaw Sr. [MD 14:143-44, citing PCLR 2:2:32]. On the same day, Bryant sold to Barnes for a valuable sum his share as a townsman of Plymouth in the land at Punckatesett [MD 14:144-45, citing PCLR 2:2:33]. On 10 November 1661, John Barnes sold to John Haward of Acushena the quarter share at Dartmouth, which he had purchased from Stephen Bryant [MD 16:181-82, citing PCLR 2:2:71].

On 26 November 1661, John Barnes sold to Jone Tilson, widow, "one half of his farm land at the place or village commonly called and known by the name of Lakenham near the town of Plymouth ... the whole said farm ... containing one hundred acres of upland and ten acres of meadow" [MD 16:183-84, citing PCLR 2:2:73].

On 24 March 1661[/2?], William Palmer of Accushenah, cooper, sold to Mr. John Barnes of Plymouth, yeoman, "all that his home lot lying and being at Accushenah aforesaid containing twenty-five acres of upland with all the house, housing and fences thereon with three acres of meadow as yet unlaid out," but not including right of commonage [PCLR

2:2:86]. On 10 August 1666, Barnes exchanged this land with Benjamin Bartlett of Plymouth, receiving in return an eleven-acre parcel lying on the southside of Plymouth [PCLR 3:74].

On 27 October 1662, John Barnes was granted "a small parcel of meadow ... lying at the upper end of the South Meadow" [PTR 1:50].

On 7 August 1666, John Barnes of Plymouth, yeoman, sold to Hugh Cole of Plymouth, shipcarpenter, "all that my share of land lying and being at Taunton or Teticutt River being the twenty-sixth part of all the uplands and meadow," being the twenty-second lot [PCLR 3:68].

In his will, dated 6 March 1667/8 and proved 29 October 1671, John Barnes bequeathed to wife Joan Barnes one half the housing and lands for life; to son Jonathan the other half of the housing and lands forever (unless he forfeit it based on conditions stated later); to grandson John Marshall land lying near Rhode Island; to "my cousin the wife of Henery Samso[n]," 40s.; to wife one-third of moveables forever (on certain conditions); to son Jonathan one-third of moveables "in case he do not demand any part of that estate that formerly I gave to my daughter Lyddyah now deceased, in case he shall so do then third shall fall unto my grandson John Marshall"; to "my grandchildren now in being together with my kinswoman Ester Ricket" one-third of moveables; wife Joan Barnes and son Jonathan Barnes to be executors [MD 4:98-100, citing PCPR 3:1:31; PCR 5:81; Stratton 447-49].

The inventory of the estate of "Mr. John Barnes lately deceased," taken 30 August 1671, totalled £226 18s. 8d., with no real estate included [MD 19:61-62; PCPR 3:1:32-36; Stratton 449-56].

On 5 March 1671/2, the court "ordered, that notice be given to Mr. Robert Marshall, that forasmuch as Mistress Jone Barnes complaineth that she can not provide for his children, now in her custody, that he, within one month or six weeks after the date thereof, take care to provide for his said children, viz: John Marshall and Robert Marshall, or otherwise the Court will take course for the disposal of them" [PCR 5:85]. On 8 March 1682/3, the court ordered the Plymouth selectmen to "inquire after and use means that what appertains to Robert Marshall may be delivered to him, and also to take into their custody whatsoever appertains to the widow, Mistress Jone Barnes, and to improve it for her support as she shall or may stand in need thereof" [PCR 6:103].

BIRTH: By about 1608 (based on date of marriage).
DEATH: Died between 6 March 1667/8 (date of will) and 30 August 1671 (date of inventory), and certainly closer to the latter date. (In an undated report to the Plymouth court of 5 March 1671/2, a coroner's jury

viewed "the corpse of Mr. John Barnes" and stated that "being before his barn door in the street, standing stroking or feeling of his bull, the said bull suddenly turned about upon him and gave him a great wound with his horn on his right thigh, near eight inches long, in which his flesh was torn both broad and deep, as we judge; of which wound, together with his wrench of his neck or pain thereof (of which he complained) he immediately languished; after about 32 hours after he died" [PCR 5:88].)
MARRIAGE: (1) Plymouth 12 September 1633 MARY PLUMMER [PCR 1:16; PM 359]. She died at Plymouth 2 June 1651 [PCR 8:13].

(2) Before 1 March 1652/3 Joan _____ (who on that day was presented at court for "slandering and defaming the children of Captain Willett and the daughter of George Watson" [PCR 3:23]). She was living on 8 March 1682/3 [PCR 6:103].

CHILDREN:
With first wife
- i MARY BARNES, b. say 1640; m. Plymouth in 1660 [day and month lost] Robert Marshall [PCR 8:22].
- ii JONATHAN BARNES, b. say 1642; m. Plymouth 4 January 1665 Elizabeth Hedges [PCR 8:31]. (Savage claims a birthdate of 3 June 1643, but no evidence for this is seen.)
- iii HANNAH BARNES, b. say 1644; living on 14 October 1651 [PCR 12:214-15]; no further record.
- iv JOHN BARNES, b. say 1646; d. Plymouth 25 December 1648 [PCR 8:5].
- v LYDIA BARNES, b. Plymouth 24 April 1648 [PCR 8:4, 290]; in his will John Barnes enjoined his son Jonathan from demanding "any part of that estate that formerly I gave to my daughter Lyddyah now deceased," which may simply refer to the cattle she had received after her mother's death; there is no indication that she married or had children.

ASSOCIATIONS: In his will John Barnes makes bequests to "my cousin the wife of Henery Samso[n]" and to "my kinswoman Ester Ricket." John Barnes had married on 12 September 1633 Mary Plummer, and HENRY SAMSON [PM 401] had married 6 February 1635/6 ANNE PLUMMER [PCR 1:16, 36]. There is no Plummer family in Plymouth Colony this early, so Mary and Anne may have come on their own or, more likely, as part of some family of a different surname. Given the dates of marriage, they would seem to be of the same age, so one might expect that they were sisters, but in that case Barnes should refer to Anne (Plummer) Samson as his sister and not cousin. Thus, Anne and Mary Plummer may have themselves been cousins, or, less likely, they may have been aunt and niece; other more distant relationships are also possible.

On 31 October 1651 at Plymouth, John Rickard married Hester Barnes [PCR 8:13]. As Hester was about the same age as the children of John Barnes, the likeliest suggestion is that she was the daughter of a brother of John Barnes. On 5 July 1666 John Barnes had a servant named Thomas Barnes [PCR 4:133], also a likely candidate to be a relative, and possibly a brother of Hester. If Hester and Thomas were siblings, and if John Barnes was their uncle, there is no evidence that their father came to New England. (See NEHGR 112:154.)

COMMENTS: John Barnes appeared in the court records constantly, giving us a detailed view of a complicated personality. He was a man of high social standing, for he was frequently referred to as "Mr.," and he was a man of wealth who engaged in mercantile activity. But there was a dark side to his character, which placed him constantly at odds with the authorities, and prevented him from taking the place in Plymouth society that should have been his based on his wealth and social standing.

His trading activities are seen on occasion as the records of normal transactions [e.g., PCR 1:9, 13, 138, 2:31, 54], but more frequently when he engaged in some practice that the General Court deemed illegal, or at least unfair. On 1 December 1640, John Barnes was presented "for exaction in taking rye at four shillings per bushel, and selling it again for five without adventure or long forbearance in one and the same place"; he was found not guilty [PCR 2:5]. On 2 March 1640/1, he was presented "for selling black & brown threads at five shillings, four pence per lb."; he was found not guilty [PCR 2:12]. (See also PCR 1:34, 167-68 and, for a case that goes into great detail, PCR 7:120-22.)

John Barnes was also in court frequently as either plaintiff or defendant in civil suits, usually over debts arising from his business activities. These cases cover a period of thirty years, from 1636 to 1667 [PCR 1:42, 168, 2:50, 108, 3:203, 4:9, 12, 79, 89, 158, 7:16, 19, 28, 29, 63, 69, 72, 76, 93, 103, 113, 117, 124, 127, 137].

Aside from these legal disputes over business activities, Barnes was occasionally in court under accusation of having slandered one of his neighbors. On 9 June 1653, he was presented for having accused Winifred Whitney of lying, but was unable to bring forth proof and acknowledged his fault in making the accusations [PCR 3:38]. On 1 March 1663/4, Samuel Allin complained that Barnes had defamed him by stating that he was one of three men who might have been the father of the child of William Newland's daughter; Barnes wrote an apology, explaining that he was merely passing on a rumor [PCR 7:114].

Evidence for his wealth may also be seen in the frequency with which he was acquiring the time of servants from other men, or otherwise involved in disputes over his servants. On 26 August 1634, "John Rouse, the servant of the said Thomas Prince, having a desire to forsake the service of his master, and to dwell with the forementioned John Barnes the remainder of his time; and also Richard Willis, servant of John Barnes aforesaid, having inclination to dwell with the said Thomas Prince," the parties so agreed [PCR 1:30]. On 4 August 1638, for £6 10s. and twenty bushels of Indian corn, John Barnes assigned to Robert Bartlett the remaining term of service of Thomas Shreive (being three years from the first day of August instant), Robert Bartlett also paying Shreive £3 6s. 8d., and Shreive agreeing to serve an additional year for another £5 [PCR 12:32]. Especially suggestive is the court case of 5 July 1666 in which "Thomas Barnes, servant unto Mr. John Barnes of Plymouth," complained of some problem in the agreement between the two parties; some kinship relation between the two men seems likely [PCR 4:133]. (See also PCR 1:129, 132, 2:38, 3:27, 39, 126.)

Another side of John Barnes may be seen in the frequency with which he was called on by others to stand surety for them when they had problems, as on 16 April 1639 when he posted bond of £20 for Richard Derby when he was accused of poisoning John Dunford [PCR 1:121]. (See also PCR 1:19, 75, 105, 2:73, 107, 3:159, 177.)

The worst of the difficulties encountered by Barnes were the frequent occasions when he was presented at court for drunkenness. The first occasion of record was on 4 December 1638 when John Barnes was "presented for inordinate drinking about four months since, and in regard the evidence thereof was not adjudged sufficient evidence, it was remitted to better proof" [PCR 1:107]. On 7 November 1643, "John Barnes, proved to be drunken, both in the Bay and at Scituate ... is fined £5" [PCR 2:66]. On 5 June 1650, "[w]e present John Barnes, of Plymouth, for being drunk. Cleared by paying the fine" [PCR 2:156].

This problem became so serious that on 1 March 1652/3 John Barnes, having been accused of drunkenness and then having come into court drunk, was fined £10 and ordered to post an additional £40 bond for his good behavior [PCR 3:22-23]. This penalty clearly had little effect, for on 6 October 1659 John Barnes was disfranchised for "frequent and abominable drunkenness" [PCR 3:167, 176]. Still John Barnes did not alter his behavior, for on 10 June 1661 the Court ordered that the "ordinary keepers of the town of Plymouth are hereby prohibited to let

John Barnes have any liquors, wine, or strong drink at any time," under penalty of 50s. fine [PCR 3:219]. (See also PCR 3:5, 129, 4:106.)

There may be some humor, however, in a few other court occurrences related to the excessive drinking. On 2 October 1637, he was to testify against a number of servants and others who were drinking at the home of Stephen Hopkins on the sabbath [PCR 1:68]. On 2 May 1648, "John Barnes, of Plimouth, is allowed by the Court to brew and sell beer unto comers and goers until the Court shall see reason to the contrary in regard of his intent to bake biscake, and for that otherwise it would be prejudicial unto him" [PCR 2:122]. On 14 September 1666, John Barnes was recorded as having brought fifty gallons of rum into Yarmouth for Elisha Hedge [PCR 4:152]; this may be the source of the false claim that Barnes had resided for some time at Yarmouth.

For other estimations of the character of John Barnes see Stratton [240-41, 447-56] and Darrett B. Rutman, *Husbandmen of Plymouth: Farms and Villages in the Old Colony, 1620-1692* (Boston 1967).

The dates of birth for the children of John Barnes as estimated above all fall into a brief range in the 1640s. However, inasmuch as Barnes first married in 1633, one or more of these children were very likely born a few years earlier than suggested here.

ROBERT BARTLETT

ORIGIN: Unknown.
MIGRATION: 1623 on the *Anne* [PCR 12:6].
FIRST RESIDENCE: Plymouth.

OCCUPATION: Wine cooper [PCLR 3:328].
CHURCH MEMBERSHIP: On 1 May 1660 at Plymouth court "Robert Bartlett appeared, being summoned in answer for speaking contemptuously of singing of psalms, and was convict of the fact" [PCR 3:185-86].
FREEMAN: In the 1633 Plymouth list of freemen in proximity to those admitted on 1 January 1632/3 [PCR 1:4]. In list of 7 March 1636/7 [PCR 1:53]. In Plymouth section of lists of freemen of 1639 and 1658 [PCR 8:174, 197].
EDUCATION: Signed all deeds by mark. His inventory included "books" valued at 7s.
OFFICES: Plymouth petit jury, 6 June 1643, 28 October 1645, 7 June 1648, 6 March 1649/50, 4 October 1653, 7 March 1653/4, 3 October

1654, 3 May 1659 [PCR 2:126, 7:35, 41, 47, 67, 70, 72, 93]. Grand jury, 5 June 1644, 2 June 1646, 17 May 1649, 7 June 1652, 8 June 1655 [PCR 2:71, 102, 3:9, 78; PTR 1:28].

Committee to lay out highways, 2 May 1637 [PCR 1:58]. Committee to lay out land, 24 May 1660 [PTR 1:41].

Plymouth surveyor of highways, 4 June 1645, 4 June 1661 [PCR 2:84, 3:215].

In Plymouth section of 1643 Plymouth Colony list of men able to bear arms [PCR 8:189].

ESTATE: In the 1623 Plymouth land division granted one acre as a passenger on the *Anne* [PCR 12:6]. In the 1627 Plymouth division of cattle "Robert Bartlet" was the twelfth person in the tenth company [PCR 12:12].

Assessed 9s. in the Plymouth tax lists of 25 March 1633 and 27 March 1634 [PCR 1:10, 27].

On 1 July 1633, it was ordered that "Mrs. Warren & Rob[er]t Bartlet mow where they did last year" [PCR 1:15]. On 28 May 1635, "Thomas Litle came before the Governor and acknowledged that he had given unto Robart Bartlet a parcel of land at the end of his lot beyond Eel River," and described himself as brother-in-law to Bartlett [PCR 1:34]. On 14 March 1635/6, it was ordered that "Mrs. Warren, Rich[ard] Church, Tho[mas] Litle, & Rob[er]t Bartlet mow where they did last year" [PCR 1:41]. On 20 March 1636/7, it was ordered that "Richard Church, Rob[er]te Bartlet, & Thomas Little, [have] hay ground where they had the last year, and to take further supply where they can find it, in places not granted to others, and Rob[er]te Bartlet to have the swamp or pit at the head of Mr. Bradford's ground" [PCR 1:56]. On 5 May 1640, "Richard Church, Rob[er]te Bartlett, Thomas Little, & Mrs. Elizabeth Warren are granted enlargements at the heads of their lots to the foot of the Pine Hills" [PCR 1:152].

On 7 February 1637, "Mrs. Elizabeth Warren of the Eele River widow for and in consideration of a marriage solemnized betwixt John Cooke the younger of the Rockey Nooke and Sarah her daughter" granted to the said John Cooke "eighteen acres or thereabouts and lying on the north side of Robert Bartlett's lot formerly also given the said Robert in marriage with Mary another of the said Mrs. Warren's daughters" [PCR 12:27]. On 11 November 1637, John Cooke exchanged this eighteen-acre parcel with Robert Bartlett for a "lot of land of like quantity lying on Duxborrow side betwixt the lots of Thomas Morton and Jonathan Brewster" [PCR 12:28].

On 9 April 1649, Richard Church sold to Robert Bartlett a "house and housing and land with all the meadow ground with the addition that he had of Goodman Kemton at the Eel River" [PCR 12:165-66].

On 7 March 1652, Robert Bartlett held a full share as a purchaser of Dartmouth [MD 4:185-88, citing PCLR 2:1:106-7].

On 30 January 1653, Samuel Hicks of Plymouth, planter, sold to Robert Bartlett of Plymouth, cooper, eleven acres of upland on the south side of Plymouth [MD 5:94-95, citing PCLR 2:1:97].

Robert Bartlett appears in a March 1651 Plymouth town list of those "that have interest and proprieties in the town's land at Punckateesett over against Road Iland" [PTR 1:37]. On 22 March 1663, the lots at "Puncateesett" were described, Robert Bartlett sharing the 24th lot with James Cole Sr. [PTR 1:67]. On 8 March 1668/9, Robert Bartlett of Plymouth, cooper, sold to John Almey of Portsmouth, Rhode Island, merchant, his share in land granted by the town of Plymouth in 1649 "lying over against Rhode Island aforesaid, at the place commonly called and known by the name of Punckateesett" [PCLR 3:328].

On 27 June 1659, Robert Bartlett of Plymouth, cooper, engaged to pay to Benjamin Foster, the son of Richard Foster, £8 when he reaches the age of twenty-one, on the condition that Bartlett would have the use of Richard Foster's land for the term of ten years; and "Mary the wife of the said Richard Foster deceased" engages to bring up the said Benjamin Foster, who is now four years old [MD 14:15-16, citing PCLR 2:2:28].

In 1660 the town of Plymouth granted to Robert Bartlett fifty acres "lying between the sea and the fern swamp between the Eelriver and Mannomett ponds" [PTR 1:43]; the bounds of this grant were described on 20 February 1662 [PTR 1:54]. On 26 January 1663, the town of Plymouth granted to those living at Eel River a quarter-mile extension on their lots, towards the pine hills [PTR 1:59]. On 21 February 1663, the town of Plymouth granted to Robert Bartlett eight acres of meadow that had been in dispute [PTR 1:61, 62]. On [blank] July 1667, the town of Plymouth granted to Robert Bartlett "a piece of swamp ... to make meadow of lying adjoining to his meadow at the Eelriver" [PTR 1:89].

On 14 July 1670, Robert Bartlett of Plymouth, wine cooper, deeded to "my son-in-law James Barnabey, cordwainer," of Plymouth and "my daughter Lydia Barnabey his wife" twenty acres "by me purchased of the said my brother-in-law Richard Church," and four acres of upland meadow added to it [MD 3:112, citing PCLR 3:297].

On 17 February 1670/1, Robert Bartlett of Plymouth, cooper, sold to Thomas Burge Jr. of Newport, Rhode Island, half his share of land at Acushena in Dartmouth and half his share of land at Pascomansucke in

Dartmouth (reserving one-third of the last named share) [MD 3:112, citing PCLR 5:118; RILE 1:140].

On 14 July 1673, "Robert Bartlett of the town of Plymouth ... wine cooper" deeded to "my son Joseph Bartlett" for love and affection "all that my farm, messuage, tenement and seat, which I now live in and am possessed of, in the township of Plymouth aforesaid, situate and being at a place or river commonly called Eel River: viz: all that my house and land there"; four acres of marsh meadow there; and two acres of fresh or upland meadow; to be entered upon by his son on the death of the grantor and his wife [MD 3:112-13, citing PCLR 3:301].

On 19 September 1676, Robert Bartlett made a nuncupative will, bequeathing to "my wife all my estate yet undisposed of whether it be in lands or moveables, goods, chattels, debts. I give all unto my wife to be absolutely at her dispose among my children" [MD 3:114, citing PCPR 3:2:87].

The inventory of the estate of Robert Bartlett, taken 29 October 1676, totalled £170 16s. 6d., of which £100 was real estate: "2 dwellinghouses and a barn, upland and meadow" [MD 3:114, citing PCPR 3:2:87]. On 6 March 1676/7, "[l]etters of administration is granted by the Court unto Mary Bartlett & Joseph Bartlett to administer the estate of Robert Bartlett, deceased" [PCR 5:220].

On 13 February 1677, "Mary Bartlett widow and late wife unto Robert Bartlett deceased" sold to "my son Joseph Bartlett" for £300 all the estate which was reserved to her use for life in the deed of gift from her husband Robert Bartlett to the said Joseph Bartlett, as well as fifty acres of upland "near a place commonly called the salt marsh ... between the Eelriver and Mannomett Ponds," fifty acres of upland lying between the land of Ephraim Morton Jr. and the land that did belong to James Barnabey deceased, a parcel of meadow on the Eelriver, and all personal estate given her by husband Robert Bartlett in his will [MD 3:115-16, citing PCLR 4:223].

BIRTH: Born by about 1604 (based on estimated date of marriage).
DEATH: Between 19 September 1676 (date of will) and 29 October 1676 (probate of will).
MARRIAGE: By about 1629 Mary Warren, daughter of RICHARD WARREN [PM 477] (on 7 March 1636/7, Elizabeth Warren, widow of Richard Warren, was made a purchaser in his stead, in part because "of the lots of lands given formerly by her unto her sons-in-law, Richard Church, Robert Bartlett, and Thomas Little, in marriage with their wives, her daughters" [PCR 1:54], and this was confirmed on 5 October 1652

[PCR 3:19]). "Mary Bartlett, widow," died at Plymouth on "March, 27:[1683] in her 73d year" [PChR 1:250].

CHILDREN:
- i BENJAMIN BARTLETT, b. say 1629; m. (1) by 1654 Susanna Jenney, daughter of JOHN JENNEY [PM 291] (in her will of 4 April 1654, Sarah Jenney, widow of John Jenney, bequeathed to "my son Benjamin Bartlett," and to Mr. Thomas Cushman "the Bible which was my daughter Susanna's" [MD 8:171-75, citing PCPR 1:17-21]); m. (2) after 4 April 1654 Sarah Brewster, daughter of Love Brewster [MF Warren 11-12, citing PCR 4:80, 173-4]; m. (3) before 21 January 1678 Sissilla _____ (named in his will of 21 August 1691 [MF Warren 11-12, citing PCLR 4:281; MQ 51:131-34]).
- ii REBECCA BARTLETT, b. say 1631; m. Plymouth 20 December 1649 William Harlow [PCR 8:8].
- iii MARY BARTLETT, b. say 1633; m. (1) Plymouth 10 September 1651 Richard Foster [PCR 8:13]; m. (2) Plymouth 8 July 1659 Jonathan Morey [PCR 8:22 (marriage contract dated 27 June 1659 [MD 14:16, citing PCLR 2:2:28a])].
- iv SARAH BARTLETT, b. say 1636; m. Plymouth 23 December 1656 Samuel Rider [PCR 8:17].
- v JOSEPH BARTLETT, b. about 1639; m. by about 1663 Hannah Pope, daughter of THOMAS POPE [MD 19:24, citing PLR 1:84; PM 362]. "March the 12, 1710 My dear wife Hannah Bartlet died being near 72 years of age, myself being six months younger than she when she died" [NEHGR 101:279 (from family Bible)]. (If the date given for the death of Hannah is 12 March 1710/1, then she was probably born in the first half of 1639, which would place her husband's birth late in 1639.)
- vi ELIZABETH BARTLETT, b. say 1641; m. Plymouth 26 December 1661 Anthony Sprague [PCR 8:23], son of WILLIAM SPRAGUE {1629, Charlestown} [GMB 3:1737].
- vii LYDIA BARTLETT, b. Plymouth 8 June 1648 [PCR 8:4, 291 (despite the fact that this is published as a birth of 1647, it is clear from the sequence of the records that it should be for 1648)]; m. (1) by about 1670 James Barnaby [PCLR 3:297]; m. (2) shortly after 30 October 1677 John Nelson [TAG 56:33-34; MF 18:1:17]. She d. Plymouth 11 September 1691 [PVR 135].

viii MERCY BARTLETT, b. Plymouth 10 March 1650/1 [PCR 8:11]; m. Plymouth 25 December 1668 John Joy of Boston [MF 18:1:18; PCR 8:32 (not Ivey)].

COMMENTS: In 1959 John G. Hunt suggested that Robert Bartlett of Plymouth was the same as a Robert Bartlett baptized at Puddletown, Dorsetshire, on 27 May 1603, and twenty years later Paul Prindle published a fuller pedigree of this Dorsetshire family, but at the moment this proposed identification remains only a possibility [TAG 35:214, 55:164-70]. Robert of Puddletown had brother Benjamin and sisters Mary, Lydia and Elizabeth, all names used by Robert of Plymouth.

Clues as to the ages of the children of Robert Bartlett are sparse, and several attempts have been made to determine the birth order of the children. Aside from the evidence of birthdates for the last two children, the date of freemanship for son Benjamin and the age at death for son Joseph, our most useful information comes from the marriage dates for the older daughters. The statement has frequently been made that Benjamin must have been born by 6 June 1633, since he was made free on 6 June 1654 [PCR 3:48]. But he had by 4 April 1654 already married and buried one wife and was soon to marry a second, which suggests a man a few years older than twenty-one in that year. If we place the birth of Benjamin in 1629, then we have a gap of about six or seven years in which to place daughters Rebecca and Mary (1629-1636), but to do this we must assume that they both married when they were about eighteen, rather than rely on our usual rule of marrying daughters at age twenty in the absence of other evidence. There would be nothing unusual about this, and the resulting sequence of births for the elder children is in agreement with the evidence. Note also that under almost any interpretation there is a gap of about six years between the births of the sixth and seventh children of this couple.

On 25 December 1635, Robert Bartlett took Richard Stinnings as an apprentice for nine years, his time to begin on 1 December 1635 [PCR 1:35]. On 4 August 1638, for £6 10s. and twenty bushels of Indian corn, John Barnes assigned to Robert Bartlett the remaining term of service of Thomas Shreive (being three years from the first day of August instant), Robert Bartlett also paying Shreive £3 6s. 8d., and Shreive agreeing to serve an additional year for another £5 [PCR 12:32].

BIBLIOGRAPHIC NOTE: The most complete treatment of Robert Bartlett and his family is in George E. Bowman's account of the descendants of RICHARD WARREN [MD 3:105-17]. This article includes abstracts of all records relating to Robert Bartlett and complete transcripts of the probate documents and some critical deeds, and is only slightly marred by a misguided effort to represent dates in both Old Style and New Style.

In 1938 the deForests published a shorter but also excellent account of this family [Moore Anc 60-72]. Paul W. Prindle included a solid version of the family in his limited edition *Ancestors and Descendants of Timothy Crosby Jr.* (Orleans, Mass., 1981), 2:342-50.

For a more recent treatment of this family, see the Mayflower Five Generations Project volume on Richard Warren, which carefully presents the evidence for the marriages of the children [MF 18:1: 3-4, 11-18].

WILLIAM BASSETT

ORIGIN: Unknown.
MIGRATION: 1621 on the *Fortune* [PCR 12:5].
FIRST RESIDENCE: Plymouth.
REMOVES: Duxbury by 1637 [PCR 1:63], Bridgewater by 1656.

OCCUPATION: Blacksmith [PCLR 3:66] (the first five lines of his inventory included blacksmith's tools, including a pair of bellows, an anvil, a vice, tongs and hammers and coal shovels, and "all the rest of the smith shop" items [PCPR 2:2:37-38]).
FREEMAN: In 1633 Plymouth list of freemen, among those admitted before 1 January 1632/3 [PCR 1:3]; also in list of 7 March 1636/7 [PCR 1:52]. In Duxbury portion of list of 1639 [PCR 8:174]. In Bridgewater portion of list of 1658 [PCR 8:202].
EDUCATION: His inventory included more than twenty books, listed by title, mostly theological [MD 16:163].
OFFICES: Deputy for Duxbury to Plymouth court, 2 June 1640, 6 June 1643, 29 August 1643, 5 March 1643/4, 7 June 1648 [PCR 1:154, 2:57, 60, 68, 123].

Plymouth coroner's jury, 2 March 1635/6 [PCR 1:39]. Grand jury, 5 June 1638, 6 June 1654 [PCR 1:87, 3:49]. Petit jury, 7 March 1636/7, 2 January 1637/8, 6 March 1637/8, 4 June 1639, 3 September 1639 [PCR 7:5, 7, 8, 12, 13].

Committee to admit newcomers to Duxbury, 7 May 1638 [PCR 1:84]. Committee to lay out land, 3 September 1638, 7 January 1638/9, 4 February 1638/9, 4 March 1638/9, 31 August 1640, 5 October 1640 [PCR 1:95, 109, 112, 115, 161, 163]. Committee on bounds between

Duxbury and Marshfield, 2 March 1640/1 [PCR 2:9, 42]. Council of war for Duxbury, 27 September 1642 [PCR 2:46]. Committee to lay out highways [PCR 3:61, 62].

Duxbury constable, 3 June 1652 [PCR 3:8].

In Duxbury portion of 1643 Plymouth Colony list of men able to bear arms [PCR 8:190].

ESTATE: In the 1623 Plymouth land division "William Bassite" received two acres as a passenger on the *Fortune* in 1621 [PCR 12:5]. In the 1627 Plymouth division of cattle, the sixth company included William Basset, Elizabeth Basset, William Basset Jr. and Elizabeth Basset Jr. [PCR 12:11].

Assessed £1 7s. in the Plymouth tax lists of 25 March 1633 and 27 March 1634 [PCR 1:10, 27].

On 1 July 1633, 14 March 1635/6 and 20 March 1636/7, William Bassett was ordered to "mow at the end of his own ground" [PCR 1:14, 40, 56].

On 23 June 1637, William Bassett of Duxbury released to Mr. Ralph Partridge "so much of the lot of his lands lying in Ducksborrow aforesaid as is now enclosed by the said Mr. Partridg" [PCR 12:18-19], and again, on 7 November 1637, a similar agreement was reached regarding land released to William Leverich and Ralph Partridge [PCR 12:25].

On 6 April 1640, Plymouth Colony granted to "William Basset of Duxburrow" one hundred acres of upland with "meadow convenient" [PCR 1:144, 146].

On 3 June 1652, William Bassett of Duxbury deeded to "his son-in-law Leiftenant Perigrine White" forty acres of upland with the meadow adjoining [MD 1:96, citing PCLR 2:1:5]. On 16 June 1656, "William Bassett Senior of Duxburrow now living at Bridgewater" made a deed of gift of his Marshfield lands to his "two sons there living viz: Perigrine White and Nathaniell Bassett" [MD 10:25-27, citing PCLR 2:1:177-78].

William Bassett and Mr. [John] Howland jointly held one share as Dartmouth purchasers, 7 March 1652 [MD 4:187, citing PCLR 2:1:107].

On 8 November 1666, William Bassett, blacksmith, of Bridgewater sold to John Sprague of Duxbury, husbandman, four lots of upland containing fourscore acres and five acres of meadow, with dwelling house, cowhouse, stable, barn, outhouse, orchard and garden; William Bassett acknowledged the deed on 7 November 1666, and, on 5 November 1666, "Mary Bassett the wife of William Bassett Sr. ... of Bridgewater" consented to the sale [PCLR 3:66, with dates in the unlikely order as given].

On 3 April 1667, William Bassett Senior made a nuncupative will, bequeathing the moveables to his wife, and the house and land to her during her life, after which it was to go to his son William's son, and bequeathing his tools to his son Joseph, and "being demanded about his books which he formerly took care about, answered he could not now do it" [MD 16:162, citing PCPR 2:2:37].

His inventory, taken 12 May 1667, totalled £123 2s. 6d., with no real estate included [PCPR 2:2:37-38]. On 5 June 1667, letters of administration were granted to William Bassett Jr. on the estate of William Bassett Sr. deceased [PCR 4:155].

On 2 June 1669, "William Bassett of Sandwich ... the eldest son and heir of William Bassett sometimes inhabitant of ... Bridgewater ... now deceased" confirmed to "Joseph Bassett of Bridgewater my youngest brother" land in Bridgewater granted him by his father in his lifetime but not legally confirmed [PCLR 3:140].

BIRTH: By about 1596 (based on estimated date of first marriage).
DEATH: Between 3 April 1667 (date of will) and 12 May 1667 (date of inventory). (The claim that William Bassett died on 4 April 1667 derives from a peculiar misreading of the probate documents, in which the date of probate is taken as 5 April rather than 5 June, and the assumption is made that the death must have occurred between the third and the fifth.)
MARRIAGE: (1) By 1623 (and probably by 1621) Elizabeth _____, probably also a passenger on the *Fortune* in 1621. She appears in no record after 1627 and may have died anytime between 1634 (birth of her last child) and and the date of her husband's second marriage.

(2) After 1651 and before 12 December 1664 Mary (Tilden) Lapham, daughter of Nathaniel Tilden and widow of Thomas Lapham (see TIMOTHY HATHERLEY [PM 234]). She was living at Bridgewater as late as 28 March 1690 [Bassett Gen 6, citing BridTR 1:320].
CHILDREN:
With first wife
- i WILLIAM BASSETT, b. Plymouth say 1624; m. by about 1652 Mary Rainsford, daughter of EDWARD RAINSFORD {1630, Boston} [NEHGR 139:299; GMB 3:1543-48].
- ii ELIZABETH BASSETT, b. Plymouth say 1626; m. Sandwich 8 November 1648 Thomas Burgess [PCR 8:6], from whom she was divorced on 10 June 1661 [PCR 3:221].
- iii SARAH BASSETT, b. Plymouth say 1628; m. by 6 March 1648/9 Peregrine White, son of WILLIAM WHITE [PCR 2:183; MF 1:101-3; PM 495].

iv   NATHANIEL BASSETT, b. say 1630; m. about 1661 Dorcas Joyce, daughter of John Joyce [TAG 43:3-5].

v   JOSEPH BASSETT, b. say 1632; m. (1) by about 1660 Mary _____ (said to be his stepsister Mary Lapham, daughter of Thomas Lapham [see NEHGR 115:85]); m. (2) Hingham 16 October 1677 Martha Hobart [NEHGR 121:200].

vi   RUTH BASSETT, b. say 1634; m. (1) by 1655 John Sprague, son of FRANCIS SPRAGUE [TAG 41:178-81, citing PCR 6:109 for evidence of marriage; PM 447]; m. (2) _____ Thomas [TAG 41:179; Robert S. Wakefield suggests that this was John Thomas of Marshfield, who died before 12 January 1691/2, and whose first wife had died 2 January 1682/3].

COMMENTS: In 1611 a William Bassett, formerly of Sandwich in England, widower of Cecily Light, was twice betrothed at Leiden in Holland. His first bride-to-be died, but he succeeded the second time [Plooij VI, VIII]. Some have held that this was the man who came to Plymouth, but this seems unlikely given the ten-year gap before the arrival in Plymouth in 1621, and the lack of evidence for children of the Plymouth man born before that date, assuming that he had been married at least twice before. It is also possible that the William Bassett of Leiden in 1611 was the father of the immigrant to Plymouth in 1621, but there is no evidence directly favoring this hypothesis. (See discussion in Stratton 242-43.)

If the two-acre grant to William Bassett in 1623 was for William and his wife Elizabeth, then the first child would not have been born until 1624, three years after William's arrival in Plymouth. It is possible (though not likely) that the marriage took place in Plymouth, and Elizabeth came on the *Fortune* as a single woman.

Savage has misread the 1627 Plymouth cattle division, somehow including daughter Sarah Bassett in this list, when in fact only two children, William and Elizabeth, were included [Savage 1:136]. Sarah must have been born soon after 1627, however, to have married by the end of 1648.

Pope claimed that William Bassett resided at Sandwich in 1650, but this would be the son of the same name [Pope 37].

D.O.S. Lowell listed a "probable" seventh child, a daughter Jane who married a Thomas Gilbert [Munsey-Hopkins 67]. This must be a simple error in which "Rossiter" was misread for "Bassett," as there was a Thomas Gilbert of Taunton who married Jane Rossiter.

Various secondary sources claim that William Bassett volunteered for service in the Pequot War, and in the index to the first volume of published Plymouth Colony records he is listed for the page on which such volunteers appear, but he does not actually appear in the list [PCR 1:61]; a number of the index entries for William Bassett actually seem to be for William Paddy.

On 6 March 1648/9, William Bassett was fined 5s. "for not mending of guns in seasonable time," and, on 9 June 1653, he was fined 10s. "for neglecting to publish and make known an order directed to him from the council of war, prohibiting provisions for being transported out of the colony" [PCR 2:137, 3:36]. On 9 August 1655 and 10 June 1661, the colony treasurer received payment of fines by William Bassett [PCR 3:93, 8:104].

WILLIAM BEALE

In the 1623 Plymouth land division William Beale was granted one acre as a passenger on the *Fortune* in 1621; he was paired with Thomas Cushman [PCR 12:5]. As he does not appear in the 1627 cattle division, he must have died or departed soon.

JOHN BEAVEN

25 July 1633: "John Beaven hath covenanted to serve Joh. Wynslow or his assigns the full term of six years, according to the nature of an apprentice, beginning June 24, 1633. And at the end of his said term, the said John Wynslow, his master, to give him twelve bushels of Indian corn, & 25 acres of unmanured land" [PCR 1:15-16].

COMMENTS: No further record.

WILLIAM BENNETT

ORIGIN: Unknown.
MIGRATION: 1632 (based on appearance in tax list of 25 March 1633 [PCR 1:11]).
FIRST RESIDENCE: Plymouth.

REMOVES: Salem 1633, Manchester by 1645.

OCCUPATION: Carpenter (William Bennett "aged about seventy-three years" deposed in a lawsuit brought at Salem Court on 27 March 1677 that "when John Winthrop Esq. was at the Salthouse 30 odd years past that I having occasion to work there upon some carpentry work sometimes for Mr. Winthrop & sometimes hewing timber for ship or vessels ..." [EQC 6:247-48]).

Innkeeper ("William Benet was licensed to keep an ordinary" on 27 November 1677 [pursuant to a certificate from Manchester town meeting dated 21 November], and had the license renewed on 24 June 1679 and on 29 June 1680 [EQC 6:370, 7:222, 401]).

FREEMAN: Oath of fidelity, 1677 [EQC 6:401].

EDUCATION: The widow's inventory included "1 great Bible and other books" valued at 15s.

OFFICES: Essex petit jury, 29 November 1659 [EQC 2:182]. Grand jury, 30 November 1669, 20 July 1675, 30 November 1675, 27 November 1677 [EQC 4:187, 6:31, 73, 345]. Coroner's jury, 1677 [EQC 6:397].

Salem fenceviewer, 4 April 1640 [STR 1:110; EQC 1:28].

Manchester constable, 25 June 1650, 24 June 1662 [EQC 1:192, 2:413]. Selectman, 1665, 1679 [EQC 3:292, 7:200, 271].

On 26 November 1667, "William Bennet was dismissed from common training paying to the use of the company of Manchester one bushel of corn per annum" [EQC 3:459]. His inventory included "household goods and wearing clothes and carpentry tools and a sword and a gun" valued at £30.

ESTATE: In Plymouth tax list of 25 March 1633, but column for assessment not filled in [PCR 1:11]; not in 1634 tax list.

In portion of 1636 Salem land grant devoted to those who were not "freemen" [i.e., not members of Salem church], but no amount given [STR 1:22]. On 28 August 1637, William Bennett was one of three men who requested land at Jeffrey's Creek, and, on 8 November 1637, he was granted 25 acres [STR 1:56, 60]. On 25 December 1637, he was granted one-half acre of marsh, for a household of three [STR 1:102].

In his nuncupative will of 20 November 1682 (probated 27 June 1683), William Bennett bequeathed to wife Jane "my now dwelling house with the lot that was given me by the town of Salem ... as also ... all my moveable goods"; "to my eldest son Moses Bennitt, only an acre of the same lot being already bounded and possessed by my son Aaron Bennitt, before date underwritten which said acre of land I will to my son

Aaron aforesaid, with his house now standing upon the said acre of land"; to son Aaron "my lot called Pickworth's lot ... he being already in possession of said lot only a strip excepted, lying next to Lee's lot that was, being about an acre of land with a small piece of salt meadow being about half an acre called by the name of the little marsh I give to my grandson John Croe"; to son Aaron "the next pond of marsh joining to my grandson John Croe"; to son Aaron marsh at Kettle Cove Pond; to grandson John Croe an acre of meadow in the mill pond; to wife Jane for life all meadow or marsh not bequeathed, "out of my moveables which above written I have given to my beloved wife Jane during her natural life I give unto my two grandchildren Aaron Croe and Abigall Croe one heifer betwixt them"; and to "my daughter Mary ten pounds to be paid out of the moveables as my wife shall see cause, and my will is that my daughter Mary shall live in the house so long as she continues unmarried without disturbance" [EQC 9:77-78]. (Samuel Leach and Robert Leach explain that when William Bennett was on his deathbed he sent for them to hear his will, and they sent for a scribe to take down the will, which the scribe began to do, but Bennett died before the will was finished, and so Samuel and Robert are testifying to what they heard; this may explain why some of the bequests are incomprehensible and seemingly contradictory.)

The inventory of the estate of "William Bennit, lately deceased in Manchester Nov. 20 1682," taken 29 December 1682, totalled £189 15s. of which £136 was real estate: "one dwelling house and orchard with other outhousing and a four and twenty acre lot belonging to it with an acre and half of marsh lying to the said lot," £65; "five and twenty acres of land with small orchard to it an acre and half of marsh belonging to it the said land called by the name of Pickworth's lot," £40; one-fourth part of a forty-acre lot by the town, £10; "one acre and half of fresh meadow in the sawmill pond and half an acre at Kettle Island," £8; "one-fourth part of the beaver dam meadow," £1; and "one-fourth part of a saw mill," £12 [EQC 9:78].

Administration of the estate of "William Bennett of Manchester dying intestate" was granted to his widow Jane on 3 April 1683 [EQC 8:439].

The inventory of the estate of "Jane Bennit ... administratrix to the estate of her husband William Bennit the said widow deceased the 27th day of April 1693," taken 8 May 1693, totalled £25 17s., of which £2 10s. was real estate: "a piece of swampy meadow," £2 10s. [EPR 303:154-55].

BIRTH: About 1604 (deposed before 27 March 1677 "aged about seventy-three years" [EQC 6:247-48]).
DEATH: Manchester 20 November 1682 [EQC 9:77].
MARRIAGE: By about 1637 (assuming she is the mother of all his children) Jane Knowles, daughter of Thomas and Jane (Conant) Knowles of East Budleigh, Devonshire [NEHGR 153:221]. She was admitted to Salem church on 18 June 1643 [SChR 12], and died at Manchester on 27 April 1693 [EPR 303:154]. (She is "my daughter-in-law Jane Bennett in New England" named in the 26 October 1657 will of Philip Wotton of East Budleigh, Devonshire [Waters 1141-42], who married the widow of Thomas Knowles.)
CHILDREN:
    i   MOSES BENNETT, b. say 1637; bp. Salem 2 July 1643 [SChR 19]; living 20 November 1682; apparently unm.
    ii   DELIVERANCE BENNETT, b. say 1639; bp. Salem 2 July 1643 [SChR 19]; m. Salem 8 October 1657 Christopher Crow (or Crowell).
    iii   AARON BENNETT, b. say 1641; bp. Salem 2 July 1643 [SChR 19]; m. (1) by 1665 Ann ____ (eldest known child b. Manchester 25 March 1665); (2) by 1708 Elizabeth _____ (in husband's will of 3 December 1708 [EPR 310:90]).
    iv   MARY BENNETT, bp. Salem 3 September 1654 [SChR 24]; living 20 November 1682, unmarried. (The baptismal record calls Mary daughter of James Bennett, but as there is otherwise no record of a James Bennett at Salem this early, and as Jane Bennett was a member of Salem church and William was not, the child would have been baptized in her name, and the entry in the published volume of church records is a simple error.)
ASSOCIATIONS: William Bennett's wife, Jane (Knowles) Bennett, was niece of ROGER CONANT [NEHGR 153:221; PM 134].

COMMENTS: Pope claims that a Jane Bennett, aged 16, who was a passenger to New England in 1635, was the wife of William Bennett [Hotten 72]; this is extremely unlikely, for it would imply a marriage in England, and we have no evidence that William returned to England, and if he had we would not expect her to be travelling alone.
    On 2 and 3 January 1632/3, "William Bennet complained of Edw[ard] Dowty to have dealt fraudulently with him about a flitch of bacon," and of other matters, which were resolved by the Court [PCR 1:7]. On 1 April 1633, William Bennett sued Edward Doty for slander, accusing

Doty of having "called him a rogue, which being proved by diverse testimonies, the jury, Josuah Pratt being foreman, found the defendant to be guilty, & amerced him in fifty shillings fine ..." [PCR 1:12].

As this is the last record of William Bennett in Plymouth, and especially since he does not appear in the tax list of 27 March 1634, he almost certainly left Plymouth shortly after winning this slander suit. That this is the same William Bennett who appeared a short time later in Salem is indicated by the removal there at the same time of others from Plymouth, including RALPH FOGG [PM 206] and FRANCIS WESTON [PM 487]. Presumably these men had become adherents of ROGER WILLIAMS [PM 503] and followed him when he left Plymouth in 1633 and returned to Salem.

William Bennett was one of those who petitioned the General Court on 13 May 1640 "to have Jeffrey's Creek & land to erect a village there," this being the area that became Manchester [EQC 7:201-2; Perley 2:172-75].

Pope misread the will of William Bennett, giving him a son John, probably based on the bequests to grandson John Crow.

BIBLIOGRAPHIC NOTE: For additional information on this family, see Dean Crawford Smith, *The Ancestry of Samuel Blanchard Ordway, 1844-1916* (Boston 1990), pp. 138-42. In 1999 John C. Brandon assembled the evidence that identified the wife of this immigrant [NEHGR 153:221].

JOHN BILLINGTON

ORIGIN: Spalding, Lincolnshire.
MIGRATION: 1620 on the *Mayflower.*
FIRST RESIDENCE: Plymouth.

ESTATE: In the 1623 Plymouth land division John Billington received three acres as a passenger on the *Mayflower* [PCR 12:4]. In the 1627 Plymouth cattle division John Billington Senior, Hellen Billington and Francis Billington were the eleventh through thirteenth persons in the seventh company, and John Billington [Jr.] was the tenth person in the ninth company [PCR 12:11, 12].

On 8 January 1637/8, "Mrs. Elinor Billington, widow," deeded to "Francis Billington my natural son ... all and singular those my land, meadows, pastures and commons with all and singular the appurtenances thereunto belonging situate, lying and being near Plain Dealing within the government of New Plymouth" [PCR 12:28-30]. On 21 September 1638, "Gregory Armestronge, Ellinor his now wife and Francis Billington her natural son" sold to "Mr. William Bradford ... one acre & a half of land lying on the north side of the lands of the said Will[ia]m Bradford upon the lowest division next the water side in the field on the north side of the town of Plymouth" [PCR 12:37-38].

BIRTH: By about 1579 (based on estimated date of marriage).
DEATH: Hanged September 1630 at Plymouth [Bradford 234; WJ 1:43].
MARRIAGE: By about 1604 Elinor _____. She married (2) between 14 and 21 September 1638 Gregory Armstrong and was living as late as 2 March 1642/3 [MF 21:3-4; PCR 12:33-34].
CHILDREN:
   i   JOHN BILLINGTON, b. say 1604; d. Plymouth between 22 May 1627 and September 1630 [PCR 12:12; Bradford 446].
   ii   FRANCIS BILLINGTON, b. about 1606 (deposed 10 July 1674 "68 years of age" [MD 2:46, citing PCR 1:81]); in the Plymouth tax list of 25 March 1633 and 27 March 1634 assessed 9s. [PCR 1:10, 27]; m. Plymouth [blank] July 1634 "Christian Eaton" [PCR 1:31]. She was CHRISTIAN (PENN) EATON, widow of FRANCIS EATON [PM 187].

COMMENTS: In his list of passengers on the *Mayflower,* Bradford includes "John Billington and Ellen his wife, and two sons, John and Francis" [Bradford 442]. John Billington signed the Mayflower Compact on 11 November 1620. In his 1651 accounting of the *Mayflower* families, Bradford reported that "John Billington, after he had been here ten years, was executed for killing a man, and his eldest son died before him but his second son is alive and married and hath eight children" [Bradford 446]. (The man murdered by Billington was JOHN NEWCOMEN [PM 344].)

In a Survey of 1650 for the manor of Spalding in Lincolnshire is a lease for three lives in which one of the lives is "Francis Billington son of John Billington." In describing the three lives involved, we are told that "Francis Billington (as it is informed) was living about a year since in New England aged forty years or thereabouts" [NEHGR 124:116-18]. The estimated age for Francis Billington is probably less accurate than his own deposition in 1674, but this record does provide an excellent clue for further research on the English origin of the family.

Among these incidents the most significant (prior to his committing homicide) was Billington's outspoken support for Lyford and Oldham in their revolt against Bradford and the rest of the Leiden contingent [Bradford 156-57].

BIBLIOGRAPHIC NOTE: The family of John Billington has been treated thoroughly by Harriet Woodbury Hodge (as revised by Robert S. Wakefield) in the twenty-first volume of the Five Generations Project of the General Society of Mayflower Descendants. They list the many occasions on which John Billington or his sons were in trouble with the Plymouth authorities in the first decade of the colony's existence [MF 21:1-4].

THOMAS BLOSSOM

ORIGIN: Leiden, Holland.
MIGRATION: 1629.
FIRST RESIDENCE: Plymouth.

CHURCH MEMBERSHIP: (See discussion below under *COMMENTS*.)
EDUCATION: His correspondence with William Bradford indicates substantial education [MHSC 3:41-42, 44; MD 5:165-67, 169-70]. This may have taken place at Cambridge, although there is no evidence of him on the university records there.
ESTATE: In the 25 March 1633 Plymouth tax list, "Widdow Blossome" was assessed 9s. [PCR 1:11]. (By the date of the 1634 list she had remarried.)

BIRTH: By about 1580 (based on date of marriage). He was probably son of Peter and Annabel (____) Blossom of Great Shelford, Cambridgeshire [TAG 63:73]. (See MD 39:181-82 for another, less likely proposed parentage for the immigrant.)
DEATH: Plymouth before 25 March 1633 [PCR 1:11].
MARRIAGE: St. Clement, Cambridge, Cambridgeshire, 10 November 1605 Anne Elsdon [TAG 63:70]. She married (2) Plymouth 17 October 1633 HENRY ROWLEY [PCR 1:16; PM 398].
CHILDREN:
    i   Child BLOSSOM, bur. Pieterskerk, Leiden, 15 February 1617 [NS] [NEA 3:2:50].

ii   Child BLOSSOM, bur. Pieterskerk, Leiden, 12 April 1617 [NS] [TAG 63:75; NEA 3:2:50].

iii   Son BLOSSOM, b. by 1620; accompanied his father on the *Speedwell* in 1620, returned to Leiden, and died there by 15 December 1625 [MD 5:166-67 (see *COMMENTS* below)].

iv   ELIZABETH BLOSSOM, b. say 1620; m. (1) Scituate 10 May 1637 Edward FitzRandolph [NEHGR 9:286]; m. (2) Piscataway, New Jersey, Capt. John Pike [TAG 63:77].

v   THOMAS BLOSSOM, b. say 1623; m. Barnstable 18 June 1645 Sarah Ewer [NEHGR 9:286; TAG 63:238-39], daughter of THOMAS EWER {1635, Charlestown} [GM 2:2:479-83]. (Florence Harlow Barclay has suggested that Sarah (Ewer) Blossom married as her second husband Nicholas Davis [TAG 64:113-18].)

vi   PETER BLOSSOM, b. after 1627 (not in 1643 list of men able to bear arms); m. Barnstable 21 June 1663 Sarah Bodfish [MD 3:53; TAG 63:239-41].

COMMENTS: In his letter to Bradford from Leiden, dated 15 December 1625 [NS], Blossom closes by stating that "God hath taken away my son, that was with me in the ship, when I went back again; I have only two children which were born since I left you" [MD 5:166-67]. This statement assists greatly in arranging the list of Blossom's children. It also seems to be the only source for the claim that Blossom was one of the passengers on the *Speedwell* in 1620, and that he and his son had to be left behind.

The claim that Thomas Blossom was deacon at Plymouth derives from Savage, but this appears to be a misreading of Prince, who was supposedly quoting Morton, but was in fact misquoting Bradford. In his history of Plymouth, Bradford included an account of the epidemic of 1633 and mentioned Thomas Blossom, Richard Masterson and Samuel Fuller as dying in that year. He refers to Samuel Fuller's services as deacon, and this was apparently transferred by Savage to Blossom [Bradford 260]. Prince quoted most of this same section, but altered the sequence, although not enough to confuse the attribution of the office of deacon, and claimed Morton as his source; he mentioned Blossom and Fuller, but not Masterson [Prince 437]. Morton also paraphrased this same passage, but noted by name only Fuller, so he cannot have been the sole source for Prince [Morton 108]. To this confusing mix we must add Morton's account of the early history of the Plymouth church, in which he explicitly states that Richard Masterson and Thomas Blossom were named deacons *after* the death of Samuel Fuller [PChR 1:83]. But Bradford's language (on which Morton must have been relying here as well) carries the clear implication that Fuller died after Masterson and Blossom, and Samuel Fuller was still alive on 1 July 1633 to receive an allocation of mowing ground [PCR 1:14], whereas Thomas Blossom was already dead by that date. In this instance Morton seems to have misinterpreted Bradford in a different way, and his claim that Masterson and Blossom were briefly deacons at Plymouth should not be accepted.

This passage also bears on the date of death for Thomas Blossom. Most of the deaths in 1633 occurred in the months of June, July and August, and it appears from Prince's version that Blossom falls within this period. But in Bradford the reference to these summer months comes several lines after the mention of Blossom, and Blossom's death is not so closely tied to Fuller's in Bradford as it is in Prince. Blossom had certainly died before 1 July 1633, as a letter of that date from Rev. Ralph Smith in Plymouth to Rev. Hugh Goodyear in Leiden refers to "Tho[mas] Bloso[m] our brother who now sleepeth" [TAG 63:77]. The tax list of 25 March 1633 includes an entry for Widow Blossom, so the death apparently took place before that date, although this list could have been altered at a later date [PCR 1:11].

BIBLIOGRAPHIC NOTE: In 1988 and 1989 John Insley Coddington and Maclean W. McLean published a lengthy article discussing the English ancestry and Leiden sojourn of Thomas Blossom and presenting five generations of male descent [TAG 63:65-77, 238-246, 64:23-31].

THOMAS BOREMAN

In the 25 March 1633 Plymouth tax list "Thomas Boreman" was assessed 9s. [PCR 1:11].

In the 15 November 1633 inventory of John Thorp of Plymouth, carpenter, "Tho[mas] Boreman" owed two pounds of beaver, valued at £1 [MD 1:159].

COMMENTS: In later years there was a Thomas Boreman of Barnstable and a Thomas Boardman of Sandwich and Yarmouth. Was either of these the Thomas Boreman of Plymouth in 1633? The more likely identification is with the Barnstable man [Otis 1:80-81; Stratton 247-48], but there are enough doubts and conflicting data to make this a far from certain conclusion.

Thomas Boreman appeared in the Barnstable section of the 1643 Plymouth Colony list of men able to bear arms [PCR 8:193], and a year or two later he married Hannah Annable, daughter of ANTHONY ANNABLE. From that point on he is consistently associated with Barnstable and died there testate in 1663 [MD 18:63; Otis 1:80-81].

Thomas Boardman is first seen with certainty on 7 August 1638, when the Plymouth court accused him of "living incontinently with Luce, his now wife, and did beget her with child before they were married together"; the court proceedings call him of Sandwich, carpenter, and make it clear that the child born to him and Luce before marriage had been born in London and left behind when he came to New England [PCR 1:93, 94]. Thomas Boardman was granted three acres of meadow at Sandwich on 16 April 1640 [PCR 1:150]. "Thomas Bordman" appeared in the Sandwich section of the 1643 Plymouth Colony list of men able to bear arms [PCR 8:192], making him clearly distinct from Thomas Boreman of Barnstable. After living in Sandwich for a few years, Thomas Boardman moved to Yarmouth, where he died in August 1689 [PCR 12:142; MD 10:101-2]. (There are three additional records, from 1637 and 1639, which cannot be confidently allocated to either man [PCR 1:61, 110, 118].)

The most interesting record comes from the Plymouth court of 13 March 1634/5, where "Thomas Boreman" agreed to carry out the construction of the fort for £30 [PCR 1:33-34]. From the court records for 1638 we know that Thomas Boardman of Sandwich and later Yarmouth was a carpenter. Was Thomas Boreman of Barnstable also a carpenter? Otis claims that he was, but does not cite any document; perhaps he was confused on this point.

If Thomas Boreman of Barnstable was not a carpenter, then we have no certain record of him prior to 1643. Does this mean that Thomas Boardman of Sandwich was the man of the 1633 records? Further research in London records might clarify this point, since we are told that he had a child by Luce in London sometime before 1638 (but probably not long before).

It should be noted further that although "Thomas Boreman" was in the 1633 tax list, he was not in the list of 27 March 1634, which may indicate that, whoever he was, he was not in Plymouth in early 1634. This could of course be a simple defect in the tax list, but until further evidence is uncovered, we make no determination here as to the later history of the Thomas Boreman who was in Plymouth in 1633.

JOHN BOWMAN

John Bowman was assessed 9s. in the Plymouth tax lists of 25 March 1633 and 27 March 1634 [PCR 1:11, 28].

COMMENTS: There is no other record in early New England for this John Bowman. The record cited by Stratton as possibly applying to this man is instead for NATHANIEL BOWMAN {1630, Watertown} [GMB 1:193-96; Stratton 249].

WILLIAM BRADFORD

ORIGIN: Leiden, Holland.
MIGRATION: 1620 on the *Mayflower*.
FIRST RESIDENCE: Plymouth.

OCCUPATION: Magistrate.
CHURCH MEMBERSHIP: As a member of the Scrooby congregation, Bradford was of course prominent also in the churches both at Leiden and Plymouth.
FREEMAN: In 1633 list of Plymouth freemen, prior to those admitted on 1 January 1632/3 [PCR 1:3]. In the list of 7 March 1636/7 [PCR 1:52]. "Mr. William Bradford" (as governor) was in the Plymouth section of the list of 1639 [PCR 8:173].
EDUCATION: Although not educated at one of the universities, Bradford could certainly hold his own with any of those who were. His library was one of the most extensive among the first generation of New Englanders, being valued at £14 3s. [MD 2:232-33], and, like many of the ministers, he had knowledge of many languages, including Hebrew [Bradford xxvii]. His education was also on display in his many writings (see *BIBLIOGRAPHIC NOTE* below).

His inventory included a detailed listing of his library, valued at £14 3s. and comprising two Bibles, thirty books or sets of books (mostly theological) listed by title and a parcel described as "three and fifty small books" [MD 2:232-33, citing PCPR 2:1:57-58]. The inventory of his widow's estate included a similar list, stated to be located in "the study," valued at £14 7s. and comprising the same listing as in her husband's inventory, with the exception of four specific titles which she no longer held [MD 3:146-47, citing PCPR 3:1:3].

OFFICES: Governor of Plymouth Colony, 1621-32, 1635, 1637, 1639-43, 1645-56 [Bradford 86; PCR 1:32, 48, 116, 140, 2:8, 33, 52, 83, 100, 115, 123, 139, 153, 166, 3:7, 30, 48, 77, 99 (note that this gives Bradford thirty-one terms as governor, an accounting at odds with a number of secondary sources)]. Assistant, 1633, 1634, 1636, 1638, 1644 [PCR 1:5, 21, 36, 79, 2:71]. Plymouth Commissioner to United Colonies, 1647-49, 1652, 1656 [PCR 2:115, 123, 139, 3:99, 9:84, 109 (elected president), 150, 10:71, 153 (elected president)].

"Mr. Bradford" appeared in the Plymouth section of the 1643 Plymouth Colony list of men able to bear arms [PCR 8:188]. His inventory included "3 matchcock muskets" valued at £2 2s., "a snaphance musket" valued at £1, "a birding piece and another small piece" valued at 18s., "a pistol and cutlass" valued at 12s., "a corslet and one headpiece" valued at £1 10s. and "1 fowling piece without a lock, 3 old barrels of guns, one pair of old bandoliers and a rest" valued at 16s. [MD 2:229-34, citing PCPR 2:1:54-59]. The inventory of his widow included "2 guns and a pair of bandoliers" valued at £1 and "a rest and some other odd things" valued at 2s. [MD 3:145-49, citing PCPR 3:1:3-5].

ESTATE: In 1623 Plymouth land division received three acres as a passenger on the *Mayflower*, and Alice Bradford received one acre as a passenger on the *Anne* [PCR 12:4, 6]. In the 1627 Plymouth cattle division "the Governor Mr. William Bradford and ... his wife Alles Bradford," William Bradford Junior and Mercy Bradford were the first four persons in the eleventh company [PCR 12:12].

Assessed £1 16s. in the Plymouth tax list of 25 March 1633 and £1 7s. in the list of 27 March 1634 [PCR 1:9, 27].

In his nuncupative will, dated 9 May 1657 and proved 3 June 1657, "Mr. William Bradford Senior being weak in body, but in perfect memory having deferred the forming of his will in hopes of having the help of Mr. Thomas Prence therein," stated that he had "disposed to John and William already their proportions of land, which they are possessed of," asked "that my son Joseph be made in some sort equal to his brethren out of my estate," made "my dear and loving wife Allice Bradford" executrix and for "her future maintenance my will is that my stock in the Kennebecke trade be reserved for her comfortable subsistence," appointed "my well-beloved Christian friends Mr. Thomas Prence, Captain Thomas Willett and Lieutenant Thomas Southworth" as supervisors, to whose wisdom he commended "some small books written by my own hand to be improved as you shall see meet; in special I commend to you a little book with a black cover, wherein there is a word to Plymouth, a word to Boston, and a word to New England, with sundry useful verses" [MD 2:228-29, citing PCPR 2:1:53].

The inventory of "the estate of Mr. Will[i]am Bradford Sr. lately deceased," taken 22 May 1657, was not totalled; it included several parcels of real estate, not all of which were valued: "the house and orchard and some small parcels of land about the town of Plymouth," £45; "one parcel at Eastham and another at Bridgwater," not valued; and "a small parcel about Sawtuckett and his purchase land at Coaksett with his rights in the town's land at Punckatessett," not valued [MD 2:229-34, citing PCPR 2:1:54-59].

In her will, dated 29 December 1669 and proved 7 June 1670, "Allis Bradford Senior of the town of Plymouth ..., widow," requested that "my body may be interred as near unto my deceased husband, Mr. William Bradford, as conveniently may be" and bequeathed to "my dear sister Mary Carpenter" moveables; to "my son Mr. Constant Southworth my land at Paomett"; to "my said son Constant Southworth and unto my son Mr. Joseph Bradford the one-half of my sheep to be equally divided betwixt them and the other half to my son Captain Will[i]am Bradford"; to "my said son Joseph Bradford" livestock; to "my honored friend Mr. Thomas Prence one of the books that were my dear husband's library, which of them he shall choose"; to "my dear grandchild Elizabeth Howland, the daughter of my dear son Captain Thomas Southworth deceased, the sum of seven pounds, for the use and benefit of her son James Howland"; to "my servant maid Mary Smith a cow calf"; residue equally divided to "my sons Mr. Constant Southworth, Captain Will[i]am Bradford and Mr. Joseph Bradford" [MD 3:144-45, citing PCPR 3:1:2].

The inventory of the estate of "Mistress Allice Bradford Senior late deceased," taken 31 March 1670, totalled £162 17s., with no real estate included [MD 3:145-49, citing PCPR 3:1:3-5].

BIRTH: Baptized Austerfield, Yorkshire, 19 March 1589/90, son of William and Alice (Hanson) Bradford [MD 7:65-66; NEHGR 84:10-11].
DEATH: Plymouth 9 May 1657 [Hull 180].
MARRIAGE: (1) Amsterdam, Holland, 10 December 1613 [NS] Dorothy May of Wisbech, Cambridgeshire [MD 9:115-17, 22:63-64; Plooij XXVII, LXX; Stratton 324-26]. She died on 7 December 1620 [Prince 165].

(2) Plymouth 14 August 1623 Alice (Carpenter) Southworth [Prince 221], daughter of Alexander Carpenter and widow of Edward Southworth (see PRISCILLA CARPENTER [PM 92] and CONSTANT

SOUTHWORTH [PM 437]). She died at Plymouth on 26 March 1670 [MD 18:68].

CHILDREN:
With first wife
   i   JOHN BRADFORD, b. say 1617; m. by 1650 Martha Bourne, daughter of Thomas Bourne [Waterman Gen 615-19, 625].

With second wife
   ii   WILLIAM BRADFORD, b. Plymouth 17 June 1624 [Prince 227, MD 30:4]; m. (1) by 1650 Alice Richards, daughter of THOMAS RICHARDS {1633, Dorchester} [GMB 3:1575-79], d. Plymouth 12 December 1671 [MD 18:68]; m. (2) by 1675 Sarah (____) Griswold, widow of Francis Griswold [NEHGR 155:245-50]; m. (3) after 7 March 1675/6 Mary (Wood) Holmes, daughter of John Wood and widow of John Holmes [PCR 5:188, 6:163; PLR 4:20, 11:156, 14:93; NEHGR 144:26-28].

   iii   MERCY BRADFORD, b. by 1627; m. Plymouth 21 December 1648 Benjamin Vermayes [PCR 8:5].

   iv   JOSEPH BRADFORD, b. about 1630; m. Hingham 25 May 1664 Jael Hobart [NEHGR 121:116], daughter of the Reverend Peter Hobart, and granddaughter of EDMUND HOBART {1633, Charlestown} [GMB 2:958-60].

COMMENTS: In his accounting of the *Mayflower* passengers, Bradford described his own family in 1620 as "William Bradford and Dorothy his wife, having but one child, a son left behind who came afterward," and in 1651 reported that "William Bradford his wife died soon after their arrival, and he married again and hath four children, three whereof are married" [Bradford 441, 444].

Although we know that Dorothy May, first wife of William Bradford, was from Wisbech, Cambridgeshire, her parentage has not been satisfactorily determined. She has been called daughter of John and Cordelia (Bowes) May [NEHGR 50:462-65], and this couple apparently did have a daughter Dorothy, but that she was the same as the wife of William Bradford remains only a supposition. Bowman debunked the story claiming that Dorothy (May) Bradford had committed suicide [MD 29:97-102, 31:105], and Stratton summarized the literature on her identity and her death [Stratton 324-26].

BIBLIOGRAPHIC NOTE: The best information on William Bradford is found in his own writings. Most important of these, of course, is his history of Plymouth Colony, and of its antecedents. In his edition of this work Samuel Eliot Morison tells the story of how the manuscript was found after having been lost for many years. He also lists all earlier editions of the history and allows that "the best edition of Bradford was edited by Worthington C. Ford."

History of Plymouth Plantation 1620-1647. By William Bradford, ed. Worthington C. Ford, 2 volumes (Boston 1912).

Of Plymouth Plantation 1620-1647, ed. Samuel Eliot Morison (New York 1952).

The Five Generations Project of the General Society of Mayflower Descendants has published the descendants of William Bradford in Volume 22 of the series, compiled by Ann Smith Lainhart and Robert S. Wakefield and published in 2004.

WILLIAM BREWSTER

ORIGIN: Leiden, Holland.
MIGRATION: 1620 on the *Mayflower*.
FIRST RESIDENCE: Plymouth.
REMOVES: Duxbury.

OCCUPATION: Publisher (in Leiden). (See R. Breugelmans, ed., *The Pilgrim Press, a bibliographical & historical memorial of the books printed at Leyden by the Pilgrim Fathers by Rendel Harris & Stephen R. Jones, With a chapter on the location of the Pilgrim Press in Leyden by Dr. Plooij, Partial reprint with new contributions by R. Breugelmans, J.A. Gruys & Keith Sprunger* [Nieuwkoop 1987].)

CHURCH MEMBERSHIP: Morison summarized Brewster's church activities prior to 1620: "One of the original members of the separatist congregation at Scrooby which became the nucleus of the Pilgrim church, he emigrated with them to Holland in 1608, and became elder and teacher of their church at Leyden" [Morison 368]. With no minister at the Plymouth church for most of the years before Brewster's death, he was the lay leader and preached to the congregation regularly, and continued in this manner after his move to Duxbury. In the course of relating the controversy surrounding John Lyford, Bradford recounts how "our reverend Elder hath labored diligently in dispensing the Word of God to us, before he came: and since, hath taken equal pains with himself, in preaching the same" [Bradford 162]. Included in the inventory of his library were "7 sermons by W B," which may have been his notes for some of his own sermons.

FREEMAN: In 1633 Plymouth list of freemen, prior to those admitted on 1 January 1632/3 [PCR 1:3]. In list of 7 March 1636/7 [PCR 1:52]. In Plymouth section of list of 1639 (annotated "dead") [PCR 8:173].

EDUCATION: Entered Peterhouse, Cambridge, 3 December 1580, but did not graduate [Venn 1:213; Morison 368]. Within the inventory of William Brewster separate listings were made of his Latin and English books, with nearly four hundred titles included; "the total of both Latin & English books amounts to the sum of £42 19s. 11d." [MD 3:27].

ESTATE: In the list of Plymouth "meersteads & garden plots of [those] which came first laid out 1620" Mr. W[illia]m Brewster is on the south side of the street, at the corner of the highway, and next to John Goodman [PCR 12:3].

In the 1623 Plymouth land division Mr. William Brewster received six acres as a passenger on the *Mayflower*, and "Pacience & Fear Brewster" received two acres as passengers on the *Anne* [PCR 12:4, 6]. In the 1627 Plymouth cattle division "Mr. Will[ia]m Brewster," Love Brewster and Wrestling Brewster were the first three names in the fifth company [PCR 12:10].

Assessed £1 7s. in the Plymouth tax lists of 25 March 1633 and 27 March 1634 [PCR 1:9, 27].

Administration on the estate of William Brewster was granted on 5 June 1644 to Jonathan Brewster and Love Brewster [MD 3:15, citing PCR 2:101]. The inventory of the estate of William Brewster, taken 18 May 1644, totalled £150 7d., with no real estate included [MD 3:15-27, citing PCPR 1:53-59].

"Whereas William Brewster late of Plymouth, gent., deceased left only two sons surviving vizt. Jonathan the eldest and Love the younger and whereas the said William died intestate for ought can to this day appear," the two sons requested William Bradford, Edward Winslow, Thomas Prence and Miles Standish to assist them in coming to an agreement, and on 20 August 1645 a division was made. Jonathan Brewster was excused the debt he had owed to his father, except £4 "in consideration of the wintering of some cattle which the said Jonathan had the summering upon the division and for the diet of Isaack Allerton a grandchild of the said Will[ia]m which he had placed with his son Love to table and because he was the first born of his father we gave him his father's arms and also a two year old heifer over and above his part of the dividables of the said estate," and Love received his father's dwelling house. The lands were divided equally, except for a dispute over the lands at Duxbury, of which sixty-eight acres went to Jonathan (along with a "dwelling house which the said Jonathan had built on the said land by leave of his said father") and forty-three acres went to Love "and the reason wherefore we gave Love the less quantity was and is because the quality of Love's land in goodness is equal to the quantity of Jonathan's as we judge" [MD 3:27-30, citing PCLR 1:198-99; PCR 12:115-17].

BIRTH: About 1566, probably at Scrooby, Nottinghamshire, son of William Brewster.
DEATH: Duxbury 10 April 1644 [MD 1:7].
MARRIAGE: By 1593 Mary _____. She died at Plymouth on 17 April 1627 [MD 1:7]. (See *COMMENTS* below for discussion of her identity.)
CHILDREN:
- i JONATHAN BREWSTER, b. Scrooby, Nottinghamshire, 12 August 1593 [MD 1:7]; m. Plymouth 10 April 1624 "Lucretia Oldam of Darby" [MD 1:8]; she was bp. All Saints, Derby, Derbyshire, 14 January 1600/1, and was sister of JOHN OLDHAM [PM 345].
- ii PATIENCE BREWSTER, b. say 1603; m. Plymouth 5 August 1624 THOMAS PRENCE [PM 374], "the ninth marriage at New Plymouth" [Prince 229].
- iii FEAR BREWSTER, b. say 1605; m. Plymouth by 1627 ISAAC ALLERTON [Bradford 218, 242; PM 10].
- iv LOVE BREWSTER, b. say 1607; m. Plymouth 15 May 1634 Sarah Collier [PCR 1:30], daughter of WILLIAM COLLIER [PM 128].
- v Child BREWSTER, bur. St. Pancras, Leiden, 20 June 1609 [NS] [Dexter 605].
- vi WRESTLING BREWSTER, b. say 1611; d. unm. after 1627 and by 1651 [Bradford 444; see GDMNH 109, MD 43:13, Waterhouse Anc 67].

COMMENTS: In his list of passengers on the *Mayflower* Bradford included "Mr. William Brewster, Mary, his wife, with two sons, whose names were Love and Wrestling" [Bradford 441]. In the accounting of 1651 we find that "Mr. Brewster lived to very old age; about 80 years he was when he died, having lived some 23 or 24 years here in the country. And though his wife died long before, yet she died aged. His son Wrestling died a young man unmarried. His son Love lived till this year 1650 and died and left four children, now living. His daughters which came over after him are dead but have left sundry children alive. His eldest son is still living and hath nine or ten children; one married who hath a child or two" [Bradford 444].

The quest for the identity of Mary, the wife of William Brewster, has attracted the attention of many genealogists, but as yet without a definitive result. For some time she had been thought to be Mary Wentworth, daughter of Thomas Wentworth of Scrooby, and in 1965 John G. Hunt presented his case in favor of this identity [TAG 41:1-5, 63], but this claim was rejected by Rubincam and others, and Hunt himself has now given up this position. He has, however, published a pamphlet claiming that she was a certain Mary Wyrrall, based on the appearance in a will of a bequest to "Mary Butho," which Hunt took be a variant of Brewster resulting from a speech defect in the person dictating the will [John G. Hunt, *Of Mary Brewster: The Identity of Mary, Wife of Elder William BREWSTER of the Mayflower Voyage of 1620 from Plymouth, England, to New Plymouth, New England* (Bowling Green, Virginia, 1984)]. Eugene A. Stratton reviewed this volume negatively in 1985 [*Detroit Society for Genealogical Research Magazine* 48:135-36], to which Hunt responded with a supplement to his pamphlet [*Of Mary Brewster, part two* (Bowling Green, Virginia, August 1985]. The maiden surname of Mary, wife of Elder Brewster, remains unknown. (Hunt has published other articles on various aspects of William Brewster's life, which, as with all of Hunt's work, need to be used with caution: "'Master Williamson' of the *Mayflower*" [NGSQ 62:88-90]; "The Mother of Elder William Brewster of the Mayflower" [NEHGR 124:250-56]; "Mary Stubbe - A Connection of Elder William Brewster?" [NEHGR 128:288-90].)

A number of other children have been proposed for William Brewster, although there is no reason to accept any of these proposals. Jacobus in 1936 disposed of the claimed connections between William Brewster of Plymouth and Francis Brewster of New Haven and his son Nathaniel [TAG 12:199-210, 13:8-21, 113-116]. Mary Walton Ferris proposed a son Edward, for whom there is no evidence [Dawes-Gates 2:151].

BIBLIOGRAPHIC NOTE: Emma C. Brewster Jones published early in this century a serviceable genealogy of the family [*The Brewster Genealogy, 1566-1907* ..., 2 volumes (New York 1908)]. Among the many versions of the family published in all-my-ancestor volumes the most complete is that of Mary Walton Ferris [Dawes-Gates 2:142-56].

The General Society of Mayflower Descendants published in its "Mayflower Families in Progress" series an accounting of the first four generations of descendants of William Brewster, prepared by Barbara Lambert Merrick, the third edition of which was published in 2000. Two additional volumes by the same compiler were published in 1999 and 2000, the first of these on the fifth-generation descendants of son Jonathan Brewster, and the second on the fifth-generation descendants of daughter Patience (Brewster) Prence.

In 1985 and 1986 Jeremy D. Bangs published a three-part article presenting and discussing all known documents naming Jonathan Brewster in Leiden [MQ 51:161-67, 52:6-16, 57-63]. Bangs examined the claim made by the Dexters that Jonathan Brewster had an earlier wife and child while residing in Leiden and determined that the records cited by the Dexters did not pertain to Jonathan Brewster.

THOMAS BRIAN

10 January 1632/3: "Thomas Brian, the servant of Samuel Eedy, was brought before the Governor, & Mr. William Bradford, Mr. John Done, Stephen Hopkins, & William Gilson, Assistants, because the said Thomas had run away & absented himself five days from his master's service, and being lost in the woods, & found by an Indian, was forced to return; and for this offence was privately whipped before the Governor & Council aforementioned" [PCR 1:7].

COMMENTS: SAMUEL EDDY had arrived in New England in 1630 and in 1633 was a resident of Plymouth.

Pope claimed that this is the same as the Thomas Briant, servant of Mr. [Isaac] Allerton, who appeared before the Massachusetts Bay court on 14 June 1642 [MBCR 2:6, 8]. Pope apparently based this identification on the name and on the connection of Allerton with Plymouth. Given the lapse of ten years between the two court records, this conclusion seems doubtful. In any case no other occurrence of the name is seen in early New England records. [See also Stratton 252.]

WILLIAM BRIDGES

ORIGIN: Unknown.
MIGRATION: 1623 on the *Anne*.
FIRST RESIDENCE: Plymouth.
REMOVES: Watertown 1630, Charlestown 1643.

RETURN TRIPS: Possibly with stepfather John Oldham in England from 1628 to 1630.

OCCUPATION: Ferryman. At Charlestown selectmen's meeting of 22 February 1646/7 "[i]t was agreed that Peter Tuft may join with his brother William Bridges to keep the ferry" [ChTR 71]. (Tufts and Bridges had married sisters, daughters of Thomas Pierce.)
CHURCH MEMBERSHIP: Admission to Watertown or Charlestown church prior to 26 May 1647 implied by freemanship (and see *COMMENTS* below).
FREEMAN: 26 May 1647 [MBCR 2:294].
ESTATE: Granted thirty-five acres in the Great Dividend in Watertown, 25 July 1636 [WaBOP 4]. Granted five acres in the Beaverbrook Plowlands, 28 February 1636/7 [WaBOP 6]. Granted five acres in the Remote Meadows, 26 June 1637 [WaBOP 8]. Granted a Farm of seventy-seven acres, 10 May 1642 [WaBOP 13].

In the Watertown Composite Inventory, William Bridges held three parcels: "homestall of five acres"; "four acres of Remote Meadows & the 9 lot"; and "a Farm of seventy-seven acres of upland in the 7 division" [WaBOP 52]. (There is no entry for William Bridges in either the Inventory of Grants or the Inventory of Possessions, so we cannot tell whether he acquired his homelot by grant from the town or purchase from an earlier owner. Of the other two parcels of land known to have been granted to William Bridges by the town, the Great Dividend parcel was held by John Brabrook in the Inventory of Possessions and the Composite Inventory [WaBOP 34, 122], and the Beaverbrook Plowlands parcel was held by Simon Eire Jr. in the same two inventories [WaBOP 46, 131].)

On 1 December 1643, "William Bridges of Charlstowne" sold to "John Bageley twenty acres of land lying in Watertowne in the first squadron & the fifteenth lot" [SLR 1:46]. (This lot in the Great Dividends had originally been granted to Henry Dengayne and was sold by Bridges to John Bigelow [WaBOP 3, 58, 139-40].)

In 1644 William Bridges petitioned General Court for a grant of land based on his service to John Oldham, but was told to look for land in a new plantation [MA Arch 45:94].

On 2 February 1648[/9?], "Peircis Bridges, widow of William Bridges," sold to "Richard Temple one dwelling house and a barn, and half an acre of ground … situate on the stinted common of Charltowne" [ChBOP 105]. On 6 May 1653, "Peircis Bridges, formerly the widow of William Bridges, deceased, but now the wife of John Harrison, of

Boston, ropemaker," sold to "Christopher Goodwinge, bricklayer, inhabitant in Charlstown, ... my house and garden, being by estimation half an acre of land," also "two cow commons on the stinted common in Charlstown" [ChBOP 127-28].

BIRTH: By about 1615 (based on receipt of land grant in Watertown in 1636, and estimated date of marriage).
DEATH: Before 6 February 1648/9, when wife Persis appears as widow [ChBOP 105]; probably during 1648.
MARRIAGE: By 1643 Persis Pierce, daughter of Thomas and Elizabeth (____) Pierce of Charlestown. (Her identity is deduced from the 1665 will of Thomas Pierce naming granddaughters Mary Bridge and Elizabeth Jefts [Tufts] living with him, and the Charlestown town record of 1646/7 calling William Bridges and Peter Tufts brothers [MPR Case #17583; ChTR 71].) Persis was born in England, probably about 1625, and came to Charlestown in 1634 with her family. "Peircis Bridges" was admitted to Charlestown church 30 November 1643 [ChChR 10]. After William Bridges's death, and no later than 6 May 1653, she had married John Harrison of Boston, ropemaker [ChBOP 127].
CHILDREN:
- i REBECCA BRIDGES, b. Charlestown 2 Feb. 1643/4 [ChVR 1:8]; d. there 30 April 1644 [ChVR 1:8].
- ii PERSIS BRIDGES, b. say 1645; m. by 1664 William Brown of Boston (eldest known child b. Boston 6 July 1664 [BVR 91; TAG 9:59]).
- iii SAMUEL BRIDGES, b. Charlestown 25 March 1647 [ChVR 1:10]; m. (1) by 1672 Hannah _____ (eldest known child b. Boston 20 May 1672 [BVR 122]); m. (2) Boston 3 December 1690 "Christian Peirse" [BVR 191], widow of Nathaniel Peirce and daughter of Anthony and Christian (Eire) Stoddard [Hale, House 739].
- iv MARY BRIDGES, b. say 1649; m. Charlestown 22 June 1668 John Knight [ChVR 1:28]. Thomas Pierce in his will of 7 November 1665 named granddaughter Mary Bridge, and Mary (Bridge) Knight twice named daughters Persis [MPR Case #17583; ChVR 1:72, 83].

ASSOCIATIONS: Stepson of JOHN OLDHAM of Plymouth and Watertown [PM 345].

COMMENTS: The evidence that ties together William's career is his petition of 1644, transcribed here in full [MA Arch 45:94]:

To the Wor[shipful] Governor the Assistants and the deputies of this present genl. Courte

The humble petition of William Bridge of Charlestown

Humbly shewing unto your Wor[ships] that whereas I came over into this Countrey with Mr. John Oldham who was my father-in-law about one & twenty yeares since & endured much hardship diverse yeares together with him not having received any recompence of him besides what my then present necessities did require, he dying in debt, I doe humbly intreate your Wor[ships] to consider that my condition and (if it shall seeme good to your Wor[ships]) to appoint unto me your pore petitioner some quantity of land by way of recompence for my sd service done to my sd father-in-law, and that the rather because I have yet had no allotment of land given me by any towne. Thus desiring the Lord to direct you
   I remaine, yours in all dutie according to God

      William Bridge

     [The] answer to this
  Wee conceive that there is no reason to grant land to any upon such considerations, as is mentioned in your petition; but rather we would advise such to look after new plantations in which they are likely to be considered
  Voted by the howse of deputyes, who desire [that] our honored Magistrates would consent to this returne
     Per Robert Bridges, by order from the howse

Consented unto by the Magistrates
   Jo: Endicott Gov[erno]r

This petition and its endorsements are undated, but in the court records is the following order, dated 11 June 1644 [MBCR 3:8]:

It is ordered (in answer to the petition of William Bridge) that this Court thinks not meet to grant land to any upon such considerations therein expressed, but advise such to look after new plantations.

Thus, the petition was probably written in early 1644, shortly after Bridges's marriage and move to Charlestown.

The claim in this petition that "I have yet had no allotment of land given me by any towne" is clearly belied by the grants recorded to him in Watertown several years before this petition. This was undoubtedly known to many members of the General Court, easily explaining the rejection of the petition by that body.

In this same connection, we note that there were a number of irregularities in the land records generated by William Bridges in Watertown. His grants in the Beaverbrook Plowlands and the Remote Meadows were five acres each, but some years later they appear in the Watertown land inventories as four acres each. The alteration in these grants was highly unusual and indicates that some special circumstance must have been involved. Furthermore, a grant of five acres would indicate a family of that size, but in 1637, when these two grants were made, William Bridges had not yet married. Finally, based on the existence of his entry in the Composite Inventory, we would expect entries for William Bridges in the Inventory of Grants, and possibly in the Inventory of Possessions, if his homestall did not come to him by direct grant from the town, but no such entries exist.

A possible expanation for all this would be that these grants of land were based on a proprietary share originally granted to John Oldham, William Bridges's stepfather. As a resident of Watertown in the early 1630s, Oldham would have received a homestall, which would have carried with it the right to later divisions of land. Oldham was killed by the Indians in July of 1636, close to the date of the granting of the Great Dividend lots. Perhaps one or more of the four Watertown grants recorded to William Bridges were actually made to "the estate of John Oldham" or "in the right of John Oldham," thus providing to William Bridges some legalistic cover for making the inaccurate claim in the petition.

In the Boston records is the birth of a son Peter to William and Mary Bridg [*sic*] in January 1643/4 [BVR 15]. Based on this and the statement above that John Oldham was father-in-law of William Bridges, earlier sources concluded that William Bridges had a first wife Mary, daughter of John Oldham, that she had son Peter, that she died soon, and that Bridges then married Persis Pierce. Two arguments allow us to eliminate wife Mary and son Peter from this family. First, there is no other record to connect William Bridges with Boston, while there is a William *Briggs* with wife Mary who has other children in Boston. Second, William

Bridges could not possibly have had a son Peter born in January 1643/4 and a daughter Rebecca born in February 1643/4.

Having cleared away these difficulties, and knowing that William Bridges's wife Persis was not a daughter of John Oldham, we must interpret "father-in-law" in this case to mean stepfather. This accords better with the petition of William Bridges, since he said that he had come over to New England in 1623 with his father-in-law, long before he was married to anyone. The subsequent conclusion is that JOHN OLDHAM must have married a widow Bridges before sailing from England, and that this wife and a young stepson William Bridges accompanied him in that year on the *Anne*.

With regard to William Bridges's church membership and freemanship, we need to examine the freeman admissions on 26 May 1647 [MBCR 2:294]. Beginning with "Ro: Chaulkly" we have a sequence of nine men made free on that date, ending with "John Wayte," who had been admitted to Charlestown church between 1 July 1645 and 3 May 1647 (assuming that Edward Harrington of the church admissions is Richard Harrington of the list of freemen) [ChChR 11]. Following these nine are names of three more men associated with Charlestown about this time, but not admitted to Charlestown church by 26 May 1647: Lawrence Dowse (admitted Boston church 22 March 1644/5 [BChR 43] and Charlestown church 21 March 1652[/3?] [ChChR 11]); William Bridges; and Edward White (admitted Roxbury church early 1640s [RChR 85] and died Charlestown by 13 January 1648[/9?] [Wyman 1015]).

If our conclusion that the Edward White who first shows up in Roxbury is the one who died in Charlestown a few years later is correct, then we have parallel sequences for Dowse and White: admitted to a church other than Charlestown and then moved to Charlestown prior to 26 May 1647, without transferring their membership to Charlestown church by that date. And if this is correct, then we conclude that men who had joined church A and then moved to town B could be submitted for freemanship by town B (or the minister of town B) before joining that church. And if all this is true, then the likely sequence for William Bridges would be that he joined Watertown church sometime before his move to Charlestown about 1643 and never got around to transferring his membership to Charlestown church.

CLEMENT BRIGGS

ORIGIN: Southwark, Surrey.
MIGRATION: 1621 on the *Fortune.*
FIRST RESIDENCE: Plymouth.
REMOVES: Weymouth by 1630.

OCCUPATION: Fellmonger [PCR 12:34-35].
EDUCATION: Made his mark to his deed of 8 October 1637 and deposition of 29 August 1638. His inventory included "books" valued at 6s.
OFFICES: His inventory included "arms 1 musket 12s. 1 small gun 10s. 1 sword 6s." [SPR 3:151-52, Case #101].
ESTATE: In the 1623 Plymouth land division, "Clemente Brigges" was granted one acre "beyond the first brook to the wood westward" as a passenger on the *Fortune* [PCR 12:5]. In the 1627 Plymouth cattle division, "Clemont Briggs" was included in the company of John Howland [PCR 12:10].

On 8 October 1637, "Clement Briggs of Wessaguscus" sold to "John Browne of Plymouth ... four acres of land of the upper end of that lot of land that appertaineth unto me the said Clement Briggs and that the said John Browne doth also agree that the said Clement Briggs shall have for him & his heirs forever the like quantity of four acres of land out of the land of the said John Browne lying at the lower end and adjoining to the residue of the land of the aforesaid Clement Briggs at Joanes River" [PCR 12:22]. On 29 August 1639, Clement Briggs sold to "Mr. Rob[er]te Heeks one acre of land in the upper fall near the Second Brook" [PCR 12:34].

In a compilation of Weymouth landholding, probably prepared about 1643, Clement Briggs held two parcels of land: "ten acres in the eastern neck first granted to him" and "two acres upon the neck at the ferry" [Weymouth Hist 1:190].

In his undated will, probated 24 October 1650, "Clemant Brigs of Waymouth" bequeathed to "my son Thomas my home lot at Plimouth 20 acres ... and my biggest iron pot"; to "my son Jonathan 3 acres of my land joining to John Rees land that is not broke up and to enter it when he is of the age of 18 years and when he is of the age of 21 years to have so much as will make the portion 3 acres one fourth part of all my lands in Waymouth and after the decease of my wife it is my will he shall have one fourth part more"; to "my son Clemat my housing and the other half of my land in Waymouth and to enter it when he is of the age of 21 years"; to "my sons Thom[as], David, John, Rememb[er] my other land at Plimouth or in Plimouth jointly and equally amongst them"; "one year after Clem[en]t do enter to the foresaid land he shall give his brother Rememb[er] 20s. and John 10s. and ... Jonathan shall give 10s. to his brother David and to brother Thom[as] 10s. in one year after he do enter to half my land"; wife to be executrix and John Rogers and Robert Tucker overseers [SPR Case #101]. (This will was not recorded until the nineteenth century, at which time the copyist misread Remember as Edmund [SPR NS 1:456].)

The inventory of the estate of Clement Briggs, taken 23 February 1648[/9?] and presented at court 28 July 1659, totalled £65 7s., of which £36 was real estate: "one dwelling house and old barn," £4; "17 acres of planting land adjoining to the said house," £18; "one share of upland upon the eastward neck," £5; "3 acres near James Smith's house," £2; "one acre of salt marsh upon the westward neck near the ferry," £4; "about an acre of marsh more on the eastward neck," £2; and "land in Plimouth and Plimoth Pattent," £1 [SPR 3:151-52, Case #101].

On 7 June 1659, Plymouth court granted to "Thomas Briggs, son of Clement Briggs, deceased," one hundred fifty acres of land and twenty acres of meadow "in the way to Deadum from Taunton" [PCR 3:164].

On 8 June 1664, "Phineas Pratte and the Elder Bates, in the behalf of the children of Clement Briggs," not having "had their proportions of land with others of this jurisdiction formerly called purchasers or old comers," asking for consideration, Plymouth court granted "unto the said Phineas Pratt and unto two of the said Clement Briggs his sons, viz:, David Briggs and Remember Briggs, three hundred and fifty acres" of land in Plymouth Colony near the Massachusetts Bay line "near unto Waymouth," assigning two-thirds of the grant to Pratt and the other third to the sons of Clement Briggs [PCR 4:68].

On 19 March 1671, twelve acres of marsh land were laid out to "the children of Clement Briggs," by order of court 29 October 1668, adjoining "their Great Lot" [PCLR 3:214; PCR 5:5].

In her will, dated 13 November 1683 and probated 11 August 1691, "Elizabeth Briggs of Weymouth" bequeathed to "my son David," £10, brass kettle, brass pot, and great Bible; to "my grandchild Clement Briggs," £15, if he renounces further claims on estate; to "my son Remember Briggs," remainder of estate, he to be executor; in a codicil of 11 November 1685, Elizabeth Briggs noted that her son David had died since the making of her will and reassigned David's bequest of £10 to her grandson Clement Briggs, and the rest of David's legacy to Remember Briggs [SPR Case #1873].

BIRTH: By about 1600 (the deposition of 1638 implies that in 1616 Briggs had already been a servant of Mr. Samuel Latham for a few years).

DEATH: By 23 February 1648[/9?] (date of inventory).

MARRIAGE: (1) By 1 March 1630/1 Joan Allen (on 1 March 1630/1, "Mr. Tho[mas] Stoughton, constable of Dorchester, is fined £5 for taking upon him to marry Clement Briggs & Joane Allen" [MBCR 1:83]). She died by 1640. (On 6 March 1637/8 at a Quarter Court at Cambridge, Clement Briggs gave a bond of £10 for the appearance of his wife at the next court; at the same court Arthur Warren was presented "for keeping company with Clement Briggs's wife, [which] was found to be true" [MBCR 1:219]. At a Quarter Court on 5 June 1638, Clement Briggs's wife was "enjoined not to come into the company of Arthur Warren" [MBCR 1:233].)

(2) By 1640 Elizabeth _____. She died between 11 November 1685 (date of codicil) and 11 August 1691 (probate of will).

CHILDREN:

With first wife

   i THOMAS BRIGGS, b. Weymouth 14 June 1633 [NEHGR 8:348]; m. by an unknown date Ann _____ [BrPR 2:64-65].

   ii JONATHAN BRIGGS, b. Weymouth 14 June 1635 [NEHGR 8:348]; m. by about 1664 Experience _____ [TAG 33:83-86].

With second wife

   iii DAVID BRIGGS, b. Weymouth 23 August 1640 [NEHGR 8:348]; d. between 13 November 1683 (date of mother's will) and 11 November 1685 (codicil to that will), apparently without issue.

   iv CLEMENT BRIGGS, b. Weymouth 1 January 1642[/3] [NEHGR 8:348]; m. by 1669 Hannah Packard (on 19 November 1669, "administration of the estate of Clement Briggs of Weymouth deceased [was] granted to Hannah Briggs his relict and Samuel Packer his father" and "100 acres of land acknowledged before the honored magistrates given by Samuell Packer with his daughter in marriage" [SPR 7:1]).

   v REMEMBER BRIGGS, b. say 1645; m. by 1686 Mary _____ (eldest known child of "Remember and Mary" b. Weymouth 4 November 1686).

   vi JOHN BRIGGS, b. say 1647; named in his father's will; no further record. (He is not named in the will of Elizabeth

Briggs, which might be evidence that he was not her son, but he was almost certainly dead before she wrote her will; if he had been a son of Clement Briggs by his first wife, he should have appeared in the Weymouth vital records for the 1630s and early 1640s. There is no evidence that he is any one of the men by the name of John Briggs later appearing in New England.)

ASSOCIATIONS: On 29 August 1638, "Clement Briggs of Weymouth, fellmonger," deposed that "about two and twenty years since this deponent then dwelling with one Mr. Samuel Lathame in Barmundsey Street in Southwarke, a fellmonger, and one Thomas Harlow then also dwelling with Mr. Rob[er]te Heeks in the same street, a fellmonger, the said Harlow and this deponent had often conference together how many pelts each of their masters pulled a week." Briggs goes on to tell in detail how many pelts had been handled a week "for the space of three or four years," possibly implying that he had in 1616 been servant to Samuel Latham since about 1612. The deposition was apparently taken at the request of ROBERT HICKS [PM 243], who may have been involved in a lawsuit in England [PCR 12:34-35].

COMMENTS: In a letter of 6 February 1631/2 from the governor and assistants of Plymouth to the governor and assistants of Massachusetts, Clement Briggs is included in a list of men who had "gone from hence, to dwell and inhabit with you" [WP 3:65]. Savage thought that Briggs first went to Dorchester and then Weymouth, based probably on the fact that Thomas Stoughton, who married Clement Briggs and Joan Allen, was a resident of Dorchester. However, at this time Weymouth (still Wessaguscus) was for administrative purposes considered a part of Dorchester, and it is more likely that Briggs went directly from Plymouth to Weymouth.

The children of Clement Briggs are distributed between his two wives based on the bequests made in the will of Clement's widow, Elizabeth (____) Briggs.

BIBLIOGRAPHIC NOTE: In 1966 Edna Anne Hannibal, with the assistance of Claude W. Barlow, published a solid genealogy of the descendants of Clement Briggs [*Clement Briggs of Plymouth Colony and His Descendants, 1621-1965* (n.p., 1966)]. This volume presents evidence supporting the interesting hypothesis that the widow of Clement Briggs was the "widow Briggs" residing in the early 1650s at Southampton [p. 4].

80   The Pilgrim Migration

RICHARD BRITTERIDGE

Richard Britteridge appears in Bradford's list of *Mayflower* passengers as one of the many single men who "died soon after ... arrival in the general sickness" [Bradford 443, 447]. He signed the Mayflower Compact on 11 November 1620. "Dec. 21 [1620], dies Richard Britteridge, the first who dies in this harbour" [Prince 168].

JOHN BROWN

ORIGIN: Dorking, Surrey [TAG 79:161].
MIGRATION: 1632.
FIRST RESIDENCE: Duxbury.

OCCUPATION: Weaver [PCLR 1:186].
FREEMAN: Took oath of fidelity at Duxbury in 1658 [PCR 8:182].
EDUCATION: Signed his will by mark.
OFFICES: In Duxbury section of 1643 Plymouth Colony list of men able to bear arms [PCR 8:189].
ESTATE: Assessed 9s. in Plymouth tax lists of 25 March 1633 and 27 March 1634 [PCR 1:10, 27].

On 8 June 1650, William Allin of Sandwich sold to John Browne of Duxbury, weaver, about thirty acres of upland in Duxbury "being one part of three of land which appertained unto the children of Peter Brown, brother unto John" [PCLR 1:186, cited in TAG 42:41]. On 13 August 1679, Ephraim Tinkham of New Plymouth sold to John Brown of Duxbury two acres of meadow "one of which I had in right of Mary my wife, daughter of Peter Brown deceased" [PCLR 5:197, cited in TAG 42:41]. On 7 November 1679, William Snow of Bridgewater sold to John Brown "all that my one third of 25 acre lots of land formerly of Peter Brown of Duxbury" [PCLR 5:197, cited in TAG 42:41].

In his will, dated 15 April 1672 and sworn 5 June 1684, "John Brown of Duxbury, planter," bequeathed "unto Pheebe my wife all my houses, lands, & cattells & moveables for term of her life, & as for cattells & moveables to be disposed of at her discretion, and at the end of her life I give this aforementioned houses & lands unto my son-in-law Josiah Wormall & unto his wife Remember my true & natural daughter, and at the end of their lives the aforementioned houses & lands I give unto John Wormall my grandchild at the decease of his father & mother, and if God so dispose that the aforesaid John Wormall be deceased before he do or may by right enjoy it then I give it equally between Pheebe & Lyddia my grandchildren" [PCPR 4:2:128].

BIRTH: Baptized Dorking, Surrey, 29 June 1600, son of William Brown [TAG 79:161].
DEATH: By 5 June 1684 (probate of will).
MARRIAGE: 26 March 1634 Phebe Harding [PCR 1:26]. She was named in her husband's will, 15 April 1672.
CHILD:
    i   REMEMBER BROWN, b. say 1648; m. by about 1668 Josiah Wormall [MD 43:154-59].
ASSOCIATIONS: Brother of PETER BROWN of Plymouth.

COMMENTS: The identification of John Brown of Duxbury as brother of Peter was published in 1957 by Donald Lines Jacobus and again in 1966 by Florence Barclay [TAG 33:214-22, 42:35-42]. More recently Gerald W. McFarland repeated this identification, and added to it an explicit argument showing why this John Brown was not the same man as the John Brown who resided in Plymouth, Taunton and Rehoboth, and served frequently as an Assistant of Plymouth Colony [NEHGR 140:331-32; GMB 2:1:420-29].

It remains to demonstrate that John Brown, brother of Peter, was the man taxed in Plymouth in 1633 and 1634, thus placing his arrival as early as 1632, and removing any evidence for the presence of the more prominent John Brown in Plymouth prior to 1635.

John Browne of Plymouth, Taunton and Rehoboth was referred to in the records as "Mr." or "gent." He had travelled to Leiden, where he met the Rev. John Robinson [Morton 171-72]. He was elected an assistant on 5 January 1635/6 [PCR 1:36] and had, along with Timothy Hatherly, been admitted as a freeman on the same day [PCR 1:4]. From that date on, he was frequently named to high office and was one of the most important men in the colony.

The tax list entries for 1633 and 1634 assess John Brown at nine shillings, the lowest amount assessed. Mr. John Browne, the assistant, would have had an estate large enough to earn a higher assessment. John Brown, brother of Peter, fits the economic profile of these tax assessments better, and we already know that he was in Plymouth at least by 1633, based on his date of marriage.

Thus, the evidence is consistent with the arrival of John Brown, brother of Peter, by 1632, in time to appear in the 1633 tax list, and of Mr. John Browne in 1635, followed by immediate admission as a freeman and election as an assistant. [For more on this John Brown, see GM 2:1:420-29.]

John Brown may have lived for some time in Plymouth before his removal to Duxbury, but the earliest records for this man (two tax lists and marriage) may have been from either town, as the colony records at this date do not differentiate among Plymouth, Duxbury and Scituate.

Since John Brown of Duxbury had arrived by 1632, there is a chance that he was the John Brown who sailed on the *Lyon* in 1632, but reasons are given in the sketch of JOHN BROWN of Watertown for thinking that he is more likely this passenger [GMB 1:255-57].

The estimated date of birth for daughter Remember is based on the crude estimate that she married by about 1668, based on her father's will which shows that she had three children by 1672. Josiah Wormall was born in Rowley in 1642. Remember was in fact probably born somewhat earlier than 1648, but still probably some years after her parents' marriage.

BIBLIOGRAPHIC NOTE: In 2004 Caleb Johnson published data that establishes with a high degree of certainty that the brothers John and Peter Brown were baptized in Dorking, Surrey [TAG 79:161].

PETER BROWN

ORIGIN: Dorking, Surrey [TAG 79:161].
MIGRATION: 1620 on the *Mayflower*.
FIRST RESIDENCE: Plymouth.

FREEMAN: In 1633 Plymouth list of freemen, ahead of those made free on 1 January 1632/3 [PCR 1:4].
EDUCATION: His inventory included "1 Bible" valued at 3s.
OFFICES: His inventory included "1 fowling piece" valued at £1 10s. and "12 oz. of shot" valued at 2s. [MD 1:79-82, citing PCPR 1:7-8].
ESTATE: In list of "meersteads & garden plots of [those] which came first laid out 1620" on south side of street next to John Goodman [PCR 1:3].

In the 1623 Plymouth land division "Peter Browen" received one acre as a passenger on the *Mayflower* [PCR 12:4]. In the 1627 Plymouth cattle division Peter Brown, Martha Brown and Mary Brown were the fourth, fifth and sixth persons in the eighth company [PCR 12:11].

"Peter Browne" was assessed 18s. in Plymouth tax list of 25 March 1633 [PCR 1:10]. "Widow Browne" was assessed 9s. in list of 27 March 1634 [PCR 1:28].

The inventory of the estate of "Peter Browne of New Plymouth deceased," taken 10 October 1633, was untotalled, and presented at court on 28 October 1633, on which date the widow, Mary Brown, was granted administration [MD 1:79-82, citing PCPR 1:7-8; PCR 1:17].

On 11 November 1633, a court of assistants at Plymouth ordered that "whereas Peter Browne died without will, having diverse children by diverse wives, his estate amounting to an hundred pounds, or thereabouts, it is ordered, that Mary, his wife, who is allowed the administratrix of the said Peter, forthwith pay down fifteen pounds for the use of Mary Browne, daughter of the said Peter, to Mr. Joh. Done, of Plymoth aforesaid, with whom the said Court have placed the said Mary for nine years; at the end whereof the said John is to make good the said fifteen pounds to her or her heirs, if in case she die. Also it is further ordered, that the said widow Mary Browne pay or cause to be paid into the hands of Mr. Will[iam] Gilson the full sum of fifteen pounds, for the use of Prisilla Browne, another of the daughters of the said Peter, the Court having placed the said Prisilla with the said Will[iam] for 12 years, at the end whereof the said Will[iam] is to make good the same unto her, as her father's legacy as aforesaid; & to that end the said John & Will[iam] either stand bound for other for performance of the several payments, as also for such other performances of meat, drink, clothing, &c., during the said term, as is meet.

"And for the rest of the estate, the widow having two children by the said Peter, together with her own 3d, it is allowed her for bringing up the said children, provided that she discharge whatsoever debts shall be proved to be owing by the said Peter, & the legacies given by the Court. For performance whereof she & Mr. Will[iam] Brewster bound in two hundred pounds" [PCR 1:18-19].

BIRTH: Baptized Dorking, Surrey, 26 January 1594/5, son of William Brown [TAG 79:161].
DEATH: Plymouth between 25 March 1633 (tax list) and 10 October 1633 (inventory).
MARRIAGE: (1) By 1626 widow MARTHA FORD, who died in 1630 or 1631 [TAG 42:35-42; PM 211].

(2) By 1631 Mary _____, who survived her husband by at least one year [PCR 1:28], but was probably dead by 1647 when one of her daughters sold land without referring to the widow's dower rights.

CHILDREN:
  With first wife
  i   MARY BROWN, b. about 1626 (and certainly before the division of cattle on 22 May 1627); m. by 27 October 1647 Ephraim Tinkham [PCLR 1:146; PCR 12:146].
  ii PRISCILLA BROWN, b. about 1628; m. Sandwich 21 March 1649 William Allen [PCR 8:9].
  With second wife Mary
  iii REBECCA BROWN, b. about 1631; m. by about 1654 William Snow [PCLR 5:197].
  iv Child BROWN, b. by 1633; d. by 1647.

ASSOCIATIONS: JOHN BROWN of Plymouth by 1632 was brother of PETER BROWN.

COMMENTS: In his list of those who came on the *Mayflower,* Bradford included Peter Browne in a group of men without families [Bradford 443]. In his accounting of the *Mayflower* passengers as of 1651, Bradford tells us that "Peter Browne married twice. By his first wife he had two children who are living and both of them married; and the one of them hath two children. By his second wife he had two more. He died about sixteen years since" [Bradford 447].

The evidence for the marriages of Peter Brown's three daughters is largely from deeds in which his land was sold by his sons-in-law, with the consent of his daughters. The earliest and best treatment in print on this point is an article published in 1966 by Florence Barclay [TAG 42:35-42, citing PCLR 1:146, 186, 5:197 (bis)]. The claim has also been made that Peter Brown of Windsor was son of the Plymouth Peter, but these same deeds, showing that each of the three daughters controlled one-third of the real estate, provide the best evidence that there was no such son, and Robert S. Wakefield argued this in greater detail in 1979 [NGSQ 67:253-54]. Barbara Merrick has argued for some estimated dates slightly different from those used here [MQ 53:10-13].

BIBLIOGRAPHIC NOTE: The seventh volume of the Five Generations Project of the General Society of Mayflower Descendants, prepared by Robert S. Wakefield and published in 1992, with a revised second edition published in 2002, covers the descendants of Peter Brown [Robert S. Wakefield, *Mayflower Families Through Five Generations: Volume Seven, Peter Brown* (Plymouth 2002)].

In 2004 Caleb Johnson published data that establishes with a high degree of certainty that the brothers John and Peter Brown were baptized in Dorking, Surrey [TAG 79:161].

MARY BUCKETT

In the 1623 Plymouth land division, "Marie Buckett," as a passenger on the *Anne* in 1623, is granted one acre "adjoining to Joseph Rogers" [PCR 12:6].

COMMENTS: She has been identified as the wife of GEORGE SOULE [PM 432]. Most writers call her Mary Becket, but the above spelling is the only contemporaneous one we have.

EDWARD BUMPAS

ORIGIN: Unknown (but see *ASSOCIATIONS*).
MIGRATION: 1621 on the *Fortune*.
FIRST RESIDENCE: Plymouth.
REMOVES: Duxbury, Marshfield by 1643.

FREEMAN: Oath of fidelity, Duxbury, 1639 [PCR 8:182].
EDUCATION: Made his mark to report of coroner's jury, 14 February 1654/5 [PCR 3:70].
OFFICES: Plymouth coroner's jury, 14 February 1654/5 [PCR 3:70].
 In Marshfield section of 1643 Plymouth list of men able to bear arms [PCR 8:196].
ESTATE: In the 1623 Plymouth land division, "Edward Bompass" received one acre as a passenger on the *Fortune* [PCR 12:5]. In the 1627 Plymouth cattle division, "Edward Bumpasse" was the twelfth person in the second company [PCR 12:9].
 Edward Bumpas was in the list of Purchasers [PCR 2:177], and, on 3 June 1662, he was one of those permitted to "look out accommodations of land, as being the first born children of this government" [PCR 4:19].
 On 26 March 1628, "Edward Bompass and Moses Simonson sold each of them an acre of ground, to Robart Hicks lying on the north side of the town" [PCR 12:7]. (This was the acre apiece granted in 1623.)
 Assessed 9s. in the Plymouth tax lists of 25 March 1633 and 27 March 1634 [PCR 1:11, 28].

On 1 July 1633, Miles Standish was to "mow the ends of the grounds belonging to Edward Bumpasse & Will[iam] Latham" [PCR 1:14]. In early 1635 Edward Bumpas sold to John Washburn "his house & palisado, standing [on] his late lot of ground which he had by William Palmer's, beyond the creek called the Eagles Nest, which lot he gave up to the company, for a lot of ground allowed him in another place by the Governor then being; and the said lot ([on] which this house standeth) was, by the consent of the Governor & Assistants given to the said John Washborne" [PCR 1:33]. On 16 September 1645, Morris Truant and Solomon Lenner of Duxbury exchanged land, Truant receiving "the house, upland and meadows" which Solomon Lenner "lately bought of Edward Bumpas" [PCR 12:113].

On 15 July 1653, "Edmond Chandeler of Duxburrow" exchanged land with Edward Bumpas of Marshfield, Chandler relinquishing all his rights to lands or meadows in "Duxburrow New Plantation commonly called and known by the Indian names of Satuckquett and Nunckatatesett and places adjacent" in return for the rights of Bumpas as "one of the thirty-four purchasers who are to have their proportions of land at the places commonly called and known by the Indian names of Cushenett and Coaksett and places adjacent" [MD 2:245-46, citing PCLR 2:1:53]. On 30 March 1655, Edward Bumpas of Marshfield (with the consent of Hannah his wife) sold to "Edmond Chandeler of Duxburrow ... all his land lying at Ducke Hill lying between the lands of John Rouse and the lands of the said Edmond Chandeler" [MD 10:73, citing PCLR 2:1:169].

BIRTH: By about 1605 (based on estimated date of marriage).
DEATH: Between 4 July 1679 and 5 March 1683/4 [TAG 43:66, citing PCR 6:20 and PPR 1:112].
MARRIAGE: By 1631 Hannah ____. She died at Marshfield on 12 February 1693 [MarVR 19; MD 5:233].
CHILDREN (first eight recorded Marshfield [MarVR 2; MD 2:4-5]):
  i   SARAH BUMPAS, b. 9 March 1631[/2]; m. Marshfield 31 March 1659 Thomas Durram [MarVR 5; MD 2:110; TAG 43:67].
  ii ELIZABETH BUMPAS, b. 9 March 1633[/4]; m. Marshfield 6 June 1653 ("first Monday in June") Joseph Rose [MarVR 1; MD 2:4; TAG 67:155].
  iii JOHN BUMPAS, b. 2 June 1636; m. by 1671 Sarah ____ (eldest known child bp. Scituate 20 August 1671 [NEHGR 57:180]).

iv   EDWARD BUMPAS, b. 15 April 1638; d. Marshfield 3 April 1693, unm. [MD 3:187; MarVR 16; TAG 43:67-68; PCR 6:20].

v   JOSEPH BUMPAS, b. 15 February 1639[/40]; m. by 1669 Wybra Glass (eldest known child b. Plymouth 2 August 1669 [PVR 667; MD 8:33, 34]), daughter of James and Mary (Pontus) Glass and granddaughter of WILLIAM PONTUS. (This identity for the wife of Joseph Bumpas seems to be based solely on the rarity of the given name of the bride.)

vi   ISAAC BUMPAS, b. 31 March 1642; no further record.

vii   JACOB BUMPAS, b. 25 March 1644; m. Scituate 24 January 1676/7 Elizabeth (Banks) Whitmer, daughter of Richard Banks and widow of William Whitmer [TAG 43:72-73; GDMNH 75; PCR 6:39-40].

viii   HANNAH BUMPAS, b. 3 April 1646; d. after 4 March 1672/3, when she was described as "a distracted person" [PCR 7:175], apparently unm. [TAG 43:68-69; PCR 4:22].

ix   PHILIP BUMPAS, b. say 1648; m. by 1686 Sarah Eaton [TAG 43:150-51, citing PLR 1:287; MF 9:9-10, 21:23-24].

x   THOMAS BUMPAS, b. say 1650; m. Barnstable in November 1679 Phebe Lovel [MD 3:72].

xi   MARY BUMPAS, b. say 1652; m. Marshfield 2 January 1682 Daniel Crocker [MarVR 16; MD 3:42].

xii   SAMUEL BUMPAS, b. Marshfield say 1654; served in King Philip's War and slain at Pawtucket 26 March 1676 [TAG 60:237; Bodge 349].

ASSOCIATIONS: In the land division of 1623, and in the tax lists of 1633 and 1634, EDWARD BUMPAS is adjacent to PHILIP DELANO. The two men at a later date held adjacent land [PCR 1:59, 66, 67]. The last three sons of Bumpas were Philip, Thomas and Samuel, names also used by Delano. These items suggest that Edward Bumpas came from Leiden with Delano in 1621, that the two may have had some association there before that date, and that Bumpas was also a member of the Walloon community there.

COMMENTS: Of the twelve children of Edward Bumpas, the births of the first eight were recorded together in Marshfield, and the births of the last four were not recorded. Since Bumpas lived first in Plymouth, then in Duxbury, and by 1643 in Marshfield, we cannot tell in which town any of the first six were born, but the last six are here assumed to be born at Marshfield.

On 7 March 1642/3, Plymouth court decreed the "northerly bounds of Marshfield," which included the proviso that the line "take in Edward Bumpass lands" [PCR 2:54]. It may be that Bumpas did not move from Duxbury to Marshfield, but merely had the town line redrawn around his property. When the line was drawn again on 23 February 1683, part of the description of the boundary was that it ran "on a straight line to the southwest side of Edward Bumpp's land, so called, where he formerly lived, at Duck Hill, taking in the said land sometimes the said Edward Bumppase's to the township of Marshfield" [PCR 6:155].

Edward Bumpas was sued for debt by Joseph Tilden on 4 October 1664 and 3 October 1665, but Tilden did not collect [PCR 7:117, 125]. As he did not have any recorded land transactions after 1655, and his estate was not entered for probate, Edward Bumpas clearly spent the later years of his life on the lower end of the economic scale.

BIBLIOGRAPHIC NOTE: The best treatment of the first few generations of the family of Edward Bumpas is that published by Florence Barclay in 1967 [TAG 43:65-75, 150-55, 211-16]. She abstracts a number of documents that are crucial to the chronology of the immigrant, his wife and children, and the specific pages for those items are often cited above; at these locations more detailed discussion may be found than is possible here.

Bompass, Bumpas, Bump, Bumpus and Allied Families, 1621-1981, revised edition (Baltimore 1985), compiled by Carle Franklin Bumpus, is less successful, but does provide information on later generations (see TAG 60:189).

EDWARD BURCHER

In the 1623 Plymouth land division, two acres were assigned to Edward Burcher as a passenger on the *Anne* in 1623. His name does not appear in the 1627 division of cattle [PCR 12:5].

John Bridge, master of the *Little James*, writing to James Sherley on 9 September 1623, related that "father Virtcher and his wife were as hearty as the youngest in the ship" [MHSP 44:180-81]. Emmanuel Altham, in his letter to his brother of about the same date, tells of "an old woman in our ship about four score years of age, which was in good health" [Three Visitors 24].

COMMENTS: The allocation of two acres indicates that Edward Burcher had a household of two persons, the second presumably being his wife. In 1648 these two acres were in the hands of Samuel Fuller and at that time sold to Matthew Fuller [PCR 12:164].

Pope (followed by Stratton [p. 257]) claimed that this Edward Burcher of Plymouth was the same as the Edward Burcham who appeared some years later in Lynn. Wakefield argues that Edward Burcher, already married in 1623, and by implication from the comments of Bridge and Altham, well advanced in years, would be too old to be the Edward Burcham next seen in Lynn in 1638 [MD 39:185-86]. The difference in spelling and the gap of fifteen years without any record would also militate strongly against this identification.

John Bridge's reference to this man as "father Virtcher" is most likely simply a respectful reference to a senior citizen rather than a statement of a genealogical connection.

Although Edward Burcher (and JOHN JENNY) are known from these letters to have sailed on the *Little James*, they are listed in the 1623 Plymouth land division as if they had come on the *Anne*, perhaps just a matter of scribal convenience.

JOHN BURSLEY

ORIGIN: Unknown.
MIGRATION: 1623.
FIRST RESIDENCE: Weymouth.
REMOVES: Barnstable 1639.

CHURCH MEMBERSHIP: No evidence of church membership for John Bursley, but, on 22 July 1643, "Mistress Bursly" joined the Barnstable church [NEHGR 9:280].
FREEMAN: Requested 19 October 1630 (as "Mr. John Burslin") and admitted 18 May 1631 (as "Mr. Jo: Burslyn") [MBCR 1:79, 366].
OFFICES: Weymouth deputy to Massachusetts Bay General Court, 25 May 1636 [MBCR 1:174]. On 8 September 1636 the General Court ordered that "whereas the town of Waimoth hath sent 3 deputies to this Court, being a very small town, at the request of the said deputies two of them were dismissed by the Court, viz: Mr. Bursley & John Upham" [MBCR 1:179]

Massachusetts Bay committee to make colony rate, 25 May 1636 [MBCR 1:175]. Committee to survey colony boundary, 20 November

1637 [MBCR 1:211]. Fined 6s. 8d. on 5 June 1638 "for absence when the Court sat in the afternoon, being jurymen" [MBCR 1:232].

Dorchester committee to assess £30 for the captain of the train band, 2 June 1634 [DTR 7].

Plymouth grand jury, 1 June 1647 [PCR 2:116].

Barnstable constable, 4 June 1645 [PCR 2:83].

ESTATE: "John Busley, gent.," was one of the group of New England men on both the first and second patents for Agamenticus [York] granted by the Council for New England, 2 December 1631 and 2 March 1631/2 [Council NE 101, 105]. There is no evidence that he ever resided on or took advantage of this grant.

"Mr. John Bursleye's inventory" was taken 21 August 1660 and totalled £115 5s., with no real estate included [MD 17:159; PCPR 2:2:63].

The following record, although ostensibly for a Thomas Bursley, must be for John, for it comes at the right time, it takes place in Barnstable, and the widow's name is Joanna: "Mr. Hinckley is appointed by the Court to treat with Joanna, the wife of Mr. Thomas Bursley, late deceased, concerning the disposing of some part of his estate unto his children, that so what is done on that behalf may be entered on the Court records," 2 October 1660 [PCR 3:201].

BIRTH: By about 1600 (based on his appearance at Weymouth in 1623).
DEATH: Barnstable before 21 August 1660 (date of inventory).
MARRIAGE: Sandwich about 28 November 1639 "Mr. Hull's daughter" [NEHGR 9:286]. She was Joanna Hull, daughter of the Reverend JOSEPH HULL {1635, Weymouth} [GM 2:3:452-60], and married (2) after 1660 DOLOR DAVIS {1634, Cambridge} [GM 2:2:292-97].
CHILDREN:
    i   Child BURSLEY, "died suddenly in the night and buried" at Barnstable 25 January 1640/1 [NEHGR 9:285].
    ii   MARY BURSLEY, bp. Barnstable 29 July 1643 [NEHGR 9:282]; m. Barnstable 25 April 1663 John Crocker [MD 3:150].
    iii JOHN BURSLEY, bp. Barnstable 22 September 1644 [NEHGR 9:283]; bur. there 27 September 1644 [NEHGR 9:285].
    iv JOANNA BURSLEY, bp. Barnstable 1 March 1645/6 [NEHGR 9:283]; m. Barnstable [blank] April 1653 [*sic*] Shubael Dimmock [MD 4:221; in the margin beside this entry and the accompanying births of children is the note

"These records perhaps 10 years too old," and so the year of this marriage was more likely 1663]. (Joanna is inadvertently called "Jemima" by Savage.)

v   ELIZABETH BURSLEY, bp. Barnstable 25 March 1649 [NEHGR 9:284]; m. (1) Barnstable [blank] November 1666 Nathaniel Goodspeed [MD 5:73]; m. (2) (as "Elizabeth Goodspeed the wid[ow] of Nath[anie]ll Goodspeed") Barnstable [blank] October 1675 Increase Clap [MD 4:120].

vi   JOHN BURSLEY, bp. Barnstable 11 April 1652 [NEHGR 9:284]; m. Barnstable [blank] December 1673 Elizabeth Howland [MD 3:53], daughter of John Howland and granddaughter of JOHN HOWLAND of the *Mayflower*.

vii   TEMPERANCE BURSLEY, b. say 1657; m. Barnstable "the beginning of December 1677" Joseph Crocker [MD 3:152].

ASSOCIATIONS: In both the 1628 assessment for the removal of THOMAS MORTON and the 1631 patent for Agamenticus, Bursley is associated with WILLIAM JEFFREYS {1623, Weymouth} [GMB 2:1082-85].

COMMENTS: Charles Francis Adams marshalled the evidence in favor of the position that John Bursley was part of the company of ROBERT GORGES, which arrived in New England in the fall of 1623 and settled at the location that was to become Weymouth [MHSP 1:16:197]. One of the most important pieces of evidence in this argument is the list of those who contributed to the expenses involved in deporting THOMAS MORTON {1622, Merrymount} [GMB 2:1299-30] in 1628, which included an entry for "Mr. Jeffrey and Mr. Burslem, £2" [Bradford LB 43].

The identity of the John Bursley of Weymouth with the man of the same name in Barnstable is based on the marriage of Bursley to the daughter of the Reverend Joseph Hull, at about the time the latter moved from Weymouth to Barnstable, and the disappearance of John Bursley from Weymouth about the time of this marriage. Both Pope and GDMNH have separate entries for the activities of this man in the two towns. That this same man was patentee of York is based on the continued association with WILLIAM JEFFREYS and with the Gorges family.

The John Bursley who resided in Exeter, Hampton and Kittery was a different man, since he was of a lower social stratum, and there were chronological conflicts between him and the Barnstable man [GDMNH 122-23; Granberry 186].

On 14 May 1634, the General Court ordered that Wessaguscus [i.e., Weymouth] should bear the charges for "Thomas Lane, late servant to John Burslyn, [who], by the providence of God, is fallen lame & impotent, & hath since remained at Dorchester" [MBCR 1:121]. This record, and the service of John Bursley on the Dorchester committee to make a rate for the pay of the captain of the train band, have led some writers to state that Bursley lived for a time at Dorchester. However, since Weymouth was in these early years an appendage of Dorchester for church and military matters [GMN 1:29], the appearance of Bursley in association with Dorchester does not require that he ever lived there.

WILLIAM BUTTON

In recounting the voyage of the *Mayflower* in 1620, Bradford recalls that "there died but one of the passengers, which was William Button, a youth, servant to Samuel Fuller, when they drew near the coast" [Bradford 59, 442, 445].

C

JOHN CANNON

In the 1623 division of Plymouth land, John Cannon is paired with William Tench as passengers on the *Fortune* in 1623, the two men receiving a total of two acres [PCR 12:5]. They do not appear in the 1627 division of cattle. In a note of 14 September 1638 in the land records, John Carman [*sic*] and William Tench were said to have transferred these two acres to John Billington [PCR 12:37]. Since Billington was hanged in 1630, the transfer must have taken place before that date, and also before the 1627 division of cattle.

COMMENTS: The land grant indicates that these men were both single; they were probably servants of some investor of the colony who had not yet arrived. Stratton suggests that they were associated with Lyford and left with him, although this is not certain [Stratton 258, 361].

Since his name is given once as Cannon and once as Carman, we cannot be sure which is correct; however, if Carman is correct, there is no evidence whatever that he is the same as either JOHN CARMAN [GMB 1:311-13] or JOHN KIRMAN [GMB 2:1133-35], both of whom arrived in Massachusetts in 1631.

PRISCILLA CARPENTER

WILLIAM WRIGHT arrived in New England in 1621, and before his death in 1633 he had married Priscilla Carpenter. We have no record that William Wright returned to England between those two dates, and if he did not, then Priscilla Carpenter must have come to Plymouth sometime prior to 1633 as a single woman.

COMMENTS: Priscilla Carpenter was born perhaps about 1598, daughter of Alexander Carpenter of Wrington, Somersetshire, and was one of five sisters who came to New England, or married men who came to New England, or both. The family of Alexander Carpenter is outlined briefly here and was best treated by Mary Lovering Holman [Scott Gen 284-85]. Further detail may be found in the sketches of the husbands or children of these women.

"Alexander Carpenter from Wrington" was on 16 December 1600 [NS] witness at the Amsterdam marriage of "Antoine Fetcher" and "Jenneken Richeman" [J. de Hoop Scheffer, *History of the Free Churchmen ...* (Ithaca NY n.d.), p. 186]. He was at Leiden by 1611 [Dexter 608]. In a letter of 19 August 1644 or 1646 to Mary Carpenter of Wrington, sister of his wife Alice (Carpenter) (Southworth) Bradford, William Bradford noted that the mother of the Carpenter sisters had recently died and he invited Mary to join them in Plymouth, which she soon did [NEHGR 14:195-96].

The years of birth of the sisters are approximated based on the ages at death of Juliann, Mary and Priscilla. These dates are all consistent with one another. Some of birthdates estimated for these women, however, make them a few years older than the norm at their first marriages, and extreme ages at death are frequently exaggerated, so it may be that all these estimated birthdates should be shifted forward by a few years.

In 1988 Janet K. Pease published some entries from the IGI that purport to relate to this family, but many of them were clearly not from the parish registers [MQ 38:190]. A year later Myrtle Hyde published the results of research that had been carried out in 1971 in the registers of St. James, Bath, and Wrington, Somersetshire [MQ 39:182-83]; these entries seem more reliable, but some discrepancies remain.

    i   JULIANN CARPENTER, b. say 1583; m. (1) Leiden 22 July 1612 [NS] GEORGE MORTON [Leiden Pilgrims 66; MD 11:193; PM 336]; m. (2) Plymouth bef. 22 May 1627 MANASSEH KEMPTON [PM 297]; d. Plymouth 19 February 1664 "aged fourscore and one year" [PCR 8:25].

    ii   AGNES CARPENTER, b. say 1585; m. Leiden 23 April 1613 [NS] SAMUEL FULLER [Leiden Pilgrims 66; MD 8:129-30; PM 217]. She died by 1617 (when Samuel Fuller married his third wife).

    iii   ALICE CARPENTER, b. say 1590; m. (1) Leiden 25 May 1613 [NS] Edward Southworth [Leiden Pilgrims 66] (father of CONSTANT SOUTHWORTH [PM 437] and THOMAS SOUTHWORTH [PM 440]); m. (2) Plymouth 14 August 1623 WILLIAM BRADFORD [MD 30:4; PM 62].

iv   MARY CARPENTER, b. say 1596; d. Plymouth unm. "20th March 1687 in 91 year" [PVR 133].

v   PRISCILLA CARPENTER, b. say 1598; m. (1) between 1629 and 1633 WILLIAM WRIGHT [PM 524]; m. (2) Plymouth 27 November 1634 John Cooper [PCR 1:32]; d. Plymouth "28th Dec. 1689 in 92d year" [PVR 133].

ROBERT CARTER

Robert Carter came to Plymouth in 1620 on the *Mayflower* as a servant of William Mullins, and "died the first winter" [Bradford 442, 445].

JOHN CARVER

ORIGIN: Leiden, Holland.
MIGRATION: 1620 on the *Mayflower*.
FIRST RESIDENCE: Plymouth.

EDUCATION: Signed the will of WILLIAM MULLINS [Waters 255; MD 1:230-32].
OFFICES: Governor from landing at Plymouth until his death in early 1621 [Bradford 76].

BIRTH: By about 1585 (based on date of first appearance in Leiden).
DEATH: "In this month of April [1621], whilst they were busy about their seed, their Governor (Mr. John Carver) came out of the field very sick, it being a hot day. He complained greatly of his head and lay down, and within a few hours his senses failed, so as he never spake more till he died, which was within a few days after. Whose death was much lamented and caused great heaviness amongst them, as there was cause. He was buried in the best manner they could, with some volleys of shot by all that bore arms. And his wife, being a weak woman, died within five or six weeks after him" [Bradford 86].
MARRIAGE: By 1609 Catherine (White) Leggatt, daughter of Alexander White. She died at Plymouth about five or six weeks after her husband, so in late May or early June 1621 [Bradford 86]. (The identification of the wife of John Carver derives from the following evidence: Alexander White in his will of 15 March 1594 named daughters Catherine, Bridget, Jane and Francis (all apparently unmarried); Eleanor White, widow of

Alexander White, in her will of 7 April 1599 named "my son Leggatt and his wife" and "their daughter Marie," along with daughters Bridget, Janie and Frances (still apparently unmarried); Bridget White married in 1604 Rev. John Robinson; and in a latter of 14 June 1620 [NS] John Robinson addressed John Carver as "My dear friend and brother, whom with yours I always remember in my best affection" [MD 43:183-86; see Bradford 42 for letter from Robinson; see also English Homes 44; Stratton 259]. Insofar as this identification rests on the letter from Robinson there may be some doubt, inasmuch as Robinson addresses others as brother, so this may reflect only a church relationship.)

CHILDREN: None recorded. (Dexter published burials of two children at St. Pancras, Leiden, one in 1609 and one in 1617, as children of John Carver [Dexter 608-9]. Dexter misread these burial records, which pertain to other families [private communication from Jeremy D. Bangs].)

ASSOCIATIONS: The ancestry given for John Carver, and the connection to Robert Carver of Marshfield, in the Carver genealogy are completely unsupported and should be discounted [Clifford N. Carver, *The Carver Family of New England* (n.p. 1935), pp. 18, 23]. Banks champions a different ancestry, citing the baptism at Doncaster, Yorkshire, on 9 September 1565 of John, son of Robert Carver [English Homes 44]. This would make Carver forty-four years old at the time of his first appearance in Leiden, and we have no other indication that Carver would have been this old at that date (unless his appointment as governor in 1620 requires it).

If John Carver's wife has been correctly identified, then he was uncle by marriage of ISAAC ROBINSON of Scituate and Barnstable [PM 391].

COMMENTS: In his account of the passengers on the *Mayflower* in 1620, Bradford records as the first family "Mr. John Carver, Katherine his wife, Desire Minter, and two manservants, John Howland, Roger Wilder. William Latham, a boy, and a maidservant and a child that was put to him called Jasper More." In the accounting of these families as of 1651 Bradford reports that "Mr. Carver and his wife died the first year, he in the spring, she in the summer," and then goes on to give the fate of their several servants [Bradford 441, 443]. John Carver signed the Mayflower Compact.

John Carver was clearly one of the most respected members of the *Mayflower* contingent [Oxford DNB]. He and ROBERT CUSHMAN [PM 158] travelled to London in the summer of 1620 to plan and prepare for the voyage of members of the Leiden congregation to America. Several letters addressed to John Carver during this period give some evidence of his activities [Bradford 42-46, 360-61, 367].

EDMUND CHANDLER

ORIGIN: Leiden, Holland.
MIGRATION: 1632.
FIRST RESIDENCE: Plymouth.
REMOVES: Duxbury.

OCCUPATION: Sayweaver, draper, pipemaker (in Leiden [Dexter 609]).
FREEMAN: In 1633 Plymouth list of freemen, ahead of those admitted on 1 January 1632/3 [PCR 1:4]. In list of Plymouth freemen of 7 March 1636/7 [PCR 1:52]. In Duxbury sections of Plymouth Colony lists of freemen of 1639 and 1658 [PCR 8:174, 198].
EDUCATION: His inventory included "a parcel of books" valued at 10s.
OFFICES: Duxbury deputy to Plymouth General Court, 4 June 1639, 29 August 1643, 5 March 1643/4 [PCR 1:126, 2:60, 68].

Plymouth petit jury, 7 June 1636, 1 September 1640, 5 October 1640 [PCR 1:42, 7:17, 18].

Duxbury representative to committee on "the nearer uniting of Plymoth & those on Duxburrough side," 11 March 1635/6 [PCR 1:41]. Duxbury representative to committee on dividing meadow, 2 October 1637 [PCR 1:67].

Duxbury constable, 3 January 1636/7, 7 March 1636/7 [PCR 1:48, 54].

His inventory included "1 sword, shotmolds, burning mark and shears" valued at 11s.
ESTATE: Land of Edmund Chandler was mentioned on 1 July 1633 [PCR 1:14]. On 20 October 1634, "Edmund Chanler" sold to John Rogers "a lot of ground adjoining to the lots of Robert Hicks, on Duxbury side, it being a lot which the said Edward bought of John Barnes" [PCR 1:31]. On 4 July 1635, Isaac Robinson sold to Joseph Bidle "half a lot of ground lying above the island creek, which the said Isaake bought of Edmond Chanler, and he of John Barnes" [PCR 1:34].

On 2 January 1636/7, "Edmond Chandler" was granted forty acres "on the east side of Moyses Symonson, where Morris formerly began to clear for Mr. Bowman" [PCR 1:47, 49]. He was granted sixty acres on Duxbury side "on the northeast side of the lands granted to Moyses

Symons," 2 April 1638 [PCR 1:82]. He was granted fifty acres with some meadow at the North River, 2 November 1640 [PCR 1:165].

On 19 July 1639, Mr. Thomas Besbeech of Duxbury sold to "Edmond Chaundler of the same one acre of land lying to the north side of the lands of the said Thomas Besbeech" [PCR 12:46]. On 8 June 1650, "Edmond Chandeler of Duxburrow" sold to John Browne of Duxbury, weaver, "an house situate in Duxburrow aforesaid and an acre of land on which the said house standeth next adjoining unto the house and land of Mr. John Rener above the path" [PCR 12:187]. On 7 June 1651, "Edmond Chandeler of Duxburrow" sold to Thomas Byrd of Scituate fifty acres at the North River, "with all the meadow land or marsh abutting upon the aforesaid fifty acres of upland" [PCR 12:207].

On 4 May 1653, James Lendal of Duxbury, tailor, sold to "Edmond Chandeler of the town aforesaid ... planter ... two acres of marsh meadow ... which was sometimes the meadow of Peeter Brown's children" [MD 2:169, citing PCLR 2:1:51]. On 15 July 1653, "Edmond Chandeler of Duxburrow" exchanged land with Edward Bumpas of Marshfield, Chandler relinquishing all his rights to any lands or meadows in "Duxburrow New Plantation commonly called and known by the Indian names of Satuckquett and Nunckatatesett and places adjacent" in return for the rights of Bumpas as "one of the thirty-four purchasers who are to have their proportions of land at the places commonly called and known by the Indian names of Cushenett and Coaksett and places adjacent" [MD 2:245-46, citing PCLR 2:1:53]. On 30 March 1655, Edward Bumpas of Marshfield (with the consent of Hannah his wife) sold to "Edmond Chandeler of Duxburrow ... all his land lying at Ducke Hill lying between the lands of John Rouse and the lands of the said Edmond Chandeler" [MD 10:73, citing PCLR 2:1:169]. On 16 June 1659, Samuel Eaton sold to "Edmond Chandeler of Duxburrow two acres of meadow lying between Mr. Kempe's land and John Rouse's" [MD 14:14, citing PCLR 2:2:27].

In his will, dated 3 May 1662 and proved 4 June 1662, "Edmond Chandeler" bequeathed to "my son Samuell Chandeler my whole share of land that is at ... Akoaksett and Cushenah"; to "my son Benjamine Chandeler ... all that tract ... of land lying in Duxburrow both upland and meadow with all the housing belonging thereunto"; to "my son Joseph Chandeler ... my whole share of land which now lieth by Taunton River"; to "my three daughters Sarah, Anna and Mary three thousand and five hundred of sugar which belongs to me at Barbadoes"; to "my three children viz: Benjamine, Josepth and Ruth Chandeler" rent due from "my son Samuell Chandeler"; the cattle that have been in the hands of "my son Samuel" to be equally divided between "my three children Benjamine, Josepth and Ruth" [MD 14:68, citing PCPR 2:2:75].

The inventory of the estate, taken 2 June 1662, totalled £38 7s. 6d., with no real estate included [MD 14:69, citing PCPR 2:2:76].

BIRTH: By about 1587 (based on estimated date of first marriage).
DEATH: Duxbury between 3 May 1662 (date of will) and 2 June 1662 (date of inventory).
MARRIAGE: (1) By about 1612 _____ _____; not seen in any record.
  (2) By about 1632 _____ _____; not seen in any record.
CHILDREN:
  With first wife
   i SAMUEL CHANDLER, b. say 1612; m. at an undetermined date a woman whose name is not known, who inherited his small estate on 5 March 1683/4 [PCR 6:124; MD 14:69]; no known children. (All records in Plymouth Colony for a Samuel Chandler prior to 1684 apply to this man [see *COMMENTS* below]; the Samuel Chandler who married three times in Dorchester must be another man.)
   ii (prob.) LYDIA CHANDLER, b. say 1614; m. Plymouth 11 December 1634 RICHARD HIGGINS [PCR 1:32; PM 249].
   iii Child CHANDLER, bur. Pieterskerk, Leiden, 26 March 1619 [NS] [Dexter 609; NEA 3:2:48-49].
  With second wife
   iv JOHN CHANDLER, b. say 1632; on 25 June 1653, John Chandler "being at sea bound for Barbados" left his entire estate to "Edmund Chandler, my father, living at New Plimouth in New England," and if his father was dead then to his brothers and sisters [BarbPR 1:70].
   v SARAH CHANDLER, b. say 1638; named in father's will, 3 May 1662; no further record.
   vi ANNA CHANDLER, b. say 1640; named in father's will, 3 May 1662; no further record.
   vii MARY CHANDLER, b. say 1642; named in father's will, 3 May 1662; no further record.
   viii BENJAMIN CHANDLER, b. say 1644; m. by 1672 Elizabeth Buck (eldest known child b. Scituate 16 February 1672[/3?]), daughter of John Buck of Scituate [MD 14:128].
   ix JOSEPH CHANDLER, b. say 1646; m. by 1673 Mercy _____ [Small Gen 1050-51, citing PCLR 3:287].

x   RUTH CHANDLER, b. say 1648; named in father's will, 3 May 1662; no further record.

ASSOCIATIONS: Probably related to ROGER CHANDLER, as both were sayworkers in Leiden, both came to Plymouth about the same time, and both removed to Duxbury [PM 101].

COMMENTS: Although we cannot place Edmund Chandler in Plymouth prior to 1632 based on New England records, he was probably one of the last group of Leiden church members who came to Plymouth in 1629 and 1630.

Edmund Chandler does not appear in the 25 March 1633 and 27 March 1634 Plymouth tax lists, even though his age, wealth and social status would lead one to expect that he should.

Records for a Samuel Chandler of Plymouth and then of Duxbury begin with appearances on the 25 March 1633 and 27 March 1634 Plymouth tax lists [PCR 1:11, 28], and continue through the 1683 estate records in Duxbury. Attempts have been made to distribute these records between two Samuel Chandlers, the elder being possibly the son of Roger Chandler seen in Leiden records, who did not survive his father, and the younger being the Samuel Chandler named in the will of Edmund Chandler. We will argue here that these records, spread over sixty years, pertain to only one Samuel Chandler, who was son of Edmund.

First, the Samuel Chandler taxed in 1633 must have been at least 21, and therefore born no later than 1612. Edmund Chandler was made a citizen of Leiden in 1613, and was therefore born no later than 1592, and perhaps earlier; he could easily have been father of a Samuel born in 1612.

Second, the records for Samuel Chandler from 1633 to 1683 do not at any point imply two persons of that name at Duxbury during these years. The designations "Sr." and "Jr." are never employed in the records.

Third, when Samuel Chandler was charged with slander against the Plymouth government in 1639, one of his bondsmen was Richard Higgins, who had married in 1634 at Plymouth Lydia Chandler. If she married at the normal age, Lydia would have been born about 1614, and so could well have been a sister of Samuel.

Fourth, on 20 May 1637 John Jenny sued Samuel Chandler for a debt of £20. "Edmond Chaundler became bail to the action, and to satisfy the debt," and, on 2 October 1637, "Edmond Chaundler undertook to pay the plaintiff" the amount remaining due [PCR 7:6].

All of these arguments are consistent with the hypothesis that Edmund Chandler had three children by a first wife: Samuel, Lydia and the child buried at Leiden in 1619.

The will of Edmund Chandler names six other children, but we have little to help us in dating them. Two of these six were sons, Benjamin and Joseph, with Benjamin always named first in the will. Three of the daughters (Sarah, Anna and Mary) are grouped together, after which the other three children were grouped together (Benjamin, Joseph and Ruth). Our arrangement of the children above assumes that these six were named in birth order and were all by a second (or later) wife.

The argument has been made that Joseph must have been born by 1641, since he was named executor by his father in 1662; but since a testator might not be planning to die immediately, this is not necessarily true. Benjamin married by about 1671, and Joseph probably sometime in the mid-1670s, so rough estimates of birthdates for these six children are assigned on this basis.

Nothing is known of the fate of the four daughters of Edmund Chandler. The grouping together of Sarah, Anna and Mary may possibly indicate that they were married by 3 May 1662, the date of their father's will.

The son John, who died testate at Barbados, would be older by some years than all of these children by the second wife, if we assume that he was twenty-one when he made his will.

On 23 January 1638/9, "Edmond Chandler, of Duxborrow, yeoman," took John Edwards as an apprentice for five years [PCR 1:110].

BIBLIOGRAPHIC NOTE: The best sustained treatment of Edmund Chandler and his family is that of Lora A.W. Underhill [Small Gen 1027-60]. Additional useful material was published by George Ernest Bowman [MD 14:65-70].

ROGER CHANDLER

ORIGIN: Leiden, Holland.
MIGRATION: 1632.
FIRST RESIDENCE: Plymouth.
REMOVES: Duxbury.

OCCUPATION: Sayworker (in Leiden).

FREEMAN: In 1633 Plymouth list of freemen, in a section which includes men admitted on 1 January 1632/3 [PCR 1:4]. In list of 7 March 1636/7. In Duxbury section of 1639 list, and possibly the man of this name in Duxbury section of the list of 1658 [PCR 1:53, 8:174, 198].

ESTATE: Assessed 9s. in the Plymouth tax lists of 25 March 1633 and 27 March 1634 [PCR 1:10, 27].

On 2 November 1640, granted twenty-five acres "northwards from Duxburrow Mill, towards Greens Harbour" [PCR 1:165]. On "the last of February 1644, Roger Chaundler of Duxborrow" sold to Francis Godfrey of Duxbury twenty-five acres "on the northern side of the freshet that runneth into Greene's Harbour where the way to Sittuate crosseth the same being on the upper side the said path" [PCR 12:109].

On 3 October 1665, "one hundred and fifty acres are granted by the Court unto the three sisters, the daughters of Roger Chandler, deceased, viz: to each of them fifty acres, lying between the Bay line and the bounds of Taunton, according to the desire of John Bundy" [PCR 4:110].

BIRTH: By about 1590 (based on date of marriage).
DEATH: Between 5 May 1646 (dispute with Kenelm Winslow) and 3 October 1665 (grant of land to his daughters in his right), and probably closer to the earlier date.
MARRIAGE: Leiden, Holland, 21 July 1615 [NS] Isabel Chilton (the groom described as "of Colchester in England") [Plooij XXI; Leiden Pilgrims 142; MD 11:129], daughter of JAMES CHILTON [PM 103].
CHILDREN:

  i SAMUEL CHANDLER, b. before 15 October 1622; not seen after Leiden census of 1622. (See discussion of Samuel Chandler, son of EDMUND CHANDLER.)
  ii SARAH CHANDLER, b. before 15 October 1622; m. about 1640 Solomon Leonard(son).
  iii MARTHA CHANDLER, b. probably late 1620s; m. by 1649 John Bundy.
  iv MARY CHANDLER, b. probably late 1620s; m. by 1653 Edmund Bruff.

ASSOCIATIONS: Probably related to EDMUND CHANDLER, as both were sayworkers in Leiden, both came to Plymouth about the same time, and both removed to Duxbury [PM 97]. There may also have been some connection with the Nathaniel Chandler who appears in the Duxbury portion of the 1643 Plymouth list of men able to bear arms, and as a soldier from Duxbury in 1645 for an expedition against the Narragansetts [PCR 2:90, 8:190].

COMMENTS: The marital history of the three daughters has been set forth in two splendid articles, one by Frederick Warner and one by Florence Barclay [TAG 27:1-6, 37:212-17]. These articles provide lengthy abstracts of deeds and other documents proving these marriages; the most important evidence derives from the sale and transfer of the one-hundred-fifty acre parcel granted to the three [unnamed] daughters of Roger Chandler in 1665. Further treatment of these three daughters and their descendants may be found in the Mayflower Society's Five Generations Project volume which includes JAMES CHILTON [MF 15:5, 8-10].

On 5 May 1646, "[u]pon hearing of the cause betwixt Roger Chaundler and Kenelme Winslow, for his daughter's clothes, which the said Kenelme detaineth, upon pretense of some further service which he required of her, whereunto the said Roger utterly refused to consent, it is ordered by the Court, that the said Kenelme Winslow shall deliver the maid her clothes without any further delay" [PCR 2:90]. Given the date of this dispute, the daughter in question must have been one of the two younger daughters, Mary or Martha.

The record immediately above is the last that can with certainty be assigned to the immigrant Roger Chandler. The Roger Chandler who appears in the Duxbury section of the 1658 list of freemen could be the Roger Chandler who later resided in Concord, consistent with the information given in the next paragraph.

Claims have been made that Roger Chandler of Concord was a son of this ROGER CHANDLER, mainly on the basis of the identity of names and on the statement by Shattuck that "Roger Chandler, and twenty others of Plymouth Colony, had a grant of four hundred acres of land in Concord in 1658" [Shattuck 367]. The specificity of the grant of land to "the three sisters, the daughters of Roger Chandler, deceased," in 1665 would seem to rule out the possibility that the immigrant was survived by any sons, but the Concord connection remains a tantalizing clue, as a number of other Plymouth residents removed to Concord about this time as well. (See Charles H. Chandler, *The Descendants of Roger Chandler of Concord, Mass., 1658* [Provo UT 1949].)

JAMES CHILTON

ORIGIN: Leiden, Holland.
MIGRATION: 1620 on the *Mayflower*.
FIRST RESIDENCE: Died before *Mayflower* reached Plymouth.

OCCUPATION: Tailor.

ESTATE: In the 1623 Plymouth land division "Marie Chilton" received an unknown number of acres (perhaps three) as a passenger on the *Mayflower* [PCR 12:4]. In the 1627 Plymouth cattle division Mary, now the wife of John Winslow, is listed as the sixth person in the sixth company [PCR 12:11].

BIRTH: About 1556 (aged 63 in 1619 [Bangs 34]), probably at Canterbury, Kent, son of Lionel Chilton by an unknown first wife [TAG 38:244].

DEATH: 8 December 1620 off Cape Cod [Prince 165].

MARRIAGE: By 1586 _____ _____. On 12 June 1609, "[blank] the wife of James Chilton" was excommunicated from St. Peter, Sandwich, Kent. [NEHGR 153:407-12]. She died at Plymouth early in 1621 [Bradford 446]. (John G. Hunt has suggested that she was Susanne Furner, James Chilton's stepsister [TAG 38:244-45], but there are serious chronological problems with this identification [NEHGR 153:408-9].)

CHILDREN:

    i   ISABELLA CHILTON, bp. St. Paul, Canterbury, Kent, 15 January 1586/7 [MF 15:3]; m. Leiden 21 July 1615 [NS] ROGER CHANDLER [Leiden Pilgrims 142; MD 11:129; PM 101].

    ii   JANE CHILTON, bp. St. Paul, Canterbury, 8 June 1589 [MF 15:3]; no further record.

    iii   JOEL CHILTON, bur. St. Martin, Canterbury, 2 November 1593 [MF 15:3].

    iv   MARY CHILTON, bur. St. Martin, Canterbury, 23 November 1593 [MF 15:3].

    v   ELIZABETH CHILTON, bp. St. Martin, Canterbury, 14 July 1594 [MF 15:3]; no further record.

    vi   JAMES CHILTON, bp. St. Martin, Canterbury, 22 August 1596 [MF 15:3]; d. by 11 September 1603.

    vii   INGLE CHILTON, bp. St. Paul, Canterbury, 29 April 1599 [MF 15:3]; thought to be the "Engeltgen Gilten" who m. Leiden 27 August 1622 [NS] Robert Nelson [Leiden Pilgrims 198; Dexter 627]; no further record.

    viii   CHRISTIAN CHILTON (dau.), bp. St. Peter, Sandwich, Kent, 26 July 1601 [MF 15:3]; no further record.

    ix   JAMES CHILTON, bp. St. Peter, Sandwich, 11 September 1603 [MF 15:3]; no further record.

x   MARY CHILTON, bp. St. Peter, Sandwich, 30 May 1607 [MF 15:3]; m. Plymouth by 22 May 1627 JOHN WINSLOW [PM 511].

COMMENTS: Until recently there was no direct evidence that James Chilton resided in Leiden, despite the marriage of one and perhaps two daughters there. Recent research in Leiden has revealed a notarial record detailing an assault on James Chilton, aged 63, and his daughter on 28 April 1619 [NS]; this assault has been interpreted as one of the reasons leading the Pilgrims to believe that they were becoming less welcome in Leiden, and therefore as a factor in the decision to leave for New England [Bangs 34].

In his list of those on the *Mayflower,* Bradford included "James Chilton and his wife, and Mary their daughter; they had another daughter that was married, came afterward" [Bradford 442]. In his accounting of the family in 1651 Bradford reported that "James Chilton and his wife also died in the first infection, but their daughter Mary is still living and hath nine children; and one daughter is married and hath a child. So their increase is ten" [Bradford 446].

The death date for James Chilton is given variously as 6, 8, or 18 December 1620. The best evidence for the date is Prince, who cites a now-lost notebook kept by WILLIAM BRADFORD [Prince 165]. The date of 18 December may have arisen when someone corrected for the 1752 calendar change, an unnecessary confusion. A month before his death James Chilton signed the Mayflower Compact.

A longstanding tradition has held that Mary Chilton was the first of the *Mayflower* passengers to step onto Plymouth Rock. Charles Thornton Libby carried out a detailed examination of this story, published as *Mary Chilton's Title to Celebrity* (Boston 1926; rpt. Warwick RI 1978). He accepted the tradition as correct.

BIBLIOGRAPHIC NOTE: JAMES CHILTON has been treated in the fifteenth volume of the Mayflower Society's Five Generations Project [MF 15:1-150].

RICHARD CHURCH

ORIGIN: Unknown.
MIGRATION: 1630.
FIRST RESIDENCE: Weymouth.

REMOVES: Plymouth 1631, Eastham 1649, Charlestown by 1652, Hingham 1654.

OCCUPATION: Carpenter [PCR 1:69]. (On 16 February 1632/3, Richard Church hired William Baker to work for him for seven months as a sawyer [PCR 1:8]. On 23 July 1633, William Mendlove bound himself apprentice to Richard Church for seven years "in the trade of carpentry" [PCR 1:15].)
FREEMAN: Requested Massachusetts Bay freemanship,19 October 1630 [MBCR 1:80] (but apparently moved away before 18 May 1631, when the first group of freemen were admitted).

Admitted Plymouth freeman 2 January 1632/3 [PCR 1:6]. In 1633 and 7 March 1636/7 Plymouth lists of freemen [PCR 1:4, 53]; and in Plymouth section of 1639 list [PCR 8:174].
EDUCATION: He made his mark as witness to a deed of 1 June 1649 [PCR 12:181]. His inventory included "books" valued at £1.
OFFICES: Plymouth petit jury, 7 June 1636, 5 October 1640, 1 March 1641/2, 1 November 1642 [PCR 1:42, 7:17, 28, 32]. Grand jury, 7 March 1636/7, 4 June 1639, 1 March 1641/2, 7 June 1642, 7 March 1642/3, 1 June 1647 [PCR 1:54, 126, 2:34, 41, 53, 116]. Appointed arbiter in a civil dispute, 7 August 1638 [PCR 7:9].

Volunteered for service in Pequot War, 7 June 1637 [PCR 1:60]. In Plymouth section of 1643 Plymouth Colony list of men able to bear arms [PCR 8:189]. His inventory included "arms & ammunition" valued at £4.
ESTATE: Assessed £1 16s. in the Plymouth tax list of 25 March 1633 and £1 7s. in the list of 27 March 1634 [PCR 1:11, 28].

Granted forty acres "at the head & on the south side of Eele River Swampe," 4 December 1637 [PCR 1:70]. On 3 June 1647, Richard Church exchanged this parcel with Manasseh Kempton, receiving in return "a parcel of land next adjoining unto the said Richard Church his lot" and also a small piece of meadow [PCR 12:144]. Granted one acre and a half of meadow "lying up the river, betwixt the two Mannamett Ponds," 7 August 1638 [PCR 1:92]. On 9 April 1649, "Richard Church senior" sold to Robert Bartlett "an house and land lying at the Eel River near Plymouth aforesaid with all the meadow land" [PCR 12:165].

On 13 July 1649, "Mr. Thomas Prence of Nawset" sold to "Richard Church ... of Nawset ..., carpenter," and Anthony Snow of Marshfield, feltmaker, "a certain tract of upland and marsh meadow in the limits of Green's Harbor *alias* Marshfeild" [PCR 12:176]. On 22 October 1650, "Richard Church sometimes of the town of Nawsett ..., carpenter," sold to John Dingley of Marshfield, smith, his half-share in this parcel of land [PCR 12:197].

On 24 January 1652[/3], Thomas Joy of Boston, carpenter, and Joan his wife sold to "Richard Church of Charlestowne, carpenter," one half the corn mill at Hingham, with one half the land and other appurtenances thereto belonging [SLR 2:77].

On 2 July 1667, Plymouth court "do admit of Richard Church to come with the ancient servants for a share of land at Saconett" [PCR 4:159]. On 29 October 1668, Richard Church was one of four men permitted to seek out "a parcel of land ... lying at Namassakett Pond" [PCR 5:5].

In his will, dated 25 December 1668 and proved 26 January 1668/9, "Richard Church of Hingham" bequeathed to "my beloved wife Elizabeth Church ... the remainder during her natural life" (after debts are paid); after her decease remainder to "be equally divided amongst my children only my son Joseph to have a double portion ... by reason of the lameness of his hand, whereby he is disenabled above the rest of my children" [SPR 6:21].

The inventory of "the estate of Richard Church of Hingham deceased," taken 1 January 1668[/9], totalled £365 14s., of which £270 was real estate: "the dwelling house with the barn, orchard & houselot containing six acres," £110; "half a tide mill," £100; "his share of the ironworks at Taunton," £50; and "2 acres of land lying by the mill," £10 [SPR 5:116].

BIRTH: About 1608 (deposed 25 August 1664 aged about 56 [PCR 4:85; MD 4:152]).
DEATH: Dedham 26 December 1668 [DeVR 11], probably on a visit to his son Caleb. In his will, written the day before his death, he calls himself of Hingham, but the witnesses are all of Dedham.
MARRIAGE: By 7 March 1636/7 [PCR 1:54; TAG 60:129-30] (and probably by 14 March 1635/6 [PCR 1:41, 56, 152]) Elizabeth Warren, daughter of RICHARD WARREN [PM 477]. She died at Hingham on 9 March 1669/70 [NEHGR 121:124].
CHILDREN:
  i ELIZABETH CHURCH, b. say 1636; m. Hingham 8 January 1657/8 Caleb Hobart [NEHGR 121:107].
  ii JOSEPH CHURCH, b. say 1638; m. Hingham 13 December 1660 Mary Tucker [NEHGR 121:111].
  iii BENJAMIN CHURCH, b. say 1640; m. Hingham 26 December 1667 Alice Southworth [NEHGR 121:121 (giving

    date of marriage but not name of bride)], daughter of CONSTANT SOUTHWORTH [PM 437].
- iv NATHANIEL CHURCH, b. say 1642; m. 1666 Sarah Barstow (on 8 June 1666, Nathaniel Church and "Sarah Barstow *alias* Sarah Church" each owed £5 to the colony treasury, presumably for fornication, as their eldest child was b. Scituate 16 December 1666 [PCR 8:116-17]).
- v CHARLES CHURCH, b. say 1644; d. Hingham 30 October 1659 "killed by the overturning of his cart" [NEHGR 121:110; TAG 60:131].
- vi CALEB CHURCH, b. say 1646; m. (1) Hingham 16 December 1667 Joanna Sprague [NEHGR 121:121], daughter of WILLIAM SPRAGUE [GMB 3:1737]; m. (2) by 8 June 1680 Deborah _____ [MLR 7:283-84]; m. (3) Watertown 6 November 1691 "Rebaca Scottoo" [WaVR 64], probably widow of John Scottow of Boston [TAG 60:135].
- vii ABIGAIL CHURCH, b. 22 June 1648 [MD 15:27, correcting PCR 8:4]; m. Hingham 19 December 1666 Samuel Thaxter [NEHGR 121:119].
- viii SARAH CHURCH, b. say 1652; m. Hingham 8 December 1674 James Burroughs [TAG 60:137, citing Hingham TR 1:33].
- ix MARY CHURCH, d. Duxbury 30 April 1662 [NEHGR 121:113].
- x DEBORAH CHURCH, bp. Hingham 22 March 1656/7 [NEHGR 121:106]; no further record. (See TAG 40:101, 60:131-32 for discussions of her possible fate.)

COMMENTS: In a letter of 6 February 1631/2 from the governor of Plymouth to the governor of Massachusetts Bay on matters of interest to the two colonies, Bradford, in listing persons who had moved from Massachusetts Bay to Plymouth, included "Richard Church [who] came likewise as a sojourner to work for the present; though he is still here resident longer than he purposed; and what he will do, neither we nor I think himself knows. But if he resolve here to settle we shall require of him to procure a dismission; but he did affirm to us at the first, that he was one of Mr. Webb's men, and freed to go for England or whither he would, the which we the rather believed because he came to us from Wessagasscusett upon the falling out with his partner" [WP 3:65].

In the settlement of a lawsuit on 3 January 1632/3, Richard Church was the assignee of William Bennett, the successful plaintiff [PCR 1:7].

Richard Church was plaintiff in civil suits in Plymouth court on 4 February 1638/9, 7 September 1642, 4 June 1652 and 3 March 1662/3 [PCR 7:11, 31, 59, 105, 108].

Richard Church was surety for Mark Mendall/Mendlove on 12 July 1637 and on 4 December 1637 [PCR 1:63, 69], on 4 June 1645 for Matthew Fuller [PCR 2:87], and on 2 March 1646/7 (as "Richard Church, of the Eale River, planter") for George Wright [PCR 2:113, 121, 127].

On 2 June 1640, several people residing at Eel River were presented for not building a bridge there according to order, and repay 50s. to Richard Church and Robert Bartlett (perhaps for undertaking some of the work themselves) [PCR 1:156].

BIBLIOGRAPHIC NOTE: The definitive article on Richard Church was published by Robert S. Wakefield in 1985 [TAG 60:129-39]. He analyzed in great detail the list of children for Richard Church, and discarded four alleged children included in many previous accounts of the family [TAG 60:138-39]. We concur in this, and differ from his treatment only in a few minor and insubstantial places: We do not include even as a possibility the questionable son Richard, for whom there is no documentation, and we differ slightly in some of the estimated dates of birth, where we place no reliance at all on LCVR.

RICHARD CLARK

Richard Clarke came to Plymouth in 1620 on the *Mayflower* and signed the Mayflower Compact. He died soon after arrival in the general sickness [Bradford 443, 447].

THOMAS CLARK

ORIGIN: Unknown.
MIGRATION: 1623 on the *Anne.*
FIRST RESIDENCE: Plymouth.
REMOVES: Boston by 1660, Plymouth by 1673 (with occasional residence in Barnstable).

FREEMAN: In 1633 Plymouth list of freemen ahead of those admitted on 1 January 1632/3 [PCR 1:4]. In list of 7 March 1636/7 [PCR 1:52]. In

Plymouth sections of lists of 1639, 1658, 29 May 1670 (as "Mr. Thomas Clarke") and 1 [blank] 1683/4 [PCR 5:274, 8:174, 197, 202].

EDUCATION: He signed his name to coroner's jury statements.

OFFICES: Deputy for Plymouth to Plymouth General Court, 5 June 1651, 8 June 1655, 3 June 1656 [PCR 2:167, 3:79, 99].

Plymouth coroner's jury, 2 March 1635/6, 29 June 1652, 3 September 1652 [PCR 1:39, 3:15, 16]. Petit jury, 7 December 1641, 1 November 1642, 9 June 1653, 4 October 1653 [PCR 7:25, 32, 65, 67].

Plymouth constable for Eel River, 1 March 1641/2 [PCR 2:34]. Surveyor of highways, 7 June 1642, 7 March 1642/3 (Eel River), 5 June 1644 (Eel River), 1 June 1647, 7 June 1648 [PCR 2:40, 53, 72, 116, 124].

Plymouth committee to procure supplies for the expedition of the Lord Protector, 6 June 1654 [PCR 3:53]. Committee to treat with the commissioners regarding the trade at Kennebecke, 2 July 1655 [PCR 3:87]. Committee to supply and accommodate the Governor and Magistrates, 3 June 1657 [PCR 3:120].

Volunteered for service in the Pequot War, 7 June 1637 [PCR 1:60]. In Plymouth section of 1643 Plymouth Colony list of men able to bear arms [PCR 8:189].

ESTATE: In 1623 Plymouth land division received one acre as passenger on *Anne* [PCR 12:6]. In 1627 Plymouth cattle division "Thomas Clarke" was the thirteenth person in the third company [PCR 12:10].

On 28 September 1629, Abraham Pierce sold one acre of land on the south side of town to Thomas Clark [PCR 12:7]. The next day, Thomas Clark sold the acre of land to William Bradford, along with another acre of land bounded by widow Warren [PCR 12:7, 8]. On 24 March 1630[/1], Ralfe Wallen sold to Thomas Clark land called Wallen's Well [PCR 12:17]. On 24 February 1633/4, Thomas Clark purchased of Ralph Wallen "so much land adjoining to the said Thomas, on the south side his dwelling, as maketh up a former moiety the said Thomas bought of the said Ralph['s] twenty acres," and "one share of meadow ground belonging to the said lot when division shall be made thereof" [PCR 1:25, 76]. On 1 February 1640/1, the court ordered that the twenty acres of land purchased by Thomas Clark from Ra[l]ph Wallen were to be laid out at the lower end of the two lots of forty acres Clark had at the Eel River [PCR 2:7].

Assessed £1 4s. in Plymouth tax list of 25 March 1633 and £1 7s. in list of 27 March 1634 [PCR 1:10, 27].

Assigned mowing ground, 1 July 1633, 14 March 1635/6, 20 March 1636/7 [PCR 1:15, 41, 57].

On 4 December 1637, a previous grant of sixty acres to Thomas Clark was confirmed and ordered to be laid out [PCR 1:70]. On 2 April 1628, all that parcel of land called Slowly Field, formerly in the tenure of Mr. Edward Winslow, was granted to Thomas Clark [PCR 1:83]. On 7 October 1639, the court granted Thomas Clark liberty to erect a house at Mannamett Pond to fodder his cattle in this winter until some lands be laid out for him there [PCR 1:135]. On 6 January 1639/40, since Thomas Clark relinquished his grant of land at "the Whoop Place" except eight acres reserved to Thomas Little, the court granted Clark eighty-five acres purchased of Nicholas Presland, to be laid out at Mannamett Ponds, "forty acres formerly granted to Thomas Little there, to be parcel thereof" [PCR 1:138].

He was listed among the fifty-eight purchasers [PCR 2:177].

On 5 March 1671/2, Thomas Clark was granted the "skirts of meadow lying upon the pond at Mannomett" [PCR 5:89].

On 18 June 1673, "Thomas Clarke of Plymouth" granted to "my wellbeloved son Andrew Clarke of Boston," shoemaker, "all that my house & ground lying & being in Boston ... which I recovered from the estate of John Nicolls by virtue of a judgment granted me at the court of Assistants sitting in Boston March the 5th 1672" [SLR 8:225-27].

(Jacobus refers to an original deed of gift, dated 6 June 1693, apparently unrecorded and now lost, which was published in Samuel C. Clarke, *Descendants of Thomas Clarke* [Boston 1869], in which Thomas Clark named his sons Andrew, William, James, Nathaniel and John [TAG 47:5].)

BIRTH: About 1599 (based on age given at death). (John Insley Coddington argued forcefully that Thomas Clark was the son of John Clark, pilot of the *Mayflower*, and that he was identical with the "Thomas son of John Clarke of Ratliff" who was baptized 8 March 1599/1600 at St. Dunstan's, Stepney, Middlesex [TAG 42:201-2]. The hypothesis is very attractive and was accepted by Jacobus [TAG 47:3], but remains underproven.)

DEATH: Plymouth 24 March 1697 (apparently 1696/7) "in his 98th year" [PVR 135; TAG 42:202].

MARRIAGE: (1) By July 1631 Susanna Ring, daughter of William and MARY (Durrant) RING [TAG 42:201-2; PM 389]. She died between 1644 (birth of youngest son) and 20 January 1664/5 (prenuptial agreement of husband with second wife).

(2) Soon after 20 January 1664/5 Alice (Hallett) Nichols [SCC 6], daughter of Richard Hallett and widow of Mordecai Nichols. She died by 25 July 1671 [SCC 8].

CHILDREN:
With first wife
- i WILLIAM CLARK, b. about 1634 (deposed 10 August 1671 aged thirty-seven [TAG 47:4, citing SJC Case #1179]); m. (1) Plymouth 1 March 1659[/60] Sarah Wolcott [PCR 8:22; PVR 662]; m. (2) Saybrook 7 March 1677/8 Hannah Griswold [SayVR 8 (also recorded Plymouth PVR 85)]; m. (3) Plymouth 3 August 1692 Abiah Wilder [PVR 85].
- ii JAMES CLARK, b. say 1636; m. Plymouth 7 October 1657 Abigail Lothrop [PCR 8:17; PVR 662], daughter of JOHN LOTHROP {1634, Scituate}.
- iii SUSANNA CLARK, b. say 1638; m. Plymouth 3 November [PCR 8:22; PVR 662] or Barnstable 1 December [MD 6:238] 1658 Barnabas Lothrop, son of JOHN LOTHROP {1634, Scituate}.
- iv JOHN CLARK, b. about 1640 (deposed 31 October 1671 aged about thirty [TAG 47:4, citing SJC Case #1179]); m. by 1668 Sarah _____ (eldest known child b. Boston 11 November 1668 [BVR 107]; see further discussion in TAG 43:19-26, 47:7, 49:143).
- v NATHANIEL CLARK, b. say 1642; m. between July 1684 (when she entered an account of the estate of her deceased husband Edward Gray [PCR 6:149-50]) and 4 June 1686 (when she sued Nathaniel Clark for divorce [PCR 6:190-92]) Dorothy (Lettice) Gray, daughter of Thomas Lettice and widow of Edward Gray.
- vi ANDREW CLARK, b. about 1644 (deposed 31 October 1671 aged about twenty-five [TAG 47:4, citing SJC Case #1179]); m. by 1672 Mehitable Scotto (eldest child b. Boston 10 July 1672 [BVR 122]; son Scotto Clark b. 1680 [MF 3:37]).

COMMENTS: Thomas Clark aspired to be a lawyer. On 2 July 1638, he was ordered to frame and offer a bill of indictment against Richard Clough for taking a waistcoat out of a suit Clough was to make for Edward Shaw [PCR 1:91]. On 5 March 1638/9, the court presented an abuse committed by Thomas Clarke, who accused Richard Cloofe of felony, but Clarke did not appear in court to prosecute the case for the King. And further, Clarke took the case of another man [Edward Shaw] and "prosecuted the said action in Court by way of barratry" [PCR 1:118].

About 1644 Robert Mendam authorized Thomas Clark of Eel River to sell a parcel of land at Duxbury [PCR 2:77]. When Tobias Taylor and John Shawe had a disagreement, the court on 7 July 1646 ordered Mr. Alden and Thomas Clark to represent Tobias and come to a settlement with the representatives of John Shawe [PCR 2:105].

On 4 December 1637, Thomas Clark was surety for Edward Shaw, who was accused of theft [PCR 1:69]. More often, Clark was a victim of theft: on 5 January 1635/6, he sued widow Warren for taking a boat of his; the court decided in favor of the defendant, but awarded the plaintiff 30s. "for other considerations" [PCR 1:36]; on 5 April 1642, the court supported Thomas Clark in his suit against Mathew Fuller [PCR 2:37]; on 5 June 1671, William Walker was charged with stealing cloth from Thomas Clark "of Boston," was sentenced to pay double for the cloth and for telling a lie about it, and was fined 10s. [PCR 5:61].

He brought suits against a number of men who owed him money, including Mr. "Gromes," 2 May 1648 [PCR 2:122], Morgan Jones in March 1668 [PCR 7:153, 154], Henry Clarke of Duxborrow, 1 July 1672 [PCR 7:171], and Samuel Knowles, of Eastham, administrator of the estate of his brother James Knowles, deceased, 31 October 1683 [PCR 7:268].

Sometimes the suits were not easily decided. On 3 December 1639, arbiters were selected to end the differences between Mr. Samuel Gorton & Thomas Clark [PCR 1:137]. On 29 October 1667, he sued the estate of Thomas Ewer, late of Barnstable, but the jury felt that the case was not clearly presented, and dismissed it [PCR 7:141]. On 5 March 1684/5, Mr. Thomas Clark brought suit against Peter, Indian, but Clark did not appear in court and Peter was freed [PCR 6:152]. "Mr. Thomas Clarke, sometimes of Boston, now of Barnstable," sued in 1667 Daniel Winge of Sandwich, administrator to the estate of Thomas Ewer, late of Barnstable, for a debt, but the jury did not understand the case, and Clarke desired to present the case again, but reconsidered and withdrew on 28 October 1684 [PCR 7:279].

On 2 October 1650, Thomas Clarke was allowed to draw and sell a cask of strong waters [PCR 2:163]. He was presented 5 October 1652 for staying and drinking at James Cole's contrary to the order of the court [PCR 3:17].

He was presented 6 March 1654/5 for charging £6 for the loan of £20, which the grand jury felt was extortion [PCR 3:75]. On 5 June 1655, he was cleared [PCR 7:73]. When Richard Clough sued Thomas Clark for slander on 4 September 1638, Clough lost [PCR 7:9]. Clark stated plainly in open court, 13 June 1660, that "G[e]orge Barlow is such an one that he is a shame and reproach to all his masters; and that he, the said Barlow, stands convicted and recorded of a lie at Newberry" [PCR 3:190].

His legal pretensions were also on display during his contentions with his second wife and her sons in the late 1660s and early 1670s, when he employed his legal Latin in arguing the precise nature of his relation with his spouse and the consequences of her actions [SCC 5-9, 98-99, 569-70; RCA 1:47].

His usefulness in court in later years included his service as overseer of the will of Mrs. Jenny. He and Samuell Jenny had some disagreement over the care and guardianship of Sarah, daughter of Samuell Jenny, that was settled 6 October 1659 [PCR 3:171]. He complained about Mr. Constant Southworth for the illegal disposal of a mare and her increase belonging to the estate of "Mistris Sarah Jeney, deceased" and came to an agreement as overseer, 1 June 1663 [PCR 4:43, 7:102]. He was also one of the administrators of the estate of Mr. "Willam Collyare," 5 July 1671 [PCR 5:68]. He acted as attorney to several of the purchasers at "Mannamoiett," 1 June 1675 [PCR 5:171].

On 5 July 1678, Thomas Clark of Plymouth, late of Boston, sued Mr. Constant Southworth, of Duxbury, for withholding one-eighth part of the yearly profits of the fishing at Cape Cod, but withdrew the action [PCR 7:213]. On 7 July 1682, he sued Samuel Smith of Eastham, for the unjust detaining of one-quarter of the profits of the fishing off the Cape, and withdrew this case also [PCR 7:249].

On 1 November 1679, "Mr. Thomas Clarke, resident at Plymouth, one of the old comers," successfully sued Mr. John Freeman, Senior, of Eastham, for pulling up a stake that was a boundary marker for Clark's land at Old Indian Field [PCR 7:218].

"Mr. Thomas Clarke, Senior," of Plymouth and William Shirtliffe wrangled repeatedly in 1681 and 1682 over the partition of land once jointly owned by Clark and William Shirtliffe's father [PCR 7:234, 237, 244, 255].

Thomas Clark was prosperous enough to employ a number of apprentices and servants. The court records mention three: on 2 September 1634, Thomas Clark took William Shetle as an apprentice for eleven years [PCR 1:31]; on 13 August, 1639, John Barnes assigned the remaining term of seven years' service of his servant Symon Trott to Thomas Clark, with Clark agreeing to pay Trott a heifer calf when six years of the term were up [PCR 1:129]; and, on 4 August 1654, Clark bought out the remaining time of Robert Ransom, servant of Thomas Dexter Jr. [PCR 3:63]. On 2 July 1655, Thomas Clark undertook to provide horses and equipment for the use of the commissioners on their journey to New Haven [PCR 3:86]. On 3 July 1656, Thomas Clark engaged to lend the country £5 of wheat to pay those who had worked on the "Joanses River bridge" [PCR 3:106]. On 7 July 1668, John Williams engaged to pay towards his wife's maintenance, payment to be made the following November "unto Mr. Thomas Clarke at Boston" [PCR 4:191].

On 12 February 1689/90, a Thomas Clark married Elizabeth Crow [PVR 86], and this has incorrectly been claimed as a third marriage for our Thomas Clark. "Elizabeth, the wife of Deacon Thomas Clerke, deceased 13th November, 1695" at Plymouth [PVR 135]. There seems to be only one Thomas Clark at Plymouth with wife Elizabeth at this time, and our Thomas was certainly not a deacon. The Thomas Clark who was a deacon is supposed to have died in 1727. If our Thomas had married Elizabeth Crow, he would have been ninety years old, and have been living as a widower for nearly twenty years when the marriage to Elizabeth Crow took place. (See also TAG 49:143 on this point.)

BIBLIOGRAPHIC NOTE: Thomas Clark is examined in a posthumously published article by Donald Lines Jacobus, incorporating his own research and that of John Insley Coddington [TAG 47:3-16].

RICHARD CLOUGH

ORIGIN: Manchester, Lancashire.
MIGRATION: 1630.
FIRST RESIDENCE: Massachusetts Bay.
REMOVES: Plymouth 1633, Massachusetts Bay 1640, New Amsterdam by 1643, Gravesend 1652.

OCCUPATION: Tailor. "Richard Clough, of Plymouth, tailor," was twice bound in £40 as defendant in lawsuits over jobs of tailoring, in which the claim was that Clough had not returned all the material given to him, 2 July 1638 and 4 September 1638 [PCR 1:91, 97].
FREEMAN: "Richard Cluffe" is in the 1633 list of Plymouth freemen, between a group of men admitted 1 January 1634/5, and Timothy Hatherly, noted as being admitted 5 January 1635[/6] [PCR 1:4]; also in list of 7 March 1636/7 [PCR 1:53].
EDUCATION: Made his signature as witness to several deeds.

OFFICES: Plymouth coroner's jury, 2 March 1635/6, 5 June 1638 [PCR 1:39, 88].

He volunteered to serve in the Pequot War, 7 June 1637 [PCR 1:61].

ESTATE: "Richard Cloufe" was assessed 12s. in the Plymouth tax list of 27 March 1634 [PCR 1:29].

On 6 October 1636, "Rich[ard] Clough" was granted five acres "at the fishing point next Slowly Field" [PCR 1:45]; on 7 November 1636, it was discovered that the place designated for this grant did not quite allow the full five acres [PCR 1:46]. "Desired lands at the South Ponds, by Josias Cooke," 7 May 1638 [PCR 1:83].

On 21 January 1647 [NS], "George Bacxter, Richard Clof and associates" were issued a patent for a "tract of land named Canarise, on the south side of Long Island ... on condition that they shall, within three years from date, settle twenty families thereon" [New York Historical Manuscripts: Dutch, Land Papers, p. 46]; the associates did not meet the terms of the patent.

In the settlement at Plymouth of the estate of Thomas Willett, a list of uncollected debts included, under date of 1649, 22 gilders, 3 stivers, due from Richard Clough [MD 33:38].

On 2 September 1652, the court at Gravesend ordered William Alldridge to pay to "Rich: Clough" a debt of ten guilders ten stivers, and permit "Richard Cloughe peacably & quietly to enjoy that parcel of land bought by the said Clough of the said Alldridge" [Gravesend TR 1:130]. On 24 January 1655, "Richard Cloughe" sold to Thomas Hall "a certain parcel of land with the housing and fencing thereunto belonging and being formerly purchased by the said Richard Cloughe of William Alldridge" [Gravesend TR 2:20].

On 7 November 1657 [NS], Thomas Hall sold to Nicholas Stillwell lot number twenty-nine in Gravesend, and also "a certain tenement with all the housing thereunto belonging ... now in the possession of Richard Cluff" [Gravesend TR 2:37].

BIRTH: About 1607 (deposed 23 July 1647 [NS] "from Manchester, aged about 40 years" [New York Historical Manuscripts: Dutch, Volume IV, *Council Minutes, 1638-1649*, p. 419]).

DEATH: After 7 November 1657 [NS] [Gravesend TR 2:37].

MARRIAGE: None recorded.

CHILDREN: None recorded.

ASSOCIATIONS: The interactions of Richard Clough with ISAAC ALLERTON [PM 10] and THOMAS WILLETT [PM 497] in New Netherland indicate that this is the same as the Plymouth Richard

Clough. After twenty-seven years of more or less continuous activity in New England and New Netherland he vanishes from the records. Given his trading connections with Virginia, it may be that he continued his migration down the eastern seaboard.

COMMENTS: On 28 September 1630, "[i]t is ordered, that all Rich[ard] Cloughe's strong water shall presently be seized upon, for his selling great quantity thereof to several men's servants, which was the occasion of much disorder, drunkenness, & misdemeanor" [MBCR 1:76].

On 5 October 1636, William Bradford won a suit for trespass against Richard Clough and three others, although he was awarded only half what he had claimed [PCR 1:44]. On 12 March 1638/9, Richard Clough was involved in a lawsuit, apparently as plaintiff, in which William Hiller was defendant [PCR 1:119].

On 1 September 1640, "Richard Cluffe, for saying, Shall I pay 12d. for the fragments which the grand jury rogues have left, he was bound to his good behavior & fined three pounds six shillings & eight pence, which was discounted by Mr. Robert Saltonstall upon account" [MBCR 1:300].

"Richard Cluff" witnessed the deposition of Thomas Farrel at New Amsterdam on 19 October 1643 [NS] [New York Historical Manuscripts: Dutch, Volume II, *Register of the Provincial Secretary*, 1642-1647, p. 169]. On 7 July 1644 [NS], "Ritchert Cloff" deposed about "Sir Edman Pleydoen, knight, residing in Virginia, [who] purchased from Philip Weyt in Kiketan"; he signed as "Richard Clouff" [New York Historical Manuscripts: Dutch, Volume II, *Register of the Provincial Secretary*, 1642-1647, pp. 236-37]. On 11 May 1645, "Ritchert Cloff" sued "Philip Weyt ... for payment for 2200 lb. of pork," to which the defendant answered that "he paid Mr. Bosseroot in Virginia" [New York Historical Manuscripts: Dutch, Volume IV, *Council Minutes, 1638-1649*, p. 264].

On 10 January 1645 [NS], "Tomas Hal and Ritchert Cloff, administrators of the estate of Francoys Lasle, deceased, have adjusted accounts with Isaack Allerton" [New York Historical Manuscripts: Dutch, Volume II, *Register of the Provincial Secretary*, 1642-1647, pp. 285-86]. On 22 September 1647 [NS], "I, Isaack Allerton, empower and appoint Jan Oghden and Ritchert Cloff to collect the debts which are due me by Luys Hulen" [New York Historical Manuscripts: Dutch, Volume II, *Register of the Provincial Secretary*, 1642-1647, p. 492].

On 15 July 1645 [NS], "Philip Geraerdi and Ritchert Cloff" sued George Collen for debt and for running away [New York Historical Manuscripts: Dutch, Volume IV, *Council Minutes, 1638-1649*, p. 272].

On 23 July 1647 [NS], "Ritchert Clof from Manchester, aged 40 years," deposed as to what "Mr. Willet ... said in the deponent's presence in the house of Isaack Allerton" [New York Historical Manuscripts: Dutch, Volume IV, *Council Minutes, 1638-1649*, p. 419].

On 5 September 1650 [NS], "Thomas Doxsey of Roade Island" made "my well-beloved friend Richard Cluffe" his attorney in all matters of debt and trade between Doxsey and Nicholas Stillwell [Gravesend TR 1:67]. On 19 October 1650 [NS], "Richard Cluffe" agreed with Lieutenant Nicholas Stillwell "for a certain lot lately purchased by the said Nicholas Stillwell of George Homes the said lot being for the proper use of Thomas Doxsey" [Gravesend TR 1:49-50]. On 24 March 1651 [NS], "Rich[ar]d Cluffe of the Munnatows [Manhattan] arrested the house & land of Thomas Doxsey of Pequett in New England for certain debts due" [Gravesend TR 1:85]. On 27 May 1651 [NS], "Mr. Robert Scott of Boston" purchased this lot from Doxsey and "is to defray all such charges the said Rich[ar]d Clough is out upon it & pay such debts he can prove due to him from Doxsey" [Gravesend TR 1:89].

On 4 December 1651 [NS], "Richard Clugh" sued "Thomas Aplegat Junior" at Gravesend over a cow that Applegate was to deliver in return for 314 lb. of tobacco [Gravesend TR 1:94].

In June 1654 "Richard Clof" sued "William Strengwits ... for having conveyed one Willem Crump from Gravesend to Virginia without the knowledge of the Magistrates against the law of this land, said Crump being indebted to him" [Berthold Fernow, ed., *The Records of New Amsterdam from 1653 to 1674 Anno Domini*, Volume I. Minutes of the Court of Burgomasters and Schepens (rpt. Baltimore 1976), pp. 203-4].

Richard Clough witnessed deeds at Gravesend on 28 April 1655 [NS], 19 May 1655 [NS] and 6 September 1656 [NS] [Gravesend TR 2:22, 23, 34]. On 25 December 1655 [NS], "Richard Cluffe," as attorney for William Hallett, sold a lot in Gravesend to Nicholas Stillwell [Gravesend TR 2:27].

HENRY COBB

ORIGIN: Unknown.
MIGRATION: 1632.
FIRST RESIDENCE: Plymouth.

REMOVES: Scituate 1634, Barnstable 1639.

OCCUPATION: Tavernkeeper. Licensed to draw wine at Barnstable, 5 June 1644 [PCR 2:73].

CHURCH MEMBERSHIP: "Goodman Cob and his wife" were members #7 and #8, admitted at the founding of Scituate church on 8 January 1634/5 [NEHGR 9:279]. "Decemb. 15, 1635 our Brother Cobb was invested into the office of a Deacon" at Scituate [NEHGR 10:37]. Ordained ruling elder of Barnstable church, 14 April 1670 [Cobb Gen, citing BarnChR 1:1].

FREEMAN: In the 1633 Plymouth list of freemen near others admitted on 1 January 1632/3 [PCR 1:4]; in 7 March 1636/7 list of freemen [PCR 1:53]. Initially entered in Scituate portion of 1639 list of Plymouth Colony freemen, then transferred to Barnstable section [PCR 8:175, 177]. In Barnstable section of 1658 and 29 May 1670 lists of Plymouth freemen [PCR 5:277, 8:200].

EDUCATION: Signed his name to coroner's jury findings [PCR 3:147]. His inventory included "books" valued at 24s.

OFFICES: Deputy for Barnstable to Plymouth General Court, 5 June 1644, 3 March 1645/6, 7 July 1646 (fined for "defect in appearance" 4s. [PCR 2:106]), 1 June 1647, 7 June 1652, 7 June 1659, 6 June 1660, 2 October 1660, 4 June 1661, 3 June 1662 [PCR 2:72, 95, 104, 117, 3:9, 162, 187, 198, 214, 4:14].

Plymouth petit jury, 4 June 1639, 3 September 1639, 3 December 1639, 3 March 1639/40, 1 September 1640, 2 March 1640/1, 17 June 1641, 7 September 1642, 6 June 1649, 6 June 1650 [PCR 7:12-15, 18, 19, 21, 32, 46, 49, 2:140]. Coroner's jury, 5 June 1658 [PCR 3:147].

Excise collector for Barnstable, 8 June 1664 [PCR 4:67].

In Barnstable section of 1643 Plymouth list of men able to bear arms [PCR 8:193]. Committee for defense of Barnstable, 10 October 1643 [PCR 2:65]. His inventory included "a gun and ammunition" valued at 20s.

ESTATE: Assessed 9s. in the Plymouth tax lists of 25 March 1633 and 27 March 1634 [PCR 1:11, 29].

In the compilation of houses in Scituate prepared by Rev. John Lothrop, "Goodman Cobbe's" house is seventh on the list, among those in place before September 1634; this is annotated "now Goodman Rowlye's" and "now Goodman Vinall's," perhaps indicating that there were two houses on this lot, or perhaps implying that Rowley purchased the house from Cobb and then sold it to Vinall. Later in the list, at position #32, among houses built in 1636, is "Brother Cobb's, on his lot," this being his second residence in Scituate, and probably the lot that he sold to Manasseh Kempton when he removed to Barnstable.

On 1 December 1640, "Henry Cob" sold to "Manasseth Kempton" of Plymouth his house in Scituate with twelve acres of upland with the parcel of meadow lying before the house and fourscore acres of upland in the fourth lot by North River, with a parcel of marsh meadow of about twelve acres [PCR 12:65].

One of five men "granted liberty to view and to purchase a tract of land at Saconeesett," 7 June 1659 [PCR 3:164, 208, 216].

In his will, dated 4 April 1678 and proved 3 June 1679, "Henery Cobb" of Barnstable, though "weak in body," bequeathed to "my son James Cobb" my great lot in Barnstable; to "my sons John, James, Gershom and Eliezer" half my lands at Suconeesett equally divided between them "and 40s. being in the hand of my son James for my son Eliezer's part"; to "Sarah my dear and loving wife during her natural life" my new dwelling house and all the rest of my lands; at Sarah's decease, to "my son Samuel" my dwelling house and two acres of upland, and an acre and a half of my marsh which I bought with his stock in partnership with my son James; to "my sons Samuel, Jonathan and Henry" residue of lands equally; to "my sons John, Gershom and Eliezer" one shilling each; to "my daughters Mary, Hannah and Patience" one shilling each; to "my daughter Sarah" my second best bed and furniture; residue to Sarah "my loving wife and sole executrix." In a codicil dated 22 February 1678[/9], he ordered that "my son Samuel" shall have only two acres of my upland after my wife's decease and all the rest of my lands equally divided between my "three sons Samuel, Jonathan and Henry"; Henry to have my house after my wife's decease and his part of the land to lie most convenient to the house, only my lands at the Island equally divided between my three sons; "my son James to dry thatch on half an acre of the Island when the English corn is taken off" [transcribed in full in Cobb Gen 14-15, citing PCPR 4:1:22-23].

The undated inventory of the estate of "Elder Henery Cobb Late of Barnstable" was untotalled, with real estate valued at £80: "a house land and meadow," £80. He also owned part of a "thachboate" [transcribed in full in Cobb Gen 16-17, citing PCPR 4:1:23].

On 2 March 1679/80, administration of the estate of Sarah Cobb was granted to Mr. Thomas Hinckley and Samuel Cobb, who were "with the advice and help of their friends and relations, to make a distribution of the estate amongst the children, still having a special respect therein to the youngest children, for their best good" [PCR 6:32].

BIRTH: By about 1607 (based on estimated date of first marriage).
DEATH: Between 22 February 1678[/9] (date of codicil) and 3 June 1679 (probate of will).
MARRIAGE: (1) By 1632 Patience Hurst, daughter of JAMES HURST (his will names Cobb grandchildren) [PM 284]. She was buried at Barnstable on 4 May 1648 "the first that was buried in our new burying place by our meeting house" [MD 3:73; PCR 8:42; NEHGR 9:285].

(2) Barnstable 12 December 1649 Sarah Hinckley [PCR 8:42; NEHGR 9:287], daughter of SAMUEL HINCKLEY {1635, Scituate} [GM 2:3:334]. She was admitted to Barnstable church 20 January 1649/50 [NEHGR 9:281] and died before 2 March 1679/80 [PCR 6:32].

CHILDREN (MD 3:73; PCR 8:42 [less complete and less accurate]):
With first wife
- i   JOHN COBB, b. Plymouth 7 June 1632; m. Plymouth 28 April 1658 Martha Nelson [PCR 8:17].
- ii   JAMES COBB, b. Plymouth 14 January 1634; m. Barnstable 26 December 1663 Sarah Lewis [MD 3:73], daughter of GEORGE LEWIS {1635, Scituate} [TAG 68:26].
- iii MARY COBB, b. Scituate 24 March 1636/7, bp. there 26 March 1637 [NEHGR 9:281]; m. Plymouth 15 October 1657 Jonathan Dunham [PCR 8:17], son of JOHN DUNHAM [TAG 30:145].
- iv   HANNAH COBB, b. Scituate 5 October 1639, bp. there 5 October 1639 [NEHGR 9:281]; m. Barnstable 9 May 1661 Edward Lewis [MD 10:250], son of GEORGE LEWIS {1635, Scituate} [TAG 68:26].
- v   PATIENCE COBB, b. Barnstable "about 15 of March" 1641/2, bp. there 13 March 1641/2 [NEHGR 9:282]; m. (1) Barnstable "beginning August 1667" Robert Parker [MD 11:100]; m. (2) after 1 June 1685 William Crocker and d. Barnstable 23 October 1727 [NEHGR 112:190-97].
- vi   GERSHOM COBB, b. Barnstable "about 10 January" 1644/5, bp. there 12 January 1644/5 [NEHGR 9:283]; bur. Swansea 24 June 1675 [PCR 8:61]; unm. (division of his estate to brothers and sisters [PCR 5:180]).
- vii ELIEZER COBB, b. Barnstable "about 30 March" 1648, bp. there 2 April 1648 [NEHGR 9:283]; residing in Barnstable in 1703, apparently unm. [Otis 1:172].

With second wife

- viii MEHITABLE COBB, b. Barnstable 1 September 1651, bp. there 7 September 1651 [NEHGR 9:284]; bur. Barnstable 8 March 1651/2 [PCR 8:42; NEHGR 9:286].
- ix SAMUEL COBB, b. Barnstable 12 October 1654; m. Barnstable 20 December 1680 Elizabeth [blank] [MD 3:73] (said to be Elizabeth Taylor, daughter of Richard Taylor [Otis 1:173]).
- x SARAH COBB, b. Barnstable 15 January 1658; bur. there 25 January 1658.
- xi JONATHAN COBB, b. Barnstable 10 April 1660; m. Barnstable 1 March 1682/3 Hope (Chipman) Huckins [MD 3:149], daughter of John Chipman and widow of John Huckins.
- xii SARAH COBB, b. Barnstable 10 March 1662/3; m. Barnstable 27 December 1686 Samuel Chipman [MD 4:121].
- xiii HENRY COBB, b. Barnstable 3 September 1665; m. Barnstable 10 April 1690 Lois Hallet [MD 3:73].
- xiv MEHITABLE COBB, b. Barnstable 15 February 1667; no further record.
- xv EXPERIENCE COBB (daughter), b. Barnstable 11 September 1671; no further record.

BIBLIOGRAPHIC NOTE: Henry Cobb and his family were treated in detail by Philip L. Cobb early in this century [*A History of the Cobb Family*, Part 1 (Cleveland 1907), cited above as Cobb Gen]. The author of this genealogy is to be commended for including full transcripts of many records for the early generations, while at the same time avoiding the many legends and traditional tales typical of volumes published in that era. (See also Otis 1:166-79.)

JAMES COLE

ORIGIN: Barnstaple, Devonshire.
MIGRATION: 1633.
FIRST RESIDENCE: Plymouth.

OCCUPATION: Shoemaker [PCLR 2:2:69].
 Innkeeper. On 7 June 1637, "James Coale of Plymouth" was fined 10s. "for selling less than a Winchester quart for ijd. ... but not in

ignorance" [PCR 1:61]. On 5 May 1640, "James Cole, of Plymouth, is prohibited by the Court to draw any wine or strong water until the next General Court, nor then neither without special license from the Court" [PCR 1:153]. On 2 June 1640, John Kerman deposed that "there was such disorder in James Cole's house, by throwing stools, & forms, & fire, until within a hour of day, or thereabouts, that they could hardly sleep, and in the morning he found them on sleep by the fire" [PCR 1:156]. On 1 September 1640, James Cole "for drawing wine without license & contrary to the express prohibition of the Court, & for his contempt & disorders suffered in his house, is fined £5" [PCR 1:162]; in the margin is the annotation "Discharged." On 7 January 1644/5, he was licensed to draw wine "if he shall agree with Mr. Done to take off those wines he now hath in his hands" [PCR 2:80]. It was ordered 9 June 1653 that "James Cole, the ordinary keeper of Plymouth," be paid "for what he expendeth in keeping the ordinary" [PCR 3:38]. On 7 June 1659, the court authorized £10 for the "repairing of the house he now liveth in, so as it may be fitted as an ordinary for the entertainment of strangers" [PCR 3:166]. On 5 March 1660/1, James Cole, senior, was fined 10s. for selling wine to the Indians [PCR 3:207]. He was fined 5s. 3 October 1665 for allowing Richard Dwelley to be drunk in his house [PCR 4:107]. On 2 March 1668/9, James Cole, senior, and Mary, his wife, were presented for selling strong liquors to an Indian, and for allowing James Clarke, Phillip Dotterich, Mary Ryder and Hester Wormall to drink on the Lord's Day [PCR 5:15]; the large fine was partly remitted on 1 June 1669 [PCR 5:21]. On 8 March 1670/1, John Sprague was fined for "highly misdemean[ing]" himself at the house of James Cole, including riding his mare into the parlor [PCR 5:53]. On 5 June 1671, "James Cole, Senior," was fined "for being found drunk the second time" [PCR 5:61]. On 29 October 1671, he was presented for suspicion of being drunk, "he pleading infirmity of body, which may make some think that sometimes he is drunk" [PCR 5:81].

FREEMAN: In 1633 Plymouth list of freemen, between those made free 1 January 1633/4, and those made free 1 January 1634/5 [PCR 1:4]. In 7 March 1636/7 Plymouth list of freemen [PCR 1:53]. In Plymouth sections of 1639, 1658 and 29 May 1670 lists of freemen [PCR 5:274, 8:174, 197].

EDUCATION: Signed his deeds.

OFFICES: Plymouth petit jury, 2 January 1637/8, 3 May 1642, 1 November 1642, 6 June 1643, 7 November 1643 [PCR 1:74, 7:29, 32, 35, 36]. Coroner's jury, 1 August 1648, 15 July 1660 [PCR 2:132, 3:196].

Plymouth constable, 1 March 1641/2, 5 June 1644 [PCR 2:34, 72]. Surveyor of highways, 1 March 1641/2, 7 June 1642, 5 June 1651, 7 June 1652 [PCR 2:34, 40, 168, 3:9].

At the end of the list of Plymouth men who will serve in the Pequot war "if they be pressed" is "James Coale," 7 June 1637 [PCR 1:61]. In Plymouth section of 1643 Plymouth Colony list of men able to bear arms (as "James Cole Sen[ior]") [PCR 8:188]. The "boat of James Cole of Plymouth," with seamen, was impressed to transport soldiers, 20 June 1654 [PCR 3:57].

ESTATE: Assessed 9s. in Plymouth tax list of 27 March 1634 [PCR 1:28].

On 2 January 1636/7, one of four men granted "seven acres apiece, to belong to their several dwelling houses in Plymouth" [PCR 1:49].

On 16 September 1641, James Cole was granted fifty acres of upland at Lakenhame Meadow, and some meadow to be laid out "upon view" [PCR 2:26]. On 27 September 1642, James Cole was granted "an enlargement at the head of his lot" [PCR 2:48].

On 9 September 1661, Samuel Dunham of Plymouth, planter, sold to "James Cole Senior of [Plymouth], shoemaker, all that his part, portion or share of land at Punckateeset" [PCLR 2:2:69].

He was first on the list when, on 3 June 1662, the court allowed that the "servants and ancient freemen shall have liberty, in case they cannot procure Saconett Necke ..., to look out some other place undisposed of, for their accommodation" [PCR 4:18]. He received one share, equivalent to about thirty acres, on the westerly side of Namasskett River, 7 June 1665 [PCR 4:94].

On [blank] March 1668, James Cole Sr. of Plymouth, yeoman, gave to "my beloved son-in-law Mr. John Almey of ... Portsmouth in Rhode Island" his entire right at Punckateeset [PCLR 3:326].

On 31 October 1673, James Cole Sr. of Plymouth "for natural love and affection" granted to "my son Hugh Cole of Swansea" his right to land at Saconnet [PCLR 3:310].

BIRTH: By about 1600 (based on date of marriage).
DEATH: After October 1678 (his son sold land as "James Cole Junior" [PCLR 4:226]). (Savage states that "he was living in 1688, very aged.")
MARRIAGE: Barnstaple, Devonshire, 1 May 1625 Mary Tibbes [Thomas Wainwright, ed., *Barnstaple Parish Register of Baptisms, Marriages and Burials, 1538 A.D. to 1812 A.D.* (Exeter 1903), cited herein as Barnstaple PR, p. 21]. She died after 7 March 1659/60 [PCR 3:181].

CHILDREN:
  i JAMES, bp. Barnstaple, Devonshire, 11 February 1626/7 [Barnstaple PR 68]; in Plymouth section of 1643 list of men able to bear arms [PCR 8:188]; m. (1) Plymouth 23 December 1652 Mary Tilson [PCR 8:14]; m. (2) by September 1698 Esther _____; m. (3) in 1700 or later Abigail _____ [TAG 67:243-45 discusses the wives and children of this man in detail].
  ii HUGH, bp. Barnstaple, Devonshire, 29 June 1628 [Barnstaple PR 70]; in Plymouth section of 1643 list of men able to bear arms [PCR 8:188]; m. Plymouth 8 January 1654[/5] Mary Foxwell [PCR 8:72, 74; TAG 64:139-41].
  iii JOHN, b. say 1630; possibly the John Cole whose inventory was taken at Portsmouth, R.I., 15 December 1676 [Scrapbook 122].
  iv MARY, b. say 1632; m. (1) by 1668 John Almy [PCLR 3:326; Scrapbook 10-11; Austin 238]; m. (2) by 28 June 1677 John Pococke [Austin 154, 238].

COMMENTS: James Cole of Saco was not part of this family [GDMNH 155].

On 2 January 1637/8, the Plymouth court noted that James Cole had been drinking excessively at the house of Mr. Hopkins [PCR 1:75].

On 2 July 1638, and again on 4 September 1638, James Cole was surety for RICHARD CLOUGH in a criminal case [PCR 1:91, 97]; in the first instance he was called "sailor," and in the second innkeeper.

On 6 September 1641, Emanuel White sued James Cole over twenty-two bushels of Indian corn, and Cole agreed to pay [PCR 7:23]. On 7 September 1641, James Cole's fine of £5 was remitted "allowing the diet of John Mynard during the time he was erecting the prison" [PCR 2:24]. On 7 December 1641, James Cole sued James Luxford and Luxford's goods were attached [PCR 7:26]. On 21 November 1644, James Cole undertook to pay 22s. for Francis Goole to William Hanbury [PCR 2:78].

On 2 October 1650, he was cleared of assaulting "William Shirtley" of Plymouth [PCR 2:162]. On 4 March 1650/1, James Cole Senior, sued James Shaw and won a 36s. judgment [PCR 7:53].

Robert Willis was up all night drinking at James Cole's before he went out fishing and accidentally drowned, as the inquest found 26 July 1652 [PCR 3:15]. On 5 October 1652, James Cole was presented for "entertaining townsmen in his house, contrary to order of court" [PCR 3:17]. On 7 March 1653/4, John Barnes sued "James Cole, Seni[o]r," for taking eleven barrels of oil on behalf of Barnes, but delivering him only ten [PCR 7:69].

On 7 March 1659/60, Thomas Lucas was fined 30s. for his "abusive and threatening speeches and turbulent carriages towards the wife of James Cole, Senior, and the child of James Cole, Junior" [PCR 3:181].

On 7 May 1662, James Cole Sr. and Joseph Ramsdens reached agreement over a debt [PCR 4:11]. On 3 May 1664, James Cole won a judgment against Henery Saunders for nonpayment of a debt [PCR 4:57]. James Cole Sr. attached a gun belonging to Joseph Billington, but the court ordered it released for Billington's goods were already attached by John Barnes [PCR 4:69-70]. On 6 February 1665/6, he was granted a judgment of £1 10s. 11d. against John Sutten [PCR 4:112].

JOB COLE

ORIGIN: Unknown.
MIGRATION: 1633 [MD 1:86].
FIRST RESIDENCE: Plymouth.
REMOVES: Duxbury, Yarmouth by 1643, Eastham by 1648.

FREEMAN: Propounded for freeman 5 March 1638/9, and admitted 3 March 1639/40 [PCR 1:117, 140]. In the 1639 list of Plymouth freemen, Job Cole is entered first in the Duxbury section, then is crossed off and added to the Yarmouth section of the same list [PCR 8:175, 176]. He is then found in the Eastham section of the lists of Plymouth freemen of 1658, 29 May 1670 and 1 [blank] 1683/4 [PCR 5:278, 8:202, 208].
EDUCATION: Signs his name as witness to a deed [PCR 12:25].
OFFICES: Deputy for Yarmouth to Plymouth General Court (apparently replaced during the year), 5 June 1644 [PCR 2:72].

Plymouth grand jury, 6 June 1643 [PCR 2:56].

Duxbury constable (replaced during the year), 2 March 1640/1 [PCR 2:9].

"Naussit" [Eastham] constable, 7 June 1648 [PCR 2:124]. Eastham surveyor of highways, 6 June 1654 [PCR 3:50].

In Yarmouth section of 1643 Plymouth list of men able to bear arms [PCR 8:194].
ESTATE: Granted "a parcel of land on Duxborrow side, when they are viewed," 4 June 1638 [PCR 1:85]. Granted forty acres upland, with some meadow, at Green's Harbor, 2 July 1638 [PCR 1:91, 135, 146].

On 2 October 1650, "Jobe Cole of ... Nawsett" sold to Thomas Chillingsworth of Marshfield, shoemaker, land at Marshfield, being about forty acres of upland and six acres of meadow [PCR 12:195].

On 13 August 1651, "Job Cole of Eastham" sold to Christopher Wadsworth of Duxborough "a house and land lying against a place called Morton's hole with meadow and fencing." Rebecca acknowledged this deed [PCR 12:216].

On 8 January 1680[/1?], Samuel Cole of Eastham sold to Samuel Smith of Eastham "all that my parcel of meadow or marsh ground lying and being in the township of Eastham ... which was granted unto my father Job Cole by the town" [PCLR 5:256].

On 5 April 1710, the Barnstable judge of probate ordered that "whereas it appears to me that there is some land & meadow laid out lying at Little Billingsate in Eastham to the name or heirs of Job Cole late of said Eastham now deceased & not yet settled or legally disposed of and it appearing to me that Rebecca Nickerson widow daughter of said deceased hath not had anything material of her deceased father's estate and was at some charge in supporting of her mother after the decease of her father the said land and meadow is therefore settled upon and ordered unto the said Rebecca Nickerson" [BarnPR 3:93].

BIRTH: By about 1609 (based on date of marriage).
DEATH: After 1683 [PCR 8:208] and before 29 December 1698 (death of widow).
MARRIAGE: Plymouth 15 May 1634 Rebecca Collier [PCR 1:30], daughter of WILLIAM COLLIER [PM 128], baptized at St. Olave, Southwark, Surrey, on 10 January 1614/5. She died at Eastham 29 December 1698, widow of Job Cole, aged about 88 [MD 6:204].
CHILDREN:
    i   DANIEL COLE, b. say 1650; at the Plymouth court in June 1672, "Daniel Cole, son of Job Cole, for cursing, fined 10s." [PCR 5:94, 8:137]; m. by about 1675 Mercy Fuller, daughter of Samuel Fuller and granddaughter of SAMUEL FULLER [TAG 75:124-29; PM 217].
    ii   REBECCA COLE, b. Eastham 26 August 1654 [PCR 8:15; MD 17:70]; m. by an unknown date Robert Nickerson.
    iii SAMUEL COLE, b. say 1656; m. by about 1680 _____ _____ [TAG 71:198-99].

ASSOCIATIONS: The will of John Cole, proved at Plymouth 7 January 1637/8, names brother Job Cole, sister Rebecca [possibly Job's wife, Rebecca Collier], Elizabeth Collier, "each of Master Collier's men," and "my brother Daniel" [MD 2:209-10]. (Partly on the basis of this document Stratton suggests that Job Cole may have been one of "Mr. Collier's men" who appear in the Plymouth tax list of 25 March 1633 [PCR 1:11; Stratton 267]. If this is the case, then Job Cole was probably included in the household of WILLIAM COLLIER [PM 128] in the tax list of 27 March 1634 [PCR 1:27], less than two months before Cole married Collier's daughter.)

In his will of 16 November 1630, Zaccheus Cole of St. Olave, Southwark, Surrey, citizen and grocer of London, made bequests to his mother Frances, to brothers Nathaniel, John and Daniel, and made brother Job executor [PCC Scroope 106, as cited in TAG 42:119-20]. The location of Zaccheus Cole in the same parish as WILLIAM COLLIER, Job Cole's future father-in-law, makes it likely that this is the correct family.

The Daniel Cole named as brother in these wills was the man of that name who appeared in Yarmouth by 1643 and married Ruth Collier, daughter of WILLIAM COLLIER.

COMMENTS: On 28 October 1633, the estate of Richard Lanckford owed Job Cole 3s. 9d. [MD 1:86]. On 18 February 1634/5, Job Cole owed the estate of Thomas Evans an unspecified amount [MD 2:89]. On 6 May 1639, the service of Thomas Gray was transferred from John Atwood to Job Cole [PCR 1:121].

Savage gave Job Cole two additional children, sons John and Job. Daniel, Job's brother, had a son John residing in Eastham, who has apparently been misplaced in the family of Job. There is no indication that there was a Job in the second generation.

The two instances in which Job Cole was replaced in office in mid-term may point to the dates of two of his removes: replaced as Duxbury constable sometime during the year after 2 March 1640/1, perhaps indicating that he had moved to Yarmouth; and replaced as Yarmouth deputy during the year after 5 June 1644, perhaps indicating that he had moved to Eastham.

WILLIAM COLLIER

ORIGIN: Southwark, Surrey.
MIGRATION: 1633 (based on date of admission to freemanship).
FIRST RESIDENCE: Plymouth.
REMOVES: Duxbury after 1639.

OCCUPATION: Grocer (in England).

FREEMAN: Admitted 1 January 1633/4 and included in list of 1633 [PCR 1:4, 21]. In list of freemen, 7 March 1636/7 [PCR 1:52]. In Plymouth section of list of 1639 (where his name is crossed out and reentered in the Duxbury section) [PCR 8:173-74]. In Duxbury sections of lists of 1658 and 29 May 1670 (where his name is crossed out and marked "deceased") [PCR 5:274, 8:198].

EDUCATION: His appointment to the committee to review the laws speaks of considerable education.

OFFICES: Plymouth Colony Assistant, 1635-37, 1639-51, 1654-65 [PCR 1:33, 36, 48, 116, 140, 2:8, 33, 52, 71, 83, 100, 115, 123, 139, 153, 166, 3:48, 77, 99, 114, 134, 162, 187, 214, 4:13, 36, 60. 90]. Plymouth Commissioner to United Colonies, 1643 [PCR 2:53, 9:8-9]. Coroner, 2 June 1646 [PCR 2:101]. Auditor, 3 July 1656 [PCR 3:104].

Plymouth Colony committee to assess colony taxes [PCR 1:26]. Committee to lay out highways, for "Duxbery side," 1 October 1634 [PCR 1:31]. Committee to view farm land, 2 March 1635/6 [PCR 1:39]. Committee to set bounds for Scituate, 6 March 1637/8 [PCR 1:80]. Committee to view North Hill and set bounds, 4 February 1638/9 [PCR 1:112]. Committee to treat with Massachusetts Bay, 7 March 1642/3, 10 June 1650 [PCR 2:53, 159]. Council of War, 27 September 1642, 10 October 1643, 1 June 1658 [PCR 2:47, 64, 3:139]. Committee to draw up the excise, 7 July 1646 [PCR 2:105]. Committee for the letting of trade, 8 June 1649 [PCR 2:144]. Committee to review the laws, 3 June 1657 [PCR 3:117].

ESTATE: "Mr. Collier's men" were assessed 18s. in Plymouth tax list of 25 March 1633 [PCR 1:11]. "Mr. Will[iam] Collier" was assessed £2 5s. in list of 27 March 1634 [PCR 1:27].

In the allocation of mowing ground on 1 July 1633, reference is made to ground "that Mr. Collier hath" [PCR 1:14].

On 5 July 1635, Mr. William Collier was granted a parcel of land in the woods called North Hill, with some "tussicke marsh ground" [PCR 1:35]. On 3 October 1662, "Mr. Collyare" complained that the records of his grant at the North Hill were lost and could not be found, and the court ordered that the land be viewed and the report of it be recorded [PCR 4:27, 39].

On 6 March 1649[/50], "William Colliar" made over his right to a ten-acre parcel of upland in "Duxborrow" to "my kinsman William Clark" [PCR 12:182].

On 16 October 1659, "William Collyare" deeded to "my son-in-law Daniell Cole of the town of Eastham ..., yeoman, all that my right, title and interest of and into the Purchase Land commonly so-called lying and being upon Cape Cod ... at Satucquett, Namscekett or Paomett both upland and meadow land with all and singular the appurtenances, rights, privileges and immunities belonging thereunto ... viz: all the woods, commons and privileges of blubber" [MD 14:89-90, citing PCLR 2:2:29].

On 2 July 1667, the court agreed to a grant of thirty or forty acres of land for "Mr. William Collyare" for "that grand child who is now serviceable unto him" [PCR 4:159]. On 2 March 1668/9, the court granted him fifty acres in the tract of land at Namassakett [PCR 5:14].

On 5 July 1671, the court appointed Gov. Mr. Constant Southworth, Mr. Thomas Clarke, and "Benjamine Barlett," or any three of them to administer the estate of "Mr. William Collyare," deceased [PCR 5:68]. On 29 October 1671, the court ordered that "Daniell Cole" was to have all such particulars out of the estate of "William Collyare" that are extant [PCR 5:80].

BIRTH: By about 1585 (based on date of marriage). On 7 June 1659, "[i]n regard that Mr. Collyare, by reason of age and much business on him, cannot attend the country's business at courts but with great difficulties, the Court have appointed the Treasurer to procure him a servant, and do allow him for that purpose the sum of £10" [PCR 3:166].
DEATH: After 29 May 1670 (in list of Duxbury freemen) and before 5 July 1671 (administration granted on estate).
MARRIAGE: St. Olave, Southwark, Surrey, 16 May 1611 Jane Clark [TAG 49:215]. She died after 28 June 1666 (when she consented to a deed made by her husband [PCLR 3:152]).
CHILDREN (unless otherwise stated, from TAG 49:215):
  i   MARY COLLIER, bp. St. Olave, Southwark, 18 February 1611[/2]; m. Plymouth 1 April 1635 THOMAS PRENCE [PCR 1:34; PM 374].
  ii HANNAH COLLIER, bp. St. Olave 14 September 1613; bur. there 31 August 1625.
  iii REBECCA COLLIER, bp. St. Olave 10 January 1614[/5]; m. Plymouth 15 May 1634 JOB COLE [PCR 1:30].
  iv SARAH COLLIER, bp. St. Olave 30 April 1616; m. Plymouth 15 May 1634 Love Brewster [PCR 1:30], son of WILLIAM BREWSTER [PM 66].
  v   JOHN COLLIER, bp. St. Olave 18 March 1616[/7]; bur. there 24 August 1618.

vi   ELIZABETH COLLIER, bp. St. Olave 9 March 1618[/9]; m. Plymouth 2 November 1637 CONSTANT SOUTHWORTH [PM 437; PCR 1:68].

vii   JOHN COLLIER, bp. St. Olave 23 March 1619[/20]; bur. there 6 August 1625.

viii   CATHEREN COLLIER, bur. St. Olave 13 January 1621[/2].

ix   JAMES COLLIER, bp. St. Mary Magdalen, Bermondsey, Surrey, 16 March 1622[/3] [TAG 51:58]; bur. St. Olave 24 August 1624.

x   MARTHA COLLIER, bp. St. Mary Magdalen, Bermondsey, 28 March 1624 [TAG 51:58]; bur. St. Olave 30 May 1625.

xi   WILLIAM COLLIER, bur. St. Olave 12 August 1625.

xii   LYDIA COLLIER, bp. St. Olave 8 March 1625[/6]; bur. there 12 March 1625[/6].

xiii   RUTH COLLIER, b. about 1628 ("Ruth Cole the wife of Daniel Cole" d. Eastham 15 December 1694 "in the sixty-seventh year of her age" [MD 6:204]); m. by 1644 Daniel Cole (eldest known child b. Eastham 15 July 1644 [MD 5:23]), brother of JOB COLE [PM 126].

ASSOCIATIONS: The will of Zaccheus Cole of St. Olave, Southwark, citizen and grocer of London, named mother Frances, brothers Nathaniel, John and Daniel Cole, and appointed brother Job Cole executor [PCC Scroope 106, as cited in TAG 42:119-20]. The New England will of John Cole about 1637 named his brothers Job Cole and Daniel Cole, his sister Rebecca (surname not stated) and "Elizabeth Collyer" (no relationship stated), and left legacies to "each of Master Collyer's men," Edward, Joseph, Arthur, Ralph and John [MD 2:209-10]. Job Cole, apprentice in New England of William Collier and then his son-in-law, was likely the brother of Zaccheus Cole. This connection and others are discussed in TAG 42:119-21.

On 19 November 1645, Nathaniel Warren, son of RICHARD WARREN [PM 477], married at Plymouth Sarah Walker [PCR 2:94]. On 7 June 1653, "Mrs. Jane Collyare in behalf of her grandchild the wife of the said Nathaniel Warren" petitioned Plymouth Court in a land dispute [MD 3:141]. John Insley Coddington has suggested that when William Collier married her, Jane Clark was a widow, and that by her Clark husband she had a daughter who married a Walker [TAG 51:92-93]. Coddington further suggested that the Sara, daughter of William Walker, who was baptized at St. Olave, Southwark, on 10 November 1622 was the grandchild of Jane Collier who married Nathaniel Warren. If this solution proves to be correct, it would also explain the 1650 land transaction in which William Collier granted to "my kinsman William Clark" [PCR 12:182].

COMMENTS: John Hunt demonstrated that "William Collyer" was apprenticed to William Russell for eight years and was entered and sworn in the Grocers' Company of London 16 August 1609. John Arnold, dyer, and William Hurdman, pewterer, were sureties for William Collier for two years beginning 15 August 1612. He became a partner in Southwark with "Mr. Monger" and was sworn a free brother of the Grocers' Company 3 March 1627/8 [TAG 42:120-21].

William Collier appears on the 1626 list of adventurers in Bradford's Letter Book [Bradford LB 26]. Bradford records of Mr. Allerton that "in the first two or three years of his employment, he had cleared up £400 and put it into a brew-house of Mr. Collier's in London, at first under Mr. Sherley's name" [Bradford 239].

Edward Winslow called "Mr. Collier" "my partner" in a 1643 letter to John Winthrop [WP 4:452]. Winslow also reported that "Mr. Collier [was] ... absent to our grief" at the vote over liberty of conscience in Plymouth Colony in 1645 [WP 5:56].

On 6 August 1637, William Morris, of Royston, in the county of Hertford, butcher, having been indentured 4 April 1637 to William Collier, gentleman, for five years, agreed to switch his service to Love Brewster of "Ducksborrow" [PCR 1:64].

William Collier subscribed to the 7 November 1639 agreement between the inhabitants of "Duxborrow" and George Pollard "late inhabitant of the town of Stokeclere, yeoman," and William Hiller of New Plymouth, carpenter [PCR 12:72-73].

On 20 December 1648, John Balden bound himself to "Mr. William Colliar of Duxburrow" for a term of five years, in return for which Collier was to give him "meat, drink and clothing, lodging and washing, and at the end of four years' service ... a heifer of two years old" [PCR 12:164].

The court of 5 June 1651 agreed that payment should be raised for "Mr. Collyar" for his service as magistrate [PCR 2:169]. They were still going about raising this money on 29 June 1652 [PCR 3:14].

He was one of the fifty-eight Purchasers [PCR 2:177].

On 6 December 1659, "Josepth Prior" was summoned to answer the charge of "Mr. William Collyares" that Prior was guilty of "pilfering and purloining practices, and other unworthy carriages relating thereunto, viz: in alluring a young maid, a kinswoman to Mr. William Collyares, to help him ... to sundry things pertaining to the said Mr. Collyare, without knowledge of or leave from Mr. Collyare or Mis[tress] Jane Collyare, his wife" [PCR 3:177]. Mr. Collier was called to the next court to prosecute the case.

CHRISTOPHER CONANT

ORIGIN: London.
MIGRATION: 1623 on the *Anne*.
FIRST RESIDENCE: Plymouth.
REMOVES: Massachusetts Bay by 1627.
RETURN TRIPS: Not seen in New England after 1630, so perhaps returned to England by then.

OCCUPATION: Grocer (in England).
OFFICES: Massachusetts Bay petit jury, 9 November 1630 [MBCR 1:81].
ESTATE: In the 1623 Plymouth land division "Christopher Connant" was granted one acre as a passenger on the *Anne* in 1623 [PCR 12:5].

BIRTH: Baptized East Budleigh, Devonshire, 13 June 1588, son of Richard and Agnes (Clarke) Conant [Conant Gen 13, 56].
DEATH: After 9 November 1630.
MARRIAGE: (1) St. Ann Blackfriars, London, 13 August 1617 Sicily Croxon. "Mrs. Cannant" was buried at St. Lawrence Jewry on 19 August 1618 "in the South Aisle near the Lower End" [NEHGR 147:239].
    (2) Shobrooke, Devonshire, 14 September 1619 "Christopher Conant, of London, merchant, and Mrs. Anne Wilton."
CHILDREN: None recorded.
ASSOCIATIONS: Brother of ROGER CONANT of Salem [PM 134].

COMMENTS: We have assumed here that all these records pertain to the same Christopher Conant. The two marriages in England would seem to belong to the brother of Roger Conant, since the first occurred in the same parish as did Roger's marriage, and the second called him of London.

In Plymouth in 1623 Christopher Conant received only one acre, implying that he did not have with him a wife or children. It may be, then, that his second wife had died soon after marriage and that Christopher was again a single man.

Since he was not in Plymouth in 1627, but was in Massachusetts Bay in late 1630, it may be hypothesized that he followed his brother Roger to Nantasket, then to Cape Ann and Naumkeag. But the mystery remains as to why he vanished so completely from the records after 1630.

ROGER CONANT

ORIGIN: London.
MIGRATION: 1624.
FIRST RESIDENCE: Plymouth.
REMOVES: Nantasket 1624, Cape Ann 1625, Salem 1626, Beverly.

OCCUPATION: Salter. On 20 January 1619/20, he signed the composition bond of his brother John as "Roger Conant, salter," implying that he was free of the Salters' Company and a Citizen of London [Conant Gen 99].
CHURCH MEMBERSHIP: "Roger Connant" is in the list of Salem church members compiled in late 1636 [SChR 5].
FREEMAN: Requested 19 October 1631 (as "Mr. Roger Conant") and admitted 18 May 1631 [MBCR 1:79, 366].
EDUCATION: "Mr. Roger Conant" was one of those chosen to consider how to lay the division of Marblehead neck so that it would not "hinder the building of a college," 18 April 1636 [STR 1:16; Morison 162].
OFFICES: Deputy to General Court for Salem, 9 May 1632 [MBCR 1:95]. Committee to lay out land for John Humphrey, 7 November 1632 [MBCR 1:102]. Committee to determine bounds between Salem and Saugus, 20 November 1637 [MBCR 1:211].

Appointed Essex magistrate, 17 May 1637 [MBCR 1:197]. Essex magistrate, 27 June 1637, 3 October 1637, 27 March 1638, 26 June 1638, 25 December 1638, 25 March 1639 [EQC 1:5-10]. Grand jury, 9 July 1644, 6 July 1647, 25 December 1649, 25 June 1650, 25 November 1651, 29 June 1652, 27 November 1655 [EQC 1:62, 114, 180, 191, 238, 253, 408]. Essex jury, 27 December 1636, 20 October 1653 (foreman) [EQC 1:4, 309]. Petit jury, 27 December 1642 (foreman), 26 December 1643 (foreman), 31 December 1644, 8 July 1645, 30 June 1646, 29 November 1653, 28 November 1654, 24 November 1657 [EQC 1:44, 57, 74, 78, 95, 313, 372, 2:58]. Essex surveyor of canoes, 27 June 1636 [EQC 1:3].

Salem selectman, 1637-41, 1650-54/5, 1657[/8]-58[/9] [STR 1:50-52, 55-59, 61-65, 67-68, 71, 73-74, 77, 79-80, 83-87, 89, 91-94, 97, 105,

112, 164-67, 169-71, 175-77, 179-80, 210, 218, 221, 223]. Salem town clerk (at least he kept the minutes of the selectmen's meeting), 11 September 1637 [STR 1:57]. Committee to draw the line between Ipswich and Salem, 27 March 1643 [STR 1:119]. Surveyor of lots, 2 January 1636[/7], 27 January 1636[/7], 20 February 1636[/7], 10 April 1637, 15 May 1654, 16 January 1656[/7], 8 March 1657/8 [STR 1:28, 35, 38, 44, 179, 195, 213]. Auditor, 12 November 1638, 20 March 1647[/8] (ordered to give an account) [STR 1:73, 154]. Director of highway repairs, 26 February 1643[/4] [STR 1:125]. Surveyor of highways, 13 June 1644 [STR 1:130]. Assessor, 22 September 1645 [STR 1:137]. Arbitrator, 16 February 1655[/6], 24 February 1656[/7], 20 June 1658 [STR 1:189, 196, 216].

ESTATE: "Mr. Connant" was one of the five prominent men to receive a two-hundred acre farm in the freeman's lands at the head of Bass River on 25 January 1635[/6] [STR 1:12, 19]. He received one acre in the Salem grant of 25 December 1637 with a household of nine persons [STR 1:103]. (This grant is in Roger Conant's hand.)

On 4 February 1638[/9], Henry Bayley requested a piece of land "next Mr. Conants house at Catt Cove" [STR 1:80]. On 7 May 1639, "Mr. Conant" received a grant of five acres of meadow "in some convenient place" [STR 1:96].

On 7 June 1664, "William Dodge, John Rayment, Roger Conant, Benjamin Balch & Peter Woodbury of Bass River in Salem" sold "each of us one acre of land unto Isaak Hull, cooper, who is also of Bass River, ... this land being in the whole five acres, lyeth near to the southeast corner of the great pond" [ELR 3:70]. On 23 March 1669/70, "Roger Connant, Jno. Rayment & Benjamin Balch of Bass River side or otherwise Beverly, planters," sold to "Isack Hull of the same place, cooper, ... nine acres of land ... part swamp and part upland ... which land lyeth near his now dwelling house" [ELR 3:70].

On 20 November 1666, "Roger Connant of Salem ..., yeoman," deeded to "my son Lott Conant of the same town ... my now dwelling house & all that my land adjoining thereto, with the orchard & all appurtenances thereto belonging ... containing about twenty acres," "also twelve acres ... adjoining on the east side," "also about ten acres of meadow lying in the great marsh against Wenham River," "also sixty acres of upland lying near Richard Dodge's farm," "also one acre of salt marsh," "also one acre of marsh at the Thatch Pond" [ELR 3:28]. On 21 November 1666, "Lott Connant of Salem" leased back to "Roger Connant & Sara his wife of the same town ... a dwelling house with an orchard or orchards & garden adjoining thereunto, containing about three acres ... and also one acre of salt marsh," for the yearly rent of "one Indian corn" [ELR 3:29]. On 20 November 1666, "Roger Conant of Salem ..., yeoman," deeded to "my son Exercise Conant ... forty-five acres of upland being situate & lying in the township of Salem toward Wenham," also "about three acres & a half of fresh meadow lying in Wenham Great meadow," "also one acre & a quarter lying at the great pond marsh" [ELR 3:30].

On 4 February 1673[/4?], "Roger Conant of Beverly ..., yeoman," deeded to "my kinsman John Conant of the same place, house carpenter, ... a certain parcel of land, containing twenty acres, situate, lying & being near Wenham great pond" [ELR 4:50]. (This "kinsman" was the grantor's grandson, son of his son Roger.)

On 28 May 1679, "Mr. Roger Conant of Beverly, *alias* Bass River," received one parcel of land in the wilderness on the eastern side of Merrimack River consisting of two hundred acres as laid out by Jonathan Danforth [MBCR 5:227].

In his will, dated 1 March 1677[/8] and proved 25 November 1679, "Roger Conant aged about eighty-five years ... though weak & feeble in body" bequeathed to "my son Exercise" one hundred and forty acres near Dunstable (a part of two hundred acres granted by the General Court), also ten acres adjoining his present homelot, also two acres of marsh at the south end of Wenham's great pond "or if my daughter Elizabeth Conant will exchange to have so much at the great marsh near Wenham," also my swamp at the head of the rails which is yet undivided, also my portion of land lying by Henry Haggat's on Wenham side, from which land he is to pay £7 toward the discharge of my legacies; to "my grandchild John Conant, son of Roger Conant," ten acres adjoining his twenty acres by the great pond, he to pay £20 toward the discharge of my legacies; to "my grandchild Joshua Conant" seventeen acres by the south side of the great marsh "and the rest to return to my executor"; to "my daughter Sarah" to her and her children, two acres between the head of the rails and Isaac Hull; to "a daughter of one Mrs. Pitts deceased ... now living in Culleton a town in Devon in old England" into the hands of Capt. Roger Clap of the Castle near Dorchester as attorney for Mrs. Pitts "for certain goods sold for the said Mrs. Pitts in London and was there to be paid many years since but it is alleged was never paid"; to "my son Lott his ten children" £20 to be equally divided; to "my daughter Sarah's children, to John £5, to the four daughters" £5 between them; to "my daughter Mary Dodge to herself £5 and £5 to her five children equally divided"; to "Exercise his children" £4 between them; to "Adoniron Veren" £3, "to his sister Hannah" 20s. and "her two children each 10s.";

to "my cousin Mary Veren wife to Hillier Veren" £3; to "the daughters of my cousin Jane Mason deceased" £3 "including Love Steevens her child a share"; to "my son Exercise" residue of moveable goods and "my gray horse and cattle"; to "Rebacka Connant my grandchild" my sheep; to "Mary Leach" one sheep; "and whereas there remains in my hands a certain portion of cattle belonging unto one Mr. Dudeny in England and by him assigned unto his nephew Richard Conant valued at £25 and now left in the hands of my son Exercise Conant that there be a rendering up of such cattle or their valuation ... unto the said Richard Conant upon seasonable demand"; "son Exercise" executor; "my son William Dodge and my grandchild John Conant Senior" overseers [EPR 3:335-37].

The inventory of the estate of "Roger Conant deceased," taken 24 November 1679, totalled £258 10s., of which £216 was real estate: "200 acres of land lying at Dunstable not improved," £60; "more land sold to Elizabeth Conant not paid for," £40; "more land 10 acres and more 10 acres 20," £40; "more land 23 acres," £59; "more two acres of meadow," £10; "swampy land," 20s.; "2 acres of land," £5; and "more land," £1 [Conant Gen 125-26; EPR 3:337].

BIRTH: Baptized East Budleigh, Devonshire, 9 April 1592, youngest of the eight children of Richard and Agnes (Clarke) Conant [Conant Gen 99].
DEATH: Beverly 19 November 1679.
MARRIAGE: St. Ann Blackfriars, London, 11 November 1618 Sarah Horton, daughter of Thomas and Catherine (Satchfield) Horton [NEHGR 147:234-39]. "Sarah Connant" is included in the list of Salem church members compiled in late 1636 [SChR 6]. She was alive in November 1660 to depose about the marriage of James Bede and the widow "Ellot" [EQC 2:265]. She is not named in her husband's will and therefore probably died before 1 March 1677/8.
CHILDREN:
    i   SARAH CONANT, bp. St. Lawrence Jewry, London, 19 September 1619; bur. there 30 October 1620.
    ii   CALEB CONANT, bp. St. Lawrence Jewry, London, 27 May 1622; d. before 11 November 1633 when administration was taken by his paternal uncle John Conant, clerk, on the estate of "Caleb Conant, late beyond seas, deceased, a bachelor" [PCC Admons 1633 folio 204].
    iii SARAH CONANT, b. New England say 1623 (named in grandmother's will in 1627 [NEHGR 147:239]); m. John Leach (apparently mother of Mary Leach called kinswoman

iv   LOT CONANT, b. about 1624 (aged "about fifty years" in his will dated 24 September 1674 [EQC 5:431]); m. Elizabeth Walton, bp. Seaton, Devonshire, 27 October 1629, daughter of Rev. WILLIAM WALTON {1635, Hingham} (her brother Nathaniel Walton names her "Elizabeth Conant" in his will [EQC 5:254; NEHGR 142:368]). She m. (2) Lynn 10 January 168[1/2] Andrew Mansfield Sr.

in will of Lot Conant [EQC 5:432], and probably the family of which Roger Conant says "my daughter Sarah, her son John, and four daughters" in his will).

v   (poss.) JOANNA CONANT, b. say 1626; for striking whom Lydia Gutch was fined on 21 February 1648/9 [EQC 1:157].

vi   ROGER CONANT, b. Salem say 1628 "being the first born child in Salem" [STR 1:98]; m. by 1661 Elizabeth Weston (her child bp. Salem 22 January 1661[/2] "upon the letter from the Church at Corke testifying of her membership there" [SChR 93]), daughter of THOMAS WESTON [PM 490].

vii   JOSHUA CONANT, b. say 1630; m. by 1657 Seeth Gardner, daughter of THOMAS GARDNER {1624, Cape Ann} [GMB 2:731-37].

viii   MARY CONANT, b. say 1632; m. (1) say 1652 John Balch, son of JOHN BALCH {1624, Cape Ann} [GMB 1:84-86] (his estate showed a large debt to Lot Conant of Marblehead and was appraised by Roger Conant [EPR 1:365]); m. (2) by 1663 William Dodge, son of WILLIAM DODGE {1629, Salem} [GMB 1:563-68] ("my son William Dodge" named in Roger Conant's will; called "Mary Balch, widow of John Balch, now wife of William Dodge" on 4 June 1679 [EQC 7:390]).

ix   ELIZABETH CONANT, b. say 1635; living unm. at the time of her father's will.

x   EXERCISE CONANT, bp. Salem 24 December 1637 [SChR 16]; m. by 1668 Sarah _____ (eldest known child bp. Beverly 14 February 1668/9).

ASSOCIATIONS: CHRISTOPHER CONANT, who received one acre in Plymouth Colony in 1623 as a passenger on the *Anne*, was Roger's brother [PCR 12:5; PM 133].

Jane (Knowles) Bennett, wife of WILLIAM BENNETT of Salem [PM 52], was niece of Roger Conant [NEHGR 153:221].

COMMENTS: Despite Roger Conant's prominence and his reputation as the leader among the Old Planters, there are a number of disquieting questions that still hover about him. Although we do not claim to have resolved these questions here, we would like to propose an interpretation that would provide a relatively simple answer.

The questions come in two groups. First, did Roger Conant reside at Plymouth when he first arrived, and was he the salter who arrived in 1624 with Rev. JOHN LYFORD and who was described uncharitably by Bradford? Second, given the great advantages available to Conant, including his many prominent connections in English Puritan circles, and his appointment in 1625 to direct the activities of the Dorchester Adventurers at Cape Ann, why did he not take a larger part in the affairs of Massachusetts Bay after the early 1630s?

Attempts to place Conant and his family on one ship or another face an inconsistency in the records that defies certain resolution. The 28 May 1671 petition of Roger Conant places his arrival in New England before May of 1623:

> The humble petition of Roger Conant of Bass River *alias* Beverly, who have been a planter in New England forty-eight years and upward, being one of the first, if not the first, that resolved and made good my settlement under God, in matter of plantation with my family, in this colony of the Massachusetts Bay, and have been instrumental, both for the founding and carrying on of the same, and when in the infancy thereof, it was in great hazard of being deserted, I was a means, through grace assisting me, to stop the flight of those few that then were here with me, and that by my utter denial to go away with them, who would have gone either for England or mostly for Virginia, but hereupon stayed to the hazard of our lives. Now my humble suit and request is unto this honorable court only that the name of our town or plantation may be altered or changed from Beverly and be called Budleigh. I have two reasons that have moved me to this request. The first is the great dislike and discontent of many of our people for this name of Beverly, because (we being but a small place) it hath caused on us a constant nickname of "beggarly" being in the mouths of many, and no order was given or consent by the people here to their agent for any name until they were sure of being a town granted in the first place. Secondly, I being the first that had house in Salem (and never had any hand in naming either that or any other town) and myself with those

that were then with me, being all from the western part of England, desire this western name of Budleigh, a market town of Devonshire and near unto the sea as we are here, in this place and where myself was born. Now in regard of our firstness and antiquity in this so famous a colony, we should humbly request this little privilege with your favors and consent, to give this name abovesaid unto our town. I never yet made suit or request unto the General Court for the least matter, tho' I think I might as well have done, as many others have, who have obtained much without hazard of life or prefering the public good before their own interest, which I praise God I have done [Conant Gen 116-17, citing MA Arch 112:217].

Hubbard would have Conant at Plymouth initially, either contradicting Conant who said he came before May 1623 or the Plymouth Colony records, which make no allotment of land to Conant in 1623 when even single women who came on the *Anne* and refugees from the failed settlement at Wessagusset received their shares by name [PCR 12:5-6].

Robert Cushman wrote to Bradford on 24 January 1623[/4] saying "the salt-man [we have sent] is a skillful & industrious man, put some to him that may quickly apprehend the mystery of it" [Bradford 373], but Bradford refers to this person in less glowing terms:

... he whom they sent to make salt was an ignorant, foolish, selfwilled fellow ... he caused them to send carpenters to rear a great frame for a large house, to receive the salt & such other uses. But in the end all proved vain. Then he laid fault of the ground, in which he was deceived; but if he might have the lighter to carry clay, he was sure then he could do it ... he could not do anything but boil salt in pans, and yet would make them that were joined with him believe there was so great a mystery in it as was not easy to be attained, and made them do many unnecessary things to blind their eyes, till they discerned his subtlety. The next year he was sent to Cape Anne and the pans were set up there where the fishing was; but before summer was out, he burnt the house, and the fire was so vehement as it spoiled the pans [Bradford 146-47].

Hubbard says:

There (Nantasket) Mr. Roger Conant, with some few others, after Mr. Lyford and Mr. Oldham were, for some offence, real or supposed, discharged from having anything more to do at

Plymouth, found a place of retirement and reception for themselves and families for a space of a year and some few months, till a door was opened for them at Cape Anne, a place on the other side of the Bay, whither they removed about the year 1625 [Hubbard 102].

He further says:

... Mr. White with the rest of the Adventurers, hearing of some religious and well-affected persons ... of which number Mr. Roger Conant was one, a religious, sober and prudent gentleman, yet surviving about Salem till the year 1680, wherein he finished his pilgrimage, having a great hand in all these forementioned transactions about Cape Anne [Hubbard 106].

From these remarks it is assumed that Hubbard was acquainted with Roger Conant and had at some time perhaps discussed the history with him. To go on,

... they pitched upon him, the said Conant, for the managing and government of their affairs at Cape Anne. The information he had of him was from one Mr. Conant, a brother of his, and well known to Mr. White; and he was so well satisfied therein, that he engaged Mr. Humphrey, the treasurer of the joint Adventurers, to write to him in their names, and to signify that they had chosen him to be their governor in that place, and would commit unto him the charge of all their affairs....

It must here be noted, that Mr. Roger Conant, on the foresaid occasion made the superintendent of their affairs [at Cape Ann], disliked the place as much as the Adventurers disliked the business; and therefore, in the meanwhile, had made some inquiry into a more commodious place near adjoining, on the other side of a creek, called Naumkeag, a little to the westward, where was much better encouragement as to the design of a plantation, than that which they had attempted upon before at Cape Anne, secretly conceiving in his mind, that in following times (as since is fallen out) it might prove a receptacle for such as upon the account of religion would be willing to begin a foreign plantation in this part of the world; to which he gave some intimation to his friends in England [Hubbard 106-7].

Hubbard would have "Mr. Roger Conant" settle briefly at Nantasket with Mr. Oldham (whom Conant certainly knew and respected, yet no direct evidence supports his presence), then choose Cape Ann "a place on the other side of the Bay (more convenient for those that belong to the tribe of Zebulon than for those that chose to dwell in the tents of Issachar), wither they removed about the year 1625" [Hubbard 102]. Hubbard further says that Mr. Roger Conant was present at Cape Ann in 1625 and helped to resolve the dispute between Capt. Standish and Mr. Hewes over the fishing stages at Cape Ann [MD 5:80].

> The dispute grew to be very hot, and high words passed between them; which might have ended in blows, if not in blood and slaughter, had not the prudence and moderation of Mr. Roger Conant, at that time there present, and Mr. Peirce's interposition, that lay just by with his ship, timely prevented [Hubbard 110-11].

These events closely parallel Bradford's history of the salter, but no one agrees on the personal traits of this individual. Hubbard again casts Conant in the role of peacemaker when Mr. Endicott came to take the reins from the old planters in 1628 and a controversy arose over the changing of the name of the settlement from "Nahumkeik" to Salem:

> the late controversy that had been agitated with too much animosity betwixt the forementioned Dorchester planters and their new agent, Mr. Endicot, and his company then sent over, being by the prudent moderation of Mr. Conant, agent before for the Dorchester merchants, quietly composed [Hubbard 109].

A possible resolution of the seeming conflict among all these accounts is that they do indeed refer to one man, Roger Conant, but as seen through different sets of eyes. If Conant were one of Hubbard's regular informants, as seems quite likely, then he could well have fed the historian with slanted versions of his part in the early history of Massachusetts Bay. Bradford, on the other hand, with no stake in Conant's reputation, was speaking his mind, even though he did not name the subject of his wrath, perhaps out of respect for the living.

This combination of great promises but little results (as reported by Bradford) and the willingness to distort his actions in hindsight (if we are interpreting correctly Conant's influence on Hubbard) may be the collection of character faults that prevented Conant from rising beyond local importance in the later history of Massachusetts Bay, despite his great early advantages.

Another point should be made here. Bradford is speaking of a salter, and we do know there was at least one other salter in Plymouth in these early years, William Hilton. But Hilton had already arrived in Plymouth in 1621 and could not have been the man sent over by Cushman in 1624. On the other hand, to suppose that Conant is not the man castigated by

Bradford we would have to assume that there were three salters in Plymouth and vicinity during this brief time, which seems an excess.

We take the position, then, that Conant arrived in 1624 (and therefore made an error of one year in his petition nearly half a century later), resided briefly at Plymouth, Nantasket and Cape Ann, and then settled Salem.

Roger Conant deposed on 29 November 1664 about being one of the first inhabitants of the town of Salem, and one of the lot layers there [EQC 3:207].

In depositions some twenty years after the fact, we learn that Roger Conant was in partnership in the 1630s with Peter Palfrey, Anthony Dike and Mr. Francis Johnson, in an enterprise to collect and ship beaver skins and other goods [EQC 1:409, 2:22-4].

On 25 June 1678, "Mr. Roger Conant, aged about eighty-six years, deposed that about six or eight years since, William Hoar's two daughters, Mary and Elizabeth, came to his house to buy apples. While he was in the cellar, he had enough canvas stolen to make a lady's apron, no one being in the house but them. Later he met one of them and asked why they had stolen his canvas, and she replied that it was not she, if anybody, it was her sister" [EQC 7:50].

On 4 June 1679, "Mr. Roger Conant, aged about eighty-seven years," deposed that sixteen years ago Benjamin Balch and Mary Balch, widow of John Balch, now wife of William Dodge, came to an agreement [EQC 7:390].

BIBLIOGRAPHIC NOTE: The basic treatment of the Conant family was published in 1887 by Frederick Odell Conant [*A History and Genealogy of the Conant Family in England and America* (Portland, Maine, 1887), cited above as Conant Gen]. Mary Walton Ferris wrote at length about Conant [Dawes-Gates 2:221-28]. The identity of the wife of Roger Conant and the consequent extensive Puritan connections of Roger Conant are explored by Robert Charles Anderson [NEHGR 147:234-39, 148:107-29]. Roger Conant cuts a romantic figure in Hawthorne's "Main Street."

WILLIAM CONNER

William Conner received one acre in the 1623 Plymouth land division as a passenger on the *Fortune* in 1621 [PCR 12:5].

COMMENTS: As he is not seen in the 1627 cattle division or any other New England record William Conner must have died or returned to England soon.

FRANCIS COOKE

ORIGIN: Leiden, Holland.
MIGRATION: 1620 on the *Mayflower*.
FIRST RESIDENCE: Plymouth.

CHURCH MEMBERSHIP: In his attempt to justify the structure and practice of the Plymouth church to an English audience, Edward Winslow included among his examples "the wife of Francis Cooke being a Walloon, [who] holds communion with the Church at Plymouth, as she came from the French, to this day, by virtue of communion of churches" [MD 27:64, from *Hypocrisie Unmasked*]. (For further information on the membership of Francis Cooke and his wife in the Walloon churches at Norwich and at Leiden, see Jeremy Dupertuis Bangs, "The Pilgrims and other English in Leiden Records: Some New Pilgrim Documents" [NEHGR 143:195-98].)

FREEMAN: In 1633 Plymouth list of freemen ahead of those admitted on 1 January 1632/3 [PCR 1:3]; in 7 March 1636/7 and 1639 lists of Plymouth freemen [PCR 1:52, 8:173]. In Plymouth section of list of freemen of 1658 [PCR 8:197].

EDUCATION: His inventory included "1 great Bible & 4 old books" valued at 10s.

OFFICES: Plymouth Colony committee to lay out the twenty-acre grants, 3 January 1627[/8] [PCR 12:14]. Committee to lay out land, 5 May 1640, 5 October 1640 [PCR 1:152, 163]. Committee to lay out highways, 1 October 1634, 2 May 1637, 1 February 1640/1, 10 June 1650 [PCR 1:31, 58, 2:7, 160]. Arbitrator in land dispute between Thomas Pope and William Shurtleff, 2 August 1659 [PCR 3:169].

Plymouth petit jury, 2 January 1637/8, 3 September 1639, 3 December 1639, 3 March 1639/40, 2 June 1640, 7 June 1642, 7 September 1642, 7 March 1642/3 [PCR 1:74, 7:7, 13, 14, 16, 31, 32, 34]. Grand jury, 5 June 1638, 2 June 1640, 7 March 1642/3, 6 June 1643 [PCR 1:87, 155, 2:53, 56]. Coroner's jury, 22 July 1648 [PCR 2:132].

Surveyor of highways 1 March 1641/2, 7 June 1642, 4 June 1645 [PCR 2:34, 40, 84].

In Plymouth section of 1643 Plymouth list of men able to bear arms [PCR 8:187]. His inventory included "2 old muskets" valued at 12s.

ESTATE: Appears on diagram of "meersteads & garden plots of [those] which came first laid out 1620," between Isaac Allerton and Edward Winslow [PCR 12:3]. In 1623 Plymouth land division received two acres as passenger on *Mayflower*, plus four acres for the rest of his family who came on the *Anne* in 1623 [PCR 12:4, 5]; some of this land had apparently been sold to William Bradford by 1639 [PCR 12:51]. In the 1627 Plymouth cattle division Francis Cooke, his wife Hester Cooke, John Cooke, Jacob Cooke, Jane Cooke, Hester Cooke and Mary Cooke were the first seven persons in the first company [PCR 12:9].

Assessed 18s. in the Plymouth tax list of 25 March 1633 and 9s. in the list of 27 March 1634 [PCR 1:10, 28].

On 3 December 1638, a small parcel of land that had been previously granted to Francis Cooke was instead granted to Thomas Prence [PCR 1:103]. On 4 February 1638/9, "a parcel of upland lying at the end of Goodman Shawe's land at Smilt River is granted to Francis Cooke" [PCR 1:112].

On 5 October 1640, Francis Cooke and John Cooke Jr. were granted a parcel of upland "provided it do not exceed two hundred acres of upland, and the meadow before it," along with a parcel of upland "containing about 10 or 12 acres" [PCR 1:163, 2:149, 164]. On 9 April 1650, Francis Cooke gave "his son Jacob Cook" all his right in one hundred acres at North River granted him 5 October 1640 [PCR 12:185]. On 17 October 1642, Francis Cooke was one of those who received six acres apiece "if it be there to be had" at North Meadow by Joanes River [PCR 2:49]. He is on the list of Purchasers [PCR 2:177].

On 3 June 1662, Francis Cooke was included in the list of those who might "look out some accommodations of land, as being the first born children of this government" [PCR 4:19].

In his will, dated 7 December 1659 and proved 5 June 1663, Francis Cooke bequeathed to "my dear and loving wife" all moveables and cattle and to "Hester my wife ... my lands both upland and meadow lands which at present I possess during her life"; "my dear wife and my son John Cooke" to be joint executors [MD 2:24-25, citing PCPR 2:2:1].

The inventory of the estate of Francis Cooke, taken 1 May 1663, totalled £86 11s. 1d. "besides the housing and land," which was not included [MD 2:26-27, citing PCPR 2:2:1-2].

On 1 March 1663/4, the court "taking notice of such evidence as hath been produced for the clearing of a controversy between John Tompson, plaintiff, and Richard Wright, in reference to a parcel of land at

Namassakett, do allow an agreement between the said parties, which was ordered here to be entered, as followeth, viz: that the said parties shall have equal share of the land allotted to Francis Cooke at Namaskett aforesaid, provided that they be equal in bearing the charge about the said land" [PCR 4:54].

On 8 June 1666, John Cooke, Jacob Cooke, Hester Wright the wife of Richard Wright and Mary Tompson the wife of John Tompson, to prevent dispute over the intent of their father Francis Cooke in his will with regard to the land at Rocky Nook, agreed to divide it into five shares, with John Cooke, the eldest son, getting two shares [PCLR 3:73].

On 5 July 1670, "[w]hereas it is evident to the Court, that a certain tract or parcel of land, called Old Cooke's Holes, lying at Jonses River meadow, was formerly granted unto Francis Cooke, of Plymouth, deceased, in the lieu of some land which is supposed would have fallen within his line at the Smelt Brooke, but is not fully settled on the said Cooke and his heirs and assigns, this Court doth by these presents fully and absolutely settle, ratify, assure and confirm the said grant of land or tract of land, being threescore acres ... unto the said Francis Cooke, his heirs and assigns forever, which said land was given by the said Francis Cooke unto Richard Wright and Thomas Michell, commonly called Old Cooke's Holes, and since his decease ratified and confirmed unto the said Richard Wright and Thomas Michell by John Cooke, the heir unto the said Francis Cooke" [PCR 5:44].

BIRTH: In or shortly after 1583 [MD 3:95-96, 8:49].
DEATH: Plymouth 7 April 1663 [PCR 8:23; MD 17:183; PVR 663].
MARRIAGE: Leiden 20 July 1603 [NS] or shortly thereafter Hester Mahieu [MD 27:145-55 (incorporating and correcting MD 8:48-50, 22:13-14); Plooij LXXIII]. She died after 8 June 1666 [PCLR 3:73].
CHILDREN:

    i   JANE COOKE, b. say 1605; m. Plymouth in 1627 or soon after EXPERIENCE MITCHELL [NEHGR 127:94-95; TAG 59:28-31; PM 324].

    ii   JOHN COOKE, bp. Leiden Walloon Church January-March 1607 [NS] [MD 27:153 (note that Bowman goes slightly astray in his comments on this baptism)]; in the Plymouth tax list of 27 March 1634 assessed 9s. [PCR 1:28]; m. Plymouth 28 March 1634 Sarah Warren [PCR 1:29], daughter of RICHARD WARREN [PM 477; MD 45:54].

    iii   Child COOKE, bur. Leiden 20 May 1608 [NS] [NEHGR 143:197].

iv   ELIZABETH COOKE, bp. Leiden 26 December 1611 [NS] [NEHGR 143:197]; no further record.

v   JACOB COOKE, b. about 1618 (deposed 14 July 1674 "aged fifty-six years or thereabout" [MD 2:45-46, citing PLR 1:81]); m. (1) Plymouth shortly after 10 June 1646 (marriage contract) Damaris Hopkins [PCR 2:27; MD 2:27-28, citing PCLR 2:1:35], daughter of STEPHEN HOPKINS [MF 6:13-14; PM 271]; m. (2) Plymouth 18 November 1669 Elizabeth (Lettice) Shurtleff [PVR 666], daughter of Thomas Lettice and widow of William Shurtleff [MF 6:13].

vi   HESTER COOKE, b. say 1624; m. Plymouth in 1644 RICHARD WRIGHT {1636, Plymouth} [PCR 2:79; see also TAG 59:165-70].

vii   MARY COOKE, b. Plymouth say 1626; m. Plymouth 26 December 1645 John Tompson [PCR 12:94].

COMMENTS: In his accounting of the passengers on the *Mayflower*, Bradford includes "Francis Cooke and his son John; but his wife and other children came afterwards" [Bradford 442]. In the summary of these families as of 1651, Bradford tells us that "Francis Cooke is still living, a very old man, and hath seen his children's children have children. After his wife came over with other of his children; he hath three still living by her, all married and have five children, so their increase is eight. And his son John which came over with him is married, and hath four children living" [Bradford 446]. Francis Cooke signed the Mayflower Compact.

On 24 December 1636, John Harmon contracted to become the apprentice of Francis Cooke for seven years [PCR 1:46].

On 7 March 1636/7, Francis Cooke sued John Browne the elder and several others, and, on 7 June 1637, Francis Cooke, having sued Mr. John Browne, was granted an execution against him [PCR 1:60, 7:5].

"Take notice of our practice at Leyden, viz. that one Samuel Terry was received from the French Church there, into communion with us; also the wife of Francis Cooke being a Walloone, holds communion with the Church at Plymouth, as she came from the French, to this day, by virtue of communion of churches" [Winslow's *Hypocrisie Unmasked* in MD 27:64].

BIBLIOGRAPHIC NOTE: In 1901 George E. Bowman prepared a genealogy of the family of Francis Cooke, in which he abstracted every record he could find for the immigrant, his wife and children [MD 3:95-105]. Lora A.W. Underhill, in her pursuit of the ancestry of Edward

Small, published in 1934 an even more detailed study of the family [Small Gen 601-45]. Mary Walton Ferris also compiled a brief account of the family of Francis Cooke [Dawes-Gates 2:238-44]. In 1989 Jeremy Dupertuis Bangs published a number of records relating to Francis Cooke and his family in Leiden [NEHGR 143:195-98].

The Five Generations Project of the General Society of Mayflower Descendants in 1996 published its account of the descendants of Francis Cooke as Volume Twelve in the series, compiled by Ralph Van Wood Jr.

JOHN COOKE

ORIGIN: Unknown.
MIGRATION: 1633.
FIRST RESIDENCE: Plymouth.

OFFICES: "John Cooke Sen[ior]" appears in the Plymouth section of the 1643 Plymouth Colony list of men able to bear arms; a line was later drawn through his name, indicating either death or removal [PCR 8:188].
ESTATE: On Plymouth tax list of 27 March 1634 "John Cooke Senior" was assessed 9s. [PCR 1:28].

On 6 February 1636/7, "three or four acres of land is granted to John Cooke the elder at the norwest side of Josua Pratt's land, & betwixt him & the brook" [PCR 1:50].

On 2 August 1653, "John Cooke senior" of Plymouth sold to Thomas Lettice of Plymouth, carpenter, for £3 a "house and garden plot on which the said house standeth being situate in Plymouth aforesaid in the north street lying and being next unto the house and garden plot in which the said Thomas Lettice now liveth" [PCLR 2:1:69, transcribed in MD 3:139].

BIRTH: Before 1607 (John Cooke, son of FRANCIS COOKE, was baptized in Leiden early in 1607, and was "Jr." to this man's "Sr.").
DEATH: After 2 August 1653.
MARRIAGE: None recorded.
CHILDREN: None recorded.

COMMENTS: Of all the records under the name John Cooke in the early decades of Plymouth Colony, the above four are the only ones that can be assigned with assurance to John Cooke Sr. Many other records are ascribed to "John Cooke Junior" or "John Cooke the younger," but many are also found without any distinctive indicator. Many of those without a rank indicator, however, including the admission to freemanship on 1 January 1633/4 [PCR 1:4, 21], seem very likely to refer to the younger John Cooke, son of FRANCIS COOKE.

John Cooke Senior was obviously a man of below average wealth and social standing. There is no indication that he was related in any way to FRANCIS COOKE.

Savage suggests that this John Cooke removed to Rehoboth, and that "perhaps he removed to Warwick." But John Cooke Sr. of Plymouth must have been older than John Cooke son of Francis, and must therefore have been born before 1607, whereas John Cooke of Warwick was probably born about 1620 [TAG 52:1-10].

JOSIAS COOKE

ORIGIN: Unknown.
MIGRATION: 1633.
FIRST RESIDENCE: Plymouth.
REMOVES: Eastham.

OCCUPATION: Tavern keeper (licensed to sell wine at Nauset, 7 June 1648 [PCR 2:125]).
FREEMAN: Admitted 3 January 1636/7 [PCR 1:48] and included in Plymouth list of freemen of 7 March 1636/7 [PCR 1:53]. In Plymouth section of 1639 list of freemen, with name later crossed out and then included in "Nawsett" [Eastham] section [PCR 8:174, 177]. In Eastham section of lists of freemen of 1658 and 29 May 1670 [PCR 5:278, 8:201].
EDUCATION: Sufficient to be town clerk. His inventory included "2 Bibles & other books" valued at 4s. The widow's inventory included "books" valued at 4s.
OFFICES: Plymouth petit jury, 7 March 1636/7, 3 March 1639/40, 1 February 1640/1, 1 September 1640, 6 July 1641, 1 March 1641/2, 7 June 1642, 1 November 1642, 5 March 1643/4, 3 March 1644/5, 6 June 1649, 7 June 1649, 9 June 1653, 25 October 1668 [PCR 2:7, 140, 7:5, 16, 17, 18, 22, 29, 31, 32, 37, 40, 46, 65, 151]. Grand jury, 5 June 1638, 3 June 1656 [PCR 1:87, 3:100]. Coroner's jury, 5 June 1638 [PCR 1:88].

Plymouth highway surveyor, 3 March 1639/40, 2 June 1640 [PCR 1:141, 155, 2:5]. Constable, 2 March 1640/1, 3 May 1641 [PCR 2:9, 15].

Deputy for Eastham to Plymouth General Court, 1 June 1647, 5 June 1651, 6 June 1654, 2 March 1657/8, 1 June 1658, 7 June 1659, 7 August

1660, 4 June 1661, 3 June 1662, 1 June 1663, 8 June 1664, 5 June 1666, 2 April 1667, 5 June 1671 [PCR 2:117, 168, 3:49, 129, 135, 162, 198, 214, 4:14, 37, 60, 122, 146, 5:55]. Auditor of treasurer's accounts, 10 June 1658, 7 June 1659, 4 June 1661, 10 June 1661, 5 June 1663, 9 June 1665 [PCR 3:164, 215, 8:93, 105, 108, 113].

Eastham selectman, 5 June 1666 [PCR 4:124]. Surveyor of highways, 7 June 1648 [PCR 2:124]. Town clerk, 7 June 1648 [PCR 2:125]. Deputed to make contracts of marriage and to administer oaths at Eastham, 8 June 1664 [PCR 4:65, 74].

Committee on dividing land at Green's Harbor, 1 June 1640 [PCR 1:153]. Committee to purchase land from the Indians, 5 June 1666 [PCR 4:131].

In Plymouth section of 1643 Plymouth list of men able to bear arms [PCR 8:188]. His inventory included "1 musket" valued at 18s., "1 sword and belt" valued at 14s., "1 old musket" valued at 14s., and "powder and shot" valued at 3s.

ESTATE: Assessed 9s. in the Plymouth tax list of 27 March 1634 [PCR 1:29].

Granted six acres, for the purpose of building in Plymouth, "these lands to belong to their dwelling houses there, & not to be sold from their houses," 7 November 1636 [PCR 1:46]. Allotted mowing ground, 20 March 1636/7, 2 July 1638 [PCR 1:57, 90]. Granted forty acres of land, 5 March 1637/8 [PCR 1:78]. Granted twenty-five acres "for Steephen Deane's children (in consideration of a lot they had on Duxburrow side)," 3 September 1638 [PCR 1:96]. Granted "a little parcel of meadow ground," 4 March 1638/9 [PCR 1:115]. Granted ten acres "in the South Meadows towards Aggawam, Colebrook Meadows," 2 November 1640 [PCR 1:166].

On 30 November 1638, "Mr. Steephen Hopkins" sold to Josias Cooke "all those his six acres of land lying on the south side of the Town Brook of Plymouth" [PCR 12:39]. On 7 May 1642, "Josuah Pratt" sold to Josias Cooke "all those his two acres of marsh meadow lying at the Wood Island" [PCR 12:81].

In an undated deed, but probably about 1644, "Josias Cooke" sold his barn and garden to Gyles Rickett Sr. [PCR 12:107]. On 26 September 1645, he sold to the same Gyles Ricket Sr. of Plymouth, weaver, nine acres of upland, six acres of it purchased from "Mr. Steeven Hopkins," and three acres purchased from "Samuell Fuller" [PCR 12:114]. In response to a petition by Mr. John Done, Josias Cooke, Richard Sparrow, and Richard Higgens, the court on 6 October 1657 consented to allow them land about thirteen English miles from Rehoboth provided they observed the orderly purchase from the native proprietors [PCR 3:123, 142, 4:67].

On 25 December 1655, "Josias Cooke of Eastham" sold to John Rickard of Plymouth twenty-five acres of upland at Fresh Lake in Plymouth [MD 10:18, citing PCLR 2:1:163]. On 25 May 1657, "Josias Cooke" with the consent of his wife sold to Thomas Sherive six acres in the New Field in Plymouth [MD 15:30, citing PCLR 2:2:42]. On 9 July 1660, at the request of "Gorg Bonum" regarding their portions in the South Meadow, "Edward Banges, Nicholas Snow and Josias Cooke do upon our certain knowledge affirm that Josias Cooke had the first portion laid out to him ... namely ten acres" [MD 15:30, citing PCLR 2:2:42].

On 3 June 1662, liberty was granted that "ancient freemen" and servants could look for lands in other places if the Saconett Neck lands could not be acquired. Josias Cooke was credited as both an "ancient freeman" and as a servant [PCR 4:18].

On 25 October 1665, "Pompino and Simon my son" sold to "Josias Cooke of Eastham ... a parcel of upland commonly called Weequasett containing sixscore acres" and six acres of meadow adjoining [PCLR 3:68]. On 11 August 1669, "Josias Cooke Sr. of Eastham, husbandman," exchanged this land with Mr. John Freeman of Eastham, gent., receiving in return twenty acres of upland and four acres of meadow at Little Billingsgate [PCLR 3:163, 194].

In his will, dated 22 September 1673 and proved 29 October 1673, "Josias Cooke senior aged about 63 years" bequeathed to "my loving wife Elizabeth" during her life, and after her decease to "my natural son Josias Cooke all my abovesaid upland and meadow, orchard, house and housing ... excepting my share of the land at Pochett Island and about two or three acres lying without the fence"; after wife's decease all moveables "to be equally divided betwixt my son Josias Cooke and my daughter Bethyah Harding, or her children after her," except the following legacies: to "my grandchild Joseph Harding all my share of land at Pochet Island"; to "my grandchildren Josiah and Maaziah Harding forty acres of upland and five or six acres of meadow in the township of Plymouth adjoining to a place called Cook's Pond"; to "my grandchild Anna Snow" several head of livestock; to "my grandchild Steven Twining a musket which was formerly his grandfather Deane's"; to "my daughter Merriam Deane" a cow and £5; to "my son Josias" wearing clothes; to "grandchild Josias Cooke my rapier, belt and musket"; to "my other grandchildren Richard Cooke and Maaziah Harding my proportion of land at Saconett"; and to "my grandchild Richard Cooke after my wife's decease my Great Bible" [PCPR 3:1:90, abstracted in MD 15:34]. On 29 October 1673, administration was granted to "Elizabeth Cook" on the estate of "Josias Cook," deceased [PCR 5:132].

The inventory of the estate of "Josias Cook of Eastham," taken 20 October 1673, totalled £104 17s. 4d., with no real estate included [PCPR 3:1:90-92].

The inventory of the estate of "Elizabeth Cook deceased the wife [*worn*] Josiah Cook," taken 3 May 1687, totalled £15 7s. 7d., with no real estate included [MD 4:179-81, citing BarnPR 1:16].

BIRTH: About 1610 ("aged about 63 years" on 22 September 1673 [PCPR 3:1:90]).
DEATH: Eastham 17 October 1673 [MD 6:203].
MARRIAGE: Plymouth 16 September 1635 "Elizabeth Dean widow" [PCR 1:35]. She was widow of STEPHEN DEANE [PM 162] and daughter of widow MARY RING [TAG 42:198; PM 389] and died at Eastham by 3 May 1687. (On 9 June 1653, "Josias Cooke, late of Eastham, at the time of his marriage with Elizabeth, his wife, sometimes the wife of Steven Dean, deceased, did engage to pay several portions unto the children of the said Steven Deane" and confirmed that he had done so [PCR 2:140, 3:37].)
CHILDREN:
  i   ANNA COOKE, b. about 1636; m. Eastham 18 January 1654[/5] Mark Snow [PCR 8:15], son of NICHOLAS SNOW [PM 428]; "Anna, the daughter of Josias Cooke, and wife of Marke Snow," d. Eastham 24 July 1656 [PCR 8:30; see also TAG 42:200, MF 6:14-15].
  ii BETHIA COOKE, b. say 1640; m. Eastham 4 April 1660 Joseph Harding [PCR 8:27; see also TAG 42:201], son of MARTHA HARDING [PM 232].
  iii JOSIAH COOKE, b. say 1643; m. Eastham 27 July 1668 Deborah Hopkins [MD 8:88], daughter of Giles Hopkins and granddaughter of STEPHEN HOPKINS [TAG 42:201; MF 6:30; PM 271].
ASSOCIATIONS: Josias Cooke has, not unsurprisingly, been claimed as a son of FRANCIS COOKE. George Ernest Bowman demonstrated that this could not be true [MD 3:97].

COMMENTS: On 24 March 1633/4, Josias Cooke was fined 6s. 8d. for an altercation with Edward Doty in which Doty "drew blood from the said Josias" [PCR 1:26]. On 12 March 1638/9, "Josias Cooke" was bondsman for William Hiller of Plymouth [PCR 1:119]. On 4 February 1638/9, "Josias Cooke" sued John Combes, gentleman, for £4 debt and won a judgment of £3 [PCR 7:11]. On 1 December 1640, he was presented with other Eastham surveyors of highways for not mending the roads in a number of places [PCR 2:5]. On 6 June 1643, Joseph Hollway sued Josias Cooke [PCR 7:34]. On 7 October 1651, "Josiah Cook of Eastham" sued John Smith Sr. of Plymouth for slander, and Smith confessed that he had "much wronged the plaintiff by his unbridled tongue in these base and false charges he had charged him withall, by a letter, and otherwise" [PCR 7:55]. On 6 July 1669, Josias Cooke delivered the letter of "William Nicarson" complaining about defamation by several Indians [PCR 7:155]. On 1 November 1679, "William Nicarson Sr." of "Mannamoyett" unsuccessfully sued "Josiah Cooke Sr. of Eastham" for taking a pair of andirons and one silver dram cup, saying that "said Cooke did under color of his office, for he said he was constable of Eastham, and showed him ... his black staff; and his demand was 6s. 7½d., which was the first part of the rate he demanded" [PCR 7:218-19].

JOHN COOMBS

ORIGIN: Unknown (but see *COMMENTS* below).
MIGRATION: 1630.
FIRST RESIDENCE: Plymouth.

FREEMAN: In 1633 Plymouth freeman's list, John Coombs is among those made free before 1 January 1632/3 [PCR 1:3]; in list of 7 March 1636/7. On 3 September 1639, Plymouth court ordered that "Mr. John Combe, for being drunken, is disfranchised of his freedom" [PCR 1:132], and, on 5 June 1644, he was readmitted to freemanship [PCR 2:71]. ("Mr. John Combe" is in the 1639 list of freemen, but his name is crossed out, accompanied by the marginal notation "Disfranchised for being drunk"; his name is then reinserted near the end of the same list [PCR 8:173, 174].)
ESTATE: On 12 October 1630, "Ralfe Wallen sold to Mr. John Coombe his house, garden plot & the fences thereto belonging" [PCR 12:18].

Assessed 12s. in Plymouth tax list of 25 March 1633 and 9s. in list of 27 March 1634 [PCR 1:10, 27].

On 24 January 1633/4, "John Coomb, gent.," exchanged with Thomas Prence "thirty acres of land near unto the high cliff, [which Coombs possessed] in the right of Sarah his wife" for "thirty acres of land near unto Wynsloes stand," and paid to Prence £20 for the housing on the land he was receiving [PCR 1:25].

On 1 July 1633, allocated mowing ground at "the watering place and thereabout" [PCR 1:14]. Allocated mowing ground on 14 March 1635/6 and 20 March 1636/7 [PCR 1:40, 56].

On 14 February 1633/4, "Joh. Coomb, gent.," sold to John Doane "a dwelling house & misted with the inclosure & outhousing thereunto belonging, next adjoining to the late dwelling house of Godbert Godbertson, on the west side thereof, & the herring weir on the east" [PCR 1:25].

On 7 November 1636, Plymouth court granted to Tristram Clark eight acres between Phineas Pratt and widow Billington, "a portion allotted formerly to Mr. John Coombe" [PCR 1:46].

On 24 June 1639, "John Combe gent." mortgaged to Thomas Prence "all that his dwelling house and twenty acres of land ... which came by his wife," and "it is also agreed upon ... that whereas there was other ten acres of land exchanged with the said Mr. Thom[as] Prence which was the said Mr. Combe's mother-in-law's if the heir when he comes to his age do not legally confirm the said exchange so made that then the said ten acres shall be and remain unto the said Thomas Prence" [PCR 12:44-45].

On 3 August 1640, Plymouth court ordered that "as it appeareth by testimony of Josuah Pratt & otherwise, that the two acres of upland lying at Wellingsly Brook, on the north side of the lots given to Godbert Godbertson, were given by the said Godbert Godbertson to John Combe, gent., & Phineas Pratt, in marriage with their wives, his daughters, the Court doth confirm the said two acres unto the said John Combe & Phineas Pratt, their heirs & assigns forever" [PCR 1:159]. On 5 August 1640, "John Combe gent. and Phineas Pratt joiner" sold to John Barnes "all those two acres of upland which they had of Goodbert Godbertson in marriage with their wives" [PCR 12:61].

On 31 December 1641, "Mr. John Combe is granted a proportion of land at the head of his ground where he now dwelleth, in consideration of a lot of land he had there formerly granted which he hath now yielded up" [PCR 2:29]. On 5 April 1642, "Mr. John Combe" sold to Mr. Thomas Prence "two acres of marsh meadow lying before the house of the said Thom[as] Prence at Joanes River" [PCR 12:78].

On 27 October 1646, Isaac Allerton assigned to his son-in-law Thomas Cushman a debt of £100 due to him from "Mr. John Combe" [PCR 2:133]. On 1 August 1648, whereas "it doth appear, that Mr. John

Combe was indebted to the estate of Cudbert Godberson ... which said estate was debtor a considerable sum to Mr. Isacke Allerton, merchant," who assigned the debt to his son-in-law Thomas Cushman, "a part of the increase" from the lands of "the said Combe" should be paid to Cushman [PCR 2:131-32, 3:98].

BIRTH: By about 1607 (based on estimated date of marriage).
DEATH: By 15 October 1646 (by which date his wife was in England, having left at least one young child behind [PCR 12:137]).
MARRIAGE: By about 1632 Sarah Priest, daughter of DEGORY PRIEST [PCR 1:159, 12:61; MF 8:2; PM 382]. On 15 October 1646, "William Spooner came before the Governor and undertook to save the town harmless from any charge that might befall by reason of a child that Mrs. Coombs left with him when she went for England, and which he undertook to keep & provide for" [PCR 12:137]; and, on 1 August 1648, the court further ordered that "the children of the said Mrs. Combe, now being with William Spooner, that the said Spooner keep them for the present, and not dispose of them for the future, without further order from the court" [PCR 2:131].
CHILDREN:
    i   JOHN COOMBS, b. say 1633; m. Boston 24 February 1661/2 Elizabeth Barlow [BVR 82]; she was widow of Thomas Barlow. (For a detailed discussion of the life of John Coombs and the marital career of his wife see TAG 46:129-34.)
    ii   FRANCIS COOMBS, b. say 1635; m. (1) by 1673 Deborah Morton (eldest known child b. Middleborough "about the middle of May" 1673 [MiddleVR]; 29 October 1673 will of John Morton names "daughter Deborah the wife of Francis Combe" [MD 24:135; MF 8:13]); m. (2) by about 1678 Mary (Barker) Pratt, daughter of John Barker and widow of Samuel Pratt [Gen Adv 4:31].

COMMENTS: Robert S. Wakefield has marshalled the arguments in favor of the hypothesis that this immigrant is the John Combs baptized 13 March 1596/7 at Hemel Hempstead, Hertfordshire, son of Francis and Jane (Pope) Combs [TAG 71:247-50].

On 8 November 1638, "John Comes ... gent." posted surety for John Smyth, and, on 4 June 1639, "John Combes ... gent." posted surety for Richard Derby [PCR 1:103, 128]. On 4 December 1638, "John Comes, gen.," was fined 3s. for nonappearance [PCR 1:104].

On 1 July 1637, "John Coomes of New Plymouth ... gent." assumed from John Holmes the remaining time of his servant, William Spooner [PCR 12:19]. On 5 April 1642, "Mr. John Combe" assigned to Mr. William Thomas for £12 the remaining time of his servant, William Launder [PCR 2:38].

Even though John Coombs was consistently referred to as "Mr." or "gent.," he was constantly embroiled in situations that would have been more appropriate for someone at the opposite end of the social spectrum. As noted above, he was disenfranchised for excessive drinking. On several occasions he was involved in cases of debt, usually as defendant, and with judgment usually against him (1 July 1634, 4 February 1638/9, 5 March 1638/9, 27 May 1639, 5 May 1640, 5 April 1642, 6 March 1642/3, 5 November 1644 [PCR 1:30, 122, 151, 2:37, 51, 7:11, 38]).

BIBILIOGRAPHIC NOTE: The descendants of John Coombs to the fourth generation in all lines are covered by the eighth volume in the Mayflower Society's Five Generations series [Robert S. Wakefield, ed., *Family of Degory Priest* (Plymouth 1994), pp. 4-5, 13-15, et seq.].

HUMILITY COOPER

In Bradford's accounting of the passengers on the *Mayflower*, the family of Edward Tilley included "two children that were their cousins, Henry Sampson and Humility Cooper" [Bradford 442]; but by 1651 "the girl Humility ... was sent for into England and died there" [Bradford 446].

In the 1623 Plymouth land division, "Humillitie Cooper" was granted one acre as a passenger on the *Mayflower* [PCR 12:4]. In the 1627 Plymouth cattle division "Humillyty Cooper" was the last person in the fifth company [PCR 12:10].

COMMENTS: Robert Leigh Ward has greatly illuminated the kinship relations of EDWARD TILLEY, JOHN TILLEY, HENRY SAMPSON and Humility Cooper, and has shown that Edward Tilley's wife was Agnes Cooper [TAG 52:198-208]. In a later article Ward published "the adult baptism of 'Humilitie,' daughter of Robert Cooper, on 17 March 1638/9 in the parish of Holy Trinity, Minories at the edge of the City of London. The entry states that she was born in Holland and was aged 19 years" [TG 6:166]. In this latter article Ward goes on to provide several generations of Cooper ancestry.

The adult baptism for Humility Cooper would mean that she was no more than a year old at the time the *Mayflower* sailed. She must have died in the twelve years between her baptism and Bradford's accounting of the *Mayflower* passengers; there is no evidence whether or not she married and had children, although Bradford gives no hint that she might have.

JOHN CRACKSTONE

ORIGIN: Leiden, Holland.
MIGRATION: 1620 on the *Mayflower*.
FIRST RESIDENCE: Plymouth.

BIRTH: By about 1573 (based on estimated date of marriage).
DEATH: Plymouth between 11 January 1620/1 and 10 April 1621 [Bradford 445].
MARRIAGE: By about 1598 _____ _____; she had probably died before 1620, and perhaps considerably earlier.
CHILDREN:
   i   ANNA CRACKSTONE, b. say 1598; m. Leiden (banns) 22 December 1618 [NS] Thomas Smith [MQ 40:117-19].
   ii   JOHN CRACKSTONE, b. say 1602; came to Plymouth in 1620; in 1623 Plymouth land division granted [probably] one acre [PCR 12:4]; in 1627 Plymouth cattle division listed as the thirteenth member of the second company [PCR 12:9]; d. Plymouth in 1627 or soon after [Bradford 445].

COMMENTS: Bradford tells us that "John Crackston and his son John Crackston" were on the *Mayflower* in 1620, and in his 1651 accounting of the *Mayflower* passengers, Bradford noted that "John Crackston died in the first mortality, and about some five or six years after his son died, having lost himself in the woods; his feet became frozen, which put him into a fever of which he died" [Bradford 442, 445]. Crackstone signed the Mayflower Compact.

On 3 March 1639/40, "The Heirs of John Crackstone" were included in a list of the Purchasers or Oldcomers, who were to receive land [PCR 2:177]. By 1652 this share of land had passed to William Bradford and William Bassett [MD 4:186].

In 1974 Robert S. Wakefield gathered all the evidence then available on John Crackstone (including all the items noted above) [MQ 40:117-

19]. Since the marriage intention for Anna Crackstone, daughter of John, called her of Colchester, an extensive search was made in the records of that city. Although a few traces of the surname were found there, no firm connection was made with any Colchester records.

Wakefield noted that none of the baptismal records for children of a Thomas Smith in Leiden subsequent to 1618 appear to be for the Thomas Smith who married Anna Crackstone.

ROBERT CUSHMAN

ORIGIN: Leiden, Holland.
MIGRATION: 1621 on the *Fortune*.
FIRST RESIDENCE: Plymouth.
RETURN TRIPS: Returned permanently to England 1621.

OCCUPATION: Grocer (in Canterbury). Woolcomber (in Leiden).
EDUCATION: Several literate and businesslike letters written by Cushman to JOHN CARVER, Edward Southworth, WILLIAM BRADFORD and to the Leiden congregation are evidence of a well-educated man [Bradford 45, 54, 107, 125, 128, 355, 361, 365, 373]. On 12 December 1621, during his brief sojourn at Plymouth, Cushman preached a sermon whose principal intent was to convince the Pilgrims to accept the terms offerred by the London merchants, and was therefore more of an economic than a theological nature. This sermon, accompanied by some additional notes by Cushman, was published in London in 1622 [Young's Pilgrim Fathers 255-68].
ESTATE: In the 1623 Plymouth division of land "Robert Cochman" received one acre as a passenger on the *Mayflower* (which he was not) [PCR 12:4].

BIRTH: Baptized Rolveden, Kent, 9 February 1577/8, son of Thomas and Elinor (Hubbard) Couchman [NEHGR 68:181].
DEATH: 1625 (on his return from England early in 1626 Miles Standish "brought them notice of the death of their ancient friend Mr. Cushman, whom the Lord took away also this year" [Bradford 180]).
MARRIAGE: (1) St. Alphege, Canterbury, Kent, 31 July 1606 Sara Reder [NEHGR 68:183]. She was buried at Pieterskerk, Leiden, 11 October 1616 [NS] [Dexter 611; Small Gen 671; NEA 3:2:49].

(2) Leiden 5 June 1617 [NS] "Mary Shingelton from Sandwich in England, widow of Thomas Shingelton" [MD 10:193; NEHGR 68:183].

She apparently died before 1621 as there is no evidence she came to Plymouth with her husband and stepson.

CHILDREN:

With first wife

i   THOMAS CUSHMAN, bp. St. Andrew, Canterbury, Kent, 8 February 1607/8 [NEHGR 68:183]; "William Beale & Thomas Cushman" received two acres in partnership in the 1623 Plymouth land division, as passengers on the *Fortune* [PCR 12:5]; in the 1627 Plymouth division of cattle, he was the sixth person in the eleventh company [PCR 12:12]; admitted freeman 1 January 1633/4 [PCR 1:4, 21]; m. by about 1636 Mary Allerton, daughter of ISAAC ALLERTON. [PM 10].

ii   Child, bur. Pieterskerk, Leiden, 11 March 1616 [NS] [Dexter 611; Small Gen 688; NEA 3:2:49].

iii   Child, bur. Pieterskerk, Leiden, 24 October 1616 [NS] [Dexter 611; Small Gen 688; NEA 3:2:49].

COMMENTS: Beginning in 1617, and continuing right up until the time of his death, Robert Cushman spent much time in London and vicinity negotiating on behalf of the Leiden congregation and later on behalf also of the settlers in Plymouth. He, JOHN CARVER [PM 95] and WILLIAM BREWSTER [PM 66] labored constantly in their dealings with a number of London merchants, arranging for the shipping and provisions for the *Mayflower* and the *Speedwell* in 1620. The details of these negotiations constitute a large portion of the story told by Bradford in his history of these years.

Cushman had planned to make the voyage across the Atlantic in 1620, but when the *Speedwell* had to be abandoned he was one of those who remained behind [Bradford 54]. This original intention of Cushman's and his many other services in behalf of the Pilgrims are undoubtedly the justification for the assignment to Cushman in 1623 of land in Plymouth as if he had been a passenger on the *Mayflower*.

On 2 November 1636, "William Hodgekins & Sara Cushman" were married at Plymouth [PCR 1:45]. Some have held that this was another child of Robert Cushman, but this remains only a surmise [see Small Gen 688-93].

BIBLIOGRAPHIC NOTE: Lora Underhill has gathered together every record known to her of the life of Robert Cushman, and in the process has compiled the best biography available of the man. Her treatment also goes into great detail on the career of his son Thomas [Small Gen 669-755, with Robert Cushman at 669-93]. Elizabeth French in 1914 published her research into the ancestry of Robert Cushman, including extensive transcripts of records of the family in Kent [NEHGR 68:181-85].

In 1995 Robert E. Cushman and Franklin P. Cole published a biography of this immigrant: *Robert Cushman of Kent (1577-1625) Chief Agent of the Plymouth Pilgrims (1617-1625)* (reviewed in MD 45:173).

D

JOHN DEACON

22 July 1631: "John Deacon servant to Edward Ashley" deposed against his master, describing how Ashley traded weapons to the Indians around Penobscot [MHSP 45:494-95].

2 March 1635/6: "A jury of twelve being impanelled and charged, in the month of February foregoing, to enquire after the death of John Deacon" reported that, "having searched the dead body, we find not any blows or wounds, or any other bodily hurt. We find that bodily weakness, caused by long fasting & weariness, by going to & fro, with the extreme of the season, were the causes of death" [PCR 1:39].

2 June 1640: Daniel Salmon presented to William Bradford (as Plymouth governor) a letter of attorney, dated 13 January 1638/9, by which "Richard Francis (*alias*) Deacon of Barlston in the County of Leicester," having been "credibly informed as well by letters as by word of mouth out of New England that my brother John Francis (*alias*) Deacon there deceased did by his last will and testament give unto me the sum of ten or twelve pounds to be paid unto me or my certain attorney by Mr. Winslow Governor of Plymouth there," appointed Daniel Salmon of Saugus to receive the bequest and give a receipt for the same; this instrument was witnessed by John Salmon and Joseph Salmon, and further attested on 1 March 1638/9 at Market Bosworth, Leicestershire [PCR 12:62].

2 July 1640: Daniel Salmon acknowledged that he had received from Mr. John Howland the legacy due to Richard Francis *alias* Deacon [PCR 12:63].

COMMENTS: John Deacon's association with both EDWARD ASHLEY [PM 20] and JOHN HOWLAND [PM 279], and the reported circumstances of his death, suggest that he was involved in the fur-trading activity on the Penobscot carried on by Plymouth Colony.

Since two of the witnesses in England to the letter of attorney were John Salmon and Joseph Salmon, it is very likely that Daniel Salmon of Lynn was also from that area. Another John Deacon arrived in New England in 1635 and settled in Lynn, and he might well be related to the John and Richard Francis *alias* Deacon recorded here.

STEPHEN DEANE

ORIGIN: Unknown.
MIGRATION: 1621 on the *Fortune*.
FIRST RESIDENCE: Plymouth.

OCCUPATION: Miller. (On 7 January 1632/3, he was granted permission by the General Court to set up his corn mill "upon the brook adjoining to the town of Plymouth" and to receive as a toll one pottle of each bushel ground; from the terms of the agreement, it is clear that Deane already had a functioning mill farther from town [PCR 1:8, 22].)
FREEMAN: In the 1633 Plymouth list of freemen, ahead of those admitted on 1 January 1632/3 [PCR 1:3].
EDUCATION: Signed deeds of 1627 and 1630 [PCR 12:7]. His inventory included "a Bible & other books" valued at £1 [MD 2:88].
OFFICES: Committee to assess taxes, 27 March 1634 [PCR 1:26].
ESTATE: In the 1623 Plymouth division of land, granted one acre "beyond the first brook to the wood westward" as a passenger on the *Fortune* [PCR 12:5]. In the 1627 Plymouth division of cattle, Stephen Deane was the twelfth person in the twelfth company [PCR 12:13].

In 1627 "Phillip Delanoy" sold to Stephen Deane "one acre of land lying on the north side the town between the first and second brook" [PCR 12:7]. On 10 February 1629[/30?], "Steven Dean" sold to "Robart Hixe ... 2 acres of land lying on the north side of the town between the first & second brook, the one being his own inheritance, the other was that he bought of Philip De le noy" [PCR 12:7]. (These would be the lots granted in 1623.)

Assessed 9s. in the 25 March 1633 Plymouth tax list and 12s. in the list of 27 March 1634 [PCR 1:10, 27].

On 10 March 1633/4, William Bradford (as administrator of Godbert Godbertson) sold to "Steven Deane" "the late dwelling house of the said Godbert, with the misted, inclosures & outhousing thereunto belonging" [PCR 1:25].

The inventory of the estate of "Steven Deans," taken 2 October 1634, totalled £87 19s. 6d., of which £42 was real estate: "the house and fens at Fresh Lake," £2; "dwelling house & garden," £20; and the mill, £20 [MD 2:87-88, citing PCPR 1:26].

On 5 April 1669, "Will[i]am Twining of Eastham ... for himself and Merriam Deane his sister and for Sussanna Snow sister to his wife; which three are the proper and joint heirs of their father Steven Deane his land" sold to Peter Warden "all the lands that belongs unto and were the purchase lands of Stephen Dean deceased" [MD 15:51, citing PCLR 3:334].

BIRTH: By about 1605 (based on estimated date of marriage).

DEATH: Plymouth between 10 March 1633/4 (purchase of Godbert Godbertson's house) and 2 October 1634 (date of inventory), and probably closer to the latter date. (Secondary sources claim that he died in September 1634, which is reasonable but not proved.)

MARRIAGE: By about 1630 Elizabeth Ring, daughter of widow MARY RING (and possibly the Elizabeth Ring, daughter of William & Marie Ring, bp. Ufford, Suffolk, 23 February 1602/3) [TAG 42:197-99; PM 389]). She married (2) Plymouth 16 September 1635 JOSIAS COOKE [PCR 1:35; PM 149].

CHILDREN:
  i   ELIZABETH DEANE, b. about 1630; m. about 1650 William Twining, son of William Twining [TAG 42:198-99].
  ii MIRIAM DEANE, b. about 1632; m. after 31 January 1692/3 John Wing, son of John Wing [TAG 42:199].
  iii SUSANNA DEANE, b. about 1634; m. (1) Eastham 4 April 1660 Joseph Rogers, son of Joseph Rogers, son of THOMAS ROGERS [PCR 8:27; TAG 42:200; MF 2:157-58; PM 396]; m. (2) Eastham 28 October 1663 Stephen Snow [MD 8:15, 31:37-41 (as George Bowman notes, the alternate marriage date for this couple must be in error); TAG 42:200], son of NICHOLAS SNOW [PM 428].

COMMENTS: The best treatment of the family of Stephen Deane may be found in John I. Coddington's article on the widow MARY RING and her children [TAG 42:193-205].

PHILIP DELANO

ORIGIN: Leiden, Holland.
MIGRATION: 1621 on the *Fortune*.
FIRST RESIDENCE: Plymouth.
REMOVES: Duxbury.

OCCUPATION: Planter [PCLR 3:330, 331]. Fisherman.
CHURCH MEMBERSHIP: "There is also one Philip Delanoy, born of French parents, came to us from Leyden to New Plymouth, who coming to age of discerning demanded also communion with us; and proving himself to be come of such parents as were in full communion with the French churches, was hereupon admitted by the church of Plymouth; and after, upon his removal of habitation to Duxburrow, where Mr. Ralph Partridge is pastor of the church, and upon letters of recommendation from the church at Plymouth, he was also admitted into fellowship with the church at Duxburrow, being six miles distant from Plymouth; and so, I dare say, if his occasions lead him, may from church to church throughout New England" [Young's Pilgrim Fathers 394-95 (from Winslow, *Hypocrisie Unmasked*, 1646)].
FREEMAN: Admitted 1 January 1632/3 [PCR 1:5]. In lists of 1633 and 7 March 1636/7 [PCR 1:4, 53]. In Duxbury sections of Plymouth Colony lists of freemen of 1639, 1658 and 29 May 1670 [PCR 5:274, 8:175, 198].
EDUCATION: Signed his deeds.
OFFICES: Plymouth grand jury, 4 June 1639, 2 June 1646, 6 June 1660, 7 June 1665, 5 June 1667, 7 June 1670, 3 June 1673, 1 June 1675, 5 June 1677, 5 June 1678, 3 June 1679 [PCR 1:126, 2:102, 3:188, 4:91, 148, 5:36, 114, 166, 230, 256, 6:11]. Petit jury, 2 January 1637/8, 4 September 1638, 5 June 1644, 7 June 1648, 6 June 1649, 7 June 1649, 7 June 1651, 4 June 1652, 9 June 1653, 7 March 1653/4, 5 March 1655/6, 5 June 1656, 25 October 1668 [PCR 7:7, 9, 37, 46, 54, 60, 65, 70, 77, 79, 150, 2:126, 140]. Arbiter, 2 May 1648, 4 October 1648, 3 July 1654 [PCR 2:122, 136, 3:62].

Appointed to committee to "view the hay grounds from the river beyond Phillip Delanoy to the South River," 20 March 1636/7 [PCR 1:55]. Surveyor, 2 May 1637, 29 October 1649, 1 June 1658, 1 December 1663 [PCR 1:58, 2:147, 3:138, 4:48].

Volunteered to serve in Pequot War, 7 June 1637 [PCR 1:61]. In Duxbury section of 1643 Plymouth Colony list of men able to bear arms

[PCR 8:189]. His inventory included "1 gun" valued at 15s. [PCPR 4:2:120].

ESTATE: In 1623 Plymouth land division "Moyses Simonson & Philipe de la Noye" were jointly granted two acres as passengers on the *Fortune* [PCR 12:5]. In 1627 Plymouth cattle division "Phillip Delanoy" was the ninth person in the first company [PCR 12:9].

In 1627 "Phillip Delanoy" sold to Stephen Deane "one acre of land lying on the north side of town between the first and second brook" [PCR 12:7]; this would be the land he had been granted in 1623.

Assessed 18s. in Plymouth tax list of 25 March 1633 and 9s. in list of 27 March 1634 [PCR 1:11, 28].

Granted forty acres in Duxbury, 2 October 1637 [PCR 1:67].

On 17 January 1653/4, Phillip Delano of Duxburow and Mary his wife sold to John Churchill and Bennaiah Pratt the house and land near Plymouth "sometimes the house and land of William Pontus and James Glasse both deceased" [MD 5:92, citing PCLR 2:1:93]. On 17 January 1653, Phillip Delano of Duxburrow and Mary his wife sold to John Churchill of Plymouth a parcel of meadow sometimes the meadow of William Pontus and James Glasse deceased, being about an acre and a half [MD 5:92-93, citing PCLR 2:1:93].

On 3 December 1659, Phillip Delano Sr. with the consent of Mary his wife sold one half his purchase lands at Coaksett or Cushena or both to William Earle [MD 11:249, citing PCLR 2:2:41]. On 13 December 1660, "Phillip Delanoy of Duxburrow ... with the consent of my wife" sold to Nicholas Byram of Weymouth "my whole right of lands in the town of Bridgewater ... viz: a full and complete purchase of uplands, meadows and swamps that is or shall be laid out or divided or remain in common" [PCLR 3:25]. On 5 June 1667, Philip Delano of Duxbury, husbandman, sold to John Russell Sr. of Dartmouth, yeoman, one-half share of the lands at Dartmouth "granted unto the said Phillip Delano ... as a purchaser or old comer" [PCLR 3:83].

On 11 April 1674, Philip Delano Sr. of Duxbury, planter, in consideration of "love and natural affection" granted "unto my true and natural son John Delano my lot of five and twenty acres at Namassakett lying upon Teticutt River in Middleborough with three acres of upland lying in Duxburrow" [PCLR 3:330]. On the same day, Philip Delano Sr. of Duxbury, planter, granted to "Thomas Delano his true and natural son the one-half of his hundred acre lot at Namassakett in the town of Middleborough, the lot to be divided betwixt his brother and him, Phillip Delano and him," also one-half the meadow land in Middleborough, one-half of five acres of meadow land at the beach lying on the southside of

Plymouth and three acres of meadow lying at the Mill River [PCLR 3:331].

On 7 July 1682, administration on the estate of "Phillip Delano of Duxburrow" was granted to Samuel Delano [PCR 6:91].

The inventory of the estate of "Phillip Delano of Duxburrow," taken 4 March 1681/2, totalled £50 13s., with no real estate included [MD 11:249, citing PCPR 4:2:120].

On 5 July 1682, a comparison was made between two memoranda purporting to reflect the intent of Philip Delano for the disposal of his estate, one dated 22 August 1681, the other "now drawn" 5 July 1682. The merged intent was agreed to mean, to "his three eldest [sons] and each of [them] know their proportions, and John hath twenty five acres more at Namassakett"; to Samuel a horse, cow, two steers, chain and cart; to Jane one cow and heifer; to Rebeckah a yearling heifer; his wife a cow and free use of one-third of the orchard and land during her life; to his three sons Phillip, Thomas and Samuel a yoke of old oxen to improve "and when their service is done, to revert wholly to Phillip and Thomas"; Thomas executor; saw and wedges to Samuel; 5s. each to his "seven eldest children, of which seven, two, viz, Phillip and Thomas, have received their proportions"; at wife's death all moveables to his four youngest children [MD 11:250-51, citing PCPR 4:2:120].

BIRTH: Baptized Walloon Church, Leiden, 7 December (or 6 November) 1603 [NS], son of Jan de Lannoy and Marie Mahieu [TAG 52:91-92, 53:172-73; see also NEHGR 143:197-98].
DEATH: Between 22 August 1681 (date of memorandum serving as will) and 4 March 1681/2 (date of inventory).
MARRIAGE: (1) Plymouth 19 December 1634 Hester Dewsbery [PCR 1:32]; she died between about 1648 and 1653.

(2) By 17 January 1653[/4] Mary (Pontus) Glass, born by 1622, daughter of WILLIAM PONTUS [MD 5:92; PM 360] ("Phillip Delanoy, who was then present, and with the consent of Mary, his wife, the other daughter of the said William Pontus," 3 May 1664 [PCR 4:58]), and widow of James Glass (on 3 March 1676/7, "Phill[i]p Delano Senr. aged 74 years or there about testifieth and saith before he married Mary Glass the relict of James Glass deceased" [MD 14:64, citing PCLR 6:93]). She was living as late as 5 July 1682 [MD 11:250-1, citing PCPR 4:2:120].
CHILDREN:
   With first wife
      i   MARY DELANO, b. say 1635; m. Plymouth 29 November 1655 Jonathan Dunham [PCR 8:17], son of JOHN

DUNHAM; she d. soon and had no children [TAG 36:243-49; PM 182].

ii PHILIP DELANO, b. say 1637; m. say 1670 Elizabeth Sampson, daughter of Abraham and _____ (Nash) Sampson (called Elizabeth Delano in her grandfather Nash's will [NEHGR 52:76; TAG 15:165-67]).

iii THOMAS DELANO, b. say 1639; m. by 1667 Rebecca Alden, daughter of JOHN ALDEN [PM 4] ("Thomas Delanoy, and his now wife, for committing carnal copulation before marriage, fined" at October Court, 1667 [PCR 8:122]).

iv ESTHER DELANO, b. say 1641; on 1 October 1661, Abraham Pierce Jr. confessed that he had falsely accused "Rebeckah Alden and Hester Delanoy" of being pregnant [PCR 4:7]; probably m. (1) by about 1670 Samuel Samson, son of Abraham and _____ (Nash) Samson, and if so m. (2) by 1679 John Soule [Muriel Curtis Cushing, *Philip Delano of the "Fortune" 1621* (Plymouth 1999), pp. 4-5].

v JOHN DELANO, b. say 1644; m. by about 1679 Mary Weston, daughter of Edmund Weston of Duxbury [NGSQ 71:41-43].

vi JONATHAN DELANO, b. about 1648 (d. Dartmouth 28 December 1720 in 73rd year); m. Dartmouth 28 February 1677/8 Mercy Warren, daughter of Nathaniel Warren and granddaughter of RICHARD WARREN [MF 18:1:39-40; PM 477].

With second wife

vii JANE DELANO, b. say 1655; living 1682 (settlement of her father's estate); no further record.

viii REBECCA DELANO, b. about 1657 (d. Plymouth 7 April 1709 "aged 52 years" [Bradford Kingman, *Epitaphs from Burial Hill, Plymouth, Massachusetts* (Brookline 1892), p. 9]); m. Plymouth 28 December 1686 John Churchill [PVR 85].

ix SAMUEL DELANO, b. say 1659 [adult 1682]; m. by 1679 Elizabeth Standish, daughter of Alexander Standish (in his will of 21 February 1701/2, Alexander named "my daughter Elizabeth Delano the wife of Samuel Delano" [MD 12:101]).

x (possibly) Daughter DELANO, b. say 1661 (included in accordance with *COMMENTS* below).

ASSOCIATIONS: In the land division of 1623, MOSES SIMONSON [PM 419] was joined with PHILIP DELANO in a grant of land, suggesting that they may both have come from Leiden. Also in the land division of 1623, and in the tax lists of 1633 and 1634, EDWARD BUMPAS [PM 85] is adjacent to PHILIP DELANO. The two men at a later date held adjacent land [PCR 1:59, 66, 67]. The last three sons of Bumpas were Philip, Thomas and Samuel, names also used by Delano. These items suggest that Edward Bumpas came from Leiden with Delano in 1621, and that the two may have had some association there before that date.

COMMENTS: In a deposition of 1641, "Phillip De Lanoe of Duxbury planter" stated that he was "aged about thirty-six years"; he at that time owned a boat that he used in catching mackerel [Lechford 420]. On 3 March 1676/7, "Phill[i]p Delano Senior" gave his age as "74 years or there about" [MD 14:64, citing PCLR 6:93].

Some sources claim that Philip Delano lived in Middleborough and Bridgewater, but this merely misinterprets his holdings of lands granted in those locations.

The number of children born to Philip Delano and their allocation between his two wives remains a vexed problem, due to the vagueness of his "will" and the almost total lack of chronological checkpoints among his children and grandchildren.

In the settlement of his estate six children are identified by name: Philip, Thomas, John, Samuel, Jane and Rebecca [MD 11:250-51]. Several additional statements assist in our analysis: Samuel was the "only son to the relict of the deceased"; house and land given to "his 3 eldest ... and John hath 25 acres more at Namassakett"; five shillings apiece to "his seven eldest"; and at wife's death moveables to "his 4 youngest children." Three additional names are known from other records: Mary (who predeceased her father, without leaving issue), Esther and Jonathan.

The bequest to the "seven eldest children" implies eight or more living in 1682, and the six named in the agreement, with Jonathan and Esther added, brings us to this number.

The grant of moveables to the four youngest at his wife's decease implies that these four were children of the second wife, and this together with the statement that Samuel was the only son of the relict leads to the conclusion that the four youngest children were Samuel and three daughters (only two of whom are known). The remaining known living children, all sons, and the daughter Mary must then be children of the first wife.

ANTHONY DIKE

ORIGIN: Unknown.
MIGRATION: 1623 on the *Anne*.
FIRST RESIDENCE: Plymouth.
REMOVES: Cape Ann, Salem.

OCCUPATION: Mariner.
CHURCH MEMBERSHIP: Although not in the list of early Salem church members, his inclusion in the "freeman's land" section of the 1636 Salem land grant indicates that he was a member of that church no later than 1636.
FREEMAN: 18 May 1631 [MBCR 1:366].
OFFICES: On 26 December 1637, "Margaret Weston challenged three of the jurymen of Salem, Jeffrey Massie, Edm[ond] Batter and Anth[ony] Dike" [EQC 1:7], and none of these men appeared on the jury list for that court session.
ESTATE: "Anthony Dixe" received a grant in the 1623 Plymouth land division as a passenger on the *Anne* [PCR 12:6].

"Antho: Dike" was granted forty acres in 1636 Salem division of land, being included among those designated freemen (original grant of twenty acres changed to forty) [STR 1;21, 22, 25]. On 16 January 1636/7, "Antho[ny] Dike" was one of eight men to "have each ½ an acre of land granted them at Winter Harbor for fishing trade, & to build on" [STR 1:33]. On 21 August 1637, "Anthony Dike" requested meadow for two or three cows, but no record was made of any action on this request [STR 1:56]. "Anth[ony] Dike" was granted one acre in the 1637 division of marshland, for a household of six [STR 1:103].

On 11 August 1673, "Anthony Dike of Salem, seaman," sold to "my father-in-law Nathaniell Pickman of Salem ... every part & parcel of land or whatsoever else did or do any ways appertain or belong unto me the abovesaid Anthony Dike, as eldest son to my father Anthony Dike deceased" [ELR 5:10]. On 30 October 1682, "John Alford of Salem ... fisherman & Charity my wife" sold to "our father-in-law Nath[anie]ll Pickman of Salem" for "diverse good considerations ... all our right, title & interest that we have or might have or of right do or might any ways belong to us or either of us in any part or parcel of the lands formerly of Anthony Dike, the father of me the said Charity, deceased" [ELR 6:67].

BIRTH: By about 1606 (based on estimated date of marriage).

DEATH: 15 December 1638: "Anthony Dick, in a bark of thirty tons, cast away upon the head of Cape Cod. Three were starved to death with the cold; the other two got some fire and so lived there, by such food as they saved, seven weeks, till an Indian found them, etc." [WJ 1:345].

MARRIAGE: By about 1631 Tabitha _____. She married (2) after 8 August 1639 Nathaniel Pittman (or Pickman) of Salem. (In the 1655 litigation against Francis Johnson, Nathaniel Pittman appears as the successor to Anthony Dike, and, on 30 March 1657, Tabitha Pittman testified regarding the last words spoken to her by "her husband Dike" just before he "was taken away at Cape Cod by the hard winter" [EQC 2:25]. On 8 August 1639, there was "granted to Nathaniell Pitman a proportion of land, near about 20 acres lying next unto the Widow Diks land on the south side of the Forrest River" [STR 1:89].)

CHILDREN:
  i   CHARITY DIKE, b. about 1631 (deposed 28 June 1681 "aged about fifty years" [EQC 8:108-9]); m. John Alford [Essex Ant 3:104; EIHC 66:323].
  ii ANTHONY DIKE, b. say 1636; m. by about 1665 Margery _____ (eldest known child b. before 1667 [Perley 1:206]); she m. (2) John Polin (antenuptial agreement dated 2 June 1680 [ELR 7:26]).

COMMENTS: Since Anthony Dike was in Plymouth for the 1623 land division and not for the 1627 cattle division, and since Anthony Dike is next seen in Salem, Savage suggests that he joined ROGER CONANT [PM 134] in the exodus from Plymouth to Cape Ann.

In the division of meadow land in Salem in 1637, Anthony Dike was granted six acres, suggesting he may have had as many as four children by that date. Only two children are known from later records.

Dike's maritime activities took him to all parts of the New England coast and constantly led him into perilous situations, leading finally to his shipwreck and death off Cape Cod in 1638.

Roger Clap records the following story of the capture and release of Anthony Dike by the pirate Dixey Bull in 1632: "They having taken one Anthony Dicks, a master of a vessel, did endeavor to persuade him to pilot them unto Virginia; but he would not. They told him that they were filled with such fear and horror, that they were afraid of the very rattling of the ropes; this Mr. Dicks told me with his own mouth" [Clap 362-63].

About the same time Dike entered into a partnership with Roger Conant, Peter Palfrey and Francis Johnson for trading in beaver in Maine; this led to extensive litigation more than twenty years later, and also provides the evidence for the name and remarriage of Tabitha, Anthony Dike's wife [EQC 1:409, 2:22-26].

In 1636 Dike was carrying freight to the Connecticut for William Pynchon [WP 3:286], and then in 1637 he took an active part in the Pequot War, appearing at Saybrook and in Narragansett Bay, bringing reports to Roger Williams and carrying a letter from Governor Vane of Massachusetts Bay [WP 3:407, 411-12; RWCorr 78-81].

Savage says that Anthony Dike "in 1637 was of Charlestown or Salem." There was an Anthony Dix, carpenter, who was an inhabitant of Charlestown in 1641, and sometime before 1652 sold a house and lot in Charlestown to Walter Allen [Wyman 294; ChBOP 136]. This could not be either Anthony Dike of Salem or his son of the same name.

That the Anthony Dix/Dike who had wife Margery in Salem by about 1665 was the son of the immigrant is supported by the probate of his estate, in which two of the appraisers were Nathaniel Pickman Sr. and Nathaniel Pickman Jr., who would be his stepfather and half-brother. (See TAG 17:163-65 for an account of Jonathan Dike, the son of this younger Anthony.)

JOHN DOANE

ORIGIN: Unknown.
MIGRATION: 1630.
FIRST RESIDENCE: Plymouth.
REMOVES: Eastham 1645.

OCCUPATION: Yeoman.
Innkeeper (on 4 June 1639, "Mr. John Done is allowed to draw wine until the next Court, that further order may be taken therein" [PCR 1:127]; on 2 June 1640, "we present Mr. Done for selling wine contrary to order made by the Court. It was mistaken by the grand inquest, and so he was discharged by the Court the 3d September 1640, and appointed by the Court to be thus erased out" [PCR 1:156]; on 7 January 1644/5, Doane agreed to let James Cole "take off those wines he now hath in his hands" [PCR 2:79-80]).
CHURCH MEMBERSHIP: On 2 January 1633/4, "Mr. John Done, being formerly chosen to the office of a deacon in the church, at the request of the church & himself was freed from the office of an Assistant in the commonwealth" [PCR 1:23].

On 18 April 1642, John Done, agent for the church of Plymouth, purchased from Mr. Ralph Smith a house, buildings and garden plots in Plymouth, also six acres of upland in the new field [PCR 12:79-80]. The same year, Doane turned this property over to "Mr. John Reynor their teacher" [PCR 12:87].

FREEMAN: In 1633 Plymouth list of freemen, ahead of those made free 1 January 1632/3 [PCR 1:3]. In list of 7 March 1636/7 [PCR 1:52]. In Plymouth section of Plymouth colony list of 1639 (as "Mr. John Done"), from which he was erased and reentered in the Eastham section of the same list [PCR 8:173, 177]. In Eastham sections of lists of 1658, 29 May 1670 and 1 [blank] 1683/4 [PCR 5:278, 8:201, 208].

EDUCATION: Appointment to committee to revise laws indicates considerable education. His inventory included "9 books, a glass bottle, a sword" and some tools valued at 13s. 6d. [BrPR 1:11].

OFFICES: Plymouth Colony Assistant, 1 January 1632/3 [PCR 1:5]. Committee to divide meadow ground, 1 July 1633, 2 October 1637 [PCR 1:14, 67]. Committee to assess taxes, 2 January 1633/4, 2 March 1635/6 [PCR 1:26, 38]. Committee to collect money for building a mill, 5 July 1635 [PCR 1:35]. Committee to regulate prices and wages, 5 January 1635/6 [PCR 1:36]. Committee to revise laws, 4 October 1636, 6 May 1639 [PCR 1:44, 121]. Committee on trade with the Indians, 7 March 1636/7 [PCR 1:54]. Committee to lay out highways, 2 May 1637, 1 February 1640/1 [PCR 1:58, 2:7]. Committee on beaver trade, 7 June 1637 [PCR 1:62].

Deputy for Plymouth to Plymouth General Court, 4 June 1639, 7 June 1642, 27 September 1642, 6 June 1643, 29 August 1643, 10 October 1643, 5 March 1643/4, 5 June 1644 (but did not attend) [PCR 1:126, 2:40, 45, 57, 59, 60, 63, 68, 72]. Deputy for Nawset [Eastham], 6 June 1649, 4 June 1650 [PCR 2:144, 154]. Deputy for Eastham, 5 June 1651, 6 April 1653, 7 June 1653, 7 June 1659 [PCR 2:168, 3:24, 32, 162]. Auditor, 7 September 1641, 3 March 1644/5 [PCR 2:24, 82].

Plymouth grand jury, 2 June 1640, 2 March 1640/1 [PCR 1:155, 2:11]. Petit jury, 7 March 1636/7, 2 October 1637, 2 January 1637/8, 6 March 1637/8, 4 September 1638, 3 March 1639/40, 5 October 1640, 6 September 1641, 7 December 1641, 3 May 1642, 1 November 1642, 5 November 1644, 3 March 1644/5, 1 March 1652/3, 2 October 1660 [PCR 3:200, 7:5, 7-9, 16, 17, 23, 25, 28, 29, 32, 38, 40, 64]. Coroner's jury, 5 June 1638 [PCR 1:88].

On 1 June 1663, the court appointed Mr. John Doane to "administer marriage in Eastham for the next year, also to administer oath to witnesses before grand enquest, and other witnesses" [PCR 4:43].

In Plymouth section of 1643 Plymouth Colony list of men able to bear arms [PCR 8:188]. On 24 January 1641/2, "Mr. John Done" was one of four men elected to head committees to supply six muskets with shot, powder and swords every Lord's day "ready for service if need require" [PCR 2:31].

(It is very likely that the following service belongs to his son of the same name: Eastham selectman, 5 June 1677, 5 June 1678, 3 June 1679, 1 June 1680, 7 June 1681, 6 June 1682, 6 June 1683, 3 June 1684, 2 June 1685 [PCR 5:230, 257, 6:10, 35, 59, 84, 108, 129, 164, 168, 186]. Eastham constable, 7 June 1676 [PCR 5:196]. Eastham highway surveyor, 5 June 1672, 3 June 1673, 5 June 1677 [PCR 5:93, 115, 232]. Deputy for Eastham to Plymouth General Court, 6 June 1682 [PCR 6:85].)

His inventory included "9 books, a glass bottle, a sword" and some tools valued at 13s. 6d. [BrPR 1:11].

ESTATE: "John Done" was assessed £1 7s. in the Plymouth tax lists of 25 March 1633 and 27 March 1634 [PCR 1:9, 27].

On 14 February 1633/4, John Coombs sold to "Joh. Done & his heirs forever a dwelling house & misted with the inclosure & outhousing thereunto belonging" [PCR 1:25].

Allotted mowing ground, 14 March 1635/6, 20 March 1636/7 [PCR 1:40, 56].

On 30 December 1636, whereas "the now dwelling house with all & singular the outhousing, lands & enclosures in the use & occupation of John Done, of Plymouth, near unto Plain Dealing, were in partnership between the said John Done & John Atwood, late of London, gent., now know ye that upon accounts between the said Joh. & John, the said John Atwood, for & in consideration of threescore pounds, hath bought out the said John Done, his heirs & assigns, so that it remaineth wholly to the said John Atwood & his heirs forever" [PCR 1:47].

On 2 October 1637, he was granted ten acres "to belong to his house at Plymouth," and one hundred acres at Jones River [PCR 1:65-66]. On 4 December 1637, he was granted ten acres [PCR 1:69]. On 4 February 1638/9, he was granted one hundred acres, partly to make up for portions of an earlier grant which he had remitted [PCR 1:111-12]. On 1 June 1640, he was granted ten acres of meadow [PCR 1:154]. On 2 November 1640, he was granted ten acres meadow in the North Meadow [PCR 1:166].

On 7 April 1642, "Mr. John Done" sold to Mr. William Bradford for four goats, a garden in Plymouth, also three acres of marsh bought of Thomas Willet [PCR 12:79].

On 19 February 1645/6, "Mr. John Done" sold to Mr. William Hanbury of Plymouth his dwelling house and garden places, barn and buildings, with all the fruit trees, the corn now growing in the garden excepted with some half dozen small fruit trees, to be given to Doane in the fall or spring [PCR 12:133-34].

On 6 October 1657, Mr. John Done and others petitioned to acquire land thirteen English miles from Rehoboth, and the court gave them permission to purchase it from the Indians [PCR 3:123]. On 1 June 1658, a portion of land was granted by the court to "Mr. John Done" and others, between Bridgewater and Weymouth [PCR 3:142]. On 5 June 1666, the court, having granted him one hundred acres of upland at "Pottamumaquate Neck" and six acres of meadow there, ordered Lt. Freeman and Josias Cooke to view and buy it for him [PCR 4:131].

On 1 April 1659, "Mr. John Done" of Eastham, yeoman, "with the consent of his wife mistress Lydia Done," sold to "Mrs. Allis Bradford Senior of Plymouth, widow, ... all that his tract and parcel of land lying at Jones River in the township of Plymouth aforesaid, being an hundred acres" of upland and meadow, which had been sold to William Bradford Senior during his lifetime but not confirmed until this date [PCLR 2:2:20]. By the time Bradford's son Joseph took this land, the boundaries were lost and it had to be re-surveyed in 1699 [PTR 1:268-69].

At an unknown date (but acknowledged 2 July 1669), "John Doan" of Eastham, husbandman, exchanged land with "Richard Higgens" of Eastham, Doane receiving three acres of meadow and Higgins receiving four acres of meadow at Billingsgate [PCLR 5:140].

On 23 December 1681, "John Done, gent., tailor, of Eastham" for "love and natural affection" gave to "my daughter Abigaill Done ... my dwelling house with all the upland about the said house," about twelve acres, with two acres of meadow, in Eastham [PCLR 5:89].

In his will, dated 18 May 1678 and proved 2 June 1686, "John Doane of Eastham, aged eighty and eight years or there about," bequeathed to "my loving wife" my dwelling house in Eastham with all the upland and meadow about it and two acres at a place called the Acres, and all personal estate for life; to "daughter Abigail Doane," the house and land at her mother's death; to "son John Doane," sole executor, twenty-seven acres of upland, eight acres at Poche Island, all my right in Eastham being a town purchaser, also one hundred acres granted by the Plymouth court "by his majesty's order invested with power to do equity and justice to his poor distressed subjects," also my great table and form; to "son Daniel Doane," the land he now lives on and twenty acres near the dry swamp and four and a half acres of meadow; to "son Ephraim

Doane" twenty acres of upland and four acres of meadow at Little Billingsgate; to "granddaughter Margaret Hicks" a trunk and a pair of sheets; residue at wife's death divided equally among all the sons and daughters [MD 3:177, citing BarnPR 1:10].

The inventory of "Mr. John Doane deceased the 21th of February 1685 aged about a hundred years," taken 21 May 1686, totalled £10 16s. 7d., with no real estate included [MD 3:178, citing BarnPR 1:11].

BIRTH: About 1590 (based on age given when he wrote his will).
DEATH: Eastham 21 February 1685[/6] [MD 3:178, citing BarnPR 1:11], "aged about a hundred years" [*sic*].
MARRIAGE: (1) By 4 December 1648 Ann ____ (and by 1625 if she was the mother of his children) (signed a deed dated 4 December 1648 [Dawes-Gates 304, citing Eastham TR]). She died by 1659.

(2) By 1 April 1659 Lydia____ [MD 13:232, citing PCLR 2:2:20]. She was living on 18 May 1678 when she was named in her husband's will, but was presumably deceased by 23 December 1681 when property he left to her in the will was deeded by him to his daughter Abigail [PCLR 5:89].
CHILDREN:
With first wife
  i   LYDIA DOANE, b. say 1625; m. Plymouth 11 September 1645 Samuel Hicks [PCR 2:88], son of ROBERT HICKS [PM 243].
  ii   ABIGAIL DOANE, b. about 1631; m. in early 1690s Samuel Lothrop of Norwich, son of Rev. John Lothrop; d. Norwich 23 January 1734/5 "in the 104th year of her age" [Norwich Hist 218, illustration of tombstone]. "Mrs. Abigail Lothrop died at Norwich Jan. 23, 1735 in her 104th year. Her father John Done and his wife came to Plymouth in 1630, and there she was born the next year. She lived single till 60 years old and then married Mr. John Lothrop [mistake for Samuel Lothrop] of Norwich, who lived ten years and then died" [Norwich Hist 578, citing *Boston Weekly Journal*]. (Ferris gives a birthdate of 13 January 1631/2, which is not found in the records and may be an inaccurate calculation based on the tombstone [Dawes-Gates 2:305].)
  iii JOHN DOANE, b. say 1635; m. (1) Eastham 30 April 1662 Hannah Bangs [MD 8:89], daughter of EDWARD BANGS [PM 23]; m. (2) Eastham 14 January 1684[/5] Rebecca Pette [MD 8:89].

    iv   DANIEL DOANE, b. about 1637 (d. Eastham 20 December 1712 in his 76th year [MD 8:3]); m. (1) by 1669 _____ _____ (eldest known child b. Plymouth 7 March 1669/70 [PCR 8:57; MD 19:111]); m. (2) after 28 July 1682 Hepsibah (Cole) Crispe. (Hepzibah Cole, daughter of Daniel Cole of Eastham, had married at Eastham 24 May 1677 George Crisp, and he had died there 28 July 1682 [MD 3:180]; in the distribution of the estate of Daniel Cole, dated 15 January 1694/5, the list of heirs included "Daniel Doan and his wife Hipsibath" [MD 23:67, citing BarnPR 1:107; see also Dawes-Gates 2:305].)

    v   EPHRAIM DOANE, b. say 1642; m. (1) Eastham 5 February 1667[/8] Mercy Knowles [PCR 8:57]; m. (2) after 1692 Mary (Smalley) Snow, daughter of JOHN SMALLEY [PM 422] and widow of John Snow [MD 34:56, citing BarnPR 2:103; GMB 3:1687-89].

ASSOCIATIONS: Twice in the 1630s John Doane acted jointly with John Atwood of London. On 8 April 1633, as agent of Mr. John Atwood of London, John Doane sold to Henry Howland the remaining time of Walter Harris [PCR 1:12-13]. Doane and Atwood had held a piece of land as partners, but on 30 December 1636, probably not long after he had arrived in New England, Atwood bought out Doane [PCR 1:47]. They do not seem to have interacted after that date.

The widow Martha Harding may have been John Doane's sister [Dawes-Gates 2:302].

COMMENTS: On 28 October 1633, "John Done" presented the inventory of Martha Harding [PCR 1:18], and, on 11 November 1633, with Stephen Hopkins, the inventory of Godbert Godbertson and Sarah his wife [PCR 1:19].

On 11 November 1633, Mary Brown, daughter of PETER BROWN, deceased, was placed with "Mr. Joh. Done" for nine years [PCR 1:18; PM 82]. On 10 October 1644, when Mary Brown had reached seventeen, her portion, which had been in Doane's hands, was ordered given to John Browne of Duxbury [PCR 2:76].

On 7 June 1636, "John Done, yeoman, entereth an account of slander, & layeth it in an £100, against Helin Billington, widow" [PCR 1:41]; the defendant was fined £5 and ordered "to be set in the stocks & be whipped" [PCR 1:42].

A "John Done," sixteen years old, sailed from London for New England on the *True Love* in 1635, and Pope thinks this is the son of the immigrant, but 1635 is close to the year of birth of the son of the immigrant, so the 1635 passenger must be someone else.

EDWARD DOTY

ORIGIN: Unknown.
MIGRATION: 1620 on the *Mayflower*.
FIRST RESIDENCE: Plymouth.

OCCUPATION: Planter [PCR 2:44, 69].
FREEMAN: In the 1633 Plymouth list of freemen, ahead of those admitted on 1 January 1632/3 [PCR 1:3], and in the list of 7 March 1636/7 [PCR 1:52]. In the Plymouth section of the list of 1639 [PCR 8:174].
EDUCATION: Signed his deeds by mark.
OFFICES: In Plymouth section of 1643 Plymouth Colony list of men able to bear arms [PCR 8:187]. His inventory included "a matchcock musket" valued at 12s. and "a watch bill" valued at 3s. [PCPR 2:1:15-16].
ESTATE: In the 1623 Plymouth division of land there are two consecutive entries for "Edward [blank]," granted one acre; one of these must be for Edward Doty [PCR 12:4]. In the 1627 Plymouth division of cattle "Edward Dolton" was the eleventh person in the fourth company [PCR 12:10].

Assessed £1 7s. in the Plymouth tax list of 25 March 1633 and 18s. in the list of 27 March 1634 [PCR 1:10, 27].

On 12 July 1637, "Edward Dotey" sold to Richard Derby "all those his messuages, houses and tenements at the High Cliff or Skeart Hill together with the four lots of lands and three other acres purchased of Josuah Pratt, Phineas Pratt and John Shawe," with an exclusion of an inner chamber in the "chief messuage ... wherein the said Edward Dotey layeth his corn" and that Doty would keep possession of the other house and three lots until he received all the £150 and reaped the crop of corn. If Richard Derby failed to return from old England or failed to have the £150 paid by harvest time, Doty could sow another crop and reap it until Derby returned or paid [PCR 12:20-21]. Apparently Derby settled for the single lot and paid £22 [PCR 12:46].

On 16 September 1641, Edward Doty was granted a forty-acre parcel of upland at Lakenham [PCR 2:26]. On 7 May 1642, "Edward Dotey" purchased one acre of upland at High Cliff from Joshua Pratt [PCR

12:81]. On 5 May 1643, "Edward Dotey" sold two lots totalling forty acres of upland to Stephen Bryan and John Shaw Jr. [PCR 12:91]. On a list entitled "Names of the Purchasers," probably dated after 26 December 1651, Edward Doty is twenty-first of fifty-eight [PCR 2:177].

In his will, dated 20 May 1655 and proved 5 March 1655/6, Edward Doty Senior of Plymouth "being sick" bequeathed "my purchase land lying at Coaksett unto my sons; my son Edward I give a double portion and to the rest of my sons equal alike," only to "my wife I leave a third during her life then after to return to my sons"; to "my loving wife ... my house and lands and meadows within the precincts of New Plymouth"; "my share of land at Punckquetest if it come to anything I give it unto my son Edward"; on 5 March 1655/6, "Faith the wife of Edward Dotten deceased" relinquished to her sons her right in lands at Coaksett [MD 3:87-88, citing PCPR 2:1:14].

The inventory of the estate of "Edward Dotten lately deceased," taken 21 November 1655, totalled £137 19s. 6d., of which £60 was real estate: "his dwelling house and his land adjoining," £25; "threescore acres of upland with the meadow adjoining to it lying in the woods," £10; "the land at Clarkes Iland," £5; and "the purchase land lying at Coakset," £20 [MD 3:88-89, citing PCPR 2:1:15-16].

In her will, dated 12 December 1675 and proved 8 June 1676, "Faith Phillips the wife of John Phillipes" of Marshfield "though weak in body" bequeathed to "my daughter Mary" £9 in "my son John's hands"; to "my daughter Elizabeth £6"; to "my daughter Mary £3 due by bill of sale"; to "my daughter Desire £6 due by my bill of sale and a warming pan." On 4 November 1676, letters of administration were granted to "John Rouse Junior of Marshfield ... in the behalf of himself his wife and sisters: viz: Desire [torn] and Mary Doten" [MD 3:89-90, citing PCPR 3:2:12].

BIRTH: By about 1599 (he was a servant on his arrival, but as he fought a duel within months of landing at Plymouth, he was more likely close to the end of his servitude rather than the beginning; he signed the Mayflower Compact, probably as an adult).

DEATH: Plymouth 23 August 1655 [PCR 8:17].

MARRIAGE: (1) Before 1635 _____ _____; not seen in any record. Her existence is implied only by Bradford's comment that Edward had "a second wife" (see *COMMENTS* below).

(2) Plymouth 6 January 1634/5 "Fayth Clarke" [PCR 1:32], daughter of Thurston Clarke. She married (2) Plymouth 14 March 1666[/7] John Phillips [PCR 4:163-64, 8:31; MD 18:56] and was buried at Marshfield on 21 December 1675 [MarVR 9].

CHILDREN:
With second wife
- i EDWARD DOTY, b. say 1636 (eldest son in father's will); m. Plymouth 25 or 26 February 1662[/3] Sarah Faunce [MD 13:204; PCR 8:23], daughter of JOHN FAUNCE [PM 201].
- ii JOHN DOTY, b. say 1638; m. (1) by 1668 Elizabeth Cooke (eldest known child b. Plymouth 24 August 1668 [PVR 5]), daughter of Jacob Cooke and granddaughter of FRANCIS COOKE {1620, Plymouth} [MF 12:54, 81-82; PM 144]; m. (2) Plymouth 22 November 1694 Sarah Jones [PNQ 3:121], daughter of Joseph Jones and great-granddaughter of RICHARD WARREN [MF 18:1:82; PM 477].
- iii THOMAS DOTY, b. say 1640; m. by 1675 Mary Churchill (by whom he had had an illegitimate child in 1672), daughter of John Churchill. Widow Mary m. (2) 8 February 1687/8 Henry Churchill. (In 1960 Florence Harlow Barclay studied the family of Thomas Doty and concluded that he married two women named Mary [TAG 36:1-7]. In 1996 Barbara Lambert Merrick reexamined the problem and concluded that Thomas Doty had only one wife and that Henry Churchill was not son of John Churchill [TAG 71:114-20]. We follow the latter article here.)
- iv SAMUEL DOTY, b. say 1642; m. Piscataway, New Jersey, 13 November 1678 Jeane Harman [NJHSP 4:4:34] (by license dated 24 October 1678 Jeane Harman, both of Piscataway, New Jersey [East Jersey Deeds 3:149; GMNJ 43:49]).
- v DESIRE DOTY, b. about 1645 (d. Marshfield 22 January 1731, aged eighty-six years [MarVR 409]); m. (1) Marshfield 25 December 1667 William Sherman [MarVR 10], son of WILLIAM SHERMAN [PM 416]; m. (2) Marshfield 24 November 1681 Israel Holmes [MarVR 16], son of WILLIAM HOLMES {1635, Scituate} [GM 2:3:392-97]; m. (3) by 1689 as his second wife Alexander Standish, son of MILES STANDISH [MD 12:48-52; PM 451].
- vi ELIZABETH DOTY, b. say 1646; m. (1) Marshfield 13 January 1674[/5] John Rowse [MarVR 8]; m. (2) Marshfield 28 January 1718/9 William Carver [MD 8:43; MarVR 35, 40].
- vii ISAAC DOTY, b. Plymouth 8 February 1648/9 [MD 15:27; PCR 8:5]; m. by about 1673 Elizabeth England (in his will of 11 January 1684[/5], Hugh Parsons of Portsmouth, Rhode

viii JOSEPH DOTY, b. Plymouth 30 April 1651 [PCR 8:12]; on 27 October 1674, accused by Elizabeth Warren of fathering her child [PCR 5:156]; m. about summer 1674 Deborah Ellis (late enough to have conceived a child with her b. 22 February 1674/5 but not so soon as to have committed adultery to conceive a child with Elizabeth Warren still unborn 27 October 1674 [TAG 36:9-11]); m. (2) Rochester 5 March 1711/2 Sarah Edwards, widow [TAG 64:152-54].

ix MARY DOTY, b. say 1653; m. after 10 July 1677 Samuel Hatch [PCR 5:239; MD 5:111-13, citing PCLR 4:345 and PLR 25:120; TAG 36:7-8].

Island, who had married Elizabeth, the widow of William England, bequeathed to "my wife's two daughters, living on Long Island, viz: Susannah Carpenter and Elizabeth Doty" [Austin 144]).

ASSOCIATIONS: Edward Doty had a complex financial relationship with Richard Derby, but not one that necessarily implies kinship.

COMMENTS: In 1988 Neil D. Thompson published a refutation of the false claim for the ancestry of Edward Doty made by Gustave Anjou [TAG 63:215].

Bradford, in his accounting of 1651, stated that Edward Doty came on the *Mayflower* as a servant of STEPHEN HOPKINS, and that in 1651 "Edward Doty by a second wife hath seven children, and both he and they are living" [Bradford 442, 447]. Doty signed the Mayflower Compact.

Doty went with his master Hopkins and more than a dozen others on the voyage of "discovery" on 6 December 1620 [Mourt 31-32].

Edward Doty is said to have been guilty of the "second offence" committed in Plymouth. As Bradford tells us, "the first duel fought in New England, upon a challenge at single combat with sword and dagger, between Edward Doty and Edward Leister, servants of Mr. Hopkins. Both being wounded, the one in the hand, the other in the thigh, they are adjudged by the whole company to have their head and feet tied together, and so to lie for twenty-four hours, without meat or drink; which is begun to be inflicted, but within an hour, because of their great pains, at their own and their master's humble request, upon promise of better carriage, they are released by the governor" [Prince 190-91, citing Bradford's lost register].

This incident set the tone for the next twenty years in which Doty was frequently in court for fighting, slandering, trespass and debt. Edward

Doty was defendant in three civil suits at the court of 2 January 1632/3, all involving hogs; he won one and lost two [PCR 1:6-7]. On 1 April 1633, Doty was sued for slander by one of the winning plaintiffs just noted, and was fined 50s. [PCR 1:12].

Still he prospered, for he had an apprentice in 1633, although an unhappy one. On 2 January 1633/4, the court settled a dispute between Edward Doty and his apprentice John Smith, reducing the time of the apprenticeship from ten years to five [PCR 1:23]. On 31 August 1638, Doty received the assignment of seven years labor of William Snow from Snow's previous master, Richard Derby [PCR 1:94].

On 24 March 1633/4, Edward Doty was fined 10s. for breaking the peace and drawing blood from Josias Cooke [PCR 1:26]. On 28 March 1634, Edward Doty won a suit against Francis Sprague [PCR 1:29].

On 7 March 1636/7, Edward Doty was found guilty of a "deceitful bargain" over a lot of land, and restored the lot to George Clarke [PCR 7:5]. The controversy continued when George Clark won damages and costs from Doty on 2 October 1637, Clark charging him with denying liberty to hold land for the term he had taken it [PCR 7:6]. Things escalated, for that same day Clark also charged Doty for assault and battery, and Doty was further fined [PCR 7:6]. Doty was sued in less sanguinary encounters between 1638 and 1651 with Richard Derby, John Shaw, widow Bridget Fuller and John Holmes over debt and trespass, and lost them all [PCR 7:10, 15, 16, 47, 48, 56]. On 7 December 1641, he successfully sued James Luxford for trespass [PCR 7:26].

On 1 February 1641/2, Thomas Symons charged "Edward Dotey" with carelessly allowing cattle put in his hands to "break into men's corn" endangering the cattle and other property, and Doty was ordered to put his cattle in a "keep" [PCR 2:33].

On 10 February 1643/4, "Edward Dotey" was one of six men directed by the town of Plymouth to build a wolftrap at Plain Dealing [PTR 1:16]. In March 1657 he was midway down the list of "those that have interest and proprieties in the town's land at Punckateeset over against Rhode Island" [PTR 1:37].

Writing in 1897 Ethan Allen Doty quotes many documents, including some that would be very helpful in refining our knowledge of this family, but which do not appear in the colony or town records. The most important of these would be receipts given by all the sons of the immigrant for their shares in his estate [*The Doty-Doten Family in America* (Brooklyn 1897), p. 28]. Perhaps these documents are privately held.

Desire, who married successively William Sherman, Isaac Holmes and Alexander Standish, was said to have been eighty-six when she died in 1731, placing her birth about 1645. But her last child with Standish was born when she would have been forty-eight by this reckoning. She was probably a few years younger than her age at death shows, but it is hard to know just where to fit her into the sequence of children.

Savage states that the immigrant had children William and Faith, in addition to the children listed above, but there is no evidence for such children. From the probate records for Edward Doty's widow we may be sure that no daughter by the name of Faith survived to adulthood. Savage also claims that Edward Doty removed to Yarmouth, but all records for him place him in Plymouth.

BIBLIOGRAPHIC NOTE: The Five Generations Project of the General Society of Mayflower Descendants has published its study of Edward Doty as Volume Eleven of the series, in three parts, compiled by Peter B. Hill. Part I, published in 1996, covered the descendants of sons Edward and John. Part II, also published in 1996, covered the descendants of sons Thomas and Samuel and daughters Desire and Elizabeth. Part III, published in 2000, covered the descendants of sons Isaac and Joseph and daughter Mary.

JOHN DUNHAM

ORIGIN: Leiden, Holland.
MIGRATION: 1632.
FIRST RESIDENCE: Plymouth.

OCCUPATION: Weaver [PCR 12:149].
CHURCH MEMBERSHIP: At the time of his death it was recorded that "He was an approved servant of God, and a useful man in his place, being a deacon of the church of Christ at Plymouth" [PCR 8:32].
FREEMAN: In 1633 Plymouth list, before those admitted on 1 January 1632/3 [PCR 1:3]. In list of 7 March 1636/7 [PCR 1:52]. In Plymouth sections of Plymouth Colony lists of 1639 and 1658 [PCR 8:174, 197].
EDUCATION: Signed his will by mark. Some education implied by service on committee to make laws.
OFFICES: Deputy for Plymouth to Plymouth Colony General Court, 4 June 1639, 2 June 1640, 27 September 1642, 10 October 1643, 5 June 1644, 20 August 1644, 28 October 1645, 7 July 1646 (fined for failing to

appear), 1 June 1647, 6 June 1649, 4 June 1650, 3 June 1652, 7 June 1653, 6 June 1654, 1 August 1654, 8 June 1655, 3 June 1656, 2 March 1657/8, 7 June 1659, 4 June 1661, 3 June 1662, 8 June 1664 [PCR 1:126, 154, 2:45, 63, 72, 74, 94, 104, 117, 144, 154, 3:3, 31, 49, 63, 79, 99, 129, 162, 187, 198, 214, 4:14, 60]. Auditor, 3 March 1644/5 [PCR 2:82]. Committee to treat with the partners about the trade [on the Kennebec], 1 October 1634 [PCR 1:31]. Committee to make laws, 16 May 1639 [PCR 1:121]. Committee to confer and "conclude with the General Court about the war," 20 September 1642 [PTR 1:11].

Plymouth grand jury, 7 March 1636/7, 5 June 1638, 1 June 1641, 1 March 1641/2, 7 March 1642/3, 6 June 1643, 7 June 1648, 4 October 1648 [PCR 1:54, 87, 2:16, 34, 45, 53, 56, 124, 134]. Petit jury, 7 June 1636, 3 March 1639/40, 5 October 1640, 2 March 1640/1, 1 June 1641, 6 July 1641, 3 August 1641, 1 November 1642, 1 March 1652/3, 6 December 1653, 3 October 1654, 4 October 1655, 5 March 1655/6, 5 October 1656, 3 May 1659 [PCR 1:42, 7:15, 17, 19, 20, 22, 32, 64, 68, 72, 75, 77, 81, 93]. Coroner's jury, 3 September 1652 [PCR 3:16].

Plymouth selectman, 1644, 1647, 1649-50 [PTR 1:18, 22, 28, 32]. Assessor, 1644, 1649-51, 1663 [PTR 1:19, 29, 31, 32, 58]. Lot layer, 1663 [PTR 1:61]. Viewer of land, 4 January 1641/2, 25 October 1649, 1 June 1658, 2 August 1659 [PCR 2:32, 145, 3:142, 169].

ESTATE: He was assessed 9s. in Plymouth tax lists of 25 March 1633 and 27 March 1634 [PCR 1:10, 27].

John Dunham was granted use of mowing ground, 14 March 1635/6, 20 March 1636/7 [PCR 1:40, 56], and granted "a parcel of upland lying at the head of his lot," 5 October 1640 [PCR 1:163]. About 1637, the General Court moved that "long since diverse lots of lands lying at Winberry Hill which should have contained twenty acres apiece were granted to John Donhame" and that Dunham, having relinquished many of them to new inhabitants, the court confirmed to him the thirty acres he had still remaining [PCR 12:27]. On 16 September 1641, "John Dunhame, the elder," was granted sixty acres of upland at Swanhold and also eight acres of meadow; his son received a grant the same day [PCR 2:26]. On 31 December 1641, he was granted a parcel of meadow and of upland at Swanhold [PCR 2:30].

On 19 January 1647[/8?], John Dunham of "New Plymouth," weaver, deeded to "my son Samuel Dunham" six acres of upland [PCR 12:149]. On 18 February 1650[/1?], "Samuell Donham" of Plymouth, planter, sold to "John Donham senior" of Plymouth, weaver, a house and land containing twelve acres, also half an acre of meadow at the watering place, also ten or twelve acres of upland at Wellingsley [PCR 12:203].

In March 1651, John Dunham was listed as a proprietor with interest in the town's land at Punckateesett "over against Rhode Island." His lot was number seventeen [PTR 1:36, 66].

On 13 June 1655, "John Dunham senior of Plymouth ... weaver" deeded to "his son-in-law Gyles Rickard Junior of Plymouth ... planter a parcel of upland ground being estimated at about twelve acres ... at Wellingsley" in Plymouth [MD 9:234-35, citing PCLR 2:1:157]. On 4 July 1658, John Dunham Sr. of Plymouth, weaver, deeded to "his son Jonathan Dunham" of Plymouth, planter, "all that his house and land that the said Jonathan Dunham now liveth on" containing fourteen acres, along with one-third of "his marsh meadow at the watering place" [MD 12:214-15, citing PCLR 2:1:212]. On 28 May 1663, John Dunham Sr. of Plymouth, weaver, deeded to "his son John Dunham the one half of all that his share, lot and portion of meadow at Winnatuxett in the township of Plymouth as also his whole portion of upland at the place forenamed" on the condition that he accept this as his whole share in his father's estate [MD 18:37-38, citing PCLR 2:2:119].

On 15 February 1658, Plymouth selectmen confirmed to John Dunham Sr. a former grant of twelve acres of land "at a place called Fresh Lake" [MD 13:146, citing PCLR 2:2:14].

On 1 June 1669, letters of administration were granted to "Abigall Dunham, Senior, widow," for the estate of "John Dunham, Senior," deceased [PCR 5:22].

In his will, dated 25 January 1668 and proved 4 June 1669, "John Dunham Senior of Plymouth" bequeathed to "my son John Dunham who is my eldest son ... I have given him his portion already ... to what I was able and beyond my ability"; to "my son Benajah Dunham and my son-in-law Stephen Wood" all my right at Agawaum and Sepecan equally; to "my son Daniell Dunham" all my land at Fresh Lake, also "all that land that lieth at home which he made use of this year which I already ordered to him"; to "my loving wife Abigaill Dunham" my now dwelling house, my orchards, with all my land not elsewhere given, all my meadow at the watering place during her life and at her death, to "my son Daniell Dunham"; to "my son Thomas Dunham" £5 paid by my son Daniel Dunham upon demand; to "all the rest of my children that are not expressed in this my last will 12d. each if they demand it"; residue to my loving wife Abigail Dunham, executrix; "my loving friends Captain Thomas Southworth and the elder Thomas Cushman and my son Samuell Dunham" overseers [MD 17:113-14, citing PCPR 2:2:53].

An inventory of the goods of "John Dunham Senior deceased," taken 16 March 1668/9, was untotalled; it included only £3 of real estate:

"house and land not prised [presumably because he had already given it to Daniel] only threescore acres of upland at Swanhold not willed away" [MD 17:114, citing PCPR 2:2:54].

BIRTH: By about 1587 (based on date of marriage), possibly son of Richard Dunham of Langford, Bedfordshire [TAG 71:132].
DEATH: Plymouth 2 March 1668/9, aged about 80 [PCR 8:32].
MARRIAGE: (1) Clophill, Bedfordshire, 17 August 1612 Susan Kaino, probably baptized Clophill 12 December 1586, daughter of "Thomas Cainehoe" [TAG 71:130-33]. She died by 1622.

(2) Leiden 22 October 1622 [NS] Abigail Balliou, daughter of Thomas Balliou [Plooij XLIX; Leiden Pilgrims 70; TAG 71:131, 133, 250]. She was living in 1669 as executrix on her husband's estate.
CHILDREN:
With first wife
  i   JOHN DUNHAM, bp. Henlow, Bedfordshire, 19 February 1614[/5] [TAG 71:132] (d. 6 April 1692 "in his 77th year" [PChR 1:275]); m. by about 1642 Mary _____ (eldest known child b. about 1642 [TAG 30:147]).
  ii HUMILITY DUNHAM, b. say 1617; living at Leiden in 1622; no further record.
  iii THOMAS DUNHAM, b. say 1619; d. by 1677 and apparently never married [TAG 30:148-51].
With second wife
  iv SAMUEL DUNHAM, b. about 1623 (d. Plymouth 20 January 1711/2 "in his 89 years of age" [MD 16:64]); m. Plymouth 29 June 1649 Martha (Beals) Falloway, daughter of John Beals and widow of William Falloway [PCR 8:8; SPR 10:297].
  v   JONATHAN DUNHAM, b. say 1625 (on a Plymouth voters list, about 1646 [PTR 1:26]; on Plymouth proprietors' list March 1651 [PTR 1:37]); m. (1) Plymouth 29 November 1655 Mary Delano [PCR 8:17], daughter of PHILIP DELANO [PM 164]; m. (2) Plymouth 15 October 1657 Mary Cobb [PCR 8:17], daughter of HENRY COBB [PM 118]. (See TAG 36:243-49 for further detail on this man, his wives and children.)
  vi ABIGAIL DUNHAM, b. say 1627; m. Plymouth 6 November 1644 Stephen Wood (or Atwood) [PCR 2:79; PVR 655].
  vii JOSEPH DUNHAM, b. say 1631; m. Plymouth 18 November 1657 Mercy Morton [PCR 8:17], who d. Plymouth 19

February 1666 [PCR 8:31]; m. (2) Plymouth 20 August 1669 Esther Wormall [PCR 8:32], daughter of Joseph and Miriam Wormall [BVR 28].

viii HANNAH DUNHAM, b. about 1634 (d. 1 April 1708 in her 74th year [PChR 1:209]); m. Plymouth 31 October 1651 Giles Rickard [PCR 8:13].
ix PERSIS DUNHAM, b. say 1635; m. (1) Plymouth 29 November 1655 Benajah Pratt [PCR 8:17]; m. (2) August 1683 Jonathan Shaw [PPR 2:18].
x BENAJAH DUNHAM, b. say 1637; m. Plymouth 25 October 1660 Elizabeth Tilson [PCR 8:22; TAG 69:38].
xi DANIEL DUNHAM, b. say 1639; m. say 1670 Hannah _____ (named in his will [PCPR 3:2:102]).

COMMENTS: John Dunham and three children (John, Humility and Thomas) were listed as living in the Zevenhuysen section of Leiden, in the close of the English church, on 15 October 1622 [NS] [Dexter 612; NEHGR 154:423], in a survey that was conveniently taken between the dates of John Dunham's betrothal and marriage to his second wife.

His cattlemark at Plymouth was "a croch on the left ear" [PTR 1:2]. On 16 July 1638, with three others, "John Dunhame" was given power to control the stock of cows for the poor at Plymouth for the next four years [PTR 1:4]. He and his son of the same name frequently dealt with cattle [PTR 1:20, 23, 27, 28]. "The cow John Dunham had was also bogged and died. And her increase killed by the wolf" [PTR 1:29]. He was chosen one of the seven men to herd and keep cattle at Sepecan [Rochester] in 1650 [PTR 1:30].

BIBLIOGRAPHIC NOTE: The definitive treatment of John Dunham, his children and grandchildren, was carried out by Florence Barclay ("Notes on the Dunham Family of Plymouth, Mass.," TAG 30:143-55). She followed this six years later with a detailed study of Jonathan Dunham, son of the immigrant [TAG 36:243-49]. As usual, she has studied all the available records and judiciously analyzed them; we follow her arrangement here, except where noted otherwise.

In 1996 Robert Leigh Ward published data demonstrating the English origin and the first marriage of John Dunham [TAG 71:130-33]. In 1998 Paul C. Reed demonstrated the fraudulence of a published pedigree for John Dunham [TAG 73:101-4].

FRANCIS EATON

ORIGIN: Bristol, England [TAG 72:301-4].
MIGRATION: 1620 on the *Mayflower*.
FIRST RESIDENCE: Plymouth.

OCCUPATION: Carpenter. His inventory included "1 tool box" and a long list of carpenter's tools.
FREEMAN: In 1633 Plymouth list of freemen, ahead of those admitted on 1 January 1632/3 [PCR 1:3].
EDUCATION: Signed deed of 30 December 1631 [PCR 12:17].
OFFICES: Appointed arbiter in dispute between William Bennet and Edward Doty, 3 January 1632/3 [PCR 1:7].

His inventory included "1 pistol, one powder horn & one shot purse" valued at 9s. and "one piece" valued at £1 14s. [PCPR 1:17; MD 1:199].
ESTATE: In the 1623 Plymouth land division granted four acres as a passenger on the *Mayflower* [PCR 12:4]. In the 1627 Plymouth cattle division, the first four members of the tenth company were Francis Eaton, Christian Eaton, Samuel Eaton and Rachel Eaton [PCR 12:12].

On 25 June 1631, Francis Eaton sold to Edward Winslow four acres in the North Field [PCR 12:16 (this was the land received in the 1623 division)]. On 30 December 1631, Francis Eaton sold to William Brewster "one share of land, containing twenty acres, lying at the place commonly called Nothingelse" in consideration of £21 12s., which would "pay his purchase for four shares"; Eaton also sold to William Brewster an additional twelve acres from the same lot [PCR 12:16]. On 8 January 1632/3, Francis Eaton sold to Kenelm and Josiah Winslow "the now dwelling house of the said Francis, with other appurtenances thereunto belonging" [PCR 1:8].

Francis Eaton was assessed 9s. in the Plymouth tax of 25 March 1633 [PCR 1:10]. There is no entry for him or his widow in the 27 March 1634 list; her remarriage to Francis Billington may have been anticipated at the time this list was compiled, so that she would have been included in his household.

Francis Eaton is included in the list of Purchasers [PCR 2:177].

The inventory of the estate of "Fr[ancis] Eaton carpenter of Plymouth," taken 8 November 1633, totalled £64 8s. 7d., with no real estate included; to the inventory was appended a long list of debts owed by Francis Eaton [PCPR 1:17-18; MD 1:197-200]. On 25 November 1633, "whereas Franc[i]s Eaton, carpenter, late of Plymouth, deceased, died indebted far more than the estate of the said Franc[i]s would make good, insomuch as Christian, his late wife, durst not administer, it was ordered, that Mr. Thomas Prence & Mr. John Doane, in the behalf of the Court, should enter upon the estate, according to the inventory brought in upon oath the day of this present, that the creditors might have so far as the estate will make good, & the widow be freed & acquitted from any claim or demands of all or any his creditors whatsoever" [PCR 1:19-20].

BIRTH: Baptized St. Thomas, Bristol, England, 11 September 1596, son of John and Dorothy (Smith) Eaton [TAG 72:303-4].

DEATH: Plymouth between 25 March 1633 (tax list) and 8 November 1633 (date of inventory). (In the allocation of mowing ground on 1 July 1633 Francis Eaton was not assigned a location, and there was granted to "Mr. Williams that which Fr[ancis] Eaton cut last year" [PCR 1:15], so Eaton may already have died by that date.)

MARRIAGE: (1) By 1619 Sarah _____, who came on the *Mayflower* and died early in 1621 [Bradford 446].

(2) About 1622 Dorothy _____, who died soon after [TAG 72:304, 308-9]. (She is thought to be the unnamed maidservant of John Carver who "married and died a year or two after [1620], here in this place" [Bradford 444].)

(3) By about 1626 CHRISTIAN PENN, a passenger on the *Anne*; she married (2) in July 1634 Francis Billington [PCR 1:31], son of JOHN BILLINGTON [PM 56].

CHILDREN:

With first wife

i SAMUEL EATON, b. late 1619 or early 1620; apprenticed 13 August 1636 to John Cooke the younger for seven years [PCR 1:43]; m. (1) by 1646 Elizabeth _____, who died between 5 October 1652 and 10 January 1660[/1] [MF 9:5]; m. (2) Plymouth 10 January 1660[/1] Martha Billington [PCR 8:22], his stepsister.

With third wife

ii RACHEL EATON, b. Plymouth about 1626 (deposed on 22 July 1648 "aged about 23 years" [PCR 2:132]; deposed on 5

	October 1652 "aged twenty-six years or thereabouts" [PCR 3:18]); m. Plymouth 2 March 1645/6 Joseph Ramsden (or Ramsdell) [PCR 2:94; MD 36:187-89].
iii	BENJAMIN EATON, b. Plymouth in March 1627/8; apprenticed 11 February 1635/6 to Bridget Fuller for fourteen years [PCR 1:36-37]; placed in service to John Winslow on 14 January 1642/3, "being about xv years in March next" [PTR 1:12]; m. Plymouth 4 December 1660 Sarah Hoskins [PCR 8:22], daughter of WILLIAM HOSKINS {1634, Plymouth} [GM 2:3:414-20].
iv	Child EATON, b. Plymouth say 1630; an idiot, living 1651 [Bradford 447].

COMMENTS: Bradford tells us that on the *Mayflower* were "Francis Eaton and Sarah his wife, and Samuel their son, a young child," and then in 1651 reports that "Francis Eaton his first wife died in the general sickness. And he married again and his second wife died, and he married the third and had by her three children. One of them is married and hath a child. The others are living but one of them is an idiot. He [Francis Eaton] died about 16 years ago. His son Samuel who came over a sucking child, is also married and hath a child" [Bradford 443, 446-47].

The four persons who earned the allotment of four acres in the 1623 land division were Francis Eaton, his deceased first wife, his second wife and his son Samuel Eaton [MQ 40:13].

BIBLIOGRAPHIC NOTE: In 1996 Robert S. Wakefield revised the earlier account of the family of Francis Eaton in the "Silver Series" of the General Society of Mayflower Descendants [MF 9]. In 1997 Neil D. Thompson published the information that confirmed earlier suggestions as to the English origin of Francis Eaton [TAG 72:301-4]. At the same time David L. Greene presented additional comments on the life and family of this immigrant [TAG 72:305-9].

JOHN EDDY

ORIGIN: Boxted, Essex.
MIGRATION: 1630 on the *Handmaid*.
FIRST RESIDENCE: Plymouth.
REMOVES: Watertown 1631.

CHURCH MEMBERSHIP: Admission to Watertown church prior to March 1632/3 implied by Winthrop anecdote [WJ 1:120].

FREEMAN: 3 September 1634 (eighth in a sequence of eleven Watertown men) [MBCR 1:369].

EDUCATION: On 29 November 1670, Watertown selectmen ordered "that John Edy senior shall go to John Fisk his house and to Georg Lorance and Willyam Preist houses to inquire about their children whether they be learned to read the English tongue and in case they be defective to warn in the said John, Georg and Willyam to the next meeting of the selectmen" [WaTR 102], and, on 3 January 1670/1, "John Edy senior and Isaak Sternes were appointed to speak with Willyam Knop about the education of his daughter and to make return how they find it as to her education and also being kept under restraint and government" [WaTR 104]. His inventory included "a chain, a small table, a parcel of books" valued at 10s.

OFFICES: Watertown selectman, 23 August 1634, 30 [Nov]ember 1635, 10 October 1636, 7 November 1670 [WaTR 1, 2, 102]. On 14 January 1655/6, with Nathaniel Treadway, "nominated to look to the orders of hogs & fences" [WaTR 44].

ESTATE: Granted Great Dividend of fifty acres at Watertown, 25 July 1636 [WaBOP 5]. Granted Beaverbrook Plowland of nine acres, 28 February 1636/7 [WaBOP 6]. Granted Remote Meadow of nine acres, 26 June 1637 [WaBOP 8]. Granted farm of one-hundred-twenty-three acres, 10 May 1642 [WaBOP 13].

In the Watertown Inventory of Grants, John Eddy held ten parcels: sixteen acre homestall; two acres of meadow; Great Dividend of fifty acres; nineteen acres and a half of upland beyond the Further Plain; nine acres of Remote Meadow; six acres of upland; two acres and one rood of marsh; one acre and a half of meadow; seven acres of plowland in the Hither Plain; and one acre and a half of meadow in Ward's Meadow [WaBOP 81].

In the Inventory of Possessions he held three parcels, which he had acquired from Emanuel White: twenty acre homestall; three acres of Remote Meadows; and Great Dividend of twenty-five acres [WaBOP 117; see also WaBOP 78].

In the Composite Inventory he held seven parcels: forty acre homestall; four acres of meadow; Great Dividend of fifty acres; Great Dividend of twenty-five acres; nineteen acres and a half beyond the Further Plain; twelve acres of Remote Meadow; and a farm of one-hundred-twenty-three acres [WaBOP 25].

In his will, dated 11 January 1677[/8?] and proved 16 December 1684, "John Eddie of Watertowne, senior," bequeathed to "my son Samuell Eddie ... my homestall being by estimation forty acres more or less with my dwelling house and barn and all the appurtenances thereunto belonging, with seven acres of meadow and upland lying right over against Widow Barnard's house," he to pay to "my son John Eddie thirty pounds," as further limited by a writing "my sons-in-law John Miriam and Thomas Orton had ... of me"; also to "my son Samuell aforesaid a lot of twelve acres of upland more or less lying and being on the top of Stonie Brook Hill"; to "my four daughters Marie Orton, Sarah Miriam, Pilgrim Steadman, Ruth Gardner, a hundred acres of upland ... being a farm lying near upland called Nonesuch ... to be equally divided between my four daughters aforesaid"; to "my two sons aforesaid Samuell and John Eddie" all moveables to be equally divided between them; "as for my dear and wellbeloved wife I have a writing under my hand and witness to it with the particulars therein mentioned what she shall enjoy after my death"; to "my son John aforesaid fourscore and five acres of land being land called by the name of farm land"; son Samuel Eddy to be executor [MPR Case #6825].

The inventory of the estate of John Eddy, taken 8 December 1684, totalled £246 7s., of which £216 was real estate: "dwelling house and barn with about forty acres of land to it," £160; "seven acres of land over against the Widow Barnard's," £30; "twelve acres of land called the township land lying near Stony Brook," £6; and "land called farm land about a hundred acres," £20 [MPR Case #6825].

On 9 February 1703/4, after a recapitulation of the grant of a farm in Watertown to John Eddy and the bequest by Eddy of that farm to his four daughters Mary Orton, Sarah Miriam, Pilgrim Steadman and Ruth Gardner, the farm was sold to Alexander Miller of Boston by John Marion Sr. of Boston, cordwainer, and Sarah his wife, Ruth Gardner, relict widow of Ezekiel Gardner late of Boston, Pilgrim Baker (formerly the said Pilgrim Steadman) of Boston, widow, Samuel Pearce of Boston, cooper, and Mary his wife, daughter of Mary Orton who is deceased, Nathaniel Baker of Boston, baker, only son of the said Pilgrim Baker, and Samuel Gardner of Boston, tailor, eldest son of Ruth Gardner; among the signers was "Pilgrim Evle" rather than Pilgrim Baker [MLR 16:126-27].

BIRTH: Baptized Cranbrook, Kent, [blank] March 1597, son of the Reverend William and Mary (Fosten) Eddy [Eddy Gen 3-15].
DEATH: Watertown 12 October 1684 "aged 90 years" [WaVR 55].

MARRIAGE: (1) By about 1622 Amy Doggett; she died after about 1645, when her youngest child was born.

(2) After 12 May 1666 Joanna (_____) Meade, widow of Gabriel Meade. She died at Watertown on 25 August 1683 ("Johanna Eddy wife of John Eddy Sen[ior] ... aged about 80 years" [WaVR 53]). (Complete proof for this identification of the second wife is lacking, but it seems likely, since in 1664 John's son Samuel had married Sarah, daughter of Gabriel Meade, in 1675 David Meade, son of Gabriel, married in Watertown, and Israel Meade, another son, was said to have gone to Watertown [DChR 171].)

CHILDREN:
With first wife
- i   JOHN EDDY, bp. Nayland, Suffolk, 9 June 1622 [Eddy Gen 15]; bur. there 8 February 1622/3 [Eddy Gen 15].
- ii JOHN EDDY, bp. Nayland 29 March 1624 [Eddy Gen 15]; d. soon.
- iii MARY EDDY, bp. Nayland 10 March 1625/6 [Eddy Gen 15]; m. by 1648 Thomas Orton (eldest known child b. Charlestown 27 August 1648 [ChVR 1:10]).
- iv SARAH EDDY, b. about 1628 (d. Boston 3 February 1709/10 in 85th year [King's Chapel 173; Eddy Gen 29], which calculates to a birth about 1625, conflicting with the baptismal date for sister Mary, who is consistently listed first among the four daughters); m. by 1651 John Marion of Boston ("John Merion and Sara his wife" admitted to Boston church 15 February 1651/2 [BChR 54] and "John Merion son of our brother John Merion" bp. Boston 22 February 1651/2 [BChR 323]). (The John Marion of Watertown who had "Mary the daughter of John & Sarah Marrian buried 24 (11) 2 mo. old" 1641 [WaVR 9] and other children born in Watertown in the 1640s must be the man of that name who later appears in Hampton [GDMNH 458].)
- v PILGRIM EDDY, b. Watertown 25 August 1634 [WaVR 3]; m. (1) Boston 22 April 1656 William Baker [BVR 56]; m. (2) by 11 January 1677 (date of father's will) Isaac Steadman; m. (3) after 5 February 1682 (when his second wife was still alive) and before 4 January 1688/9 (when he died) Sylvester Eveleth [NEHGR 134:301; MLR 16:126-27].
- vi JOHN EDDY, b. Watertown 16 February 1636 [WaVR 4]; living on 6 August 1702 when his brother Samuel in his will directed his two sons "to take the full care to provide and

maintain my brother John Eddi during his natural life" [Eddy Gen 30-31], which suggests that John Eddy was then incompetent, and perhaps had been all his life. (The John Eddy who married Sarah Woodward and died in 1694 was son of Samuel, and therefore nephew of this John.)

vii BENJAMIN EDDY, bur. Watertown in 1639 [WaVR 6].

viii SAMUEL EDDY, b. Watertown 30 September 1640 [WaVR 8]; m. Dorchester 31 [*sic*] November 1664 "Sarah Mede" [DVR 21], daughter of GABRIEL MEADE {1637, Dorchester}.

ix ABIGAIL EDDY, b. Watertown 11 October 1643 [WaVR 11]; not mentioned in father's will; no further record.

x RUTH EDDY, b. say 1645; m. by 1671 Ezekiel Gardner (eldest known child of "Ezekiel & Ruth Gardner" b. Boston 1 August 1671 [BVR 118]).

ASSOCIATIONS: Brother of SAMUEL EDDY of Plymouth [PM 194], of Abigail (Eddy) Benjamin, wife of JOHN BENJAMIN {1632, Cambridge} [GMB 1:160-64], and of Anna (Eddy) Wines, wife of BARNABAS WINES {1634, Watertown} [Eddy Gen 13-22].

COMMENTS: On 29 November 1630, John Winthrop, in a letter to his wife in England, wrote about the recent arrival of the *Handmaid* at Plymouth, and reported that "Edy of Boxted, who came in her, told me a fortnight since that he had many letters in the ship for me" [WP 2:319]. William Bradford wrote to John Winthrop on 6 February 1631/2 on a number of matters of mutual interest to the two colonies, and spoke of "diverse gone from hence, to dwell and inhabit with you," among whom was "John Eedy" [WP 3:65].

In March 1632/3 Winthrop reported that "[o]ne John Edye, a godly man of Watertown congregation, fell distracted, and, getting out one evening, could not be found; but, eight days after, he came again of himself. He had kept his strength and color, yet had eaten nothing (as must needs be conceived) all that time. He recovered his understanding again in good measure, and lived very orderly, but would, now and then, be a little distempered" [WJ 1:120].

On 22 September 1648, a balance was drawn in the accounts between William Hudson Sr. and Lewis Kidby, and one of the items was "for cost given by the Court against his uncle Edey," 3s. [Aspinwall 235]. John Eddy of Watertown was uncle to Lewis Kidby, since Amy Doggett, wife of John Eddy, was sister of Susan Doggett who had married Lewis Kidby, father of the Lewis Kidby of Boston in 1648 [Doggett Gen 16;

Eddy Family Association Bulletin 4:118-22]. In a letter written from Hamburg on 25 September 1649 to John Winthrop Jr., John Doggett Sr. explained that he had included this letter in another "to my brother Jno. Edy not doubting that he will be careful to convey it unto you" [WP 5:370; see also WP 6:170, 286].

John Eddy was clearly known to the Winthrops before they left England. Eddy was in Nayland in the mid-1620s, just to the south of Groton, and then apparently moved across the county line to Boxted, Essex, the parish of Rev. GEORGE PHILLIPS {1630, Watertown} [GMB 3:1446-50].

SAMUEL EDDY

ORIGIN: Cranbrook, Kent.
MIGRATION: 1630 on the *Handmaid*.
FIRST RESIDENCE: Plymouth.
REMOVES: Swansea by 1681.

OCCUPATION: Tailor. On 26 June 1678, the town of Plymouth allowed five shillings to "Goodman Edey viz: Samuell Edey for work done by him in time of the war in making clothes for soldiers" [PTR 1:157].
CHURCH MEMBERSHIP: Samuel Eddy and his wife were both members of the Plymouth church, as evidenced by the inclusion of their death dates in the records of that church.
FREEMAN: Admitted 1 January 1633/4 [PCR 1:5]. In 1633 and 7 March 1636/7 Plymouth lists of freemen, and in Plymouth sections of 1639, 1658 and 29 May 1670 lists of freemen [PCR 1:4, 53; 5:274; 8:174, 197].
OFFICES: In Plymouth portion of 1643 Plymouth Colony list of men able to bear arms [PCR 8:188].
ESTATE: On 9 May 1631, Experience Mitchell sold to Samuel Eddy "his dwelling house, garden plot & fence, with all things nailfast in the same," reserving a portion of the garden plot [PCR 12:18].

Assessed 9s. in Plymouth tax lists of 25 March 1633 and 27 March 1634 [PCR 1:10, 28].

Granted three acres "next to the lands of Joh. Dunham the elder," 7 November 1636 [PCR 1:46].

On 6 July 1638, Samuel Eddy sold to Richard Clough for forty bushels of Indian corn "all that his house and garden in Plymouth wherein the said Samuel now dwelleth" [PCR 12:31]. On the same day, Nicholas Snow sold to Samuel Eddy for the same amount "all that his house & garden adjoining with the fence in & about the same in Plymouth wherein the said Nicholas now dwelleth" [PCR 12:31].

Granted "six acres of upland lying on the northwest side of Fresh Lake, about the fishing place, and thirty acres of upland at the Narrogansett Hill, and four acres of meadow, or else half the meadow ground there to it," 16 September 1641 [PCR 2:26].

On 7 March 1642[/3?], John Allen sold to Samuel Eddy "all that his house, barns & buildings with the lands thereunto belonging lying at Willingsly and Woeberry Plain" [PCR 12:90]. On 3 March 1645[/6?], Samuel Eddy sold to John Tompson "all that his house situate at the Spring Hill in Plymouth with the garden place adjoining and three acres of upland ... lying in the Newfield" [PCR 12:134]. On 20 March 1647[/8?], "Samuell Eedy" sold to Experience Mitchell of Duxbury "one acre of marsh meadow" [PCR 12:151].

As early as March 1651 Samuel Eddy had "interest and proprieties in the town's land at Punckateesett over against Road Island," and, on 22 March 1663/4, he and Thomas Savory were jointly recorded as the holders of Lot #3 on "Puncateesett Necke" [PTR 1:36, 63]. On 14 July 1667, Samuel Eddy was granted six acres of meadow "lying at the South Meadow Brook" [PTR 1:89, 281]. On 5 August 1672, "the swamp at Wellingsley lying up the brook" was granted to "the neighbors there," being five men including "Samuell Eedey" [PTR 1:127].

"Samuell Eedey" was one of five men "desiring some proportions of land to accommodate them for their posterities, the Court giveth liberty unto them to look out a tract of land for that purpose, and if found convenient it shall be confirmed unto them for the ends aforesaid," 7 June 1659 [PCR 3:164], and was in the list of those permitted to "look out some accommodations of land, as being the first born children of this government," 3 June 1662 [PCR 4:19].

On 20 February 1662, Thomas Savory of Plymouth, planter, deeded to Samuel Eddy of Plymouth, tailor, "all that his whole right part and portion of the land belonging to the town of Plymouth aforesaid commonly called and known by the name of Punckateesett, and places adjacent lying over against Road Iland," in exchange for "a parcel of upland and meadow belonging to the said Samuell Eedey lying at the four mile brook in the township of Plymouth aforesaid, as also a parcel of upland being six acres lying and being at or near Fresh Lake in the township of Plymouth" [MD 17:244-45, transcribing PCLR 2:2:111].

On 24 March 1662, "Samuell Eedey senior" of Plymouth, tailor, granted "unto his two sons viz: Zacariah Eedey and Obadiah Eedey all that his share lot and portion of land which he hath in the land granted and confirmed by the court in June last past before the date hereof, unto sundry persons, lying near unto Namassakett," to be equally divided between them, reserving "unto his own use six acres of the upland of the said lot of land," this six acres to belong to sons Zachariah and Obadiah at his death, and that they permit him to winter three cows on their share of the land; "it was mutually agreed before the ratification of the premises by and between the said Samuell Eedey and Zachariah Eedey that in case Caleb Eedey shall desire a quarter part of the abovesaid land he shall have it"; acknowledged 26 February 1672 [MD 18:34-35, transcribing PCLR 2:2:116; see also MD 18:37].

On 7 March 1671[/2], Samuel Eddy of Plymouth, tailor, sold to Steven Bryant Senior of Plymouth, husbandman, "all that my one share of land be it more or less divided and undivided that I have in a certain share or tract of land called the Major's Purchase lying at or near Namassakeesett Pond"; acknowledged by Samuel Eddy and Elizabeth his wife on the same day [PCLR 3:217].

On 16 February 1673/4, the town of Plymouth noted that "land which Samuell Ryder bought of Samuell Eedey lying at Mannomett Ponds" was still common land, according to the records searched [PTR 1:138].

BIRTH: Baptized Cranbrook, Kent, 15 May 1608, son of William and Mary (Fosten) Eddy [Eddy Gen 22].
DEATH: Swansea 12 November 1688 "in his 87th year" [*sic*] [PChR 262].
MARRIAGE: By 1637 Elizabeth ____. She died at Swansea on 24 May 1689 "in her 82nd year at the end of it" [PChR 265]. (Elizabeth has been called sister of Thomas Savory of Plymouth, based on relationships stated in deeds [Eddy Gen 22]. Unfortunately for this argument, one of these deeds does not state the connection; the deed from Thomas Savory to Samuel Eddy of 20 February 1662 does not refer to Eddy as "brother-in-law" [MD 17:244-45; PCLR 2:2:111]. The later deed, by the widow of Thomas, does refer to "our brother-in-law Samuel Eddy" [PCLR 4:311], so the identification certainly remains possible. Note also that Eddy and Savory were granted land jointly in 1664 [PTR 1:63], although these lots were all granted to pairs of individuals, not necessarily related.)
CHILDREN:
    i   JOHN EDDY, b. Plymouth 25 December 1637 (calc.) [PCR 2:82]; m. by 1659 Hepzibah Doggett (eldest known child b. 3 May 1659 [Gen Adv 3:84]), daughter of JOHN DOGGETT {1630, Watertown} [GMB 1:568-70].

ii ZACHARIAH EDDY, b. about 1639 [PCR 2:112-13]; m. (1) Plymouth 7 May 1663 Alice Padduck [PVR 663], who d. Swansea 24 September 1692 [SwVR 212]; m. (2) after 1692 Abigail (_____) Smith, widow of Jeremiah/Dermot Smith (in his will of 4 November 1718, Zachariah Eddy named wife Abigail, and, in her will of 2 January 1720, she named her Smith children [Eddy Gen 34, 37, citing BrPR 3:488, 693]).

iii CALEB EDDY, b. about 1643 [PCLR 2:1:39]; m. Swansea 6 December 1671 Elizabeth Bullock [SwVR 22].

iv OBADIAH EDDY, b. say 1645; m. by 1669 Bennet Ellis, daughter of John and Elizabeth (Freeman) Ellis [NEHGR 119:172-73].

v HANNAH EDDY, b. Plymouth 23 June 1647 [PCR 8:4]; no further record.

ASSOCIATIONS: Brother of JOHN EDDY of Watertown [PM 189], of Abigail (Eddy) Benjamin, wife of JOHN BENJAMIN {1632, Cambridge} [GMB 1:160-64], and of Anna (Eddy) Wines, wife of BARNABAS WINES {1634, Watertown} [Eddy Gen 13-22]. Relation to John Eddy of Taunton unknown [Eddy Gen 879], but this John Eddy married Susannah Padduck, sister of the Alice Padduck who married Zachariah, son of Samuel Eddy.

COMMENTS: There is no passenger list for the *Handmaid* in 1630, but inasmuch as Samuel Eddy was certainly in Plymouth by 1630 [PCR 12:18] and his brother John Eddy is explicitly stated to have come on that vessel [WP 2:319], we conclude that Samuel Eddy also came to New England on the *Handmaid*.

On 10 January 1632/3, "Thomas Brian, the servant of Samuell Eedy," was punished for running away [PCR 1:7].

On 3 April 1645, "Samuell Eddy hath put his son, John Eddy, to dwell with Francis Goulder, and Katherne, his wife, until he shall accomplish the age of xxi years, (being seven years of age the xxvth of December last past,) the said Francis, and Katherne his wife, finding unto the said John, their servant, meat, drink, and apparel during the said term" [PCR 2:82-83].

On 2 March 1646/7, "[w]hereas Samuell Edeth, & Elizabeth, his wife, of the town of Plim[outh] aforesaid, having many children, & by reason of many wants lying upon them, so as they are not able to bring them up as they desire, and out of the good respect they bear to Mr. John Browne, of Rehoboth, one of the Assistants of this government, did both of them jointly desire that he, the said Mr. Browne, would take Zachery, their son, being of the age of seven years, & bring him up in his employment of husbandry, or any business he shall see meet for the good of their child till he come to the age of one & twenty years," which Browne agreed to do [PCR 2:112-13].

On 4 March 1652, Samuel Eddy and his wife Elizabeth made a similar deal with Mr. John Browne for their son Caleb "being of the age of nine years" [MD 2:30-31, transcribing PCLR 2:1:39].

On 7 October 1651, the grand jury presented "Elizabeth Eeddy, Seni[or], of the town of Plym[outh], for laboring, that is to say, for wringing and hanging out clothes, on the Lord's day, in time of public exercise" [PCR 2:173]. On 1 May 1660, "Elizabeth Eedey was summoned to this Court, and appeared, to make answer for her travelling on the Lord's day from Plymouth to Boston; and affirmed that she was necessitated to go on that day, in regard that Mistris Saffin was very weak and sent for her, with an earnest desire to see her in her weakness, with some other pleas of like nature. The Court considering some circumstances in her answer, although they saw not a sufficient excuse for her fact therein, saw cause to admonish her, and so she was discharged of the Court" [PCR 3:186].

Because Samuel Eddy was designated "senior" in one record (24 March 1662 [MD 18:34-35]) and Elizabeth Eddy was also called "senior" once (7 October 1651 [PCR 2:173]), the suggestion has been made that the couple had children named Samuel and Elizabeth, but there is no other evidence for this.

Samuel Eddy appeared in three lists, which appear to be compilations of those who had voted in Plymouth town meetings, about 1646, 1647 and 1668 [PTR 1:22, 25, 101]. Samuel Eddy regularly hired one of the cows that were maintained for the town's poor [PTR 1:4, 19, 20, 27, 28].

_____ ELY

From Bradford's list of persons on the *Mayflower*: "There were also other two seamen hired to stay a year here in the country, William Trevor, and one Ely. But when their time was out they both returned" [Bradford 443].

THOMAS ENGLISH

From Bradford's list of persons on the *Mayflower*: "John Allerton and Thomas English were both hired, the latter to go master of a shallop here.... But they both died here before the ship returned" (i.e., during the winter of 1620/1) [Bradford 443].

COMMENTS: Dexter claimed that a Thomas England who witnessed a marriage at Leiden in 1613 was the same as this Thomas English, and he was followed in this by Banks [Dexter 614; English Homes 53].

JOHN FAUNCE

ORIGIN: Unknown.
MIGRATION: 1623 on the *Anne*.
FIRST RESIDENCE: Plymouth.

FREEMAN: In the 1633 list of Plymouth freemen "John Phance" appears in the midst of many persons admitted on 1 January 1632/3 [PCR 1:4]. In the 7 March 1636/7 list of Plymouth freemen [PCR 1:52]. In Plymouth section of 1639 list of Plymouth Colony freemen [PCR 8:174].
EDUCATION: His inventory included "an old Bible" valued at 6s.
OFFICES: Plymouth petit jury, 6 March 1637/8, 4 September 1638 [PCR 7:8, 9].

In Plymouth section of 1643 Plymouth Colony list of men able to bear arms [PCR 8:189].
ESTATE: In the 1623 Plymouth land division Manasseh Kempton and John Faunce were jointly granted two acres as 1623 passengers on the *Anne* [PCR 12:5]. In the 1627 Plymouth cattle division "John Fance" was the eleventh name in the first company, led by Francis Cooke [PCR 12:9].

John Faunce was one of the Purchasers of 1627 [PCR 2:177].

Assessed 9s. in the 25 March 1633 and 27 March 1634 Plymouth tax lists [PCR 1:10, 28].

Allotted hay ground, 14 March 1635/6, 20 March 1636/7 [PCR 1:40, 56].

On 5 January 1637[/8], "Manasseth Kempton of New Plymouth, yeoman, doth acknowledge that he hath freely and absolutely given and confirmed unto John Faunce all that lot of land whereon the said John Faunce doth now dwell containing twenty acres or thereabouts" [PCR 12:26].

With seventeen other men, granted six acres of meadow as his share "in the South Meadows towards Aggawam, Colebrook Meadows," 2 November 1640 [PCR 1:166].

On 1 November 1647, George Bonum sold to John Faunce "that lot of land that lyeth next me at the Eel River with the housing and fencings thereabouts"; Manasseh and Jane Kempton witnessed the deed [MD 10:17-18, citing PCLR 2:1:161].

The inventory of John Faunce, taken 15 December 1653, totalled £27 10s. 6d., with no real estate included; the most valuable item listed was "a weaver's loom, stays and tackling," valued at £2 10s. [PCPR 1:120]. On 7 March 1653/4, "letters of administration was granted unto Patience Faunce, to administer on the estate of John Faunce, deceased" [PCR 3:46].

On 29 October 1668, "Thomas Faunce appeared in the Court, and being of full age was taken notice of by the Court, and owned and acknowledged to be the right heir apparent to the lands of John Faunce, Senior, sometimes of Plymouth, in New England, deceased" [PCR 5:6].

BIRTH: By about 1608 (based on estimated date of marriage).
DEATH: Plymouth 29 November 1653 [NEHGR 116:188-89, reinterpreting PCR 8:16, which gives the year as 1654].
MARRIAGE: By about 1633 Patience Morton, daughter of GEORGE MORTON [PM 336]. She married (2) after 9 June 1660 Thomas Whitney [MD 14:234; NEHGR 116:189]. She died at Plymouth on 16 August 1691 in "the 77 year of her age" [MD 16:62; PVR 135].
CHILDREN:
  i   PRISCILLA FAUNCE, b. about 1633 (d. Plymouth 15 May 1707 "near 74 years of age" [PVR 136]); m. by 1653 Joseph Warren, son of RICHARD WARREN [PM 477] (eldest known child b. Plymouth 23 September 1653 [PCR 8:33]; in his will of 4 May 1689, Joseph Warren requested "my brother Thomas Faunce" to be helpful to his widow in settling the estate [MD 4:16]).
  ii MARY FAUNCE, b. say 1638; m. Plymouth 15 July 1658 William Harlow [PCR 8:21].
  iii PATIENCE FAUNCE, b. say 1641; m. Plymouth 20 November 1661 John Holmes [PCR 8:22], son of JOHN HOLMES [PM 265].
  iv SARAH FAUNCE, b. say 1643; m. (1) Plymouth 26 February 1662[/3] Edward Doty [PCR 8:23], son of EDWARD DOTY [PM 177]; m. (2) Plymouth 26 April 1693 John Buck [PVR 86].
  v   THOMAS FAUNCE, b. about 1647; m. Plymouth 13 December 1672 Jane Nelson [PCR 8:33].

vi   ELIZABETH FAUNCE, b. 23 March 1648/9 [PCR 8:5]; d. Plymouth 3 March 1649/50 [PCR 8:8].
vii   MERCY FAUNCE, b. 10 April 1651 [PCR 8:12]; m. Plymouth 29 December 1667 Nathaniel Holmes [PCR 8:31], probably son of JOHN HOLMES [PM 265].
viii   JOSEPH FAUNCE, b. 14 May 1653 [PCR 8:15]; m. Plymouth 3 January 1677[/8] Judith Rickard [PCR 8:68; NGSQ 30:136-37, 184].

ASSOCIATIONS: The defective entry in the 1623 Plymouth land division has "Manasseh & John Faunce" receiving two acres as passengers on the *Anne* in 1623, but "Kempton" has been omitted after "Manasseh." This has given rise to references to a non-existent "Manasseh Faunce" (see Phantom File), but when corrected is suggestive in other ways. Within four years after their association at the time of the land division, Manasseh Kempton had married the widow of GEORGE MORTON, and then six years after that Faunce married Kempton's stepdaughter. Faunce was nearly two decades younger than Kempton, and it may be that he came over in 1623 as Kempton's servant.

COMMENTS: Banks derived John Faunce from Stow Maries, Essex, citing only "Banks Mss." [Topo Dict 52]. DeForest, however, stated that Banks also suggested the neighboring parish of Purleigh, Essex, "merely because the name Faunce is an unusual one and he was only able to find it in and around Perleigh" [Moore Anc 244]. Apparently no one has explored this clue any further.

Savage created an extra child by interpreting the 29 November 1654 death date as applying to a non-existent son John, rather than to the immigrant himself.

BIBLIOGRAPHIC NOTE: A good account of John Faunce was published by DeForest in his usual meticulous way [Moore Anc 244-47]. Rachel Barclay added some useful notes in 1962 [NEHGR 116:188-91].

THOMAS FLAVELL

In the 1623 Plymouth division of land, "Thomas Flavell & his son" were granted two acres as passengers on the *Fortune* (1621), and "Goodwife Flavell" one acre as a passenger on the *Anne* (1623) [PCR 1:5].

COMMENTS: As this family is not found in the 1627 division of cattle, or in any other New England records, we must assume that they all died, or, more likely, returned to England.

Willison gave Flavell's wife's name as Elizabeth, and was followed in this by Robert S. Wakefield, in his analysis of the 1623 land division [Saints 449; MQ 40:58], but there is no documentary support for this name. Elsewhere Flavell's wife's name is given as Anne [Gen Bull 1:173], but this would seem to be a confusion with the name of the ship on which she arrived.

MOSES FLETCHER

ORIGIN: Leiden, Holland.
MIGRATION: 1620 on the *Mayflower.*
FIRST RESIDENCE: Plymouth.

OCCUPATION: Smith [Leiden Pilgrims 91].

BIRTH: By about 1564 (based on date of first marriage).
DEATH: Plymouth early 1621 [Bradford 447].
MARRIAGE: (1) St. Peter, Sandwich, Kent, 30 October 1589 Mary Evans [NEHGR 128:161]. She died between April 1609 (baptism of last known child) and December 1613 (remarriage of husband).

(2) Leiden, Holland, 21 December 1613 [NS] Sarah (_____) Denby, widow of William Denby [Plooij XVII; Leiden Pilgrims 91; NEHGR 128:161]; no further record.

CHILDREN (all baptisms from St. Peter, Sandwich [NEHGR 128:162]):
With first wife
  i   MARY FLETCHER, bp. 4 January 1589/90; no further record.
  ii JOHN FLETCHER, b. say 1592; m. Leiden 5 December 1618 [NS] Josina Sachariasdaughter [Leiden Pilgrims 91; NEHGR 128:163].
  iii CATHERINE FLETCHER, bp. 1 September 1594; no further record.
  iv RICHARD FLETCHER, bp. 2 January 1596/7; no further record.
  v   PRISCILLA FLETCHER, bp. 24 March 1599/1600; m. (1) Leiden 4 April 1626 [NS] Thomas Coit [Leiden Pilgrims 91]; m. (2) Leiden 1 June 1637 [NS] Help/Solomon Terry

	[Leiden Pilgrims 92; NEHGR 128:162]; m. (3) Leiden 19 July 1652 [NS] Jan Jans Vermout [Leiden Pilgrims 92].
vi	MOSES FLETCHER, bp. 10 October 1602; bur. 21 April 1603.
vii	ELIZABETH FLETCHER, bp. 8 April 1604; m. (1) Casper Barnaart; m. (2) Leiden 21 May 1636 [NS] Michiel Voorchoren [Leiden Pilgrims 91; NEHGR 128:163].
viii	JANE FLETCHER, bp. 8 February 1606/7; no further record.
ix	MOSES FLETCHER, bp. 2 April 1609; no further record.
x	JUDITH FLETCHER, bur. 6 November 1609.

COMMENTS: Moses Fletcher was employed as sexton of St. Peter, Sandwich, for a number of years in the first decade of the seventeenth century. He was excommunicated from that church three times in 1609 and 1610. On two of these occasions the offense was the participation in an illegal burial, and on the second of these two occasions the person buried was Judith Fletcher, daughter of Moses [NEHGR 153:407-10].

According to William Bradford's accounting of 1651, Moses Fletcher sailed on the *Mayflower*, signed the Compact, and "died soon after ... arrival in the general sickness," leaving "no posterity here" [Bradford 443, 447].

Robert S. Wakefield unearthed almost everything we know about the career of Moses Fletcher in Leiden, and most of this sketch has been gleaned from his article ["The Search for the Descendants of Moses Fletcher," NEHGR 128:161-69]. This article traces some lines of descent beyond the second generation, and suggests the possibility of tracing living descendants. Since this article appeared, a few descendants have been admitted to the Mayflower Society [MQ 53:289, 61:26-27].

EDMOND FLOOD

In the 1623 Plymouth land division, Edmond Flood was granted one acre as a passenger on the *Anne* [PCR 12:5]. In the 1627 Plymouth division of cattle, "Edward Fludd" was entered as the twelfth person in the tenth company, but his name was then crossed out and replaced by Robert Bartlett [PCR 12:12].

COMMENTS: Since Flood's name was entered in the 1627 list but then crossed out, and does not appear in any other New England record, he must have died or departed Plymouth about this time.

RALPH FOGG

ORIGIN: London.
MIGRATION: 1633.
FIRST RESIDENCE: Plymouth.
REMOVES: Salem 1634.
RETURN TRIPS: In England from late 1647 to early 1649. Returned to England permanently after 1652.

OCCUPATION: Skinner. Made free of the Skinners Company of London, 16 October 1623 (courtesy of Leslie Mahler). Engaged in the beaver trade in New England, 3 December 1645 [Aspinwall 11-12].
CHURCH MEMBERSHIP: Admission to Salem church prior to 3 September 1634 implied by freemanship. "Ralph Fogge" is in the list of Salem church members compiled in late 1636, with the later annotation "excommunicated" [SChR 5].
FREEMAN: In 1633 list of Plymouth freemen, "Raph Fogge" appears between group made free 1 January 1632/3 and group made free 1 January 1633/4, and then the name was crossed out [PCR 1:4].

Massachusetts Bay, 3 September 1634 [MBCR 1:369].
EDUCATION: His services as clerk of Salem court indicate considerable education.
OFFICES: Ordered to collect fines by Salem court, 27 December 1636 [EQC 1:4].

On 1 January 1645/6, "Mr. Ralph Fogge to have ten pounds out of the fines yearly for his attendance on the court, besides his fees, which 'do of right belong to his places of trust'" [EQC 1:91]. These positions included secretary of the court from 1640 to 1647 [EQC 1:19, 52, 62, 68, 73, 76, 81, 119] and marshal of Salem in 1647 [EQC 1:115]. (See SAMUEL ARCHER {1630, Salem} for discussion of the office of marshal [GMB 1:50-53; GMN 10:321-22, 328].)

On "9:5:1647 [9 July 1647], Rafe Fogge presented for speaking falsely and dealing corruptly in his place, taking pay of diverse persons and demanding it again; and some having paid twice for one and the same thing, he demanded it the third time; ... also for forging a paper that he said before was torn out of Mr. Gutch's book" [EQC 1:132-33]. The court ordered on 11 July 1649 that "Mr. Fogge to appear at next session of court, upon complaint of the clerk and marshal that the account said Fogge gave in at his departure contained many errors" [EQC 1:172]. On 13 November 1649, the court ordered "Mr. Fogge to answer to debts given in under his hand as due the country which diverse persons have denied to be due. Some persons appeared before the court and denied the whole and others a part of what was charged to them. Mr. Fogge to pay the costs of the twenty-three persons who appeared in court, to settle the accounts of all who denied that they owed the country" [EQC 1:180].

Salem town clerk, 1636 to 1647 [STR 1:6, 18]. On 6 February 1636/7, the town of Salem ordered that, in the absence of a "print house" in town, all those who had questions about town orders should "repair to Mr. Raph Fogge who keepeth the records of said orders, where they may satisfy themselves in every particular order as aforesaid" [STR 1:36]. On 20 February 1636/7, it was ordered by the freemen of Salem "that Mr. Ralph Fogg in consideration of his pains in entering the lands that are granted to the inhabitants into the town book for recording of them shall have for every 20 acres 9d., for every 30 acres 12d., for 40 [acres] 15d., for 50 [acres] & so upward 1s. 6d." [STR 1:37]. On 3 April 1637, "the order concerning repairing unto me Raph Fogg for the viewing of town orders is repealed." On the same day the following item was entered and then lined out: "Whereas Mr. Ralph Fogg hath heretofore been taken off his own employments especially in planting time to attend upon the town occasions to his great prejudice, it was agreed that what I did for the town that I should be paid & it being so formerly ordered this preceding order is needless" [STR 1:42]. (See also STR 1:43, 48, and for his signature see STR 1:46.) On 17 May 1647, Salem selectmen ordered that "William Auger shall take notice of births & deaths & marriages according to an agreement of court conferred upon Raph Fogge of Salem who now we conceive unfit for that place" and that "Samuell Archard shall be marshall of the Court of Salem" [STR 1:148].

Salem committee on fustian spinsters, 14 September 1640 [STR 1:106]. Fenceviewer, 11 October 1640/1, 4 April 1641 [STR 1:108, 111]. Committee on providing for blacksmith, 4 December 1643 [STR 1:121]. Committee to audit constables' accounts, 22 September 1645 [STR 1:137, 145].

Admitted to Ancient and Honorable Artillery Company in 1644 [HAHAC 1:140-41]. On 30 June 1646, "Mr. Ralph Fogg excused from training" [EQC 1:96].

ESTATE: On 1 July 1633, "[t]he watering place and thereabout" in Plymouth was allotted to Mr. Fogg for mowing [PCR 1:14].

On 28 October 1633, Plymouth court ordered that "a misted that was granted formerly to Richard Warren, deceased, & forfeited by a late order, for want of building, the said misted was granted to Mr. Raph Fogg & his heirs forever, provided the said Raph within twelve months build a dwelling house upon the same" [PCR 1:18]. On 2 January

1633/4, Plymouth court ordered that "the small parcel of land lying in form of an island upon Newharbour Marsh, on the north side the river, & called by the name of Susanna, be granted to Raph Fogge & his heirs forever" [PCR 1:24].

In the Plymouth tax list of 27 March 1634 "Raph Fogge" was assessed 12s. [PCR 1:28].

In the 1636 Salem land division "Raph Fogg" was granted eighty acres in the freeman's section [STR 1:20, 26]. In the 25 December 1637 division of meadow at Salem "Mr. Fogg" received one acre of marsh, for a household of six [STR 1:103].

On 9 January 1636/7, it was "agreed for the avoiding of absurdities and for the doing of justice that Raph Fogg should have five acres of the eight acres long since appointed, & now lately by Mr. Connant & Jno. Woodbury measured out, as part of eight acres that they measured where of Raph Fogg is to let them have" [STR 1:28]. This incomplete entry was crossed out, and on the same day "there is granted to Ralph Fogge 5 acres of land part of his ten acres, beyond Castle Hill near the South River" [STR 1:29]. On 25 December 1637, "granted to Ralph Fogge 8 acres of meadow lying in the Great Marsh" [STR 1:62]. On 5 February 1643/4, granted to "Raph Fogge the swamp next to William Lord's ground excepting that part of it which is granted to other men" [STR 1:124].

On 11 March 1645/6, Robert Moulton and Michael Shafflyn, agents for Mr. Townsend Bishop, sold to "Mr. Ralph Fogg of Salem ... the new messuage or dwelling house of the said Mr. Bishop's standing by the rocks near Captain Hathorne's house in Salem" [ELR 1:2]. On 2 July 1650, "Raph Fogg" entered his "caveat against all bargains made since his troubles (without his consent) of any of his lands or houses" [ELR 1:7]. On 24 June 1651, "Mr. Ralf Fogg" sued George Ropes for "detaining an acre of marsh to the value of £5. Verdict for plaintiff, his title to the land good" [EQC 1:229].

On 20 March 1656[/7], Thomas Venner of London, cooper, sold to "Ralph Fogg of London, skinner, a certain parcel of land ... being part of that plot of land whereon I built my warehouse or workhouse in Boston ... upon which parcel of land aforesaid, the said Ralph Fogg did build when I built up my warehouse"; on 1 March 1656[/7], "Ralph Fog of London skinner" assigned this parcel of land to John Lowle of Boston, cooper [SLR 2:302, 315a].

On 28 May 1674, John Fogg, Ezekiel Fogg and David Fogg, "being the sons & all the children of Ralph Fogg, citizen & skinner of London, formerly of New England, & late of Plimouth, in the County of Devon, in old England, deceased," being in Boston, received a letter from their mother, Susanna Fogg, widow of Ralph Fogg, dated 21 March last, telling of the death of their father Ralph Fogg about the 15th of March last, and passing on Ralph Fogg's wish that son John should have his lands in Salem, son Ezekiel his share of Sagadahoc Patent, & son David his land at Plymouth, and the brothers agreed to this [ELR 4:79].

On 2 January 1674/5, "John Fogg of Barnstable in the county of Devon, gent., son & heir to Ralph Fogg, citizen & skinner of London, formerly of Salem in New England, & late of Plimouth in Old England, deceased," sold to "my brother Ezekiel Fogg, citizen & skinner of London & now of New England, merchant ... one small tract of land situate & lying in the town of Salem, near the meetinghouse, ... formerly belonging to Mr. Ralph Fogg citizen & skinner of London late deceased," one acre and a half, and one acre in the common commonly called Capt. Trask's plain [ELR 4:123]. On 25 May 1676, "Ezekiell Fogg, citizen & skinner of London & now of New England, merchant," sold to John Maston Jr. of Salem, carpenter, "one small tract of land situate & lying in the town of Salem, near the meetinghouse, ... formerly belonging to Mr. Ralph Fogg citizen & skinner of London late deceased"; mention was made of "Anna, wife of Ezekiel" [ELR 5:21].

BIRTH: About 1600 (deposed in 1640, probably in November, "aged about forty years" [Lechford 335]).
DEATH: Plymouth, England, about 15 March 1673/4 [ELR 4:79].
MARRIAGE: By about 1628 Susanna Draper, daughter of Edward and Susanna (Banks) Draper (in his will of 20 May 1630, "John Bancks citizen and mercer of London" included bequests to "the children of my sister Susan Draper," to "my sister Dame Catherine Barnardiston," to "Susan Foge, the wife of Raffe Foge, the daughter of my sister Susan Draper," to "John Foge her son" and to "my sister Susan Draper the wife of Edward Draper, girdler, and her two daughters Susan Foge and Mary Draper" [Waters 653-54, citing PCC 84 Scroope]; in her will of 25 February 1632/3, "Dame Katherine Barnardiston" included bequests to "Susan Fogg and Mary Draper, daughters of my sister Susan Draper," to "Ralfe Fogg the husband of my niece" and to "John Fogg her eldest son" [Waters 742-43, citing PCC 25 Russell]). "Susana Fogge" is in the list of Salem church members compiled late in 1636, with the later annotation "removed" [SChR 6]. She was living at Plymouth, England, on 21 March 1673/4 [ELR 4:79].

CHILDREN:
  i JOHN FOGG, b. by about 1628 (sold land at Salem 20 February 1648/9 [ELR 1:7, 8]; one parcel sold "with the consent of his mother," but no consent mentioned in sale of another parcel the same day); m. by 1 August 1665 Grace _____ (living at Barnstaple, England, at the time) [ELR 1:118]; living at Barnstaple, England, 2 January 1674/5 [ELR 4:123].
  ii EZEKIEL FOGG, bp. Salem 1 April 1638 [SChR 16]; m. by 25 May 1676 Ann _____; living in New England 25 May 1676 [ELR 5:21].
  iii DAVID FOGG, bp. Salem 15 March 1639/40 [SChR 17]; living 2 January 1674/5 [ELR 4:79].

COMMENTS: In 1981 Eugene Stratton noted that Ralph Fogg and JOHN STRATTON {1628, Cape Porpoise} [GMB 3:1782-85] were business partners in New England, and that they were very likely the "Straton and Fogge" who were investors in the *Friendship* and the *White Angel* on their voyages to Plymouth [NEHGR 135:288-89; Lechford 333-36; Bradford 390].

On 28 February 1649/50, "Ralfe Fogge, for lying in face of open congregation on a Lord's day, slandering the church, and after the meeting was ended complaining to the honored Governor of wrong that he had done him both in church and court, saying that the Governor was the grand jury, and the grand jury, the Governor. To confess it next Lord's day as follows: 'I Ralfe Fogge do acknowledge that I did very wickedly and sinfully in that I did in the face of the congregation deny that either the church or any one particular member did ever make known to me any one particular for the which the church proceeded against me the which in saying I did very falsely slander the church of Christ and that I did very sinfully in saying that the Governor had done me wrong and that he was the grand jury and the grand jury was him for all which I am very sorry.' If he refuse to make this confession, ordered that he stand at the whipping post half an hour after lecture with a paper in his hat on which in capital letters shall be written, 'For slandering of the church and for abusing of the Governor.' Mr. Downing and Capt. Hathorne to see it done, and in case he 'stands not quietly with his back to the post that then the constable is to bind him to it'" [EQC 1:185-86].

____ FORD

ORIGIN: Unknown.
MIGRATION: 1621 on the *Fortune*.
FIRST RESIDENCE: Plymouth.

ESTATE: In the 1623 Plymouth land division "Widow Foord" received four acres as a 1621 passenger on the *Fortune* [PCR 12:5]. By the time of the 1627 Plymouth cattle division the widow Ford had married PETER BROWN, and she appeared as the fifth person in the fifth company, and her children John Ford and Martha Ford as the seventh and eighth persons in that company [PCR 12:11].

BIRTH: By about 1592 (based on estimated date of marriage).
DEATH: Plymouth between 11 December 1621 (Winslow's letter [Young's Pilgrim Fathers 235-36]) and late 1623 (wife appears as "Widow Foord" in land division).
MARRIAGE: By about 1617 Martha ____. She married (2) Plymouth by 1626 PETER BROWN [PM 82]. She had two children with Peter Brown and died by 1630 [TAG 42:39-40].
CHILDREN:
    i   JOHN FORD, b. say 1617; d. (or left Plymouth) between 5 January 1640/1 [PCR 2:6] and 1643 (not in 1643 Plymouth list of men able to bear arms) [TAG 42:39].
    ii   MARTHA FORD, b. about 1619 (d. Plymouth 20 December 1683 "in her 64th year" [PChR 1:250]); m. Plymouth 29 October 1640 William Nelson [PCR 1:153; TAG 56:32-35].
    iii Son FORD, b. Plymouth 9 November 1621; d. soon.

COMMENTS: The grant to the family of four acres in 1623 is subject to a number of interpretations. Barclay assumed that it encompassed the widow and three children, the husband having died by that date. Wakefield held instead that the grant was for the widow Ford, her deceased husband, and children John and Martha, the child born in 1621 shortly after landing having already died [MQ 40:55]. A third possibility is that the son John *was* the child born immediately after landing in 1621, and that the grant was for the two parents and the only two children of those parents. This would make John Ford only nineteen when he was granted land in 1640 [PCR 1:165], so if a person receiving a grant of land in Plymouth at this time was necessarily twenty-one, then this arrangement could not work.

BIBLIOGRAPHIC NOTE: In 1966 Florence Barclay treated this family definitively, and the conclusions presented here on the Ford children and what is known about the immigrant head of family follow that article [TAG 42:35-42]. Barclay's most important conclusions were that the husband of Martha and the father of these three children sailed on the *Fortune* and arrived at Plymouth where he soon died, and that William Ford of Marshfield was not a part of this family.

Robert S. Wakefield also wrote about this family, with the emphasis on the daughter Martha and her Nelson descendants [TAG 56:32-35].

EDWARD FOSTER

ORIGIN: Unknown.
MIGRATION: 1632.
FIRST RESIDENCE: Scituate.

CHURCH MEMBERSHIP: Joined Scituate church as member #10, 8 January 1634/5 [NEHGR 9:279]. Invested as deacon of Scituate church, 22 February 1637/8 [NEHGR 10:37].
FREEMAN: Admitted 3 January 1636/7 [PCR 1:48]. In list of 7 March 1636/7 [PCR 1:53]. In Scituate section of 1639 list of Plymouth Colony freemen (with annotation "dead") [PCR 8:175].
EDUCATION: Signed deed of 2 June 1643 [PCR 12:183-84]. His inventory included "3 Bibles with other books" valued at £6 [MD 6:249].
OFFICES: Deputy for Scituate to Plymouth General Court, 4 June 1639, 2 June 1640, 1 June 1641 [PCR 1:126, 155, 2:16].

Plymouth grand jury, 7 March 1636/7 [PCR 1:54]. Petit jury, 3 January 1636/7, 4 September 1638, 3 March 1639/40 [PCR 1:96, 7:4, 9, 16].

Committee to assess charges for sending soldiers against the Pequots, 7 June 1637 [PCR 1:62]. Scituate member of colony committee to survey highways, 5 March 1638/9 [PCR 1:117]. Committee to lay out lands at Scituate, 30 November 1640 [PCR 1:168].

In Scituate section of 1643 Plymouth list of men able to bear arms [PCR 8:191]. His inventory included "1 fowling piece, 1 sword & belt" valued at £1 [MD 6:249].
ESTATE: Assessed 9s. in Plymouth tax of 25 March 1633 and the same amount on the tax list of 27 March 1634 [PCR 1:11, 28].

Edward Foster was one of nine men who had built houses at Scituate prior to September 1634 [NEHGR 10:42].

As one of the freeman of Scituate who petitioned Plymouth court for a grant of land, he was included among those who were given "all that upland & neck of land lying between the North & South Rivers," along with some meadow, 1 January 1637/8 [PCR 1:72]. One of a committee of eight Scituate men granted "a plantation called Seppekann, and the lands thereabouts, for the seating of a township for a congregation there," 22 January 1638/9 [PCR 1:108]. (These two grants were reflections of the schism in the Scituate church that led to the departure of Rev. John Lothrop and his party for Barnstable later in 1639.)

On 2 June 1643, Edward Foster of Scituate sold to George Russell of Hingham "my lot of land both marsh land & upland lying in Scituate at the first herring brook ... both upland be it sixteen, eighteen or twenty acres more or less and marsh land be it ten acres more or less" [PCR 12:183-84].

In his will, dated 24 November 1643, "Edward Foster" bequeathed to "my loving wife Lettice Foster (whom I do make my sole executrix)" all cattle and all moveables ("except my books which I dispose of to my son Timothy Foster"), and also "the use of my house or housing and all my lands ... which lyeth at three several places, one at the North River, one at the Stony Brook, one at the Second Cliff" until "my son Timothy Foster" is twenty-one, and then he to get one-third, and another third to go to "the infant yet unborn whether it be male or female," and the remaining third to go to son Timothy at the death of wife Lettice; if both children die without issue then "I shall leave the ordering of it to the discretion of those faithful overseers ... Mr. Tymothy Hatherley[,] father Richard Sillis[,] Edmond Eddenden & brother Isack Robinson" [MD 6:248-49, citing PCPR 1:60].

The inventory of the estate of Edward Foster, taken 22 February 1643/4, totalled £42 3s., including no real estate [MD 6:249-50, citing PCPR 1:60].

On 5 June 1644, "Mr. Tymothy Hatherley is authorized by the Court to take the oaths of the witnesses for Edward Foster's will, and the executrix her oath to the inventory, and to return them to the Court, that they may be recorded" [PCR 2:73]. On 20 August 1644, "Mr. Tymothy Hatherley, Richard Sillis, Edmond Eddenden deposed by order of Court to the last will & testament of Edward Foster, and a true inventory exhibited upon their oaths this Court" [PCR 2:75].

BIRTH: By about 1610 (based on date of marriage).
DEATH: Between 24 November 1643 (date of will) and 22 February 1643/4 (date of inventory).

MARRIAGE: At Mr. Cudworth's [Scituate] by Captain Standish 8 April 1635 Lettice Hanford [NEHGR 9:286], baptized at Alverdiscott, Devonshire, 8 June 1617, daughter of Jeffrey and Eglin (Hatherley) (Downe) Hanford [TAG 17:49-50]. She was admitted to Scituate church (as "Goody Foster") 25 December 1636 [NEHGR 9:280]. She married (2) by about 1650 Edward Jenkins [Stevens-Miller 485-86].

CHILDREN:

   i   TIMOTHY FOSTER, bp. Scituate 7 March 1635/6 [NEHGR 9:281]; bur. there 5 December 1637 [NEHGR 9:285].

   ii   TIMOTHY FOSTER, bp. Scituate 22 April 1638 [NEHGR 9:281]; m. (1) Dorchester 13 October 1663 Ruth (Tileston) Denton, daughter of Thomas Tileston and widow of Richard Denton [DVR 21]; m. (2) Dorchester 9 March 1681[/2?] Relief (Holland) Dowse, daughter of John Holland and widow of John Dowse [DVR 24].

   iii ELIZABETH FOSTER, b. Scituate 1644, posthumously; m. (1) Scituate 9 November 1665 Ephraim Hewett; m. (2) Hingham 17 January 1681/2 James Ray [Hingham Hist 2:359, 3:123].

ASSOCIATIONS: The wife of EDWARD FOSTER was daughter of Eglin (Hatherley) (Downe) (Hanford) Sillis, wife finally of Richard Sillis of Scituate, and sister of TIMOTHY HATHERLEY [GM 2:3:205-7; PM 234; Stevens-Miller 485-89]. The three sisters of Lettice (Hanford) Foster were Susanna (Hanford) Whiston, whose first husband was JOHN WHISTON of Scituate [PM 493], Margaret (Hanford) Robinson, wife of ISAAC ROBINSON of Barnstable [PM 391], and Elizabeth (Hanford) Wade, wife of Nicholas Wade of Scituate, and the brother of these sisters was Thomas Hanford of Norwalk, Connecticut.

COMMENTS: On 7 June 1637, "Edward Foster, of Scituate, for selling less than a Winchester quart for 2d., in regard it was ignorantly done, the fine was assessed but at 12d." [PCR 1:61].

Pope says that Edward Foster moved to Barnstable in 1638/9, with Lothrop and others, but all further records for Foster are in Scituate. Since he was connected by marriage to the family of Timothy Hatherley, his loyalties in that direction were apparently stronger than his loyalties to the church.

Savage states that the Timothy baptized in 1638 died soon and another was born in 1640, but no evidence for this appears.

The marriage in Plymouth on 11 October 1639 of Samuel Tompkins and Lettis Foster is suggestive, but no relation with Edward Foster or his wife is evident [PCR 1:134].

GEORGE FOSTER

In his will of 30 July 1633, SAMUEL FULLER of Plymouth made provision for several young persons from Massachusetts Bay who had been placed in his care after his visit to that area in 1630 [PM 217]. Among these was "George Foster being placed with me upon the same terms by his parents still living at Sagos," he to be restored to his mother [MD 1:25].

COMMENTS: There is no record of a Foster family in Lynn in the early 1630s. Savage suggested that George might belong to the family of Christopher Foster who did reside in Lynn, but there is no record of him in New England prior to his appearance (along with a wife and three children aged five and under) on a 1635 passenger list [Hotten 92-93]. It may be that George Foster and his parents soon left New England without making any further mark on the records. Another possibility is that George Foster's mother had remarried and his parents were a mother and stepfather of a different surname.

EDWARD FULLER

ORIGIN: Leiden, Holland.
MIGRATION: 1620 on the *Mayflower*.
FIRST RESIDENCE: Plymouth.

ESTATE: In the 1623 Plymouth division of land Samuel Fuller Junior received three acres as a passenger on the *Mayflower* [PCR 12:4]. (This allocation would be for himself, and for his mother and father who died at Plymouth during the first winter.)

BIRTH: Baptized Redenhall, Norfolk, 4 September 1575, son of Robert Fuller [NEHGR 55:192].
DEATH: Plymouth shortly after 11 January 1620/1 [Bradford 446].
MARRIAGE: By about 1605 _____ _____. She died at Plymouth shortly after 11 January 1620/1 [Bradford 446].
CHILDREN:
    i   MATTHEW FULLER, b. say 1605; m. by about 1630 Frances _____ [TAG 61:198-99; MF 4:5-6]. (Although he wrote before the demonstration that Matthew was son of Edward, Paul Prindle prepared an excellent account of Matthew

Fuller and his family [*Ancestry of Elizabeth Barrett Gillespie* ... (n.p. 1976), pp. 157-62].)

ii SAMUEL FULLER, b. about 1608; as "Samuell Fuller Junior" he is the third person in the eighth company (and in the household of his uncle Samuel Fuller) in the 1627 Plymouth division of cattle [PCR 12:11]; "Sammell Fowller" appears in the 1633 list of Plymouth freemen, just ahead of those admitted on 1 January 1634/5 [PCR 1:4]; assessed 9s. in the Plymouth tax list of 27 March 1634 [PCR 1:28]; m. Scituate 8 April 1635 Jane Lothrop, daughter of Rev. JOHN LOTHROP {1635, Scituate} [NEHGR 9:286].

ASSOCIATIONS: Brother of SAMUEL FULLER of Leiden and Plymouth.

COMMENTS: The evidence that Edward Fuller resided in Leiden prior to coming to New England was published in 1985 by Jeremy D. Bangs [MQ 51:58, citing "R.A. 79, L, folio 172 verso"].

In his list of passengers on the *Mayflower,* Bradford included "Edward Fuller and his wife, and Samuel their son" [Bradford 442]. In the accounting of the *Mayflower* families made in 1651, Bradford reported that "Edward Fuller and his wife died soon after they came ashore, but their son Samuel is living and married and hath four children or more" [Bradford 446].

The question of the paternity of Matthew Fuller was examined exhaustively by Bruce C. MacGunnigle, Robert M. Sherman and Robert S. Wakefield in 1986, and they came to the conclusion that Matthew was a son of EDWARD FULLER [TAG 61:194-99]. They also noted that the evidence connecting EDWARD FULLER and SAMUEL FULLER to Robert Fuller of Redenhall, Norfolk, is not so strong as might be desired, leaving open the possibility that future research might lead to a different ancestry for the two brothers [TAG 61:194]. Extensive data on the Fullers of Redenhall and vicinity were published in 1901 by Francis H. Fuller [NEHGR 55:192-96, 410-16].

In his third volume treating early settlers on the Penobscot, Philip Howard Gray sets forth a completely new structure for the family of Edward Fuller, including children not previously suspected [*Penobscot Pioneers*, Volume 3 (Camden, Maine, 1993), pp. 62-66]. Gray employs a style of logic and argumentation not normally found in the genealogical literature, and his conclusions are not adopted here.

BIBLIOGRAPHIC NOTE: Bruce C. MacGunnigle has published the definitive treatment of Edward Fuller and his descendants in the fourth volume of the Five Generations Project of the General Society of Mayflower Descendants.

SAMUEL FULLER

ORIGIN: Leiden, Holland.
MIGRATION: 1620 on the *Mayflower*.
FIRST RESIDENCE: Plymouth.

OCCUPATION: Surgeon (see *CHURCH MEMBERSHIP* below). His inventory included "a surgeon's chest with the things belonging to it" valued at £5.
CHURCH MEMBERSHIP: In 1629 Samuel Fuller visited Salem, principally in his role as surgeon, but while there he consulted with Endicott about the organization and practices of the Plymouth church, a discussion that undoubtedly affected the founding of the Salem church in that year [Bradford LB 46-48]. He went on a similar mission to Massachusetts Bay in 1630 [Bradford LB 56-59]. In 1633 Bradford commented on the epidemic that took many of the Plymouth colonists, and specifically "in the end, after he had much helped others, Samuel Fuller who was their surgeon and physician and had been a great help and comfort unto them. As in his faculty, so otherwise being a deacon of the church, a man godly and forward to do good, being much missed after his death" [Bradford 260].
FREEMAN: "Samuel Fuller senior" appears early in the 1633 list of Plymouth freemen, before those admitted 1 January 1632/3 [PCR 1:3].
EDUCATION: Sufficient to act as a surgeon. He wrote three polished letters to Bradford in 1630 [Bradford LB 56-59]. His inventory included about thirty books valued at £3 2s. 6d.; they were mostly Bibles and other religious volumes, but there were also his "physic books," some dictionaries and other practical books [MD 2:8].
OFFICES: Plymouth tax assessor for rate of 25 March 1633 [PCR 1:9].
 His inventory included "2 fowling pieces & a musket" valued at £2 [MD 2:9].
ESTATE: In the 1623 Plymouth division of land Samuel Fuller received two acres as a passenger on the *Mayflower*, and "Brigett Fuller" received one acre as a passenger on the *Anne* [PCR 12:4, 6]. In the 1627 Plymouth division of cattle Samuel Fuller, his wife Bridget Fuller and Samuel

Fuller Junior were the first three persons in the eighth company [PCR 12:11]. (This "Samuel Fuller Junior" was not son of Samuel but of his brother Edward [MD 39:85].)

"Sam[uel] Fuller, Senior" was assessed 18s. in the 25 March 1633 Plymouth tax list, and "Widow Fuller" was assessed 9s. in the list of 27 March 1634 [PCR 1:9, 28].

"Mrs. Fuller" was allocated hay ground, 14 March 1635/6, 20 March 1636/7 [PCR 1:40, 56]

In his will, dated 30 July 1633 and proved 28 October 1633 [PCR 1:18], "Samuel Fullere the elder ... sick & weak" bequeathed "the education of my children to my brother Will Wright & his wife, only that my daughter Mercy be & remain with goodwife Wallen"; "if it shall please God to recover my wife out of her weak estate of sickness, then my children to be with her or disposed by her"; "there is a child committed to my charge called Sarah Converse, my wife dying as afore I desire my brother Wright may have the bringing up of her" and if he refuse then "I commend her to my loving neighbor & brother in Christ Thomas Prence," whosoever takes her to bring her up in the fear of God as their own "which was a charge laid upon me per her sick father when he freely bestowed her upon me"; "whereas Eliz[abeth] Cowles was committed to my education by her father & mother still living at Charles Towne" she to be conveniently apparelled and returned to her father or mother or either of them; "George Foster being placed with me upon the same terms by his parents still living at Sagos" he to be restored to his mother; to "Samuel my son my house & lands at the Smeltriver"; "my house & garden at town be sold & all my moveables there & at the Smeltriver (except my cattle) together with the present crop of corn ... except ... such as [my overseers] shall think meet in the present education of my two children Samuell & Mercy"; "two acres of land that fell unto me by lot ... to Samuell my son"; two acres of land "given me by Edward Bircher ... at Strawberry Hill if Mr. Roger Williams refuse to accept of them as formerly he hath done ... also one other acre by Mr. Heeks" to Samuel; "my cousin Samuell go freely away with his stock of cattle & swine without any further reckoning"; all the swine be sold "except my best hog which I would have killed this winter for the present comfort of my children"; whereas "I have disposed of my children to my Brother Will[iam] Wright & Prisilla his wife ... in case my wife die he enter upon my house & land at the Smelt River, & also my cattle not disposed on together with my two servants Thomas Symons & Rob[er]t Cowles for the remainder of their several terms to be employed for the good of my children"; in case "my said brother Will[iam] Wright or Prisilla his wife die, then my said children Samuell & Mercy together with the said joint charge committed to the said Will[iam] & Prisilla be void except my overseers or the survivor of them shall think meet"; a cow calf to the Church of God at Plymouth use to be determined by the Deacons; "to my sister Alice Bradford" 12s. for a pair of gloves; any debt due from Capt. Standish "I give unto his children"; a pair of 5s. gloves to "Mr. Joh. Winthrop, Govr. of the Massachusets"; to "my brother Wright" one cloth suit; the two pounds of beaver owed by Capt. John Endecott "I give it to his son"; when "my children come to age ... my overseers make a full valuation of that stock of cattle & the increase thereof & that it be equally divided between my children, and if any die in the meantime, the whole to go to the survivor or survivors," they to enjoy their portions at the age of discretion "not at any set time or appointment of years"; "my brother Wright" to have the refusal of the purchase of cattle; to "John Jenny & Joh. Wynslow" each a 5s. pair of gloves; to "Mrs. Heeks" 20s.; to "old Mr. William Brewster my best hat & band which I have never wore"; "if my children die, that then my stock be thus distributed: first that what care of pains or charge hath been by any about my children be fully recompensed"; next "as it may redound to the Governing Elder or Elders of this Church at Plymouth ... as my overseers shall think meet"; to "Rebecca Prence" 2s. 6d. for a pair of gloves; "my kinsman Sam[uel] Fuller now in the house with me enjoy whatsoever lands I am now possessed of except my dwelling house at town or whatsoever shall be due to me or them" if my children die before their full age, also "my rufflet cloak & my stuff suit I now wear"; "I institute my son Samuell my executor and because he is young & tender, I enjoin him to be wholly ordered by Edw[ard] Wynslow, Mr. Wil[liam] Bradford & Mr. Tho[mas] Prence" overseers, they to have 20s. each; to "Mercy my daughter one Bible with a black cover with Bezaes notes"; the rest of "my books to my son Samuel, which I desire my Brother Wright will safely preserve for him"; "when my daughter Mercy is fit to go to school ... Mrs. Heeks may teach her as well as my son"; whatsoever "Mr. Roger Williams is indebted to me upon my book for physic, I freely give him"; if "my wife" recover, she to have the education of the children; if the overseers die, then some other of the church be appointed; "whereas the widow Ring committed the oversight of her son Andrew to me at her death, my will is that Mr. Tho[mas] Prence one of my overseers, take the charge of him." The will was followed by a list of debts acknowledged by Samuel Fuller "upon his death bed" including "Henry Wood ... an old debt due at Leyden" and "an herbal belonging to Joh. Chew of Plymouth in old England" [MD 1:24-29, citing PCPR 1:1-3].

The inventory of the estate of "Samuel Fuller the elder" was presented at court 2 January 1633/4 and totalled £212 16s. 6d. "besides the books & the country house," with £25 in real estate: "a dwelling house &c. in the town," £15; and "the country house," £10 [MD 2:8-10, citing PCPR 1:22-24].

BIRTH: Baptized Redenhall, Norfolk, 20 January 1580, son of Robert Fuller [NEHGR 55:192].
DEATH: Between 30 July 1633 (date of will) and 28 October 1633 (probate of will).
MARRIAGE: (1) Alice Glascock, who died by 1613.
(2) (as "Samuel Fuller, say-weaver, from London in England, widower of Alice Glascock") Leiden 24 April 1613 [NS] "Agnes Carpenter, single woman, from Wrington in England" [Plooij XIV; Leiden Pilgrims 95; MD 8:129-30], daughter of Alexander Carpenter (see PRISCILLA CARPENTER [PM 93]). She was buried at Leiden on 3 July 1615 [NEA 3:2:49].
(3) (as "Samuel Fuller, say-weaver, from England, widower of Anna Carpenter") Leiden 27 May 1617 [NS] "Bridget Lee, single woman, also from England, accompanied by Josephine Lee, her mother" [Plooij XXX; Leiden Pilgrims 96; MD 8:129-30]. She died after 2 May 1667 [MD 39:86].
CHILDREN:
  i Child FULLER, bur. Leiden 29 June 1615 [NS] [Dexter 615].
  ii (poss.) BRIDGET FULLER, b. say 1619; m. Plymouth 30 September 1641 Henry Sirkman [PCR 2:23]. (The temptation is strong to place Bridget in this family; we are told that Samuel Fuller had "a child which came afterwards," apparently meaning after both parents had arrived [Bradford 442]. Samuel did not, however, name her in his will.)
  iii MERCY FULLER, b. after 22 May 1627 (not in 1627 division of cattle); named in father's will; living at time of Bradford's accounting of 1651 [Bradford 445]; no further record.
  iv SAMUEL FULLER, b. about 1629; m. (1) _____ _____; m. (2) between 11 April 1663 and 2 May 1667 Elizabeth (Nichols) Bowen, daughter of John Nichols and widow of Thomas Bowen [MD 39:86-87].

ASSOCIATIONS: Brother of EDWARD FULLER (see his sketch for a comment on the accepted ancestry of these two men). Through his second wife related to WILLIAM BRADFORD [PM 62], WILLIAM WRIGHT [PM 524] and others (see PRISCILLA CARPENTER).

COMMENTS: In his list of passengers on the *Mayflower* Bradford included "Mr. Samuel Fuller and a servant called William Button. His wife was behind, and a child which came afterwards" [Bradford 442]. In his 1651 accounting of *Mayflower* passengers Bradford reported that "Mr. Fuller his servant died at sea; and after his wife came over he had two children by her, which are living and grown up to years; but he died some fifteen years ago" [Bradford 445].

BIBLIOGRAPHIC NOTE: In 1996 the Five Generations Project of the General Society of Mayflower Descendants published an account of Samuel Fuller and his descendants, revised by Margaret Harris Stover and Robert S. Wakefield from the edition prepared earlier by Katharine Warner Radasch and Arthur Hitchcock Radasch [MF 10].

G

RICHARD GARDINER

Richard Gardiner came to Plymouth in 1620 on the *Mayflower* and signed the Mayflower Compact [Bradford 443]. In the 1623 Plymouth land division "Richard Gardener" was granted one acre [PCR 12:4], but he does not appear in the 1627 cattle division.

According to Bradford, "Richard Gardiner became a seaman and died in England or at sea" [Bradford 447]. In a letter of May 1624 Emmanuel Altham, then at Plymouth, reported to James Sherley that Governor Bradford would "provide me a sufficient man for master, notwithstanding Richard Gardiner hath earnestly requested it, claiming it as his due by place, but some say not by sufficiency. I will say no more concerning him because I know you shall understand it by others; only thus much I must needs say: that so far as he could, he was willing to help us with the ship. And now he takes it somewhat unkindly that, seeing the Company have sent our ship's company assurance for their wages, that he is not intimated therein" [Three Visitors 47-48].

WILLIAM GILSON

ORIGIN: Unknown.
MIGRATION: 1632.
FIRST RESIDENCE: Scituate.

CHURCH MEMBERSHIP: "Mr. Gilsonn and his wife" were admitted to Scituate church on 8 January 1634/5 as founding members #2 and #3 [NEHGR 9:279].
FREEMAN: In 1633 Plymouth list of freemen among those admitted prior to 1 January 1632/3 [PCR 1:3]. In list of freemen of 7 March 1636/7 [PCR 1:52]. In Scituate section of list of 1639 (annotated "dead") [PCR 8:175].
EDUCATION: His inventory included "1 Bible & 10 other books" valued at 6s. [MD 3:161].

OFFICES: Plymouth assistant, 1633 [PCR 1:5]. Plymouth colony assessor, 27 March 1634, 7 June 1637 [PCR 1:26, 61, 62]. Committee on trade, 1 October 1634 [PCR 1:31].

Plymouth grand jury, 7 March 1636/7, 2 October 1637 (fined 20s. for nonappearance, but fine remitted 6 March 1637/8) [PCR 1:54, 67].

His inventory included "3 fowling pieces & a musket" valued at £2 [MD 3:161].

ESTATE: William Gilson was assessed 12s. in the Plymouth tax list of 25 March 1633, and £1 7s. in the tax list of 27 March 1634 [PCR 1:9, 27].

"Mr. Gillsonn" had built a house at Scituate before the arrival of Rev. John Lothrop in September 1634 [NEHGR 10:42].

In his will, dated 26 January 1639[/40] and proved 3 March 1639[/40], "William Gilson although weak in body" made "his wife Frances Gilson" whole executrix and bequeathed to "his cousin John Dammen" all his land at the third Cliff when the next crop is taken off, except that which is sown with rye; to "his cousin Hannah Dammen" £20; to "his cousin Daniel Romeball" 40s.; to "Mr. John Lathorpe" £5. In a nuncupative codicil dated "seven days before he died," "Mr. William Gilson" told Edward Foster "in his own house lying upon his sick bed" that he would do nothing more for "his cousin John Dammen." Foster deposed about "understanding what he was minded to give his cousin John Dammen, which as I did conceive was not much considering that he had been a long time his servant and was his kinsman too, & he having no children" [MD 3:160, citing PCPR 1:35].

On 3 March 1639/40, whereas "Mr. Gilson, of Scituate, is lately deceased, & that Edward Foster, who should have proved his will, and Mr. Gilson's wife, who should have exhibited an inventory of his goods, were both dangerously sick, a commission is granted to Mr. Tymothy Hatherley, Will[ia]m Hatch, & Henry Cobb, to take the probate of the said will & inventory by sufficient witnesses, and to return the same the next Court" [PCR 1:141].

The inventory of "Mr. Will[ia]m Gilson who died at Scituate the first day of February 1639," taken 12 March 1639[/40], totalled £229 3s. 2d., including no real estate [MD 3:160-62, citing PCPR 1:35].

On 7 June 1649, four leading citizens of Scituate, in response to a petition from "John Damman" of Scituate, deposed that "whereas William Gillson, late of Seteeat, deceased, in his lifetime did require earnestly of the townsmen aforesaid several parcels of land for accommodation of the said William Gilson, but being required of him by us whose names are underwritten the reason of his desire of so much land, being ancient & having no issue of his body to inherit the same after him, his answer was, that he had brought over with him into New England two of his sister's children from their parents, and was bound in conscience both to take care & to provide for them as if they were his own; and we conceive that the land was granted unto him according unto his desire in that behalf" [PCR 2:142-43]. On 24 May 1649, Isaac Robinson testified that "I do remember that Mr. Gillson's plea with us for land was, that although he had no children of his own, yet that he had two of his sister's children, which he looked upon as his own, & so did desire to leave them something after his days was ended; and so for John Damman I have heard Mr. Gillson say that he should have his land after his wife's days were ended; and I have likewise heard Mr. Gillson's wife acknowledge it, & further that she would not wrong the said John & Hanna of what was her husband's will about the lands, yet she would not for some reasons have the said John & Hanna know her husband's will in that business for the present" [PCR 2:143]. On 8 June 1649, "proclamation was made that if any could lay any just claim or title to the lands of William Gillson, deceased, that they should come in and should be heard; but no claim or title was challenged" [PCR 2:143].

BIRTH: By 1610 (based on first evidence of marriage, but almost certainly much older, as he was described as "ancient" at the time he was asking for grants of land from the town [PCR 2:142-3]).
DEATH: Scituate 1 February 1639/40 (from his inventory).
MARRIAGE: By 8 January 1634/5 Frances _____ [NEHGR 9:279]. Perhaps deceased at the time of the controversy over her husband's land, in June 1649, but the language of Isaac Robinson's deposition of 24 May 1649 would seem to imply that she was still alive on that date [PCR 2:141-43].
CHILDREN: None recorded.
ASSOCIATIONS: From the several papers arising from the controversy over the settlement of Gilson's estate, we learn that he had brought over from England his sister's children, John and Hannah Damon. "Cousin" Daniel Rumble later resided in Salem.

COMMENTS: On 1 July 1633, Plymouth court ordered that "unless Mr. Gilson, John Shaw, & the rest that undertook the cutting of the passage between Green's Harbor & the bay finish it before the first of October next ensuing, according to covenant, they be amerced in ten pounds; but if any of them will do it, the fine to be exacted of the rest, & they paid for their labor" [PCR 1:13-14].

On 11 November 1633, in the settlement of the estate of PETER BROWN [PM 82], his daughter Priscilla was placed with William Gilson for twelve years, and he was given £15 for the use of Priscilla, which was to be returned at the end of her time [PCR 1:18-19]. On 28 October 1645, having finished "the term she was to dwell with W[illia]m Gilson," she chose her uncle JOHN BROWN as her guardian [PCR 2:89; PM 80]; this would imply that she continued to serve with Gilson's widow after his death.

GODBERT GODBERTSON

ORIGIN: Leiden, Holland.
MIGRATION: 1623 on the *Anne.*
FIRST RESIDENCE: Plymouth.

OCCUPATION: Hatter.
CHURCH MEMBERSHIP: "As for the Dutch, it was usual for our members that understood the language and lived in or occasionally came over to Leyden, to communicate with them ... I could instance also divers of their members that understood the English tongue, and betook themselves to the communion of our church, went with us to New England, as Godbert Godbertson, &c." [Young's Pilgrim Fathers 392-93].
FREEMAN: Included in the 1633 Plymouth list of freemen, ahead of those admitted 1 January 1632/3 [PCR 1:3].
EDUCATION: His inventory included "a writing table of slate" valued at 4d., "a great Bible" valued at 10s., "Communion of Saints in French" valued at 6d. and "Dod on the Commandments" valued at 1s. [MD 1:155].
OFFICES: His inventory included "one fowling piece" valued at £1, "a pistol" valued at 1s. and "another pistol" valued at 5s. [MD 1:154-57].
ESTATE: In the 1623 Plymouth land division "Cudbart Cudbartsone" received six acres as a 1623 passenger on the *Anne* [PCR 12:6]; this grant was for Godbert himself, his wife Sarah, their son Samuel, Sarah's deceased husband Degory Priest, and Sarah's two Priest daughters. In the 1627 Plymouth cattle division "Godber Godberson," "Sarah Godberson," "Samuell Godberson," "Marra Priest" and "Sarah Priest" were the seventh through eleventh persons in the second company [PCR 12:9].

Assessed 18s. in the 25 March 1633 Plymouth tax list [PCR 1:9].

On 1 July 1633 it was ordered that "Goodman Cutberd" mow "at Wellingly, & that he mowed the last year" [PCR 1:14].

On 28 October 1633, Phineas Pratt "was referred to further hearing ... about the goods of Godbert Godbertson & Zara, his wife" [PCR 1:18]. On 11 November 1633, Phineas Pratt was "appointed to take into his possession all the goods & chattels of Godbert Godbertson & Zarah, his wife, & safely to preserve them, according to an inventory presented upon oath to be true & just by Mr. Joh. Done & Mr. Steph[en] Hopkins" [PCR 1:19].

The inventory of the estate of "Godbert Godbertson & Zarah his wife who died without will" was taken 24 October 1633; the inventory was not totalled, but the debts exceeded the assets; the last item was "The dwelling house & fence & garden," £14 [MD 1:154-57, citing PCPR 1:11-13].

On 2 December 1633, William Bradford was appointed to discharge the debts of "Godbert Godbertson & Zarah his wife," and "whereas the greatest part of his debts are owing to Mr. Isaack Allerton, of Plymouth, merchant, late brother of the said Zarah, the said Isaack hath given free leave to all other his creditors to be fully discharged before he received anything of his particular debts to himself, desiring rather to lose all rather than other men should lose any" [PCR 1:20]. On 10 March 1633/4, William Bradford as administrator sold to Steven Deane "the late dwelling house of the said Godbert, with the misted, inclosures, & outhousing thereunto belonging" [PCR 1:25].

On 3 August 1640, the court confirmed two acres of upland at Wellingsly Brook, given by Godbert Godbertson to "John Combe, gent., and Phineas Pratt, in marriage with their wives, his daughters [i.e., stepdaughters]" [PCR 1:159].

BIRTH: By about 1592 (based on date of first marriage).
DEATH: Plymouth between 1 July 1633 (grant for mowing) and 24 October 1633 (date of inventory).
MARRIAGE: (1) Leiden 27 May 1617 [NS] Elizabeth Kendall [Plooij XXX; Leiden Pilgrims 101]. She died before 25 October 1621 (date of Godbert's betrothal to his second wife).

(2) Leiden 13 November 1621 [NS] or soon after (date of third banns) Sarah (Allerton) (Vincent) Priest [Plooij XLVII; Leiden Pilgrims 101]. She was widow first of John Vincent and second of DEGORY PRIEST, and was sister of ISAAC ALLERTON. She died "without will" within a short time of her husband [MD 1:154].

CHILD:
With second wife
  i SAMUEL GODBERTSON, b. Leiden about 1622; placed himself as an apprentice to Richard Higgins, tailor, for seven years, 1 April 1634 [PCR 1:29]; remainder of apprenticeship, until 1 April 1641, transferred to John Smalley, 31 August 1639 [PCR 1:129]; apparently m. by about 1657 _____ _____. (The only evidence that Samuel Godbertson, son of Godbert Godbertson, married is the death at Middleborough on 17 April 1699 of "Samuell Cutbird aged about 42 years" [MiddleVR 1:3], who was born at the right time to be son of Samuel Godbertson.)

ASSOCIATIONS: Through his second wife Godbertson was stepfather of the daughters of DEGORY PRIEST [PM 382] and was brother-in-law to ISAAC ALLERTON [PM 10].

COMMENTS: According to both his marriage records Godbert Godbertson was of "Eastland," meaning presumably that region around Danzig, now part of Poland.

JOHN GOODMAN

John Goodman came to Plymouth in 1620 on the *Mayflower*, signed the Compact, and is listed by Bradford as one of seven men who "died soon after their arrival in the general sickness" [Bradford 443, 447].

On 12 January 1620/1, John Goodman and Peter Brown, while cutting thatch, became lost in the woods, spent a night in the open, and found their way back to the rest on the 13th. Goodman's feet were damaged, and "it was a long while after ere he was able to go," and on the 19th he "went abroad to use his lame feet" [Mourt 45-47].

In the 1623 Plymouth land division, John Goodman received a grant, presumably one acre, as a passenger on the *Mayflower* [PCR 12:4].

COMMENTS: Bradford's statement that someone died in "the general sickness" should mean that the death occurred in the winter of 1620/1, so there may be a simple clerical error in the 1623 compilation. Another possibility (suggested by Robert S. Wakefield in private correspondence) is that John Goodman was related to some other Plymouth resident who in 1623 made good a claim to Goodman's right to an acre of land. John Goodman had certainly died by 1627, since he is not in the 1627 cattle division. (See Stratton 297 for discussion of attempts to identify John Goodman with other men of similar names.)

ROBERT GORGES

"About the middle of September [1623] arrived Captain Robart Gorges in the Bay of the Massachusets, with sundry passengers and families, intending there to begin a plantation; and pitched upon the place Mr. Weston's people had forsaken. He had a commission from the Council of New England, to be general Governor of the country, and they appointed for his counsel & assistance Capt. Francis West, the aforesaid admiral, Christopher Levite, Esquire, and the Governor of Plymouth for the time being." He took advantage of his fourteen-day stay with the Plymouth people, being blown from his course by a storm. He correctly accused Mr. Weston of taking the "many pieces of great ordnance" meant for New England and selling them beyond the seas. Weston and Gorges clashed, with Gorges "in great indignation & distemper, and vowed that he would either curb him, or send him home for England." His ship stayed at Plymouth and fitted itself for Virginia "and with her returned sundry of those from hence which came over on their particular, some out of discontent and dislike of the country, others by reason of a fire that broke out and burnt the houses they lived in and all their provisions...."

After less than a year "[t]he Governor [Gorges] and some that depended upon him returned for England, having scarcely saluted the country in his government, not finding the state of things here to answer his quality and condition.... The Gov[erno]r brought over a minister with him, one Mr. Morell, who, about a year after the Gov[erno]r returned, took shipping from hence" [Bradford 133-38].

COMMENTS: The account given above by Bradford forms the basis of the longer, definitive story of Robert Gorges and his brief stay in New England written by Charles Francis Adams [Three Episodes 131-55]. Robert Gorges was baptized 15 November 1595 at St. James, Clerkenwell, Middlesex, son of Sir Ferdinando Gorges, a leading force in the Council for New England [see GDMNH 273-76 for brief accounts of the several members of the Gorges family associated with New England (including Robert), and Raymond Gorges, *The Story of a Family ... Being a History of the Family of Gorges* (Boston 1944), pp. 128-29, for more on the Gorges family in general].

RICHARD GREENE

In 1622 THOMAS WESTON [PM 490] sent to New England "Master Richard Greene, brother-in-law to Master Weston, who from him had charge in the oversight and government of his colony, [and who] died suddenly at our plantation [Plymouth], to whom we gave burial befitting his place, in the best manner we could" [MD 26:16 and Young's Pilgrim Fathers 299, both reprinting Edward Winslow, *Good Newes from New England* (London 1624)].

COMMENTS: Charles Francis Adams weaves into his account of the early history of Massachusetts Bay the few facts available on this man [Three Episodes 55, 59, 60, 62, 163].

H

JOHN HAMPDEN

In *Good Newes from New England* Edward Winslow wrote of a March 1622/3 visit to see Massasoit, who was then ill:
> the Governor again laid this service upon myself, and fitted me with some cordials to administer to him; having one Master John Hamden, a gentleman of London, who then wintered with us, and desired much to see the country, for my consort, and Hobbamock for our guide. So we set forward, and lodged the first night at Namasket, where we had friendly entertainment.
>
> The next day, about one of the clock, we came to a ferry in Conbatant's country, where, upon discharge of my piece, diverse Indians came to us from a house not far off. There they told us that Massassowat was dead, and that day buried.... Considering now, that he being dead, Conbatant was the most like to succeed him, and that we were not above three mile from Mattapuyst, his dwelling-place ... I thought no time so fit as this to enter into more friendly terms with him ... [and so] I resolved to put it in practice, if Master Hamden and Hobbamock durst attempt it with me; whom I found willing to that or any other course might tend to the general good. So we went towards Mattapuyst.

Coming to Conbatant's village, it was discovered that Massasoit had not died, and Winslow, Hamden and Hobbamock hurried to Puckanokick where they found Massasoit very ill. Under Winslow's ministrations, graphically described, Massasoit recovered miraculously and returned the favor by revealing a plot to attack the English [Good News 314-17].

Phineas Pratt's adventure in the wilderness took place this same month. Pratt was making his way through the woods to warn the Plymouth settlers of a plan of attack being contemplated by the Indians, and as he neared Plymouth and "was running down a hill I [saw] an English man coming in the path before me. Then I sat down on a tree & rising up to salute him said, 'Mr. Hamdin, I am glad to see you alive.' He said 'I am glad & full of wonder to see you alive; let us sit down, I see you are weary'" [MHSC 4:4:484; MD 4:91-92].

COMMENTS: Alexander Young strenuously resisted the idea that the John Hampden who "wintered with us" was the celebrated English politician, as was suggested by Belknap. Young argued that Hampden was at the parliament assembled in January 1621 and dissolved in 1622, and was well aware that a new parliament would soon be called. Given his position and prestige, it seemed unlikely to Young that Hampden would go off on a pleasure jaunt at that juncture in English politics. Young further found the silence of other writers on colonial soil inexplicable should this Hampden have been the patriot [Young's Pilgrim Fathers 314-15].

The possibility that John Hampden, the parliamentarian, did come to New England should not be rejected so categorically. Many of the Puritan leaders in Parliament had a strong interest in New England, and one can imagine John Hampden having the curiosity to make such a trip. If he did come to New England, there should be a gap in his English career of several months in late 1622 and early 1623. If he can be placed unequivocally in England during this time, then the visitor to New England must be some other John Hampden.

An extensive treatment of the life of John Hampden, the parliamentarian, may be found in John Adair, *A Life of John Hampden the Patriot (1594-1643)* (London 1976).

MARTHA HARDING

ORIGIN: Unknown.
MIGRATION: 1632.
FIRST RESIDENCE: Plymouth.

ESTATE: "Widow Harding" was assessed 9s. in the Plymouth tax list of 25 March 1633 [PCR 1:11].

On 28 October 1633, "John Done presented an inventory of the goods & chattels of Martha Harding, deceased, who, in the behalf of her son, was allowed the administrator of the said Martha" [PCR 1:18]. The inventory totalled £20 18s. 6d. and included no real estate [MD 1:82-3, citing PCPR 1:8]. The estate showed disbursements to "her husband's brothers in England, to one eight pounds to another nine pounds to another three pounds." "This Martha Harding died without will leaving one son in the custody of Mr. Joh Done the administrator of the said Martha" [MD 1:83, citing PCPR 1:9].

BIRTH: By about 1612 (based on estimated date of marriage, and probably some years earlier).
DEATH: Plymouth between 25 March 1633 (tax assessment) and 28 October 1633 (administration of estate).
MARRIAGE: By about 1632 _____ Harding, who presumably died in England before his widow and son sailed for New England.
CHILD:
   i   JOSEPH HARDING, b. by 1632; m. Eastham 4 April 1660 Bethiah Cooke [PCR 8:27], daughter of JOSIAS COOKE [PM 149].

ASSOCIATIONS: It is likely that Martha Harding was sister to JOHN DOANE [PM 171], who administered her estate and took her son, Joseph, into his household after her death. Joseph Harding was complained of on 3 June 1652 for "carrying an Indian's gun unto the smith to be mended in his uncle's name" [PCR 3:10], and it is assumed by some that the uncle mentioned here would be JOHN DOANE.

COMMENTS: There were others by the name of Harding in early Plymouth, but with no obvious connection to Martha Harding: John, born by 1627 (in Duxbury section of 1643 Plymouth list of men able to bear arms [PCR 8:190]); Phebe who married 26 March 1633 John Brown [PCR 1:26]; and Winifred who married 22 November 1639 Thomas Whiton [PCR 1:134].

WALTER HARRIS

Walter Harris appears as one of sixteen names on a passenger list of 7 March 1631/2, taken at the port of London; also on this list were John Smalley and "Edmond Wynsloe," the latter returning from one of his business trips to England, having apparently recruited Harris and Smalley [Hotten 149].

8 April 1633: "Whereas Walter Harris had bound himself by indenture to serve Mr. John Atwood of London, under the command of Mr. John Done of New Plymouth, for the space of five years, the said John Done hath sold all right, title & claim to the said service to Henry Howland, by consent of the said Walter, for & in consideration of fourteen pounds

sterling, to be paid at three several payments, viz: the first in hand, the second in November next ensuing, & the third in November, anno 1634, in merchantable commodities, as corn or swine, as they shall be worth at the several times of payment" [PCR 1:12-13].

COMMENTS: No further record of Walter Harris is seen. Some sources identify this Walter Harris with the man of that name who appears later in Dorchester, and then New London, but this cannot be the case. The Dorchester man already had a family, including sons born in the 1620s; this is supported by the passenger list recently discovered by Coldham, for the ship *Speedwell*, sailing from Weymouth 22 April 1637, which includes an entry for "Walter Harris, his wife, six children & three servants" [Coldham 185]. Such a man would not have come to Plymouth in 1632 as a servant.

TIMOTHY HATHERLY

ORIGIN: St. Olave, Southwark, Surrey.
MIGRATION: 1623 [Morton 65].
FIRST RESIDENCE: Plymouth.
REMOVES: Scituate.
RETURN TRIPS: Returned to England soon after arrival in 1623, then made annual trips to New England in 1631, 1632, 1633 and 1634, settling permanently in New England in 1634.

OCCUPATION: Feltmaker (in England). Merchant.
CHURCH MEMBERSHIP: "Mr. Hetherly and his wife" joined Scituate church on 11 January 1634/5 as members #15 and #16 [NEHGR 9:279]. After Rev. John Lothrop left Scituate and took his church with him, Hatherly was the leader of that faction in Scituate that invited Charles Chauncy to be their minister, in opposition to the faction headed by WILLIAM VASSALL {1630, Boston} [GMB 3:1871-75], which invited William Wetherell [GMN 5:12-13].
FREEMAN: Admitted on 5 January 1635/6 [PCR 1:4]. In Plymouth list of 7 March 1636/7 (designated "gen[erosus]") [PCR 1:52]. In 1639 list of Plymouth colony freemen, both as an Assistant and at the head of the Scituate section [PCR 8:173, 175]. In Scituate section of 1658 list of Plymouth freemen [PCR 8:198]. (Morison states incorrectly that Hatherly, on his trip to New England in 1632, became a freeman of Massachusetts Bay [Bradford 383].)

EDUCATION: Timothy Hatherly cosigned with James Sherley a letter dated 19 March 1629/30, but there is no way to tell how much he contributed to the composition of the document [Bradford 384-87]. His inventory included "a library of books" valued at £4 7s. and "2 Bibles, 1 Testament and a small book" valued at £1 4s.

OFFICES: Plymouth Colony Assistant, 1636-1637, 1639-57 [PCR 1:36, 48, 116, 140, 2:8, 33, 52, 71, 83, 100, 115, 123, 139, 153, 166, 3:7, 30, 48, 77, 99, 114]. (Elected Assistant in 1638, but refused the office [PCR 1:79, 86]. Elected Assistant in 1658, but "not sworn" [PCR 3:134].) Treasurer, 1640 [PCR 1:140]. Commissioner for Plymouth to the United Colonies, 1646, 1651 [PCR 2:100, 166, 9:61, 192].

Committee to "lay out the most convenientest way from Plymouth to Scittuate," 6 June 1654 [PCR 3:5]. Committee to resolve dispute over church rate at Rehoboth, 8 June 1655 [PCR 3:81]. Committee on the Kennebec trade, 5 March 1655/6 [PCR 3:96]. Committee to revise colony laws, 3 June 1657 [PCR 3:117]. Appointed to "administer marriage at Scittuate as occasion shall require," grant warrants and administer oaths, 2 October 1658, 7 June 1659, 13 June 1660, 10 June 1662, 1 June 1663 [PCR 3:152, 166, 192, 4:22, 43].

On 3 June 1652, the court "ordered Mr. Hatherley that he take course that the military company of Scittuate do train according to order this year, and that he see that some fit persons be joined with the constables of Scittuate, to take view of their ammunition, and to see that they have powder and shot according to order" [PCR 3:11]. Council of war, 2 June 1646, 6 April 1653, 12 May 1653, 1 June 1658 [PCR 2:100, 3:26, 28, 138].

ESTATE: "Mr. Hatherlie's two men" were assessed 18s. in the Plymouth tax list of 25 March 1633, and in the list of 27 March 1634 they were entered, but no assessment was included [PCR 1:10, 27].

On 25 March 1633, "Tymothy Hatherly, merchant of London," sold to Edward Holman and John Barnes, both of Plymouth, one heifer apiece, each valued at £13 [PCR 1:8, 9].

On 1 July 1633, it was ordered that "the whole tract of land between the brook at Scituate, on the norwest side, and Conahasset be left undisposed of till we know the resolution of Mr. James Sherley, Mr. John Beauchamp, Mr. Rich[ard] Andrews, & Mr. Tymothy Hatherly, as also that portion of land lately made choice of by Mr. Hatherly aforesaid" [PCR 1:13].

Reverend John Lothrop listed "Mr. Hatherlye's" house first among the nine that were already built when Lothrop arrived at Scituate "about [the] end of September 1634" [NEHGR 10:42].

On 1 November 1640, "John Lothrope, Pastor of the Church of Barnestable," sold to "Tymothy Hatherley of Scituate, gentleman," one dwelling house with barn and outhouses, uplands, marsh ground, a quarter of a mile eastward from Scituate, "the marsh ground containing twenty acres more or less, part whereof is an island" [PCR 12:66-67]. On 23 November 1639, "Tymothy Hatherley of the Plantation of Scituate ..., gentleman," sold to Christopher Blakewood of Scituate, planter, that property just purchased from Lothrop [PCR 12:67-68]. On 22 January 1640[/1], "Tymothy Hatherley, planter," of Scituate, sold to Thomas Ensigne, planter, of Scituate, land called "First Cliff" being eighteen acres of upland and twenty acres of marsh; this deed was signed by "Tymothy Hatherley and Susan Hatherly" [PCR 12:70].

On 24 February 1640[/1?], "Tymothy Hatherley of Scituate" deeded to "Egline Hanford of Scituate" five acres of land in Scituate "given to the said Egline Hanford the 27th day of September" in the year 1634 [PCR 12:71-72]. On 1 December 1646, "Timothy Hatherly of Seteaat in the government of New Plymouth ... gentleman" being one of four associates deeded land by Mr. William Bradford to the north of Scituate Brooke, known "by the Indians or natives by the name of Conahaset *alias* Cohaset," and being possessed of three of the four parts of this land, sold to Charles Chansy, pastor of the church of "Seteaat," and various other men, all of "Seteaat" [PCR 12:158-160]. In a retrospective deed dated 6 March 1650[/1?], "Mr. Timothy Hatherley" of Scituate, gentleman, stated that he had, in the year 1645, sold to Mr. John Floyde of Scituate, merchant, his house, barn, orchard and homelot in Scituate, with the marsh and upland and meadow, formerly the right of Samuell Hinckley, except twenty-four acres, which Hatherly sold in 1645 to Thomas Clapp of Scituate [PCR 12:204-5].

On 6 June 1654, in "regard of sundry contentions and entanglements betwixt Mr. Hatherly and some of the inhabitants of the town of Scittuate, the Court doth grant unto Mr. Hatherley, for to satisfy the partners at Conahassett, a certain competency of land out of the bounds of any particular township on the westerly side of the town of Scituate aforesaid" [PCR 3:52-53]. On 3 July 1656, there was "granted unto Mr. Timothy Hatherley a tract of land, to begin at Accord Pond, on the south side of the line, and to run three miles southerly towards the Indian Head Pond, and to be laid out three miles square" [PCR 3:103-4, 165, 4:31, 46, 99].

(Additional land transactions, many speculative, are recorded in the Plymouth Colony and Scituate town land records [PCLR 2:1:49, 65, 121, 157, 2:2:2, 4; 3:11, 35, 92-97, 102-5, 305-6; ScitTR *passim*].)

Timothy Hatherly

In his will, dated 20 December 1664 and proved 30 October 1666, Timothy Hatherly bequeathed to "my wife Lydia Hatherly my house I now dwell in with the rest of the housing ... with all the land I die possessed of during her natural life," also "my silver plate with all my pewter and brass that I do not otherwise dispose of by will," also "what moveables soever are in my parlor and parlor chamber ..., also all my linen ..., [also] my gray mare two cows and two oxen and my cart with all my wearing clothes"; to "Edward Jenkens his wife and children £12"; to "Nicholas Wade his wife and children £12 ... also one great brass kettle"; to "Sussanna the wife of Willam Brookes and her children £12 and acquit her of her first husband's debt to me, as also one copper kettle with three ears"; to "Timothy Foster £5 and to Elizabeth Foster £3"; to "Mr. Thomas Hanford" £10; to "Fear Robinson now the wife of Samuell Baker 40s. and to the other three children of Isacke Robinson John Isacke and Mercye" 40s. each; to "Lydia Garrett my wife's daughter three acres of land part of which her house stands on ... and £5 ... and likewise acquit all former accounts and reckonings between she and I from the beginning of the world to this day"; "to the four children of the said Lydia Garrett" 40s. at age twenty-one; to "Gorge Sutton his wife and children £5"; to "the wife of Will[i]am Bassett my wife's daughter £5"; to "the widow Preble my wife's daughter 50s."; to "Lydia Lapham an heifer worth 50s. or 50s. in goods"; to "Thomas Lapham 30s."; to "Stephen Tilden £5 to be paid when his service is expired"; to "Lydia Hatch the daughter of William Hatch" £8 at age twenty-one or marriage; residue to "my trusty and well-beloved friend Joseph Tildin" executor [MD 16:158-160, citing PCPR 2:2:34].

Joseph Tilden, refusing to be executor of the estate of Timothy Hatherly, was on 31 October 1666 appointed to be adminstrator of the estate [PCR 4:138], and letters of administration were granted on 5 June 1667 [PCR 4:155].

The inventory of the personal estate of Timothy Hatherly, taken 9 November 1666, totalled £224 12s. 8d., with no real estate included [MD 16:163, citing PCPR 2:2:38-40].

BIRTH: Baptized Winkleigh, Devonshire, 29 September 1588, son of Robert and Ellinor (____) Hatherly [M&JCH 18:74; see also Stevens-Miller Anc 490].
DEATH: Scituate 24 October 1666 (as "Mr. Thmoty [*sic*] Hatherlee").
MARRIAGE: (1) St. Olave, Southwark, Surrey, 26 December 1614 Alice Collard [English Homes 146]. She died by 1634.

(2) By 11 January 1634/5 Susan _____ [NEHGR 9:279]. She died after 22 January 1640/1, when she joined Timothy in a deed (and after 3 March 1640/1, if she also acknowledged this deed, which she may have done) [PCR 12:70].

(3) After 1641 Lydia (Huckstep) Tilden, widow of NATHANIEL TILDEN {1635, Scituate} [Joseph Neal Anc 55-59]. She was living in 1670 [Joseph Neal Anc 59, 61].

CHILD:

With first wife

　i　NATHANIEL HATHERLY, bp. St. Olave, Southwark, 16 July 1618 [English Homes 146]; no further record.

ASSOCIATIONS: Lothrop's church record states that "Egglin Handford, Mr. Hatherley's sister, joined November 21, 1635." She was Eglin (Hatherly) (Downe) Hanford, baptized at Winkleigh, Devonshire, on 8 June 1586 [M&JCH 18:74] and called "Eylin Hanver" in the will of their mother in 1637 [Stevens-Miller Anc 490; NEHGR 52:76]. As the widow of Jeffrey Hanford of Alverdiscott, Devonshire, she came, aged forty-six, with her daughters, Margaret and Elizabeth on the *Planter*, arriving in Boston in June 1635 [Hotten 56; GM 2:3:205-7]. She had in all four daughters and a son, all of whom came to New England: Susanna, who m. (1) JOHN WHISTON [PM 493] and (2) William Brooks; Lettice, who m. (1) EDWARD FOSTER [PM 212] and (2) Edward Jenkins; Margaret, who m. ISAAC ROBINSON [PM 391]; Elizabeth, who m. Nicholas Wade; and Thomas, who m. (1) Hannah Newberry and (2) Mary (Miles) Ince [Stevens-Miller Anc 485-89].

Hatherly's servant, Ephraim Tinkham, who may have accompanied him in the *Charles* 5 June 1632, is believed to have been the one baptized at Barnstaple, Devonshire, on 23 February 1617/8 [PCR 1:31; MQ 60:222-24].

COMMENTS: In the reorganization of Plymouth Colony's financial affairs in 1627, Timothy Hatherly became one of the four London Associates, and in the years ensuing figures frequently in colony business [Bradford *passim*]. Before coming over in 1634 to reside permanently at Scituate, Hatherly withdrew from this position, although he acted as agent for the other three associates in acquiring a grant of land near the Massachusetts Bay line [Bradford 252, 304].

Timothy Hatherly is described as of the parish of St. Olave, Southwark, feltmaker, in an indenture dated 20 April 1629 with John Irish [SJC #3597].

While in England between 1623 and 1631, Hatherly was one of the group of merchants who looked over, and frequently worsened, the business affairs of the planters at Plymouth. Then in 1631 he began a pattern, which lasted for four years, of coming to New England early in the year, and then returning to England after a few weeks or months. He is called merchant, and was initially more interested in trade than in settlement, but soon he began to make preparations to stay in New England permanently.

Hatherly came again to New England in 1631 on the *Friendship*, landing at Boston on 14 July 1631, carrying letters for Governor Winthrop [WJ 1:70; WP 3:27, 32; Bradford 227-233 (Bradford places the arrival of this ship in 1630, but his chronology for 1630 and 1631 is muddled, and most of the events placed by him in 1630 actually took place in 1631)]. Hatherly made a voyage downeast to look into his fishing affairs, and then in the fall returned to England [Bradford 231-33].

Winthrop reports on 5 June 1632 the arrival at Boston of the *Charles* of Barnstaple, with "Mr. Hatherly, the merchant," aboard [WJ 1:94], and Bradford tells us under 1632 that "Mr. Hatherly came over again this year, but upon his own occasions, and began to make preparation to plant and dwell in the country" [Bradford 252].

Hatherly cannot have stayed for long in New England in 1632, for we find that he was in England in December of that year [WP 3:104] and, on 22 February 1632/3, he arrived again at Plymouth on the *William* [WJ 1:119; WP 3:93, 98-99, 116 ("These letters [received] per the ship Mr. Trevore master, Mr. Hatherly, merchant, arrived at New-Plymouth")]. He apparently returned again to England quite soon, for on 6 August 1633 Francis Kirby, writing from London, stated that "We expect Mr. Hatherly per the next West Country ship, and by him I hope to receive letters" [WP 3:135]. The implication is that Hatherly was already in England, at some West Country port, and was expected momentarily in London.

There is no record of Hatherly's return to New England in 1634, but he first appears again on the Plymouth record on 1 July 1634 as a plaintiff in a civil suit, and again on 23 July 1634 when he turned over to John Winslow his servant Ephraim Tinkham [PCR 1:30, 31]. He now became a permanent resident of the colony; on 11 January 1634/5, Hatherly joined the church at Scituate [NEHGR 9:279] and, on 5 January 1635/6, he was made a freeman of Plymouth Colony and was elected Assistant [PCR 1:36].

BIBLIOGRAPHIC NOTE: Mary Lovering Holman published in 1948 a brief account of the Hatherly family and of the affiliated Hanford family [Stevens-Miller Anc 485-91]. This summary included an abstract of the will of the immigrant.

A lengthy biographical sketch of Hatherly was published in 1929 by Harvey Hunter Pratt [*The Early Planters of Scituate* (Scituate 1929), pp. 284-305].

WILLIAM HEARD

In the 1623 Plymouth land division, William Heard was granted one acre as a passenger on the *Anne* in 1623 [PCR 12:6]. As he does not appear in the 1627 cattle division, he must have died or departed soon.

JOHN HEWES

ORIGIN: Unknown.
MIGRATION: 1632.
FIRST RESIDENCE: Scituate.

OCCUPATION: Planter.
FREEMAN: Requested admission 6 March 1637/8 [PCR 1:79], and admitted 3 December 1639 [PCR 1:137]. In Scituate sections of 1639, 1658 and 29 May 1670 Plymouth Colony lists of freemen [PCR 5:275, 8:175, 198].
EDUCATION: Signed his deeds by mark.
OFFICES: Plymouth coroner's jury, 3 May 1653 [PCR 3:28].

Scituate surveyor of highways (as "John Hewes Sr."), 7 June 1652, 7 June 1653 [PCR 3:9, 32]. Constable, 7 June 1659 [PCR 3:163].

In Scituate portion of 1643 Plymouth Colony list of men able to bear arms [PCR 8:191].
ESTATE: Assessed 9s. in the Plymouth Colony tax lists of 25 March 1633 and 27 March 1634 [PCR 1:11, 28].

Although no record survives of any original town grant from Scituate to John Hewes, his name does appear as an abutter in a number of other early land grants, beginning as early as 10 October 1634 [ScitTR 1:235, 237-39, 241-42].

Built a "small plain palisado house" in Scituate before September 1634, then built a second house "on his lot" in 1636, after which the first house was sold to [John] Cooper [NEHGR 10:42-43].

On 4 August 1650, Humphrey Johnson of Scituate, planter, sold to "John Hewes senior of Scittuate ... planter ... all that my dwelling house and barn together with twenty acres more or less of upland on which the said house and barn standeth; which said house and land was sometimes the land and house of John Williames Junior of Scittuate" [PCR 12:200-2]. On 10 January 1650[/1], John Hewes Sr. of Scituate, planter, sold to William Randall of Scituate sixty acres of upland and eleven acres of marsh in Scituate; on 29 May 1654, "Joane the wife of John Hewes" relinquished dower [MD 15:179-81, transcribing PCLR 2:50]. On 22 April 1658, "John Hewes senior of Scituate ... planter" sold to Joseph Coleman Sr. of Scituate, shoemaker, "all that my now dwelling house, barn and other housing ... with all my upland and meadow land thereunto belonging," including two parcels of upland of twenty and ten acres, and twenty-three acres of meadow; Joanna the wife of John Hewes consented [PCLR 3:182].

On 13 June 1657, "Abigaill Hatch, widow, formerly the wife of William Hatch," describing herself also as "Abigaill Hatch of Scituate ... spinster," sold to "John Hewes my father ... my dwelling house and barn, and all the land in my possession belonging thereunto," being thirteen acres of upland and meadow land and another five acres of meadow, given to her husband by her husband's father [PCLR 3:167]. On 14 June 1669, at Weymouth, "Abigaile King" petitioned the Plymouth General Court to confirm her 1657 sale of land of her former husband, William Hatch, to her father; her daughter Phebe Hatch is now "near sixteen years of age" and is otherwise provided for; Samuel Butterworth and William Chard attest to the accuracy of this petition, and ask that the land be confirmed to "the said Abigaill King's father, John Hewes, and grandfather to the said Phebe Hatch" [PCLR 3:167]. On 27 May 1669, "John Hewes of Scituate" sold to Jeremiah Hatch of Scituate, planter, the land which he had purchased from his daughter in 1657; Joanna the wife of John Hewes consented [PCLR 3:168].

In his will, dated 6 February 1671 and proved 22 February 1674, "John Hewes of Scituate" bequeathed to "my son John Hewes" a horse and a cloak; to "Jeremiah Hatch my son-in-law" rest of wearing clothes; and residue to "Joannah my well beloved wife," she to be sole executrix [MD 34:112, citing PCPR 3:1:149].

On 28 June 1677, "John Hewes of Watertown ... weaver" sold to Thomas Coleman of Scituate "one parcel of upland lying and being in

Scituate," containing five acres (bounded on the east by "a swamp given by the freemen of Scituate unto John Hewes and Joseph Coleman Senior"); also "all my right, title, claim and interest unto or in the aforesaid swamp which is the east bounds of the abovenamed five acres of upland"; also "the privilege of the house lot in the common" [PCLR 4:110-11].

BIRTH: By about 1608 (based on estimated date of marriage).
DEATH: Scituate between 6 February 1671 (date of will) and 22 February 1674 (probate of will).
MARRIAGE: Late 1632 or early 1633 Joan _____; on 1 April 1633 the Plymouth court ordered "John Hews & Jone his wife adjudged to sit in the stocks because the said Jone conceived with child by him before they were publicly married, though in the time of contract" [PCR 1:12]. She died after 6 February 1671 (when she was named in her husband's will).
CHILDREN:
  i ABIGAIL HEWES, b. say 1633; m. (1) by 1653 William Hatch ("Phebe the daughter of William Hatch" was bp. Scituate 19 March 1653/4 [NEHGR 57:84; Joseph Neal Anc 118]); m. (2) Weymouth 14 October 1658 John King (the bride's surname in the published version of this marriage record is given as "Haty," presumably a simple misreading of the terminal "ch").
  ii MARY HEWES, b. say 1637; m. Scituate 29 December 1657 Jeremiah Hatch [MD 2:34; Joseph Neal Anc 115].
  iii JOHN HEWES, b. about 1653 (d. Lexington 15 December 1721, aged 68 [NEHGR 126:5]); m. Watertown 9 March 1676[/7] Ruth Sawtell [WaVR 41; NEHGR 126:5; Bond 296].

ASSOCIATIONS: In various land transactions John Hewes and his son were involved with Joseph Coleman and one of his sons.

COMMENTS: For more than fifteen years, beginning in 1640 [ScitTR 1:243], there were two adult men by the name of John Hewes in Scituate. In the 1643 list of men able to bear arms, the Scituate section had two men of that name [PCR 8:191]; a John Hewes took the oath of fidelity at Scituate on 15 January 1644 [PCR 8:183], when the subject of this sketch was already a freeman; and in deeds of 1650 and 1658 the subject of this sketch called himself "John Hewes Sr." Deane apparently thought this second John Hewes was son of the first, for he speaks of "his son John, who had been a freeholder, died 1661, leaving no family here."

Deane's claim that the younger John Hewes died in 1661 apparently derived from a town record of 28 July 1661, which refers to land "[g]iven formerly unto John Hewes Junior" [ScitTR 1:252]. But the will of John Hewes contradicts this, for in 1671 he makes a bequest to his son John, who could not, therefore, have died in 1661.

If this second John Hewes did in fact die in 1661 or thereabouts (although the vital records do not reflect this), and if the son of the elder John Hewes was born about 1653, then there would be a period in the 1660s and 1670s when there was only one adult John Hewes in Scituate, and in fact we do find that in the deed of 1669 John Hewes is not distinguished as "Sr." ("John Hewes Sr." and "John Hewes Jr." are in the list of rates for the Indian purchase at Scituate [PCR 7:130]. This list appears in the records near entries dated 1666, but is on its own page and is described as "here recorded for special reason." There are other entries in this list that do not make sense if they are intended for 1666, so the date would seem to be some years earlier, and the two men by the name of John Hewes are the two early contemporaries, and not the father and son.)

In the deed of 1677 John Hewes of Watertown relinquished his "right, title, claim and interest" that he had in a piece of swamp granted to "John Hewes and Joseph Coleman Senior." We have seen that the elder John Hewes was in other matters associated with this Joseph Coleman, and it would appear that the Watertown man is ceding his right to this part of his father's estate. The two men by the name of John Hewes in Scituate from 1643 to 1658 are therefore not known to be related to one another.

Deane calls John Hewes, the subject of this sketch, "the Welshman" [Scituate Hist 283], and is followed in this by Savage. The evidence for this is in a town record of 28 February 1693/4, regarding encroachments made by "Joseph Collman or his brother ... under pretense of a lot of lands they had bought called the Welshman's Lot." The committee appointed to investigate found "an old stone wall that was reported to be made by John Huse viz: the aforesaid Welshman" [ScitTR 1:284-85]. This apparently refers to the land described in the deed of 28 June 1677 [PCLR 4:110-11], and so identifies this immigrant as the Welshman.

ROBERT HICKS

ORIGIN: London.
MIGRATION: 1621 on the *Fortune*.
FIRST RESIDENCE: Plymouth.

OCCUPATION: Fellmonger (in England).
FREEMAN: In the 1633 list of Plymouth freemen, among those admitted before 1 January 1632/3 [PCR 1:3]. In list of 7 March 1636/7 [PCR 1:52]. In the Plymouth section of the 1639 Plymouth Colony list of freemen (with the annotation "dead") [PCR 8:173].
EDUCATION: His inventory included "3 books" valued at 8s. [MD 8:144]. His widow, Margaret, signed her will.
OFFICES: His inventory included "a part of a pair of bandoliers" valued at 6d. [MD 8:143].
ESTATE: In the 1623 Plymouth division of land, "Robart Hickes" was granted one acre as a passenger on the *Fortune*, and his wife and children were granted four acres as passengers on the *Anne* [PCR 12:5, 6]. In the 1627 Plymouth division of cattle, Robert Hicks, Margaret Hicks, Samuel Hicks, Ephraim Hicks, Lydia Hicks and Phebe Hicks were the sixth through eleventh persons in the twelfth company [PCR 12:13].

Assessed 18s. in the Plymouth tax list of 25 March 1633 and 12s. in the list of 27 March 1634 [PCR 1:9, 27]. "Robert Hickes" was thirty-seventh on the list of Purchasers [PCR 2:177].

On 10 February 1629[/30], "Steven Dean sold to Robart Hixe 2 acres of land lying on the north side of the town ... the one being his own inheritance, the other was that he bought of Philip De le noy" [PCR 12:7]. On 29 August 1638, Clement Briggs sold to "Mr. Rob[er]te Heeks one acre of land in the upper fall near the second brook" [PCR 12:34]. On 9 December 1639, "Mr. Rob[er]te Hicks" leased to "John Smyth five acres ... at the Reed Pond" [PCR 12:51]. On 13 July 1639, George Sowle sold to "Rob[er]te Hicks of Plymouth ... all those his two acres of lands lying at the place called the watering place on the south side of the town of Plymouth" [PCR 12:45]. On 20 July 1639, John Barnes of Plymouth, yeoman, sold to "Mr. Rob[er]te Hicks of the same ... all those four acres of meadow ground lying at the High Pines which he bought of John Winslowe" [PCR 12:45].

On 11 February 1639[/40], "Mr. Robert Hicks of Plymouth, planter," sold to "Samuell Hicks his eldest son all that his house, outhouses and garden place situate in Plym[outh] aforesaid together with four acres of lands lying in the field on the south side of the said town of Plymouth and eight acres of lands or thereabouts ... together with all the meadow ground lying at the High Pines and Island Creek containing seven acres" and three cows [PCR 12:54].

On 7 April 1642, "Mr. Rob[er]te Hicks" sold to "Mr. William Bradford ... two acres of marsh meadow lying at the High pines" [PCR

12:79]. On 7 May 1642, "Mr. Robert Hicks" sold to "Will[ia]m Brett of Duxborrow ... seven acres of upland lying at Island Creek" [PCR 12:80]. On the same day, "Mr. Robert Hicks" sold to "Mr. John Reynor ... three acres of marsh meadow lying at the High Pines" [PCR 12:80]. On 9 October 1645, "Mr. Rob[er]te Hicks" sold to "Georg[e] Partrich all that parcel of marsh meadow ... containing two acres" [PCR 12:115].

In his will, dated 28 May 1645 and proved 15 May 1648, "Robert Hicks of Plymouth ... being full of infirmities of body" bequeathed to "my son Ephraim all that my dwelling house barn and buildings with the gardens ... in Plymouth," also "all those three fields one lying on the north side of the said town of Plymouth ..., the second which I lately purchased of Mr. John Aldin and the third called the south field"; "but my mind and will is that my executrix hereafter named shall have and enjoy three rooms in the said house during her life she keeping herself unmarried, viz: the hall and chamber over and cellar underneath, and also that my said son Ephraim shall pay her the thirds of the said lands during her life and widowhood"; to "my said son Ephraim all my lands lying at Iland Creek on Duxbery side except two lots of upland of twenty acres apiece lying next unto Mr. Kemp's lands, which I hereby give and bequeath unto John Banges my grandchild"; to "my executrix ... the rents of the said land not set and let forth for six years yet to come if she shall so long live, but all the rest of my lands ... I give unto my said son Ephraim"; "I give unto John Reyner the son of Mr. John Reyner our teacher fifty acres of the purchased lands accruing ... to me as a purchaser of my share of lands lying at Seawams or Secunck if the said Mr. John Reyner his father do remain at Plymouth"; to "Samuell my eldest son" fifty acres; to "my said son Ephraim" fifty acres; to "John Watson" fifty acres; to "John Bangs" fifty acres; to "the younger of Mr. Charls Chancy's sons which his wife had at one birth when he dwelt at Plymouth" fifty acres; to "my said son Ephraim" household goods; to the Town of Plymouth one cow calf; to "William Pontus" 20s.; to "John Faunce" 20s.; to "Nathaneell Morton" 20s.; to "Thomas Cushman" 20s.; "Margaret my loving wife" sole executrix and residue; Mr. John Howland, Mannasses Kempton and Thomas Cushman overseers; to John Howland and Mannasses Kemton 10s. each for a remembrance; to Joshua Prat "a suit of my wearing clothes with a pair of shoes and stockings"; to Samuell Eddy a pair of wearing stockings; to "my said son Ephraim ... my four oxen, paying my loving wife ... the thirds of the profits of the lands as is before mentioned ... and to draw her twenty loads of wood yearly to her house in Plymouth during her life" [MD 8:144-46, citing PCPR 1:70].

The inventory of the estate of "Mr. Robert Hicks deceased the 24th of May 1647 taken the fifth of July in the year aforesaid also exhibited upon oath the 4th of May 1648" totalled £39 13s., with no real estate included [MD 8:143-44, citing PCPR 1:69].

On 23 January 1648, John Rogers of Duxbury bought the rent of lands improved by Mr. Robert Hicks now deceased from Ephraim Hicks of Plymouth [PCR 12:155-56].

On 1 May 1660, "G[e]orge Watson," on behalf of his son John Watson and nephew John Bangs, requested that, because "Samuel Hickes" was mistakenly entered in the court records as purchaser of lands at Cushenah and Accoaksett, and it should have been "Mr. Robert Hickes," it be corrected; the matter was referred to a later court [PCR 3:186]. On 3 October 1662, "Samuell Hickes" was offered an equal division with others in the lands of Mr. Robert Hicks at Accushena, and Coaksett, but he declined [PCR 4:27]. Margaret and Samuel could not agree on the division of goods in Robert's estate and the matter was taken to court on 7 June 1661 [PCR 3:217].

On 7 October 1662, "Margarett Hickes of Plymouth, widow, as sole executrix to my husband Mr. Robert Hickes," confirmed his bequest of fifty acres to "Elnathan Chauncye the younger of the twins of Mr. Charles Chauncye" [MD 17:240-41, citing PCLR 2:2:107].

On 22 March 1663[/4], "Mistress Hickes" and "Sam[uel] Hickes" were granted Lot 7 in the Plymouth lands at "Puncateesett Necke" [PTR 1:64].

In her will, dated 8 July 1665 and proved 6 March 1665/6, "Margarett Hickes widow of the town of Plymouth" bequeathed to "my son Samuell Hickes" £5; to "my daughter-in-law Lydia Hickes" 30s.; to "my son Samuel's children" 10s. each "there being seven of them"; said legacies to be paid by "son Samuell Hickes" from his debt "he having already received a large portion of that which God hath given me not only in lands but also in goods and chattels which was not only my husband's and son Ephraim's estate formerly but also given to me by will at my son Ephraim's death"; to "my grandchild John Banges" 40s.; residue to "the children of my son-in-law Gorg Watson and my loving daughter that is deceased Phebe Watson," also said estate to be "at the dispose of my son-in-law Gorg Watson"; "my son-in-law Gorg Watson and my friend Captain Southworth" overseers [PCPR 2:2:32, abstracted in MD 16:157-58].

The inventory of the estate of "Mistress Margarett Hickes," taken 5 March 1665[/6], totalled £53 12s. 6d. and included no real estate [PCPR 2:2:33, abstracted in MD 16:158]. On 6 March 1665/6, "Gorge Watson" was granted administration on the estate of "Mistress Margarett Hickes, deceased" [PCR 4:117].

BIRTH: By about 1578 (based on estimated date of marriage).
DEATH: Plymouth 24 May 1647 (from inventory). (Savage and Pope both give this date as 24 March, apparently based on the abstract of the inventory published in 1850 [NEHGR 4:282]. On the original the month of death is in the upper right corner of the page, and is worn, so that only "Ma" can now be read on microfilm. Bowman saw this as May, and his reading is followed here.)
MARRIAGE: By 1603 Margaret _____. She died at Plymouth between 8 July 1665 (date of will) and 6 March 1665/6 (probate of will).
CHILDREN (first eight baptized at St. Mary Magdalen, Bermondsey, Surrey [TAG 51:58]):
   i   THOMAS HICKS, bp. 19 February 1603/4; bur. 23 April 1604.
   ii   JOHN HICKS, bp. 12 October 1605; no further record.
   iii   SARA HICKS, bp. 25 October 1607; bur. 24 February 1617/8.
   iv   RICHARD HICKS, bp. 17 September 1609; no further record.
   v   SAMUEL HICKS, bp. 18 August 1611; m. Plymouth 11 September 1645 Lydia Doane [PCR 2:88], daughter of JOHN DOANE [PM 171].
   vi   LYDIA HICKS, bp. 6 September 1612; m. by about 1633 EDWARD BANGS [PM 23].
   vii   PHOEBE HICKS, bp. 15 March 1614/5; m. by about 1636 George Watson (their daughter Phebe m. Jonathan Shaw on 22 January 1656 [PVR 662]).
   viii   MARY HICKS, bp. 11 May 1617; bur. 14 September 1619.
   ix   EPHRAIM HICKS, b. Plymouth about 1625; m. Plymouth 13 September 1649 Elizabeth Howland [PCR 8:8], daughter of JOHN HOWLAND [PM 279]; Ephraim Hicks d. 12 December 1649 "a violent death" [PCR 3:202] and his widow m. (2) Plymouth 10 July 1651 John Dickenson [PCR 8:13].

COMMENTS: The major breakthrough on this family was made when Robert S. Wakefield discovered additional baptismal entries in the St. Mary Magdalen, Bermondsey, register [TAG 51:57-58].
    Several sources give Robert Hicks two wives: Elizabeth Morgan and Margaret Winslow. No record has been found of any marriage for Robert

Hicks, and his only known wife was Margaret; the argument that Margaret was a Winslow has little basis [TAG 54:31-34].

Clement Briggs of Weymouth, fellmonger, deposed 29 August 1638 that

> about two and twenty years since this deponent then dwelling with one Mr. Samuell Lathame in Barmundsey Streete in Southwarke a fellmonger and one Thomas Harlow then also dwelling with Mr. Rob[er]te Heeks in the same street a fellmonger the said Harlow and this deponent had often conference together how many pelts each of their masters pulled a week. And this deponent deposeth and saith that the said Rob[er]te Heeks did pull three hundred pelts a week and diverse times six or seven hundred & more a week in the killing seasons, which was the most part of the year (except the time of Lent) for the space of three or four years. And that the said Rob[er]te Heeks sold his sheep's pelts at that time for 40s. a hundred to Mr. Arnold Allard, whereas this deponent's Mr. Samuell Lathame sold his pelts for 50s. per hundred to the same man at the same time and Mr. Heeks pelts were much better ware [PCR 12:35].

On 13 July 1639, Robert Hicks of Plymouth, "citizen & leatherseller of London," by a bill dated 6 July 1618 was indebted to Thomas Heath, citizen & cooper of London, for £180, which amount was demanded by letter of attorney made by Hannah Cugley but Hicks showed an acquittance of all debts to Heath, having paid it long ago [PCR 12:43].

On 6 March 1649[/50], administration of the estate of Ephraim Hickes was granted to Margaret Hicks and Thomas Willet [PCR 2:148]. The nuncupative will made by Ephraim to Mr. Thomas Southworth was set aside, Ephraim being "not in a capacity in regard of his said manner of death to make a legal will" [PCR 3:202]. The court ordered that Ephraim's estate be set aside for the benefit of his mother, "Mistress Margaret Hickes," but the order was not recorded, and Margaret had to go back to court many years later, on 3 December 1660, to insist it be recorded [PCR 3:203].

BIBLIOGRAPHIC NOTE: In 1938 Louis Effingham deForest compiled a comprehensive summary of all that was known about Robert Hicks at that date [Moore Anc 295-308]. (This summary includes children Elizabeth and Daniel, for whom there is no evidence.)

RICHARD HIGGINS

ORIGIN: Unknown.
MIGRATION: 1632.
FIRST RESIDENCE: Plymouth.
REMOVES: Eastham 1645, Piscataway 1670.

OCCUPATION: Tailor (on 1 April 1634, he took Samuel Godbertson as apprentice to learn trade of tailor [PCR 1:29]; in a deed acknowledged on 25 March 1669 he calls himself "Richard Higgens of Eastham ... tailor" [PCLR 3:147]).
FREEMAN: In 1633 Plymouth list of freemen after those admitted 1 January 1634/5 [PCR 1:4]. In Plymouth Colony list of 7 March 1636/7 [PCR 1:53]. In Plymouth section of 1639 Plymouth Colony list of freemen; his name was then erased and "Rich[ard] Higgenson" was added to the "Nawsett [Eastham]" section of the same list [PCR 8:174, 177]. In Eastham section of 1658 list of freemen [PCR 8:201]. (He was not in the 29 May 1670 list of Plymouth freemen.)
OFFICES: Plymouth Colony committee on highways, 2 May 1637 [PCR 1:58]. Committee on bounds between Barnstable and Yarmouth, 11 March 1657/8 [PCR 3:175]. Committee on Kennebec trade, 13 June 1660 [PCR 3:195].

Plymouth Colony petit jury, 4 September 1638, 7 September 1642, 7 March 1642/3, 5 March 1643/4, 1 June 1647 [PCR 2:117, 7:9, 32, 34, 37]. Grand jury, 5 June 1644 [PCR 2:71]. Coroner's jury, 24 December 1667 [PCR 4:176].

Deputy for Eastham to Plymouth General Court, 1647, 1653, 1655, 1657, 1658, 1660, 1665 [PCR 2:117, 3:32, 80, 115, 135, 187, 4:90].

Eastham selectman 1666, 1667, 1668 [PCR 4:124, 146, 182]. Surveyor of highways, 5 June 1651 [PCR 2:168].

In Plymouth section of 1643 Plymouth Colony list of men able to bear arms [PCR 8:189].
ESTATE: Assessed 9s. in the Plymouth tax list of 25 March 1633 and 12s. in the list of 27 March 1634 [PCR 1:11, 28].

On 7 October 1633, Thomas Little sold to "Richard Higgens ... his now dwelling house & misted" [PCR 1:16]. On 13 January 1633/4, John Barnes sold to "Rich[ard] Higgens ... one dwelling house & 20 acres of land, being lately in the possession of Edw[ard] Holman," part of the consideration being "20 acres of land at Scituate" [PCR 1:24].

On 4 March 1638/9, "Richard Higgens" was granted "forty acres of upland lying at the southeast side of the great South Pond, and two parcels of marsh ground for meadow, lying southwest from the said upland" [PCR 1:115]. On 30 November 1640, "[w]hereas it appeareth that twenty acres of land were formerly granted long since to Richard Higgen, at Mannamett Ponds, the court doth now confirm the same unto him" [PCR 1:168].

On 11 June 1640, "John Smaly & Richard Higgens have exchanged two parcels of meadow land with each other, viz: one acre that the said John Smaly had at Blewfish River with Richard Higgens for a parcel of meadow ground granted him at Warrens Wells containing by estimation two acres" [PCR 12:59]. On 3 March 1644[/5], "Richard Higgens" sold to "Gyles Rickett half an acre of marsh meadow ... lying at Hobbs Hole" [PCR 12:107]. On 18 August 1645, "Richard Higgens" sold to "John Churchwell all that his dwelling house, outhouses and buildings with the garden and orchard situate near Browne's Rock together with the uplands thereunto adjoining and all his lands at Wooberry together with his meadow at South ponds and at Colebrook meadows towards Aggawam" [PCR 12:111-12].

Katharine Chapin Higgins quotes extensively from, and also summarizes, much information about the landholding of Richard Higgins, both at Eastham and Piscataway, referring to Eastham town records, Plymouth Colony deeds, and Piscataway town records [Higgins (1918) pp. 32-36; Higgins (1924) pp. 5-7].

Richard Higgins died within a few years of his arrival in New Jersey, and no will has survived, but his widow is called executrix of his estate [PCLR 5:139]. The widow acquired much land in the period after Richard's death and before her marriage to Isaac Whitehead [Higgins (1918) pp. 38-41].

BIRTH: By about 1609 (based on date of first marriage).
DEATH: Piscataway after 20 November 1674 [PCLR 4:165] and before 1 June 1675 [PCR 5:169-70].
MARRIAGE: (1) Plymouth 11 December 1634 Lydia Chandler (Eastham records give this date as 23 November, but the Plymouth record is clearly to be preferred), probably daughter of EDMUND CHANDLER [PM 97]. She died probably shortly after the birth of Benjamin in 1640, and certainly before Richard Higgins remarried.

(2) Eastham [blank] October 1651 Mary (____) Yates, widow of John Yates of Eastham [MD 8:13]. She survived her second husband and married (3) at Piscataway as his second wife Isaac Whitehead, she having recanted her intention to marry Samuel Moore Sr. of Woodbridge

[NYGBR 47:21]. She was living in 1702 when her son Thomas allowed her a life tenancy in part of his home [NYGBR 47:22].

CHILDREN:

With first wife

i   JONATHAN HIGGINS, b. Plymouth July 1637 [PCR 8:27]; m. (1) Eastham 9 January 1660 Elizabeth Rogers [MD 6:15, 7:16; MF 2:161]; m. (2) by 1680 Hannah Rogers [NEHGR 123:147-48; MF 2:163; NYGBR 46:393]. (The two wives of Jonathan Higgins were sisters, a situation that was considered incestuous by the Puritans and strenuously discouraged; but the evidence presented by Anne Borden Harding in 1969 indicates that in this instance the two wives were sisters [NEHGR 123:147-48].)

ii   BENJAMIN HIGGINS, b. Plymouth June 1640 [PCR 8:27]; m. Eastham 24 December 1661 Lydia Bangs [MD 8:12], daughter of EDWARD BANGS [PM 23].

With second wife

iii   MARY HIGGINS, b. Eastham 27 September 1652 [PCR 8:27; MD 8:13]; m. William Looker of Elizabethtown, New Jersey, and was supported as "a lame and distracted woman the wife of one Wm. Looker, late of Elizabeth Towne, brewer," by her mother and brother Eliakim Higgins [NYGBR 47:24]. (Claims that she had an earlier husband who was a Bradford have no basis.)

iv   ELIAKIM HIGGINS, b. Eastham 20 October 1654 [PCR 8:27; MD 8:14]; m. Piscataway 15 May 1684 Alice Newbould [NJHSP 4:4:36; NYGBR 46:394; Monnette 227].

v   JADIAH HIGGINS, b. Eastham [blank] March 1656/7 [PCR 8:27; MD 8:14]; m. 12 May 1684 Mary Newbold [NYGBR 46:394 (source not stated; place of marriage not noted)].

vi   ZERA HIGGINS, b. Eastham [blank] June 1658 [MD 8:14]; m. Piscataway 25 December 1680 Elizabeth Oliver [NJHSP 4:4:36; NYGBR 46:394; Monnette 227].

vii   THOMAS HIGGINS, b. Eastham [blank] January 1661 [MD 8:14]; m. Piscataway 9 July 1690 Elizabeth Hull [NJHSP 4:4:36; NYGBR 46:394; Monnette 227].

viii   LYDIA HIGGINS, b. Eastham [blank] July 1664 [MD 8:14]; no further record.

ix   REBECCA HIGGINS, b. say 1666; m. Piscataway 28 April 1683 Thomas Martin [NJHSP 4:4:36; NYGBR 46:394; Monnette 227].

    x   RUTH HIGGINS, b. say 1671; m. (1) Woodbridge 23 April 1692 Isaac FitzRandolph [Monnette 249]; m. (2) 1695 Stephen Tuttle [NYGBR 46:394, 47:31 (accounting for her first husband's estate as "Ruth Tuttle")].

    xi   SARAH HIGGINS, b. say 1673; m. Woodbridge 26 October 1693 Samuel Moore [NYGBR 46:394; Monnette 249 (says 1702 or 1693)].

ASSOCIATIONS: The contention that the first wife of Richard Higgins was daughter of EDMUND CHANDLER is based in part on the frequent early interactions of Higgins with Chandler and his son Samuel. Richard Higgins was with Edmund Chandler creditor of estate of Godbert Godbertson, 1633 [MD 1:157]; with Samuel Chandler, creditor of estate of John Thorpe, 1633 [MD 1:160]; and surety for Samuel Chandler in court case of 3 December 1639 [PCR 1:137-38].

In 1639 John Smalley took over from Richard Higgins the apprenticeship of Samuel Godbertson (both men were tailors) [PCR 1:129-30]. The association between Smalley and Higgins continued in 1640 with an exchange of Plymouth land [PCR 12:59]. Higgins and Smalley migrated about the same time to Piscataway, and continued together in land transactions there.

COMMENTS: Two hypotheses have been set forth on the English origin of Richard Higgins. Orra E. Monnette published one, which was based on family papers, as verified by Gustave Anjou. This proposal was refuted in 1918 and 1924 by Katharine Chapin Higgins, and the ever-gullible Monnette was clearly taken in by the ever-mendacious Anjou.

The alternate suggested origin, that the immigrant was the Richard Higgins who was apprenticed as a tailor in 1627, is at least possible and has some attractions, but is far from being proved.

The claim that Higgins came in 1623 cannot be true, since he did not participate in any of the land grants made to this group of immigrants. The claim that he came in 1629 on the *Talbot* is not impossible, but is not supported by any documentary evidence.

Higgins was a member of the 1644 committee to explore settlement of Eastham, but his actual move probably dates from his sale of Plymouth land in 1645. His last records in Eastham are in 1669, and he does not appear in the 29 May 1670 Plymouth Colony list of freemen, so he apparently moved to Piscataway in late 1669 or early 1670.

A son William is recorded in Plymouth vital records as born 15 December 1654, an impossible date given the birthdate for Eliakim; this William is not seen again, and is probably an erroneous entry. Rebecca is called daughter of Richard and Mary in her marriage record in 1683; given this date of marriage she must have been born in Eastham, even though there is no record of her birth there. The last two children, Ruth and Sarah, were presumably born after the move to Piscataway; they are included as children of Richard and Mary since they have the surname Higgins in their marriage records, and Thomas Higgins is co-administrator with Ruth on the estate of her first husband.

BIBLIOGRAPHIC NOTE: All substantial research on Richard Higgins was published between 1915 and 1926. Orra E. Monnette had published a lengthy article in 1915 and 1916 ["Richard Higgins of Plymouth and Eastham, Mass., and Piscataway, N.J., and Some of His Descendants," NYGBR 46:387-94, 47:20-32]. In 1918 Mrs. Katharine Chapin Higgins published privately *Richard Higgins: A Resident and Pioneer Settler at Plymouth and Eastham, Massachusetts, and at Piscataway, New Jersey and His Descendants* (Worcester MA), and followed this in 1924 with a *Supplement* [cited herein as Higgins (1918) and Higgins (1924)]. This round of publication terminated in 1926 with an editorial note in NYGBR incorporating Monnette's objection to Chapin's (and Bartlett's) rejection of his (and Anjou's) suggested English connection [NYGBR 57:298-99].

Other items published more recently have not added to our knowledge of Richard Higgins [John Ralph Higgins, "The Higgins Genealogy: Twelve Generations: From Massachusetts to California: 1632-1972" (Los Gatos, California, 1972); Vivian Higgins Morse, *An American Family and its Ancestor Predecessors* (Baltimore 1973); and Anne Farrell Higgins Wood, "The Story of Many Descendants of the Brothers Ichabod and Richard Higgins: 1603-1979" (n.p. 1979)].

THOMAS HIGGINS

1 January 1633/4: "At the same Court, Tho[mas] Higgens, having lived an extravagant life, was placed with John Jenny for eight years, to serve him as an apprentice, during which time the said John competently to provide for him, & at the end thereof to give him double apparel, 12 bushels of corn, & 20 acres of land" [PCR 1:21].

COMMENTS: Pope has this man marry at Eastham 3 November 1648 the widow of Hugh Tilley [Pope 229]. This is in fact the second marriage of Thomas Huckins of Barnstable, who is first of record in 1643 [PCR

8:193]. It is possible that this latter man is the Thomas Higgins of 1634, having finished his apprenticeship; but given the different spelling of the name, and the gap of nine years without any record of either name, it seems more likely that we have two different people.

JOHN HILL

Governor William Bradford and the Assistants of Plymouth Colony wrote on 6 February 1631/2 to their Massachusetts Bay counterparts saying "Now there are diverse gone from hence, to dwell and inhabit with you, as Clement Brigges, John Hill, John Eddy, Daniel Ray, etc., the which if either you, or they desire their dismissions, we shall be ready to give them" [WP 3:65].

COMMENTS: CLEMENT BRIGGS went to Weymouth [PM 76], JOHN EDDY went to Watertown [PM 189] and DANIEL RAY went to Salem [PM 385]. With many John Hills in evidence in the 1630s, it is difficult to determine which, if any of them, the Plymouth man might be. While the Dorchester John Hill appearing as an abutter in 1633/4 is a strong possibility [DTR 5], no firm identification is made here.

WILLIAM HILTON

ORIGIN: London.
MIGRATION: 1621 on the *Fortune.*
FIRST RESIDENCE: Plymouth.
REMOVES: Piscataqua, Dover 1628, Kittery 1648, York 1651.

OCCUPATION: Tavern keeper and ferry operator (at Kittery). On 27 June 1648, "Mr. William Hilton being licensed for to keep the ordinary at the mouth of the river of Pascataquack and that none other shall keep any private ordinary there, nor to sell wine, beer nor liquor upon any pretence" [MPCR 1:125]. On 16 October 1649, "Mr. William Hilton presented for not keeping victual and drink at all times for strangers and inhabitants, admonished" [MPCR 1:135]. On 15 October 1650, "for as much as the house at the river's mouth where Mr. Shapleigh's father first built and Mr. William Hilton now dwelleth; in regard it was first house there built and Mr. Shapleigh intendeth to build and enlarge it, and for further considerations, it is thought fit it should from time to time be for a house of entertainment or ordinary with this proviso, that the tenant be such a one as the inhabitants shall approve of" [MPCR 1:147].

CHURCH MEMBERSHIP: In his discussion of the controversy surrounding Rev. JOHN LYFORD [PM 309] and his followers, Hubbard noted that "the first occasion of quarrel with them was, the baptizing of Mr. Hilton's child, who was not joined to the church at Plymouth" [Hubbard 93-94]; this event apparently took place in 1624.

FREEMAN: 19 May 1642 [MBCR 2:292]. "Mr. W[illia]m Hilton" was among the residents of York who on 22 November 1652 subjected themselves to Massachusetts Bay government and took the freeman's oath [MBCR 4:1:129].

EDUCATION: William Hilton wrote several competent, if poorly spelled, letters [NEHGR 21:179; WP 3:119, 120-21, 449]. Committee to "examine the book delivered in by Mr. Bellingham, & compare it with the book of records, & return their objections & thoughts thereof to this house in writing," 7 June 1644 [MBCR 3:6].

OFFICES: Deputy for Dover to Massachusetts Bay General Court, 7 March 1643/4, 29 May 1644, 14 May 1645 (disguised as "William Heath") [MBCR 2:54, 66, 3:2, 10].

York grand jury, 11 March 1651, 28 June 1655 [MPCR 1:159, 2:40]. Jury, 25 November 1650 [MPCR 1:155]. Committee to divide land, 19 March 1651/2, 28 June 1655 [MPCR 1:178, 2:38]. Arbiter, 15 October 1650 [MPCR 1:144].

York alderman, 1652 [YLR 1:2:14-15]. Selectman, 1653, 1654 [GDMNH 335].

ESTATE: In the 1623 Plymouth division of land William Hilton received one acre as a passenger on the *Fortune* and "William Hilton's wife & 2 children" received three acres as passengers on the *Anne* [PCR 12:5, 6].

On 30 June 1656, administration on the estate of William Hilton was granted to Richard White "the said Whitte having married his widow" [MPCR 2:51]. White posted a £100 bond as administrator [MPCR 2:54].

On 31 May 1660, Massachusetts Bay General Court, in "answer to a petition of Willjam Hilton, humbly craving the Court's allowance & confirmation of a deed of gift of six miles square of land lying on the River Pennieconaquigg, being a rivulet running into the River Penacooke, with two miles of the best meadow lying on the northeast side of Pennacook, given to his father & him in the year 1636 by Tahanto, the sagamore there; & the Court, having considered the contents of this petition, judge meet not to grant the same, but considering the petitioner's grounds for the approbation of the Indian's grant, do judge meet to grant that three hundred acres of the said land be set out to the petitioner by a committee chosen by this Court, so as that it may not prejudice any plantation; and this as a final end of all future claims by virtue of such grant from the Indians" [MBCR 4:1:430].

BIRTH: By about 1591 (based on estimated date of marriage), son of William Hilton of Northwich, Cheshire [GDMNH 334].

DEATH: Between 28 June 1655 (when he was appointed to a committee [MPCR 2:38]) and 30 June 1656 (by which date the widow had remarried [MPCR 2:47]).

MARRIAGE: (1) By 1616 _____ _____, who came with two children to Plymouth in 1623 on the *Anne*. She died by about 1636.

(2) By about 1636 Frances _____, born about 1618 (deposed on 27 February 1687/8, aged about seventy, regarding events that had taken place forty-six years earlier involving William Hilton [NEHGR 31:181, citing York Court Files]). She survived him and married again by 30 June 1656 Richard White [MPCR 2:74]. (In a footnote in his MPCR series, Charles Thornton Libby remarked: "This woman's [Frances's] court records serve to illustrate the social distinctions of the period. While married to Mr. William Hilton she was always entitled 'Mistress,' even when called into court for rude behavior, but after his death and upon her marriage to Goodman Richard White, she promptly dropped to 'Goody'" [MPCR 1:267].)

CHILDREN:

With first wife

i ELIZABETH HILTON, bp. Northwich 27 June 1616 [GDMNH 335]; bur. there 1 August 1616 [GDMNH 335].

ii WILLIAM HILTON, bp. Northwich 22 June 1617 [GDMNH 335]; m. (1) by 1641 Sarah Greenleaf, daughter of Edmund Greenleaf (eldest known child b. Newbury June 1641; in his will of 22 December 1668, Edmund Greenleaf made a bequest to "my grandchild Elizabeth Hilton" [Pillsbury Anc 590, citing SPR 7:112]); m. (2) Charlestown 16 September 1659 Mehitable Nowell [ChVR 1:38], daughter of INCREASE NOWELL {1630, Charlestown} [GMB 2:1342-46]. (See NEHGR 124:88-108 for his activities as an explorer.)

iii MARY HILTON, bp. Northwich 11 May 1619 [GDMNH 335]; apparently the second of Hilton's two children who arrived at Plymouth in 1623; no further record. (See *COMMENTS* below.)

iv   JOHN HILTON, b. about 1624, perhaps the child whose baptism caused such strife in Plymouth; did not marry [GDMNH 332]. (There is no assurance that the child born shortly after the family's arrival in Plymouth was named John, but there does not appear to be any other child who would have been born at this date.)

With second wife

v   MAGDALENE HILTON, b. say 1636; m. (1) by 1656 James Wiggin; m. (2) Newbury (int.) 14 May 1698 Henry Kenning. (On 30 June 1656, "Magdeline Wiggin the wife of James Wiggin" was presented at York Court for "reporting that she saw William Moore & her mother Frances Whitte in the act of adultery" [MPCR :52]. The claim that this marriage took place by 1646 [GDMNH 335] seems to be a simple typographical error.)

vi   MAINWARING HILTON, b. by 1646 [YLR 2:33]; m. by about 1671 Mary Moulton, daughter of THOMAS MOULTON {1637, Newbury} (on 4 July 1671, administration was granted to "Tho[mas] Mowlton of the estate of Mannering Hilton his son-in-law lately deceased" [MPCR 2:214]; eldest child of daughter Magdalen b. York 24 September 1691 [NEHGR 110:60]).

vii   AGNES HILTON, b. say 1647; m. by 1667 Arthur Beale (apparently based on his occupation of Hilton land and subsequent activity in association with Mainwaring Hilton and Richard White [YLR 2:33]).

viii   WILLIAM HILTON, b. about 1653 (aged twenty-four December 1677 [GDMNH 336, citing unknown source]); m. by 1678 Ann ____ [GDMNH 336, 531].

ASSOCIATIONS: His brothers EDWARD HILTON {1628, Dover} [GMB 2:947-51] and Richard Hilton came to Piscataqua.

COMMENTS: In a letter written in November 1621, soon after his arrival at Plymouth, and published the following year by Captain John Smith, William Hilton wrote to a cousin in England saying "Our company are for the most part very religious honest people, the word of God sincerely taught us every Sabbath, so that I know not anything a contented mind can here want. I desire your friendly care to send my wife and children to me, where I wish all the friends I have in England" [Philip L. Barbour, ed., *The Complete Works of Captain John Smith (1580-1631) in Three*

Volumes (Williamsburg, Virginia, 1986), pp. 430-31; Young's Pilgrim Fathers 250-51; NEHGR 31:179].

William's wife and two children (son William and daughter Mary) arrived in 1623. A third child was born soon, probably in 1624, and Rev. JOHN LYFORD's baptism of this child was the opening shot in a series of disruptions at Plymouth revolving around Lyford and JOHN OLDHAM [PM 345].

William Hilton and his family soon left Plymouth, but his place of residence in the next few years is not certain, and is intertwined with the career of his brother EDWARD HILTON. A useful document in this regard is the petition of William Hilton, eldest son of the immigrant William Hilton. Although the petition itself is not dated, it was discussed at court in Massachusetts Bay in late May and early June of 1660. William Hilton tells us that "your petitioner's father came over into New England about the year Anno Domini 1621; & your petitioner came about one year & an half after, and in a little time following settled ourselves upon the River of Pischataq[ua], with Mr. Edw[ard] Hilton, who were the first English planters there" [SJC Case #362; NEHGR 36:41-42]. The petition goes on to claim land up the Merrimack River, which had been granted to William Hilton Senior and William Hilton Junior by the local Indian sachem; the petition was only partially successful.

Edward Hilton settled on the Piscataqua sometime between 1625 and 1628 [GMB 2:950], and the petitioner is here claiming that the Hilton brothers made the settlement simultaneously. One possibility, then, is that William Hilton left Plymouth in later 1624 or early 1625, after the baptism incident, and joined his brother Edward about that time in settling what would become Dover. This would not require any residence between Plymouth and Dover.

Noyes, Libby and Davis state that Hilton "left Plymouth and joined [David] Thomson at Little Harbor with the purpose of starting salt works," and apparently did this in partnership with GILBERT WINSLOW [GDMNH 334-35, 765 (no documentary evidence provided); PM 510]. This would provide William Hilton and his family with a home prior to the arrival of Edward Hilton, assuming the latter did not come so early as 1625.

John T. Hassam demonstrated that the immigrant William Hilton had two sons by that same name. The deposition of 1660 was made by the elder of these two sons, who lived in Newbury and Charlestown. A deposition of 1683 proves the younger son William of the immigrant William, for on 30 May 1683 two men testified that "Willia[m] Hilton now resident in York ... was commonly known, & reputed, to be the son of William Hilton Senior deceased, & formerly lived in York" [YLR 3:125; NEHGR 31:184, 36:40].

Mary Hilton *alias* Downer who married Thomas Sears and Abel Huse has sometimes been placed in this family, but she had children at an age far too advanced to be the Mary Hilton, daughter of William, who was baptized in 1619 [GDMNH 333]. Her parentage remains a mystery.

Noyes, Libby and Davis note that "(b)esides the wife who followed him to Plymouth, and Frances, possibly a widow with children when he married her about 1651, there may have been others," suggesting that "if one of his wives should prove to have been a Winslow it would explain his letter writing with Edward Winslow, his association with John Winslow, his removal to Piscataqua with Gilbert Winslow and the marriage of two of John Winslow's sons to his relations" [GDMNH 335 (without, unfortunately, documentary support for the Winslow associations)].

There is no date of death for the first wife of William Hilton, and we do not know when he married Frances, so the distribution of his children among his wives is difficult. We assume here that the first wife did not survive long in this country, and that the last four children were all with Frances. Magdalene, who calls Frances her mother, need not have been a Hilton, but since this name also suggests a Winslow connection, and since Libby makes such a point of the low social status of Frances, one might question the exact nature of this relation as well. For the moment we leave the problem in this unsatisfactory state.

Sometime before March 1639, William Hilton had participated in an exploratory expedition up the Merrimack [WP 4:101].

On 16 October 1649, Mrs. Hilton was presented and admonished for fighting and abusing her neighbors with her tongue. At the same court Mr. William Hilton was presented for breach of the Sabbath in carrying of wood from the woods and for failing to keep food and drink on hand for strangers and inhabitants [MPCR 1:135].

On 15 March 1649/50, Mr. William Hilton brought cases against Hatevell Nutter, Thomas Hanscom and Robert Mendam [MPCR 1:138]. He was still suing Hanscom and Mendam on 11 March 1651[/2] [MPCR 1:156]. On 15 October 1650, Mr. William Hilton and Frances his wife were sued by Mr. Georg Moncke for slander [MPCR 1:145]. On 11 March 1651[/2], Jeremy Sheires reviled Mr. William Hilton when Hilton was foreman of the jury, and Sheires was fined £2 [MPCR 1:160]. On 14 October 1651, Mr. William Hilton posted bail for Clement Campion, sued Thomas Way for debt, and sued Michaell Powell for debt [MPCR 1:169].

On 30 June 1653, "William Hilton Senior" sued Samuell Allcocke for cutting and carrying away his timber [MPCR 2:11]. On 25 October 1653, Mr. William Hilton Senior sued Ann Mason of London and, in a separate action, sued Sir Ferdinando Gorges, for damage done against him [MPCR 2:19].

On 28 June 1655, the court found Frances Hilton, the wife of William Hilton, guilty of "railing at her husband and saying he went with Joane [*sic*, John in the blotter] his bastard to his three halfe penny whores and that he carried a cloak of profession for his knavery." For this offense she was sentenced to have "twenty lashes upon the bare skin, only the execution thereof upon her husband's request to be respited upon her good behavior until the next county court, except any just complaints come in against her. In the meantime, which if they do unto authority then the punishment to be inflicted upon her by order of the commissioners of York at what time they shall see cause to order it" [MPCR 2:43-44].

At the same court in which Richard White became William Hilton's administrator, White also brought a charge of slander against Rice Jones for an offense against his wife, Frances White [MPCR 2:47]. As the court dragged on, Frances White was countersued for "causelessly abusing" the wife of Rice Jones with opprobrious and disgraceful speeches and was sentenced to acknowledge her offence in court, 3 July 1656 [MPCR 2:50]. On 6 July 1657, Joan Andrews was presented for "threatening Goody Whitte at York in a profane manner saying that she would swear herself to the devil but she would be avenged of her" [MPCR 2:56].

On 30 July 1656, "Magdeline Wiggin the wife of James Wiggin" was presented for saying she saw "William Moore & her [step]mother Frances Whitte" in the act of adultery [MPCR 2:52].

On 5 July 1658, complaints were heard about Richard White and his wife fighting and quarrelling together [MPCR 2:63]. On 3 July 1660, Richard White and his wife Frances White were presented for allowing men to be drunk in their house on the Sabbath and for not attending public meeting, and for "common lying and backbiting of their neighbors & slandering them & for their great disorder in falling out & fighting one with another & for beating company in their house & for beating Mistress Gunnison & Joseph Davesse his servants, & Ric[hard] Whitte for being drunk several times" [MPCR 2:91]. On 1 July 1673, Richard White was paying fines for himself and his wife [MPCR 2:260]. On 6

July 1675, they were presented for not attending the public worship [MPCR 2:307].

Noyes, Libby and Davis list as a possible first child of this William Hilton a John Hilton who was buried at Northwich on 26 November 1610. This seems unlikely, as six more years would pass before another child was known to have been born to this William.

BIBLIOGRAPHIC NOTE: In 1877 John T. Hassam published "Some Descendants of William Hilton" and in 1882 "The Dover Settlement and the Hiltons" [NEHGR 31:179-87, 36:40-46]. Although these articles contain some errors (and in fact the second corrects some items in the first), they are filled with useful information on both brothers.

JOHN HOCKING

John Hocking traded on the Kennebec in the early 1630s. George Ludlow received from Mr. William Hilton the goods of "Mr. John Hockings" on 2 August 1632, which included nine rugs, eight men's coats, two "papowes coates," nine shirts and four hogsheads of bread [YLR 1:60]. (The receipt was recorded in 1657 for no obvious purpose.)

Little is known about him, other than his murder in 1634, and the legal and political wrangling that ensued. Hocking was at Piscataqua as an agent of Lord Brooke and Lord Saye and Sele, who had purchased the Piscataqua plantation. In April of 1634 he attempted to trade with the Indians on the Kennebec, a trade that rightly belonged to Plymouth, according to their patent. The Plymouth men tried to force Hocking's boat downriver, Hocking shot and killed one of the Plymouth men (Moses Talbot), and another Plymouth man immediately shot and killed Hocking.

A graphic account with noble and ignoble speeches was given by Governor Thomas Prence who stated that after attempting once to cut the second anchor cable, the Plymouth canoe was sent out a second time with "John Irish, Thomas Savory, William Rennoles" and Moses Talbot, "who accordingly went very readily." Hocking came on deck

> with a carbine & a pistol in his hand & presently presented his piece at Thomas Savory but the canoe with the tide was put near the bow of the bark, which Hocking seeing presently put his piece almost to Moyses Talbott's head, which Mr. Howland seeing called to him desiring him not to shoot his man but take himself for his mark ... saying he stood very fair but Hocking

would not hear nor look towards our bark but presently shooteth Moyses in the head, and presently took up his pistol in his hand but the Lord stayed him from doing any further hurt by a shot from our bark himself was presently struck dead being shot near the same place in the head where he had murderously shot Moyses [MD 2:11].

Bradford described the continued fallout in both the Bay, Plymouth, and in England, complaining that it was written to Lord Saye and Lord Brooks in terms

as much as they could to exasperate them in the matter, leaving out all the circumstances, as if he had been killed without any offence of his part, concealing that he had killed another first, and the just occasion that he had given in offering such wrong; at which their Lordships were much offended, till they were truly informed of the matter [Bradford 262-68].

Winthrop tells us that word reached Massachusetts Bay on 3 May 1634, and there followed some months of argumentation among Massachusetts Bay, Plymouth and Piscataqua; one of the participants was "a kinsman of the said Hocking," otherwise unidentified [WJ 1:155-56, 162-63, 165-66, 173-74].

In a letter to Sir Nathaniel Rich under date of 22 May 1634, Winthrop gave a subdued account of the "sad accident which lately fell out between our neighbors of Plimouth and some of the Lord Saye his servants at Pascat[aqua]." Ever the politician, Winthrop's concern was for the effect news of the event had on various ears.

Upon the report of this we were much grieved that such an occasion should be offered to our enemies to reproach our profession and that such an injury should be offered to those honorable persons who for love of us and for furtherance of our beginnings here, had so far engaged themselves with us.... I would entreat you to intercede with the Lords for them, that the injury and discourtesy may be passed by [WP 3:167-68].

WILLIAM HOLBECK

William Holbeck came on the *Mayflower* as servant to William White, and died soon after landing [Bradford 442-45].

COMMENTS: Banks notes that the "name of Holbeck is found in St. Andrew's parish, Norwich, where the Rev. John Robinson had a curacy before his removal to Leyden. He is to be credited as one of the Leyden contingent" [English Homes 59]. The surname "Hollebeek" is found among Flemish refugees in Leiden (private communication from Jeremy D. Bangs).

EDWARD HOLMAN

ORIGIN: Unknown.
MIGRATION: 1623 on the *Anne*.
FIRST RESIDENCE: Plymouth.

OCCUPATION: Seaman.
OFFICES: Volunteered to serve in Pequot War, 1637 [PCR 1:61]. In Plymouth section of 1643 Plymouth Colony list of men able to bear arms [PCR 8:188].
ESTATE: In the 1623 Plymouth division of land "Edw[ard] Holman" received one acre as a passenger on the *Anne* [PCR 12:6]. In the 1627 Plymouth division of cattle "Edward Holdman" is the twelfth person in the fourth company [PCR 12:10].

In the Plymouth tax list of 26 March 1633 Edward Holman was assessed 18s. [PCR 1:11], but he did not appear in the list of 27 March 1634.

On 1 October 1638, a "garden place next to Mr. Done is granted to Edward Holman, provided that he do erect a house thereupon within two months now next ensuing, or else the garden place to be forfeited" [PCR 1:99]. On 7 May 1639, Edward Holman sold to Robert Waterman "all that his garden place situate & being in the new street in Plym[outh]" [PCR 12:42]. On 7 November 1639, Edward Holman sold to John Barnes "all those his two acres of meadow assigned the said Edward and laid forth for him at the Turkey Point" [PCR 12:49].

On 17 April 1644, "Edward Holman and Amy his wife" sold to William Browne "all those their six acres of upland lying in the New Field on the west side the lands of Andrew Ring" [PCR 12:113]. Edward Holman was one of the Purchasers [PCR 2:177] and as a result he had "one whole share" in the Dartmouth lands [MD 4:188].

On 4 January 1661[/2], "Edward Holman ... of Plymouth ... seaman" sold to Hugh Cole of Plymouth, ship carpenter, "the one half of my lot share or portion of land commonly called the Purchase land, lying and being at a place Acushenah, Coaksett and places adjacent" [MD 16:208-9, citing PCLR 2:2:79]. In an undated deed (acknowledged 17 June

1667), Edward Holman of Plymouth, seaman, sold to Mr. John Almey of Portsmouth, Rhode Island, one-quarter share of a lot of Purchase Land at Ponagansett in Dartmouth [PCR 4:287]. On 23 April 1675 (acknowledged 3 May 1675), "Edward Holman in the Colony of Plymouth, seaman," confirmed a sale made twenty-eight years earlier to "Thomas Clark then of Plymouth" of "all that my lot of land lying and being ... at and up Mannomet Pond brookside" [PCR 4:21].

BIRTH: Say 1605 (probably came as a boy in his teens, servant of John Jenny).
DEATH: After 3 May 1675 [PCLR 4:21].
MARRIAGE: By 1644 Amy (Glass) Willis, daughter of James and Mary (Cogan) Glass and widow of Richard Willis [NEHGR 111:172-73, 177]. She is seen as wife of Holman only in the deed of 1644 [PCR 12:113], and was presumably dead by 24 January 1648[/9] when "Edward Holman of Plymouth" arranged for the apprenticeship of "Richard Willis the son-in-law of Edward aforesaid" with Gyles Rickard [PCR 12:157].
CHILDREN: None recorded. (George E. McCracken, in his treatment of the Cogan family, gave Edward Holman a son Edward, born in 1647, for whom there is no evidence [NEHGR 111:177].)
ASSOCIATIONS: Throughout his years in Plymouth, Edward Holman maintained an ambivalent relationship with John Barnes. On 25 March 1633, in separate transactions, each bought a heifer from Timothy Hatherly [PCR 1:8-9]. On 10 January 1633/4, Holman sold to Barnes a shallop, a house and twenty acres [PCR 1:24]. On 4 October 1636, both Holman and Barnes were presented at court for Sabbath-breaking [PCR 1:44], and, on 20 March 1636/7, Barnes and Holman were linked together in the annual allotment of hayground [PCR 1:56]. On 30 November 1640, the two men were ranged against one another in two disputes that reached the court, one over two acres of land and the other over ownership of a boat [PCR 1:167-68]. Richard Willis, whose widow Holman married by 1644, had been a servant of Barnes. Many years later, on 2 February 1657/8, "John Barnes complained against Edward Holman for entertaining John Wade, his servant, and for carrying the said Wade to Duxbury in his boat, without his master's consent." Shortly after this, on 2 March 1657/8, Barnes was brought before the court on a repeat offense of drunkenness, and in the court entry immediately following, Holman was admonished for lying to the court, although there is no certain link here [PCR 3:126, 129].

Holman also had a briefer connection with John Jenny. They shared hayground on 14 March 1635/6 [PCR 1:40], and then, on 26 August

1636, the two men were engaged in a dispute before court, in which it is stated that Holman had been in Jenny's service [PCR 1:43].

COMMENTS: Edward Holman clearly existed on the fringes of Plymouth society. He was fined on various occasions for drunkenness and Sabbath-breaking, and was also brought before the court on 7 December 1641 to answer for taking items from a shipwreck, which should have been reported to the authorities [PCR 2:29, 31]. A few months later, on 1 March 1641/2, the court recorded "Edward Holman's demands for his pains about a chest of goods found at Mannamoyit" [PCR 2:35]. On 1 June 1647, Thomas Prence sued "Edward Holeman & Nicolas Hodges" in an action of trespass [PCR 2:117] and, on 7 March 1653/4, Holman sued John Jourdaine "for making sale of a parcel of land belonging to the said Edward Holman" [PCR 7:68]. On two occasions (4 May 1652 and 9 June 1653), he was ordered not to keep company with Martha, the wife of Thomas Shrive [PCR 3:6, 37]; by this time Holman's wife Amy was almost certainly dead. Also, Holman was never made a freeman, and did not serve the colony in any civil capacity. His only recorded positive contribution was his offer to serve against the Pequots in 1637.

On the passenger list of the *Lyon* in 1632 is a man whose name has been read by Savage, Hotten and Coldham as "Edward Holmar." Pope, Banks and others make this out to be Edward Holman of Plymouth returning from a trip to England. Most of the other passengers on this vessel in 1632 were family men from Essex, a description that does not seem to fit Edward Holman, so this identification cannot be sustained at this point.

JOHN HOLMES

ORIGIN: Unknown.
MIGRATION: 1632.
FIRST RESIDENCE: Plymouth.

OCCUPATION: Messenger; marshal.
FREEMAN: Admitted 1 January 1634/5 (and added to 1633 list) [PCR 1:4, 32]. In list of Plymouth freemen, 6 March 1636/7 [PCR 1:53]. In Plymouth section of 1639 Plymouth Colony list of freemen [PCR 8:174].
EDUCATION: Sufficient to hold office of marshal.

OFFICES: On 4 December 1638, "Mr. John Holmes is sworn messenger for the whole government" [PCR 1:105] and he served in that capacity until at least 1643 [PCR 2:6]. On 5 March 1638/9, "John Holmes, the messenger, [was] presented for taking five shillings for serving of a warrant," and was discharged [PCR 1:118]; he was also presented at the same court for "sitting up in the night, or all the night, drinking inordinately, when he was sent about public business" and for "abusing other men's names to procure wine to drink amongst others inordinately." On 3 January 1643/4, "Mr. John Holmes, the Messenger," submitted his accounts for the preceding three years, indicating that the colony owed him £10 9s. 8d. [PCR 2:51]. The court on 7 October 1651 recorded a "note of what is due unto Mr. Holmes, the marshal, from Duxburrow, of his wages there" [PCR 7:51]. (The messenger was the equivalent of the marshal in Massachusetts Bay, an office that would later be called marshal in Plymouth, and would in time become the county sheriff [GMN 10:25-26, 32].)

Plymouth petit jury, 4 October 1636, 4 September 1638 [PCR 1:44, 96].

In Plymouth section of 1643 Plymouth Colony list of men able to bear arms [PCR 8:188].

ESTATE: Assessed 18s. in Plymouth tax lists of 25 March 1633 and 27 March 1634 [PCR 1:10, 28].

"Mr. Holmes" was allotted hay ground between Mr. Smith and James Hurst on 14 March 1635/6 and on 20 March 1636/7 [PCR 1:40, 56].

On 16 October 1632, "Mr. John Holmes" purchased a house and six acres adjoining Reed Pond from William Palmer [PCR 12:18]. On 5 February 1637/8, Mr. John Holmes "desired enlargement above his house, & the wood to be stayed from felling & carrying away" [PCR 1:76]. On 7 August 1638, "Mr. John Holmes requested 10 or 12 acres of lands at his lot's end, to be viewed & laid him forth; as also a little parcel of meadow at the Reed Pond" [PCR 1:93]. On 26 July 1638, Mr. John Holmes was given six shares of a cow [PTR 1:4]. On 1 October 1638, "Mr. John Holmes is granted ten acres of land, lying at his lot end" [PCR 1:99]. On 31 December 1641, "Mr. John Holmes is granted forty acres of upland at Narrogansett Hill, lying betwixt the highway and Derby's Ponds" [PCR 2:30].

At an unknown date (probably in 1644), "Mr. John Holmes of Plymouth, messenger," sold to Experience Mitchell of Duxbury "all those his two acres of marsh meadow lying next unto the meadow of Experience Michell aforesaid" [PCR 12:109].

BIRTH: By about 1611 (based on estimated date of marriage).
DEATH: After 7 October 1651 [PCR 7:51].
MARRIAGE: By about 1636 Sarah _____. She died at Plymouth on 18 August 1650 [MD 16:235]
CHILDREN:
   i   JOHN HOLMES, b. say 1636; m. (1) Plymouth 20 November 1661 Patience Faunce [PCR 8:22], daughter of JOHN FAUNCE [PM 201]; m. (2) about 1681 Patience (Bonham) Willis, widow of Richard Willis [NGSQ 74:87-89].
   ii   (prob.) NATHANIEL HOLMES, b. about 1643 (died 25 July 1727 in his eighty-fourth year [NGSQ 74:87, citing gravestone]); m. Plymouth 29 December 1667 Mercy Faunce [PCR 8:31; NGSQ 74:89-91], daughter of JOHN FAUNCE [PM 201].

COMMENTS: On 1 April 1633, John Holmes "was censured for drunkenness, to sit in the stocks, & amerced in twenty shillings fine" [PCR 1:12]. He was cited on other occasions for drunkenness [PCR 1:118, 132].

On 27 March 1637, "William Spooner of Colchester," Essex, indentured himself to "John Holmes of New Plymouth in America gent." for a term of six years [PCR 12:19]. John Holmes took Dorothy Temple into his service in 1639, relieving Stephen Hopkins of his contractual agreement to keep her as a servant [PCR 1:111-13].

John Holmes was defendant in civil suits on 2 January 1637/8, 3 March 1639/40, 5 October 1640 and 7 March 1642/3 [PCR 1:162, 7:7, 16, 17, 33]. On 7 October 1651, "Mr. John Holmes" sued Joseph Warren (for battery) and Edward Doty (for trespass and assault), and prevailed in both cases [PCR 7:56].

BIBLIOGRAPHIC NOTE: In 1986 Eugene A. Stratton published a detailed article on this John Holmes and his descendants [NGSQ 74:85-110, 203-23]. Stratton collected all known records for Holmes, and analyzed carefully a number of problems, including his English origin, his date of death, and the correct list of his children.

WILLIAM HOLMES

ORIGIN: Unknown.
MIGRATION: 1632.

FIRST RESIDENCE: Plymouth.
REMOVES: Duxbury by 1639, Boston by 1649.
RETURN TRIPS: To England 1641 to serve in Civil War, and return to New England by 1645.

OCCUPATION: Soldier.
FREEMAN: "Lieutenant Will[iam] Holmes" in 1633 Plymouth list of freemen prior to those admitted 1 January 1632/3 [PCR 1:3]. In list of 7 March 1636/7 [PCR 1:52]. In Duxbury section of Plymouth Colony list of freemen of 1639 (with his name later crossed out) [PCR 8:174].
EDUCATION: He signed his will.
OFFICES: Arbiter, 5 January 1640/1 [PCR 2:6].

On 2 March 1635/6, the court ordered that "Captain Myles Standish and Lieutenant Will[iam] Holmes be employed in teaching the use of arms at the town of Plymouth & Duxburrow ... and that the said lieutenant have likewise the charge of the guard at town," each to be paid £20 annually [PCR 1:38]. On 7 March 1636/7, it was "referred to the Governor, Treasurer, and Assistants, to agree with Lieutenant Holmes to exercise the inhabitants of the colony in the use of arms" [PCR 1:54]. On 7 June 1637, "Lieutenant William Holmes is elected to go leader of the said company" against the Pequots [PCR 1:60].
ESTATE: Not in the tax lists of 1633 and 1634.

To have mowing ground "against his ground," 1 July 1633 [PCR 1:14], and "between Mr. Smith & James Hurst," 14 March 1635/6 and 20 March 1636/7 [PCR 1:40, 56].

On 1 October 1638, the "thirty acres of lands formerly granted to Lieutenant Will[ia]m Holmes, lying at Iland Creeke, is now confirmed unto him by the Court," and "one hundred acres of lands are granted unto Lieutenant Will[ia]m Holmes, lying at the North River" [PCR 1:99-100]. On 6 April 1640, "Captain Standish and Mr. Alden are to view the meadow lying by the lands granted to Lieutenant Will[ia]m Holmes, and to allow him a proportion thereof to his upland there" [PCR 1:145].

In his will, dated 12 November 1649 and proved 30 November 1649, "Major William Homes being sick of body" bequeathed to "my loving kinswomen Margarett Homes & Mary Homes now residing at the Iland of Antigo and daughter of my deceased brother Thomas Homes ... all my estate ... equally divided between them ... all the lands, goods, chattels, debts and demands which I now have ... in New England"; to "my sister-in-law Margarett Webb *alias* Homes the late wife of my said brother Thomas Homes and to Rachell Homes and Bathsheba Homes two other daughters of my said brother all now living in London, if they or any of them do hereafter come over into New England all my farm with the appurtenances ... in New England ... late in the possession of William Brooke ... half ... to the said Margarett Webb *alias* Homes during her natural life and after her decease to the said Rachell & Bathsheba Homes ... half ... to the said Margarett Webb *alias* Homes for & towards the maintenance & bringing up of the said Rachell & Bathsheba until they and either of them shall attain the age of sixteen years or be married" and if they do not come over, then to remain to "my kinswomen Margarett & Mary Homes"; "arrears due ... for being a soldier and commander in the army and service of the king and parliament" to belong to his four nieces if they pursue it; to "my loving and kind kinsman Job Hawkyns of Boston in New England" £20; "my very good friends James Penn, Robert Scott" executors [SPR 1:445; PCPR 2:1:60-63].

On 30 May 1654 and 1 June 1654, James Penn, Isabel Simpkins, Nicholas Simpkins and Leonard Buttles, all of Boston, made depositions describing the debts incurred by William Holmes while in Boston, mostly at taverns, and the payment of those debts by Job Hawkins "his kinsman" [PCPR 2:1:62-63].

On 6 June 1654, whereas "a right is claimed by Jobe Hawkins, of Boston, unto the land of Major William Holmes, deceased, which land lieth at the North River, in the township of Marshfield, ... which right is claimed as due debt, as also by a legacy of forty pounds given to him in the last will and testament of the said Major Holmes, the Court have ordered, upon consideration of the premises, that the said Jobe Hawkins or his assigns may enter upon the said land, and possess and enjoy the same until any other shall come and shew a clearer right" [PCR 3:51]; this judgment was reiterated on 2 March 1657/8, with some conditions added [PCR 3:131].

BIRTH: By about 1610 (based on estimated date of freemanship).
DEATH: Boston between 12 November 1649 (date of will) and 30 November 1649 (probate of will).
MARRIAGE: None recorded.
CHILDREN: None recorded.
ASSOCIATIONS: Aside from the survivors of his brother Thomas Holmes named in his will, William Holmes was also related in some unexplained way to Job Hawkins of Boston.

COMMENTS: On 31 October 1632, when Governor John Winthrop and his party were leaving Plymouth, Lt. [William] Holmes escorted this group on its way north [WJ 1:110]. In October 1633 William Holmes took part in the Plymouth Colony expedition to establish a trading post on the Connecticut River [WJ 1:135].

WILLIAM BAKER [PM 21] was bailed out by "Sergeant [*sic*] Homes" but escaped, according to a 28 February 1637/8 letter of Roger Williams to John Winthrop [WP 4:15; RWCorr 145]. Williams followed up on the matter, reporting that having Mr. Allen of Hartford and "Lieftenant Holmes" overnight at his home, Holmes informed him that he had recaptured William Baker several months later [WP 4:31; RWCorr 155, 158]. Holmes had dealings with the Indians and the Dutch, as reported by Edward Winslow [WP 4:453-54].

On 4 December 1638, "Lieutenant Will[ia]m Holmes [was] presented for inordinate drinking in the Bay, which was not directly proved, & so he was discharged by order of the Court" [PCR 1:107].

On 6 July 1641, Lt. William Holmes unsuccessfuly sued James Luxford [PCR 2:22, 7:21].

Another William Holmes appeared at Scituate as early as 1638 [PCR 1:98, 110, 2:24, 38, 8:182, 190; NGSQ 74:103], removed some years later to Marshfield and died there in 1678, aged 86, but his records are easily distinguished from those of the Lieutenant. William Holmes of Scituate was sometimes designated "Senior," although he did not have a son William; this was done presumably to distinguish him from the Lieutenant, whose farm was in Scituate, although his residence was at Duxbury.

WILLIAM HONYWELL

"Will[iam] Honywell" agreed to serve Thomas Prence for seven years, beginning from 24 June 1633, at the end of which time he would get twenty-five acres of land and twelve bushels of Indian corn [PCR 1:16].

On 28 February 1639/40, the terms of the indenture were adjusted, with Honywell to stay with Thomas Atkinson, and to relinquish his claim to the corn at the end of his service, but still to get the land [PCR 1:139].

1 June 1641: "William Honywell is to have the lands due to him for his service laid forth or assigned him at Joanes River, or some other convenient place" [PCR 2:16].

6 March 1665/6: "William Honywell, having been committed to jail on suspicion of buggery with a beast, at this court was examined ..., and

stiffly denied it; and whereas no sufficient evidence appeared to convict him of the said fact, he was set at liberty" [PCR 4:116].

COMMENTS: These are the only records for William Honywell, indicating that he had arrived as a servant by 1633, completed his term of service, and acquired land. Since William Honywell does not appear in the 1643 list of men able to bear arms, or in any other Plymouth Colony record, the William Honywell who appears in the unfortunate incident of 1665/6 is almost certainly a different person than the immigrant of 1633.

JOHN HOOKE

John Hooke came on the *Mayflower* as servant to Isaac Allerton and "died with the first" [Bradford 441, 444]. "Jan de Houck" was apprenticed to Allerton at Leiden on 7 January 1619 [NS] [NEHGR 143:207].

STEPHEN HOPKINS

ORIGIN: London.
MIGRATION: 1620 on *Mayflower*.
FIRST RESIDENCE: Plymouth.

OCCUPATION: Tanner and merchant.
FREEMAN: In the 1633 list of Plymouth freemen Stephen Hopkins is included among the assistants [PCR 1:3]. In list of Plymouth Colony freemen, 7 March 1636/7 (as "Steephen Hopkins, gen.") [PCR 1:52]. In the Plymouth section of the 1639 Plymouth Colony list of freemen (as "Mr. Steephen Hopkins," annotated "dead") [PCR 8:173].
EDUCATION: He signed his will. His inventory included "diverse books" valued at 12s. [PCPR 1:63].
OFFICES: Assistant, 1633-36 [PCR 1:5, 21, 32, 36].
   Volunteered for service in the Pequot War, 1637 [PCR 1:61].
ESTATE: In the 1623 Plymouth division of land "Steven Hobkins" received six acres as a passenger on the *Mayflower* [PCR 12:4]. In the 1627 Plymouth division of cattle Stephen Hopkins, his wife Elizabeth Hopkins, Gyles Hopkins, Caleb Hopkins and Deborah Hopkins are the first five persons in the seventh company, and Damaris Hopkins is the thirteenth person in the eighth company [PCR 12:11, 12].

In the Plymouth tax list of 25 March 1634 Stephen Hopkins was assessed £1 7s. and in the list of 27 March 1634 £1 10s. [PCR 1:9, 27]. "Steven Hopkins" was one of the Purchasers [PCR 2:177].

On 1 July 1633, "Mr. Hopkins" was ordered to mow where he had mowed the year before [PCR 1:15], followed by similar orders on 14 March 1635/6 and 20 March 1636/7 [PCR 1:41, 57].

On 5 February 1637/8, "Mr. Stephen Hopkins requesteth a grant of lands towards the Six Mile Brook" [PCR 1:76].

On 7 August 1638, "[l]iberty is granted to Mr. Steephen Hopkins to erect a house at Mattacheese, and cut hay there this year to winter his cattle, provided that it be not to withdraw him from the town of Plymouth" [PCR 1:93].

On 17 July 1637, "Steephen Hopkins of Plymouth, gent.," sold to George Boare of Scituate, yeoman, "all that his messuage, houses, tenements, outhouses lying and being at the Broken Wharfe towards the Eele River together with the six shares of lands thereunto belonging containing six acres" [PCR 12:21]. On 30 November 1638, "Mr. Steephen Hopkins" sold to Josias Cooke "all those his six acres of land lying on the south side of the Town Brook of Plymouth" [PCR 12:39]. On 8 June 1642, William Chase mortgaged to "Mr. Stephen Hopkins ... all that his house and lands in Yarmouth containing eight acres of upland and six acres more lying at the Stony Cove" [PCR 12:83].

On 1 June 1640, "Mr. Hopkins" was granted twelve acres of meadow [PCR 1:154, 166].

In his will, dated 6 June 1644 and proved 20 August 1644, Stephen Hopkins "of Plymouth ... weake yet in good and perfect memory" directed that he be buried "as near as conveniently may be to my wife, deceased," and bequeathed to "son Giles Hopkins" the great bull now in the hands of Mrs. Warren; to "Steven Hopkins my son Giles his son" 20s. in Mrs. Warren's hands; to "daughter Constanc[e] Snow, wife of Nicholas ... my mare"; to "daughter Deborah Hopkins" cows; to "daughter Damaris Hopkins" cows; to "daughter Ruth" cows; to "daughter Elizabeth" cows; to "four daughters Deborah, Damaris, Ruth and Elizabeth Hopkins" all the moveable goods; if any of the daughters die, their share to be divided equally among the survivors; to "son Caleb heir apparent" house and lands at Plymouth, one pair of oxen and hire of them and all the debts "now owing unto me"; daughters to have free recourse to use of the house in Plymouth while single; "son Caleb" executor; Caleb and Captain Standish joint supervisors [PCPR 1:61].

The inventory of the estate of Stephen Hopkins, taken 17 July 1644, was untotalled, with no real estate included [PCPR 1:62-63].

On 28 October 1644, "Caleb Hopkins son and heir unto Mr. Steephen Hopkins of Plymouth deceased" deeded to "Gyles Hopkins of Yarmouth, planter, one hundred acres of those lands taken up for the Purchasers of Satuckquett which said lands do accrue unto the said Steephen as a Purchaser" [PCR 12:104].

BIRTH: By about 1579 (based on estimated date of first marriage).
DEATH: Plymouth between 6 June 1644 (date of will) and 17 July 1644 (probate of will).
MARRIAGE: (1) By 1604 Mary _____. She was buried at Hursley, Hampshire, 9 May 1613 [TAG 73:169].
(2) St. Mary Matfellon, Whitechapel, London, 19 February 1617/8 Elizabeth Fisher. She died at Plymouth sometime in the early 1640s before her husband, who desired to be buried near her; Bradford indicated that both she and her husband had lived in Plymouth above twenty years.
CHILDREN:
With first wife
- i ELIZABETH HOPKINS, bp. Hursley, Hampshire, 13 May 1604 [TAG 73:170]; living on 12 May 1613 [TAG 73:165]; no further record.
- ii CONSTANCE HOPKINS, bp. Hursley, Hampshire, 11 May 1606 [TAG 73:170]; m. Plymouth by 1627 NICHOLAS SNOW [PM 428] (in the 1627 Plymouth division of cattle "Nickolas Snow" and "Constance Snow" were the sixth and seventh persons in the seventh company, which was headed by Stephen Hopkins [PCR 12:11]).
- iii GILES HOPKINS, bp. Hursley, Hampshire, 30 January 1607/8 [TAG 73:170]; m. Plymouth 9 October 1639 Catherine Whelden [PCR 1:134; TAG 48:5].

With second wife
- iv DAMARIS HOPKINS, b. say 1618; probably d. at Plymouth before the birth of her sister of the same name.
- v OCEANUS HOPKINS, b. at sea between 16 September and 11 November 1620; died by 1627.
- vi CALEB HOPKINS, b. Plymouth say 1624; "became a seaman & died at Barbadoes" between 1644 and 1651 [Bradford 445].
- vii DEBORAH, b. Plymouth say 1626; m. Plymouth 23 April 1646 as his first wife Andrew Ring [PCR 2:98; TAG 42:202-5], son of widow MARY RING [PM 389].

viii DAMARIS HOPKINS, b. Plymouth say 1628; m. Plymouth shortly after 10 June 1646 Jacob Cooke [MD 2:27-8], son of FRANCIS COOKE [PM 144]. (Since this Damaris was still bearing children in the early 1670s, she cannot be the same as the Damaris who came on the *Mayflower*.)

ix RUTH HOPKINS, b. Plymouth say 1630; d. after 30 November 1644 and by spring 1651 [Bradford 445]; unm.

x ELIZABETH HOPKINS, b. Plymouth say 1632; believed to have died by 6 October 1659 when her property was appraised "in case Elizabeth Hopkins do come no more" [MD 4:114-19]; unm.

COMMENTS: Caleb Johnson's discovery [TAG 73:161-71] of the family of Stephen Hopkins in Hursley, Hampshire, at last definitively eliminates the suggestion that Stephen Hopkins was son of Stephen Hopkins, a clothier, of Wortley, Wooten Underedge, Gloucestershire [MF 6:3, citing "[t]he Wortley historian"].

Johnson's discovery also strengthens the argument that this was the same Stephen Hopkins who was the minister's clerk on the vessel *Sea Venture,* which met with a hurricane in 1609 while on a voyage to Virginia [TAG 73:165-66]. One of one hundred and fifty survivors marooned on Bermuda, he fomented a mutiny and was sentenced to death, but "so penitent he was and made so much moan, alleging the ruin of his wife and children in this his trespass," that his friends procured a pardon from the Governor [MF 6:3, citing William Strachey's account]. (This episode is one of the underlying sources for Shakespeare's *The Tempest.*)

A brief docket item in official English records raises tantalizing possibilities. On 20 September 1614, a letter was sent "to Sir Thomas Dale Marshall of the Colony in Virginia, to send home by the next return of ships from thence Eliezer Hopkins" [*Calendar of State Papers, Domestic Series, of the Reign of James I, 1611-1618* (London 1858), p. 253; *Calendar of State Papers, Colonial Series, 1574-1660* (London 1860), p. 17]. Examination of the original of this record by Michael J. Wood verifies that this is the correct reading, and the docket item does not refer to Stephen Hopkins. (The letter itself apparently does not survive.)

In his listing of the *Mayflower* passengers Bradford included "Mr. Stephen Hopkins and Elizabeth his wife, and two children called Giles and Constanta, a daughter, both by a former wife. And two more by this wife called Damaris and Oceanus; the last was born at sea. And two servants called Edward Doty and Edward Lester" [Bradford 442]. Stephen Hopkins signed the *Mayflower* Compact. In his accounting of this family in 1651 Bradford reported that "Mr. Hopkins and his wife are now both dead, but they lived above twenty years in this place and had one son and four daughters born here. Their son became a seaman and died at Barbadoes, one daughter died here, and two are married; one of them hath two children, and one is yet to marry. So their increase which still survive are five. But his son Giles is married and hath four children. His daughter Constanta is also married and hath twelve children, all of them living, and one of them married" [Bradford 445].

In June 1621 Steven Hopkins and Edward Winslow were chosen by the governor to approach Massasoit, and Hopkins repeated this duty as emissary frequently thereafter [Mourt 60; Bradford 87].

Despite his social standing and his early public service, Stephen Hopkins managed to run afoul of the authorities several times in the late 1630s. On 7 June 1636, while an Assistant, he was fined for battery of John Tisdale, whom he "dangerously wounded" [PCR 1:41-42]. On 2 October 1637, he was fined for allowing drinking on the Lord's day and the playing of "shovell board" [PCR 1:68] and, on 2 January 1637/8, he was "presented for suffering excessive drinking in his house" [PCR 1:75]. On 5 June 1638, he was "presented for selling beer for 2d. the quart, not worth 1d. a quart" [PCR 1:87]; for this and other similar infractions he was on 4 September 1638 fined £5 [PCR 1:97]. He dealt harshly with his pregnant servant Dorothy Temple and only the intercession of John Holmes freed him from being held in contempt of court [PCR 1:111-13]. On 3 December 1639, he was presented for selling a looking glass for 16d. when a similar glass could be bought in the Bay for 9d. [PCR 1:137].

BIBLIOGRAPHIC NOTE: In 1992 John D. Austin published an excellent and extensive account of Stephen Hopkins and his descendants as the sixth volume in the Five Generations Project of the General Society of Mayflower Descendants [cited herein as MF6]. In 1998 Caleb Johnson published his discovery of the baptismal place of the children of Stephen Hopkins and his first wife [TAG 73:161-71].

HENRY HOWLAND

ORIGIN: Fenstanton, Huntingdonshire.
MIGRATION: 1632.

FIRST RESIDENCE: Plymouth.
REMOVES: Duxbury 1636.

FREEMAN: In the 1633 list of Plymouth freemen Henry Howland appears immediately before those admitted on 1 January 1632/3 [PCR 1:4]. In the 6 March 1636/7 list of Plymouth Colony freemen [PCR 1:52]. In the Duxbury sections of the 1639 and 1658 lists of Plymouth freemen (with his name erased from the 1658 list) [PCR 8:174, 198]. (See *COMMENTS* for disenfranchisement in 1659.)

EDUCATION: He signed his will. His inventory included "books" valued at 10s. [PCPR 3:1:27].

OFFICES: Plymouth grand jury, 7 June 1645, 4 June 1650, 2 October 1650, 7 June 1653, 3 June 1657 (refused to serve) [PCR 2:84, 155, 162-63, 3:32, 115]. Petit jury, 7 March 1636, 2 October 1637, 2 January 1637/8, 4 June 1639, 3 September 1639, 7 July 1646, 6-7 June 1649, 29 October 1649, 10 June 1650, 7 October 1651, 4 June 1652, 5 March 1655/6, 5 October 1656 [PCR 2:140, 160, 7:5, 7, 12, 13, 42, 46, 56, 60, 77, 81].

Duxbury highway surveyor, 3 June 1656, 3 June 1668 [PCR 3:100, 4:181].

His inventory included "2 guns with one old rapier" valued at £2 15s. [PCPR 3:1:27].

ESTATE: In the Plymouth tax list of 25 March 1633 assessed 9s. and in the list of 27 March 1634 assessed 18s. [PCR 1:11, 28].

On 27 July 1640, William Renolds sold to Henry Howland of Duxbury five acres of upland in Duxbury and one acre of marsh meadow lying at the east end thereof, with all rights [PCR 12:60-61]. On 6 June 1650, Henry Howland granted to Experience Mitchell access to a spring on the border of his property [MD 1:97-98, citing PCLR 2:1:9].

In his will, dated 28 November 1670 and proved 8 March 1670/1, Henry Howland bequeathed "all my housing both dwelling house and barn, with all my lands both upland and meadow ... within the township of Duxburrow ... unto my son Joseph Howland only during my wife's life she shall have and enjoy the new room to herself for her own use"; to "my son Joseph Howland four oxen and two heifers and one horse with all the tackling ... also a bed with things belonging thereunto, as also my fowling piece"; "my son Joseph Howland out of the forementioned houses and lands and cattle shall pay or cause to be paid unto my son Zoeth Howland £20 ... as also 12d. apiece to all his brothers and sisters and their children now surviving"; to "my daughter Sarah two heifers and two steers and one mare now running at Ponaganset, as also one bed and bedding thereunto belonging"; to "my son John one musket"; to "my daughter Elizabeth one cow"; "my old mare now running at Ponagansett unto my son Samuell Howland"; to "my son Joseph Howland two acres of meadowland ... at ... Gurnett's Nose marsh"; to "my daughter Mary 10s."; to "my daughter Abigaill 10s. to be paid by my son Joseph who is to sell a barrel of cider and to pay it out of that"; to "my two sons John and Samuell each of them a barrel of cider"; to "my loving wife Mary Howland" residue [MD 19:32-33, citing PCPR 3:1:26].

The inventory of "Henery Howland of Duxburrow late deceased," taken 14 January 1670/1, totalled £141 4s., with no real estate included [MD 19:33, citing PCPR 3:1:27].

In her will, dated 8 May 1674 and proved first 26 April 1674 and second 8 April 1675, Mary Howland "sometimes the wife of Hennery Howland now deceased" bequeathed to "my daughter Abigaill Young" £1; to "my son Zoeth Howland" £1; to "my son John Howland my house at Ponagansett"; to "my daughter Mary Cudworth" £1; to "my son Samuel Howland" £1; to "my daughter Sarah Denis" £1; to "my daughter Elizabeth Allin" £1; and to "my son Joseph Howland" the residue [PCPR 3:2:10].

BIRTH: Probably Fenstanton, Huntingdonshire, by about 1603 (based on estimated date of marriage), son of Henry Howland [TAG 14:214-15].
DEATH: Duxbury 1 January 1670/1 [NGSQ 75:113, endnote 3].
MARRIAGE: By about 1628 Mary _____ (assuming that she was the mother of all his children). "Mary Howland who had been the wife of Hennery" died at Duxbury 16 June 1674. (The claim that Mary was a Newland is unsupported [NGSQ 75:105].)
CHILDREN:
    i   ABIGAIL HOWLAND, b. say 1628; m. Plymouth 13 December 1648 John Young [PCR 8:5].
    ii   ZOETH HOWLAND, b. say 1631; m. by 1657 Abigail _____ (eldest known child b. 5 October 1657 [RIVR 7:64]). (The marriage date is printed as "Dec. 1656," with the bride's surname not given [RIVR 7:21]; this may be a record created by calculation, and the original should be examined.)
    iii SAMUEL HOWLAND, b. about 1638 (described as "near 70 years old" in 8 July 1707 [NGSQ 75:112, citing Bristol County Court of General Sessions 1702-1714:121]); m. by about 1673 Mary Sampson, daughter of Abraham Sampson (eldest known child b. about 1673 [NGSQ 75:112]) [TAG 15:165-67].

iv JOHN HOWLAND, b. say 1641; m. Duxbury 29 January 1684/5 Mary Walker; d. Freetown before 8 August 1687 ([BrPR 1:2]). (His wife was apparently dead, as administration was granted to his brother Samuel; his inventory included £3 10s. in "women's apparel".)

v MARY HOWLAND, b. say 1643; m. by 1665 James Cudworth (eldest known child b. Scituate 3 June 1665 [NGSQ 75:110, citing records of Pembroke Monthly Meeting]), son of JAMES CUDWORTH {1634, Scituate} [GM 2:2:249-58].

vi SARAH HOWLAND, b. about 1645 (d. Portsmouth 2 October 1712, aged about sixty-seven years [NGSQ 75:216]); m. Portsmouth, Rhode Island, 19 November 1672 Robert Dennis [NGSQ 75:216].

vii ELIZABETH HOWLAND, b. say 1647; m. by about 1669 Jedidiah Allen (eldest known child b. 30 August 1669 or 1670 [NGSQ 75:111, citing Sandwich Monthly Meeting]).

viii JOSEPH HOWLAND, b. say 1649 (evidently not a minor when his father wrote his will); m. Hampton 4 May 1683 Rebecca Hussey [NGSQ 75:217, citing Salem Monthly Meeting 3:1].

ASSOCIATIONS: Brother of JOHN HOWLAND [PM 279] and Arthur Howland [NGSQ 71:84].

COMMENTS: On 22 December 1657, Henry Howland, for entertaining Quaker meetings at his house, was summoned to appear at the next court [PCR 3:126]. On 2 March 1657/8, he was fined 10s. for entertaining a meeting at his house contrary to the order of the court [PCR 3:129].

On 7 June 1659, "Henry Howland of Duxburrow" as a Quaker "or manifest encourager of such" is on a list to lose freemanship and is ordered to appear in August to be convicted and censured [PCR 3:167]. On 6 October 1659, Henry Howland was disenfranchised for being an "abettor and entertainer of Quakers" [PCR 3:176].

On 1 May 1660, Henry Howland was accused of entertaining another man's wife in his house after complaint was made to him by the husband, and for permitting a Quaker meeting in his house, and for entertaining a foreign Quaker contrary to the order of the court. The first charge he "stiffly denied" but he was convicted of the other two and fined [PCR 3:186]. He was twice fined on 2 October 1660 for entertaining Quaker meetings [PCR 3:201].

We differ slightly from Wakefield and Sherman [NGSQ 75:107] in the birth sequence and estimate of birth dates for the children of Henry

Howland. The assumption has been made that all the sons were of age when the father made his will, but this makes some of them older than the norm when they marry. Even this arrangement leaves an apparent gap of about seven years between the first two children (Abigail and Zoeth) and the remaining six. These first two children may well have been born in England, and there is the possibility that they were by an earlier wife and not by Mary.

BIBLIOGRAPHIC NOTE: The parentage and parish of origin of the three Howland brothers were reported in 1938 by Clarence A. Torrey [TAG 14:214-15]. A definitive article on what is known to date about Henry Howland was published in 1987 by Robert S. Wakefield and Robert M. Sherman [NGSQ 75:105-16, 216-225].

JOHN HOWLAND

ORIGIN: Fenstanton, Huntingdonshire.
MIGRATION: 1620 on the *Mayflower*.
FIRST RESIDENCE: Plymouth.

FREEMAN: In the 1633 list of Plymouth freemen John Howland is near the head of the list, among the Assistants [PCR 1:3]. In the 6 March 1636/7 list of Plymouth Colony freemen [PCR 1:52]. In the Plymouth sections of the 1639, 1658 and 29 May 1670 lists of Plymouth Colony freemen [PCR 5:274, 8:173, 197].
EDUCATION: His inventory included "1 great Bible and Annotations on the 5 Books of Moses" valued at £1 and "Mr. Tindall's Works, Mr. Wilson's Works, 7 more books" valued at £1.
OFFICES: Plymouth Colony Assistant, 1 January 1632/3, 1 January 1633/4, 1 January 1634/5 [PCR 1:5, 21, 32].

Deputy for Plymouth to Plymouth Colony General Court, 1 June 1641, 28 October 1645, 1 June 1647, 7 June 1648, 8 June 1649, 4 June 1650, 5 June 1651, 3 June 1652, 7 June 1653, 7 March 1653/4, 6 June 1654, 1 August 1654, 8 June 1655, 3 June 1656, 1 June 1658, 4 June 1661, 1 June 1663, 1 June 1666, 5 June 1667 [PCR 2:16, 94, 117, 123, 144, 154, 167, 3:8, 31, 44, 49, 63, 79, 99, 135, 214, 4:37, 122, 148].

In charge of the fur trading post at Kennebec, 1634 [MD 2:10-11]. Committee on the fur trade, 3 October 1659 [PCR 3:170].

In the Plymouth section of the 1643 Plymouth Colony list of men able to bear arms (as "John Howland Sen.") [PCR 8:187].

ESTATE: In the 1623 Plymouth division of land John Howland received four acres as a passenger on the *Mayflower* [PCR 12:4]. In the 1627 Plymouth division of cattle John Howland, his wife Elizabeth Howland, John Howland Junior and Desire Howland were the first four persons in the fourth company [PCR 12:10].

In the Plymouth tax list of 25 March 1633 John Howland was assessed 18s., and in the list of 27 March 1634 £1 4s. [PCR 1:9, 27]. John Howland was a Purchaser [PCR 2:177].

On 4 December 1637, "forty acres of land are granted to Mr. John Howland, lying at the Island Creeke Pond at the western end thereof, with the marsh ground that he useth to mow there" [PCR 1:70]. On 5 November 1638, the "island called Spectacle, lying upon Green's Harbor, is granted to Mr. John Howland" [PCR 1:102, 110, 168]. Granted six acres of meadow "at the North Meadow by Jones River," 17 October 1642 [PCR 2:49].

In his will, dated 29 May 1672 and proved 6 March 1672/3, "John Howland Seni[o]r of the town of New Plymouth ... being now grown aged, having many infirmities of body upon me," bequeathed to "John Howland my eldest son besides what lands I have already given him, all my right and interest to that one hundred acres of land granted me by the court lying on the eastern side of Taunton River"; to "my son Jabez Howland all those my upland and meadow that I now possess at Satuckett and Paomett"; to "my son Jabez Howland all that my one piece of land that I have lying on the southside of the mill brook"; to "Isaac Howland my youngest son all those my uplands and meadows ... in the town of Middlebery and in a tract of land called the Major's Purchase near Namassakett Ponds which I have bought and purchased of William White of Marshfield"; to "my said son Isacke Howland the one half of my twelve acre lot of meadow that I now have at Winnatucsett River"; to "my dear and loving wife Elizabeth Howland the use and benefit of my now dwelling house in Rockey Nooke in the township of Plymouth ... with the outhousing lands ... uplands and meadow lands ... in the town of Plymouth ... excepting what meadow and upland I have before given to my sons Jabez and Isacke Howland during her natural life"; to "my son Joseph Howland after the decease of my loving wife Elizabeth Howland my aforesaid dwelling house at Rockey Nooke"; to "my daughter Desire Gorum 20s."; to "my daughter Hope Chipman 20s."; to "my daughter Elizabeth Dickenson 20s."; to "my daughter Lydia Browne 20s."; to "my daughter Hannah Bosworth 20s."; to "my daughter Ruth Cushman 20s."; to "my grandchild Elizabeth Howland the daughter of my son John Howland 20s."; "these legacies given to my daughters [to] be paid by my executrix"; to "my loving wife Elizabeth Howland my debts and legacies being first paid, my whole estate," she to be executrix [MD 2:70-73, citing PCPR 3:1:49-50].

The inventory of "Mr. John Howland lately deceased," taken 3 March 1672/3, totalled £157 8s. 8d. [MD 2:73-77, citing PCPR 3:1:51-54]. After the inventory, the appraisers noted that "the testator died possessed of these several parcels of land following": "his dwelling house with the outhousing, uplands and meadow belonging thereunto lying at Rockey Nooke in the town of New Plymouth," "a parcel of meadow at Jones River meadow," "the one half of a house and a parcel of meadow and upland belonging thereunto lying and being at Colchester in the aforesaid township," "a parcel of meadow and upland belonging thereunto lying near Jones River bridge in the town of Duxburrow," "one house and 2 shares of a tract of land and meadow that lyeth in the town of Middleberry that was purchased by Captain Thomas Southworth of and from the Indian Sachem Josias Wampatucke," and "2 shares of a tract of land called the Major's Purchase lying near Namassakett ponds" [MD 2:77, citing PCPR 3:1:54]. (See also PCR 5:108, 110, 127.)

In her will, dated 17 December 1686 and proved 10 January 1687/8, "Elizabeth Howland of Swanzey ... being seventy nine years of age" bequeathed to "my eldest son John Howland the sum of £5 ... and my book called *Mr. Tindale's Works* and also one pair of sheets & one pair of pillowbeers and one pair of bedblankets"; to "my son Joseph Howland my stilliards and also one pair of sheets and one pair of pillowbeers"; to "my son Jabez Howland my featherbed & bolster that is in his custody & also one rug & two blankets that belongeth to the said bed & also my great iron pot & pothooks"; to "my son Isaack Howland my book called *Willson on the Romanes* & one pair of sheets & one pair of pillowbeers & also my great brass kettle already in his possession"; to "my son-in-law Mr. James Browne my great Bible"; to "my daughter Lidia Browne my best featherbed & boulster two pillows & three blankets & a green rug & my small cupboard one pair of andirons & my lesser brass kettle & my small Bible & my book of Mr. Robbinson's Works called *Observations Divine & Moral* & also my finest pair of sheets & my holland pillowbeers"; to "my daughter Elisabeth Dickenson one pair of sheets & one pair of pillowbeers & one chest"; to "my daughter Hannah Bosworth one pair of sheets & one pair of pillowbeers"; to "my granddaughter Elizabeth Bursley one pair of sheets and one pair of pillowbeers"; to "my grandson Nathanael Howland (the son of Joseph Howland) ... my lot of land with the meadow thereto adjoining ... in the township of Duxbury near Jones River Bridge"; to "my grandson James

Browne one iron bar and one iron trammell now in his possession"; to "my grandson Jabez Browne one chest"; to "my granddaughter Dorothy Browne my best chest & my warming pan"; to "my granddaughter Desire Cushman four sheep"; "my wearing clothes linen and woollen" and the residue to "my three daughters Elisabeth Dickenson, Lidia Browne and Hannah Bosworth to be equally divided amongst them"; "my loving son-in-law James Browne and my loving son Jabez Howland" executors [MD 3:54-57, citing BrPR 1:13-14].

BIRTH: By about 1592 (based on age at death), son of Henry and Margaret (_____) Howland of Fenstanton.
DEATH: Plymouth 23 February 1672/3 "above eighty years" [PCR 8:34].
MARRIAGE: Plymouth by about 1624 Elizabeth Tilley, baptized Henlow, Bedfordshire, 30 August 1607, daughter of JOHN TILLEY [PM 462]. She died at Swansea 22 December 1687, aged eighty [SwVR 27].
CHILDREN:

i   DESIRE HOWLAND, b. say 1624; m. by 1644 John Gorham (eldest known child b. Plymouth 2 April 1644 [MD 5:72]).

ii JOHN HOWLAND, b. Plymouth 24 February 1626[/7] [Sewall 463]; m. Plymouth 26 October 1651 Mary Lee [PCR 8:13].

iii HOPE HOWLAND, b. say 1629; m. by 1647 John Chipman (eldest known child b. Plymouth 24 June 1647 [PCR 8:4]) [THQ 60:2:8-13].

iv ELIZABETH HOWLAND, b. say 1631; m. (1) Plymouth 13 September 1649 Ephraim Hicks [PCR 8:8], son of ROBERT HICKS [PM 243]; m. (2) Plymouth 10 July 1651 John Dickerson [PCR 8:13; THQ 60:3:13-19].

v   LYDIA HOWLAND, b. say 1633; m. by about 1655 James Brown, son of JOHN BROWN {1635, Plymouth} [GM 2:1:420-29].

vi HANNAH HOWLAND, b. say 1637; m. Swansea 6 July 1661 Jonathan Bosworth [SwVR 23], son of JONATHAN BOSWORTH {1633, Cambridge} [GMB 1:187-91].

vii JOSEPH HOWLAND, b. say 1640; m. Plymouth 7 December 1664 Elizabeth Southworth [PCR 8:25], daughter of THOMAS SOUTHWORTH [PM 437].

viii JABEZ HOWLAND, b. about 1644 (deposed on 19 July 1680 aged 36 years [SJC #1915]); m. by 1669 Bethiah Thatcher, daughter of Anthony Thatcher (eldest known child b. Plymouth 15 November 1669 [PVR 668; NYGBR 42:154]).

ix RUTH HOWLAND, b. say 1646; m. Plymouth 17 November 1664 Thomas Cushman [PCR 8:25], son of Thomas Cushman.

x ISAAC HOWLAND, b. Plymouth 15 November 1649; m. by 1677 Elizabeth Vaughn, daughter of George Vaughn [TAG 23:24-26].

ASSOCIATIONS: Brother of HENRY HOWLAND [PM 275] and Arthur Howland [NGSQ 71:84].

COMMENTS: In his list of passengers on the *Mayflower,* Bradford tells us that John Howland was one of the "manservants" of JOHN CARVER [Bradford 441; PM 95]. During a particularly bad storm on the crossing John Howland (characterized by Bradford as "a lusty young man") went above deck and was swept overboard, but

> it pleased God that he caught hold of the topsail halyards which hung overboard and ran out at length. Yet he held his hold (though he was sundry fathoms under water) till he was hauled up by the same rope to the brim of the water, and then with a boat hook and other means got into the ship again and his life saved. And though he was something ill with it, yet he lived many years after and became a profitable member both in church & commonwealth [Bradford 59].

In his 1651 accounting of the family of John Carver, Bradford reported that "[h]is servant John Howland married the daughter of John Tilley, Elizabeth, and they are both now living, and their eldest daughter hath four children; and their second daughter one, all living, and other of their children marriageable" [Bradford 444].

In an undated deposition we learn that in April 1634 John Hocking came to Kennebec and challenged the rights of the Plymouth men to their exclusive trade in that place. Mr. John Howland, in charge of the trading post, went out in their bark with several other men and warned Hocking off, but was taunted and defied. Howland "bid three of his men go cut his cable [Hocking's anchor]," but the flow of the stream was too strong and Howland called them back and added Moses Talbot to the crew. Hocking, seeing that their intent was to cut the cable, "presently put his piece almost to Moyses Talbott's head, which Mr. Howland seeing called to him desiring him not to shoot his man but take himself for his mark saying his men did but that which he commanded them and therefore desired him not to hurt any of them, if any wrong was done it was himself that did it and therefore called again to him to take him for his mark saying he stood very fair, but Hocking would not hear nor look towards our bark, but presently shooteth Moyses in the head, and presently took up his pistol in his hand but the Lord stayed him from doing any further hurt by a shot from our bark himself was presently struck dead being shot near the same place in the head where he had murderously shot Moyses" [MD 2:10-11].

BIBLIOGRAPHIC NOTE: Because of the multitude of descendants of John Howland, through all ten of his children, the publication of the first five generations of descent from John Howland will occupy many volumes. Elizabeth Pearson White has prepared the first two volumes in this series: *John Howland of the* Mayflower: *Volume 1, The First Five Generations, Documented Descendants Through his first child Desire^2 Howland and her husband Captain John Gorham* (Camden, Maine, 1990) and *John Howland of the* Mayflower: *Volume 2, The First Five Generations, Documented Descendants Through his second child John^2 Howland and his wife Mary Lee* (Camden, Maine, 1993).

In her first volume White argued that John Howland lived for several years in Maine, and that three of his children were born there. Robert S. Wakefield has gathered the evidence to show that this could not have been the case [MD 42:15-16].

JAMES HURST

ORIGIN: Leiden, Holland [NEHGR 154:423].
MIGRATION: 1631.
FIRST RESIDENCE: Plymouth.

OCCUPATION: Tanner.
CHURCH MEMBERSHIP: Deacon of the Plymouth church, 21 March 1647 [PCR 12:153].
FREEMAN: In 1633 Plymouth list of freemen prior to those admitted 1 January 1632/3 [PCR 1:3]. In 7 March 1636/7 list of freemen [PCR 1:52].
OFFICES: Deputy for Plymouth to Plymouth Colony General Court, 1 June 1647 [PCR 2:117]. In Plymouth sections of lists of 1639 and 1658 [PCR 8:174, 197].

Plymouth petit jury, 7 June 1636, 7 March 1636/7, 2 October 1637, 6 March 1637/8, 4 June 1639, 3 September 1639, 3 December 1639, 3 March 1639/40, 6 July 1641, 3 August 1641, 7 December 1641, 1 March 1641/2, 3 May 1642, 7 June 1642, 7 March 1642/3, 6 June 1643, 3

March 1644/5, 28 October 1645, 7 July 1646, 2 March 1646/7, 6 March 1648/9, 6 June 1649, 7 June 1649, 29 October 1649, 6 March 1649/50, 2 October 1650, 4 March 1650/1, 2 March 1651/2 [PCR 1:42, 2:111, 140, 7:5, 7, 8, 12-16, 22, 25, 28, 29, 31, 34, 35, 40-42, 45-47, 52, 53, 58]. Grand jury, 5 June 1638, 2 June 1640 [PCR 1:87, 155]. Coroner's jury, 1 August 1648 [PCR 2:132].

Plymouth highway committee, 23 July 1634 [PCR 1:31]. Arbiter, 5 January 1640/1 [PCR 2:6]. Lotlayer, 27 September 1642 [PCR 2:48].

His inventory included "a fowling piece" valued at £1 [PCPR 2:1:66].

ESTATE: Assessed 9s. in Plymouth tax lists of 25 March 1633 and 27 March 1634 [PCR 1:11, 29].

On 1 January 1637/8, James Hurst was granted additional land near his house [PCR 1:72]. On 2 November 1640, James Hurst received "the meadow that Goodman Cooke should have had" [PCR 1:167]. James Hurst received a share in the Dartmouth lands [MD 4:187].

In his will, dated 10 December 1657 and proved 2 March 1657[/8], "James Hurst of Plymouth" bequeathed to "wife Garteud Hurst my dwelling house at Plymouth with all my land thereunto belonging and all outhousing" for her life, "and at her decease all the abovesaid particulars I bequeath to my grandchild John Cobb"; "my wife [to] have and enjoy all my goods and cattles"; to "my grandchild Gershom Cobb ... all my right of land at Punckatessett"; to "my grandchild John Cobb forty acres of my land at Coaksett or Cushenett and to my grandchildren James Cobb, Gershom Cobb & Eliezer Cobb twenty acres apiece of my land at Coaksett or Cushenett"; to "my three grandchildren Mary Dunham, Hannah Cobb and Patience Cobb 20s. apiece"; "my wife" sole executrix; "my loving friends Mr. Cushman and Gyles Rickard Senior" supervisors [MD 14:228, citing PCPR 2:1:65].

The inventory of the estate of "James Hurst of New Plymouth lately deceased," taken 24 December 1657, totalled £97 6s., of which £36 was real estate: "the dwelling house and outhouses, meadow ground, uplands that lies within the town of Plymouth," £20; "land lying against Road Island belonging to Plymouth," £1; and "the share of Purchase land lying at Coaksett," £15 [MD 14:228, citing PCPR 2:1:66].

The inventory of the estate of "Garthern Hurst widow deceased," taken 30 May 1670, totalled £13 5s. 11d.; an accounting of "Grandmother Hurst's debts" was prepared after her death [PCPR 3:1:18; Scrapbook 68, 90-91].

BIRTH: About 1582 (based on stated age at marriage).
DEATH: Plymouth between 10 December 1657 (date of will) and 24 December 1657 (date of inventory).
MARRIAGE: Amsterdam, Holland, 4 October 1608 [NS] Gertrude Bennister ("Jacobus Hurste from Rekfort (Retford), bombazine-weaver, 26 years, and Geertrud Bennister from Rekford (Retford), 23 years" [J. deHoop Scheffer, *History of the Free Churchmen* ... (Ithaca, New York, n.d.), p. 190]. She died before 30 May 1670 when her inventory was taken.
CHILDREN:
  i JOHN HURST, b. say 1610; in Leiden census of 1622 [NEHGR 154:423]; no further record.
  ii PATIENCE HURST, b. say 1612; in Leiden census of 1622 [NEHGR 154:423]; m. by 1632 HENRY COBB [PM 118].

COMMENTS: In 1622 James Hurst, his wife and two children were living in the close of the English church in Leiden [NEHGR 154:423].

James Hurst first appears in a dated record in the tax list of 25 March 1633, and from his position in the first list of freemen, he must have attained that status before 1 January 1632/3. But his arrival can be placed even earlier based on the birth of his first grandchild. His only known child, Patience, married Henry Cobb, and their first child was born in Plymouth on 7 June 1632, which would place the marriage of Henry and Patience no later than September 1631. Although it is possible that the marriage took place in England, followed by migration to Plymouth in 1632, it seems more likely that Henry Cobb and Patience Hurst met in Plymouth, so that her father would have arrived in Plymouth by 1631. Given the record of his marriage in Amsterdam, he may well have been at Leiden, which would make it likely that he was part of the last contingent of the Leiden congregation that came over in 1629 and 1630.

After fifteen years of regular duty as a juryman, James Hurst came into court on 7 March 1653/4 and, along with three other men, sued Samuell Sturtivant and Edward Gray "in an action of trespass on the case, to the damage of ten pounds, for destroying a certain parcel of hay" belonging to the four plaintiffs; the court found for the plaintiffs [PCR 7:68].

I

JOHN IRISH

ORIGIN: "Clisdon, Somersetshire."
MIGRATION: 1630.
FIRST RESIDENCE: Plymouth.
REMOVES: Duxbury.

OCCUPATION: Laborer [SJC Case #3597]. Roper [MD 14:91]. Planter [PCLR 3:305; BrLR 1:382].
EDUCATION: Signed his deeds by mark.
OFFICES: Volunteered to serve in the Pequot War, April 1637 [PCR 1:61]. In the Duxbury section of the 1643 Plymouth Colony list of men able to bear arms [PCR 8:189].
ESTATE: On 5 April 1641, John Rowse testified that John Irish and Henry Wallis made a covenant that the "longer liver of them should have each other's five acres of land lying by the Stony Brooke in Duxborrow." Irish as the survivor was consequently granted the land at Wallis's death [PCR 2:12-13]. On 11 June 1641, John Irish traded his ten acres of upland on the north side of Stony Brooke and two acres of marsh meadow adjoining, for the dwelling house and garden and fruit of William Hiller in Duxbury [PCR 12:74].

On 5 March 1643/4, the court ordered that "John Irish is to have his twenty-five acres of land due for his service, made up by Duxborrow men, because it is agreed upon formerly that such servants as are to have lands by their covenants at the expiration of their term are to be provided for in the towns where they live or are received as inhabitants" [PCR 2:69].

On 29 September 1658, John Irish of Duxbury was given liberty to "make enquiry and search out a portion of land to accommodate him according to his indenture" [PCR 3:149]. On 3 June 1662, John Irish appeared on the list of "servants and ancient freemen" who were given liberty to find land at Saconett Neck or some other place [PCR 4:18].

On 7 December 1659, John Irish of Duxbury, roper, "with the consent of Elizabeth his wife," sold to "Guydo Bayley" of Bridgewater, planter, "all that his share, lot and portion in the lands and township of Bridgwater" [MD 14:91, citing PCLR 2:2:30b].

On 20 December 1673, John Irish of Duxbury, planter, deeded to "Elias Irish my true and natural son ... my whole share and portion of land at or about Saconnet ... belonging unto me the said John Irish as an ancient servant" [PCLR 3:305]. On 20 March 167[3/]4, John Irish Sr. of Duxbury, planter, deeded to "John Irish his true and natural son" his right to land in Saconnet; on 23 March 1673/4, John Irish Sr. and his wife Elizabeth Irish acknowledged the deed [BrLR 1:382]. On 5 March 1677/8, division was ordered on a parcel of land at Saconett "which was the land of John Irish deceased, and by him bequeathed to his two sons, Elias Irish and John Irish Junior, his brother" [PCR 5:252]. (How these two actions are to be reconciled is not evident.)

BIRTH: By about 1611 (if he was eighteen at the indenture date).
DEATH: By 5 March 1677/8 [PCR 5:252].
MARRIAGE: By about 1644 Elizabeth _____. She died at Little Compton on 28 August 1687 [DSGRM 47:155]. (Claims that she was Elizabeth Risley have no basis.).
CHILDREN:
   i   ELIZABETH IRISH, b. say 1644; m. by about 1664 Philip Washburn, son of JOHN WASHBURN [PM 480] (on 8 December 1708, "John Washband of Plymouth ... yeoman" sold to Samuel Bradford of Duxbury "all that my twenty acres of upland ... in the township of Duxborough aforesaid being lot upon which my honored grandfather John Irish deceased formerly dwelt being near Duxborough Mill & commonly known by the name of Irish's Orchard" and one acre of meadow "which was also my said grandfather's" [PLR 10:1:466; MD 15:247-53, 16:248-53]).
   ii   JOHN IRISH, b. say 1647; m. (1) by about 1672 Elizabeth _____ (said to be Savory) [DSGRM 47:155]; m. (2) 1 May 1708 Priscilla (Southworth) Talbot, daughter of Edward Southworth and widow of Samuel Talbot [NEHGR 54:181; TAG 60:131-32, 138-39, 78:1-8, 256-64].
   iii   ELIAS IRISH, b. say 1649; m. Taunton 26 August 1674 Dorothy Witherill [PCR 8:65]. (On 30 October 1677, William Witherell of Taunton was granted administration on the estate of Elias Irish [PCR 5:247].)

COMMENTS: In an indenture dated 20 April 1629, "John Irish of the parish of Clisdon in the county of Summersett, laborer," agreed with TIMOTHY HATHERLY [PM 234] of the parish of St. Olave in Southwark to "dwell, serve, remain & abide with the said Timothy Hatherly or his assigns at the town of Plimouth called New England from the day of the date of these presents unto the end & term of five years from thence next ensuing" [SJC Case #3597].

There is no Clisdon parish in Somersetshire. George E. Irish attempted to show that Cliddesden (also spelled Clisdon) in Hampshire was meant, but his argument is not convincing [Irish Bio 11-12].

John Irish must have been one of "Mr. Hatherlie's two men" who appeared in the Plymouth tax lists of 25 March 1633 and 27 March 1634 [PCR 1:10, 27]. The other may have been Ephraim Tinkham.

John Irish was one of those who sawed at JOHN HOCKING's anchor cable when the trader challenged the Plymouth men at Kennebec with fatal results [MD 2:11; PM 261-62]. (His name in this document has been misread as "Frish.")

Several sources claim that John Irish had a daughter Lydia who married someone named Gray and moved to France. This suggestion stretches credulity more than most.

BIBLIOGRAPHIC NOTE: Two genealogies of the family of John Irish have appeared in the last few decades. In 1964 Willis Luther Irish and Stella Bertha (Putnam) Irish produced an account of the descendants of John Irish that had a brief treatment of the immigrant [*Descendants of John Irish The Immigrant 1629-1963 and Allied Families* (Freeport, Maine, 1964), cited above as Irish Gen]. In 1991 George E. Irish published a volume devoted totally to the life of the immigrant [*John Irish: His Life and Ancestors, 1086-1677* (Baltimore 1991; supplement, Melbourne Beach, Florida, 1993), cited above as Irish Bio].

In the 1991 volume George E. Irish reaches several dubious conclusions, a number of which are overturned in the Supplement. In particular, his proposed parentage for the immigrant is shown in the Supplement to be incorrect. The Supplement shows that a pedigree supposedly taking the Irish family back to the time of William the Conqueror [Irish Gen 7-8] was created out of thin air by changing the family name on a pedigree of the Irton family [Supplement, Appendix 6.1AA].

J

JOHN JENNY

ORIGIN: Leiden, Holland.
MIGRATION: 1623 on the *Little James*.
FIRST RESIDENCE: Plymouth.

OCCUPATION: Brewer. Miller. On 5 March 1638/9, "Mr. John Jenney [was] presented for not grinding corn serviceable, but to great loss & damage, both in not grinding it well, as also causing men to stay long before it can be ground, except his servant be fed ... and also for not keeping his stampers going, which is much to the detriment of all" [PCR 1:118]. On 20 August 1644, "Mrs. Jenney, upon the presentment against her, promiseth to amend the grinding at the mill, and to keep the mortars clean, and bags of corn from spoiling and loosing" [PCR 2:76].
CHURCH MEMBERSHIP: "As for the Dutch, it was usual for our members that understood the language and lived in or occasionally came over to Leyden, to communicate with them, as one John Jenny, a brewer, long did, his wife and family, &c. and without any offense to the church" [*Hypocrisie Unmasked* 392; see also MD 27:63 (which has "London" instead of "Leyden")].
FREEMAN: In the 1633 Plymouth list of freemen, among those made free before 1 January 1632/3 [PCR 1:3]. In list of 7 March 1636/7 [PCR 1:52]. In Plymouth section of 1639 Plymouth Colony list of freemen, among the Assistants (annotated "dead") [PCR 8:173].
EDUCATION: The inventory of the estate of John Jenny included a "small globe," 2s. 6d., and a Bible and other books, £1 1s. The inventory of the estate of Sarah Jenny included "a [p]salme booke 1s.," "Cartwright on the Remise 6s.," "Downham's Workes 6s.," "four old bookes 6d.," "Mr. Ainsworth on Genesis & Exodus 2s. 6d." and "a great Bible & a small one 11s.," and she made her mark to her will.
OFFICES: Plymouth Assistant, 1637, 1638, 1639, 1640 [PCR 1:48, 79, 116, 140]. Deputy for Plymouth to Plymouth Colony General Court, 1 June 1641 [PCR 2:16]. Committee to assess colony, 2 January 1633/4, 2 March 1635/6 [PCR 1:26, 38]. Committee to lay out highways, 1

October 1634 [PCR 1:31]. Committee to control wages and prices, 5 January 1635/6 [PCR 1:36]. Committee on reuniting Plymouth and Duxbury, 14 March 1635/6 [PCR 1:41]. Committee on revising laws, 4 October 1636 [PCR 1:44]. Committee to apportion haygrounds, 20 March 1636/7 [PCR 1:55]. Committee to survey meadows, 5 May 1640 [PCR 1:152]. Committee on providing soldiers against the Indians, 27 September 1642 [PCR 2:45].

Plymouth coroner's jury, 2 March 1635/6 [PCR 1:39].

In Plymouth section of 1643 Plymouth Colony list of men able to bear arms [PCR 8:188].

ESTATE: In the 1623 Plymouth land division "John Jenings" was granted five acres as a 1623 arrival [PCR 12:5]. In the 1627 Plymouth cattle division "John Jene ... his wife Sarah Jene" and Samuell, Abigall and Sara Jene were the first five persons in the twelfth company [PCR 12:13].

John Jenny was assessed £1 16s. in the 25 March 1633 Plymouth tax list and £1 7s. in the list of 27 March 1634 [PCR 1:9, 27]. John Jenny was a Purchaser [PCR 2:179]. On 7 March 1652, "Mrs. Jennings" received one share in the Dartmouth lands [MD 4:187, citing PCLR 2:1:106-7].

Assigned as hayground for the year "the grounds from Joh. Wynslow downward to Mr. Allerton's house, or the creek there," 14 March 1635/6 [PCR 1:40]. On 20 March 1636/7, assigned hayground "where he had the last year, and to edge more upon the sedgy place, that there may be hay also got there for the team of the town" [PCR 1:56].

In 1635 "Mr. John Jeney" sold to George Watson "the dwelling house & garden with all the appurtenances thereunto belonging, which was sometimes Richard Maisterson's" [PCR 12:51].

On 6 January 1636/7, it is "agreed that the six acres of the lands of John Jenney, and the two acres of Mrs. Fuller, lying at Strawberry Hill, enclosed by Mr. Raph Smyth, shall be yielded up unto them this year, that they may improve them to the setting of corn; provided that the said John Jenney shall erect a dwelling house near or upon the said six acres, which are to belong unto the said house as long as it shall be a dwelling" [PCR 1:50].

On 5 March 1637/8, "one hundred and fifty acres of lands are granted unto Mr. John Jenney, lying on the east side of the Six Mile Brook, in the way to Namascutt, to be a farm belonging to the town of Plymouth, and to be called by the name of Lakenhame. And whereas there was not enough found on the east side of the said brook, the Court granted unto him a certain neck which is bounded as followeth, viz: by Lakenham

Brook on the one side, and with a swamp on the other side, with a small brook in it" [PCR 1:77].

On 2 April 1638, as part of a grant to Gabriell Fallowell, "the residue of the lands reserved for the mill, whereof the five or six acres aforesaid is a part, is, with Mr. Jenny's consent, granted to Gabriell Fallowell; and Mr. Jenney hath other lands granted to him in lieu thereof at Lakenhame" [PCR 1:82].

On 29 August 1638, "Web Adey" sold to "Mr. John Jenney all that his house and garden place adjoining situate in Plymouth together with the three acres of lands in the new field thereunto belonging" [PCR 1:35]. On 24 January 1638[/9], "Mr. John Jenney" sold to John Howland "all that his house, barns & outhouses at Rockey Nook together with all the lands thereunto belonging laid forth for the said Mr. Jenney's shares with that which was Phillip Delanoy's allowed him for want of measure and the five acres of meadow adjoining," receiving as partial compensation "three acres of lands of the said John Howland lying at Caughtaughcanteist Hill" [PCR 12:41, 42]. On 10 June 1639, "Richard Cluffe of Plymouth, tailor," sold to "Mr. John Jenney of the same ... all that his house & garden with the fence about the same all that the said Richard Cluff bought of Samuell Eddy" [PCR 12:44].

On 16 September 1641, "Mr. John Jenney is granted as much more upland as will make his farm at Lakenhame two hundred acres, and when that is used, then to have more added to it, in lieu of some land he hath yielded up at the town to Gabriell Fallowell" [PCR 2:26].

In his will, dated 28 December 1643 and proved 5 June 1644, John Jenny of New Plymouth bequeathed to "my eldest son Samuell Jenney" a double portion of all his lands; to "Sarah my loving wife" for life "my dwelling house and mill adjacent with all the lands thereunto belonging"; and to the rest "of my said children John, Abigall, Sarah and Susann" a single portion; "whereas Abigail my eldest daughter had somewhat given her by her grandmother and Henry Wood of Plymouth aforesaid is a suitor to her in way of marriage my will is that if she the said Abigaile will dwell one full year with Mr. Charles Chauncey of Scittuate before her marriage ... that then my said daughter Abigall have two of my cows and my full consent to marry with the said Henry Wood" [MD 6:169-70, citing PCPR 1:50].

The inventory of the estate of "Mr. John Jenney," taken 25 May 1644, totalled £108 3s. 3d., with no real estate included; a list of debts owed by the estate was appended [MD 6:171-74, citing PCPR 1:50-52].

In her will, dated 4 April 1654 and proved 5 March 1655/6, "Mrs. Sarah Jeney of Plymouth being sick and weak in body," thinking it "good to dispose of some small things that is my own proper goods leaving my husband's will to take place," bequeathed to "my daughter Pope" a bed and household goods and "further I bequeath to my daughter Sarah Pope all my wearing clothes to dispose of them to my daughter Abigaill Wood and to my grandchild Sarah Wood for their use as they have need excepting two of my petticoats which have not been worn which I give to my daughter Sarah Pope for her pains"; to "my son Samuell Jeney and to my daughter Abigaill Wood my mare equally to be divided between them"; to "my son Benjamin Bartlett all my ... cattle ... in the hands of Joseph Warren at the Eel River"; "my sheep be kept together till my legacies be paid"; to "the teacher Mr. John Reyner one ewe lamb"; to "the Elder Mr. Thomas Cushman one ewe lamb and the Bible which was my daughter Susanna's"; to "my loving friend Goodwife Clarke" one ewe lamb; "also I give one ewe lamb to Thomas Southworth." In a codicil dated 18 August 1655, she bequeathed "that which is my own since the death of my husband I give to my two daughters and the children of my son Samuel, excepting what I give as followeth, one colt I give to the three daughters of my children viz: Sarah Wood, Susanna Pope and Sarah Jeney if she come hither to abide, or else not to have any part of this colt or anything else of my estate"; "if my son Samuel take away his children that are now here with me, then my will is that none of them shall have anything of mine ... but it shall be reserved for the two boys if they do well when they come to age"; "I give unto Benjamine Bartlett only the starred cow which is at Thomas Pope's recalling whatsoever else is mentioned in my former will"; to "my daughter Sarah Pope" household goods; "my loving friends Capt. Standish, Elder Cushman, Thomas Clarke and Thomas Pope" overseers [MD 8:171-72, citing PCPR 2:1:17-18].

The inventory of the estate of "Mrs. Sarah Jeney," taken 18 February 1655[/6], totalled £248 5s. 8d., of which £131 was real estate: "the land & meadow at Lakenham," £7; "all the land at Strawberry Hill and meadow at the Salthouse Beach," £14; "the Purchasers' land," £10; and "the mill with the land belonging to it and dwelling house," £100 [MD 8:173-75, citing PCPR 2:1:18-21].

BIRTH: By about 1589 (based on date of marriage). (In his marriage record, he was stated to be of Norwich.)
DEATH: Between 28 December 1643 (date of will) and 25 May 1644 (date of inventory).

MARRIAGE: Leiden 1 November 1614 [NS] Sarah Cary, of Monk's Soham, Suffolk [Plooij XX; Leiden Pilgrims 135]. She died at Plymouth between 18 August 1655 (codicil to will) and 5 March 1665/6 (probate of will).

CHILDREN:
  i SAMUEL JENNY, b. about 1616 ("my eldest son" [father's will]; apprenticed for four years in 1633, so perhaps twenty-one in 1637); m. (1) after 1637 Susanna Wood [NEHGR 69:188-89; TAG 35:70-72]; m. (2) by 1657 Anne Lettice (eldest known child b. Plymouth 22 November 1657 [TAG 35:72]; in his will of 1678 Thomas Lettice of Plymouth bequeathed to "my three daughters," one of whom was "Anne the wife of Samuel Jenney" [MD 14:64, citing PCPR 4:2:11]).
  ii Child JENNY, bur. Leiden 1618 [Dexter 619].
  iii ABIGAIL JENNY, b. say 1621 ("eldest daughter" [father's will]); m. Plymouth 28 April 1644 Henry Wood [PCR 2:79; MD 48:13-20].
  iv Son JENNY, b. 1623 aboard *Little James*; d. before the 1627 Plymouth cattle division.
  v SARAH JENNY, b. say 1625; m. Plymouth 29 May 1646 THOMAS POPE [PCR 2:98; PM 362].
  vi JOHN JENNY, b. by 1627 (in 1643 list of men able to bear arms [PCR 8:188]); named in father's will but not in mother's will; no further record.
  vii SUSANNA JENNY, b. say 1634; m. by 1654 Benjamin Bartlett, son of ROBERT BARTLETT [PM 42].

COMMENTS: Emmanuel Altham, master of the *Little James*, writing in September 1623 to his brother Sir Edward Altham, told of "one goodwife Jennings [who] was brought abed of a son aboard our ship and was very well" [Three Visitors 24]. (Since Samuel Jenny was apprenticed in 1633 for a term of four years, and since he volunteered for service in the Pequot War in 1637, he could not have been the son born aboard ship in 1623.)

Nathaniel Morton, in reporting the arrival of the *Little James*, noted that one of "the principal passengers that came in her was Mr. John Jenny, who was a godly, though otherwise a plain man, yet singular for publicness of spirit, setting himself to seek and promote the common good of the plantation of New Plimouth; who spent not only his part of this ship (being part owner thereof) in the general concernment of the plantation, but also afterwards was always a leading man in promoting the general interest of this colony. He lived many years in New England, and fell asleep in the Lord, anno 1644" [Morton 66].

On 25 July 1633, "John Smith hath covenanted to serve John Jenny the full term of seven years, after the manner of an apprentice" [PCR 1:16]. On 1 January 1633/4, "Tho[mas] Higgens, having lived an extravagant life, was placed with John Jenny for eight years, to serve him as an apprentice" [PCR 1:21].

On 26 August 1636, "Edw[ard] Holman complaining of Joh. Jenny to the Governor & Assistants, for that the said John would not make payment for a piece he, the said Edw[ard], lost in his service; but the thing being heard, the said John was acquitted" [PCR 1:43].

John Jenny seems to have had a brief feud with Samuel Chandler. On 20 May 1637, Jenny complained "against Samuell Chaundler, in an action upon the case to the damage of £20, whereupon a parcel of beaver of the defendants was arrested aboard the said Mr. Jenney's bark" [PCR 7:6]. On 2 June 1640, "Samuell Chaundler complains against John Jenney, gent., in an action of trespass upon the case, to the damage of £40," and the jury found for Chandler [PCR 7:15-16]. In 1642 and 1643 John Jenny had a dispute with Joseph Ramsden [PCR 2:38-39, 57, 7:33-34].

On 4 September 1638, "Mr. John Jenney presented for digging down the highway before his mill, to the endangering of man and beast" [PCR 1:98].

On 24 January 1641/2, "Mr. John Jenney" purchased a one-sixteenth share in a bark of 40 or 50 tons soon to be built [PCR 2:31].

BIBLIOGRAPHIC NOTE: A brief account of John Jenny was published by Mary Lovering Holman in 1919 [Scott Gen 286-88]. A more comprehensive treatment may be found in the manuscript collections of Bertha Winifred Clark at the New England Historic Genealogical Society.

K

MANASSEH KEMPTON

ORIGIN: London.
MIGRATION: 1623 on the *Anne.*
FIRST RESIDENCE: Plymouth.

OCCUPATION: Yeoman. Planter.
CHURCH MEMBERSHIP: In England, Manasseh Kempton had belonged to Separatist congregations in Colchester and in London and was closely affiliated with Henry Jacob [TAG 67:132-35; Burrage 1:319, 2:299].
FREEMAN: In 1633 Plymouth list of freemen, before those admitted on 1 January 1632/3 [PCR 1:3]. In list of 7 March 1636/7 [PCR 1:52]. In the Plymouth section of the Plymouth Colony lists of freemen of 1639 and 1658 [PCR 8:173, 197].
EDUCATION: He made his mark to deeds [PCR 12:204] and to an agreement [PCR 3:211].
OFFICES: Deputy for Plymouth to Plymouth Colony General Court, 4 June 1639, 2 June 1640, 18 January 1643/4, 5 June 1644, 20 August 1644, 28 October 1645, 3 March 1645/6, 7 July 1646, 7 June 1648, 8 June 1649, 4 June 1650, 5 June 1651, 6 June 1660, 2 October 1660 [PCR 1:126, 154, 2:68, 72, 74, 94, 104, 123, 144, 154, 167, 3:187, 198].

Plymouth grand jury, 7 March 1636/7, 5 June 1638 [PCR 1:54, 87]. Petit jury, 3 March 1639/40, 1 June 1641, 6 September 1641, 7 December 1641, 7 June 1642, 6 June 1643, 5 November 1644, 5 October 1652 [PCR 7:15, 20, 23, 25, 31, 35, 38, 62].

Plymouth Colony committee "to treat with the now partners ... concerning the trade," and committee to lay out highways for "Plymouth side," 1 October 1634 [PCR 1:31]. Committee to regulate prices and wages, 5 January 1635/6 [PCR 1:36]. Committee to reunite Plymouth and Duxbury, 14 March 1635/6 [PCR 1:41]. Committee to allocate hay grounds, 20 March 1636/7 [PCR 1:55]. Committee to make laws, 6 May 1639 [PCR 1:121]. Committee to lay out land, 16 September 1641 [PCR 2:25].

Plymouth assessor, 3 March 1634/5, 1 March 1635/6, 20 September 1642, 9 October 1643, 21 November 1644, 4 November 1648, [blank] November 1649, 4 November 1650, 25 November 1651 [PCR 1:33, 38; PTR 1:11, 16, 19, 28, 29, 31, 32].

Committee to confer about the war, 26 and 27 September 1642 [PTR 1:11; PCR 2:45]. In Plymouth section of 1643 Plymouth Colony list of men able to bear arms [PCR 8:189].

ESTATE: In the 1623 Plymouth land division "Manasseh [Kempton] & John Fance" were granted two acres jointly, as passengers on the *Anne* [PCR 12:5]. In the 1627 Plymouth cattle division "Manases Kempton" and "Julian Kempton" were the eighth and ninth persons in the eleventh company and shared the benefit of a heifer and two she-goats brought over in the *Anne* [PCR 12:12-13].

Assessed 18s. in Plymouth tax lists of 25 March 1633 and 27 March 1634 [PCR 1:9, 27].

Permitted to mow "at the Iland Creeke abutting upon Stephen Tracie's ground & Edmund Chandler's," 1 July 1633, "against the fence of the said George [Soule], & against the fence of Thomas Little," 14 March 1635/6, and "at Joanes River where Mr. Bradford and Constance Southerne do get hay," 20 March 1636/7 [PCR 1:14, 41, 56].

On 5 January 1637/8, "Manasseth Kempton" of New Plymouth, yeoman, gave twenty acres "whereon the said John Faunce doth now dwell" to Faunce [PCR 12:26]. On the same day, "Manasseth Kempton of New Plymouth, yeoman," gave twenty acres "whereon the said Nathaniel doth now dwell" to Nathaniel Morton [PCR 12:26]. (These two parcels of land would be the twenty-acre shares received by Manasseh Kempton and his wife in the "second division" of land at Plymouth, authorized on 3 January 1627/8 [PCR 12:13].)

On 2 July 1638, "Manasseth Kempton ... & the rest of the neighborhood there request enlargement at the end of their lots where they dwell" [PCR 1:90]. On 1 June 1640, "Manasseth Kempton is granted an enlargement at the head of his ground, to extend up into the woods as far as Nathaniel Morton's ten acres last granted him," and also granted a piece of meadow [PCR 1:154]. On 1 December 1640, Henry Cobb sold his house in Scituate, with twelve acres of upland and a parcel of meadow and eighty acres of upland in the fourth lot, and a twelve acre parcel of marsh to "Manasseth Kempton" [PCR 12:65].

On 2 November 1640, "Manasseth Kempton" was granted ten acres "in the South Meddows towards Aggawam, Colebrook Meddowes" [PCR 1:166]. On 8 April 1645, "Manasseth Kempton of New Plymouth ...., planter," sold to Joseph Tilden of Scituate, yeoman, eighteen acres on

Cooper's Island and an eighteen acre marsh [PCR 12:105]. On 26 February 1645/6, his nephew Ephraim Kempton, having taken a bond to hold his uncle "Manasseth" harmless for any debts of the estate of Ephraim Kempton Sr., gave his goods to Mr. William Paddy, merchant, as security for the bond [PCR 12:125-26]. On 3 June 1647, "Manasseth Kempton" exchanged with Richard Church parcels of land in Plymouth near the swamp [PCR 12:144].

On 23 October 1643, Peregrine White of Marshfield sold to "Mannasses Kempton of Plymouth ... planter ... all those his uplands and meadows lying at the Eel River in Plymouth Township aforesaid lately assigned and confirmed unto the said Peregrine by Mr. Edward Winslow in the public court held at Plymouth the twenty-eight of September Anno Domini 1642" [MD 18:33-34, citing PCLR 2:2:114]. On 14 February 1659[/60], "Mannasses Kempton of Plymouth yeoman do ... make over the abovesaid deed unto Ephraim Morton my son-in-law," reserving some portions of meadow for himself [MD 18:34; PCLR 2:2:115].

On 22 February 1650/1, "Mannasses Kemton of Plymouth, planter," deeded to his "son-in-law Ephraim Morton" a parcel of land and a parcel of meadow at Sagaquas and his part and right in the land at Satuket. In case Morton's brothers wished to settle on the land, Kempton ordered that it be divided equally among them [PCR 12:204]. On 22 June 1651, Edward Bangs of Eastham, yeoman, and Rebecca his wife, sold to "Mannasses Kemton" of Plymouth, yeoman, forty acres of upland in Plymouth [PCR 12:209]. Kempton was one of those having an interest in the lands at Puncktateesett near Rhode Island in March 1651, sharing lot #34 with Nathaniel Morton [PTR 1:36, 69]. Manasseh Kempton was one of the Dartmouth Purchasers [MD 4:187].

On 4 January 1660[/1], "Mannasses Kemton of Plymouth" deeded to "his son-in-law Nathaneell Morton of Plymouth ... two acres of fresh meadow" in Plymouth, as well as the use of Kemptons's "marsh meadow at the Island Creek in the Township of Duxburrow" [MD 15:31, citing PCLR 2:2:44].

On 20 February 1660[/1], "Mannasses Kemton of Plymouth" deeded to William Harlow of Plymouth "two acres of fresh meadow lying in the meadow commonly called the south meadow," and on the same day he deeded to "his son-in-law Nathaneell Morton Sr." of Plymouth "all that his part, portion or share of land belonging to him as a townsman of the town of Plymouth which said land is commonly called and known by the name of Punckateesett" [MD 15:184-85, citing PCLR 2:2:54]. On 21 February 1660[/1], "Mannasses Kemton" of Plymouth, yeoman, deeded to Ephraim Morton of Plymouth "the one half of all that his lot or share of land commonly called the purchase land lying and being at Acushena, Coaksett and places adjacent both upland and meadow" [MD 15:185, citing PCLR 2:2:55].

On 12 July 1661 or 1662, "Mannasses Kemton of Plymouth" gave permission for "his son-in-law John Morton of Plymouth" to make use of "his marsh meadow at the Island Creek in the township of Duxburrow" [MD 17:108, citing PCLR 2:2:98].

In a letter dated 6 November 1661, Manasseh Kempton gave to the church of Eastham a parcel of land in that town [PCLR 3:104].

On 27 June 1662, "Mannasses Kempton" of Plymouth, yeoman, deeded to "his son-in-law Nathaniel Morton Sr." of Plymouth, yeoman, "a certain parcel of upland ground lying and being in the township of Plymouth aforesaid at a place called Hobshole *alias* Wellingsly ... the said parcel of upland ground which was the land of Samuell Jeney and by him sold unto John Rickard and by him sold unto the said Mannasses Kemton" [MD 17:104, citing PCLR 2:2:94]. On the same day, Captain Thomas Southworth of Plymouth sold to "Mannasses Kemton and Nathaniell Morton both of Plymouth aforesaid, yeomen, ... all that his parcel of upland ground lying and being at Hobshole *alias* Wellingsley"; Kempton then gave his half share of these lands to Abraham Jackson of Plymouth [MD 17:104-5, citing PCLR 2:2:95].

On 24 July 1662, "Mannasses Kemton of ... Plymouth ... yeoman" sold to "Richard Higgens" of Eastham "twelve acres of upland ground lying at Nausett in the township of Eastham aforesaid with six acres of meadow ..., with two acres of meadow at the harbor's mouth, with two acres of meadow at Billingsgate," and on the same day he sold to Lieutenant Joseph Rogers of Eastham "forty acres of upland ... at a place called Barly Neck in the township of Eastham" [MD 17:166-67, citing PCLR 2:2:99-100]. On 1 October 1662, "Mannasses Kemton of ... Plymouth ... yeoman" sold to John Smalley of Eastham "two acres of marsh meadow ... in the Township of Eastham aforesaid near unto the now dwelling house of the said John Smalley; between other meadow of his on each side thereof the which said two acres of meadow ... was sometimes the meadow of Mr. Will[i]am Bradford," and on the same day he sold to John Bangs of Eastham "one acres [*sic*] and three-quarters of marsh meadow ... in the Township of Eastham aforesaid at a place commonly called and known by the name of Namskekett; which was sometimes the meadow of Mr. Will[ia]m Bradford deceased and a part of his purchase land there" [MD 17:239-40, citing PCLR 2:2:106].

On 2 May 1665, the "supervisors of the estate of Mannasses Kempton Sr. deceased came into the court and owned that Joseph Harding of

Eastham hath made payment to the successors of the said Mannasses Kempton for two acres of marsh meadow which the said Joseph Harding bought of the said Mannasses Kempton lying at the great meadow" in Eastham [PCLR 3:27].

BIRTH: Baptized Berwick-upon-Tweed, Northumberland, 26 February 1589/90, son of George Kempton [TAG 67:134].
DEATH: Plymouth 14 January 1662/3 [PCR 8:23].
MARRIAGE: By 1627 Juliana (Carpenter) Morton, widow of GEORGE MORTON; she died at Plymouth on 19 February 1664/5 "aged fourscore and one years" [PCR 8:25]. (See PRISCILLA CARPENTER [PM 93].)
CHILDREN: None recorded.
ASSOCIATIONS: His younger brother Ephraim Kempton came to Plymouth by 1642 [TAG 67:134; PCR 2:89, 3:17, 114].

COMMENTS: On 13 February 1639/40, Henry Coggan of Barnstable sold to Manasseh Kempton the remaining years of service of James Glass, servant to the said Henry [PCR 1:139].

On 29 May 1643, "Manasseh Kempton" contributed 6d. to purchase drumheads at Plymouth [PTR 1:14]. On 10 February 1643/4, he was on the committee to build a wolftrap at Broken Wharf [PTR 1:16]. In 1644 he was one of those in the "Ele" River company who were to gather in case of war [PTR 1:17].

Sometime in 1646 the Plymouth inhabitants were divided up into "teams." The portion of the list that explains the significance of the teams is torn and destroyed. "Mannasses Kemton" headed a team consisting of Samuel Dunham, Ephraim Morton and Thomas Morton [PTR 1:33].

BIBLIOGRAPHIC NOTE: In 1992 Dean Crawford Smith published evidence establishing the English origin of the Kempton brothers, including biographical details on both brothers before migration [TAG 67:132-35]. In 1996 Dean Crawford Smith published a large body of data on the Kempton family in England and a line of descent from Manasseh's younger brother Ephraim [Kempton Anc 1-117].

L

RICHARD LANCKFORD

In the Plymouth tax list of 25 March 1633 Richard Lanckford was assessed 9s. [PCR 1:10]. (This was the smallest amount assessed, and was the rate for about half those on the list.)

On 28 October 1633 "was presented, upon the oath of Joshua Pratt, an inventory of the goods of Rich[ard] Lanckford, late deceased, Edward Wynslow administering upon the same" [PCR 1:18].

The inventory of "the goods of Rich[ard] Lanckford deceased who died the 14th of September," taken by Joshua Pratt and Edward Foster and presented at court on 28 October 1633, totalled £13 16s. 5d., all in personal goods, with £11 11s. 5d. in debts against the estate. The estate included 10s. 6d. in books: "20 small books & 2 singing ps[alm] books," 7s. 6d.; "Aynsworth on Exodus," 1s. 6d.; and "Bifield's works," 1s. 6d. [MD 1:83-86, transcribing PCPR 1:9-11].

COMMENTS: Lanckford's appearance in the tax list means that he was certainly in New England by 1632, but he may well have been one of those who came directly to Plymouth in 1629. He was one of several who died in the sickness of 1633.

JOHN LANGMORE

Sailed to Plymouth in 1620 on the *Mayflower*, as servant of Mr. CHRISTOPHER MARTIN [PM 315], and "died in the first infection, not long after the arrival" [Bradford 442, 445].

WILLIAM LATHAM

William Latham came to Plymouth in 1620 on the *Mayflower* as a servant to John Carver. In early 1651, in his accounting of the family of John Carver, Bradford reports that "His servant boy Latham, after more than 20 years' stay in the country, went into England and from thence to the Bahama Islands in the West Indies; and there with some others was starved for want of food" [Bradford 441, 444].

In the 1627 Plymouth division of cattle William Latham was the seventh person in the eleventh company [PCR 12:12].

In a Plymouth tax list of 25 March 1633, William Latham was assessed 9s. and the same amount on 27 March 1634 [PCR 1:11, 28].

In the inventory of Francis Eaton, dated 8 November 1633, "Will[i]am Lathan" appeared as a creditor, being owed £1 8s. [MD 1:200]. On 5 June 1638, "William Lathame" was fined 40s. "for entertaining of John Phillips into his house contrary to the act of the Court" [PCR 1:87]. He had a crop of Indian corn with John Phillips of Duxbury, as seen in a 6 July 1638 deed [PCR 12:31].

On 26 December 1639, "Will[ia]m Lathame of Duxborrow, planter," sold to Ralph Partrick his dwelling house, twenty acres of land and one acre of meadow [PCR 12:54].

In a deposition of about 8 July 1641, "William Latham of Duxbury planter aged 32 years" gave evidence in a case involving John Moses and Thomas Keyser [Lechford 421].

On 28 October 1645, "William Lathame" joined Roger Cooke in a complaint against John Barker and Ann, his wife, for Ann burning their house accidentally [PCR 7:41].

COMMENTS: William Latham's name does not appear in the 1623 Plymouth division of land; Robert S. Wakefield suggests that he may have been included in the household of William Brewster [MQ 40:9].

EDWARD LEISTER

Edward Leister came to Plymouth on the *Mayflower* in 1620, as one of Stephen Hopkins's two servants. According to Bradford, "Lester, after he was at liberty, went to Virginia and there died" [Bradford 442, 445]. He signed the Mayflower Compact on 11 November 1620.

1621 "June 18. The second offense is the first duel fought in New England, upon a challenge at single combat with sword and dagger, between Edward Doty and Edward Leister, servants of Mr. Hopkins. Both being wounded, the one in the hand, the other in the thigh, they are adjudged by the whole company to have their head and feet tied together, and so to lie for twenty-four hours, without meat or drink; which is begun to be inflicted, but within an hour, because of their great pains, at their own and their master's humble request, upon promise of better carriage, they are released by the governor" [Prince 190-91; Young's Pilgrim Fathers 201].

COMMENTS: Following STEPHEN HOPKINS [PM 271] in the 1623 division of land are two men with first name Edward but without surnames; these must be his two servants, EDWARD DOTY [PM 177] and Edward Leister. But Leister is not in the 1627 division of cattle, so he must have left for Virginia between those two dates. He does not appear in the February 1623/4 list of those in Virginia living and dead, or in the February 1624/5 Virginia muster of inhabitants.

THOMAS LITTLE

ORIGIN: Unknown.
MIGRATION: 1632.
FIRST RESIDENCE: Plymouth.
REMOVES: Marshfield before 1662.

EDUCATION: Sufficient to fill the office of "Keeper of the Colony of New Plymouth books" [SJC #1960].
OFFICES: Plymouth grand jury, 8 June 1664 [PCR 4:61].
   Marshfield constable, 3 June 1662 [PCR 4:16].
   In Plymouth section of 1643 Plymouth Colony list of men able to bear arms [PCR 8:189].
ESTATE: Assessed 18s. in Plymouth tax lists of 25 March 1633 and 27 March 1634 [PCR 1:11, 28].
   On 4 March 1647, five acres of upland meadow in Plymouth "at a brook commonly called the Indian Brook" were granted to Thomas Little "so long as ... himself or any of his posterity shall remain within the limits of the township of Plymouth" [PTR 1:23-24, 38]. On 25 December 1655, the town granted to Thomas Clark "five acres of meadow lying in the same meadow with Thomas Little, Tho[mas] Little's being first laid

out according to his grant in the town book" [PTR 1:207]. In 1664 Jonathan Morey expressed a desire "to have the meadow land granted to him that was sometimes Thomas Little's being upon the Indian Brook beyond Mannomett Ponds" [PTR 1:76].

On 2 August 1652, "Thomas Little sometimes inhabitant of the town of Plymouth" (with the consent of his wife Ann) sold to Richard Foster of Plymouth, planter, "all that his house and land lying and being at the Eelriver in the township of Plymouth aforesaid whereon the said Thomas Little formerly lived" [MD 1:98-99, citing PCLR 2:1:11].

On 3 June 1662, Thomas Little's rights to a farm he purchased in Marshfield, formerly belonging to Major William Holmes, were spelled out [PCR 4:16].

On 3 October 1665, Thomas Little, by virtue of land "he surrendered at Manomett Ponds," and Josias Keane, by virtue of "his great neccesity," were allowed to look for land, and if they found it, the court would grant them one hundred acres each [PCR 4:110]. Perhaps they failed to find unclaimed land, for, on 3 October 1665, Mrs. Rachel Davenport, as attorney to her husband Mr. Humphrey Davenport and in her own right as heir of Major William Holmes, sued Little and Keane for £600 for "detaining estate of lands and building on them" [PCR 7:126-27]. On 6 February 1665/6, Mrs. Rachel Davenport and her arbitrator referred the case against Thomas Little to the determination of the court [PCR 4:113] and the court replied on 1 May 1666 that Little should pay Davenport £15 [PCR 4:119-20].

On 29 October 1668, the court registered the claim of "Experience Michell, Henery Sampson, Richard Church and Thomas Little" to a parcel of land at Namassakett Pond, and declared that "none shall interpose to deprive them of it until the court purchases it and settles it on them" [PCR 5:5].

In his will, dated 17 May 1671 and proved 1 July 1672, Thomas Little Sr. bequeathed to "my loving wife all my housing and all my land, upland and meadow on that side of the brook I now dwell, except only the meadow I purchased of Thomas Tildin and Morris Trewant"; to "my sons Isacke and Ephraim the land on the other side of the brook"; "and all my land at Namassakett upland and meadow to my two younger sons Thomas and Samuell, except only one single share of upland I purchased of Jacob Mitchell which I bequeath to my grandchild John Jones except I do better provide for him"; to "my son Ephraim one feather bed with all meet furniture ... to be disposed to the said Ephraim at the time of his marriage"; to "Thomas and Samuel either of them a featherbed"; "my whole stock of cattle of all sorts ... equally divided amongst all my children"; residue to "my wife"; "my two eldest sons Isacke and Ephraim shall disburse out of their own estates, either of them £10 to help Thomas and Samuell in their buildings at Namassakett when they shall have occasion"; "and if I should sell my single share of land at Namassakett it is my will that my grandchild John Jones shall have forty acres of land out of the land of Thomas and Samuell and at my wife's decease Ephraim shall enjoy my housing, but the upland and meadow on that side to be equally divided between Isacke and Ephraim"; "Sarah Bonney shall have convenient apparel and a cow at the time of her departure out of her service" [MD 4:162-63, citing PCPR 3:1:46].

On 14 August 1672, administration of the estate of Thomas Little of Marshfield was granted to Anna Little his widow [PCR 5:101].

The inventory of the estate of Thomas Little, taken 4 April 1672, was untotalled, with no real estate included [MD 4:163, citing PCPR 3:1:47].

BIRTH: By about 1608 (based on date of marriage).
DEATH: Buried Marshfield 12 March 1671[/2] [NEHGR 8:191; MarVR 427].
MARRIAGE: Plymouth 19 April 1633 Ann Warren [PCR 1:13], born about 1612 (deposed on 6 June 1672 "aged sixty years or thereabouts" [MD 2:178]), daughter of RICHARD WARREN [PM 477]. She died after 19 February 1675/6 (named in son Thomas's will of that date [MD 4:164, citing PCPR 3:1:165]).
CHILDREN:

    i   ABIGAIL LITTLE, b. say 1634; m. by about 1656 as his first wife Josiah Keene (only surviving child, son Josiah, m. about 1681 [MF 18:1:18-19]; "my grandfather Josiah Keen married with Abigil Lettle" [MD 28:5, citing Hezekiah Keene's account book]).

    ii   RUTH LITTLE, b. say 1636; d. after 19 February 1675/6 (named in brother Thomas's will of that date [MD 4:164, citing PCPR 3:1:165]); apparently unm.

    iii   HANNAH LITTLE, b. say 1638; m. Scituate 25 January 1661[/2] Stephen Tilden [PCR 8:29], son of NATHANIEL TILDEN {1635, Scituate} [Joseph Neal Anc 63-64].

    iv   PATIENCE LITTLE, b. say 1640 (d. Hingham 25 October 1723 "aet. 84 years" [Hingham Hist 2:387]); m. Weymouth 11 November 1657 Joseph Jones (Thomas Little bequeathed to "grandson John Jones").

    v   MERCY LITTLE, b. say 1644; m. Marshfield last of November 1666 John Sawyer [MarVR 5]. He m. (2)

Marshfield 23 [blank] 1694 Rebecca (Barker) Snow, daughter of ROBERT BARKER [PM 29] and widow of Josiah Snow [MarVR 19].

vi   ISAAC LITTLE, b. about 1646 (d. Marshfield 24 November 1699 aged about 53 years [MarVR 388]); m. by 1674 Bethia Thomas, daughter of Nathaniel and Mary (_____) Thomas (eldest known child b. 1674 [MF 18:1:86]; on 1 March 1674/5, Isaac Little consented to the settlement of the estate of Nathaniel Thomas [PCR 5:158-59]).

vii   EPHRAIM LITTLE, b. Plymouth 17 May 1650 [PCR 8:10]; m. 22 November 1672 Mary Sturtevant, daughter of Samuel Sturtevant [MD 34:145-49].

viii   THOMAS LITTLE, b. say 1654; d. Pawtucket 26 March 1676 in King Philip's War [TAG 60:240]. In his will, dated 19 February 1675[/6] and proved 31 May 1676, "Thomas Little Senior" bequeathed to "my loving brother Samuel," to "each of my sisters, that is to say Ruth, Hannah, Patience and Mercye," and to "my loving mother," and referred to "the ten pounds which Isack and Ephraim were to pay unto me by my father's will" [MD 4:164, citing PCPR 3:1:165].

ix   SAMUEL LITTLE, b. about 1656 (deposed 18 March 1689/90 aged "thirty three years or thereabouts" [MD 2:248]); m. Marshfield 18 May 1682 Sarah Gray, daughter of Edward Gray [MarVR 19; MF 15:37].

COMMENTS: Thomas Little is included in a list of those attending town meeting in Plymouth about 1646 [PTR 1:22]. On 26 October 1647, Thomas Little of "the Yele [Eel] River" acknowledged a £20 debt to the court and king [PCR 2:120].

Thomas Little seems to have been absent from Plymouth, and from Plymouth Colony, from about 1652 to 1662. In his deed of 2 August 1652, he tells us he no longer resides in Plymouth, but does not tell us where he does live. The Weymouth vital records call Patience Little the daughter of Thomas Little of Cambridge at her marriage to Joseph Jones in 1657, but Thomas Little does not appear in published Cambridge records.

On 7 February 1664/5, William Shurtliff sued Thomas Little for carrying off trees Shurtliff had felled and squared. Major Alden and Joseph Beedle were to settle the bounds and Little to return the trees, but final judgment to await the return of the bounds [PCR 4:79]. On 9 June 1665, Thomas Little was fined £1 10s "for disclosing grand jury proceedings" [PCR 4:101, 8:114, 116]. On 7 March 1664/5, sometime constable William Holmes successfully sued Thomas Little for £5 in damages for misleading Holmes into unjustly attaching the belongings of Nathaniel Winslow [PCR 7:122-23].

The birth order and estimated dates of birth for the daughters of Thomas Little derive from the assumption that, in his will of 19 February 1675[/6], Thomas Little, the son of the immigrant, named his four surviving sisters in their birth order, and from the further assumption that the age at death given for Patience (Little) Jones should be interpreted as meaning "in 84th year."

BIBLIOGRAPHIC NOTE: The family and descendants of Thomas Little are treated in detail in Volume Eighteen of the Five Generations Project of the General Society of Mayflower Descendants, devoted to the descendants of RICHARD WARREN.

ROBERT LONG

"Robart Long" received one acre in the 1623 Plymouth land division, having arrived in 1623 as a passenger on the *Anne*; he was grouped with Patience and Fear Brewster [PCR 12:6].

COMMENTS: The fact that Long was grouped with two children of WILLIAM BREWSTER [PM 66] may indicate that he was a servant of Brewster, or possibly a relative. Since he is not in the 1627 division of cattle, Long must have died or removed before that date.

JOHN LYFORD

ORIGIN: Levalleglish, parish of Loughgall, county Armagh, Ireland.
MIGRATION: 1624 (perhaps on the *Charity*).
FIRST RESIDENCE: Plymouth.
REMOVES: Nantasket, Salem, Virginia 1627.

OCCUPATION: Minister.
CHURCH MEMBERSHIP: Lyford was expected to minister to the congregation at Plymouth, which he apparently did for a short span of time, after which he and some like-minded persons (including JOHN

OLDHAM [PM 345]) separated themselves, which led to their banishment.

EDUCATION: Although not recorded as a student at Cambridge or Oxford, John Lyford was certainly well educated. Perhaps he, like his son, attended Trinity College, Dublin, whose records are not complete.

ESTATE: The will of "John Liford" of "Sherby [i.e., Shirley] Hundred in Virginia, clerk," was probated in the Prerogative Court of Ireland in 1632 [Sir Arthur Vicars, ed., *Index to the Prerogative Wills of Ireland, 1536-1810* (Dublin 1897), p. 286]. (This will would have been destroyed in 1922.)

"Ruth Leyford" of Hingham and "Mordicay Lyford" of Hingham both acquitted "Edmund Hubbert senior" their "stepfather" for a legacy of two hundred pounds of tobacco given them by their "father John Leyford by his last will and testament" (21 October 1641 and 3 June 1642 respectively [SLR 1:27]).

BIRTH: By about 1590 (based on estimated date of marriage).
DEATH: Virginia about 1628 (having gone from Salem "to Virginia, where he shortly after died" [Bradford 169]).
MARRIAGE: By about 1617 Sarah _____, born about 1586 (deposed 1 August 1639 aged "about fifty-three years" [WP 4:137]). She perhaps married second _____ Oakley, or else this was her maiden name to which she reverted before marrying next at Charlestown 10 October 1634 EDMUND HOBART {1633, Charlestown} [GMB 2:958-60] ("Edmond Hubberd Senior and Sarah Oakeley widow did join in marriage before me," Increase Nowell [WP 3:174]; "And also I have seen a sufficient register of the marriage of the said Edmund and Sarah, testifying that they were lawfully married at Charlestown in New England upon the tenth day of October in the tenth year of his said Majesty's reign" [Lechford 140, 142]). She died at Hingham on 23 June 1649 ("Mother Hobart died in the evening being Saturday, buried on the Sabbath" [NEHGR 121:22]).
CHILDREN:
    i   OBADIAH LYFORD, b. say 1617 (in 1635 "Obadiah Liford" was a scholar at Trinity College, Dublin [George Dames Burtchaell and Thomas Ulick Sadler, eds., *Alumni Dublinienses* ..., new edition, with supplement (Dublin 1935), p. 501]); evidently died without surviving issue by 1639 when his brother Mordecai was called his "brother and next heir" [WP 4:137].

ii   RUTH LYFORD, b. say 1619 (adult 1641 [SLR 1:27]); m. 19 April 1643 James Bates [NEHGR 121:15; Hingham Hist 38-39].

iii   MORDECAI LYFORD, b. say 1621 (adult 1642 [SLR 1:27]); no further record.

iv   (possibly) MARTHA LYFORD, b. say 1628; m. by 1650 Samuel Lincoln [NYGBR 60:115-17 (for this hypothesis to work, Martha would have to be born at about the time her father died, since her last child was born in 1674)].

COMMENTS: Plymouth Colony's trials and tribulations with Rev. John Lyford dominate Bradford's historical account for late 1624 and early 1625 [Bradford 147-69].

The third eminent person ... was the minister which they sent over, by name Mr. John Lyford, of whom & whose doing I must be more large.... When this man first came ashore, he saluted them with that reverence & humility as is seldom to be seen, and indeed made them ashamed, he so bowed and cringed unto them, and would have kissed their hands if they would have suffered him; yea, he wept & shed many tears, blessing God that had brought him to see their faces; and admiring the things they had done in their wants, &c. as if he had been made all of love, and the humblest person in the world. And all the while (if we may judge by his after carriages) he was but like him mentioned in Psalm 10.10.... They gave him the best entertainment they could (in all simplicity), and a larger allowance of food out of the store than any other had.... He made a large confession of his faith, and an acknowledgement of his former disorderly walking, and his being entangled in many corruptions, which had been a burden to his conscience, and blessed God for this opportunity of freedom ... things seemed to go very comfortably and smoothly on amongst them, at which they did much rejoice, but this lasted not long, for both Oldom [JOHN OLDHAM] and he grew very perverse, and showed a spirit of great malignancy ... so as there was nothing but private meetings and whisperings amongst them; they feeding themselves & others with what they should bring to pass in England by the faction of their friends there, which brought others as well as themselves into a fool's paradise ... yet outwardly they still set a fair face of things.

At length when the ship was ready to go, it was observed Liford was long in writing, & sent many letters, and could not forbear to communicate to his intimates such things as made them laugh in their sleeves.... The Governor and some other of his friends knowing how things stood in England and what hurt these things might do, took a shallop and went out with the ship a league or two to sea, and called for Liford's and Oldum's letters.... He found above twenty of Lyford's letters, many of them large and full of slanders & false accusations, tending not only to their prejudice, but to their ruin & utter subversion [Bradford 147].

After some weeks with no response to the letters, Lyford and Oldham continued about their business, but, with no warning, one day set up a separate church and began to carry out their design. The Governor called a court and charged the two and read copies of some of the letters "at which he [Lyford] was struck mute" and the Governor asked him "if he thought they had done evil to open his letters; but he was silent, & would not say a word, well knowing what they might reply." Lyford was put under house arrest. "In conclusion, he was fully convicted, and burst out into tears, and confessed he feared he was a reprobate, his sins were so great that he doubted God would not pardon them, he was unsavory salt, &c.... After their trial & conviction, the court sentenced them to be expelled," Oldham immediately, and Lyford had "liberty to stay six months" [Bradford 219]. Lyford reverted to the humblest of men "so as they began again to conceive good thoughts of him upon this his repentance, and admitted him to teach amongst them as before ... but that which made them all stand amazed in the end ... that after a month or two ... secretly he wrote a second letter to the Adventurers in England in which he justified all his former writings" [Bradford 221].

Lyford's wife went to the Plymouth deacons and told them "he had a bastard by another before they were married, and she having some inkling of some ill carriage that way, when he was a suitor to her, she told him what she heard, and denied him. But she not certainly knowing the thing, otherwise than by some dark and secret mutterings, he not only stiffly denied it, but to satisfy her took a solemn oath there was no such matter. Upon which she gave consent and married with him; but afterwards it was found true and the bastard brought home to them" [Bradford 167].

On 1 August 1639, "Sarah Hubbard wife of Edmund Hubbard of Hingham in New England, planter, aged about fifty-three years sometimes the wife of John Lyford, clerk, deceased and mother of

Obadiah Lyford, clerk, deceased and of Mordecai Lyford sworn saith upon her oath that the said Mordecai who hath this day chosen the said Edmund Hubbard to be his guardian is brother and next heir of the said Obadiah" [WP 4:137].

Lechford tells us more:
> Edmund Hubbard of Hingham in New England planter and Sarah his wife sometime wife of John Lyford clerk deceased, Obadiah Lyford, clerk, deceased and Mordecai Lyford his brother and heir free land in the County of Tyrone. And the lease of Leballeglishe.... And also I have seen a sufficient register of the marriage of the said Edmund and Sarah, testifying that they were lawfully married at Charlestown in New England upon the tenth day of October in the tenth year of his said Majesty's reign [Lechford 140, 142]

On 6 August 1639, Edmund Hubbard of Hingham, planter, guardian of Mordecai Lyford brother and heir of Obediah Lyford, clerk, deceased, and Sarah wife of the said Edmund, gave their power of attorney to "our well beloved & trusty friends William Bladen alderman of the city of Dublin and John Fisher citizen of the same city" to demand any inheritance due to Mordecai, particularly rents from lands in County Tyrone and the lease at "Leballeglish in the county of Ardmagh" so that the Hubbards need not "be compelled to travel forth of the jurisdiction of the Massachusetts Bay in New England" [Lechford 142-44].

No doubt in relation to this case in some way, Lechford also recorded
> That Sarah Hubbard wife of Edmund Hubbard of Hingham in New England sometimes wife of John Lyford Clerk, sometime minister at Levelgkish near Laughgaid in the county of Ardmagh Deceased is alive &c. [Lechford 263].

The correct, modern name for the Irish locality in which Lyford resided was Levalleglish in the parish of Loughgall, county Armagh, a parish which is on the border of county Tyrone.

M

EDMUND MARGESSON

Edmund Margesson came to Plymouth in 1620 on the *Mayflower*, "died soon after ... arrival in the general sickness," and "left no posterity here" [Bradford 443, 447].

CHRISTOPHER MARTIN

ORIGIN: Billericay (Great Burstead), Essex.
MIGRATION: 1620 on the *Mayflower*.
FIRST RESIDENCE: Plymouth.

OCCUPATION: Merchant.
CHURCH MEMBERSHIP: He refused to kneel at holy communion at Easter, 1612 [Martin Bio 10]. On 3 March 1619/20, Christopher Martin of Billericay was cited for "suffering his son to answer me ... that his father gave him his name" [NEHGR 21:77, citing Archdeaconry Court of Chelmsford].

BIRTH: By about 1582 (based on date of marriage).
DEATH: Plymouth 8 January 1620/1 ("Saturday the 6th of January [1620/1] Master Marten was very sick, and, to our judgment, no hope of life. So Master Carver was sent for to come aboard to speak with him about his accounts; who came the next morning" [Mourt 43-44]; "January 8 this day dies Mr. Christopher Martin" [Prince 182]).
MARRIAGE: Great Burstead, Essex, 26 February 1606/7 Mary (____) Prowe[r], widow of ____ Prowe[r] [Martin Bio 3 and plate facing 10]. She died in Plymouth the first winter.
CHILD:
    i NATHANIEL MARTIN, bp. Great Burstead 26 February 1609[/10] [Martin Bio 3]; apparently alive at Great Burstead in 1620 [Martin Bio 7].

ASSOCIATIONS: Christopher Martin's servant, [stepson] SOLOMON PROWER [PM 383], was cited in the Archdeaconry Court of Chelmsford for answering improperly "unless I would ask him some questions in some catechism" [NEHGR 21:77]. This unfortunate Solomon died Christmas Eve 1620 at Plymouth: "December 24, this day dies Solomon Martin [*sic*], the sixth and last who dies this month" [Prince 168].

COMMENTS: As a stranger to the Leiden company, Christopher Martin, stated by Bradford to be "from Billerica in Essex," was chosen as the "treasurer agent" for the *Mayflower* and *Speedwell* and provided supplies in a very overbearing and brash manner [Bradford 44]. Cushman wrote "Mr. Martin saith he neither can nor will give any account of it, and if he be called upon for accounts he crieth out of unthankfulness for his pains & care, that we are suspicious of him, and flings away, & will end nothing. Also he so insulteth over our poor people, with such scorn and contempt, as if they were not good enough to wipe his shoes" [Bradford 55].

In his listing of the passengers on the *Mayflower*, Bradford included "Mr. Christopher Martin and his wife and two servants, Solomon Prower and John Langmore," and in his accounting of this family in 1651 we learn that "Mr. Martin, he and all his died in the first infection, not long after arrival" [Bradford 442, 445].

Mr. Christopher Martin who was active in the early settlement of Virginia must have been a different man, as he was still of record in Virginia when the *Mayflower* man was already dead [private communication from William Thorndale].

BIBLIOGRAPHIC NOTE: In 1982 R.J. Carpenter published a pamphlet that thoroughly traces what is known of Christopher Martin in English court and ecclesiastical records [*Christopher Martin, Great Burstead and The Mayflower* (Chelmsford, Essex, 1982), cited above as Martin Bio].

RICHARD MASTERSON

ORIGIN: Leiden, Holland.
MIGRATION: 1629.
FIRST RESIDENCE: Plymouth.

OCCUPATION: Wool-comber [Leiden Pilgrims 186].

CHURCH MEMBERSHIP: Excommunicated at Sandwich, Kent, on 17 January 1613[/4], for "affirming that the form of God's worship in the Church of England ... is a corrupt & unlawful worship and repugnant to the scriptures" [NEHGR 154:358]. Member of Robinson's church in Leiden [Bradford 260; Bradford LB 22].

Masterson was described as "having been officious with part of his estate for public good, and a man of ability, as a second Stephen, to defend the truth by sound argument, grounded on the Scriptures of truth" [PChR 83]. He was not likely made a deacon of Plymouth church, for the same reasons as discussed with THOMAS BLOSSOM [PM 58].

ESTATE: On 22 July 1634, "Mary the late wife of the said Richard and William Brewster (both of Plymouth) ... being the guardians of Nathaniell & Sarah the children of the said Richard deceased" made a power of attorney to three Leiden residents to sell a house owned by "Richard Masterson late of the City of Leiden deceased" [MD 29:19-20].

On 22 October 1650, "Mr. Raph Smith of Ipswich in N[ew] Eng[land]," for "Mary his wife (sometime formerly wife of Rich[ard] Masterson of Leidon)," made "Mr. Hugh Goodyeare of Leidon in Holland" his attorney to collect "all rents [and] arrearages due unto the aforesaid Mary for a certain house or tenement situate upon the uppermost graft near the quackle brigg in Leiden aforesaid" [Aspinwall 331-32].

BIRTH: By about 1594 (based on date of marriage).
DEATH: Plymouth 1633 [Bradford 260].
MARRIAGE: Leiden, Holland, 23 November 1619 [NS] Mary Goodall [Plooij XXXVIII; Leiden Pilgrims 186], born about 1590 (aged sixty in 1650 [NEHGR 144:24]). She married (2) before 1 July 1633 Rev. RALPH SMITH [PM 425]. She died in 1659 [NEHGR 144:24, citing D. Plooij, *The Pilgrim Fathers from the Dutch Point of View* (New York 1932), 116].
CHILDREN:
    i NATHANIEL MASTERSON, b. about 1620 (deposed aged about 43 in February 1671/2 [GDMNH 467, citing SJC #1073]; this age must be a year or two high if Nathaniel's birth occurred after the marriage to Mary Goodall); m. Ipswich 31 July 1657 Elizabeth Cogswell, daughter of JOHN COGSWELL {1635, Ipswich} [GM 2:2:137-40].
    ii SARAH MASTERSON, b. say 1625; m. by 1645 John Wood (or Atwood) [NEHGR 144:25-26].

COMMENTS: On 4 September 1618, Sabin Staresmore wrote to Mr. Carver saying "as for my own present condition, I doubt not but you well understand it ere this by our brother Masterson, who should have tasted of the same cup, had his place of residence & his person been as well known as myself" [Bradford 358-59].

From Leiden on 30 November 1625, "Richard Maisterson" and four others wrote to Bradford at Plymouth regretting that they must remain apart since to join them would be "prejudicial" to the Plymouth people at that time [MD 5:169-70].

Although Masterson first showed up in Plymouth records in 1633, at the time of his death, he was probably one of those who came from Leiden in 1629 or 1630.

In 1633 Bradford wrote that "[i]t pleased the Lord to visit them this year with an infectious fever of which many fell very sick and upward of twenty persons died, men and women, besides children, and sundry of them of their ancient friends which had lived in Holland, as Thomas Blossom, Richard Masterson, with sundry others" [Bradford 260].

BIBLIOGRAPHIC NOTE: In 1990, as part of her investigation of the history of a seventeenth-century sampler, Ruth Wilder Sherman examined closely the family of Richard Masterson, and also went on to provide details on his daughter Sarah who married John Wood *alias* Atwood [NEHGR 144:22-28].

In 2000 Michael R. Paulick published an article which included many ecclesiastical records from Sandwich, Kent, for this immigrant, and suggested that Masterson was shuttling back and forth between Sandwich and Leiden in the second decade of the seventeenth century [NEHGR 154:353-69].

WILLIAM MENDLOVE

Three consecutive actions of the Plymouth court, all dated 23 July 1633, relate to William Mendlove [PCR 1:15]:

> Will[iam] Mendlove, the servant of William Palmer, whipped for attempting uncleanness with the maid servant of the said Palmer, & for running away from his master, being forcibly brought again by Penwatechet, a Manomet Indian.

Will[iam] Mendlove bound to serve Richard Church the full term of seven years in the trade of carpentry, wherein the said Richard sufficiently to instruct & teach him, & at the expiration of his term to give him two suits of apparel.

William Palmer sold the time of service he had in William Mendlove to Richard Church, for & in consideration of three pounds sterling, to be paid in money or corn, in November next ensuing.

COMMENTS: In "The Migrations of Mark Manlove (ca. 1617-1666) in New England, Virginia, and Maryland" (TAG 61 [1985-86]:71-76), George Russell argues that the William Mendlove of the records above is the same as Mark Manlove who appears in Plymouth in 1637. While this hypothesis is plausible, it is not proven, and the career of Mark Manlove may be followed in Russell's article. William Mendlove's service should have run to 1640 based on the evidence above, but Mark Manlove was not in service when he first appeared in 1637.

ROBERT MENDUM

ORIGIN: Unknown.
MIGRATION: 1630.
FIRST RESIDENCE: Plymouth.
REMOVES: Duxbury by 1639, Kittery 1644.

OCCUPATION: Tavern keeper (licensed at Kittery 21 October 1645 [MPCR 1:90]). On 27 June 1648, it was "ordered that Robert Mendam is for to sell the wine and beer that is now in his house & afterwards to surcease" [MPCR 1:125-26]. On 16 October 1649, "Robert Mendam [was] presented for letting a company of fishermen to be drunk in his house about a fortnight ago, and also a master of a voyage so drunk that he could hardly go or speak" and "for giving public entertainment and drawing wine and beer contrary to a general court order and a town order," for which he was fined £10, immediately abated to 40s. [MPCR 1:134-35]. On 15 October 1650, "[i]t is ordered that Robert Mendam shall be permitted to keep an ordinary or house of entertainment for the term of one year from the date hereof, with this proviso, that the major part of the inhabitants of the River of Pascataquacke be therewith content" [MPCR 1:147].

FREEMAN: Oath of fidelity at Duxbury, 1639 [PCR 8:182].

"Robert Mendum" was one of those from Kittery who signed the petition to Massachusetts Bay for protection in 1662 [MPCR 1:199].

OFFICES: "Rob[er]te Mendall" volunteered for service in the Pequot War, 1637 [PCR 1:61].

York grand jury, 29 June 1654, 28 June 1655, 12 July 1658, 1 July 1661, 9 July 1667, 1 July 1679 [MPCR 1:291, 2:30, 40, 70, 108, 355]. Petit jury, 11 March 1651/2, 30 June 1656, 28 December 1665 [MPCR 1:157, 258, 2:48]. Arbiter, 16 October 1647 [MPCR 1:113].

Kittery constable, 1652, 1654, 1663, 1666 [MPCR 1:266, 2:6, 31, 133].

His inventory included "a firelock musket" valued at 14s. and "a long fowling piece" valued at 20s. [YLR 5:1:15].

ESTATE: On 2 October 1637, a "proportion of land is granted to John Carew, about the lands granted to Rob[er]te Mendall, containing ten acres" [PCR 1:67]. On 7 January 1638/9, "Jonathan Brewster & Will[ia]m Basset are appointed to lay forth Rob[er]te Mendlove's & John Carew's land, and the garden place for John Rowe" [PCR 1:109].

On 19 October 1639, "Rob[er]te Mendall of Duxborrow" sold to John Phillips "all that his dwelling house & outhouses and all the lands thereunto belonging ... with two acres of meadow ... [p]rovided that if the said John Phillips do fail to make payment of the first payment at the day and place aforesaid that then the bargain to be void" [PCR 12:48].

On 5 November 1644, whereas "there was a suit commenced by Arthur Howland against Rob[er]te Mendam for the sum of six pounds, for goods which the said Rob[er]te Mendam's wife brought for the said Arthur Howland out of England, and did not deliver them, but sold them, and converted the money to her own use, as was proved in court; and whereas the said Rob[er]te Mendam hath authorized Thomas Clarke, of the Eele River, to sell a parcel of land the said Rob[er]te Mendam hath at Duxborrow, viz: ten acres of upland, and two acres of meadow, the which the said Thomas Clark had performed for him, and made sale thereof unto Will[ia]m Hiller, of Duxborrow, for one Dutch cow, valued at six pounds, and hath confirmed the same unto the said Will[ia]m Hiller ...; and that the said Arthur Howland commenced his suit as aforesaid by attaching the said cow," the court granted judgment upon the cow to Howland and confirmed the land to Hiller [PCR 2:77-78; see also PCR 7:38, 12:109-10, 139-40].

On 21 September 1647, "Robert Mendam of Pascataquacke" purchased Thomas Crockett's house and four acres [YLR 1:12].

On 15 July 1654, Robert Mendum of Kittery and his wife sold to Mr. Hugh Gunnison "my two houses & land upon the point where now Mr. Gunnison dwelleth with all my right and interest there, and also my land on the west side of the mouth of Spruce Creek where Robert Mendum and John White did plant, with all the land that was given by the townsmen unto Robert Mendum" [MPCR 1:253].

On 20 May 1681, "Jonathan Mendum now of Kittery ... together with my father Robert Mendum" sold to Nicholas Weeks of Kittery land on the east side of Spruce Creek, all done "with the consent of my father," but Robert did not sign [YLR 3:112].

In his will, dated 1 May 1682 and proved 18 May 1682, "Robert Mendum ... weak in body" bequeathed to "my son Jonathan Mendum" all the housing and land belonging to it during his life and after his death, to his two younger sons, Jonathan and David Mendum; if either dies before he comes of age, then the survivor to have the whole, and if both die, then "my grandson Robert Mendum shall have it"; to "my grandson Robert Mendum" all my land in Spruce Creek; to "my son & daughter Mendum" ten of my cattle; to "my three grandchildren aforesaid" five cattle apiece; "my son & daughter to have the improvement of all both land and stock till my grandchildren come to age"; to "my grandson Robert Muchamore" a heifer delivered by my son Jonathan when he comes of age; "my son Jonathan" sole executor; "bury me in my field by my last wife"; "my honored friend Richard Martyn Esqr." overseer [YLR 5:1:14-15].

The inventory of the estate of "Robert Mendum of Kittery deceased," taken 16 May 1682, totalled £336 2s. (plus £10 4s. 6d. in debts owed to the estate), of which £150 was real estate: "the dwelling house & all the outhouses with all the land adjoining thereunto being about seventy acres," £100; and "the land in Spruce Creek by report one hundred acres," £50. [YLR 5:1:15].

BIRTH: About 1602 (aged about fifty in April 1654 and seventy-six in 1676 [GDMNH 475, citing unidentified sources]).
DEATH: Between 1 May 1682 (date of will) and 16 May 1682 (date of inventory).
MARRIAGE: (1) By 1639 Mary _____ [PCR 1:132]. She probably died by 1658.
(2) (perhaps) By 1658 Judith (_____) _____, mother of Nicholas Weeks's wife, Judith [GDMNH 476; EQC 2:117]. In 1702 Mary Woodman deposed that her mother-in-law Mendum wanted her father-

in-law Mendum to give Nicholas Weeks a deed to certain land, but he said he never would [GDMNH 476; see YLR 3:112].

CHILDREN:
  With first wife
  i   SARAH MENDUM, b. say 1647; m. by 1667 James Muchmore (if she was his only wife, they were absent from meeting and were presented by the grand jury on 1 October 1667 [MPCR 1:334]; father's will names her son Robert, a minor in 1682) [GDMNH 500].
  ii JONATHAN MENDUM, b. by 1650 (witness to deed, 4 April 1664 [YLR 2:2]; adult by July 1672 [MPCR 2:239]); m. by about 1675 Mary Raynes (see *COMMENTS* below). She m. (2) by August 1693 John Woodman [MPCR 4:134, 147-49].

ASSOCIATIONS: Robert Mendum (whose name is also given as Mendall or Mendlove) had dealings with William Hiller, who also was associated with Mark Manlove/Mendlove (see sketch of WILLIAM MENDLOVE above).

COMMENTS: On 3 September 1639, "Mary, the wife of Rob[er]te Mendame, of Duxborrow, for using dalliance diverse times with Tinsin, an Indian, and after committing the act of uncleanness with him, as by his own confession by several interpreters is made apparent, the Bench doth therefore censure the said Mary to be whipped at a cart's tail through the town streets, and to wear a badge upon her left sleeve during her abode within this government; and if she shall be found without it abroad, then to be burned in the face with a hot iron; and the said Tinsin, the Indian, to be well whipped with a halter about his neck at the post, because it arose through the allurement & incitement of the said Mary, that he was drawn thereunto" [PCR 1:132].

Occasionally court was held at "Mendam's" at Kittery [MPCR 1:115, 154].

On 6 July 1646, "Robert Medam" was sued by Widow Billing "concerning a cellar" [MPCR 1:95]. Perhaps this had something to do with the parcel of land which, on 27 June 1648, "John Treworgye" affirmed he had sold to Robert Mendam, "which his cellar is built thereon and from his cellar unto his new house which now he hath built" [MPCR 1:131]. On 15 March 1650[/1], Nicholas Shapleigh successfully sued "Robert Mendam" for having his cellar on Shapleigh's land and for cutting wood on Shapleigh's land; Mendum's appeal was granted but only under condition that "Robert Mendam is not to demolish, diminish or make any waste, or any defacing of any edifice thereon" [MPCR 1:139, 167].

On 18 October 1647, "Robert Mendam" was presented for beating his wife, but he contested it and the case was dropped [MPCR 1:119]. On 27 June 1648, he was in court attaching goods of William Waldron, deceased, held by Mr. Edward Godfrey, 27 June 1648 [MPCR 1:124]. On 11 March 1651[/2], Mr. William Hilton successfully sued "Robert Mendam" and "Thomas Hanscome" for trespass [MPCR 1:156]. On 14 October 1651, Capt. Paul Whitt sued Robert Mendum in an action of trespass [MPCR 1:166].

On 16 October 1651, "Goody Mendum" was presented for abusing Mrs. Gullison [i.e., Gunnison] "in words" and she was fined 2s. 6d. for calling Hugh Gullison and John Davis "x x the devils" (evidently language too rich for the editors) [MPCR 1:164-65]. On 18 October 1651, Goody Mendum was again presented for cursing and saying "the devil take Mr. Gullison and his wife"; this time she was fined £5 [MPCR 1:165].

How Robert Mendum's second wife knew enough about William Norman to accuse him in court on 14 October 1651 of never having had a legal divorce from his wife in England is unknown [MPCR 1:169].

"Mary Mendam, at the complaint of Grace Dimond & her husband, John Dymond, who depose they stand in fear of life, so Robert Mendam her husband is bound in recognizance of £40 that she shall keep the peace and be of a bearing both to the parties grieved and others 5 December 1651"; she was found guilty of assault and battery and fined 40s. and costs [MPCR 1:173, 175]. On 18 March 1651[/2], Goody Mendum was presented for saying Mr. Shapley was "a base knave" and for looking upon "Miss Shapleigh to be some peddler's trull" and for saying she [Mendum] would kill her child and for saying she looked at Mr. Godfrey "to be a dissembling man"; her husband, Robert Mendum, gave a bond of £10 for her good behavior [MPCR 1:176].

"Robert Mendum" deposed on 29 June 1658 that "twelve or thirteen years since, Thomas Crockett and Thomas Beeson did fall timber and saw upon the neck of land over against Thomas Crockett's field" [YLR 2:1].

The estimation of the marriage date of about 1675 for son Jonathan is based on a number of factors [GDMNH 475, 577-78]. He had three children at the time of his father's will in 1682, sons Robert, Jonathan and David. In 1701 son Robert had been absent for ten years and presumed dead; if he had been born about 1676 he would have been about fifteen in 1691, a likely age to make a sea voyage from which he did not return. Son Jonathan received a grant of land in 1699 and had married by 1702, which would be consistent with a year of birth of about 1678. The third son, David, could then be born about 1680 and satisfy the bequests in the will of the immigrant. The elder Jonathan Mendum was born by 1650, making him at least twenty-five in 1675. The elder siblings of Mary Raynes, the wife of the elder Jonathan Mendum, were born in the late 1640s and early 1650s, which would suggest that she would have been born in the mid-1650s. This would be consistent with a marriage about 1675.

DESIRE MINTER

Desire Minter came to Plymouth in 1620 on the *Mayflower,* in the household of JOHN CARVER [PM 95]. "Desire Minter returned to her friend and proved not very well and died in England" [Bradford 441, 443-44].

COMMENTS: Jeremy D. Bangs suggests that Desire Minter may have been daughter of William and Sarah (Willett) Minter of Leiden [NEHGR 143:209]. If Desire Minter is related to the Minters of Leiden, then she would also be connected with THOMAS WILLETT [PM 497].

In Bradford's list, Desire appears immediately after John Carver and his wife, and before a number of other persons specifically described as servants, which might indicate that she was somehow a relative of the Carvers. Note also that Bradford says that "Desire Minter returned to her friend." The OED indicates that friend could at this time mean relation or kinsman, citing Shakespeare: "But she I mean is promised by her friends, Unto a youthful gentleman of worth" (*The Two Gentlemen of Verona* III.1.106-7). See the sketch of JOYCE BRADWICK for the same usage [GMB 1:215]; perhaps the word at this time also had the meaning of "guardian."

EXPERIENCE MITCHELL

ORIGIN: Leiden, Holland.
MIGRATION: 1623 on the *Anne.*
FIRST RESIDENCE: Plymouth.
REMOVES: Duxbury by 1639, Bridgewater between 1684 and 1689.

FREEMAN: In 1633 Plymouth list of freemen in close proximity to those admitted 1 January 1632/3 [PCR 1:4]. In Plymouth Colony list of 7 March 1636/7 [PCR 1:53]. In Duxbury sections of lists of freemen dated 1639, 1658, 29 May 1670, and [blank] March 1683/4 [PCR 5:274, 8:174, 198, 203].

EDUCATION: His inventory included "books" valued at 14s. [MD 4:152, citing PPR 1:45]. He signed his will.

OFFICES: Plymouth petit jury, 5 October 1640, 5 June 1644, 1 June 1647, 7 June 1648, 6 June 1649, 7 June 1649, 4 June 1652 [PCR 2:117, 126, 140, 7:17, 37, 46, 60]. Grand jury, 7 June 1659 (fined for refusing to serve), 5 June 1666, 5 June 1677 [PCR 3:163, 4:123, 5:230]. Coroner's jury, 7 May 1662 [PCR 4:12].

Duxbury surveyor of highways, 1 June 1658 [PCR 3:136].

In Duxbury section of 1643 Plymouth Colony list of men able to bear arms [PCR 8:189]. His inventory included "in my brother Johns hand one cow, one short gun & a small iron kettle" valued at £2 12s. [MD 4:152, citing PPR 1:45].

ESTATE: In the 1623 Plymouth land division, George Morton and Experience Mitchell together received eight acres [PCR 12:6]. In the 1627 Plymouth cattle division, "Experience Michaell" was the tenth person in the first company with Francis Cooke [PCR 12:9].

On 9 May 1631, Experience Michell sold to Samuell Eddy his dwelling house and part of his garden plot [PCR 12:18].

Assessed 18s. in Plymouth tax list of 25 March 1633 and 9s. in list of 27 March 1634 [PCR 1:10, 27]. He was forty-ninth on the list of Purchasers [PCR 2:177].

In an undated entry, but probably in 1645, Mr. John Holmes of Plymouth, messenger, sold to Experience Mitchell of Duxbury two acres of marsh meadow [PCR 12:109]. On 20 March 1647, "Samuel Eedy" sold to Experience Mitchell one acre of marsh meadow [PCR 12:151].

On 1 July 1650, Andrew Ringe of Plymouth sold to Experience Mitchell two acres of marsh meadow in Duxbury at Blewfish River [PCR 12:189]. On 20 November 1650, William Paybody of Duxbury, planter, sold to Experience Mitchell of Duxbury, planter, a house and ten acres of land at Blewfish River in Duxbury [PCR 12:198].

On 3 October 1662, Experience Mitchell was one of a group nominated for consideration for lands on the northerly bounds of Taunton "if any be left over" [PCR 4:27]. On 8 June 1664, he was part of a group permitted to look for land between Bridgewater and the Bay line [PCR 4:67]. On 7 June 1665, Experience Mitchell was fifth on a list of twenty-four shares of land on the westerly side of Namasskett River "for his children," no one to possess above two shares [PCR 4:94]. On 5 June 1666, he again had liberty to look for land [PCR 4:132]. On 3 June 1668, he was granted land near Mattapoisett River [PCR 4:185]. On 29 October 1668 and 1 June 1669, the court arranged for Experience Mitchell and others to have land at Namassakett [PCR 5:5, 20].

In his will, dated 5 December 1689 [*sic*] and proved 4 September 1689, "Experience Mitchell now living in the town of Bridgwater" bequeathed to "my son Edward Mitchell ... all my lands both upland and meadow lying in the town of Duxbury at the place where I formerly dwelt"; if "my wife Mary Mitchell shall survive me I require my son Edward to take care of her" if she wished to live in Bridgewater, but if "she rather incline to live at Duxbury" then half the rent of the land at Duxbury to be given her during her life; "my son Edward shall have the sole dispose of it as to the letting of it out for the house I acknowledged it to be his," he also to receive household goods; to "my son John I have formerly given him his portion of land and my will is that he rest satisfied ... which was fourscore acres of upland and four acres of meadow lying at Namatakeesit" and the moveables in his hands, "one cow, a short gun, a small iron kettle I give unto my grandson Experience and the remainder I give unto my son John"; "as for my land lying in the town of Middlebury I give it to my daughters Mary Shaw, Sarah Haward and Hannah Haward and to my grandson Experience Mitchell the son of my son John to be equally divided"; to "my daughter Mary Shaw 20s."; to "Hannah Haward 40s."; "and if my stock stand I give to my grandson Thomas Mitchell one cow and to my granddaughter Mary Mitchell one cow"; "I leave the dispose of my granddaughter Mary Mitchel with my son Edward and Joseph Bartlett"; residue of moveables and chattels to "my son Edward Mitchell," executor [MD 4:150-51, citing PPR 1:44-45; Small Gen 518-20].

The inventory of the estate of Experience Mitchell of Bridgewater, taken 14 May 1689, totalled £21 17s., including no real estate [MD 4:152, citing PPR 1:45; Small Gen 520-21].

BIRTH: By about 1603 (based on estimated date of marriage).
DEATH: By 14 May 1689 (date of inventory).
MARRIAGE: (1) By about 1628 Jane Cooke, daughter of FRANCIS COOKE [PM 144]. She died before 1641, and perhaps some years earlier.

(2) By about 1641 Mary _____. She died after about 1662 (birth of last child).

CHILDREN:
With first wife
- i ELIZABETH MITCHELL, b. say 1628; m. Plymouth 6 December 1645 John Washburn [PCR 2:94], son of JOHN WASHBURN [PM 480].
- ii THOMAS MITCHELL, b. say 1630; living on 1 August 1672 [MD 3:104, citing PCLR 3:234; MF 12:35-36]. (In 1936 Merton Taylor Goodrich argued that this Thomas Mitchell was the man of that name who appeared on Block Island by 1678 and had a family there [TAG 12:93-99; see also NEHGR 82:457-58, which does not make this claim]. Others who have agreed with this position are G. Andrews Moriarty [TAG 19:226] and Robert S. Wakefield [MD 38:187-89].)
- iii MARY MITCHELL, b. say 1632; m. (1) Plymouth 24 December 1652 James Shaw [PCR 8:14], son of JOHN SHAW [PM 413]; m. (2) after 6 December 1684 John Jenney [MF 12:74; BrLR 3:61].

With second wife
- iv SARAH MITCHELL, b. Plymouth about 1641 (aged "about ninety years" in December 1731 [Plymouth County Court Records 2:125]); m. by 1661 John Hayward [PNQ 3:102], son of THOMAS HAYWARD {1635, Cambridge} [GM 2:3:288-94].
- v JACOB MITCHELL, b. say 1643; m. Plymouth 7 November 1666 Susanna Pope [PCR 8:31], daughter of THOMAS POPE [PM 362]. (On 5 March 1677/8, Experience Mitchell, Edward Mitchell and Joseph Bartlett were made guardians of the children of Jacob Mitchell [PCR 5:188, 252].)
- vi EDWARD MITCHELL, b. say 1645; m. (1) about 1668 Mary Hayward ("and lived with her forty years without children" [TAG 59:31]); m. (2) Plymouth 26 August 1708 Alice Bradford [PVR 89].
- vii JOHN MITCHELL, b. say 1650; m. (1) Duxbury 14 December 1675 Mary Bonney, daughter of THOMAS BONNEY {1635, Charlestown} [GM 2:1:340-43]; m. (2) Duxbury 14 January 1679[/80] Mary Lathrup; m. (3) Duxbury 24 May 1682 Mary Prior.
- viii HANNAH MITCHELL, b. say 1662; m. by 1682 Joseph Hayward (eldest known child b. Bridgewater 20 March 1682/3).

ASSOCIATIONS: Thomas Mitchell, nephew of Experience Mitchell, wrote two letters to his relatives in New England, one dated 23 April

1661 [NS], and the other in 1689 [PNQ 3:101-4]. In the earlier of these two letters he asks his uncle Experience, "to present my respects and my sisters' and their husbands' to my Aunt Jean Gunn and my cousin Joseph." Jean Gunn remains unidentified and no record of her has been found in New England.

COMMENTS: In 1973 John B. Threlfall pointed out the likelihood that Jane Cooke was not the mother of all the children of Experience Mitchell, with daughter Elizabeth and son Thomas as the only two who could be certainly ascribed to this mother [NEHGR 127:94-95]. Ten years later Robert S. Wakefield emphasized the same points, with the additional point that Jane (Cooke) Mitchell must have died before Bradford prepared his accounting of *Mayflower* families early in 1651 [TAG 59:28-31].

Both Threlfall and Wakefield note the possibility that daughter Mary was also a child of Jane (Cooke) Mitchell. The dates assigned above indicate a gap of nearly a decade between Mary and the next child of Experience Mitchell, with all later children following at more or less normal intervals. This chronological analysis places Mary in the same sequence as Elizabeth and Thomas and separates her from the other children. Although the evidence is not as strong as that for Elizabeth and Thomas, we feel more strongly than Threlfall or Wakefield that Mary was a daughter of Jane (Cooke) Mitchell.

Barbara Lambert Merrick has argued that the rest of the children of Experience Mitchell are not with his first wife [MD 49:144-45].

In this connection it should also be noted that the last child, Hannah, seems to be considerably younger than all the others, raising the possibility that Mary was the third wife of Experience rather than the second.

In 1980 John B. Threlfall presented a document showing that on 3 April 1633 Mary Smedley and Mary Mitchell of Amsterdam "(where their husbands and children remain)" wished to return from England where they had been visiting friends. Mary Mitchell was described as the wife of Thomas Mitchell, and Threlfall suggested that Thomas was a brother of Experience [TAG 56:97-98].

On 20 June 1654, Experience Mitchell, Miles Standish, John Alden and Philip Delanoy were ordered to settle the bounds between Arthur Howland and Thomas Doggett [PCR 3:62].

BIBLIOGRAPHIC NOTE: Lora A.W. Underhill prepared a lengthy treatment of Experience Mitchell as part of her examination of the Small and allied families [Small Gen 507-98].

ELLEN MORE
JASPER MORE
MARY MORE

In Bradford's accounting of the passengers on the *Mayflower*, in the family of John Carver was "a child that was put to him called Jasper More," who died before the spring of 1621 "of the common infection" [Bradford 441, 443].

The family of William Brewster in 1620 included "a boy ... put to him called Richard More, and another of his brothers" [Bradford 441]. Thirty years later, in summarizing the Brewster family, Bradford reported that "Richard More's brother died the first winter" [Bradford 444].

In the family of Edward Winslow in 1620 was "a little girl ... put to him called Ellen, the sister of Richard More," who died "soon after the ship's arrival" [Bradford 441, 444].

COMMENTS: The parish register of Shipton, Shropshire, contains the following baptisms of four children of Samuel Moore of Larden (the fourth of which gave the mother's name as Catherine) [NYGBR 36:213-19, 291-301]:

>Ellinor, bp. 24 May 1612
>Jasper, bp. 8 August 1613
>Richard, bp. 13 November 1614
>Mary, bp. 16 April 1616

In 1959 Anthony Wagner came upon a document that told an interesting story about these children. In 1610 Samuel Moore married Catherine Moore, his third cousin, and Wagner noted that "it looks as if the marriage was arranged to keep Larden in the More family." After some years Samuel discovered that his wife had maintained an adulterous relation with one Jacob Blakeway, who was the father of some if not all of the children. After considerable difficulty, Samuel

Moore managed to divorce Catherine, and, wanting to start a family of his own, he arranged for Catherine's four children to be put in the care of JOHN CARVER [PM 95] and ROBERT CUSHMAN [PM 158], who would transport them into Virginia, maintain them for seven years, and then provide them with fifty acres of land [NEHGR 114:163-68]. At the end of this article, Wagner listed a number of other possibilities for research into the legal battle between Samuel and Catherine Moore, most of which have not been examined. Wagner also published an outline of various royal descents for the More children [NEHGR 124:85-87].

The document printed by Wagner refers to "the four children of the petitioner Katharine More," and in the baptismal records are two boys and two girls. The list prepared by Bradford explicitly names Ellinor (Helen), Jasper and Richard, and refers to the fourth child only as Richard's brother. One possibility is that after the passage of three decades Bradford's memory had erred, and the fourth More child on the *Mayflower* was Mary, the last child, baptized in 1616. Alternatively, Catherine More may have had a fifth child, a boy, not recorded at Shipton. This would of course require that the daughter Mary had died by July 1620. The close spacing between births of the first three children implies that the More family was employing a wetnurse, and so another child might have been born in 1615.

RICHARD MORE

ORIGIN: Shipton, Shropshire.
MIGRATION: 1620 on the *Mayflower*.
FIRST RESIDENCE: Plymouth.
REMOVES: Salem 1637.
RETURN TRIPS: To England after 1627 and returned June or July 1635 in the *Blessing*; travelled to Virginia or Maryland in the early 1640s [NGSQ 62:168].

OCCUPATION: Mariner. On 26 November 1674, Thomas Smith "deposed that about the beginning of August last, he was on board the ship *Friendship* of Salem, Richard Moore, master" [EQC 5:444].

Tavernkeeper. On 29 September 1674, "Capt. Richard More was licensed to keep an ordinary and to sell beer and cider, but not wine or liquors, for a year" [EQC 5:400].

CHURCH MEMBERSHIP: Admitted to Salem church on 27 February 1642/3 [SChR 11].

FREEMAN: 28 February 1642/3 [EQC 1:50].

EDUCATION: He signed his name to deeds but Christian made her mark.

OFFICES: Perhaps some of the considerable petit jury and grand jury service in Essex County pertained to this Richard More, although there was another man of this name in Lynn contemporaneously [EQC 3:154, 4:292].

ESTATE: In the 1627 Plymouth division of cattle Richard More was the fourth person in the fifth company headed by William Brewster [PCR 12:10].

On 1 November 1637, "Richard Moore of Ducksborrow, yeoman," sold all his property in Duxbury to Abraham Blush [PCR 12:22-23].

On 3 October [1649], James Hyndes of Salem sold to Richard Moore one dwelling house on the south river side with three-quarters of an acre adjoining and ten acres of upland in the south field [ELR 1:16]. On 20 September 1659, Richard Moore of Salem, mariner, mortgaged to Henry Shrimpton of Boston one dwelling house with three-quarters of an acre, with the yard, warehouse and stable in Salem [ELR 1:69]. On 13 September 1655, John Horne of Salem sold to Richard Moore of Salem one dwelling house and an acre of land [ELR 2:82A].

On 7 July 1662, "Mr. Richard Moore and Mary Chichester, wife of William, came into court and acknowledged their free act and deed in exchanging a piece of land of about seven poles that lay on the north side of said Marie's ground for so much lying on the east side of said ground, as the fence now stands" [EQC 2:432].

On 11 July 1664, Henry Bartholomew of Salem, with the consent of his wife Eliza, sold to Richard More of Salem a dwelling house and an acre of land in Salem [ELR 2:82A]. On 20 January 1667[/8], Richard More of Salem, mariner, sold to Edward Grove of Salem, sailmaker, half an acre, "which More has by an execution against John Prescott" [ELR 3:27]. On 10 January 1670[/1], Richard More of Salem, mariner, and Christian his wife, sold to Thomas Pitman of Marblehead, husbandman, ten acres in Marblehead [ELR 3:107]. On 21 September 1658, Richard Moore of Salem, mariner, sold to William Flint of Salem, husbandman, ten acres in the south field [ELR 3:127]. On 27 September 1671, Richard Moore Sr. of Salem, mariner, sold to William Browne Jr. of Salem, half an acre in Salem [ELR 3:127 (and re-recorded 3:174)].

On 30 August 1673, "Richard More of Salem, mariner," with the consent of Christian his wife, sold his rights as a purchaser at Swansea to Samuel Shrimpton of Boston [PCLR 3:303].

On 10 June 1675, Richard More of Salem for "natural affection" deeded to "Caleb More & Richard More my sons and my daughters Susanna & Christian More ... my dwelling house in Salem where I now live with all out houses etc. and all moveables quick and dead" [ELR 4:114].

On 4 June 1684, Richard More Sr. of Salem deeded for natural affection and "more especially for & in consideration of marriage betwixt him the said Samuel Dutch and my daughter Susannah his now wife" land in Salem where Samuel Dutch's house then stood and a quarter of an acre where a highway ran through part of More's orchard [ELR 6:123].

On 9 October 1687, Richard More Sr. of Salem, mariner, sold to John Higginson Jr. of Salem, merchant, a parcel of flats and wharf land in Salem south of "my now dwelling house" [ELR 8:9]. On 17 December 1687, Richard More of Salem, mariner, mortgaged to Mr. Phillip Cromwell of Salem, slaughterer, a small parcel of land in Salem containing the out kitchen and leanto [ELR 8:15]. On 15 May 1688, Richard More Sr. of Salem, mariner, sold to William Browne Esq. and Mr. Benjamin Browne, both of Salem, "my homestead which I am now possessed of ... in Salem ... excepting the piece of land I mortgaged to Philip Cromwell" [ELR 8:85].

On 14 August 1688, Richard More Sr. and Richard More Jr., both of Salem, mariners, sold to Peter Osgood of Salem, tanner, sixty poles of ground in Salem, part of the houselot [ELR 8:93].

On 10 July 1688, Richard More Sr. of Salem, mariner, deeded to "my son Richard More Jr." part of "my dwelling house called by new room or long room with the garden enclosed and the cellar under it" [ELR 8:95]. On 10 May 1690, Richard More of Salem deeded the land he had mortgaged in 1687 to Philip Cromwell, slaughterer [ELR 8:150].

BIRTH: Baptized Shipton, Shropshire, 13 November 1614, the repudiated son of Samuel and Catherine Moore of Larden [MD 22:77].
DEATH: Salem between 19 March 1693/4 and 20 April 1696 [MD 22:49, 78], "aged 84 years" [MD 4:198, 22:49].
MARRIAGE: (1) Plymouth 20 October 1636 Christian Hunter [PCR 1:45], daughter of Thomas and Susan (Gentleman) Hunter [TAG 78:241-44]. She was born say 1615 and died Salem 18 March 1676, "aged 60 years" [MD 3:198]. She was twenty years old when she came on the *Blessing* in 1635 [TAG 40:77].

(2) By 1678 Jane (_____) Crumpton, widow of Samuel Crumpton who was slain at Muddy Brook Bridge on 18 September 1675, in the

company of THOMAS LOTHROP {1633, Salem} [Bodge 137; GMB 2:1201-6]. On 23 May 1678, "Richard More, as husband of the relict of Samuel Crumpton," sued Christopher Lattimore for debt [EQC 7:111]. She died at Salem on 8 October 1658, "aged 55 years" [MD 3:198].

CHILDREN:
With first wife
- i SAMUEL MORE, bp. Salem 6 March 1641/2 [SChR 18]; living 1651 [Bradford 444] but no further record.
- ii THOMAS MORE, bp. Salem 6 March 1641/2 [SChR 18]; living 1651 [Bradford 444] but no further record.
- iii CALEB MORE, bp. Salem 31 March 1644 [SChR 20]; d. Salem 4 January 1678/9, "aged 34 years" [MD 3:199]; unm.
- iv JOSHUA MORE, bp. Salem 3 May 1646 [SChR 21]; living 1651 [Bradford 444] but no further record.
- v RICHARD MORE, bp. Salem 2 January 1647/8 [SChR 21]; m. by 1673 Sarah _____ [MD 3:199].
- vi SUSANNA MORE, bp. Salem 12 May 1650 [SChR 22]; m. (1) say 1675 Samuel Dutch (her father witnessed her bond as administratrix of Samuel's estate 19 March 1694 [MD 22:77]); m. (2) by 1696 Richard Hutton [EPR Case #8426]; m. (3) (int.) Wenham 11 April 1714 John Knowlton. (The best account of the Dutch family was published by Walter Goodwin Davis in 1947 [Phoebe Tilton Anc 87-107].)
- vii CHRISTIAN MORE, bp. Salem 5 September 1652 [SChR 23]; m. Salem 31 August 1676 Joshua Conant.

COMMENTS: In his accounting of the *Mayflower* passengers, Bradford included in the household of William Brewster "a boy [that] was put to him called Richard More" [Bradford 441]. In 1651 Bradford wrote that "Richard More's brother died the first winter, but he is married and hath four or five children, all living" [Bradford 444]. Richard More was one of four children of Samuel and Katherine More, whose bitter divorce made the *Mayflower* voyage a welcome answer to the problem of placement of their unwanted children. Sir Anthony Richard Wagner has provided us with the first and most accurate account of the English background of Richard More and his siblings [NEHGR 114:163-68 and 124:86-87]. More recently Donald Harris has presented much of this same material, placing it in historical context, but adding little about More himself [MD 43:123-132, 44:11-20, 109-118].

A "Richard More of Salem in New England" married on 23 October 1645 at St. Dunstans, Stepney, Middlesex, at a time when Richard More of Salem was certainly married. Unless we are prepared to accept Richard More of Salem as a bigamist, there must have been, at least for a brief time, two Richard Mores in Salem.

The bell taken at Port Royal, Nova Scotia, was brought to Salem "in Capt. Moor's ketch" [EQC 7:310-12].

On 25 January 1641/2, John Stacy sued Richard More for killing his swine [EQC 1:30]. On 1 January 1645/6, Thomas Tuck testified that Richard Moore "made a well upon the common for his own use the last summer, being very dry and water scarce upon the neck. Tuck hired a cow, which came to drink at the well, and the water being very low the cow broke her neck" [EQC 1:93].

On 29 June 1654, the administrators of the estate of Richard Hollingsworth acknowledged a judgment to Capt. Traske and another to Rich[ard] Moore [EQC 1:359].

In June 1661 when William Shakkerley, master of the bark *Hopewell*, complained that it was insufficient for a voyage to Newfoundland, the court commissioned Richard More, master, and others to examine it [EQC 2:313]. On 30 September 1665, Robert Starr deeded to Capt. Richard More and Mr. Philip Cromwell as guardians to "my three children Robert, Richard and Susanna" a house "given to me by my father-in-law Richard Hollingsworth as a portion with my wife ... for the use and benefit of my three children" [ELR 3:139].

For the 27 June 1665 court, Richard More, aged "about fifty years," deposed in a case between Symond Crosby and Henry Roads [EQC 3:256]. On 15 January 1665[/6], Bartholomew Roes Jr. at "Charlestown in Carolina" authorized payment to "Capt. Richard Moore" of 673 pounds of "good Muschovadee Sugar" [ELR 3:101]. On 24 January 1666[/7], Richard More executed a bill of lading for the ship *Swan* carrying tobacco on account of Col. Augustine Warner of Virginia [ELR 3:5]. On 3 March 1668/9, Richard More deposed regarding the law and customs for the entry of vessels into Maryland [SJC #907].

BIBLIOGRAPHIC NOTE: In 1997 the Five Generations Project of the General Society of Mayflower Descendants published a revised version of the family and descendants of Richard More, compiled by Robert Moody Sherman, Robert S. Wakefield and Lydia Dow Finlay [MF 15:151-87]. In 1901 George Ernest Bowman published several depositions given by Richard More late in his life, regarding events that had happened in his early New England years; this article also included photographs and transcriptions of a number of early tombstones [MD 3:193-201].

In 2002 David Lindsay published *Mayflower Bastard: A Stranger Among the Pilgrims* (New York 2002), a biography of Richard More, which takes great liberties with the available evidence [TAG 77:318-19].

BENNETT MORGAN

"Benet Morgan" was granted one acre in the 1623 Plymouth land division as a passenger on the *Fortune* in 1621 [PCR 12:5]. He was not in the 1627 cattle division, and so had presumably died or returned to England by that date.

He was certainly in England in November 1624 when, as "Bennet Morgan of Plymouth, New England, sailor aged 27," he deposed in the Admiralty proceeding of *William Stevens & Thomas Fell v. The Little James* [English Adventurers 17; NGSQ 63:295].

WILLIAM MORRELL

In his account of events in 1623, Bradford reports that ROBERT GORGES [PM 229] "brought over a minister with him, one Mr. Morrell, who about a year after the Governor [Gorges] returned, took shipping from hence. He had I know not what power and authority of superintendency over other churches granted him, and sundry instructions for that end, but he never showed it or made any use of it. (It should seem he was in vain.) He only spoke of it to some here at his going away. This was in effect the end of a second plantation in that place [Wessagussett]" [Bradford 138; see also Ford 1:336-40].

COMMENTS: William Morrell matriculated at Cambridge at Easter 1611, sizar from Magdalene College, received his B.A. in 1614/5, was ordained deacon at Peterborough on 23 May 1619 and priest on 24 May 1619 [Venn 3:214].

Charles Francis Adams provides the best description of William Morrell's brief stay in New England. Adams thinks that Morrell left in the spring of 1625, and that his departure was not the end of the plantation at Wessagusset [Three Episodes 156-59; MHSP 16:194-206].

Upon his return to England, Morrell wrote a poem containing his observations of the countryside and the native population; he presented this poem in Latin with an English translation, and it was published in London with the title *New-England or A Briefe Enarration of the Ayre,*

Earth, Water, Fish and Fowles of that Country with A Description of the Natures, Orders, Habits, and Religion of the Natives (London 1625) [MHSC 1:1:125-39].

GEORGE MORTON

ORIGIN: Leiden.
MIGRATION: 1623 in the *Anne*.
FIRST RESIDENCE: Plymouth.

OCCUPATION: Merchant.
EDUCATION: Considering his son's literary accomplishments, it is likely that George was literate as well.
ESTATE: In the 1623 Plymouth land division George Morton was paired with Experience Mitchell, as passengers on the *Anne*, in a grant of eight acres [PCR 12:6]. By the time of the 1627 Plymouth cattle division, George Morton's widow, Juliana, had married Manasseh Kempton, and she and four of her children, Nathaniel, John, Ephraim and Patience Morton, were included in the company of William Bradford [PCR 12:13]. A fifth child, Sarah Morton, was the eleventh person in the company of Francis Eaton [PCR 12:12].

George Morton received one share in the Dartmouth lands [MD 4:187]; as he was long dead when this division was made, the grant was presumably to his heirs.

BIRTH: By about 1587 (based on date of marriage).
DEATH: Plymouth June 1624 [Prince 310].
MARRIAGE: Leiden 23 July 1612 [NS] Juliana Carpenter, daughter of Alexander Carpenter, the groom stated to be "of York in England" [MD 11:93; Plooij XII; Leiden Pilgrims 66, 195 (the second and third of these published sources have misread the day of marriage)]. She married (2) by 1627 MANASSEH KEMPTON [PM 297] and died at Plymouth on 19 February 1664 "aged fourscore and one year" [PCR 8:25].
CHILDREN:
    i   NATHANIEL MORTON, b. say 1613; in the Plymouth tax lists of 25 March 1633 and 27 March 1634 assessed 9s. [PCR 1:11, 28]; m. Plymouth 25 December 1635 Lydia Cooper [PCR 1:35].

ii   PATIENCE MORTON, b. about 1615 (d. Plymouth 16 August 1691 "being entered into the 77 year of her age" [MD 16:62; PVR 135]); m. by 1633 JOHN FAUNCE [PM 201].

iii   JOHN MORTON, b. say 1617; m. by 1649 Lettice _____ (eldest known child b. Plymouth 11 December 1649 [PCR 8:8]). She m. (2) about 1674 Andrew Ring, son of MARY RING [TAG 42:203; PM 389].

iv   SARAH MORTON, b. say 1620; m. Plymouth 20 December 1644 George Bonham [PCR 2:79].

v   EPHRAIM MORTON, b. by 1623; m. Plymouth 18 November 1644 Ann Cooper [PCR 2:79].

ASSOCIATIONS: Through his marriage to Juliana Carpenter, George Morton was brother-in-law to SAMUEL FULLER [PM 217], WILLIAM BRADFORD [PM 62] and WILLIAM WRIGHT [PM 524], and was uncle to CONSTANT SOUTHWORTH [PM 437} and EDWARD SOUTHWORTH [PM 440] (see PRISCILLA CARPENTER [PM 93]).

In 1957 John G. Hunt published a speculative piece suggesting a distant collateral connection between WILLIAM BRADFORD and George Morton [NEHGR 111:68].

COMMENTS: George Morton's son Nathaniel wrote a history of Plymouth Colony called *New England's Memorial* and says about the *Anne*

> Two of the principal passengers that came in this ship were Mr. Timothy Hatherly and Mr. George Morton.... The latter of the two forenamed, namely Mr. George Morton, was a pious, gracious, servant of God, and very faithful in whatsoever public employment he was betrusted withal, and an unfeigned well willer, and according to his sphere and condition, a suitable promoter of the common good and growth of the plantation of New Plimouth; laboring to still the discontents that sometimes would arise amongst some spirits by reason of the difficulties of these new beginnings but it pleased God to put a period to his days soon after his arrival in New England, not surviving a full year after his coming ashore. With much comfort and peace he fell asleep in the Lord, in the month of June, anno 1624 [Morton 63-64].

THOMAS MORTON

ORIGIN: Unknown (but possibly Leiden).
MIGRATION: 1621 on the *Fortune*.
FIRST RESIDENCE: Plymouth.

ESTATE: In the 1623 Plymouth land division Thomas Morton was granted one acre as a passenger on the *Fortune* in 1621 and Thomas Morton Junior was granted one acre as a passenger on the *Anne* in 1623 [PCR 12:5, 6]. In the 1627 Plymouth cattle division Thomas Morton Junior was the sixth person in the company of John Howland, while Thomas Morton Sr. was entered as the thirteenth member in the company of Samuel Fuller, but his name was crossed out and another substituted [PCR 12:10, 12].

BIRTH: By about 1592 (based on estimated date of marriage).
DEATH: Probably in 1627 (since his name was entered in the cattle division of that year and then deleted).
MARRIAGE: By about 1617 _____ _____; she is not seen in any New England record.
CHILD:
    i   (probably) THOMAS MORTON, b. say 1617 (sold land in 1639 [PCR 12:56]); in Plymouth section of 1643 Plymouth Colony list of men able to bear arms [PCR 8:189]; m. by about 1645 Rose _____ ("Roas, the wife of Thomas Morton," d. Plymouth 31 [*sic*] November 1685 [PVR 134]).

ASSOCIATIONS: These two Thomases may have been father and son, although this is not certain. The elder Thomas was quite possibly the witness to the marriage of George Morton and Juliana Carpenter in Leiden on 6 July 1612 [NS] [MD 11:193]. When the younger Thomas Morton sold land on 16 March 1639, the deed originally had attached to it the statement that the acknowledgement of the instrument "was conditional that if Manasseth Kempton and his wife & the said Thom[as] Morton's friends did consent to it then to stand firm" [PCR 12:56]; Manasseh Kempton had married the widow of George Morton, suggesting that the younger Thomas Morton was in some way related to George (who had also arrived on the *Anne*), perhaps as nephew. Thomas the elder could, of course, be brother to George Morton and Thomas the younger could be nephew, without the two Thomases being father and son. (This discussion agrees for the most part with the conclusions set

WILLIAM MULLINS

ORIGIN: Dorking, Surrey.
MIGRATION: 1620 on the *Mayflower*.
FIRST RESIDENCE: Plymouth.

OCCUPATION: Shoemaker (based on the contents of his estate).
ESTATE: On 23 July 1621, administration on the estate of William Mullins was granted to "Sare Blunden *alias* Mullins filie naturali et legitime dicti defuncti" [Sara Blunden *alias* Mullins, natural and legitimate daughter of the said deceased] [MQ 34:10; Waters 254-55; MD 1:230-32 (all citing PCC 68 Dale)].

In his will (probably nuncupative), dated 2 April 1621 and proved July 1621, William Mullins directed that from the £40 in the hand of Goodman Woodes "I give my wife £10, my son Joseph £10, my daughter Priscilla £10, and my eldest son £10, also I give to my eldest son all my debts, bonds, bills (only that £40 excepted in the hands of Goodman Wood) ... with all the stock in his own hands"; to "my eldest daughter I give 10s. to be paid out of my son's stock"; "the goods I have in Virginia as followeth, to my wife Alice half my goods & to Joseph and Priscilla the other half equally divided"; "I have twenty-one dozen of shoes and thirteen pair of boots which I give into the Company's hands for £40 at seven years ... or as my overseers shall think good"; "and if they like them at that rate at the divident I shall have nine shares whereof I give as followeth, two to my wife, two to my son William, two to my son Joseph, two to my daughter Priscilla, and one to the Company"; "if my son William will come to Virginia I give him my share of land"; to "my two overseers Mr. John Carver and Mr. Williamson, 20s. apiece to see this my will performed desiring them that he would have an eye over my wife and children to be as fathers and friends to them, also to have a special eye to my man Robert which hath not so approved himself as I would he should have done" [MQ 34:10; Waters 254-55; MD 1:230-32 (all citing PCC 68 Dale)].

BIRTH: By about 1572 (based on marriage date of parents), son of John and Joan (Bridger) Mullins [MF 16:1:16].

DEATH: Plymouth 21 February 1620/1 ("February 21. Die Mr. William White, Mr. William Mullins, with two more" [Prince 184]).

MARRIAGE: By 1593 Alice _____ (assuming she is the mother of all the children). She died at Plymouth in the first winter.

CHILDREN:
    i   WILLIAM MULLINS, b. say 1593; m. (1) by 1618 _____ _____ [MQ 39:83]; m. (2) Boston 7 May 1656 Ann (_____) Bell [BVR 56], widow of Thomas Bell. (William Mullins was in Duxbury by 1637, died apparently early in 1674, and had a daughter who married three times but had no children [MD 7:37-48, 179-83].)
    ii   JOSEPH MULLINS, b. say 1596; d. Plymouth in the first winter.
    iii   SARAH MULLINS, b. say 1598; m. by 1621 _____ Blunden [PCC 68 Dale].
    iv   PRISCILLA MULLINS, b. say 1603; m. by about 1623 JOHN ALDEN [PM 4].

COMMENTS: In his accounting of the passengers on the *Mayflower,* Bradford included "Mr. William Mullins and his wife and two children, Joseph and Priscilla; and a servant, Robert Carter" [Bradford 442]. In the listing of the fate of these passengers in 1651 he reported that "Mr. Mullins and his wife, his son and his servant died the first winter. Only his daughter Priscila survived, and married with John Alden; who are both living and have eleven children. And their eldest daughter is married and hath five children" [Bradford 445].

BIBLIOGRAPHIC NOTE: A summary of what is known about the English background of William Mullins is incorporated in the Five Generations Project volume on John Alden [MF 16:1:14-19]. In 2004 Caleb Johnson published some records from Dorking, Surrey, for this immigrant [TAG 79:161].

N

SAMUEL NASH

ORIGIN: Unknown.
MIGRATION: 1632.
FIRST RESIDENCE: Plymouth.
REMOVES: Duxbury by 1639.

FREEMAN: In the 1633 list of Plymouth freemen, without date of admission, but in a sequence of men mostly admitted in January 1632/3 [PCR 1:4]. In Plymouth Colony list of freemen of 7 March 1636/7 [PCR 1:53]. In Duxbury section of Plymouth Colony lists of freemen of 1639, 1658, and 29 May 1670 [PCR 5:274, 8:174, 198].

OFFICES: On 4 June 1652, "Lieutenant Samuell Nash was chosen and approved by the Court to serve in the office of chief marshal, according to the extent of the said office already entered, and is to have for his wages 20 marks per annum, besides his ordinary fees allowed by the Court" (followed by a schedule of fees); Nash was the first to hold this position after the office of messenger was divided into "chief marshal" and "under marshal" [PCR 3:12]. (For some insight into the range of duties of the chief marshal, see PCR 3:94, 4:121, 135, 6:39, 70, 79, 7:226, 8:147, 150; GMN 10:321-22, 328.)

Deputy for Duxbury to Plymouth General Court, 6 April 1653 [PCR 3:23]. Committee to lay out land, 1 December 1663, 3 May 1664, 7 June 1665, 9 June 1665 [PCR 4:48, 58, 96, 102].

Plymouth petit jury, 3 September 1639, 3 December 1639, 3 March 1644/5, 7 July 1646, 1 June 1647, 7 June 1648, 7 October 1651, 4 June 1652 [PCR 2:117, 126, 7:13, 14, 40, 42, 56, 60]. Grand jury, 5 June 1638, 1 June 1641, 7 June 1642 [PCR 1:87, 2:16, 41].

Duxbury highway surveyor, 2 March 1640/1 [PCR 2:9].

Volunteered for service against the Pequots, 1637 [PCR 1:61]. In Duxbury section of 1643 Plymouth Colony list of men able to bear arms [PCR 8:189].

Sergeant for military company for Plymouth, Duxbury and Marshfield, 29 August 1643 [PCR 2:61]. Sergeant Nash was at the head of six Duxbury men who were sent against the Narragansetts, 15 August 1645; as "Sergeant, now Lieutenant Nash," he was paid £2 10s. for this service [PCR 2:90, 91]. In October 1645 he was chosen Lieutenant by Duxbury [PCR 2:88]. His inventory included "one gun" valued at 12s. [PCR 6:126].

Council of war, 2 October 1658 [PCR 3:153]. Committee to "draw up a form of commission for military officers," 10 June 1662 [PCR 4:21].

ESTATE: Assessed 9s. in the 25 March 1633 Plymouth tax list and the same amount in the list of 27 March 1634 [PCR 1:10, 27].

In his will of 2 June 1681, probated in 1685, Samuel Nash bequeathed to "my daughter Martha Clark my dwelling house, orchard, outhousing, meadows & improved upland" during her natural life; to "my deceased grandson Samuel Sampson's two sons, viz: Samuel Samson & Ichabod Samson, all my housing, orchard, meadows & upland" equally divided between them after decease of said daughter; to "said daughter & Elizabeth Dillano & Mary Howland my granddaughters" the residue to be equally divided between them; daughter Martha to be executrix; "loving friends John Soule & Thomas Dillano" to be overseers [PCPR 4:2:112].

During his lifetime, "Lieutenant Samuell Nash, of Duxberry, being aged, and not in a capacity to live and keep house of himself, hath therefore put his estate into the hands of William Clarke, of Duxburrow, that thereby he may have a comfortable livelihood." To this end, an inventory of his estate was taken on 18 June of an unstated year; the estate totalled £17 18s. 3d., to which was added £1 12s., with a reference to "the disposing of his house and land during his lifetime." This collection of documents was presented at Court on 5 March 1683/4, with the annotation that "the abovewritten account to be the real due of Martha Clarke, the wife of William Clarke, of Duxburrow, in compensation of her pains & care in looking to her father, Samuell Nash, late deceased" [PCR 6:125-26].

BIRTH: About 1602 (deposed 6 July 1682 "aged eighty years or thereabouts" [PCR 7:257]).
DEATH: After 6 July 1682 (date of deposition [PCR 7:257]) and before 5 March 1683/4 (date of distribution [PCR 6:125-26]). (Samuel Nash was alive when his inventory was taken; the date of this document could be as late as 18 June 1683.)
MARRIAGE: By about 1625 _____ _____. This marriage must have taken place in England, and both of the known children would also have been born in England. As we have no record of a wife for Samuel Nash

in Plymouth Colony, she may well have died before the family came to New England.

CHILDREN:
   i   Daughter NASH, b. say 1625; m. by 1645 ABRAHAM SAMPSON {1638, Duxbury}; she died by about 1655 [TAG 15:165-67, 63:207-10].
   ii   MARTHA NASH, b. say 1630; m. by about 1650 William Clark of Duxbury; no issue [TAG 15:165-67].

COMMENTS: The statement has appeared in print more than once that Esther, wife successively of Samuel Sampson and John Soule, was a daughter of Samuel Nash [NEHGR 52:76; MD 3:121], but this is an error, based on losing a generation by misreading the will of Samuel Nash [NEHGR 56:205].

On 25 July 1641, "Samuell Nash of Weymouth in New England shoemaker" made a power of attorney to "Enoch Lunt of Weymouth in NE blacksmith" [Lechford 430], and the question has been raised whether this is the Duxbury man residing briefly in Weymouth [Weymouth Hist 4:421]. In fact the names of both parties to this transaction have been misread; they should be James Nash (who was a shoemaker of Weymouth) and Enoch Hunt (who was a blacksmith of Weymouth). The power of attorney names various parishes in Cambridgeshire in England, and so provides powerful clues for finding the English origin of James Nash and perhaps Enoch Hunt.

Raymon Meyers Tingley published records purporting to claim that Samuel Nash had a sister Elizabeth who married Thomas Symons [Tingley-Meyers 371]. As with so much in this source, these records are totally fabricated, and the conclusions of Tingley have no value.

BIBLIOGRAPHIC NOTE: The children of Samuel Nash are definitively identified by Clarence Almon Torrey in his brilliant article "A Nash-Sampson-Delano-Howland Problem" [TAG 15:165-67]. Robert S. Wakefield returns to this problem from the perspective of identifying all the children of Abraham Sampson by both wives, and adds some insights of his own [TAG 63:207-10].

JOHN NEWCOMEN

In 1630 JOHN BILLINGTON of Plymouth [PM 56] "waylaid a young man, one John New-comin, about a former quarrel and shot him with a gun, whereof he died." After consultation with Winthrop and others in Massachusetts Bay, the Plymouth authorities tried Billington, found him guilty, and executed him in September 1630 [Bradford 234].

COMMENTS: John G. Hunt has published a highly speculative identification of the origins of this John Newcomen, based partly on an argument by elimination, and partly on the now discredited theory that the wife of WILLIAM BREWSTER [PM 66] was Mary Wentworth [NEHGR 113:68-69]. Although the proposed identification is not impossible, there is simply not enough evidence for Hunt's theory. (We should also be alert to the possibility that "New-comin" is not a surname, but an indication that the murder victim was newly arrived at Plymouth, and his surname was unknown to Bradford. Not surprisingly, THOMAS MORTON {1622, Merrymount} [GMB 2:1299] makes a punning use of the name, employing this sense of the word [New English Canaan 216].)

ELLEN NEWTON

In the 1623 Plymouth land division, Ellen Newton was granted one acre as a passenger on the *Anne* in 1623 [PCR 12:6].

COMMENTS: Before 1627 she had married JOHN ADAMS of Plymouth [PM 1], and after his death in 1633 she married KENELM WINSLOW [PM 518].

AUSTEN NICHOLAS

In the 1623 Plymouth land division, Austen Nicholas was granted one acre as a passenger on the *Fortune* in 1621 [PCR 1:5].

COMMENTS: As Nicholas is not found in the 1627 divison of cattle, or in any other New England record, he must have died soon or returned to England.

O

JOHN OLDHAM

ORIGIN: Derby, Derbyshire.
MIGRATION: 1623 on the *Anne* [PCR 12:6].
FIRST RESIDENCE: Plymouth.
REMOVES: Nantasket 1624, Watertown 1630.
RETURN TRIPS: Returned to England 1628, and back to New England 1630.

OCCUPATION: Trader.
FREEMAN: 18 May 1631 (as "Mr. John Oldeham") [MBCR 1:366].
EDUCATION: Could certainly read and write, since he sent many letters to England at the time of his connivance with Reverend JOHN LYFORD, but Bradford complains "he was so bad a scribe as his hand was scarce legible" [Bradford 151].
OFFICES: "Mr. Oldeham" was one of two delegates sent by Watertown to the General Court to consult on raising money, 9 May 1632 [MBCR 1:95]. Watertown deputy to General Court, 14 May 1634 [MBCR 1:116]. Committee to survey land at Mount Wollaston for enlargement of Boston, 14 May 1634 [MBCR 1:119]. Committee to oversee powder and shot, "Mr. Oldham for Waterton & Meadford," and committee to set out bounds of towns, 3 September 1634 [MBCR 1:125]. Committee to examine defacing of colors by John Endicott, 6 May 1635 [MBCR 1:145].
ESTATE: In 1623 Plymouth land division "Mr. Ouldom & those joined with him" were granted ten acres as passengers on the *Anne* in 1623 [PCR 12:6]. Three of those "joined with him" were his sister Lucretia, his wife (unnamed) and his stepson, William Bridges. The other six remain unidentified, although there were probably some servants among them.

On 1 April 1634, "There is five hundred acres of land granted to Mr. Jo: Oldham, lying near Mount Feakes, on the northwest of Charles River" [MBCR 1:114]. This land was later laid out to Mr. Craddock, near "Mount Feake" [MBCR 1:330] and, on 18 March 1647, "Nicholas

Davison of Charlstowne, attorney to Mrs. Rebecca Cradock *alias* Glover, sole executrix of Matthew Craddock deceased, granted to Thomas Mayhew, merchant, this same five hundred acres of land [SLR 1:91].

Presumably the proprietary share held by WILLIAM BRIDGES [PM 70] in the late 1630s in Watertown had earlier been held by Oldham, which would mean that he had been granted by the town a houselot and one or two other parcels of marsh or arable land.

On 28 July 1636, the Massachusetts Bay General Court issued orders to Watertown in Connecticut [i.e. Wethersfield] "to seize and inventory Mr. Oldham's goods for payment of his debts" [WJ 2:423]. Oldham's was the first estate probated in Connecticut, where an unsatisfactory inventory was presented at the court of 10 September 1636. After much wrangling, a satisfactory inventory was delivered to the court on 6 February 1639/40, which showed £504 9s. 3d. in debts, and £136 66s. 21d. [*sic*] in assets. A year later, on 6 January 1640/1, the accounts had still not been settled; the suggestion was made that the paperwork be sent to the Bay in case anyone there wished to make a claim, and nothing more is heard of the matter [CCCR 1:43; Manwaring 1:25-28].

BIRTH: Baptized All Saints, Derby, Derbyshire, 14 July 1592, son of "William Ouldam."

DEATH: July 1636 near Block Island [WP 1:225].

MARRIAGE: By 1623 _____ (_____) Bridges, mother of WILLIAM BRIDGES, later seen at Watertown and Charlestown; her date of death is unknown. In 1624, when John Oldham was expelled from Plymouth, "his wife and family had liberty to stay all winter or longer" [Bradford 157]. She may have predeceased her husband, since no provision was made for her in his estate proceedings.

CHILDREN: None recorded.

ASSOCIATIONS: His sister Lucretia Oldham, bp. All Saints, Derby, Derbyshire, 14 January 1600/1, married at Plymouth (as "Lucretia Oldam of Darby") on 10 April 1624 Jonathan Brewster [MD 1:8]. John and Thomas Oldham, aged twelve and ten, passengers to New England in 1635 on the *Elizabeth & Ann*, were probably his kinsmen, perhaps nephews [Hotten 78].

COMMENTS: John Oldham was a fascinating personality, with many talents, and the ability to influence others, both favorably and unfavorably. During his time in New England, totalling not much more than a decade, he managed to involve himself in three important episodes in early Massachusetts history: the revolt of the Reverend JOHN

LYFORD and others against the Pilgrims at Plymouth; conflict with the Massachusetts Bay Company over its patent; and his death at the hands of the Indians in 1636, which precipitated the Pequot War. Each of these incidents will be discussed briefly here, with references for further reading.

Not long after Oldham's arrival in Plymouth, Bradford tells us, he began to stir up trouble among the discontented [Bradford 148-57, 165-66]. This activity increased in 1624, with the arrival of the Reverend John Lyford, who soon began to exert his Church of England views against the church organized at Plymouth. For Oldham the upshot was that he was banished from Plymouth about the middle of 1624, perhaps in July or August. His movements between then and his return to England are shadowy, and have been described in various ways, not all accounts agreeing. Bradford at one point says that Oldham commenced a trip to Virginia, which failed, but later says that he travelled to Virginia and returned to New England by the time of the arrival of Winthrop, but says nothing about the return to England. Adams, writing more than two centuries later, places Oldham at Nantasket (Hull) for much of this time (and not at Cape Ann), but without providing documentation [Three Episodes 183-93]. At any rate, Oldham was soon back in the good graces of the leaders at Plymouth, and in June of 1628 he was assigned the task of escorting THOMAS MORTON back to England [Three Episodes 207-8; GMB 2:1299].

This leads directly to the second of Oldham's major conflicts. Taking Morton back to England, he had to deliver him to Sir Ferdinando Gorges, and this gave Oldham the opportunity to gain from the Council of New England (then controlled by Gorges and Captain John Mason) a grant for much of the land at the bottom of Massachusetts Bay, which had just been granted by the King to the Massachusetts Bay Company. Exactly what Oldham had in mind is not clear, but he was apparently trying to trade this grant for some influence in the Massachusetts Bay Company. The progress of these negotiations can be followed in the court records and letters of the Company, and ultimately Oldham failed in his larger purpose (although the mere existence of his patent apparently forced the settlement of Charlestown in 1629 as a pre-emptive strike) [MBCR 1:28, 29, 34, 39, 388, 389, 398; Three Episodes 212-17]. He did, however, obtain a grant of five hundred acres in Watertown, perhaps a token compensation for his forlorn grant from Gorges, and he did become a leading citizen of Watertown in his few years in residence there. In Plymouth and Massachusetts Bay, Oldham had overreached himself and aroused the ire of the leaders, but eventually, in each instance, he regained their confidence and made a useful contribution to both settlements.

As may be seen in the correspondence of the Winthrop family, John Oldham was active in his business of coastal trading early in 1636, mostly about Long Island Sound and Narragansett Bay [WP 3:235, 244, 256, 258, 276], and about the same time he had obtained a grant of Prudence Island in Narragansett Bay from Canonicus [WP 3:502]. On 20 July 1636 JOHN GALLOP [GMB 2:725-28], another coastal trader, was sailing in the vicinity of Block Island and Fisher's Island, and saw a shallop that he recognized as Oldham's, but he could see only Indians on board. Winthrop tells the story of Oldham's gruesome death in great detail [WJ 1:225ff.], but only one point need detain us here. Winthrop tells us that Oldham "had been long out a trading, having with him only two English boys, and two Indians of Narragansett." Bradford, in his much briefer account of this episode, says that "two little boys that were his kinsmen were saved, but had some hurt" [Bradford 166]. These two kinsmen were apparently Thomas and John Oldham, passengers to New England on the *Elizabeth & Ann* in 1635 (then 12 and 10 respectively), presumably nephews of John Oldham. But there may be some doubt whether the two boys who were with Oldham on his last trading voyage were John and Thomas Oldham. Winthrop, who is usually more reliable in matters of this sort, does not state a relationship; and in some notes that Winthrop took of some court actions that did not get recorded in the official records of the General Court, we find that, on 11 August 1636 (less than a month after Oldham's death), the court dealt with "[blank] a boy of Mr. Oldham's, whom he bought of [blank] for £8, we restored to his old master for £4, in regard he had no clothes, and had spent the most of the summer with Mr. Oldham, etc." [WJ 2:423]. This unnamed boy would not be one of Oldham's kinsmen, but it does seem that he was with Oldham on some of his trading missions, and perhaps on the last one.

BIBLIOGRAPHIC NOTE: Bond wrote at length about John Oldham, especially in his second edition [Bond 382, 861-64]. A recent treatment by Threlfall adds information on the maternal ancestry of the immigrant [GMC26 215-22].

P

WILLIAM PALMER

ORIGIN: Unknown.
MIGRATION: 1621 on the *Fortune*.
FIRST RESIDENCE: Plymouth.
REMOVES: Duxbury.

OCCUPATION: Nailer. His inventory included a bellows, anvil, vice and all the tools necessary for nailmaking [MD 2:150].
FREEMAN: In the 1633 Plymouth list of freemen ahead of those admitted on 1 January 1632/3 [PCR 1:3]. In 7 March 1636/7 list [PCR 1:52].
EDUCATION: His inventory included "1 Bible" valued at 12s., "1 book called Practise of Christianity" valued at 1s. 6d., and "1 catechism" valued at 4d.
OFFICES: Appointed to lay out highways for Duxbury side, 1 October 1634 [PCR 1:31]. Petit jury, 2 May 1637 [PCR 1:58].

His inventory included "3 swords and 1 rapier" valued at 14s., "1 brush & 1 powder horn" valued at 1s. 6d., "18lb. of bullets & 7lb. of shot" valued at 4s. 2d., "1 shot bag" valued at 2s. and "1 fowling piece" valued at 18s. [MD 2:150].
ESTATE: In the 1623 Plymouth division of land William Palmer received two acres as passenger on the *Fortune*, and "Franc[e]s wife to Wil[liam] Palmer" received one acre as passenger on the *Anne* [PCR 12:5, 6]. In the 1627 Plymouth division of cattle William Palmer, Frances Palmer and William Palmer Junior were the eighth, ninth and tenth persons in the seventh company [PCR 12:11].

William Palmer was assessed £1 7s. in the Plymouth tax list of 25 March 1633, and 18s. in the list of 27 March 1634 [PCR 1:10, 28].

In his will, dated 7 November 1637 and proved 4 December 1637, "William Palmer of Ducksborrow, nailer, being ill in body," named "my loving friends Mr. William Bradford, Mr. Edward Winslowe and Mr. Thomas Prence my executors"; "whereas I have married a young woman who is dear unto me I desire them to deal well with her but my desire is that my estate consisting of land, household goods, ... may be sold and turned into money all except such moveables as my executors think meet to give her for her personal comfort. Next my estate being wholly sold my desire is that my wife may not have less than one third and if she be with child then another third to be preserved and improved by my executors for that child as mine heir and that if in case she be not with child, then I would have mine executors as in conscience they are persuaded out of the remainder of my estate deal with Rebecca my grandchild and Moyses Rowley whom I love, but not so as to put into their father or mother's hands but preserve it for them till they come to years of discretion"; "somewhat to Stephen Tracy"; "somewhat towards the meeting house at Plymouth"; "young Rowley to be placed with Mr. Partridge that he might be brought up in the fear of God and to that end if his father suffer it I give to Mr. Patridge £5"; "in case my son Henry or daughter Bridgett be living, if they demand it, I give them 40s. apiece if they be living." Further "it was the will of the testator that his wife should be ruled by her ancient Mr. Edward Winslow in her marriage if she look to partake in any part of this estate, otherwise not" [MD 2:147-48, citing PCPR 1:28].

The inventory of "all the moveable goods of Will[ia]m Palm[e]r the elder, taken 13 November 1637, totalled £111 12s. 4d. [MD 2:148-52, citing PCPR 1:28-29].

BIRTH: By about 1581 (based on estimated date of first marriage).
DEATH: Duxbury between 7 November 1637 (date of will) and 13 November 1637 (date of inventory]).
MARRIAGE: (1) By about 1606 Frances _____. She arrived on the *Anne* in 1623 and had died by 1637.

(2) By 1637 Mary _____. She married (2) by 20 October 1646 Robert Paddock [PCR 2:109; TAG 32:42-43]. She married (3) Plymouth 24 March 1650/1 Thomas Roberts [PCR 8:11; TAG 32:44].
CHILDREN:
   With first wife
- i   HENRY PALMER, b. say 1606; in case he "be living" in his father's will; no further record. (This man was not the Henry Palmer who later appeared in Wethersfield [TG 17:167-69, 175-85.)
- ii   BRIDGET PALMER, b. say 1608; in case she "be living" in her father's will; no further record.
- iii   Daughter PALMER, b. say 1610; probably m. by about 1630 HENRY ROWLEY [PM 398].

iv   WILLIAM PALMER, b. say 1612; assessed 9s. in the Plymouth tax list of 27 March 1634 (immediately after the entry for "Will[iam] Palmer," his father) [PCR 1:28]; admitted freeman on 1 January 1634/5 (and appended to the 1633 list of freemen, and then deleted from the same list) [PCR 1:4, 32]. "William Palmer, Junior, & Elizabeth Hodgekins were married the 27 of March" 1634 at Plymouth [PCR 1:26]. She m. (2) by 2 January 1637/8 John Willis [PCR 7:7].

With second wife

v   WILLIAM PALMER, b. Duxbury 27 June 1634 [*sic*, probably 1638] (posthumous) [PCR 8:25]; m. say 1662 Susanna _____ [TAG 32:44-45 and sources cited there].

COMMENTS: On 23 July 1633, William Mendlove, the servant of William Palmer, was whipped for attempting to force his affections on the maid servant of the same Palmer, and for running away from his master and having to be brought back "forcibly" by Penwatechet, a Manomet Indian; Palmer sold his service to Richard Church [PCR 1:15]. On 25 July 1633, William Palmer, nailer, of Plymouth, purchased the time of Robert Barker, the apprentice of the late John Thorpe, and promised to teach him the trade of "nailing & at the end of his time to give him only two suits of apparel" [PCR 1:16].

On 2 January 1637/8, Mr. Hopkins was presented for allowing excessive drinking in his house. "Old Palmer" was one of the three men said to have been drunk there, and "widow Palmer" and "widow Palmer's man" were two of the witnesses [PCR 1:75].

On 2 January 1637/8, "John Willis and Elizabeth his wife complains against Mr. Will[ia]m Bradford, Mr. Edward Winslow, & Mr. Thomas Prince, executors of the last will and testament of William Palmer, Senior, deceased, in an action upon the case to the damage of £20, for a lot of land the complainant pretended he had right unto by the marriage of his wife, who had formerly been the wife of William Palmer the younger, son of the said William the elder. The jury found for the defendants, and gave them 12d. damage, and the charges of the Court" [PCR 7:7]. (This suit provides the evidence for the early death of the elder of the two sons named William born to the immigrant, and for the remarriage of the widow of this son to John Willis.)

BIBLIOGRAPHIC NOTE: In 1956 Florence Barclay produced the definitive article on William Palmer, resolving many of the outstanding problems, outlining the careers of the two sons of the immigrant named William, and pointing out several errors in Savage, particularly the mixing of William (b. 1612) with the man of that name who went to Newtown, Long Island [TAG 32:39-45]. In 1976 Paul Prindle also published a brief account of William Palmer [Gillespie Ancestry 354-56].

Carlton A. Palmer Jr, has published several articles attempting to outline the three Williams and their wives and arriving at conclusions contrary to those of Florence Barclay [*The Augustan Society Omnibus* 9:101-3, 107; MQ 50:188-90]. Unfortunately, his misunderstanding of the meaning of "son-in-law" undermines his own arguments.

CHRISTIAN PENN

In the 1623 Plymouth land division Christian Penn received one acre as a passenger on the *Anne* in 1623 [PCR 12:6].

COMMENTS: Within a year or two after arrival Christian Penn had married FRANCIS EATON [PM 187], and after his death Francis Billington, son of JOHN BILLINGTON [PM 86].

WILLIAM PHIPS

In his deposition of 19 July 1631 regarding the activities of EDWARD ASHLEY [PM 20], JOHN DEACON [PM 161] stated that "Thomas Willett and William Fipps are better acquainted with his unlawful traffic" [MHSP 45:495].

31 August 1636: "William Phips, the late servant of the partners, hath sold unto Josiah Wynslow, his heirs, &c., all that portion of land which is due unto him by his service of apprenticeship, now completely ended, for & in consideration of the sum of fifty shillings received" [PCR 1:43].

4 February 1638/9: "Josias Winslow having bought fifty acre of land of Will[ia]m Phybs, which was due to him for his service, according to his covenant, which was affirmed unto by Mr. Thomas Willet, who had often times seen the said covenant, the court doth grant him 25 acres, to be laid forth for him in some convenient place, to be in full satisfaction of the said 50 acres" [PCR 1:111].

COMMENTS: These three records tell a brief story, in which William Phips was in the service of the Plymouth Colony fur trade in Maine for some years in the early 1630s, received a grant of land at the end of his servitude, sold the land to Josiah Winslow, and left New England.

JOHN PICKWORTH

ORIGIN: Unknown.
MIGRATION: 1631.
FIRST RESIDENCE: Massachusetts Bay.
REMOVES: Plymouth 1631, Salem by 1632, Manchester.

OFFICES:]. On 24 June 1656, he was sworn constable of Manchester [EQC 1:424].

On 28 February 1642/3, "John Pickworth [was] presented for absence from watch," but was acquitted [EQC 1:51]. His inventory included "a fowling piece" valued at £1 5s. [EPR 1:429].

ESTATE: In the Salem land division of 1636 "John Pikworth" received twenty acres in the non-freeman's section of the grant [STR 1:24]. In the division of marsh and meadow of 25 December 1637 he was granted three-quarters of an acre, with a household of five [STR 1:102].

On 28 August 1637, John Pickworth requested "a parcel of land at Jeffries Creeke" [STR 1:56], and, on 8 November 1637, he was allowed twenty-five acres there [STR 1:60]. On 20 November 1639, he was granted "3 or 4 acres of meadow to the land formerly granted him" [STR 1:92].

In his will, dated 27 June 1663 and proved 25 November 1663, "John Peckworth" bequeathed to "my well beloved wife An Peckworth" to have entire estate during her widowhood, and to have her thirds if she remarry; after her death or remarriage, to "my eldest son John Peckworth ... the house, meadow & 25 acres of land with the part of the neck that lyeth between Abraham Wh[i]tyare and myself"; to "my three sons Samuel, Joseph & Beniemen" the "30 acres bought of Robert Morgan with the meadow that belongeth to it"; to "my son Samuel" the "6 acres that lyeth upon the neck next to Robert Leach's lot"; "my part of the sawmill" to wife as above, son Samuel to run it and share in the profits; to "my two eldest daughters Ruth Masterson & [Karen?] Collen" 40s. apiece; to "my youngest son Beniemen & my youngest daughter Abegell" one cow calf [EPR 1:428-29; Essex Ant 11:157].

The inventory of the estate of John Pickworth, taken 25 August 1663, totalled £168 4s., of which £85 was real estate: "house with the meadow and lands, 25 acres," £35; "more land and meadow," £16; "a piece of meadow at Kettell Island," £4; and "a share of the sawmill," £30 [EPR 1:429].

In her will, dated 10 May 1682 and proved 10 April 1683, "the widow Ane Pickworth of Manchester" bequeathed to "my two daughters Ruth Masters and Rachell Sible" clothes and furniture, including a bed "left me by my son John Pickworth"; to "my son Joseph Pickworth['s] daughter Ane Pickword"; to "my grandchild Ane Killem the daughter of John Killem"; and to "my daughter Rachell Sible['s] youngest daughter her name being Ane Sibblie" [EPR Case #21848]. Her inventory was taken on 28 June 1683 and totalled £32 7s. [EPR 302:45].

On 26 June 1683, the estate of "John Pickworth Senior deceased" was distributed to Ruth Masters, Rachell Sibly, Joseph Pickworth, Samuel Pickworth (son of Samuel Pickworth deceased) and "Hannah Kellum deceased her children" [EPR 302:45].

BIRTH: By about 1606 (based on estimated date of marriage).
DEATH: Between 27 June 1663 (date of will) and 25 August 1663 (date of inventory).
MARRIAGE: By 6 February 1631/2 Anne _____ [WP 3:65]. "Anne Pickworth" was admitted to Salem church 30 September 1638 [SChR 7]. She died between 10 May 1682 (date of will) and 10 April 1683 (probate of will).
CHILDREN:
    i   RUTH PICKWORTH, b. say 1633, bp. Salem 14 October 1638 [SChR 17]; m. by 1654 Nathaniel Masters, grandson of JOHN MASTERS {1630, Watertown} [GDMNH 467; GMB 2:1234-36]. (On 29 June 1654, "Nathaniell Masters [was] presented for his wife being with child by him before they were married, the act having been committed in Pequott Harbor. Certificate of the fact to be sent to that town for trial in that jurisdiction" [EQC 1:360].)
    ii ANNA PICKWORTH, b. say 1635, bp. Salem 14 October 1638 [SChR 17]; m. by 1660 John Killam (eldest known child b. Wenham 29 April 1660), son of AUSTIN KILLAM {1637, Salem} [EIHC 49:215].
    iii JOHN PICKWORTH, b. say 1637, bp. Salem 14 October 1638 [SChR 17]; d. before 26 June 1677, apparently unm. [EPR 3:138, 302:8].

iv   SAMUEL PICKWORTH, b. say 1640; m. Salem 3 November 1667 Sarah Marston.

v   JOSEPH PICKWORTH, bp. Salem 12 February 1642/3 [SChR 19 (father's name given as "Jonathan")]; m. by 1668 Abigail Elithorpe, daughter of Thomas Elithorpe [TAG 31:20-21].

vi   RACHEL PICKWORTH, bp. Salem 3 May 1646 [SChR 21]; m. by 1675 John Sibley (eldest known child b. Manchester 20 August 1675).

vii   BENJAMIN PICKWORTH, bp. Salem 2 July 1648 [SChR 21]; m. by 1681 Elizabeth _____; he was thought to have died before 26 June 1677, perhaps at sea [EPR 3:138], but lived until 20 August 1681, on which date he made his will and bequeathed to "my dear & loving wife Elezebeth Pickworth" money and tobacco (the wording of the bequest implying that Elizabeth is not in New England), and she to return £15 of this "to New England to be disposed of among my relations, that is to say to my brother Joseph Pickworth a part, to my brother Natha[niel] Masters a part & to my sister Rachealle Siblle a part"; to "my dear mother the widow Ane Pickworth [illegible] pounds"; and to "my cousin Samuell Pickworth son of my brother Samuell Pickworth deceased" his right to his share of his father's land [EPR Case #21849].

viii   SARAH PICKWORTH, bp. Salem 6 October 1650 [SChR 23]; no further record.

ix   ABIGAIL PICKWORTH, bp. Salem 2 October 1652 [SChR 23]; named in father's will (27 June 1663); no further record.

COMMENTS: In the letter of 6 February 1631/2 from the Governor and Assistants of Plymouth to the Governor and Assistants of Massachusetts, one of those who had come from Massachusetts Bay to Plymouth, and then returned to Massachusetts, was "John Pickworth, he came but as a sojourner to work for a few weeks, in which time he got a wife, and so is long since returned double, and hath no cause to complain, except he hath got a bad wife" [WP 3:65].

On 27 December 1636, Thomas G[r]ay was "presented for defaming John Pikworth" [EQC 1:4]. On 30 March 1641, George Williams sued John Pickworth regarding some trees [EQC 1:26]. On 1 July 1657, "Major Hathorne brought in fines against Edw[ard] Pitford and John Pickworth for being drunk" [EQC 2:50].

On 26 June 1660, "Jno. Pickworth Sr. and his sons, John, Samuell and Joseph, [were presented] for a breach of the peace in fighting with Jno.

Norman Sr. and John Norman Jr., Thomas Bushop and Norman's servant. Dismissed" [EQC 2:225]. On 28 November 1660, Samuel Friend, constable of Manchester, reported that he had issued a summons to "John Peckworth Sr. and his sons Samuell and Joseph; as for his son John he is not in this plantation" [EQC 2:226].

ABRAHAM PIERCE

ORIGIN: Unknown.
MIGRATION: 1623 on the *Anne.*
FIRST RESIDENCE: Plymouth.
REMOVES: Duxbury after 1643.

FREEMAN: In the 1633 list of Plymouth freemen, between those admitted on 1 January 1632/3 and those admitted 1 January 1633/4 [PCR 1:4]. In Plymouth Colony list of 7 March 1636/7 [PCR 1:53]. In the Plymouth section of the 1639 list of Plymouth Colony freemen, then deleted and added to Duxbury section [PCR 8:174-75]. In the Duxbury sections of the 1658 and 29 May 1670 Plymouth Colony lists of freemen [PCR 5:275, 8:178].
OFFICES: Coroner's jury, February 1635/6 [PCR 1:39].

In Plymouth section of 1643 Plymouth Colony list of men able to bear arms; his name was lined through and then added to the Duxbury section [PCR 8:187, 190].
ESTATE: Abraham Pierce was one of the two servants of Mr. [John] Pierce in the 1623 Plymouth division of land who received an acre of land apiece as passengers on the *Anne* [PCR 12:6; TAG 54:164-66]. In the 1627 Plymouth division of cattle "Abraham Peirce" was the twelfth person in the third company [PCR 12:10]. He was the thirty-first person on the list of Purchasers [PCR 2:177].

On 20 January 1627, Abraham Pierce sold to Capt. Miles Standish two shares in a red cow for two ewe lambs [PCR 12:15].

On 28 September 1629, Abraham Peirce sold to "Thomas Clarck one acre of land lying on the south side of the town abutting on Hobs-hole" (the land he received in the 1623 land division) [PCR 12:7].

In the 25 March 1633 and 27 March 1634 Plymouth tax lists assessed 9s. [PCR 1:10, 28].

On 5 December 1637, Abraham Pierce sold to Josuah Pratt a house and garden place in Plymouth [PCR 12:24]. On 8 June 1643, Abraham

Pierce sold to Thomas King forty acres of upland and meadow on the south side of the North River [PCR 12:95].

Prior to 31 July 1646, "Abraham Pearse" exchanged a lot of land with Joseph Rogers at Stony Brook and also leased two acres of meadow to William Merick for two years and an agreement was reached as to the further term of the lease and the division of wheat grown on the land [PCR 12:136].

On 13 June 1660, three acres of meadow were granted to Abraham Pierce Senior, lying on the north side of the brook at Namassakesett [PCR 3:194]. On 4 June 1661, the court confirmed that Abraham Pierce and several other men had liberty to purchase land at Saconeesett [PCR 3:216]. On 4 June 1668, "Abraham Pearse Senior of Duxburrow" sold to Thomas Hatch "one whole share of land or purchase which was granted unto me ... lying and being at Saconessett" [PCLR 3:113].

On 3 June 1673, "Abraham Peirse, Junior," made over to "his brother Isacke Peirse" twenty acres of upland and two acres of meadow, part of the land and meadow of "his father Abraham Peirse deceased, he dying intestate," the land falling to Abraham Peirse Junior as his proper right. Abraham Peirse Junior also gave 20s. apiece to "his three sisters, viz: Rebeckah Wills, Mary Baker, and Allice Baker," the court giving him administration on the estate [PCR 5:116-17].

BIRTH: By about 1605 (assuming he was eighteen when he arrived in 1623).
DEATH: By 3 June 1673 [PCR 5:116-17].
MARRIAGE: By 1638 Rebecca _____. She does not appear to have survived him since her son made no acknowledgment of or provision for her dower. "Alice, daughter of Abraham Peirce of Plimoth, being brought hither by Goody Scudder, his wife's sister and here baptized July 21, 1650" [NEHGR 9:284]. "Goody Scudder" was evidently the wife of John Scudder of Barnstable. Her first name may have been Hannah. That her sister took her youngest child implies that either Rebecca was ill, unable to nurse, or deceased following the birth.
CHILDREN:
    i   ABRAHAM PIERCE, b. [blank] January 1638[/9?] [PVR 2 (entered at his death in 1718)]; m. (1) by about 1665 Hannah Baker (in his will, dated 4 March 1692/3, Francis Baker made a bequest to "my daughter Hannah Pearse" [MD 31:107; CCL 106:7, citing BarnPR 2:30]); m. (2) Scituate 29 October 1695 Hannah _____ (said to be Hannah Glass).

ii ISAAC PIERCE, b. say 1641; living 1673 [PCR 5:116-17]; no further record.
iii REBECCA PIERCE; b. say 1643; m. by 1673 Samuel Wills [PCR 5:116-17].
iv MARY PIERCE, b. say 1645; m. by about 1670 Nathaniel Baker ("Samuel Baker the son of Nathanell Baker was 4 years old the 29th of October 1674" [YarVR 1:126; MD 2:207]).
v ALICE PIERCE, bp. Barnstable 21 July 1650 [NEHGR 9:284]; m. by 1672 John Baker (eldest known child b. 31 May 1672 [YarVR 1:126; MD 2:207]).

ASSOCIATIONS: Abraham Pierce may be related in some way to Mr. John Pierce of London [TAG 54:164-66].

On 13 November 1730, "Caleb Pearce" of Yarmouth, planter, appointed "my uncle Isaac Pearce of Easthem," planter, his attorney to recover any right he might have in land "descending to me from my greatgrandfather Abraham Pearce" of Duxbury, deceased, especially his right in "a plantation or other estate in the government of the Island of Barbadoes formerly belonging to & in the possession of Thomas Pearce late of said Barbadoes, deceased, & by him given to my greatgrandfather Abraham Pearce ... & from him descending to my grandfather Abraham Pearce of said Duxborough late of Pembroke ... and from him descending to my father John Pearce of the town of Pembroke abovesaid deceased & so to myself" [MD 9:162-63, citing a document in private hands]. The great-grandfather of Caleb Pearce was Abraham Pierce the immigrant, and so this power of attorney provides a powerful clue that should assist in finding the English origin of Abraham.

COMMENTS: On 7 September 1642, the court ordered that "the difference betwixt Mr. Will[ia]m Hanbury and Abraham Perse about the lugging and killing Mr. Hanburie's swine" was to be settled by Mr. William Paddy and John Howland, for William Hanbury, and Stephen Tracy and John Cooke the younger, for Pierce [PCR 2:44]. The settlement was unsuccessful for, on 7 November 1643, William Hanbury sued Abraham Pierce for trespass, and Pierce countersued for trespass and charged Mr. William Hanbury with assault and battery. The court ordered that Hanbury pay 3s. 4d. and court charges for this latter offense [PCR 7:35].

In the 1643 list of men able to bear arms, Abraham Pierce happened to be listed immediately before "the blackamore," clearly a separate entry for another man in the original, but unfortunately run together by

Pulsifer or Shurtleff to read "Abraham Pearse, the blackamore" [PCR 8:187]. Those not referring to the original could easily be misled into believing that "Abraham Pearse" had an African origin, but in 1983 Richard L. Ehrlich and James W. Baker demonstrated conclusively that this could not be [MQ 49:57-67; see also Stratton 337].

On 2 March 1651/2, Abraham Pierce was presented for "slothful and negligent spending the Sabbath and not frequenting the public assembly." He was warned to amend and excused [PCR 3:5].

On 15 June 1660, a "James Peirse" was killed by lightning in Plymouth Harbor [PCR 3:195-96]. Stratton states that this was a son of Abraham Pierce [Stratton 337], but James is clearly called "of Boston," and he and his companions were not acquainted with Plymouth Harbor, so there would not seem to be any relationship between Abraham and James.

WILLIAM PITT

In the 1623 division of Plymouth land, William Pitt shared a two-acre grant with William Wright, as passenger on the *Fortune* in 1621 [PCR 12:5].

COMMENTS: Pitt is not in the 1627 division of cattle, or in later Plymouth Colony records, so he must have died or departed soon. No connection is seen with later New England men by the name of William Pitt.

MARY PLUMER

John Barnes married Mary Plumer at Plymouth on 12 September 1633 [MD 13:86; PCR 1:16].

COMMENTS: Note that on 6 February 1635/6, Henry Samson married Anne Plumer, also at Plymouth [MD 13:87; PCR 1:36]. See JOHN BARNES [PM 35] and HENRY SAMSON [PM 401].

WILLIAM PONTUS

ORIGIN: Leiden, Holland.
MIGRATION: 1632.
FIRST RESIDENCE: Plymouth.

OCCUPATION: Fustian-worker (from Leiden marriage record).
FREEMAN: In 1633 Plymouth list of freemen ahead of those admitted 1 January 1632/3 [PCR 1:3]. In 7 March 1636/7 list of Plymouth Colony freemen [PCR 1:52], and in Plymouth section of 1639 list [PCR 8:174].
EDUCATION: Signed his will by mark.
OFFICES: Plymouth petit jury, 7 June 1636, 7 March 1636/7, 4 September 1638 [PCR 1:42, 96, 7:5].
ESTATE: On 5 February 1637/8, William Pontus requested "6 acres of lands to be laid to his house as near as conveniently may be" [PCR 1:76]. On 5 March 1637/8, "[w]hereas, by a General Court long since" William Pontus was granted two lots totalling forty acres upon which he built a house, and has since, "for the more commodious receipt of people into the town of New Plymouth," relinquished all but five acres of the forty, these five acres are confirmed to William Pontus, and he is granted six more acres "towards the New Field" [PCR 1:78-79].

On 31 December 1641, "Will[ia]m Pontus is granted two acres of upland to his half acre of meadow in the woods beyond his house about Agawam Path" [PCR 2:29 (a Plymouth town meeting, recorded in the colony records)].

On 19 January 1647[/8?], Samuel Dunham of Plymouth sold to James Glass of Plymouth six acres of upland that had been given to Samuel by his father John Dunham, who had reserved timber rights on the land; to complete the transaction John Dunham released to James Glass the timber rights in return for "a small moiety of land belonging unto William Pontus aforesaid being estimated at about half an acre" [PCR 12:150].

In his will, dated 9 September 1650 and proved 4 March 1652/3, William Pontus bequeathed to "my eldest daughter Mary ... my dwelling house with all my lands, goods and all things else whatsoever," except "unto my other daughter Hannah twenty shillings sterling as an addition to her portion which ... I have already given her"; "my son-in-law James Glasse" to be executor. On 4 March 1652/3, John Dunham testified that he heard Pontus say "that he had given unto his son-in-law, John Churchill, and Hannah, his wife, one third part of his meadow at the watering place near Plymouth," and that the other daughter, the widow Mary Glass, consented [MD 11:92, citing PCPR 1:1:114].

The inventory of the estate of William Pontus, 20 February 1652/3, totalled £12 17s., of which £8 was real estate: "his house and land," £8 [MD 11:92-94]. (See PTR 1:3 for a description of the location of the house of William Pontus using reference points of 1889.)

BIRTH: By about 1585 (based on date of marriage).
DEATH: Plymouth 9 February 1652/3 [PCR 8:14].
MARRIAGE: Leiden 4 December 1610 [NS] Wybra Hanson [Plooij IV; Leiden Pilgrims 203]. She died after 15 December 1633 (when she was named as a creditor in the estate of JOHN THORP [PM 459; MD 1:160]).
CHILDREN:
    i   MARY PONTUS, b. Leiden by 15 October 1622; m. (1) Plymouth 31 October 1645 James Glass [PCR 2:88; NEHGR 111:178]; m. (2) by 17 January 1653[/4] PHILIP DELANO [PM 164].
    ii HANNAH PONTUS, b. say 1624; m. (1) Plymouth 18 December 1644 John Churchill [PCR 2:79]; m. (2) Plymouth 25 June 1669 Giles Rickard [PCR 8:32; see TAG 30:145].
ASSOCIATIONS: JOHN DUNHAM [PM 182] had also lived in the Zevenhuysen section of Leiden and presumably came to Plymouth at the same time as William Pontus, at which time the two men were granted adjacent parcels of land for their homelots. This may betoken no more than decades of neighborliness, but a kinship connection may also be indicated.

COMMENTS: Pope says that Pontus was "from near Dover, England," but the marriage record says only from England, and then adds (as translated) "living in the Marendorp near Douveren," which may explain the confusion. His bride is also said to be from England.

On 15 October 1622, William Pontus lived in the Zevenhuysen section of Leiden with his wife and daughter, was a woolcarder, and was "too poor to be taxed" [Dexter 629]. This daughter is assumed to be Mary, described in the will of William Pontus as "my eldest daughter."

The appearance of William Pontus in the 1633 list of Plymouth freemen, early enough to have been admitted no later than 1632, and his former residence in Leiden, lead to the conclusion that he was probably on one of the last two ships known to have brought members of the Leiden congregation, in 1629 or 1630. His absence from the 1633 and

1634 tax lists indicates that his estate had not improved since 1622, and his absence from the 1643 list of men able to bear arms suggests that he was already sixty, and so perhaps born a few years before 1585, as estimated above.

On 6 February 1638/9, "John Dunhame and Will[ia]m Pontus do undertake to procure the herring weir repaired and drawn and what they agree for with any that shall do the work shall be paid by the whole town according to each in proportion of shares" [PTR 1:5]. On 25 March 1640, "Will[ia]m Pontus, Thomas Lettice and John Greemes shall repair the herring weir and draw it and deliver the shares" for the ensuing three years [PTR 1:7].

In 1644 and 1648 William Pontus wintered one of the cows that was kept for the poor [PTR 1:19, 27]. The cattle mark of William Pontus was a "swallow cropped upon the [word lost] and a snip cut out upon the outside of the right ear" [PTR 1:1].

BIBLIOGRAPHIC NOTE: In 1938 L. Effingham deForest prepared a full account of the family of William Pontus [Moore Anc 423-28].

THOMAS POPE

ORIGIN: Unknown.
MIGRATION: 1632.
FIRST RESIDENCE: Plymouth.
REMOVES: Dartmouth by about 1670.

OCCUPATION: Cooper.
FREEMAN: In 1638 list of those of Plymouth who took the oath of fidelity [PCR 8:181].
EDUCATION: Signed his deeds, but made his mark to his will.
OFFICES: Plymouth constable, 4 June 1645 [PCR 2:83]. Surveyor of highways, 5 June 1651, 7 June 1652 [PCR 2:168, 3:9].

Volunteered to serve in Pequot War, 7 June 1637 [PCR 1:61]. In Plymouth section of 1643 Plymouth Colony list of men able to bear arms [PCR 8:188]. His inventory included "2 guns" valued at £2 10s. [MD 18:131].
ESTATE: Assessed 9s. in the Plymouth tax lists of 25 March 1633 and 27 March 1634 [PCR 1:10, 28].

On 6 October 1636, granted five acres "at the fishing point next Slowly Field" [PCR 1:45]; on 7 November 1636, it was discovered that the place designated for this grant did not quite allow the full five acres [PCR 1:46]. On 2 November 1640, granted five acres "in the South Meddows towards Aggawam, Colebrook Meddowes" [PCR 1:166].

On 29 August 1640, Thomas Pope sold to George Bonam "all that his house and land thereto belonging containing five acres and the enlargement since and all the fence in and about the same" [PCR 12:61]. On 30 October 1652, Thomas Pope of New Plymouth, cooper, acquitted George Bonum of all debts owed to Pope [MD 1:132-33, citing PCLR 2:1:13].

On 17 May 1658, Thomas Pope of New Plymouth, cooper, sold to Joseph Warren a parcel of marsh meadow at Eel River [MD 12:213-14, citing PCLR 2:1:212]. On 24 March 1661, Thomas Pope of Plymouth, cooper, sold to Robert Ransome "all the right, title and interest he hath in his land at Lakenham ... both upland and meadow" in exchange for "twenty-five acres of upland which lyeth with a parcel of upland belonging to Jonathan Pratt lying and being at a place called Acushenah with two acres of meadow which is yet unlaid out at Acushenah aforesaid" [MD 17:42, citing PCLR 2:2:86].

On 5 July 1677, Thomas Pope of Dartmouth, cooper, made a deed of gift to "Seth Pope my eldest son" of "all that my one-half share or portion" at Saconett [PCLR 4:140].

On 31 October 1680, Thomas Pope of Dartmouth, cooper, sold to Charles Stockbridge of Scituate, cooper, "all that my one fourth or quarter part of a grist or corn mill" in the town of Plymouth, along with one-fourth of the implements and the three acres of land associated with the mill, and also "one small piece of land containing twenty-six rods" [PCLR 5:187]. On 2 November 1680, "Thomas Pope Senior and Seth Pope both of the town of Dartmouth" sold to David Lake their share in the grant of land at Saconnet, divided and undivided, the divided part amounting to one hundred acres [PCLR 5:78].

In his will, dated 9 July 1683 and proved 2 November 1683, Thomas Pope bequeathed to "my son Seth as an addition to what I have formerly given him ten shillings in money, also I give unto my grandson Thomas Pope all that my twenty-five acres of upland and two acres of meadow lying and being on the west side of Acushenett River"; "my son Seth shall ... pay three pound sterling unto my grandson Jacob Michell when he comes to age of twenty-one years"; to "my daughter Deborah Pope five pound in money and to each of my other daughters five pound apiece in money, also my meadow lying at the South Meadows in Plymouth or the value of it I give to be equally divided amongst all my sons and daughters"; to "my son Isacke all my seat of land where I now dwell with all the meadows belonging thereunto," except that if he die before twenty-one years without an heir, this land to go to "the sons of my son Seth"; son Isaac to be residuary legatee [MD 18:130, citing PCPR 4:2:50].

The inventory of "Thomas Pope of the town of Dartmouth late deceased," taken 4 August 1683, totalled £274, of which £130 was real estate: "the housing and the seat of land belonging thereunto," £100; "25 acres of upland and 2 acres of meadow lying on the west side of Cushenett River," £10; and "7 acres of upland and 7 acres of meadow at Plymouth," £20 [MD 18:131, citing PCPR 4:2:51].

BIRTH: By about 1612 (based on date of first marriage). (According to Savage, "In 1675, he was 67 yrs. old" [Savage 3:459], but no source is cited.)
DEATH: Dartmouth between 9 July 1683 (date of will) and 4 August 1683 (date of inventory).
MARRIAGE: (1) Plymouth 28 July 1637 Anne Fallowell [PCR 1:63], daughter of Gabriel and Catherine (Finney) Fallowell. She died before 29 May 1646 (and probably soon after the birth of daughter Hannah).

(2) Plymouth 29 May 1646 Sarah Jenny [PCR 2:98], daughter of JOHN JENNY [PM 291]. She died before 9 July 1683 (date of husband's will).
CHILDREN:
   With first wife
   i   HANNAH POPE, b. about 1639 (died 12 March 1710[/1?], aged 71 [NEHGR 101:279 (from family Bible)]); m. by about 1663 Joseph Bartlett, son of ROBERT BARTLETT [PM 42; MD 19:24, citing PLR 1:84].
   With second wife
   ii SUSANNA POPE, b. about 1647; m. Plymouth 7 November 1666 Jacob Mitchell [PCR 8:31], son of EXPERIENCE MITCHELL [PM 324].
   iii SETH POPE, b. Plymouth 13 January 1648/9 [PCR 8:5]; m. (1) by 1675 Deborah Perry (eldest known child b. Dartmouth 23 October 1675), daughter of Ezra Perry [NEHGR 115:86-90]; m. (2) Rebecca ____ (Rebecca Pope, widow of Seth Pope, Esq., was buried at Dartmouth on 25 January 1741, in her 79th year).
   iv THOMAS POPE, b. Plymouth 25 March 1651 [PCR 8:12]; no further record.

v   JOHN POPE, b. Plymouth 15 March 1652/3 [PCR 8:14]; d. July 1675 [PCR 5:205].
vi SARAH POPE, b. about 1656; m. (1) Barnstable 13 November 1676 Samuel Hinckley [MD 6:98, 10:11-16]; m. (2) Barnstable 17 August 1698 Thomas Huckins [MD 6:139, 10:11-16].
vii JOANNA POPE, b. say 1658; m. Dartmouth 5 March 1682 John Hathaway.
viii ISAAC POPE, b. about 1664; m. by 1687 Alice Freeman (eldest known child b. Dartmouth 23 December 1687), daughter of Edmund and Margaret (Perry) Freeman [TAG 40:108-10, citing BarnPR 2:190].

COMMENTS: Savage claimed that daughter "Susanna ... being called in 1663 *eldest* daughter of said Pope by wife Sarah requires us to believe that another daughter followed." However, the use in the seventeenth century of what we would now call the superlative did not require that more than one daughter was intended; this is seen frequently in probate documents of the period, in which a son is called eldest when he is also the only son [TAG 69:86].

Pope included "Son Isaac, not yet 2 years old," the age being apparently a simple typographical error for "21."

On 6 October 1659, Thomas Lettice sued Thomas Pope for abusive carriages [PCR 3:173]. On 5 October 1663 Thomas Pope and Gyles Rickard Sr. were presented for striking each other [PCR 4:48]. On 7 June 1670, Thomas Pope was fined for vilifying the ministry [PCR 5:39].

JOSHUA PRATT

ORIGIN: Unknown.
MIGRATION: 1623 on the *Anne*.
FIRST RESIDENCE: Plymouth.

FREEMAN: In 1633 Plymouth list of freemen prior to those admitted 1 January 1632/3 [PCR 1:3]. In the 7 March 1636/7 list of freemen (immediately preceding Phineas Pratt) [PCR 1:52]. In Plymouth section of 1639 Plymouth Colony list of freemen [PCR 8:174].
EDUCATION: His inventory included "a great Latin Bible" valued at 9s., "a part of another Bible and other old books" valued at 23s. and "2 old psalm books" valued at 1s.

OFFICES: Messenger and constable, 1 January 1633/4, 7 March 1636/7, 5 June 1638 [PCR 1:21, 54, 86]. Constable of Plymouth, 3 January 1636/7, 6 March 1637/8, 4 December 1638 [PCR 1:48, 80, 105]. Assessor, 3 March 1634/5, 1 March 1635/6 [PCR 1:33, 38].

Plymouth petit jury, 1 April 1633 (foreman), 3 September 1639, 3 december 1639, 3 March 1639/40, 1 September 1640, 5 October 1640, 2 March 1640/1, 1 June 1641, 6 July 1641, 3 August 1641, 1 November 1642, 7 March 1642/3, 6 June 1643, 7 November 1643, 5 June 1644, 28 October 1645, 7 July 1646, 1 June 1647, 2 March 1646/7, 7 June 1648, 3 October 1648, 4 October 1648, 6 March 1648/9, 6 June 1649, 7 June 1649, 29 October 1649, 6 March 1649/50, 2 October 1650, 4 March 1650/1, 7 June 1651, 2 March 1651/2, 5 October 1652, 1 March 1652/3, 6 December 1653, 5 June 1655 [PCR 1:12, 2:111, 117, 126, 134, 140, 7:13, 14, 16, 17, 19, 20, 22, 32, 34-37, 41-43, 45-47, 52-54, 58, 62, 64, 68, 73]. Grand jury, 1 June 1641 [PCR 2:16]. Coroner's jury, 29 June 1652 [PCR 3:15].

Committee to divide meadow ground, 1 July 1633 [PCR 1:14]. Committee to view Morton's Hole, 14 March 1635/6 [PCR 1:41]. Arbiter, 5 October 1636 [PCR 1:44]. Committee to view the hay grounds (as "The Messenger"), 20 March 1636/7 [PCR 1:55]. Sealer of weights and measures and measurer of land, 4 December 1638 [PCR 1:105]. Committee to view planting land for the first division at Yarmouth, 5 March 1638/9 [PCR 1:117]. Committee to view the ungranted meadows at Green's Harbor, 5 May 1640 [PCR 1:151]. Committee to view the meadows about Edward Doty's, 5 May 1640 [PCR 1:152]. Committee on laying out highways, 1 February 1640/1 [PCR 2:7].

In Plymouth section of 1643 Plymouth Colony list of men able to bear arms [PCR 8:188].

ESTATE: In 1623 Plymouth land division, paired with Phineas Pratt as recipients of two acres as passengers on the *Anne* [PCR 12:6]. In 1627 Plymouth cattle division, twelfth person in first company [PCR 12:9].

On 7 November 1636, Josuah Pratt received six acres [PCR 1:46]. With his consent, this land was granted to Mrs. Bridgitt Fuller, widow, 6 February 1636/7 [PCR 1:50]. On 7 May 1638, "Josuah Pratt" was granted the enlargement of a garden place [PCR 1:84]. On 26 July 1638, "Josuah Pratt" had four shares in the black heifer [PTR 1:4]. On 5 November 1638, "Josuah Pratt" was granted six acres of land at the east end of Mr. Doane's land "except the Governor make choice of it for himself" [PCR 1:102]. On 2 November 1640, "Josuah Pratt" was granted five acres of meadow in Colebrook Meadows [PCR 1:166]. On 16 September 1641, "Josuah Pratt" was granted a garden place about the house he purchased of Thomas Savory at "Squerrell" [PCR 2:27]. He was twenty-fifth on the list of the purchasers [PCR 2:177].

On 5 December 1637, "Abraham Perse" sold to "Josuah Pratt a house and a garden place in Plymouth next to Ady Webb's house" [PCR 12:24]. On 7 May 1642, "Josuah Pratt" sold to Edward Doty "one acre of upland lying at the high cliff" and to Josias Cooke "two acres of marsh meadow lying at the Wood Island" [PCR 12:81].

On 7 March 1652[/3?], Joshua Pratt was listed as holding "one whole share" in the Purchasers' Land at Acushena and Coaksett (Dartmouth) [MD 4:187, citing PCLR 2:1:107].

On 5 October 1656, administration on the estate of Joshua Pratt, deceased, was granted to Bathsheba Pratt [PCR 3:108].

The inventory of the estate of Joshua Pratt, presented at court on 6 October 1656, totalled £18 11s. 3d., with no real estate included [PCR 3:108; PCPR 2:1:41; MD 14:113].

In a 22 March 1663 list of the owners of lots on "Puncateesett Necke," Joshua Pratt was paired with Gyles Rickard Jr. (presumably a delayed entry of a grant made during Pratt's lifetime) [PTR 1:63].

BIRTH: By about 1605 (based on estimated date of marriage).
DEATH: Between 5 June 1655 (when he served on a petit jury [PCR 7:73]) and 5 October 1656 (date of administration).
MARRIAGE: By about 1630 Bathsheba _____ (assuming she was the mother of all his children). She married (2) Plymouth 29 August 1667 "John Doged [Doggett] of Martha's Vineyard" [MD 8:31] (see JOHN DOGGETT {1630, Watertown} [GMB 1:568-70]).
CHILDREN:
    i   BENAJAH PRATT, b. say 1630; m. Plymouth 29 November 1655 Persis Dunham [MD 8:17], daughter of JOHN DUNHAM [TAG 30:145; PM 182]. (The death record for Benajah Pratt, as published, reads "Benajah Prat, March, 17: in his s[worn]" [PChR 249], entered in a place that would make the date 17 March 1682/3. This might be supposed to mean that he was sixty years old or more, which would place his birth about 1622. Were this true he would be a full decade older than his siblings, and he should be accounted for in the 1627 Plymouth division of cattle. The more likely explanation is that the worn entry has been misread and the word that has been read as beginning with "s" actually begins with "f" for some age in the fifties.)

ii HANNAH PRATT, b. say 1632; m. Plymouth 18 March 1651[/2?] William Spooner [MD 8:13] (as his second wife [PCR 8:5]).

iii JONATHAN PRATT, b. say 1637; m. (1) Plymouth 2 November 1664 Abigail Wood [PCR 8:25]; m. (2) Taunton 3 March 1689/90 Elizabeth (White) Hall [NEHGR 13:252], daughter of Nicholas White and widow of Samuel Hall (on 29 October 1698, Elizabeth Pratt, widow, of Taunton, receipted for her legacy from the estate of her father, Nicholas White [BrPR 2:11; TAG 17:196]).

iv BATHSHEBA PRATT, b. about 1639 (deposed in 1661 aged 22 [Wyman 773, apparently citing Middlesex Court Files]); m. Charlestown [blank] December 1662 "Josua Ris" [ChVR 1:42; Wyman 773, 808], son of ROBERT ROICE {1632, Boston} [GMB 3:1599-1600].

ASSOCIATIONS: Joshua Pratt and PHINEAS PRATT [PM 369] have many times been called brothers. Though there is no direct evidence of this relationship, much circumstantial evidence points in that direction. They received joint grants in the 1623 Plymouth division of land, and they were listed consecutively in the 1639 Plymouth list of freemen. Bathsheba, the daughter of Joshua, married in Charlestown, where her uncle Phineas Pratt was living at the time; she may have been placed in his household after her father's death.

Since we know that Phineas Pratt came in 1622 as one of THOMAS WESTON's men, and not in 1623 on the *Anne* as indicated in the 1623 land division, we might wonder whether Joshua also came in 1622 in the same manner. Although this is possible, it seems unlikely, for otherwise we would expect that Phineas, in his narrative of his trials and tribulations that first winter in New England, would have made mention of his brother.

COMMENTS: On the assumption that Joshua Pratt married in Plymouth, the range of families that might have supplied his wife Bathsheba is quite limited. There is no Bathsheba in any family listed in the 1627 Plymouth cattle division, yet Joshua was married by about 1630. This suggests strongly that his wife was a member of one of the families that arrived in Plymouth in late 1629 and early 1630, many of which had come from Leiden. Joshua's elder son Benajah married the daughter of JOHN DUNHAM, one of these late arrivals from Leiden, and Dunham had named a younger son Benajah, some years after the birth of Benajah Pratt, but more than fifteen years before the marriage of Benajah Pratt to

Persis Dunham. Jonathan is apparently another name used by both Dunham and Pratt.

Some sources claim that Joshua Pratt's wife was named Bathsheba Fay. There is no evidence for this, and no Fay family in Plymouth who might have supplied such a wife. This false claim apparently arises from the misinterpretation of the marriage in Marlborough, Massachusetts, of John Pratt and Bathsheba Fay on 4 January 1715/6.

On 5 November 1638, for some unseen offence, "Josuah Pratt" of Plymouth, yeoman, was fined £10 and was "released" [PCR 1:101].

On 3 August 1640, "Josuah Pratt" deposed regarding two acres of upland at Wellingsly Brook that were given by Godbert Godbertson to John Combe, gentleman, and Phineas Pratt, in marriage with their wives (Godbertson's stepdaughters) [PCR 1:159].

PHINEAS PRATT

ORIGIN: Unknown.
MIGRATION: 1622 on the *Sparrow*.
FIRST RESIDENCE: Weymouth.
REMOVES: Plymouth 1623, Charlestown 1648.

OCCUPATION: Joiner. (His inventory included a "holdfast," which implies ther existence of a bench for woodworking [MD 4:139].)
FREEMAN: In the 1633 Plymouth list of freemen ahead of those admitted on 1 January 1632/3 [PCR 1:4]. He appears immediately following Joshua Pratt on the 7 March 1636/7 list of Plymouth freemen [PCR 1:52]. In Plymouth section of 1639 list of freemen, but his name is crossed out and noted "gone," presumably when he left for Charlestown [PCR 8:174].
EDUCATION: He was author of the remarkable *Declaration*, which showed him to be an intelligent man with an eye for detail. He signed his will, and his inventory included 8s. in books.
OFFICES: Plymouth coroner's jury, 2 March 1635/6 [PCR 1:39]. Petit jury, 2 October 1637 [PCR 7:7].

In the Plymouth section of the 1643 Plymouth Colony list of men able to bear arms [PCR 8:187].
ESTATE: In 1623 Plymouth land division, paired with Joshua Pratt as recipients of two acres as passengers on the *Anne* in 1623 [PCR 12:6]. In 1627 Plymouth cattle division, thirteenth person in company of Francis Cooke [PCR 12:9].

Assessed 9s. (the minimum amount) in the Plymouth tax lists of 25 March 1633 and 27 March 1634 [PCR 1:10, 27].

On 10 March 1633/4, "Phineas Prat, joiner, in the behalf of Marah his wife," exchanged thirty acres near the high cliff with Mr. Thomas Prence, for another thirty acres at Winslow's [PCR 1:26]. On 14 March 1635/6, Phineas Pratt was to have hayground "between Fr[ancis] Billington and his own house" and, on 20 March 1636/7, he was granted the same hay ground he and Mr. Coomes had the last year [PCR 1:40, 56]. On 1 June 1640, Phineas Pratt was granted five acres of meadow [PCR 1:154]. On 2 November 1640, he was granted six acres in the north meadow by Joanes River [PCR 1:166]. On 5 August 1640, he joined John Combe, gentleman, in selling the acre that came to him from Godbert Godbertson in marriage to Godbertson's step-daughter [PCR 12:61]. On 26 August 1646, "Phineas Prate of Plimoth, joiner," sold to John Cooke Jr. of Plymouth, planter, "all that his house & housing and garden place and orchard ... and fifty acres of upland, two acres of meadow at Joanes River ... [and] six acres of upland meadow"; Mary, his wife, consented to this sale, as did "Samuell Cudberte" [PCR 12:137-38]. He was twenty-eighth on the list of purchasers [PCR 2:177].

On 5 June 1658, the court allowed "Phenias Prat" to look for a tract of land to accommodate himself and his posterity [PCR 3:139]. Phineas Pratt and Elder Bates (in behalf of the children of Clement Briggs) petitioned the court, and the court ordered on 8 June 1664 that since Briggs and Pratt had not received their proportions of land as other "Purchasers" had, two of Briggs's sons and Pratt were to have three hundred and fifty acres granted to them [PCR 4:68]. On 7 June 1665, "Pheneas Pratt and James Lovell" were granted "a certain parcel of meadow ... lying on the westerly side of Phenias Pratt's land that was granted unto him the last June Court ... to be equally divided betwixt them" [PCR 4:97]. On 1 January 1672/3, Phineas and Mary Pratt of Charlestown sold to John Shaw Sr. of Weymouth the land granted to them by the court on 8 June 1664 and 7 June 1665 [PCLR 3:271].

On 30 June 1676, "Phineas Pratt aged eighty-one years" deposed "that the lands formerly which I did live upon and did enjoy at Plimouth ... containing twenty acres ... was granted by the Court unto Mr. John Combs" [MD 2:46, citing PLR 1:81].

On 20 May 1648, George Bunker sold to "Phinias Prat" a house and garden in Charlestown [ChBOP 99]. Phineas Pratt drew lot #54 in the 1 March 1657/8 division of wood and commons on Mystic Side [ChBOP 77]. On 21 January 1662/3, Phineas Pratt and wife Mary sold to John Smith a woodlot in Charlestown [MLR 10:136].

In payment for his history of the early settlement titled *A Declaration of the Affairs of the English People That First Inhabited New England*, the General Court on 7 May 1662 granted him three hundred acres "where it is to be had, not hindering a plantation" [MBCR 4:2:56]; on 20 October 1664, this land was laid out "east of Merremack River, near the upper end of Nacooke Brook, on the southeast of it" [MBCR 4:2:154-55]. In October 1668 Phineas Pratt again petitioned the General Court asking for further assistance [MHSC 4:4:487-88; MD 4:134-35], but this petition went unanswered. Although the General Court declined his request, the selectmen of Charlestown provided amply for him for the rest of his life [MD 4:135-36, citing Charlestown Town Orders 3:96, 100, 205, 4:2, 16, 17].

In his will, dated 8 January 1677[/8] and proved 15 June 1680, "Phinias Pratt of Charlstown ... joiner, being very aged and crazy of body," bequeathed to "my beloved wife Mary Pratt all my moveable goods and 40s. a year to be paid out of my land in Charlestowne and the use of the garden for term of her life"; "this 40s. is to be paid by my son Joseph Pratt for and in consideration of the having of my land and my wife is to have a convenient room of my son Joseph with a chimney in it to her content to live in for term of her life, without molestation or trouble, but if my son Joseph doth not perform this will that then my wife Mary Pratt shall have the one half of the land to her disposing for her best comfort; it is to be understood that the one half which the new house standeth on is given to Joseph upon the condition of providing of a convenient room for me and my wife for term of our lives and this other half for the paying of the 40s. a year"; residue at the death "of my wife it shall be equally divided among all my children" [MPR Case #12762; MD 4:139].

The inventory of the estate of "Phinias Prat of Charlstown, deceased," taken 21 May 1680, totalled £40 16s. 6d., of which £24 was real estate: "a parcel of land," £18; and "cow common in Charlstown stinted common," £6 [MPR Case #12762; MD 4:139-40].

The town of Charlestown supported the widow Pratt with a small annual stipend, as seen in town orders dated 5 February 1683/4 and 7 March 1686/7 [MD 4:137, citing Charlestown Town Orders 4:56, 84].

On 31 July 1738, the court's commissioners examined the estate of Phineas Pratt and determined that a share be given to each of the children, including the heirs of sons John and Peter, who were then dead. Although most of the other children were also deceased at that date, they were not so noted. The children listed were John, Samuel, Daniel, Peter, Mary, Joseph, Aaron and Mercy [MD 4:138].

BIRTH: About 1593 (deposed 30 June 1674 aged "eighty-one years or thereabouts" [MD 2:46, citing PLR 1:81], but see the inscription on his tombstone, which would make him slightly older).

DEATH: Charlestown 19 April 1680 ("Pinas Pratt [Senr.], of Charlstowne, joiner, died Apr. 19, 1680 [one of the 1st Planters in New England]" [ChVR 1:110]. The inscription on his tombstone is frequently quoted: "Fugit Hora. Here lies the body of Phinehas Pratt ag[e]d about 90 y[ea]rs dec[ease]d April the 19 1680 & was one of the first English inhabitants of the Massachusets Colony" [MHSC 4:4:476].

MARRIAGE: By about 1633 Mary Priest, daughter of DEGORY PRIEST and Sarah (Allerton) (Vincent) Priest [PM 382], and step-daughter of GODBERT GODBERTSON [PM 226]. (On 3 August 1640, "Josuah Pratt" deposed regarding two acres of upland at Wellingsly Brook that were given by Godbert Godbertson to JOHN COOMBS, gentleman [PM 153], and Phineas Pratt, in marriage with their wives, his [Godbertson's] step-daughters [PCR 1:159]. On 11 November 1633, Phineas Pratt was appointed to "take into his possession all the goods and chattels of Godbert Godbertson & Zarah, his wife, & safely to preserve them" [PCR 1:19].) She is likely the "Widow Pratt lately died" at Charlestown in July 1689 [MD 4:136, citing Charlestown Town Orders 4:93].

CHILDREN:

i MARY PRATT, b. about 1633 (d. Cambridge 11 February 1702[/3] "in her 70th year"); m. Cambridge 1 March 1655[/6] John Swan.

ii JOHN PRATT, b. say 1635; m. by 1664 Ann Barker (eldest known child b. Kingstown, Rhode Island, 13 November 1664 [RIVR 7:70]), daughter of John Barker [Macdonough-Hackstaff 425]. (See MD 3:1-7 for a discussion of the later life of this John Pratt and of his children.)

iii SAMUEL PRATT, b. say 1637; m. by 1668 Mary Barker, daughter of John Barker [Gen Adv 4:31-32]. She married as her second husband Francis Coombs, son of JOHN COOMBS [PM 153].

iv DANIEL PRATT, b. say 1641; m. by about 1680 Anna _____ [MF 8:9].

v PETER PRATT, b. say 1643; m. Lyme, Connecticut, 5 August 1679 Elizabeth (Griswold) Rogers [LymeVR 255], and daughter of Matthew and Anna (Wolcott) Griswold and widow of John Rogers [MF 8:11].

vi   MERCY PRATT, b. say 1645; m. 1667 Jeremiah Holman (eldest known child b. Cambridge 12 November 1667 [MF 8:10]).

vii   JOSEPH PRATT, b. say 1647; m. Charlestown 12 January 1674/5 "Dorcas Foldgier" [ChVR 1:89], daughter of Peter Folger.

viii   AARON PRATT, b. about 1654 (d. 23 February 1735/6, aged eighty-one [Cohasset VR 221]; this estimated year of birth is not impossible, but the age at death may be misstated); m. (1) say 1684 Sarah Pratt, daughter of Joseph Pratt [Small Gen 910-11]; m. (2) Reading 4 September 1707 Sarah (Wright) Cummings, daughter of Joseph Wright and widow of Abraham Cummings [Parker-Ruggles 208-9].

ASSOCIATIONS: See JOSHUA PRATT for a discussion of the likelihood that he and Phineas Pratt were brothers [PM 365].

COMMENTS: According to his *Declaration*, Phinehas Pratt was one of ten men who came to the new world on behalf of THOMAS WESTON [PM 490], in the ship *Sparrow* in 1622. They arrived far up the coast at "Damorall's Cove" where they attempted to acquire a pilot, but none among the fishing ships there nor the Indians would assist them. Sailing down the coast, they recognized Plymouth when a round of celebratory ordnance greeted them. Two further ships with Weston's men followed and by August 1622 the settlement of Wessagusset [Weymouth] was commenced. Unfortunately, they spent their time building fortifications and were soon starving.

On learning of the intent of some Indians to wipe out the English at both Wessagussett and Plymouth, Pratt determined to travel on foot to Plymouth to warn the settlement and look for help. Pursued through the snow, he lost his way, and consequently lost his pursuers who better knew the path. Arriving nearly exhausted "running down a hill I [saw] an English man coming in the path before me. Then I sat down on a tree & rising up to salute him said, 'Mr. Hamdin, I am glad to see you alive.' He said, 'I am glad & full of wonder to see you alive: let us sit down, I see you are weary'" [MD 4:91-92]. Miles Standish and his company, now amply warned, set out on a preemptive attack, which warded off the anticipated danger. Phineas made his home at Plymouth for a quarter of a century thereafter.

On 5 November 1644, "Thomas Bunting, dwelling with Phineas Pratt, hath, with and by the consent of the said Phineas, put himself as a servant to dwell with John Cooke, Junior ... during the term of eight years ... the said John Cooke having paid the said Phineas for him one milch cow ... and 40s. in money and is to lead the said Phineas two loads of hay yearly during the term of seven years" [PCR 2:78].

BIBLIOGRAPHIC NOTE: The full text of Phineas Pratt's remarkable narration was published in 1858 [MHSC 4:4:476].

Rodney MacDonough prepared in 1902 a comprehensive biography of Phineas Pratt [MacDonough-Hackstaff 382-423; MD 4:87-98, 129-140]. The eighth volume of the Five Generations Project of the General Society of Mayflower Descendants, covering the descendants of Degory Priest, includes information on the children, grandchildren and greatgrandchildren of Phineas Pratt; our estimation of the ages of the children of Phineas Pratt differs slightly from the estimations made in this study.

THOMAS PRENCE

ORIGIN: All Saints Barking, London [EIHC 17:103-4].
MIGRATION: 1621 on the *Fortune.*
FIRST RESIDENCE: Plymouth.
REMOVES: Duxbury by 1637, Eastham 1644, Plymouth by 1665.

FREEMAN: In the 1633 Plymouth list of freemen Thomas Prence was just after the Assistants, and ahead of those admitted on 1 January 1632/3 [PCR 1:3]. "Thomas Prence, gen.," is in the 7 March 1636/7 list of Plymouth freemen [MBCR 1:52]. In the list of Assistants at the head of the 1639 list of Plymouth Colony freemen, but as this list was revised and annotated his name was included in the "Nawsett" portion of the list [PCR 8:173, 177]. In Eastham section of 1658 list of Plymouth freemen, and in Plymouth section of list of 29 May 1670 [PCR 5:274, 8:201]
EDUCATION: His inventory included a long list of books valued at £14 2d., including two great Bibles and "100 of psalm books." Most of the books were theological, but other titles included *New England's Memorial*, Culpepper's *London Dispensatory* and Blunt's *Law Dictionary* [MD 3:208-9]. There were also "1 midwife's book" and "44 school books" [MD 3:212, 213].
OFFICES: Plymouth Governor, 1 January 1633/4, 6 March 1637/8, 3 June 1657, 1 June 1658, 7 June 1659, 6 June 1660, 4 June 1661, 3 June 1662, 1 June 1663, 8 June 1664, 7 June 1665, 5 June 1666, 5 June 1667, 3 June 1668, 1 June 1669, 7 June 1670, 5 June 1671, 5 June 1672 [PCR

1:21, 79, 3:115, 134, 162, 187, 214, 4:13, 36, 60, 90, 122, 147, 179, 5:17, 34, 54, 90]. Assistant, .1 January 1634/5, 5 January 1635/6, 3 January 1636/7, 5 March 1638/9, 3 March 1639/40, 2 March 1640/1, 1 Maarch 1641/2, 7 March 1642/3, 5 June 1644, 4 June 1645, 2 June 1646, 1 June 1647, 7 June 1648, 6 June 1649, 4 June 1650, 5 June 1651, 3 June 1652, 7 June 1653, 6 June 1654, 8 June 1655, 3 June 1656 [PCR 1:32, 36, 48, 116, 140, 2:8, 33, 52, 71, 83, 100, 115, 123, 139, 153, 166, 3:7, 30, 48, 77, 99]. Treasurer, 3 January 1636/7 [PCR 1:48]. Council of War, 7 June 1637, 2 June 1646, 1 June 1658 [PCR 1:60, 100, 3:138; PTR 1:16]. Commissioner for Plymouth to the United Colonies, 4 June 1645, 4 June 1650, 7 June 1653, 1 August 1654, 8 June 1655 (replaced), 3 June 1656, 3 June 1657, 1 June 1658, 4 June 1661 (President), 3 June 1662, 1 June 1663, 7 June 1670, 5 June 1671, 5 June 1672 (President) [PCR 2:83, 153, 3:30, 67, 77, 99, 115, 135, 4:36, 5:34, 55, 90, 9:31, 78, 113, 153, 178, 197, 254, 271, 290, 352].

In Plymouth section of 1643 Plymouth Colony list of men able to bear arms [PCR 8:188]. His inventory included "2 firelock muskets" valued at £2, "2 powder horns and a brush" valued at 2s. and "a broken box in it powder and bullet" valued at 6d. [MD 3:207, 209].

ESTATE: In the 1623 Plymouth division of land Thomas Prence received one acre as a passenger on the *Fortune* [PCR 12:5]. In the 1627 Plymouth division of cattle Thomas Prince, Patience Prince and Rebecca Prince are the tenth, eleventh and twelfth persons in the fifth company [PCR 12:10].

In the Plymouth tax list of 25 March 1633 Thomas Prence was assessed £1 7s. [PCR 1:9]. He was omitted from the list of 27 March 1634. His cattle mark was three marks on the outer side of the ear [PTR 1:2]. On 1 July 1633, 14 March 1635/6 and 20 March 1636/7, "Tho[mas] Prence" was granted mowing rights [PCR 1:14, 40, 56].

On 20 March 1633/4, "[w]hereas John Coomb, gent., is possessed of thirty acres of land near unto the high cliff, in the right of Sarah his wife, the said John & Sarah have exchanged the same with Mr. Tho[mas] Prence for other thirty acres of land near unto Wynsloe's stand" [PCR 1:25].

On 6 March 1636/7, "Mr. Thomas Prence" was granted "a parcel of land ... lying between the two cedar swamps" [PCR 1:51]. On 5 February 1637/8, "Mr. Thomas Prince" was granted "[a]ll the lands remaining betwixt Mr. Burnes land at Greenes Harbor and a little creek or certain passage of water running through betwixt the two rivers of Greenes Harbor and South River" [PCR 1:77]. Granted "the garden place betwixt the Spring Lane and Mr. John Reynor's," 2 April 1638 [PCR

2:83]. Granted "ten acres of land in some convenient place about the town," 5 November 1638 [PCR 1:102]. Granted "a parcel or tongue of land about an acre & a half broad at Smilt River, lying betwixt the river & the lands of Mr. Thomas Prince," 3 December 1638 [PCR 1:103]. Granted "the parcel of ground betwixt John Barnes garden and Georg[e] Watson's field," 2 December 1639 [PCR 1:136]. Granted "an enlargement at the head of his lot at Jones River," 16 September 1641 [PCR 2:26]. Granted six acres "at the North Meadow by Jones River," 17 October 1642 [PCR 2:49].

On 24 October 1650, "Mr. Thomas Prenc[e] of the town of Nawsett" sold to "John Cook Junior of Plymouth ... two acres of marsh meadow" [PCR 12:197-98].

On 11 July 1649, Mr. Thomas Prence of Nawset, gentleman, sold to Jacob Cooke of Plymouth, planter, forty acres of upland in Rocky Noocke with three acres of marsh [PCR 12:175]. On 13 July 1649 Mr. Thomas Prence of Nawset, gentleman, sold to Richard Church of Nawset, carpenter, and to Anthony Snow of Marshfield, feltmaker, upland and marsh at Marshfield and forty acres of upland received by grant dated 5 February 1647 [PCR 12:176].

On 13 June 1655, Thomas Prence of Eastham sold to "Mr. Edward Buckley" of Marshfield five acres of marsh in Marshfield [MD 9:234, citing PCLR 2:1:155]. On 12 July 1655, Thomas Prence of Eastham sold to John Browne of Rehoboth "my half share with other purchasers situate and being near Rehoboth and Sowamsett" [MD 10:16, citing PCLR 2:1:159]. On 31 August 1658, Thomas Prence sold to John Cooke of Plymouth two acres of marsh meadow at Jones River [MD 13:44, citing PCLR 2:2:6].

On 5 February 1665, the town of Plymouth granted Mr. Thomas Prence six acres of upland meadow on the west side of Jones River meadow and, on 16 March 1667[/8], twelve acres more there [PTR 1:83, 97].

On 8 December 1662, Thomas Prence deeded to "my son [i.e., stepson] Samuell Freeman and Mercye his wife the house and land Samuel now dwelleth in" [PCLR 3:201]. On 20 September 1664, Thomas Prence deeded to John Freeman of Eastham "all that his upland and meadow lying on the southeast side of great Namskekett, viz: a parcel of upland containing eight acres ... with five acres of meadow," also two acres of meadow with ten acres of upland [PCLR 3:28]. On 14 November 1669, Thomas Prence exchanged one hundred acres "of upland lying upon Pachague Neck on the southerly side of Teticutt River" with "Mrs. Alice Bradford the executrix of Mr. William

Bradford," receiving in return "a half share of Purchase Land at Satuckett, be it forty-five acres more or less, and also the one-half of twenty-five acres of meadow" [PCLR 3:171]. On 2 May 1670, Thomas Prence of Plymouth, gent., sold to Thomas Paine of Eastham, cooper, "all my one-half share of Purchase Land at Paomett," with the consent of "Mrs. Prence" [PCLR 5:480]. On 25 July 1672, Thomas Prence, Esquire, Governor of New Plymouth, deeded to John Freeman Sr. of Eastham "one parcel of land containing thirty acres," "another parcel of land containing eight acres ... of swamp and upland," "one other parcel of marshland, containing twenty-four acres," "also forty acres of upland," "also [another] forty acres of upland," "also fifteen acres of upland," and "also five acres of upland" [PCLR 3:278].

In his will, dated 13 March 1672/3 and proved 5 June 1673, "Thomas Prence being at present weak in body" bequeathed to "Mary my beloved wife ... such household goods of any kind as were hers before we married, returned to her again, after my decease, and if any of them be much impaired or be wanting, that she shall make it good out of my estate in such goods as she desireth"; to "my said loving wife my best bed and the furniture thereunto appertaining, and the court cupboard that now stands in the new parlor with the cloth and cushion that is on it, and an horse and three cows such as she shall make choice of, and four of my best silver spoons, and also during her natural life, I give her the rents and profits of my part of the mill at Satuckett, and of the lands adjoining, and my debts and legacies being first paid, I do further give unto my said wife a full third part of my personal estate that remains"; to "my daughter Jane the wife of Marke Snow my silver tankard"; to "my daughter Mary Tracye a silver wine cup and a dram cup"; to "my daughter Sarah Howes my biggest beer bowl"; to "my daughter Elizabeth Howland my silver salt"; to "my grandchild Theophilus Mayo and to the heirs of his body lawfully begotten, the one half of my lands and meadows at or near Namassakett in the township of Middleberry"; "I give unto my grandchild Sussanna Prence the daughter of my deceased son Thomas Prence, the other half of my above mentioned lands and meadows at Middleberry aforesaid"; in the absence of an heir of these grandchildren, the abovesaid lands to revert to "my daughters, or such of them as shall be then surviving, or their heirs if all my daughters should be dead"; "to my said grandchild Theophilus, and to his heirs forever, my part of the mill and lands adjacent at Satuckett after the decease of my wife, and this I give for his encouragement to proceed in learning"; residue divided among "my seven daughters, Hannah, Marcye, Jane, Mary, Elizabeth, Sarah and Judith, and my above mentioned grandchild

Susanna Prence"; Mary "my beloved wife sole executrix"; "my loving friend Major Josias Winslow to be helpful therein." A codicil to the will bequeathed to "Mr. John Freeman *Speed's Cronicle* and *Wilson's Dictionary* and the abridgement, and *Simpson's History of the Church* and *Newman's Concordance*"; to "my daughter Elizabeth Howland a black heifer"; to Lydia Sturtivant a little yellow heifer; to "my daughter Jane a bed, and another bed to my daughter Elizabeth Howland"; to "my grandson Theophilus Mayo all my books fit for him in learning, and if he carry it well to his grandmother I then give him a bed"; also "I desire my brother Thomas Clarke to be helpful to my wife as need may require" [MD 3:204-6, citing PCPR 3:1:58-59].

The inventory of "Thomas Prence Esqr. lately deceased," taken 23 April 1673, totalled £422 10s. 7d. [MD 3:206-16, citing PCPR 3:1:60-70]. Real estate was listed at the end of the inventory, but unvalued: "one hundred acres of land lying in the town of Middleberry at or near Winnapaukett pond and the brook going from it"; "one share of meadow lying in a certain tract of meadow called the Major's meadow that lieth upon Namassakett River, betwixt the pond and the weir"; "one hundred acres of land lying on the northerly side of Teticutt River"; "a considerable tract of land that lieth on the easterly side of Namassakett River between Winnapauckett pond and a tract of land called the Major's purchase"; "eight acres of land on the westerly side of Namassakett River"; "a grant of ten or twelve acres of land and a small parcel of meadow at Jones River meadow in the township of Plymouth"; "ten acres of land lying on the south side of a cart way that goeth to Lakenham, called Prence bottom in Plymouth"; "the one half of fifty or sixty acres of land and three acres of meadow between him and Major Winslow in Middleberry"; "twenty acres of land and three acres of meadow at Tonsett in the township of Eastham"; "eight acres of land lying on Pochey Island in the aforesaid Eastham"; and "one fourth part of a mill at Satuckett and lands adjoining to it" [MD 3:215-16].

On 10 June 1673, John Freeman, Jonathan Sparrow, John Tracy, Mark Snow, Jeremiah Howes, Arthur Howland and Isaac Barker receipted to "our mother-in-law Mrs. Mary Prence late wife and executrix to our father Thomas Prence Esquire deceased" for their shares of the estate of Thomas Prence [MD 33:97-100 (with photograph of the unrecorded original)].

On 10 June 1676, Josiah Winslow, Esquire, "attorney for ... Susanna Prence at Catheren Gate near the Tower in London ..., singlewoman," and John Freeman in the right of Mary his wife and as attorney for "Mary Prence, relict and executrix of the last will and testament of the honored Thomas Prence, late Governor ... deceased," and of Jonathan Sparrow and Hannah his wife, Marke Snow and Jane his wife, and Jeremiah Howes and Sarah his wife, daughters of the said Thomas Prence, and John Tracye and Mary his wife, Arthur Howland and Elizabeth his wife, and Isacke Barker and Judith his wife, daughters also of the said Thomas Prence, sold to Constant Southworth, treasurer and agent of Plymouth Colony, "all that our dwelling house, messuage or tenement" in Plymouth "at a place commonly called Plain Dealing"; signed by Josiah Winslow, John Freeman, John Trasye, Arthur Howland and Isack Barker [PCLR 4:124].

BIRTH: About 1600 (based on age at death), son of Thomas Prence, carriage-maker, of Lechlade, Gloucestershire. In his will, dated 31 July 1630 and proved 14 August 1630, Thomas Prence, carriage-maker, of Lechlade, Gloucestershire, left a legacy to his son Thomas Prence "now remaining in New England in the parts beyond the seas" [EIHC 7:103-4, citing PCC 70 Scroope].

DEATH: Plymouth 29 March 1673, in his 73rd year ("Thomas Prence, Esquire, Governor of the jurisdiction of New Plymouth, died the 29th of March, 1673, and was interred the 8th of April following. After he had served God in the office of Governor sixteen years, or near thereunto, he finished his course in the 73 year of his life. He was a worthy gentleman, very pious, and very able for his office, and faithful in the discharge thereof, studious of peace, a wellwiller to all that feared God, and a terror to the wicked. His death was much lamented, and his body honorably buried at Plymouth the day and year above mentioned" [PCR 8:34; see also MD 3:203-4]).

MARRIAGE: (1) Plymouth 5 August 1624 Patience Brewster [Prince 229], daughter of WILLIAM BREWSTER [PM 66]. She died late in 1634 (in a letter to his son John Winthrop Jr. dated 12 December 1634, John Winthrop reported that "the pestilent fever hath taken away some at Plimouth, among others Mr. Prence the governor his wife" [WP 3:177]).

(2) Plymouth 1 April 1635 Mary Collier [PCR 1:34], daughter of WILLIAM COLLIER [PM 128]. She died perhaps by 1644.

(3) After 1 July 1644 (when she witnessed Rev. George Phillips's will as Apphia Freeman in Watertown [NEHGR 3:78]) and certainly some considerable time before 8 December 1662 (when Thomas gave land to her son) Apphia (Quick) Freeman, former wife of SAMUEL FREEMAN {1630, Watertown} [GMB 1:698-700], daughter of William Quick of London [TAG 11:178].

(4) After 26 February 1665[/6] and by 1 August 1668 Mary (_____) Howes, widow of Thomas Howes [MD 6:157-65, 230-35]. She died on 9 December 1695 [MD 6:230, citing YarTR 3:328].

CHILDREN:

With first wife

- i REBECCA PRENCE, b. say 1625 (living at time of cattle division in 1627 [PCR 12:10]); m. Plymouth 22 April 1646 Edmund Freeman [PCR 2:98], son of EDMOND FREEMAN {1635, Lynn} [GM 2:2:576-82].
- ii THOMAS PRENCE, b. say 1627 (in the 1627 Plymouth division of cattle is a second Thomas Prence, inserted at the end of the tenth lot; this may be the son Thomas Prence, born at about the time this list was compiled, and added separately from his family); m. _____ _____ (an appendix to the fifth edition of Morton's Memorial refers to letters from the widow and daughter of this Thomas Prence, in London, to his father, the immigrant [pp. 424-25]; these letters have apparently never been published, but copies of some of them are held by the Massachusetts Historical Society).
- iii HANNAH PRENCE, b. say 1629; m. (1) Eastham 13 February 1649/50 Nathaniel Mayo [PCR 8:26]; m. (2) by 1671 Jonathan Sparrow [MD 14:193-203], son of RICHARD SPARROW [PM 443].
- iv MERCY PRENCE, b. say 1631; m. Eastham 13 February 1649/50 John Freeman [PCR 8:26], son of EDMOND FREEMAN {1635, Lynn} [GM 2:2:576-82].

With second wife

- v JANE PRENCE, b. Duxbury 1 November 1637 [MD 6:230]; m. Eastham 9 January 1660[/1] Mark Snow [PCR 8:28], son of NICHOLAS SNOW [PM 428].
- vi MARY PRENCE, b. say 1639; m. by about 1661 John Tracy [Tracy Gen 26].

Perhaps with third wife

- vii JUDITH PRENCE, b. say 1645; m. (1) Plymouth 28 December 1665 Isaac Barker [PCR 8:31], son of ROBERT BARKER [PM 29]; m. (2) after 1693 William Tubbs [PPR 1:168; PLR 2:123].
- viii ELIZABETH PRENCE, b. about spring 1647 [WP 5:169]; m. Marshfield 9 December 1667 Arthur Howland [MarVR 10], son of Arthur Howland [NGSQ 71:90-91].

ix SARAH PRENCE, b. about 1648 ("departed this life March the 3d 1706 in the 60th year of her age," tombstone, Yarmouth, which conflicts with YarVR [NEHGR 59:217]); m. by about 1669 Jeremiah Howes (birth of child estimated by child's date of marriage), her stepbrother [MD 6:233; NEHGR 59:217-18].

COMMENTS: For many years it was believed that Prence had married only three times and that his last wife was "Mary" Freeman, but this was corrected in 1904 by Ella Florence Elliott, who divided the erroneous construct into its proper wholes, revealing divorcee Apphia Freeman and widow Mary Howes as Prence's last two of four wives [MD 6:230-35].

Establishing the probable date of marriage for Apphia and Thomas Prence has significant implications for the parentage of Prence's last three children. Apphia is last seen as a Freeman 1 July 1644, about a year before the birth of Prence's seventh child, and at the end of a six-year hiatus in the birthdates of his children. She is called "Mrs. Freeman" as late as 15 October 1646 in a deed where she appears as an abutter, but this does not necessarily imply that she had not remarried by this date, since obsolete bounds were often used in such descriptions [SLR 1:78].

In a letter dated at Plymouth 8 June 1647, Thomas Prence wrote to John Winthrop that "since my parting company [with you] I have almost met with Jacob's trial in his travel between Bethel and Ephrath: God's having been heavy upon my wife and that for diverse months and is not yet removed" [WP 5:169]. In Genesis 35:16-19 Jacob's favorite wife Rachel died between Bethel and Ephrath after giving birth to a son she named Benoni, but he called Benjamin. Prence here is referring to the birth of his own daughter Elizabeth, apparently a difficult childbirth.

On 6 March 1637/8, having been elected governor, Thomas Prence was excused from the requirement that the governor live in Plymouth, and was permitted to retain his residence in Duxbury [PCR 1:79]. When he was again elected governor, in 1657, he was allowed to maintain his residence in Eastham, but in 1663 the court ordered that the governor's house at Plymouth be enlarged, and by 1665 Prence again became a resident of Plymouth [Dawes-Gates 2:684].

BIBLIOGRAPHIC NOTE: Perhaps due to the fact that Thomas Prence had no grandsons that carried the Prence surname, little attention has been directed to this family. A brief account of his family was prepared in 1852 by David Hamblen and a more substantial treatment was published in 1931 by Mary Walton Ferris [Dawes-Gates 2:682-94].

DEGORY PRIEST

ORIGIN: Leiden, Holland.
MIGRATION: 1620 on the *Mayflower*.
FIRST RESIDENCE: Plymouth.

OCCUPATION: Hatter (when admitted as a citizen of Leiden) [Leiden Pilgrims 216].
ESTATE: In the 1623 Plymouth land division "Cudbart Cudbartsone" received six acres as a passenger on the *Anne* in 1623 [PCR 12:6]; four of these six shares would be for the deceased Degory Priest, his widow Sarah and his two daughters. In the 1627 Plymouth cattle division "Marra Priest" and "Sarah Priest" were the tenth and eleventh persons in the second company, just after their mother and stepfather [PCR 12:9].

BIRTH: About 1579 (aged about forty in 1619 [Dexter 630]).
DEATH: Plymouth 1 January 1620/1 [Prince 287].
MARRIAGE: Leiden 4 November 1611 [NS] "Sara Vincent, widow of Jan Vincent" [Plooij IX; MD 7:129-30; Leiden Pilgrims 216]; Priest is said to be of London. She was sister of ISAAC ALLERTON [PM 10] and married (3) Leiden 13 November 1621 or soon after (betrothed 25 October 1621 [NS]) GODBERT GODBERTSON [Plooij XLVII; Leiden Pilgrims 101; PM 226].
CHILDREN:
    i   MARY PRIEST, b. say 1612; m. by about 1630 PHINEAS PRATT [PM 369].
    ii SARAH PRIEST, b. say 1614; m. by about 1632 JOHN COOMBS [PM 153].

COMMENTS: Bradford included "Digory Priest" in his list of those on the *Mayflower*, and in his accounting of 1651 said that Priest "died soon after ... arrival in the general sickness," but "had his wife and children sent hither afterwards, she being Mr. Allerton's sister" [Bradford 443, 447].

In 1957 John G. Hunt published the 1582 baptism for a "Digorius Prust" in Hartland, Devonshire [NEHGR 111:320]; although there is nothing to connect this with Degory Priest of London, Leiden and Plymouth, it is a useful clue.

BIBLIOGRAPHIC NOTE: Degory Priest and his descendants have been given full and definitive treatment in the eighth volume of the Five

Generations project of the General Society of Mayflower Descendants, compiled by Mrs. Charles Delmar Townsend, Robert S. Wakefield and Margaret Harris Stover, and edited by Robert S. Wakefield (Plymouth 1994).

SOLOMON PROWER

Solomon Prower sailed to Plymouth in 1620 on the *Mayflower*, as servant of Mr. CHRISTOPHER MARTIN (his stepfather) [PM 315], and "died in the first infection, not long after the arrival" [Bradford 442, 445].

R

JAMES RAND

"James Rande" was granted one acre in the 1623 Plymouth land division as a passenger on the *Anne* in 1623 [PCR 12:5]. As he was not in the 1627 cattle division, he must have died or returned to England prior to that date.

ROBERT RATTLIFE

In the 1623 Plymouth land division "Robart Rattlife" was granted two acres as a passenger on the *Anne* in 1623 [PCR 12:6].

COMMENTS: In the published version of the land division the amount granted to Rattlife is included in square brackets, probably indicating some doubt about the reading. Savage, in fact, says that Rattlife was given four acres. Wakefield accepts the two acre amount, and interprets this to mean that Rattlife had his wife with him [MQ 40:60]. Since Rattlife does not appear in the 1627 cattle division, he must have died or departed soon.

DANIEL RAY

ORIGIN: Unknown.
MIGRATION: 1630.
FIRST RESIDENCE: Plymouth.
REMOVES: Salem 1631.

OCCUPATION: Seaman [ELR 8:121-22].
EDUCATION: He made his mark to an inventory in 1658 [EPR 1:288].
OFFICES: Essex grand jury, 30 December 1645 [EQC 1:89, STR 139]. Jury, 27 June 1636, 27 December 1636, 28 March 1637 [EQC 1:3-5].

Petit jury, 27 December 1642, 26 June 1649, 24 June 1651 [EQC 1:44, 169, 229].

Salem selectman, 1636-37 [STR 34, 44]. Assessor, February 1639[/40] [STR 97]. Tythingman, 7 June 1644 [STR 131]. Constable, 1639 [STR 154].

ESTATE: On 9 June 1630, Anthony Annable sold to Daniel Ray a dwelling house and "garden plot & fence" [PCR 12:17].

In the 1636 Salem land division he received one hundred and sixty acres in the freeman's land [STR 20]. In the 25 December 1637 division of meadow at Salem, he received one acre for a household of seven [STR 1:102].

On 15 July 1647, William Hathorne and Richard Davenport sold to John Putnam Sr., "Richard Huchesson" and "Danyell Ray" of Salem and John Hathorne of Lynn their two farms of about 280 acres apiece, each containing 260 acres of upland and 20 acres of meadow [ELR 2:55; see also ELR 2:28].

On 24 June 1662, "Whereas there hath been a will begun to be made by Daniell Rea of Salem, lately deceased, but he not being able to finish it, whereby great inconvenience is like to arise to his children, if it be left as it is" the children came to an agreement, which the court approved: "that his son Joshua Rea shall have the improvement of the whole farm, where he lives, & when his son Daniel is grown up to the age of twenty-one years, he shall have half the farm, & his father to have the other half, during the term of his own life, & also of his wife's widowhood, in case she should outlive him, and then that half also to be his son Daniel's, & so the said Daniel then to have the whole farm"; "Joshua Rea shall have the use & improvement of the seventeen acres of land lying on Salem North River, until his two daughters, Rebecca & Sarah, expressed in the will, shall attain to the age of sixteen years, & then they to have the land with the improvement of the same equally divided betwixt them"; "Joshua Rea shall have also the one acre and half on the South River's side in Salem as his proper right"; "his son Thomas Lothrop & his wife shall have the farm commonly called Captain Damport's farm"; "our mother shall have the thirds of all of this estate during her life"; residue to be disposed of by the court [EPR 1:375-76; EQC 2:413-14].

On the same day, "Joshua Ray was appointed administrator of the estate of Danyell Ray, deceased, who died intestate," and "Joshua Ray, son of the deceased, was to have £25 and Capt. Tho[mas] Lothrop, said Daniel's son-in-law, was to have all the rest of the estate, provided he keep and maintain his mother, the widow, during her life" [EQC 2:413].

The inventory of the estate of Daniell Ray, presented 26 June 1662, totalled £239 19s. 4d., of which £180 was real estate: "seventeen acres of land in the north field," £25; "an acre & a half of salt marsh upon the South River," £5; "a farm of one hundred sixty acres of upland and ten acres of meadow," £150 [EPR 1:376; EQC 2:415].

On 20 December 1688, Joshua Rea of Salem, proper heir and only son of Daniel Rea, "my father, being deceased in the year 1662," deeded to his son Daniel Rea land which "my father Daniel Rea, seaman, late of Salem, now deceased," purchased of Captain Richard Davenport in 1647 in partnership with John Putnam Sr., Richard Hutcheson and John Hathorne, and which "the said partners a short time after divided ... amongst themselves," which "I did allow my brother-in-law Thomas Lawthrop and his wife a personal right to use & dispose of that part which did belong to me ... my said brother-in-law & sister Lawthrop now being deceased, both their right to use and dispose" being past [ELR 8:122].

BIRTH: By about 1597 (based on date of marriage).
DEATH: Before 24 June 1662 [EPR 1:375-76; EQC 2:413].
MARRIAGE: By 1637 (and by about 1627 if she was the mother of both children) Bethiah _____. "Bethiah Raye" was admitted to Salem church on 1 October 1637 [SChR 7]. She was living in 1662 when THOMAS LOTHROP, son-in-law, was to keep and maintain his mother, widow of Daniel Ray, during her life [EQC 2:413]. She probably died before Lothrop, since no provision was made for her in his estate. (The suggestion was made that BETHIA JONES, initially of Boston, may have become wife of Daniel Ray when she moved to Salem [GMB 2:1111]. Since this move did not take place until 1631 (or later), this suggestion would require either that the two children of Daniel Ray be a few years younger, or that Daniel Ray had an earlier wife.)
CHILDREN:
   i JOSHUA RAY, b. by about 1627; m. Salem 26 February 1651[/2] Sarah Walters.
   ii BETHIA RAY, b. say 1630; m. (1) before 1652 (when he returned to England and told his mother that he had no children and was not likely to have any [EQC 6:170]) THOMAS LOTHROP {1633, Salem} [GMB 2:1202-6]; m. (2) by June 1676 Joseph Grafton [EQC 6:170]; m. (3) by 1685 William Goodhue. Bethia Goodhue, wife of Deacon [William] Goodhue, d. Ipswich 6 December 1688.

ASSOCIATIONS: Sarah (Dennis) Gott died following the birth of her daughter, Sarah, and Thomas Lothrop's wife, Bethiah (Ray) Lothrop, called the dead woman "my cousin" [EQC 6:95]. Sarah Dennis was the daughter of Edward Dennis and his wife, Sarah _____. The elder Sarah married second Abner Ordway.

COMMENTS: The leading men of Plymouth wrote to the leading men of the Bay on 6 February 1631/2 concerning the matter of persons moving back and forth between the two jurisdictions. "Now there are diverse gone from hence, to dwell and inhabit with you, as Clement Brigges, John Hill, John Eedy, Daniell Ray, etc., the which if either you, or they, desire their dismissions, we shall be ready to give them, hoping you will do the like in the like cases, though we have heard something otherwise" [WP 3:65].

On 27 December 1642, Daniel Ray and other men were fined for keeping their cattle in the common corn fields [EQC 1:49]. Several times subsequently his livestock got loose and he was fined [EQC 1:56, 70, 72, 83].

On 21 January 1639/40, "John Luvet Daniel Ray's servant desireth accommodation" [STR 98]. On 11 July 1644, James Thomas "servant to Daniell Ray" was ordered severely whipped for "stubbornness and disobedience to his master" [EQC 1:68].

On 21 February 1648[/9], "Danyell Rumball" and "John Rowden" were both fined for "defaming Danyell Raye" [EQC 1:157]. On 22 February 1648[/9], "Ruben Guppie" was ordered fined or to sit in the stocks for "defaming Danyell Ray" [EQC 1:158].

Both Savage and Pope have misread the will of Daniel Ray and have turned his granddaughters Rebecca and Sarah into daughters.

In the 1637 grant of meadow Daniel Ray was credited with a household of seven, but we have identified only four above. No clues have been found which would help in identifying the remaining three persons.

WILLIAM RICHARDS

William Richards appears in the Plymouth tax lists of 25 March 1633 and 27 March 1634, the assessments in both cases being 9s. [PCR 1:11, 28].

6 February 1636/7: "Six acres of land where William Richards dwelt is granted unto Nathaniell Sowther" [PCR 1:50].

COMMENTS: Deane tentatively and incorrectly claims this William Richards as a resident of Scituate by 1636, and a landholder there in 1639 [Scituate Hist 331]. He further identifies this man as the William Richards of Weymouth in 1640 and later [MBCR 1:300; Savage 3:535]. The only evidence in favor of this position is the identity of names.

JOHN RIGSDALE

"John Rigsdale and Alice his wife" were passengers to Plymouth in 1620 on the *Mayflower*, and they both died in the first sickness, during the winter of 1620/1 [Bradford 442, 446].

COMMENTS: Pope, with his usual orthographic indifference, notes an Alice Rickdall who joined the church at Dorchester about 1639, and on this slight basis suggests a possible relationship.

MARY RING

ORIGIN: Leiden, Holland.
MIGRATION: 1629 or 1630.
FIRST RESIDENCE: Plymouth.

EDUCATION: She signed her will. The inventory included "1 Bible. 1 Dod. 1 Plea for Infants. 1 Ruin of Rome. 1 Troubles of the Church of Amsterdam. 1 Garland of Virtuous Dames. 1 psalmbook. 1 Pennery. 1 pair hinges" valued at 4s.
ESTATE: In her undated will, proved 28 October 1633, "Mary Ring being sick in body" bequeathed to "Andrew my son all my brass and pewter ... my new bed & bolster ... two white blankets, one red blanket with the best coverlet ... & the curtains ... three pair of my best sheets & two pair of my best pillowbeers ... one diaper tablecloth & one diaper towel & half a dozen of napkins ... all my woollen cloth unmade except one piece of red which my will is that my daughter Susan shall have as much as will make a bearing cloth and the remainder I give unto Stephen Deane's child"; to "my son Andrew my bolster next the best ... my trunk & my box & my cupboard ... all my cattle ... half the corn which groweth

in the yard where I dwell and the other half I give unto Stephen Deane"; "the rest of my corn in other places I give to Andrew my son"; to "Steph[en] Deane my [illegible] to make him a cloak"; "timber that I lent to Mr. Winslow that cost me a pound of beaver, besides a piece more than they had of me"; to "my son Andrew all my shares of land that is due to me or shall be ... all my tools ... the money that is due to me from the Governor 40s. as also the 40s. of commodities I am to have out of England ... I give unto him also except the green say which I give unto Stephen Deane's child to make her a coat"; "one piece of new linen I give unto my son Andrew"; to "my daughter Susan Clarke my bed I lay upon with my gray coverlet & the ticks of the two pillows, but the feathers I give unto my son Andrew"; "one ruff I had of Goodman Gyles I give to my daughter Eliz. Deane"; residue "unto my daughters" equally divided; to "my son And[rew] all my books, my two pair of pothooks & my trammel, one coarse sheet to put his bed in, & all the money that is due to me from Goodman Gyles ... the piece of black stuff"; "the goods I give my two daughters are all my wearing clothes, all my wearing linen"; to "Mrs. Warren one wooden cup with a foot as a token of my love"; "the cattle I give my son be kept ... for him by Stephen Deane, or at the discretion of my overseers to take order for them for the good of the child"; "to Andrew my son all my handkerchiefs buttoned or unbuttoned ... one silver whistle"; "my will is that Andrew my son be left with my son Stephen Deane, and do require of my son Deane to help him forward in the knowledge & fear of God, not to oppress him by any burdens but to tender him as he will answer to God"; overseers "my loving friends Samuell Fuller & Thomas Blossom"; "my overseers see that those goods which I have given unto my son Andrew be carefully preserved for him until such time as they shall judge it meet to put them into his own hands"; "if my overseers shall see it meet to dispose of my son Andrew otherwise than with his Brother Deane, that then my son Deane shall be willing to consent unto it"; "I give unto Andrew a linen cap which was his father's, buttons for his handkerchief unbuttoned I leave for him"; "Andrew my son shall pay all my debts and charges about my burial" [MD 1:29-31, citing PCPR 1:4-5].

The inventory of the goods of "Mary Ring deceased" was "presented with the will of the said Mary by Thomas Prence whom Samuell Fuller requested to perform his charge & trust committed in behalf of the said Andrew & the said Thomas acknowledgeth to accept in public court the overseers of the will being both deceased & the child young"; the inventory was untotalled and included no real estate [MD 1:31, citing PCPR 1:5-6].

BIRTH: By about 1589 (based on estimated date of marriage).
DEATH: Plymouth 15 or 19 July 1631 (preamble to her will [MD 1:29]).
MARRIAGE: By about 1609 William Ring, who died at Leiden between 1620 and 1629 [TAG 42:196].
CHILDREN:
- i ELIZABETH RING, b. say 1609; m. (1) by about 1630 STEPHEN DEANE [PM 162]; m. (2) Plymouth 16 September 1635 JOSIAS COOKE [PCR 1:35; PM 149].
- ii SUSANNA RING, b. say 1611; m. by July 1631 THOMAS CLARK [PM 109].
- iii ANDREW RING, b. about 1618 (d. 22 February 1692/3 in his 75th year [PChR 275; MD 4:193 (which explains why PVR 135 has the year of death wrong)]); m. (1) Plymouth 23 April 1646 Deborah Hopkins, daughter of STEPHEN HOPKINS [PCR 2:130; PM 271]; m. (2) about 1674 Lettice (____) Morton, widow of John Morton (son of GEORGE MORTON) [TAG 42:203; PM 336].

COMMENTS: John Insley Coddington discussed this family at length in 1966 [TAG 42:193-205]. He found two potentially relevant entries in the Ufford, Suffolk, parish register: the marriage on 21 May 1601 of "Marie Durante of Ufford single woman" to Wyllyam Ringe of Petistrey, singleman [TAG 42:193], and the baptism on 23 February 1602/3 of Elizabeth, their daughter [TAG 42:194]. Coddington stressed the unproven nature of the connection between the Ufford family and the Rings of Leiden. While the marriage date for Marie Durante and Wyllyam Ringe is comfortable, daughter Elizabeth seems to have been as much as ten years older than usual at marriage and would have been nearly a decade older than her second husband. If the Ufford family is the one that came to New England, it is possible that the 1602/3 baptism is for a daughter Elizabeth who died young and the wife of Deane and Cooke is a subsequent daughter of the same name.

ISAAC ROBINSON

ORIGIN: Leiden, Holland.
MIGRATION: 1631 [Sewall 463].
FIRST RESIDENCE: Plymouth.
REMOVES: Scituate 1636, Barnstable 1639, Falmouth by 1664, Tisbury by 1671, Barnstable 1701.

OCCUPATION: Innkeeper. On 7 February 1664/5, Isaac Robinson was approved to keep an ordinary at Saconeesett "since there is great recourse to and fro by travellers to Martin's Vineyard and Nantucket" [PCR 4:80].

CHURCH MEMBERSHIP: "Isaac Robinson and my son Fuller joined [Scituate church] having their letters dismissive from the church at Plimoth unto us," 7 November 1636 [NEHGR 9:280].

FREEMAN: In 1633 list of Plymouth freemen between those admitted 1 January 1633/4 and those admitted 1 January 1634/5 [PCR 1:4]. In 7 March 1636/7 list of Plymouth Colony freemen [PCR 1:52]. In the Scituate section of the 1639 Plymouth Colony list of freemen; his name was then erased and reentered in the Barnstable section of the same list [PCR 8:175, 177]. In Barnstable section of 1658 Plymouth Colony list of freemen [PCR 8:200].

On 7 March 1659/60, the court "taking notice of sundry scandals and falsehoods in a letter of Isacke Robinson's, tending greatly to the prejudice of this government and encouragement of those commonly called Quakers, and thereby liable ... to disenfranchisement, yet we at present forebear the censure until further inquiry be made into things" [PCR 3:183]. On 6 June 1660, Isaac Robinson "for being a manifest opposer of the laws of this government expressed by him in a letter directed the Governor and otherwise" is disenfrancised of the freedom of the corporation. An interlineation following says, there being some mistake in this, Isaac Robinson is re-established and by general vote of the court, accepted again [PCR 3:189]; this interlineation may have been made as late as 1673, for Isaac Robinson is not in the 29 May 1670 list of Plymouth freemen, and, on 4 July 1673, Plymouth Court "voted Mr. Isacke Robinson to be re-established in the privilege of a freeman of this corporation" [PCR 5:126].

EDUCATION: Sufficient to write a letter to Plymouth Colony authorities in support of the Quakers. Presumably educated by his father.

OFFICES: Deputy for Barnstable to Plymouth General Court, 28 October 1645, 5 June 1651 [PCR 2:94, 168]. Tax collector, 7 July 1646, 1 June 1647, 7 June 1648 [PCR 2:105, 116, 125].

Plymouth petit jury, 2 March 1640/1 [PCR 7:19]. Coroner's jury, 5 June 1658 [PCR 3:147].

(Isaac Robinson does not appear in the 1643 Plymouth Colony list of men able to bear arms.)

ESTATE: Assessed 9s. in Plymouth tax list of 27 March 1634 [PCR 1:29].

In his list of houses built in Scituate, Rev. John Lothrop included among those erected in 1636 "Isaac Robinson's ... now Goodman Twisden's," and as the first built in 1637 "Isaac Robinson's new house" [NEHGR 10:42-43].

On 4 June 1660, the court gave Isaac Robinson and others permission to purchase land at or near Saconeesett [PCR 3:216]. On 5 June 1666, Isaac Robinson and others were granted fifty acres each of upland at Pausatuke Neck, with six acres of meadow [PCR 4:128], and, on 7 June 1668, the court confirmed a certain neck of land with meadow adjoining at Passuntaquanuncke Neck to Isaac Robinson and two others [PCR 4:189]. On 8 November 1669, Isaac Robinson of Saconeesett, husbandman, sold to John Jenkins land in Saconeesett; Isaac's wife Mary acknowledged this deed [TAG 56:147, citing PCLR 3:154].

On 20 December 1666, "Isacke Robinson Senior of Barnstable, planter," posted a bond of £4 with Joseph Tilden of Scituate, yeoman, as security for the receipt of a legacy of forty shillings "given and bequeathed unto ... Isaac Robinson Junior by the last will and testament of Mr. Timothy Hatherley deceased" [PCLR 3:102].

On 9 June 1683, the court granted Isaac Robinson's petition to look out for land for his accommodation [PCR 6:110].

In November 1701 Isaac Robinson sold his homelot at Tisbury to his son Isaac and removed to his daughter's in Barnstable [TAG 18:46].

BIRTH: About 1610 (aged 92 years, 4 April 1702 [Sewall 463]), son of Rev. John and Bridget (White) Robinson.

DEATH: At Barnstable in 1704 (so stated in all secondary sources, but no evidence supplied). (On 4 April 1702, Samuel Sewall wrote "Visit Mr. [Isaac] Robinson, who saith he is 92 years old, is the son of Mr. [John] Robinson pastor of the church of Leyden, part of which came to Plimo[uth]. But to my disappointment he came not to New England till the year [1631] in which Mr. [John] Wilson was returning to England after the settlement of Boston. I told him was very desirous to see him for his father's sake, and his own. Gave him an Arabian piece of gold to buy a book for some of his grandchildren" [Sewall 463-64].)

MARRIAGE: (1) Scituate 26 September 1636 Margaret Hanford, daughter of Eglin (Hatherly) (Downe) Hanford [GM 2:3:205-7] and niece of TIMOTHY HATHERLY [PM 234] ("Isaac Robinsonn and Margaret Handford contracted at Mr. Hetherlye's June 27, 1636" [NEHGR 9:286]) [Stevens-Miller Anc 485-87]. "The wife of Isaac Robinsonn buried [at Barnstable] June 13, 1649, and a maid child born of her before the ordinary time buried the week before" [NEHGR 9:285].

(2) By 1651 Mary _____ [TAG 56:147, citing PCLR 3:154]. She died after 8 November 1669 [PCLR 3:154].

CHILDREN:

With first wife

   i   SUSANNA ROBINSON, bp. Scituate 21 January 1637/8 [NEHGR 9:281]; no further record.

  ii   JOHN ROBINSON, bp. Barnstable 5 April 1640 [NEHGR 9:282]; m. Barnstable "about the middle of May" 1667 Elizabeth Weeks [MD 12:153].

 iii   ISAAC ROBINSON, bp. Barnstable 7 August 1642 [NEHGR 9:282]; d. before 22 October 1668 ("he tried to fetch two geese from a pond full of weedy grass and was entangled" [PCR 5:7]). (He is said to have had wife Anne, but the evidence for this is not seen. There may be some confusion with his younger half-brother who assumed his name, and did have a wife named Anne.)

 iv   FEAR ROBINSON, bp. Barnstable 26 January 1644/5 [NEHGR 9:283]; m. by 1664 Rev. Samuel Baker (in his will of 20 December 1664, TIMOTHY HATHERLY bequeathed to "Fear Robinson now the wife of Samuel Baker" [MD 16:159; see also NEHGR 142:123-25]).

  v   MERCY ROBINSON, bp. Barnstable 4 July 1647 [NEHGR 9:283]; m. Falmouth 16 March 1669 William Weekes (the bride's name given as "Mary Robenson" as published).

 vi   Daughter ROBINSON, prematurely born June 1649 and buried a few days before her mother [NEHGR 9:285].

With second wife

 vii   ISRAEL ROBINSON, bp. Barnstable 5 October 1651 [NEHGR 9:284] (later called Isaac in honor of his deceased elder half-brother); m. Anne Cottle [TAG 18:47; Martha's Vineyard Hist 3:107, 419].

viii   JACOB ROBINSON, bp. Barnstable 15 May 1653 [NEHGR 9:284]; m. (1) Mary _____; m. (2) by 1714 Experience Rogers. (These two marriages are presented in all sources without documentation [Martha's Vineyard Hist 3:419, 423; TAG 18:47]).

 ix   PETER ROBINSON, b. say 1655; m. (1) by about 1688 Mary Manter, daughter of John Manter [Martha's Vineyard Hist 3:284]; m. (2) say 1698 Experience _____ (she could not have been daughter of John Manter Jr. [TAG 18:47]).

ASSOCIATIONS: JOHN CARVER was uncle by marriage to Isaac Robinson [PM 95].

COMMENTS: On 24 May 1649, Isaac Robinson testified that he heard Mr. Gilson say that he wanted to leave his land to two of his sister's children (John and Hannah Damman), whom he looked upon as his own, and that he heard Gilson's wife acknowledge it and say she wouldn't wrong them [PCR 2:143].

On 1 March 1658/9, Isaac Robinson and Gyles Rickard Sr. complained on behalf of two children of Henery Coggen, deceased [PCR 3:156]. Perhaps as a result of this, John Coggen, one of these children, chose Mr. Isaac Robinson as one of his guardians [PCR 3:160-61]. On 8 April 1664, he was discharged as guardian [PCR 4:77].

Some sources include a son Thomas born in March 1657, but there does not seem to be any evidence for this child. This is in part based on the existence of a Thomas Robinson of Guilford, who cannot have been a son of Isaac [TAG 18:47].

BIBLIOGRAPHIC NOTE: In 1941 Mary Lovering Holman presented the ancestry of Isaac Robinson, treated the immigrant himself and followed a line of descent from Isaac [TAG 17:207-15, 18:45-55]. Amos Otis and Charles Edward Banks also prepared brief biographical sketches of Isaac Robinson [Otis 2:228-31; Martha's Vineyard Hist 2:West Tisbury:60-62].

_____ ROGERS

In 1628 William Bradford reported that "Mr. Allerton brought over a young man for a minister to the people here, whether upon his own head or at the motion of some friends there I well know not. But it was without the church's sending, for they had been so bitten by Mr. Lyford as they desired to know the person well whom they should invite amongst them. His name was Mr. Rogers; but they perceived upon some trial that he was crazed in the brain, so they were fain to be at further charge to send him back again the next year, and lose all the charge that was expended in his hither bringing.... After his return he grew quite distracted, and Mr. Allerton was much blamed that he would bring such a man over, they having charge enough otherwise" [Bradford 210-11].

COMMENTS: The surviving accounts of the Plymouth Company for 1628 show a debt of £3 11s. 4d. "paid for Mr. Rogers's passage, 20s.[,] his diet 11 weeks at 4s. 8d." [MHSC 3:1:199].

THOMAS ROGERS

ORIGIN: Leiden, Holland.
MIGRATION: 1620 on the *Mayflower*.
FIRST RESIDENCE: Plymouth.

ESTATE: In the 1623 Plymouth land division Joseph Rogers was granted two acres as a passenger on the *Mayflower* (for himself and his deceased father) [PCR 12:4]. In the 1627 Plymouth cattle division Joseph Rogers was the fifth person in the eleventh company [PCR 12:12].

Sons Joseph and John were each assessed the minimum 9s. in the 25 March 1633 rate [PCR 1:11].

On 6 April 1640, "Joseph Rogers and John Rogers, his brother," were granted fifty acres of upland each at the North River [PCR 1:144].

BIRTH: By about 1572 (based on date of marriage), son of William and Eleanor (____) Rogers of Watford, Northamptonshire [TG 10:143].
DEATH: Died Plymouth soon after arrival, probably in January or February 1620/1.
MARRIAGE: Watford, Northamptonshire, 24 October 1597 Alice Cosford, daughter of George Cosford [TG 10:140].
CHILDREN (baptized Watford, Northamptonshire [TG 10:140]):
    i   THOMAS ROGERS, bp. 24 March 1598/9; bur. 27 May 1599.
    ii (possibly) RICHARD ROGERS, bp. 12 March 1599/1600; bur. 4 April 1600.
    iii JOSEPH ROGERS, bp. 23 January 1602/3; m. by 1633 Hannah ____ (assuming she was his only wife; eldest known child of Joseph Rogers b. 6 August 1633 [MD 16:238]); appears in 1633 list of Plymouth freemen in vicinity of others admitted on 1 January 1632/3 [PCR 1:4]; assessed 9s. in the Plymouth tax lists of 25 March 1633 and 27 March 1634 [PCR 1:11, 28].
    iv JOHN ROGERS, bp. 6 April 1606; assessed 9s. in the Plymouth tax list of 25 March 1633 [PCR 1:11]; m. Plymouth 16 April 1639 Anna Churchman [PCR 1:120].

v ELIZABETH ROGERS, bp. 26 December 1609; living at Leiden in 1622; perhaps came later to New England and married there [TAG 52:110-13; Bradford 446].

vi MARGARET ROGERS, bp. 30 May 1613; living at Leiden in 1622; perhaps came later to New England and married there [TAG 52:110-13; Bradford 446].

COMMENTS: In his listing of the passengers on the *Mayflower* Bradford includes "Thomas Rogers and Joseph his son; his other children came afterwards," and in his accounting of these families as of 1651 Bradford tells us that "Thomas Rogers died in the first sickness but his son Joseph is still living and is married and hath six children. The rest of Thomas Rogers's came over and are married and have many children" [Bradford 442, 446].

Robert S. Wakefield and Jeremy D. Bangs have discussed the 1622 poll tax for Leiden which revealed Thomas Rogers's widow and children living in the Over 't Hoff quarter of Leiden [TAG 52:110-13; NEHGR 154:432-33]. Since the widow, son John and daughters of Thomas Rogers were not in the land division of 1623 or the cattle division of 1627, they presumably came to Plymouth with the last of the Leiden contingent in 1629 or 1630.

BIBLIOGRAPHIC NOTE: In 1998 Clifford Stott demonstrated the English origin of Thomas Rogers [TG 10:138-49]. In 2000 the Five Generations Project of the General Society of Mayflower Descendants published a revised edition of the Thomas Rogers volume, originally compiled by Alice A.W. Westgate and revised by Ann T. Reeves.

_____ ROWLAND

In the Plymouth tax list of 25 March 1633, _____ Rowland was assessed 9s. [PCR 1:11].

COMMENTS: Pope identifies this man with a William Rowland who had a suit in Plymouth Court in 1640, but no such suit is found in the court records of Plymouth or of Massachusetts Bay. Savage raises the possibility that the man taxed in 1633 was a John Rowland seen by him in Hingham, but without date or reference.

Since no entry for _____ Rowland is found in the 1634 tax list, the more likely explanation is that Pope and Savage are both wrong, and

_____ Rowland left New England in 1633, or perhaps was among the many who died in that year.

HENRY ROWLEY

ORIGIN: Unknown.
MIGRATION: 1632.
FIRST RESIDENCE: Plymouth.
REMOVES: Scituate 1634, Barnstable 1640.

CHURCH MEMBERSHIP: "Goodman Rowly and his wife" were founding members of the Scituate church, 8 January 1634/5 [NEHGR 9:279].
FREEMAN: Admitted 1 January 1634/5, and subsequently added to the list of 1633 [PCR 1:4, 32]. In the list of 7 March 1636/7 [PCR 1:53]. In the 1639 list of freemen, Henry Rowley appears under Scituate (lined out) and under Barnstable [PCR 8:175, 177]. In Barnstable section of 1658 and 29 May 1670 lists of freemen [PCR 5:277, 8:200].
OFFICES: Deputy for Barnstable to Plymouth Colony General Court, 29 August 1643 [PCR 2:59].

Plymouth petit jury, 6 June 1650 [PCR 7:49]. Coroner's jury, 22 October 1668 [PCR 5:7].

Barnstable constable, 2 March 1640/1, 1 June 1641 [PCR 2:9, 15]. Surveyor of highways, 2 June 1646, 1 June 1647, 7 June 1653 [PCR 2:102, 115, 3:33].

In Barnstable section of 1643 Plymouth list of men able to bear arms [PCR 8:193].
ESTATE: "_____ Rowly" was assessed 9s. in the Plymouth tax list of 25 March 1633 and 18s. in the list of 27 March 1634 [PCR 1:11, 28].

"Goodman Rowlye" had built a house by the time of Rev. John Lothrop's arrival in Scituate in September 1634; he later acquired a house built by Henry Cobb, and built a second house on his own lot [NEHGR 10:42]. On 1 January 1637/8, Henry Rowley was one of the freemen of Scituate who complained that their proportions of land were too small to subsist upon and with the others received upland, neck, and meadow between the North & South Rivers [PCR 1:72]. He was an original grantee of Seppekann, 22 January 1638/9 [PCR 1:108].

The inventory of the estate of "Henery Rowley of Saconeesett deceased," exhibited at Plymouth court in July 1673, consisted of a debt of £29 due from Jonathan Hatch "upon the repurchase of a parcel of land which the said Hatch sold to the said Henery Rowley with that limitation provided" [MD 24:137, citing PCPR 3:1:93; Scrapbook 101].

BIRTH: By about 1605 (based on estimated date of marriage).
DEATH: Between 29 May 1670 [PCR 5:277] and July 1673 (presentation of inventory).
MARRIAGE: (1) By about 1630 _____ _____, probably daughter of WILLIAM PALMER of Plymouth [PM 349; TAG 32:40-41 (but see *COMMENTS* below)]. She died by 1633.

(2) Plymouth 17 October 1633 Anne (Elsdon) Blossom ("Anna, the late wife of Tho: Blossome") [PCR 1:16; TAG 63:74; PM 58].
CHILDREN:
  With first wife
   i   SARAH ROWLEY, b. say 1630; m. Barnstable 11 April 1646 Jonathan Hatch [MD 5:171].
   ii MOSES ROWLEY, b. say 1632; m. Barnstable 22 April 1652 Elizabeth Fuller [PCR 8:47], daughter of Matthew Fuller [MF 4:10-12].

COMMENTS: Florence Barclay, in her article on WILLIAM PALMER of Plymouth, supplied the evidence in favor of the position that the mother of Moses Rowley was a daughter of William Palmer (see also PCR 3:45-46); she thought that Sarah Rowley who married Jonathan Hatch was a daughter of Henry Rowley, but not necessarily with the Palmer wife (which would imply yet another wife before the presumed _____ Palmer) [TAG 32:40-41].

There are many unresolved problems with this identification. Moses Rowley, who was certainly a son of Henry, married in 1652, which should place his birth no later than 1632, and probably somewhat earlier. Was Moses Rowley born in England or at Plymouth? If he was born at Plymouth, then Henry Rowley must have arrived before 1632, the earliest date that we may assume from surviving records. Since Rowley was not in Plymouth in 1627, he could have come in 1629 or 1630 when additions were made to the Plymouth population; but if this were the case he would have had to marry William Palmer's daughter immediately after getting off the boat, and even this just barely leaves enough time for Moses to be born by 1630, say, and it makes it almost impossible for Sarah Rowley also to have been born in Plymouth as a child of the Palmer wife. On the other hand, Rowley may have married _____ Palmer in England, in which case both Moses and Sarah could be children of this wife, born in England. The terms of William Palmer's will make it clear that he had at least two other children who are never seen in other New England records, Henry and Bridget. There are other possibilities.

Apparently through inattention, Pope assigned the marriage and children of Moses Rowley to the latter's father, Henry.

With ANTHONY ANNABLE, Henry Rowley was bondsman for William Kersley of Barnstable on 7 December 1641 [PCR 2:28].

BIBLIOGRAPHIC NOTE: In 1906 Homer W. Brainard published a lengthy account of Henry Rowley and his descendants [NYGBR 37:57-66, 97-103, 203-8, 251-56]. More recently Paul Prindle prepared a briefer study of the immigrant and a line of descent through his son Moses [Gillespie Anc 392-404]. Both of these authors include a third child for Henry, a son Joseph "living at Barnstable, 1655," and "said to have gone to Barbados" [NYGBR 37:58; Gillespie Anc 394], but neither provides documentation for this statement. Perhaps a record for Moses has been misread as for a Joseph who did not exist.

S

HENRY SAMSON

ORIGIN: Henlow, Bedfordshire.
MIGRATION: 1620 on the *Mayflower*.
FIRST RESIDENCE: Plymouth.
REMOVES: Duxbury.

FREEMAN: In the 1633 Plymouth list of freemen Henry Samson appears immediately after two men admitted on 5 January 1635/6, and before a man admitted on 2 March 1635/6 [PCR 1:4]. In the 7 March 1636/7 list of freemen [PCR 1:53]. In the Duxbury sections of the Plymouth Colony lists of 1639, 1658 and 29 May 1670 [PCR 5:275, 8:175, 198].
EDUCATION: He signed his will and his deeds by mark. His inventory included "arms, wearing clothes and library" valued at £4 10s [MD 2:143].
OFFICES: Plymouth grand jury, 1 June 1641, 6 June 1649, 4 June 1650, 2 October 1650, 7 June 1659, 1 June 1663 [PCR 2:16, 140, 155, 162, 3:162, 4:37]. Petit jury, 5 November 1644, 4 June 1645, 7 July 1646, 7 June 1649, 7 October 1651, 2 March 1651/2, 5 October 1652, 7 March 1653/4, 4 October 1655, 3 March 1662/3, 25 October 1668, 29 October 1670 [PCR 7:38, 41, 42, 46, 56, 58, 62, 70, 75, 108, 150, 163]. Coroner's jury, 8 December 1669 [PCR 5:29].

Duxbury constable, 4 June 1661 [PCR 3:215]. Tax collector, 5 June 1667, 3 June 1668 [PCR 4:150, 183]. Arbiter, 2 May 1648, 4 October 1648 [PCR 2:122, 135-36]. Surveyor, 29 October 1649, 10 June 1650 [PCR 2:147, 160].

On 7 June 1637, he volunteered for the Pequot War [PCR 1:61]. In the Duxbury section of the 1643 Plymouth Colony list of men able to bear arms [PCR 8:189]. His inventory included "arms, wearing clothes and library" valued at £4 10s [MD 2:143].
ESTATE: In the 1623 Plymouth division of land "Henerie Samson" received one acre as a passenger on the *Mayflower* [PCR 12:4]. In the 1627 Plymouth division of cattle "Henri Samson" is the fifth person in the fifth company [PCR 12:10].

On 1 January 1637/8, Henry Samson received a grant of the "overplus on the south side of the lands besides Henry Howland's three shares" [PCR 1:72]. On 6 April 1640, he was granted the common lying at the head of his lot [PCR 1:144]. On 2 November 1640, Henry Samson received fifty acres with some meadow at the North River [PCR 1:165].

Prior to 26 October 1647, Kenelm Winslow had sold some land to "Henry Sampson" [PCR 2:119]. On 27 October 1647, Ephraim Tinkham and Mary his wife sold to "Henry Sampson of Duxborough" one-third part of a lot that had belonged to Peter Browne in Duxbury [PCR 12:146].

Henry Samson was one of the fifty-eight purchasers [PCR 2:177]. On 3 October 1662 and on 8 June 1664, he was one of the men allowed to look for lands [PCR 4:27, 67]. On 7 June 1665, he was on the list of those with lands granted to them on the westerly side of Namasskett River "for his children" [PCR 4:94, 5:5]. On 2 July 1667, Henry Samson was granted liberty to "look out land to accommodate his children" [PCR 4:160].

On 24 December 1668, "Henery Samson" of Duxbury sold to Edward Gray of Plymouth Lot #19 at Namassakett [PCLR 3:237]. On 17 April 1682, Henry Samson of Duxbury, yeoman, sold to Seth Pope of Dartmouth, cooper, "all that my seven acres of meadowland which was my interest in the undivided meadows at Cokesett" in Dartmouth [PCLR 5:207]. On 18 December 1684, Henry Samson of Duxbury, yeoman, sold to Joseph Russell of Dartmouth, husbandman, "all that my fifty acres of upland" in Dartmouth, with four acres and a half of meadow adjoining, with "one-eighth part of one whole share of undivided land excepting 25 acres and one-thirtieth part of undivided land already sold out of the said eighth part of undivided lands" [PCLR 5:292].

In his will, dated 24 December 1684 and proved 5 March 1684/5, "Henery Sampson of Duxburrow" bequeathed to "my son Stephen one-third part of my whole purchase of land lying and being in the township of Dartmouth"; to "my son John one-thirds of my whole purchase of lands lying and being within the township of Dartmouth"; to "my son James the remaining part of the other third of my land lying within the township of Dartmouth" (part of this third having been sold to Joseph Russell, the proceeds of which went to James); to "my son James one shilling"; to "my son Caleb one shilling"; to "my daughter now the wife of Roberd Sprout one shilling"; to "my daughter Hannah now the wife of Josias Holmes one shilling"; to "my daughter now the wife of John Hanmore ten shillings"; to "Mary my daughter now the wife of John Summers one shilling"; to "my daughter Dorcas now the wife of Thomas

Bony one shilling"; son Stephen to be executor; "my trusty and honored friend Mr. Wiswall" to be overseer [MD 2:142-43, citing PCPR 4:2:94-95].

The inventory of the "estate of the late deceased Henery Sampson of Duxberrow," taken 24 February 1684/5, totalled £106 14s., of which £70 was real estate: "land in Dartmouth," £70 [MD 2:143-44, citing PCPR 4:2:95].

BIRTH: Baptized Henlow, Bedfordshire, 15 January 1603/4, son of James and Martha (Cooper) Samson [TAG 52:207].
DEATH: Duxbury between 24 December 1684 (date of will) and 5 March 1684/5 (probate of will).
MARRIAGE: Plymouth 6 February 1635/6 ANNE PLUMMER [PCR 1:36]. She died after 24 December 1668 [PCLR 3:237] and before 24 December 1684 (date of husband's will).
CHILDREN:
  i   STEPHEN SAMSON, b. say 1638; m. by 1686 Elizabeth _____ (eldest known child, son Benjamin, d. Kingston 19 April 1758 in 72nd year) [MF 20:1:8-9, 27].
  ii JOHN SAMSON, b. say 1640; d. between 1702 and 1718, unm. [TAG 28:5].
  iii ELIZABETH SAMSON, b. say 1642; m. by 1662 Robert Sprout (eldest known child b. Scituate 15 July 1662).
  iv JAMES SAMSON, b. say 1644; m. by 1679 Hannah (_____) Wait, widow of Samuel Wait [MF 20:1:7-8].
  v   HANNAH SAMSON, b. say 1646; m. Duxbury 20 March 1665[/6?] Josiah Holmes.
  vi Daughter SAMSON, b. say 1648; m. by 1682 (but probably some years earlier) John Hanmore [MF 20:1:5].
  vii MARY SAMSON, b. say 1650; m. by 1684 (but probably some years earlier) John Summers [MF 20:1:5-6].
  viii DORCAS SAMSON, b. say 1652; m. by 1684 (but probably some years earlier) Thomas Bonney [MF 20:1:6-7], son of THOMAS BONNEY [GM 2:1:340-43].
  ix CALEB SAMSON, b. say 1654; m. (1) by about 1686 Mercy Standish, daughter of Alexander Standish (eldest known child b. about 1686 [MF 20:1:33]; in his will of 21 February 1701/2, Alexander Standish made a bequest to "Mercy Samson the wife of Caleb Samson" [MD 12:101, citing PPR 1:362]); m. (2) Duxbury 30 January 1728/9 Rebecca (Bartlett) (Bradford) Stanford, daughter of Benjamin Bartlett

and widow of William Bradford and Robert Stanford [MF 20:1:9-10].

ASSOCIATIONS: Robert Leigh Ward's article outlines the connections among EDWARD TILLEY [PM 461], JOHN TILLEY [PM 462], HUMILITY COOPER [PM 156] and Henry Samson [TAG 52:198-208].

COMMENTS: Bradford says the passengers on the *Mayflower* included "Edward Tilley and Ann, his wife, and two children that were their cousins, Henery Samson and Humility Cooper" [Bradford 442], and in his accounting of 1651 he tells us that "the youth Henry Sampson is still living and is married and hath seven children" [Bradford 446].

There are few chronological clues to help us in arranging the children of Henry Samson. There were nine children and we know from Bradford that seven of them were born by 1651. The first daughter known to be married was Elizabeth, who had a child born in 1662, and Hannah was married just a few years later. As Elizabeth and Hannah are listed first and second among the daughters in their father's will, it may be that he named them in birth order. In the absence of other guideposts, we will make the same assumption about the sons. Thus, the birth order of the children presented above derives from these assumptions, placing the children at approximately two-year intervals after the marriage of Henry Samson. This is certainly not the only possible arrangement, but it is consistent with the available evidence.

On 5 January 1640/1, Henry Samson was assigned the remainder of Phillip Davis's indenture from John Cooke. Davis was to serve Samson for the remainder of the eleven years and two months since Davis's arrival in New England [PCR 2:6].

BIBLIOGRAPHIC NOTE: In 1952 Florence Barclay studied the family of Henry Samson, and arrived at some useful conclusions, with special emphasis on his son Caleb [TAG 28:5-8]. In 1976 Robert Leigh Ward published records that demonstrated the parentage of Henry Samson, and his likely connection with EDWARD and JOHN TILLEY [TAG 52:198-208]. In 1980 Ward added to Samson's ancestry by identifying his grandfather [TAG 56:141-43], and in 1985 he further extended the ancestry of this group of immigrants [TG 6:166-86].

In 2000 the Five Generations Project of the General Society of Mayflower Descendants published its account of the first four generations of descendants of Henry Samson, compiled by Robert Moody Sherman and Ruth Wilder Sherman and edited by Robert S. Wakefield [MF 20:1].

ANTHONY SAVORY

In 1633 Plymouth list of freemen in proximity to those admitted on 1 January 1632/3 [PCR 1:4]. In Plymouth list of freemen of 7 March 1636/7 [PCR 1:53]. In Plymouth section of 1639 Plymouth Colony list of freemen (annotated "dead") [PCR 8:174].

In a 1642 record of cows, Joshua Pratt, Thom[as] Savory and Anthony Savory shared a heifer [PTR 1:9].

COMMENTS: Stratton says that Anthony "apparently died in the 1630s" [Stratton 348-49]; however, since he appeared in a Plymouth town record in 1642 but was not in the 1643 list of men able to bear arms, he may well have died in late 1642 or early 1643. Anthony Savory was presumably related in some manner to THOMAS SAVORY.

A.W. Savary found the marriage in Salisbury, Wiltshire, on 10 December 1630 of Anthony Savery and Mary Shepperd; he held that this was a marriage for the immigrant to New England, and that it was his widow who married in Plymouth in 1661 Joseph Ramsden [NEHGR 66:367]. There seems little reason to believe this.

THOMAS SAVORY

ORIGIN: Unknown.
MIGRATION: 1633.
FIRST RESIDENCE: Plymouth.

OCCUPATION: Planter. Undermarshal.
EDUCATION: Signed his deeds and agreements. His inventory included, at the head of a long list of moveables, "1 Bible and psalm book & 3 other books" [PCPR 3:1:172].
OFFICES: On 4 June 1652, "Thomas Savory is indented with by the Court to serve in the office of under marshal, or executioner, according to the terms and nature of his said office already entered, and is to have 20 nobles per annum, besides his ordinary fees allowed by the Court" [PCR 3:12, 94].

On 7 June 1670, "Thomas Savory was dismissed from his office of undermarshal, having been found several times unfaithful in the performance of his said office," but after pleading by himself and others he was reinstated on 7 July 1670 [PCR 5:40, 44].

In the Plymouth section of the 1643 Plymouth Colony list of men able to bear arms [PCR 8:188]. His inventory included "2 short pikes and powder and shot" valued at 5s. [PCPR 3:1:172].

ESTATE: On 16 September 1641, "Josuah Pratt is granted a garden plot about the house he hath bought of Thomas Savery, at Squèrrell" [PCR 2:27].

On 20 February 1662, Thomas Savory of Plymouth, planter, granted to "Samuell Eedey" of Plymouth, tailor, "all that his whole right and portion" at Punckateesett, in exchange for "a parcel of upland and meadow ... lying at the Four Mile Brook" in Plymouth and "a parcel of upland being six acres lying and being at or near Fresh Lake" in Plymouth [MD 17:244-45, citing PCLR 2:2:111].

On 7 June 1665, "Thomas Savory for his children," along with four other men, was granted one share in the Major's Purchase, "to have thirty acres apiece out of the best of it, and commoning proportionable" [PCR 4:95; see also Stratton 288]. On 4 July 1673, Plymouth court "had measured unto Thomas Savory and Benjamin Eaton sixty acres of upland in the land called the Major's Purchase, near Namassakett" [PCR 5:129].

On 10 July 1667, Thomas Savory of Plymouth, planter, sold to "Sacaryah Eedey" of Plymouth, planter, "all that my share of land granted to me lying and being near Whetstone's Vinyards in a certain tract of land commonly called Major's Purchase containing thirty acres of upland"; Thomas Savory signed the deed, and Ann Savory consented to the sale, making her mark [PCLR 3:81].

In his will, dated 6 April 1674 and proved 7 March 167[5/]6, "Thomas Savory Senior" bequeathed to "Anne my dearly beloved wife all that estate that I have that is to say my house and lands, both my lands and meadows, with all my moveables in the house and belonging to the house, or all that appears to be mine from any other"; "I desire my dear wife to consider my son Aron at her decease, if she have anything left and the reason why I give all to my wife is because I have little all my debts being paid. I leave her sole administrator and executor" [PCPR 3:1:172].

The inventory of the estate of "Thomas Savory lately deceased at Plymouth," taken 28 January 1675[/6], was untotalled; the real estate was "his house and land, upland and meadow, and orchard, and the upland nine acres lying at home and six acres lying at the fishing point and threescore acres lying at 4 Mile Brook and four acres of meadow lying at the Four Mile Brook" valued at £12 [PCPR 3:1:172].

On 7 March 1675/6, "[l]etters of administration [were] granted unto Anne Savory, widow, to administer of the estate of Thomas Savory, Senior, deceased" [PCR 5:189].

On 22 March 1677, "Anne Savory widow" of Plymouth deeded to "my two sons Anthony Savory and Aron Savory" both of Plymouth, planters, "all that my lot and share of land" in Plymouth "at a place called Four Mile Brook which lot of land fell to my husband Thomas Savory deceased by exchange with our brother-in-law Samuell Eedey aforesaid, tailor, ... and given and willed to me the said Anne Savory by my said husband as appears by his last will and testament," about threescore acres of upland, with the meadow belonging thereto [PCLR 4:311].

BIRTH: By about 1617 (assuming he was at least sixteen when employed in the Plymouth fur trade on the Kennebec).
DEATH: Plymouth between 6 April 1674 (date of will) and 28 January 1675[6] (date of inventory).
MARRIAGE: By about 1645 Ann/Annis _____. She died after 22 March 1677 [PCLR 4:311].
CHILDREN:
- i BENJAMIN SAVORY, b. about March 1645 [MD 5:90-91, 12:133]; living on 2 March 1657[/?8] [MD 12:133]; no further record.
- ii THOMAS SAVORY, b. about March 1648 [MD 3:139-41]; d. at Pawtucket in King Philip's War, 26 March 1676 [TAG 60:241].
- iii MOSES SAVORY, b. Plymouth 22 January 1649[/50] [PCR 8:8]; d. Plymouth 9 June 1650 [PCR 8:10].
- iv SAMUEL SAVORY, b. Plymouth 4 June 1651 [PCR 8:12]; m. by 1678 _____ _____ (eldest known child b. Plymouth 3 July 1678 [PCR 8:67]).
- v JONATHAN SAVORY, b. Plymouth 4 March 1652[/3] [PCR 8:14]; no further record.
- vi MARA SAVORY, b. Plymouth 7 April 1654 [PCR 8:16]; no further record.
- vii ANTHONY SAVORY, b. say 1656; living on 22 March 1677 [PCLR 4:311]; no further record. (In his article of 1887 A.W. Savary thought that this Anthony was the one who married on 2 February 1703 Margaret Price [NEHGR 41:382], but in 1893, "according to my more mature

opinion," he decided that this groom must be of a later generation, son of Samuel [Savery Fam 26].)

viii AARON SAVORY, b. say 1658; living on 22 March 1677 [PCLR 4:311]; no further record (unless he is the Aaron Savery whose will was proved in Bristol County in 1717 [BrPR 3:359; NEHGR 41:380]).

ASSOCIATIONS: Probably related to ANTHONY SAVORY who was present in Plymouth from 1632 to 1642.

Either Thomas Savory or his wife was related to SAMUEL EDDY [PM 194] (see his sketch for further discussion).

COMMENTS: Thomas Savory was a member of the Plymouth party, led by JOHN HOWLAND [PM 279], involved in the fur trade on the Kennebec in 1634 when JOHN HOCKING [PM 261] and Moses Talbot were killed [MD 2:11].

On 4 October 1636, "Tho[mas] Savery [was] found guilty of drunkenness, & [the jury] thought meet he should be whipped" [PCR 1:44]. On 7 March 1659/60, "Thomas Savory, for being drunk, fined five shillings" [PCR 3:181].

On 3 November 1653, John Shaw Sr. of Plymouth and Alice Shaw his wife agreed with "Thomas Savory and Annis Savory his wife" that they would take "their son Beniamine" until the age of twenty-one "he being nine years old in March next," and if John Shaw or Alice Shaw should die before the end of this term of years, then Benjamin would go with their son Jonathan Shaw, who would teach him a trade and also teach him to read and write; the agreement was terminated on 4 March 1657[/8] [MD 5:90-91, citing PCLR 2:1:91]. On 2 March 1657[/8], Thomas Savory of Plymouth and Stephen Bryant Sr. of Plymouth agreed that Bryant would take "his son Benjamine Savory" as a servant until age twenty-one "he being thirteen years old this present month" [MD 12:133, citing PCLR 2:1:207].

On 2 August 1653, "Thomas Savory Senior of Plymouth and Ann his wife" agreed with Thomas Lettice of Plymouth, carpenter, "that their son Thomas Savory Junior aged five years or thereabouts on the 15th day of March last past" would stay with Lettice until the age of twenty-one, to be instructed in carpentry [MD 3:139-41, citing PCLR 2:1:71].

On 7 May 1661, "Ann, the wife of Thomas Savory, was presented before the Court to answer for being at home on the Lord's day with Thomas Lucas at unreasonable time, viz:, in the time of public exercise in the worship of God, and for being found drunk at the same time under an hedge, in uncivil and beastly manner, was sentenced by the Court as followeth, viz: for her accompanying of the said Lucas at an unreasonable time as aforesaid, she was sentenced to sit in the stocks during the pleasure of the Court, which accordingly was performed and executed; and for her being found drunk as aforesaid, fined five shillings; and for prophaning the Lord's day, fined ten shillings, according to the laws in such cases provided" [PCR 3:212].

On 1 March 1663/4, "Richard Willis and Joseph Savery [were] fined 3s. 4d. for breaking the peace towards each other" [PCR 4:50]. A.W. Savary thought that this was another son of Thomas [NEHGR 41:380], but based on this single isolated record, we can only say this is a possibility.

Reasonable evidence is available for the ages of all the children except Anthony and Aaron. They are placed here as the youngest, but they might possibly have been the eldest. Thomas Savory's request that his widow have special regard for Aaron might mean that he was in some way incapacitated.

Thomas Savory and his wife were from time to time in trouble with the courts, and he was never a freeman, yet he was for many years entrusted with the duties of undermarshal. This may tell us as much about the nature of that office as it does about the character of Thomas Savory.

BIBLIOGRAPHIC NOTE: In 1887 A.W. Savary published a lengthy article on "The Savery Families of America" [NEHGR 41:369ff.] and in 1893 he followed this up with a book on the family, which in its early sections differed little from the article six years earlier [*A Genealogical and Biographical Record of the Savery Families (Savory and Savary) and of the Severy Family (Severit, Savery, Savory, and Savary)* ... (Boston 1893), cited above as Savery Fam]. Stratton also gives a detailed account of this immigrant [Stratton 348-50].

RICHARD SEARS

ORIGIN: Unknown.
MIGRATION: 1633.
FIRST RESIDENCE: Plymouth.
REMOVES: Marblehead by 1637, Yarmouth by 1639.

OCCUPATION: Husbandman.

FREEMAN: Oath of fidelity at Yarmouth, 1639 [PCR 8:185]. Propounded for freemanship, 3 June 1652 [PCR 3:7]. Admitted a freeman, 7 June 1653 [PCR 3:31]. In the Yarmouth sections of the 1658 and 29 May 1670 lists of freemen [PCR 5:274, 8:200].

EDUCATION: His inventory included "1 Great Bible and other books" valued at £1 3s. [PCPR 3:2:54]

OFFICES: Deputy for Yarmouth to Plymouth General Court, 3 June 1662 [PCR 4:14].

Plymouth grand jury, 7 June 1652 [PCR 3:9].

Yarmouth assessor, 1 March 1658/9 [PCR 3:155]. Constable, 6 June 1660 [PCR 3:188].

In Yarmouth section of 1643 Plymouth Colony list of men able to bear arms [PCR 8:194].

ESTATE: Assessed 9s. in Plymouth tax list of 25 March 1633 [PCR 1:11]. Not included in the list of 27 March 1634.

On 1 January 1637/8, "Richard Seeres" was included in a Salem tax list for the "inhabitants of Marblehead" [STR 1:63]. On 14 November 1638, "Rich[ard] Sears" was granted four acres at Marblehead "where he had planted formerly" [STR 1:74].

On 23 November 1664, "Allis Bradford the widow of William Bradford" sold to "Richard Sares" of Yarmouth, husbandman, two tracts of twenty acres each "at a place commonly called ... Sasuet," one of which had been the lot of William Bradford deceased and the other of which had been the lot of Experience Mitchell [MD 34: 23, citing PCLR 3:18].

In his will, dated 10 May 1667 and proved 5 March 1675/6, "Richard Sares of Yarmouth" bequeathed to "Sylas Sares my younger son ... all my land, that is all the upland upon the Neck where his house stands in which he now dwells ... after mine and my wife's decease," provided that "my son-in-law Zachery Paddock" shall have the house where he dwells and two acres within the above tract "during the life of Deborah his now wife"; also to "the said Sylas Sares" a tract of meadow and half of "my land called Robins as is undivided"; to "my elder son Paule Sares all the rest and remains of my lands whatsoever"; to "Dorothy my wife" all lands and goods during her natural life, she to be sole executrix, and "do entreat my brother Thacher with his two sons as friends in trust" as overseers; to "my son-in-law Zachery Paddock" two acres from land called Robins before it is divided between Silas and Paul Sears, and this two acres, along with the two acres mentioned above, to go to Ichabod Paddock, son of Zachary, at the death of Zachary's wife; in the codicil, dated 3 February 1675/6, Richard Sears bequeathed to "my eldest son

Paul Sares ... the house which I now live in" and various moveables; on 5 March 1675/6, "John Thacher" deposed that "myself and my brother" witnessed the codicil, and that when "my uncle signed this appendix, ... he asked me to new draw the whole will and to leave out of the new draft the legacy of land that is give to Ichabod Paddock, for saith he I have answered it in another way," but Thacher never did produce this new draft [PCPR 3:2:53-54].

The inventory of the estate of "Richard Sares," taken 8 October 1676 and presented at court on 15 November 1676 by "Dorethy Sares the relict of Richard Sares and Paul Sares his eldest son," was untotalled; the real estate was "his house and lands," valued at £220 [PCPR 3:2:55; PCR 5:213].

BIRTH: About 1595 (based on age at death).
DEATH: Yarmouth 5 September [1676] "age 81y 4m" [YarVR 126].
MARRIAGE: By about 1637 Dorothy Jones. She was born about 1603, daughter of George and Agnes (_____) Jones of Dinder, Somerset [TAG 58:244-46]. "Cady [i.e., Goody] Seares was buried the 19th of March [16]78[/9]" at Yarmouth [YarVR 125].
CHILDREN:
    i   PAUL, b. about 1637 (d. Yarmouth 20 February 1707/8 in 70th year [gravestone]); m. by 1659 Deborah _____ (eldest known child aged thirteen on 3 July 1672 [YarVR 1]). (She may be daughter of George Willard.)
    ii   DEBORAH, b. about 1639 (d. Yarmouth 17 August 1732 "within about one month of 93 years of age" [YarVR 155]); m. by 1661 Zachariah Paddock (eldest known child aged seventeen on 2 February 1678 [YarVR 6]).
    iii   SILAS, b. say 1641; m. by about 1665 Anna _____, probably daughter of James Bursell of Yarmouth (on 1 November 1676, "widow Emett Bursell" and "Silas Saers" were granted administration on the estate of "James Bursell of Yarmouth," the court having agreed that "his three daughters are joint heirs thereof" [PCR 5:212]).
ASSOCIATIONS: Dorothy (Jones) Sears, wife of Richard, was sister of RICHARD JONES {1635, Dorchester} and of Elizabeth (Jones) Thatcher, wife of ANTHONY THATCHER {1635, Newbury} [TAG 58:244-46].

COMMENTS: Although the earliest record of Richard Sears in Marblehead is in 1637, he may have moved there as early as 1634, since he is in the 1633 Plymouth tax list, but not in the list of 1634.

On 2 October 1650, with a large number of other men, "Richard Seares" brought an action against William Nickerson for slander [PCR 7:50].

BIBLIOGRAPHIC NOTE: Various publications of the middle of the nineteenth century set forth an English pedigree for Richard Sears, and partly on the basis of this pedigree assigned to Richard Sears a son Knyvett Sears. In 1886 Samuel Pearce May carefully examined and analyzed this pedigree and found it to have no merit; he further demonstrated that the proposed son Knyvett did not exist [NEHGR 40:261-68]. Four years later May published a genealogy of the family [*The Descendants of Richard Sares (Sears) of Yarmouth, Mass., 1638-1888* (Albany 1890)].

In 1948 Donald Lines Jacobus prepared a brief account of the family of Richard Sears [Brainerd Anc 257-58].

EDWARD SHAW

On 3 January 1632/3, William Bennett, in suing Edward Doty, stated that he had "employed the servant of the said Edward one month in sawing of boards with Edw[ard] Shaw" [PCR 1:7].

William Corvannel (Corrannell, Cornelly) charged "Edward Shawe of Ducksborrow" with stealing 15s., as a result of which, on 4 December 1637, Shaw was required to put up bond of £40, with Thomas Clark as his surety, and, on 2 January 1637/8, he was found guilty and sentenced to be whipped and branded on the shoulder [PCR 1:68, 69, 74]. Mark Mendlove was indicted and convicted as Shaw's accessory. On the same day that Shaw was convicted, William Corvannel was indicted for receiving back from Shaw the money supposedly stolen, prior to Shaw's trial, and not informing the court [PCR 1:75].

On 2 July 1638, Richard Clough was charged by Thomas Clark with stealing cloth from Edward Shaw [PCR 1:91-92].

On 3 December 1638, "Edward Shaw is hired with Roberte Bartlett for a year from the first of December 1638 for £8 10s. sterling, to be paid in money" [PCR 1:104].

COMMENTS: In 1633 Edward Shaw was apparently a servant of William Bennett, just as the latter was leaving Plymouth Colony. In 1638 Shaw became servant of Robert Bartlett. The association with Thomas Clark in the interim suggests that Shaw may have been Clark's servant during that period.

Since Edward Shaw was associated with MARK MENDLOVE [PM 318], and since Shaw is not seen in New England records after 1638, it may be that he followed Mendlove's example and removed to a more southerly colony [TAG 61:71-76].

Savage, citing earlier authorities, suggested that Edward Shaw of Duxbury might be the same as the Edward Shaw who later appeared at Saco. This is possible, but there is no direct evidence for or against this hypothesis.

JOHN SHAW

ORIGIN: Unknown.
MIGRATION: 1627.
FIRST RESIDENCE: Plymouth.

OCCUPATION: Planter.
FREEMAN: In 1633 Plymouth Colony list among those admitted before 1 January 1632/3 [PCR 1:3]. In list of 7 March 1636/7 [PCR 1:52]. In Plymouth sections of Plymouth Colony lists of freemen of 1639 and 1658 [PCR 8:174, 197].
EDUCATION: He made his mark to deeds.
OFFICES: Plymouth petit jury, 4 September 1638, 1 June 1641, 6 September 1641, 3 May 1642, 5 March 1643/4, 5 June 1644, 3 October 1648, 4 October 1648 (as "John Shaw Senior"), 29 October 1649 [PCR 2:134, 7:9, 20, 23, 29, 37, 43, 46]. Coroner's jury, 22 July 1648 [PCR 2:132].

Plymouth highway surveyor (for Jones River), 7 March 1642/3, 5 June 1644 (as "John Shawe Senior") [PCR 2:53, 72].

In 1643 Plymouth list of men able to bear arms (followed in order by his sons James and John and his son-in-law Stephen Bryant) [PCR 8:187].
ESTATE: In 1627 Plymouth cattle division, first person in sixth company [PCR 12:11].

On 8 July 1630, John Winslow sold to John Shaw "all his arable land that is lying in that tract of land that is commonly called Knave's Acre otherwise named Woodbee"; part of the consideration was "all the meadow ground that butteth at the upper end of the said arable land" [PCR 12:15].

Assessed 18s. in 25 March 1633 Plymouth tax list and 9s. in 27 March 1634 list [PCR 1:10, 28]. He was one of the purchasers [PCR 2:177].

On 14 January 1636/7, "John Shaw is allowed to enlarge at the end of his lot lying at Black Brooke" [PCR 1:48]. On 2 October 1637, "John Shaw" was one of three men "to have enlargement of lands next unto the lands abutting above their lots at Playne Dealing, to the northward" [PCR 1:65], and these are probably the same lots referred to on 2 April 1638 and 4 February 1638/9 [PCR 1:82, 112]. On 2 April 1640, "John Shawe of Plymouth, planter," sold to William Kemp of Duxbury two acres and a half of meadow [PCR 12:57]. On 17 October 1642, he received four acres of meadow at North Meadow by Jones River [PCR 2:49].

On 3 November 1653, John Shaw Sr. and Alice Shaw his wife agreed with Thomas Savory and Annis Savory his wife, all of New Plymouth, that the Savorys' son, Benjamin, aged nine years old, would live with the Shaws until he was twenty-one, and the Shaws would pay him £5 at the end of his service, and if John or Alice died, Benjamin was to serve out his time with Jonathan Shaw, the son of John Shaw, and Jonathan was to teach him a trade, writing and reading, and give him two suits of apparel [MD 5:90-91, citing PCLR 2:1:91]. On 4 March 1657[/8], Jonathan was cleared of this engagement by mutual consent of all the persons "that are now alive" (reflecting the fact that Alice had died in the interim) [MD 5:91].

On 28 December 1653, Mr. John Winslow of Plymouth sold to John Shaw Sr. of Plymouth, planter, a two-acre parcel of marsh meadow in Green Harbor Marsh [MD 5:91-92, citing PCLR 2:1:91].

On 31 December 1656, John Shaw Sr. of Plymouth deeded to "my son Jonathan Shaw all that my house and land I am now possessed of and live upon in the township of Plymouth aforesaid containing twenty and five acres of upland ... provided ... I reserve an interest in my orchard during my life and at my decease to be my said son Jonathan's ... reserve unto myself liberty to employ or improve some small spot of upland for the planting of tobacco ... during my life ... [also] unto my said son Jonathan all my meadow land fresh or salt in any place belonging to me, in particular three acres of marsh meadow bought of Mr. John Winslow ... and six acres more or less of fresh meadow lying on the south arm of Joanes River ... one-quarter part of my purchase land" [MD 10:33-34, citing PCLR 2:1:186].

On 26 March 1658, John Shaw Sr. of Plymouth, planter, deeded to "his son Sergeant James Shaw of New Plymouth ... all the one-half of his land at Coaksett or Cushena ... provided that in case John Shaw the son of the said John Shaw Senior shall come within the term of four years beginning from the first of March 1657 and from that time fully to be expired that then the said John Shaw Jr. shall have the one-half of that half of the land given unto James Shaw aforesaid" [MD 10:34-35, citing PCLR 2:1:206].

On 30 January 1663[/4], John Shaw Sr. of Plymouth deeded to "my son-in-law Stephen Bryant of Plymouth ... all that my whole share of land allotted unto me near unto Namassakett ... also ... another portion of land called by the name of Rehoboth ... formerly granted unto me lying upon the south side of the Smelt River ... be it forty acres more or less"; to "my son James Shaw the one half of my purchase land at Cushena, and the one-fourth part of my said lot at Cushena I give unto my son Jonathan Shaw, and the other fourth part of my said Purchase lands to my son-in-law Stephen Bryant ... also my purpose and will is that my daughter Abigaill Bryant after my decease shall have my bed and all the furniture thereunto belonging, as also my chest with whatsoever else doth any ways appertain to me" [MD 10:35, citing PCLR 3:57].

BIRTH: By about 1597 (based on estimated date of marriage).
DEATH: After 30 January 1663[/4] [MD 10:35].
MARRIAGE: By 3 November 1653 [MD 5:90-91] (and by about 1622 if she was the mother of his children) Alice _____. She died at Plymouth on 6 March 1654/5 [PCR 8:17; PVR 661].
CHILDREN:
With first wife
   i   JOHN SHAW, b. by about 1622 (bought land 1643 [PCR 12:91]); apparently still living on 26 March 1658 [MD 10:34-35], but presumed to be dead on 30 January 1663[/4] when his brother James received the double portion due to the eldest son [MD 10:35].
   ii   ABIGAIL SHAW, b. say 1626; m. by about 1647 Stephen Bryant (eldest known child b. by about 1647 [NEHGR 153:426]).
   iii   JAMES SHAW, b. say 1627; m. Plymouth 24 December 1652 Mary Mitchell [PCR 8:14], daughter of EXPERIENCE MITCHELL [PM 324].
   iv   JONATHAN SHAW, b. say 1631; m. (1) Plymouth 22 January 1656/7 Phebe Watson [PCR 8:17], daughter of GEORGE

WATSON [PM 483]; m. (2) August 1683 Persis (Dunham) Pratt, daughter of JOHN DUNHAM [PM 182] and widow of Benajah Pratt [TAG 30:145].

COMMENTS: On 1 July 1633, Plymouth Court ordered that "unless Mr. Gilson, John Shaw, & the rest that undertook the cutting of the passage between Green's Harbour & the bay finish it before the first of October next ensuing, according to covenant, they be amerced in ten pounds; but if any of them will do it, the fine be exacted of the rest, & they paid for their labor" [PCR 1:13].

John Shaw brought several actions against his Plymouth neighbors for trespass, 3 March 1639/40, 1 September 1640 [PCR 7:15, 18]. Kenelm Winslow and Mr. William Hanbury brought actions against Shaw, 7 December 1641 and 7 September 1642, respectively [PCR 7:24, 31].

BIBLIOGRAPHIC NOTE: In 1997 Jonathan A. Shaw published a comprehensive account of this immigrant and his descendants to the fourth generation [NEHGR 151:259-85, 417-37].

WILLIAM SHERMAN

ORIGIN: Unknown.
MIGRATION: 1632.
FIRST RESIDENCE: Plymouth.
REMOVES: Duxbury by 1638, Marshfield by 1644.

OCCUPATION: Yeoman.
FREEMAN: In list of those in Duxbury who took the oath of fidelity in 1639 [PCR 8:182].
EDUCATION: Signed his deeds by mark.
OFFICES: Plymouth grand jury, 3 June 1657 [PCR 3:115].

Duxbury highway surveyor, 5 June 1644 [PCR 2:72]. Marshfield highway surveyor, 7 June 1652 [PCR 3:9].

In Duxbury section of 1643 Plymouth list of men able to bear arms [PCR 8:189]. (Toward the end of the Marshfield section of this same list is an entry for "[blank] Sherman," who may be this same William who moved to Marshfield in 1643 or 1644 [PCR 8:196].)
ESTATE: Assessed 9s. in the Plymouth tax list of 25 March 1633 [PCR 1:11], but absent from the list of 27 March 1634.

On 17 November 1637, James Davis of Plymouth, sailor, sold to William Sherman of Plymouth "all that his lot of lands lying near the lands granted to Mr. John Weekes containing by estimation five acres" [PCR 12:24].

On 5 February 1637/8, "Will[ia]m Sherman is granted a garden place on Ducksborrow side, & five acres of lands at Pouder Poynt, if it can be there had" [PCR 1:76]. On 1 April 1639, William Sherman requested land [PCR 1:120]. On 6 April 1640, William Sherman "is granted a meadstead about the Stony Brooke, in Duxborrow, and the said Will[ia]m & John Washborne to have such accommodations of land as may be spared in the place where they desire" [PCR 1:145]. On 1 June 1640, along with six other men, he was granted four acres in Duxbury [PCR 1:153]. On 2 November 1640, he was granted "twenty acres, his houselot to be part thereof, ... northward from Duxborrow Mill, towards Greens Harbour" [PCR 1:165].

On 4 June 1648, "[d]ifferences depending between William Sherman and John Barker about the bounds of their lands, the Court do appoint and request Captain Myles Standish and Mr. Aldin, and to be accompanied with Joshua Prat, to set at right such differences as are betwixt them" [PCR 2:127-28].

On 3 June 1662, William Sherman was one of the "servants and others that are ancient freemen" who were granted land by the General Court [PCR 4:18].

On 9 June 1673, William Sherman Senior of Marshfield, yeoman, deeded to "my natural son Samuell Sherman" of Marshfield a parcel of land and meadow "whereon I now dwell" together with "one half or moiety of the marsh and meadow land appertaining to my said lot" [PCLR 4:88]. On 5 February 1673[/4?], William Sherman Senior of Marshfield, planter, deeded to "my natural and well beloved son John Sherman of Marshfield ... all my right ... unto one share of a certain parcel or tract of land lying and being at and near Saconett" [PCLR 4:408]. On 15 August 1676, William Sherman Senior of Marshfield deeded to "my natural and well beloved son William Sherman of Marshfield ... all that my dwelling house and land ... upland and meadow" in Marshfield [PCLR 4:167].

BIRTH: By about 1613 (based on date of marriage).
DEATH: Buried Marshfield 25 October 1679 [MarVR 9].
MARRIAGE: 23 January 1638[/9] Prudence Hill [PCR 1:110].

CHILDREN:
    i   WILLIAM SHERMAN, b. say 1642; m. Marshfield 25 December 1667 Desire Doty [MarVR 10], daughter of EDWARD DOTY [PM 177].
    ii   SAMUEL SHERMAN, b. say 1644; m. (1) by about 1674 Sarah Doggett, daughter of THOMAS DOGGETT {1637, Concord} (in his will of 20 January 1689, Thomas Doggett bequeathed to "daughter Sarah Sherman's children" [Gen Adv 3:90, citing PPR 1:154]); m. (2) by 1688 Hannah _____ (eldest known child b. Marshfield 20 February 1688[/9] [MD 9:183]).
    iii   JOHN SHERMAN, b. Marshfield 23 February 164(6) [MarVR 2] (d. Marshfield 5 November 1723, aged 77 [MD 13:110]); m. Boston 25 October 1677 Jane Hatch [MarVR 16], daughter of Walter Hatch [Joseph Neal Anc 120-21].
    iv   Daughter SHERMAN, b. say 1648; m. by 1666 Edward Stephens (eldest known child b. Marshfield 18 December 1666 [MarVR 6]; in a deed of 19 May 1688, Samuel Sherman refers to "a parcel of upland formerly granted & given by my father W[illia]m Sherman deceased unto his grandson W[illia]m Stevens of Marshfield" [PLR 8:39]; in his will of 2 November 1689, Edward Stephens makes "my loving brother John Sherman" his overseer [PPR 1:59]).

COMMENTS: William Sherman appears on the tax list of 25 March 1633, but not in the list of 27 March 1634, and not in any other Plymouth Colony record for the next five years. This might be interpreted in a number of ways, including the possibilities that William Sherman returned to England, or that we are dealing with two different men of the same name. Were the gap much greater than five years, we would lean toward the latter solution, but in the absence of further evidence have concluded that only one William Sherman is represented by these records. This conclusion is reinforced by the colony grant of land to William Sherman as one of the "servants and others that are ancient freemen."

On 5 March 1638/9, William Sherman was presented "for drinking tobacco contrary to order" [PCR 1:118].

A William Sherman is mentioned in the records of the Massachusetts Bay Company on 26 February 1628/9 [MBCR 1:25], and some have thought that this might be the immigrant to Plymouth. It is more likely, however, that the William Sherman of the 1628/9 record was one of the many tradesmen supplying goods for the ships bound for Salem, rather than being himself an immigrant.

BIBLIOGRAPHIC NOTE: A comprehensive and well-documented account of the family of William Sherman was published in 1936 by Mary Lovering Holman [*Descendants of William Sherman of Marshfield, Massachusetts* (Brookline, Massachusetts, 1936)].

MOSES SIMONSON

ORIGIN: Leiden, Holland.
MIGRATION: 1621 on the *Fortune*.
FIRST RESIDENCE: Plymouth.
REMOVES: Duxbury.

OCCUPATION: Yeoman.
CHURCH MEMBERSHIP: "Moses Symonson, because a child of one that was in communion with the Dutch church at Leyden, is admitted into church fellowship at Plymouth in New England, and his children also to baptism, as well as our own" [Young's Pilgrim Fathers 393].
FREEMAN: In 1633 Plymouth list of freemen after those admitted 1 January 1634/5 [PCR 1:4]. In the list of 7 March 1636/7 [PCR 1:53]. In the Duxbury sections of the Plymouth Colony lists of freemen of 1639, 1658, 29 May 1670 and early 1683/4 [PCR 5:275, 8:175, 198, 203].
EDUCATION: Signed a number of his deeds, but by 1678 was making his mark.
OFFICES: Plymouth petit jury, 25 October 1668 [PCR 7:150].
 Duxbury highway surveyor, 3 June 1657, 3 June 1662 [PCR 3:116, 4:15].
 In the Duxbury section of the 1643 Plymouth Colony list of men able to bear arms [PCR 8:189].
ESTATE: In the 1623 Plymouth land division "Moyses Simonson & Philipe de la Noye" jointly received two acres [PCR 12:5]. In the 1627 Plymouth cattle division Moses Simonson was the eighth person in the first company (headed by Francis Cooke) [PCR 12:9].
 On 26 March 1628, Moses Simonson sold one acre to Robert Hicks [PCR 12:7].
 "Moses Symons" was assessed 9s. in Plymouth tax lists of 25 March 1633 and 27 March 1634 [PCR 1:11, 28].

On 13 December 1660, "Moses Simons of Duxburrow ... with the consent of my wife Sarah" sold to "Nicholas Byram of Weymouth ... my whole right of lands in Bridgwater town" [MD 34:85, citing PCLR 3:24].

On 3 June 1662, Moses Simonson was twenty-fifth on the list of those granted land "as being the first born children of the government," receiving two tracts of land [PCR 4:19].

On 31 October 1664, "Moses Symons of Scittuate" sold to Joseph Coleman Sr. of Scituate, shoemaker, half of forty acres of land at Coaksett which was sometimes the land of "my father Moses Symons of Duxburrow"; acknowledged by Patience, wife of Moses Symons Jr. [PCLR 3:183].

On 20 April 1669, "Moses Simons" of Duxbury, planter, deeded to "John Simons his true and natural son all that his dwelling house, outhouses and buildings, land, meadow and upland, orchards and gardens" in Duxbury, containing forty acres of upland and three acres of meadow, "with two acres of meadow ... at little wood island in the great marsh" [PCLR 3:139]. On 30 December 1674, "Moses Simons of Duxburrow ..., yeoman, ... in consideration of a marriage heretofore consummated between John Soule of Duxburrow aforesaid and my eldest daughter Rebeckah," deeded to them "all my purchased lands at Namaskett" [MD 19:96, citing PCLR 4:43]. On 4 December 1678, "Moses Simmons Senior" of Duxbury, yeoman, deeded to "my son Aron Simmons" of Scituate "all that my one-half share of land, with upland and meadow lands divided and undivided ... that I have as a purchaser or old comer" in Dartmouth [PCLR 4:219].

In his will, dated 17 June 1689 and proved 15 September 1691, "Moses Simmons" bequeathed to "my daughter Mary the wife of Joseph Alden," £4; to "my son Aaron," £4; to "my daughter Elizabeth now the wife of Richard Dwelley," 5s.; to "my daughter Sarah now the wife of James Nash," £2 10s.; to "my son John," £4, he to be executor [MD 31:60, citing PPR 1:106].

The inventory of the estate of Moses Simmons, taken 10 September 1691, totalled £33 11s., with no real estate included [MD 31:60, citing PPR 1:107].

BIRTH: By about 1605 (assuming that he was a young servant when he arrived in New England).
DEATH: Between 17 June 1689 (date of will) and 10 September 1691 (date of inventory).
MARRIAGE: By about 1637 Sarah _____ (and certainly by 13 December 1660 [MD 34:85]).

CHILDREN:
  i REBECCA SIMONSON, b. say 1637 (called "eldest daughter" by father); m. by 1657 John Soule (eldest known child, Rebecca (Soule) Weston, d. Plympton 18 November 1732 "in her 76th year"), son of GEORGE SOULE [PM 432].
  ii MOSES SIMONSON, b. say 1639; m. by 1664 Patience Barstow (by 27 July 1664, "Will[i]am Barstow Senior of Scittuate" had given to "my son Moses Simons" a small tract of land [PCR 4:68-69]), daughter of WILLIAM BARSTOW {1635, Watertown} [GM 2:1:174-80].
  iii MARY SIMONSON, b. say 1641; m. by about 1660 Joseph Alden, son of JOHN ALDEN [PM 4; MD 31:60].
  iv JOHN SIMONSON, b. say 1644; m. Duxbury 16 November 1669 Mercy Pabodie, daughter of William Pabodie [MF 16:1:59-61] and granddaughter of JOHN ALDEN [PM 4].
  v SARAH SIMONSON, b. say 1649; m. by 1669 James Nash (eldest known child b. Weymouth 21 April 1669).
  vi ELIZABETH SIMONSON, b. say 1651; m. after 1673 [PCR 5:116] and before 1689 Richard Dwelly (father's will).
  vii AARON SIMONSON, b. say 1653; m. Scituate 24 December 1677 Mary Woodworth, daughter of WALTER WOODWORTH [PM 521].

ASSOCIATIONS: In the land division of 1623 Moses Simonson was paired with PHILIP DELANO [PM 164] in a grant of land, suggesting that they may have come together from Leiden.

There was a THOMAS SYMONS [PM 457] in Plymouth by 1633, and several authors have attempted to squeeze him into the family of Moses Simonson, but there is no evidence that he belongs. The most egregious attempt in this direction was perpetrated in 1935 by Raymon Meyers Tingley, who fabricated documents, including an alleged deposition made by Thomas, and managed to make Thomas both son and brother of Moses [Tingley-Meyers 371-72].

COMMENTS: On 3 June 1673, Richard Sutton of Roxbury brought suit against "Moses Symonds," Sarah his wife, and Elizabeth their daughter, saying that Elizabeth had promised to marry him, but her parents prevented it. The court refused the engagement but ordered "Symonds" to pay Sutton £3 [PCR 5:116].

Pope included in the sketch of the immigrant an abstract of the will of his son Moses, who predeceased his father.

BIBLIOGRAPHIC NOTE: In 2004 Jeremy D. Bangs published a number of intriguing records for the family of Simon Mosesz. of Leiden and explored the possibility that he might be father of the subject of this sketch. Although such a connection is possible, it is far from proven [NEA 5:3:54-55].

JOHN SMALLEY

ORIGIN: Unknown.
MIGRATION: 1632 on the *William & Francis* [Hotten 149].
FIRST RESIDENCE: Plymouth.
REMOVES: Eastham 1645, Piscataway by 1670.

OCCUPATION: Tailor. "Memorandum, the last day of August, 1639, that Richard Higgens for & in consideration that John Smalley shall teach Samuell Godbertson the trade of a tailor, as far as in him lieth, & principally employ him therein" [PCR 1:129-30].
FREEMAN: Propounded 7 September 1641 as "John Smaley" [PCR 2:24] and admitted 1 March 1641/2 [PCR 2:33]. (His name appears toward the end of the Plymouth section of the 1639 Plymouth Colony list of freemen, presumably added upon his admission to freemanship in 1642, then is crossed out and appears again in the Eastham section [PCR 8:174, 177].) In the Eastham section of the 1658 Plymouth Colony list of freemen [PCR 8:201].
EDUCATION: He signed a deed and as a witness to the deeds of others.
OFFICES: Plymouth coroner's jury, 5 June 1638 [PCR 1:88, 4:176]. Grand jury, 6 June 1654, 6 June 1660, 7 June 1665 [PCR 3:49, 188, 4:91]. Petit jury, 7 June 1642, 7 March 1642/3, 6 June 1643, 5 March 1643/4, 8 June 1654, 2 October 1662, 5 June 1666 [PCR 7:31, 34, 35, 37, 70, 105, 4:125].

Eastham constable, 1 June 1647 [PCR 2:115]. Surveyor of highways, 6 June 1649 [PCR 2:139].

In the Plymouth section of the 1643 Plymouth Colony list of men able to bear arms [PCR 8:188].

Piscataway magistrate, 26 August 1673 [Small Gen 1:28].
ESTATE: On 5 February 1637/8, he was granted a garden place at Willingsly and seven acres of land on Woberry Plaine [PCR 1:76]. On 2 July 1638, mention is made of his request, with three others, for swamp land at Willingsby Brooke [PCR 1:90].

On 11 June 1640, John Smalley and Richard Higgens exchanged two parcels of meadow of one acre each [PCR 12:59].

On 2 November 1640, "John Smaley" was granted five acres in the south meadows [PCR 1:166]. On 31 December 1641, he was granted five acres of meadow in Cole Brooke Meadow [PCR 2:30].

On 21 March 1644[/5], John Smalley sold to Edmond Tilson all his house and housing and garden place at Wellingsly with the uplands, all his meadow at Warren's Wells and Colebrook meadows [PCR 12:108].

On 1 June 1658, "John Smally" was one of five named men (along with others unnamed) granted "a portion of land ... lying betwixt Bridgwater and Waymouth" [PCR 3:142]. On 3 June 1662, he was on the list of "servants and ancient freemen" to have land [PCR 4:18]. On 3 October 1662, he was one of those to be considered, with others, for land on the northerly bounds of Taunton [PCR 4:27].

In the Piscataqua section of the 1685 East Jersey quitrent roll, "Jno. Smalley Senior" held 118½ acres, having received a patent in 1675 [page 7].

On 16 July 1689, John Smalley of Piscataway "in consideration of the natural affection and fatherly consideration I have & bear unto my well beloved and dutiful son Isaac Smallee of the same ... having had large experience of his filial love and endeavors towards his aged parents in making our lives comfortable to us in this our pilgrimage hitherto ... grant and confirm unto my said son Isaac Smalley all & singular my goods chattels, debts, household stuff, brass, pewter, bedding ... excepting my arms (viz:) my sword & gun & my wearing apparel, which I have given to my son John Smalley after my decease, to my daughter Hanah Banges 1s., to my son John Smallie's two sons John & Jonathan one yearling heifer between them, and to my daughter Mary Snowe's three eldest daughters 5s. apiece ... my loving wife Ann Smallie shall have one cow to dispose of according to her will & pleasure ... if the said Isaac Smally should die before his said father & mother John & Ann Smally or the longer liver of them both, then it shall or may be lawful, and the said John & Ann Smally or either of them hath full power & authority to reenter and to take into their possession & custody & dispose of any of the goods & chattells above mentioned" [Small Gen 1:29-31, citing East Jersey LR F:395-97]. This testamentary deed was "proved" 23 June 1697.

BIRTH: By about 1613 (based on date of marriage).
DEATH: Piscataway 30 July 1692 [Small Gen 1:29 (source not cited)].

MARRIAGE: Plymouth 29 November 1638 Ann Walden [PCR 1:103]. She died at Piscataway on 29 January 1693/4 [NJHSP 4:4:42].

CHILDREN:
- i HANNAH SMALLEY, b. Plymouth 14 June 1641 [PCR 8:27]; m. Eastham 23 January 1660[/1] John Bangs [PCR 8:28], son of EDWARD BANGS [PM 23].
- ii JOHN SMALLEY, b. Plymouth 8 September 1644 [PCR 8:27]; m. Piscataway 18 October 1676 Lydia Marten [NJHSP 4:4:39].
- iii ISAAC SMALLEY (twin), b. Eastham 11 December 1647 [PCR 8:27]; m. (1) Piscataway 20 February 1683/4 Esther Wood [NJHSP 4:4:40]; m. (2) Piscataway 18 March 1702/3 Mary White [NJHSP 4:4:40].
- iv MARY SMALLEY (twin), b. Eastham 11 December 1647 [PCR 8:27]; m. Eastham 19 September 1667 John Snow [MD 7:17], son of NICHOLAS SNOW [PM 428].

ASSOCIATIONS: In 1639 John Smalley took over from RICHARD HIGGINS [PM 249] the apprenticeship of Samuel Godbertson (both men were tailors) [PCR 1:129-30]. The association between Smalley and Higgins continued in 1640 with an exchange of Plymouth land [PCR 12:59]. Both men moved to Eastham and then to Piscataway at about the same times.

COMMENTS: On 28 November 1664, John Smalley brought one gallon of liquor into the town of Eastham [PCR 4:100].

On 5 March 1667/8, a coroner's jury inquired into the death of "a child about five or six years old, which was kept by John Smalley, Senr., of Eastham being found dead in the woods, about six or seven miles from the house of John Smalley abovesaid, we do all judge, that it came by his death by straying away, lost its right path to get home again, and was killed by the cold" [PCR 4:177].

Since John Smalley does not appear in the 1670 Plymouth Colony list of freemen, he had apparently already moved to Piscataway by that date.

JOHN SMITH

25 July 1633: "John Smith hath covenanted to serve John Jenny the full term of seven years, after the manner of an apprentice, beginning the 24 of June, this present year; at the expiration whereof, the said John Jenny

to give him twelve bushels of Indian corn, & twenty-five acres of land" [PCR 1:16].

2 January 1633/4: "whereas John Smith, being in a great extremity formerly, to be freed of the same bound himself as an apprentice to Edward Dowty for the term of ten years, upon the petition of the said John the Court took the matter into hearing, & finding the said Edw[ard] had disbursed but little for him, freed the said John from his covenant of ten years, & bound him to make up the time he had already served the said Edward the full term of five years; and at the end thereof, the said Edward to give him double apparel, & so be free of each other" [PCR 1:23].

COMMENTS: By the terms of their service, these two Plymouth records seem to be for two distinct John Smiths. No evidence allows identification with any later John Smith of New England.

The next man of this name to appear in Plymouth Colony was John Smith, laborer, who married Bennett Morecock on 7 December 1638 [PCR 1:103, 107, 127]; he might be one of the two servants recorded above, but he might also be a third John Smith.

RALPH SMITH

ORIGIN: Unknown.
MIGRATION: 1629.
FIRST RESIDENCE: Nantasket.
REMOVES: Plymouth 1629, Manchester by 1645, Ipswich by 1652, Boston by 1660.

OCCUPATION: Minister. On 17 April 1629, the Governor and Assistants of the Massachusetts Bay Company wrote to John Endicott that "Mr. Raph Smith, a minister, hath desired passage in our [ships], which was granted him before we understood of his difference of judgment in some things from our ministers. But his provisions for his voyage being shipped before notice was taken thereof, through many occasions wherewith those entrusted with this business have been employed, and forasmuch as from hence it is feared there may grow some distraction amongst you if there should be any siding, though we have a very good opinion of his honesty, we shall not, hope, offend in charity to fear the worst that may grow from their different judgments.

We have therefore thought fit to give you this order, that unless he will be conformable to our government, you suffer him not to remain within the limits [our] grant" [MBCR 1:390]. (Perhaps the word "we" has been omitted before the word "hope" above.)

CHURCH MEMBERSHIP: Admitted to Salem church 14 November 1647 (with later annotation of "dismissed" [SChR 12]).

FREEMAN: In 1633 Plymouth list of freemen prior to those admitted 1 January 1632/3 [PCR 1:3]. "Raph Smyth, gen.," in Plymouth list of 7 March 1636/7 [PCR 1:52]. "Mr. Raph Smyth" in Plymouth section of 1639 list of freemen [PCR 8:173].

EDUCATION: Matriculated at Cambridge from Christ's College, July 1610; B.A. 1613-14 [Venn 4:106; Morison 401]. His inventory included "books as the price [on the] first leaf of them appears appraised by Hezekiah Usher Junior" valued at £13 7s., "more found since in books" valued at 16s., and "3 other books" valued at 13s. 4d.

OFFICES: Plymouth representative to committee to revise colony laws, 4 October 1636 [PCR 1:44].

ESTATE: On 1 July 1633, the land mowed by "Mr. Smith" last year was again his to mow [PCR 1:15]. On 14 March 1635/6, "Mr. Smith" was allowed to mow where John Barnes and Kanelm Wynslow mowed last year [PCR 1:40]. On 6 January 1636/7, land enclosed by "Mr. Raph Smyth" was to be used for the setting of corn [PCR 1:50]. He was allowed to mow the hay ground again the next year [PCR 1:56].

On 4 December 1637, "Mr. Raph Smyth and William Fallowell" are to have proportions of land to their houses in Plymouth, out of the lands lying betwixt the town of Plymouth and the new field reserving a portion of the mill there [PCR 1:69]. On 2 November 1640, he received eight acres at Colebrook meadows [PCR 1:166].

On 18 April 1642, "Mr. Raph Smyth" sold to John Doane "all that his house and buildings and garden plots thereunto adjoining scituate in Plymouth together with the six acres of upland lying in the new field" [PCR 12:79-80].

On 15 July 1648, Ralph Smith and Mary Smith "granted to Nathanaiell Masterson our lands in Wellingsley with our house there"; on the same day Nathaniel Masterson refers to the marsh meadow that he "bought of his father-in-law Mr. Smith" [MD 1:136, citing PCLR 2:1:19].

On 10 March 1652, Mr. Ralph Smith occupied land in Ipswich adjacent to land sold by Nathaniel Bishop to John Wyatt [Hammatt Papers 30].

The inventory of the estate of "Mr. Smith," taken 16 April 1661, totalled £37 4s. 4d., with £2 7s. 4d. added later; no real estate was included [SPR 4:14].

On 18 April 1661, administration of the estate of the late Mr. Ralph Smith was granted to "Nathaniell Masterson his late wife's son, that lived a long time with him, and was serviceable to him for the most part of his time" [SPR 4:14].

BIRTH: About 1590 (based on matriculation at Cambridge).
DEATH: At Boston "Mr. Ralph Smith Pastor of the Church of Plymouth died the first of March" 1660/1 [BVR 80].
MARRIAGE: (1) By 1629 _____ _____ [Bradford 222]. She died by 1633.

(2) By 1 July 1633 Mary (Goodall) Masterson, widow of RICHARD MASTERSON [PM 316].
CHILDREN: None recorded. (Bradford tells us that when he arrived he had with him a "wife and family" [Bradford 222]. This may mean that he had children by his first wife; but he also had servants with him, and these would constitute a family, so there need not have been children.)

COMMENTS: Bradford reported that in 1629 there was "one Mr. Ralph Smith and his wife and family that came over into the Bay of the Massachusetts, and sojourned at present with some straggling people that lived at Nantasket. Here being a boat of this place, putting in there on some occasion, he earnestly desired that they would give him and his passage for Plymouth, and some such things as they could well carry, having before heard that there was a likelihood he might procure house room for some time till he should resolve to settle there if he might, or elsewhere as God should dispose, for he was weary of being in that uncouth place and in a poor house that would neither keep him nor his goods dry. So, seeing him to be a grave man and understood he had been a minister, though they had no order for any such thing, yet they presumed and brought him. He was here accordingly kindly entertained and housed, and had the rest of his goods and servants sent for, and exercised his gifts amongst them and afterwards was chosen into the ministry and so remained for sundry years" [Bradford 222-23]. In 1636 Bradford further noted that "[t]his year Mr. Smith laid down his place of ministry, partly by his own willingness as thinking it too heavy a burden, and partly at the desire and by the persuasion of others" [Bradford 292-93]. (See also PChR 63-64, 73.)

In 1632, reporting on church practice at Plymouth, Winthrop says that Mr. Smith was part of the customary discussion in the afternoon, in which Mr. Roger Williams would pose a question to which "the pastor, Mr. Smith, spake briefly" [WJ 1:109]. In 1634 Mr. Bradford, Mr. Winslow and Mr. Smith, their pastor, came to Boston by water to confer with some of our magistrates and ministers about their "case of Kenebeck" (the killing of Moses Talbot and JOHN HOCKING [PM 261]) [WJ 1:162]. In 1635 when Mr. Norton was put by contrary winds into Plymouth, though he had been headed to the Bay, Mr. Smith "gave over his place, that he [Norton] might have it," but Norton would not stay [WJ 1:209].

On 1 September 1640, Ralph Gorham successfully sued Ralph Smith for trespass [PCR 7:17]; on 2 March 1640/1, Ralph Smith successfully sued Ralph Gorham for slander and defamation [PCR 7:19].

About 1645 Winthrop noted that "[t]he village at Jeffry's creek was named Manchester, and the people there (not being yet in church state) had procured Mr. Smith (sometimes pastor of the church of Plimouth) to preach to them" [WJ 2:310].

NICHOLAS SNOW

ORIGIN: Unknown.
MIGRATION: 1623 on the *Anne*.
FIRST RESIDENCE: Plymouth.
REMOVES: Eastham.

OCCUPATION: Carpenter (his inventory begins with a long list of "cooper's tools" and "carpenter's tools & other things" [MD 3:169-70]).
FREEMAN: In 1633 Plymouth list of freemen, in close proximity to those admitted on 1 January 1632/3 [PCR 1:4]. In list of 7 March 1636/7 [PCR 1:52]. In Plymouth section of 1639 Plymouth Colony list of freemen, then erased and moved to Eastham section of list [PCR 8:174, 177]. In Eastham sections of Plymouth Colony lists of freemen of 1658 and 29 May 1670 [PCR 5:278, 8:201].
EDUCATION: His inventory included "a parcel of old books" valued at 4s., "a psalm book" valued at 1s. and "1 book" valued at 1s. [MD 3:172, 173].
OFFICES: Deputy for Eastham to the Plymouth Colony General Court, 7 June 1648, 4 June 1650, 3 June 1652, 3 June 1657 [PCR 2:123, 154, 3:9, 115].

Plymouth petit jury, 2 October 1637, 6 March 1637/8, 3 March 1639/40, 1 September 1640, 1 June 1641, 3 August 1641, 7 March 1642/3, 6 June 1643 [PCR 7:7, 8, 16, 17, 20, 23, 34, 35]. Grand jury, 5 June 1638 [PCR 1:87]. Coroner's jury, 5 June 1638 [PCR 1:88].

Committee to lay out highways, 23 July 1634, 1 February 1640/1 [PCR 1:31, 2:7]. Committee to lay out lands, 5 May 1640 [PCR 1:151].

Plymouth surveyor of highways, 3 March 1639/40, 2 June 1640 [PCR 1:141, 155].

Eastham surveyor of highways, 1 June 1647, 7 June 1653, 5 June 1671 [PCR 2:115, 3:33, 5:58]. Excise collector, 7 June 1648 [PCR 2:125]. Constable, 3 June 1662 [PCR 4:15]. Selectman, 7 June 1670, 5 June 1671, 5 June 1672, 3 June 1674, 1 June 1675 [PCR 5:35, 57, 92, 143, 164].

In Plymouth section of 1643 Plymouth Colony list of men able to bear arms [PCR 8:189]. His inventory included "1 small gun" valued at 12s., "1 rapier" valued at 3s., "1 barrel of a gun" valued at 10s., "2 pounds of powder" valued at 3s. and "5 pounds of shot and bullets" valued at 1s. 8d. [MD 3:170, 173].

ESTATE: In the 1623 Plymouth land division granted an unknown number of acres (but almost certainly one) at Hobes Hole near the Eel River as a passenger on the *Anne* [PCR 12:6]. In the 1627 Plymouth cattle division "Nickolas Snow" and Constance Snow were the sixth and seventh persons in the seventh company (headed by Stephen Hopkins) [PCR 12:11].

Assessed 18s. in the Plymouth tax list of 25 March 1633 and 12s. in the list of 27 March 1634 [PCR 1:10, 27].

Assigned mowing ground, 20 March 1636/7 [PCR 1:57]. Requested more hay ground, 2 July 1638 [PCR 1:90]. He was one of the purchasers [PCR 2:177].

On 7 May 1638, Nicholas Snow was one of a group of men desiring "lands towards the Six Mile Brooke" [PCR 1:83], and, on 7 August 1638, he requested "5 or 6 acres of land lying on the north side the lands granted lately to Mr. Atwood" [PCR 1:93]. On 6 July 1638, Nicholas Snow sold to Samuell Eddy his house and garden in Plymouth where he "now dwelleth" [PCR 12:31].

Granted ten acres meadow in the South Meadows, 2 November 1640 [PCR 1:166]. About March 1645/6 Nicholas Snow sold his house and buildings and upland, with two acres of meadow at High Pines and ten acres of upland meadow at Colebrook meadows, totalling fifty-two acres to Thomas Morton [PCR 12:134]. On 10 March 1645[/6], Nicholas Snow sold one acre to Nathaniel Morton [PCR 12:135]. In an account of liquors brought into Eastham, dated 28 November 1664, Nicholas Snow was responsible for one and a half gallons of liquor [PCR 4:100].

In his will, dated 14 November 1676 and proved 5 March 1676/7, "Nicholas Snow of Eastham being weak and infirm of body" bequeathed to "my son Marke Snow" all twenty acres of upland lying at Namskekitt where his house now stands, and two acres of meadow and all that broken marsh at Namscekett and two thirds of "my great lot at Satuckett"; to "my son Joseph Snow I give that other third part of my great lot at Satuckett, and two acres and an half of meadow lying at Namscekett near the head and an neck of upland"; to "my son Steven Snow I give twenty acres on the southside of my great lot at Pochett, and ten acres of my little lot at Satuckett ... an acre and an half of meadow at the boat meadow ... and that part of my meadow at the great meadow that lyeth between Josiah Cooke and the Eel Creek"; to "my son John Snow I give all that my land at Paomett purchased or unpurchased ... and all my right and title or privilege there"; to "my son Jabez Snow I give all this my land lying between my house and my son Thomas Paine's, and seven acres at the Bass pond ... and an half acre of marsh at the end of it and six acres of upland at the Herring pond, and an acre and half of meadow at Silver spring ... and that part of my house he lives in as long as my wife or I do live ... and two acres of meadow at the Great Meadow"; to "my son Jabez I give that my four acres of meadow at Billingsgate due to me yet unlaid out"; "my meadow about my house I give to my son Jabez"; to "my loving wife Constant Snow all my stock of cattle, sheep, horses, swine, whatsoever, to be at her disposal for the comfort and support of her life, with all the moveable goods I am possessed of and after her decease, stock and moveables to be equally divided amongst all my children ... the use and disposal of the part of my house she now dwells in during her lifetime, and after her decease to be my son Jabez Snow's"; to "my loving wife that ten acres of upland at Pochett and twenty on Billinsgate Iland, for her disposal for the comfort of her life, but if she need it now, and leave it undisposed, I give it then to my son Steven Snow"; "twenty acres of upland at Billingsgate if my wife leave it undisposed, then to be my son Jabez Snow's"; to "the church of Eastham for the furniture of the Table of the Lord, with pewter or other necessaries, I say I do give 10s. out of my estate after my wife's decease" [MD 3:167-69, citing PCPR 3:2:71-72].

The undated inventory of the estate of Nicholas Snow of Eastham totalled £102 10s. 9d., with no real estate included [MD 3:169-74, citing PCPR 3:2:73-77].

On 6 March 1676/7, letters of administration were granted to Constant Snow, Mark Snow and John Snow, on the estate of Nicholas Snow, deceased [PCR 5:220].

BIRTH: Possibly the Nicholas Snow, son of Nicholas Snow, baptized St. Leonard Shoreditch, Middlesex, 25 January 1599/1600 [TAG 14:229].
DEATH: Eastham 15 November 1676 [MD 6:203].
MARRIAGE: By 1627 Constance Hopkins, daughter of STEPHEN HOPKINS [MF 6:9-10; PM 271]. "Constant Snow which was the wife of Nicholas Snow" died at Eastham "about the middle of October" 1677 [MD 6:203].
CHILDREN:

 i   MARK SNOW, b. Plymouth 9 May 1628 [MD 7:14]; m. (1) Eastham 18 January 1654[/5] Anna Cooke [MD 7:14], daughter of JOSIAS COOKE [PM 149]; m. (2) Eastham 9 January 1660[/1] Jane Prence [MD 7:14], daughter of THOMAS PRENCE [MF 6:14-15; PM 374].

 ii   MARY SNOW, b. say 1630; m. say 1650 Thomas Paine (called "my son" in Nicholas Snow's will; she was probably the "one married" in 1651 as described by Bradford).

 iii   SARAH SNOW, b. say 1632; m. Eastham 25 February 1654 William Walker [PCR 8:15].

 iv   JOSEPH SNOW, b. say 1634; m. say 1670 Mary _____ [NEHGR 47:83].

 v   STEPHEN SNOW, b. say 1636; m. (1) Eastham 28 October 1663 Susanna (Deane) Rogers, widow of Joseph Rogers and daughter of STEPHEN DEANE [MD 8:15, 31:37-41 (as George Bowman notes, the alternate marriage date for this couple must be in error); TAG 42:200; PM 162]; m. (2) Eastham 9 April 1701 Mary Bigford [MD 6:14].

 vi   JOHN SNOW, b. say 1638; m. Eastham 19 September 1667 Mary Smalley [MD 7:17], daughter of JOHN SMALLEY [PM 422].

 vii   ELIZABETH SNOW, b. say 1640; m. Eastham 13 December 1665 Thomas Rogers [MD 6:14], son of Joseph Rogers and grandson of THOMAS ROGERS [MF 2:160; PM 396].

 viii   JABEZ SNOW, b. say 1642; m. say 1670 as her first husband Elizabeth _____ [NEHGR 47:83].

 ix   RUTH SNOW, b. say 1644; m. Eastham 10 December 1666 John Cole [PCR 8:57].

x Child SNOW, b. say 1646; living 1651 [Bradford 445]; no further record.
xi Child SNOW, b. say 1648; living 1651 [Bradford 445]; no further record.
xii Child SNOW, b. say 1650; living 1651 [Bradford 445]; no further record.

COMMENTS: Bradford, in describing the family of STEPHEN HOPKINS in 1651, stated that "His daughter Constanta is also married and hath twelve children, all of them living and one of them married" [Bradford 445]. (In 1893 Mrs. M.L.T. Alden suggested that two of the children who are implied by Bradford's accounting but do not otherwise appear in the records were Hannah and Rebecca "on the authority of Davis's Landmarks of Plymouth. Both married Rickards" [NEHGR 47:83]; she cites no evidence.)

In January 1634/5 the Plymouth court noted that "The servant of Nicolas Snow was willing to serve out his time with John Cooper, according to the tenor of his indenture" [PCR 1:33]. This servant was not the same as Twiford West who, after brief service with Nicholas Snow, agreed on 12 February 1635/6 to return to Edward Winslow, with whom he had originally made his indenture [PCR 1:37].

Nicholas Snow and others were presented 1 December 1640 for failing to mend the highways [PCR 2:5].

BIBLIOGRAPHIC NOTE: In 1893 Mrs. M.L.T. Alden published a substantial article on Nicholas Snow and his children [NEHGR 47:81-84, 186-89, 48:71-73]. In 1948 Donald Lines Jacobus prepared an account of Nicholas Snow and a line of descent through his son Stephen [Brainerd Anc 270-72].

GEORGE SOULE

ORIGIN: Unknown.
MIGRATION: 1620 on the *Mayflower*.
FIRST RESIDENCE: Plymouth.
REMOVES: Duxbury.

FREEMAN: In the 1633 Plymouth list of freemen, ahead of those admitted on 1 January 1632/3 [PCR 1:4]. In list of 7 March 1636/7 freemen [PCR 1:52]. In the Duxbury sections of the 1639, 1658 and 29 May 1670 Plymouth Colony lists of freemen [PCR 5:275, 8:175, 198].

EDUCATION: Signed his name as witness to the will of John Barnes of Plymouth, 6 March 1667/8 [MD 4:98, citing Scrapbook 56]. Signed his will. His inventory included "books" valued at £1 [MD 2:83].

OFFICES: Deputy for Duxbury to Plymouth Colony General Court, 27 September 1642, 28 October 1645, 3 March 1645/6, 7 July 1646, 4 June 1650, 5 June 1651, 7 June 1653, 7 March 1653/4, 6 June 1654 [PCR 2:46, 3:31, 44, 49, 94, 95, 104, 154, 167].

Plymouth grand jury, 7 March 1642/3, 6 June 1643 [PCR 2:53, 56]. Jury, 3 June 1656, 3 March 1662/3 [PCR 3:102, 7:108]. Petit jury, 1 June 1647 [PCR 2:117].

Committee to grant land, 5 May 1640, 4 June 1645 [PCR 1:151, 2:88]. Committee to "draw up an order concerning disorderly drinking of tobacco," 20 October 1646 [PCR 2:108]. Committee on magistrates and deputies, [blank] October 1650 [PCR 11:155]. Committee on boundaries, 1 June 1658 [PCR 3:138].

Volunteered for Pequot War, 7 June 1637 [PCR 1:60]. His inventory included "a gun" valued at 15s. [MD 2:83].

ESTATE: In the 1623 Plymouth division of land received one acre as a passenger on the *Mayflower* [PCR 12:4]. In the 1627 Plymouth division of cattle George Sowle, Mary Sowle and Zakariah Sowle were the eleventh, twelfth and thirteenth persons in the ninth company [PCR 12:12].

Assessed 9s. in the Plymouth tax lists of 25 March 1633 and 27 March 1634 [PCR 1:10, 27]. He was on the list of purchasers [PCR 2:177].

On 1 July 1633, he was permitted to "mow for a cow near his dwelling house" [PCR 1:15]. On 20 March 1636/7, he was allowed the hay ground where he got hay the year before [PCR 1:56]. On 4 December 1637, George Soule was granted a garden place "on Ducksborrow side" [PCR 1:69]. On 7 May 1638, one acre of land was granted to George Soule "at the watering place" in lieu of another acre that was taken from him for other use, and also two acres of stony marsh at Powder Point were granted to him [PCR 1:83]. On 13 July 1639, George Soule sold to Robert Hicks two acres at the watering place on the south side of Plymouth [PCR 12:45]. On 2 November 1640, George Soule was granted "the meadow he desires" at Green's Harbor [PCR 1:165].

On 4 May 1658, George Soule was granted five acres of meadow [PCR 3:134]. On 22 January 1658 and 17 July 1668, George Soule gave his Dartmouth propriety to his sons Nathaniel and George as a single undivided share [PCLR 3:123, 245].

On 23 July 1668, "G[e]orge Soule Senior of Duxburrow ..., planter,... with the consent of Mary my wife," deeded to "Francis Walker husband to my daughter Elizabeth half my whole share of lands at Namassakett both upland and meadow" [MD 27:39-40, citing PCLR 3:126]. On 26 January 1668[/9], "G[e]orge Soule of Duxburrow" deeded to "Patience Haskall his true and natural daughter and unto John Haskall her husband all that his half share of land at Namassakett both upland and meadow ... having given the other half share formerly unto Francis Walker" [MD 27:40, citing PCLR 3:153]. On 12 March 1668[/9], "George Soul of Duxburro ..., husbandman," deeded to "my daughter Elizabeth wife unto Francis Walker ... the moiety or half share of all my purchase or purchases lying and being as before expressed in the place commonly called Namascutt"; "wife Mary Soul" relinquished her dower rights [MD 27: 40-41, citing PLR 10:2:327].

In his will, dated 11 August 1677 and proved 5 March 1679/80, "G[e]orge Soule Senior of Duxberry ... being aged and weak of body" confirmed that he had formerly given by deeds "unto my two sons Nathaniel and G[e]orge all my lands in the township of Dartmouth ... [and] I have formerly given unto my daughters Elizabeth and Patience all my lands in the township of Middlebery"; to "my daughters Sussannah and Mary," 12d. apiece; "forasmuch as my eldest son John Soule and his family hath in my extreme old age and weakness been tender and careful of me and very helpful to me, and is likely so to be while it shall please God to continue my life here, therefore I give and bequeath unto my said son John Soule all the remainder of my housing and lands whatsoever"; to "my son John Soule all my goods and chattels whatsoever"; "my son John Soule to be my sole executor." In a codicil dated 20 September 1677, "G[e]orge Soule" indicated that if "my son John Soule" were to disturb "my daughter Patience or her heirs" in the peaceable possession of lands he had given her in Middleborough, then "my gift to my son John Soule shall be void" and "my daughter Patience shall have all my lands at Duxburrey and she shall be my sole executrix ... and enter into my housing lands and meadows at Duxburrow" [MD 2:81-83, citing PCPR 4:1:50].

The inventory of the estate of George Soule of Duxbury, taken 22 January 1679[/80], totalled £40 19s., of which £25 was real estate: "dwelling house, orchard, barn and upland," £20; and "meadow land," £5; John Soule appended a long list of charges against the estate, including an item "for diet and tendance since my mother died which was three year the last December" [MD 2:83-84, citing PCPR 4:1:51].

BIRTH: By about 1602 (based on estimated date of marriage).
DEATH: Between 20 September 1677 (codicil to will) and 22 January 1679[/80] (date of inventory), and probably closer to the latter date.
MARRIAGE: By 1627 MARY BUCKETT (in the 1627 Plymouth division of cattle George Soule had wife Mary and son Zachariah; Mary has been identified by many writers as Mary Buckett of the 1623 land division on that basis that no other Mary was available in the limited Plymouth population of the earliest years). She died about December 1672 (son John Soule indicated in an account of 1676 that "my mother died which was three year the last December" [MD 2:83-84]).
CHILDREN:
- i ZACHARIAH SOULE, b. by 1627; m. by 1663 Margaret _____ [Scrapbook 20].
- ii JOHN SOULE, b. about 1632 (deposed 8 March 1705/6 aged "about seventy-four years" [MD 5:46, citing PLR 7:35]); m. (1) by about 1656 Rebecca Simonson (eldest known child, Rebecca (Soule) Weston, d. Plympton 18 November 1732 "in her 76th year"), daughter of MOSES SIMONSON [PM 419]; m. (2) by 1679 Esther (Delano) Samson, daughter of PHILIP DELANO [PM 164] and widow of Samuel Samson [TAG 15:165-67; TG 1:233; MF 3:7].
- iii NATHANIEL SOULE, b. between say 1634 and 1646 (adult by 1667/8 [PCR 3:178]); before 4 March 1673/4 fathered a child with an unnamed Indian woman and ordered to pay ten bushels of corn to her for the keeping of the child [PCR 5:163]; m. by 1681 Rose _____ (eldest known child b. Dartmouth 12 January 1681[/2]).
- iv GEORGE SOULE, b. about 1639 (deposed 1 March 1672/3 "aged 34 years or thereabouts" [RICT 3:28]); m. by about 1665 Deborah _____ (eldest known child b. by 1665 [MFIP Soule 5]).
- v SUSANNA SOULE, b. say 1641; m. by 1662 Francis West (eldest known child b. by 1662 [MFIP Soule 6]).
- vi MARY SOULE, b. about 1643 (in 1653 bound out for seven years or eight if she did not marry [MD 1:214]); m. by 1665 John Peterson (eldest known child b. by about 1665 [MFIP Soule 6]).

vii ELIZABETH SOULE, b. say 1645 (fined for committing fornication 3 March 1662/3 [PCR 5:34]; sued Nathaniel Church 5 October 1663 for refusing to marry her [PCR 7:111]; ordered whipped 2 July 1667 for committing fornication a second time [PCR 5:162]); m. by 23 July 1668 Francis Walker [MD 27:39-40, citing PCLR 3:126].

viii PATIENCE SOULE, b. say 1647; m. Middleboro January 1666[/7] John Haskell [MiddleVR 1:1].

ix BENJAMIN SOULE, b. say 1649; fell with Capt. Pierce 26 March 1676 during King Philip's War [Bodge 350]; unm.

COMMENTS: Bradford, in his list of passengers of the *Mayflower*, included George Soule as one of "two men-servants" of Mr. Edward Winslow [Bradford 441]. In 1651 Bradford summed up the group headed by Winslow, saying that one of the servants died, "but his man, George Soule, is still living, and hath eight children" [Bradford 444].

On 3 January 1636/7, George Soule and Nathaniel Thomas sued and countersued each other over two heifers [PCR 7:4].

On 3 June 1662 "Gorg Soule" was on a list of freemen desiring to look for additional land "being the first born children of this government" [PCR 4:19].

On 5 March 1667/8, George Soule Sr. stood surety with his son John for the good behavior of his son Nathaniel Soule who had verbally abused Mr. John Holmes, teacher of the church at Duxburrow [PCR 4:178].

BIBLIOGRAPHIC NOTE: In 1980 the General Society of Mayflower Descendants published a genealogy of five generations of descent from George Soule as the third volume in its series of silver volumes [John E. Soule and Milton E. Terry, *Mayflower Families Through Five Generations, Volume Three: George Soule* (Plymouth 1980), ed. Anne Borden Harding]. This is a seriously flawed volume, which should not be relied upon. George E. McCracken and Neil D. Thompson published lengthy reviews pointing out some of the problems [TG 1:225-58; TAG 57:57-58]. Between 2000 and 2003 the General Society of Mayflower Descendants replaced the 1980 volume with a series of four volumes in its *Mayflower Families in Progress* series, revised by Robert S. Wakefield and Louise Walsh Throop, with the first four generations of descendants in the first of the four volumes.

CONSTANT SOUTHWORTH

ORIGIN: Unknown.
MIGRATION: 1628.
FIRST RESIDENCE: Plymouth.
REMOVES: Duxbury.

FREEMAN: Admitted 2 January 1637/8 [PCR 1:74]. In Duxbury sections of Plymouth Colony lists of freemen of 1639, 1658 and 29 May 1670 [PCR 5:274, 8:175, 198].
EDUCATION: His inventory included "several sorts of books" valued at £4 15s. and "books, spoons & small things" valued at 10s. [PCPR 4:1:19].
OFFICES: Plymouth Assistant, 7 June 1670, 5 June 1671, 5 June 1672, 3 June 1673, 3 June 1674, 1 June 1675, 7 June 1676, 5 June 1677, 5 June 1678 [PCR 5:34, 55, 90, 112, 143, 163, 194, 229, 256]. Colony treasurer, 7 June 1659, 6 June 1660, 4 June 1661, 3 June 1662, 1 June 1663, 8 June 1664, 7 June 1665, 5 June 1666, 5 June 1667, 3 June 1668 [PCR 3:162, 187, 214, 4:14, 37, 60, 90, 122, 147, 180, 185]. Council of war, 1 June 1658, 2 October 1658, 2 April 1667, 2 July 1667 [PCR 3:138, 153, 4:145, 164-66].

Deputy for Duxbury to Plymouth Colony General Court, 1 June 1647, 8 June 1649, 4 June 1650, 5 June 1651, 3 June 1652, 6 April 1653, 7 June 1653, 7 March 1653/4, 6 June 1654, 8 June 1655, 3 June 1656, 1 June 1658, 7 June 1659, 6 June 1660, 2 October 1660, 4 June 1661, 3 June 1662, 1 June 1663, 8 June 1664, 7 June 1665, 5 June 1666, 5 June 1667, 3 June 1668, 1 June 1669 [PCR 2:117, 144, 154, 167, 3:8, 23, 31, 44, 49, 79, 99, 135, 162, 187, 198, 214, 4:14, 37, 60, 90, 122, 148, 180, 5:17].

Plymouth grand jury, 5 June 1644 [PCR 2:71].

Committee to supply towns and soldiers, 6 June 1654 [PCR 3:53]. Committee to organize the mending of bridges, 7 August 1655, 27 July 1664, 1 May 1666 [PCR 3:87, 4:69, 119]. Committee to consider the trade at Kennebeck, 8 June 1649, 5 March 1655[/6], 3 October 1659, 13 June 1660 [PCR 2:144, 3:96, 170-71, 195]. Committee to divide lands and settle ways, 4 June 1645, 3 June 1656, 6 October 1659, 1 May 1660, 13 June 1660, 2 October 1660, 5 February 1660/1, 1 June 1663 [PCR 2:88, 3:102, 174, 186, 193, 201, 204, 4:42]. Committee to oversee the building of a house of correction, 1 June 1658 [PCR 3:137]. Committee to negotiate the ownership of Hogg Island with Rhode Island, 1 March 1658/9 [PCR 3:157]. Committee to settle the bounds of Taunton, 6

October 1659 [PCR 3:172]. Committee to settle the bounds of Sandwich and Plymouth, 1 June 1663 [PCR 4:40]. Committee to oversee the purchase of lands from Indians, 3 October 1665 [PCR 4:109, 113]. Committee to revise laws, 5 June 1678 [PCR 5:263].

Duxbury constable, 2 March 1640/1, 1 June 1641, 5 June 1644 [PCR 2:9, 15, 3:116]. Duxbury invoicer of liquors, powder, shot and lead, 10 June 1662 [PCR 4:23].

In Duxbury section of 1643 Plymouth Colony list of men able to bear arms [PCR 8:190]. Ensign, 7 July 1646 [PCR 2:105]. His inventory included "6 guns, 1 rapier, 1 cutlass, 1 tuck [a type of rapier], 1 pair of stillyards, powder, shot & flints" valued at £3 13s. [PCPR 4:1:19].

ESTATE: On 6 October 1636, land was granted to Mr. William Bradford "for Constant & Thomas Southward, the land now in occupation of George Sowle" [PCR 1:45]. On 6 April 1640, "Constant Southwood and Thomas Southwood, his brother ... [were] granted fifty acres apiece of upland ... at the North River, with proportionable meadow ground" [PCR 1:144, 146]. On 10 November 1646, William Hillier of Duxbury, carpenter, sold to Constant Southworth of Duxbury, planter, his right in "the mill at Duxbury standing upon Stonie River being in partnership between him and Georg[e] Pollerd late of Duxbury," being a half share [PCR 12:139]. On 2 February 1646[/7], Constant Southworth sold to William Bradford of Plymouth "all his lands & meadows lying at the Island Creek" [PCR 12:141]. On 26 February 1648, "Constant Sowthworth of Duxbery and Thomas Sowthworth of Plymouth his brother" sold to Francis Godfrey of Duxbury, carpenter, one hundred acres of land at the North River [PCR 12:163]. On 7 June 1665, "a competency" of land at Namasskett was granted to four men, including "Mr. Constant Southworth" [PCR 4:95].

In his will, dated 20 February 1678[/9] and proved 7 June 1679, Constant Southworth Esq. of Duxbury bequeathed to "my dear and loving wife Elizabeth Southworth for and during the term of her natural life my dwelling house with the outhousing and mill belonging unto it and all my uplands and meadows" in Duxbury or Marshfield, along with £50 and some furniture; to "my son Edward Southworth after the decease of my aforesaid wife Elizabeth my aforesaid dwelling house with the outhousing and mill belonging to it and all my upland and meadows" in Duxbury and Marshfield, along with £12; to "my son Nathaniell Southworth the one half of my share of lands that lyeth near Taunton called by the name of the freemen's lands"; to "my three daughters Marcye Freeman, Allice Church and Mary Alden my other one-half of the freemen's land"; to "my daughter Elizabeth Southworth" moveables "provided that she do not marry Willam Vobbes," otherwise to have 5s.; to "my daughter Presilla Southworth" moveables; to "my son Willam Southworth" moveables; to "my grandson Constant Freeman all those my lands and meadows that I have at a place commonly called Pawomett" in Eastham; to "my sons Edward and Nathaniell and daughters Elizabeth and Presilla equally all my part of the profits that shall or may arise by the fishing at the Cape," wife Elizabeth to be sole executrix and residuary legatee, to be assisted by sons Edward and Nathaniel [PCPR 4:1:18].

The inventory of the estate of "Constant Southworth Esq. of the town of Duxburrow ... deceased," taken 15 March 1678/9, totalled £367 13s. 2d. A list of real estate, without valuation, was appended: "about twenty-five acres of land in the town of Duxburrow whereon standeth his dwelling house and barn and one grist mill"; "a parcel of land at the North Field the quantity we know not"; "several parcels of meadow lying in the towns of Duxburrow and Marshfield about 12 acres"; "one share of land in a place commonly called the freemen's land near Taunton"; and a "parcel of land and meadow at a place commonly called Paomett in the town of Eastham" [PCPR 4:1:19-20].

BIRTH: By about 1612 (based on date of marriage), son of Edward and Alice (Carpenter) Southworth.
DEATH: Duxbury 11 March 1678/9.
MARRIAGE: Plymouth 2 November 1637 Elizabeth Collier, daughter of WILLIAM COLLIER [PCR 1:68; PM 128]. She died after 20 February 1678/9 (date of husband's will).
CHILDREN:
    i   MERCY SOUTHWORTH, b. say 1640; m. Eastham 12 May 1658 Samuel Freeman [MD 6:201], son of SAMUEL FREEMAN {1630, Watertown} [GMB 1:698-700].
    ii   PRISCILLA SOUTHWORTH, b. say 1642; m. (1) Bristol 1 March 1689 Samuel Talbot [TAG 78:1-8, 256-64]; m. (2) 1 May 1708 John Irish, son of JOHN IRISH [NEHGR 54:181; TAG 60:131-32, 138-39; PM 287].
    iii EDWARD SOUTHWORTH, b. say 1644; m. Duxbury 16 November 1671 Mary Pabodie, daughter of William Pabodie and granddaughter of JOHN ALDEN [PM 4].
    iv ALICE SOUTHWORTH, b. say 1646; m. 26 December 1667 Benjamin Church, son of RICHARD CHURCH [NEHGR 121:121 (giving date of marriage but not name of bride); PM 105].

v   NATHANIEL SOUTHWORTH, b. about 1649 (d. Middleborough 14 January 1710[/1] in his 62nd year [MD 21:25]); m. Plymouth 10 January 1672 Desire Gray [PCR 8:33].

vi   MARY SOUTHWORTH, b. say 1654; m. by 1674 David Alden, son of JOHN ALDEN.

vii   WILLIAM SOUTHWORTH, b. about 1659 (d. Little Compton 25 June 1719 in his 60th year [NEHGR 115:264]); m. (1) by 1681 Rebecca Pabodie, daughter of William Pabodie and granddaughter of JOHN ALDEN (eldest known child b. Little Compton 18 April 1681 [RIVR 4:Little Compton:168]; "Rebeka the wife of Captain William Southworth ... departed this life Dec the 25th in the 43d year of her age. 1702" at Little Compton [NEHGR 115:264]); m. (2) Saybrook 14 (or 15) November 1705 Martha (Kirtland) Blague [SayVR 58], widow of Joseph Blague

viii   ELIZABETH SOUTHWORTH, b. say 1661; m. Bristol 12 May 1685 Samuel Gallup [MD 42:9-10, citing RIVR 6:Bristol:22].

ASSOCIATIONS: Constant Southworth was brother to THOMAS SOUTHWORTH, and both were sons of the second wife of WILLIAM BRADFORD [PM 62]. Various attempts have been made to extend their pedigree beyond their father Edward, but none has yet been successful [NEHGR 17:240; Ancestral Roots 15; Magna Charta Sureties 109].

COMMENTS: On 7 June 1648, Constant Southworth was allowed to sell wine in Duxbury [PCR 2:125]. On 1 March 1652/3, Constant Southworth was appointed supervisor of the will and estate of James and Mary Lendall, and the eldest child of that couple also chose him to be her guardian [PCR 3:22]. On 10 June 1662, he deposed regarding the settlement of Satuckett bounds [PCR 4:20]. Constant was frequently involved with the ordering of his neighbors' estates and debts, particularly in his capacity as Treasurer for the Colony [PCR 3:21, 149, 7:135-37, 140, 144, 147, 149, 192].

THOMAS SOUTHWORTH

ORIGIN: Unknown.
MIGRATION: 1628.
FIRST RESIDENCE: Plymouth.

FREEMAN: Propounded 7 September 1642 (as "Thomas Southwood") [PCR 2:45] and admitted 7 March 1642/3 (as "Thomas Southwood") [PCR 2:52] (and appended to Plymouth section of 1639 list of freemen as a result [PCR 8:174]). In Plymouth section of 1658 Plymouth Colony list of freemen (as "Lt. Tho[mas] Southworth") [PCR 8:197].

EDUCATION: He wrote a response from the court 9 June 1665 with indifferent spelling [PCR 4:100]. His inventory included "books" valued at £1 4s.

OFFICES: Commissioner for Plymouth to United Colonies, 7 June 1659, 6 June 1660, 4 June 1661, 3 June 1662, 8 June 1664, 7 June 1665, 5 June 1666, 5 June 1667, 3 June 1668, 1 June 1669 [PCR 3:162, 187, 4:14, 37, 60, 90, 122, 147, 180, 5:7, 17, 10:213, 238, 254, 312, 323].

Plymouth Assistant, 3 June 1652 (not sworn), 7 June 1653 (not sworn), 3 June 1657, 1 June 1658, 7 June 1659, 6 June 1660, 4 June 1661, 3 June 1662, 1 June 1663, 8 June 1664, 7 June 1665, 5 June 1666, 5 June 1667, 3 June 1668, 1 June 1669 [PCR 3:7, 30, 114, 134, 162, 187, 214, 4:13, 36, 60, 90, 122, 147, 179, 5:17]. Assistant at Kennebeck, 29 March 1655 [PCR 3:75]. Council of War, 6 April 1653, 1 June 1658, 2 October 1658, 2 April 1667 [PCR 3:26, 28, 138, 153, 4:142].

Deputy for Plymouth to Plymouth Colony General Court, 3 June 1652, 6 April 1653, 7 June 1653, 7 March 1653/4 [PCR 3:8:23, 31, 44].

Plymouth petit jury, 5 March 1643/4, 6 March 1648/9, 29 October 1649, 6 March 1649/50, 6 March 1654/5 [PCR 3:75, 7:37, 45-47]. Grand jury, 5 June 1644 [PCR 2:71]. Coroner's jury, 26 July 1652, 3 September 1652 [PCR 3:15, 16].

Committee to dispose of lands, 25 October 1649 [PCR 2:145]. Committee to examine the "writing lately sent out of the Bay," 7 June 1653 [PCR 3:33]. Committee to set differences between the Indians, Yarmouth and Barnstable [PCR 3:117]. Committee to view lands, 6 October 1659, 5 March 1660/1 [PCR 3:174, 209]. Committee to treat with Plymouth assessors, 6 December 1659 [PCR 3:179]. Authorized to purchase land of the Indians, 3 October 1665, 30 October 1667 [PCR 4:109, 113, 167].

Plymouth selectman, 18 February 1649/50 [PTR 1:29]. Constable, 7 March 1642/3 [PCR 2:53]. Surveyor of highways, 5 June 1644 [PCR 2:72]. Master of the watch, 22 June 1644 [PTR 1:15, 18].

In Plymouth section of 1643 Plymouth Colony list of men able to bear arms [PCR 8:188]. Lieutenant, 7 March 1647/8 [PCR 2:121]. Lieutenant of troops raised for the Dutch war, 3 May 1653 [PCR 3:29]. Captain of the military company of Plymouth, 2 August 1659, 4 June 1661 [PCR 3:169, 214].

ESTATE: On 6 October 1636, land was granted to Mr. William Bradford "for Constant & Thomas Southward, the land now in occupation of George Sowle" [PCR 1:45]. On 6 April 1640, "Constant Southwood and Thomas Southwood, his brother ... [were] granted fifty acres apiece of upland ... at the North River, with proportionable meadow ground" [PCR 1:144, 146]. On 28 October 1641, William Bradford deeded to "my son-in-law Thomas Southworth" a dwelling house & garden with seven acres of upland and two acres of meadow [PCR 12:77]. On 17 October 1642, "Thomas Southwood" was granted four acres at North Meadow by Joanes River [PCR 2:49]. On 19 April 1643, he was levied half a peck of corn for the keep of cows [PTR 1:13]. On 26 February 1648, "Constant Sowthworth of Duxbery and Thomas Sowthworth of Plymouth his brother" sold to Francis Godfrey of Duxbury, carpenter, one hundred acres of land at the North River [PCR 12:163]. On 22 February 1650[/1], Lieutenant Thomas Southworth was granted twelve acres of meadow at Winnituxett [PTR 1:206].

On 3 June 1662, "Captain Thomas Southworth" was one of the "sundry ancient freemen of the town of Taunton" allowed to look for land [PCR 4:20]. On 7 June 1665, "a competency of land" at Namasskett was granted to "Mr. John Alden, Captain Thomas Southworth and Mr. Constant Southworth" [PCR 4:95].

In his will, dated 18 November 1669 and proved 1 March 1669/70, "Captain Thomas Southworth" bequeathed to "my daughter Elizabeth Howland all my housing and lands both upland and meadow within the township of Plymouth"; to "daughter Elizabeth and unto her husband Joseph Howland" "all my other lands out of the township of Plymouth" to pay debts of the estate; "my rapier and belt to my son-in-law Joseph Howland"; to Thomas Faunce 40s.; to Deborah Morton 40s.; to "William Churchill" a sheep; "that lot and half of land which is at the Eel River which was exchanged by Mr. Will[i]am Bradford deceased with John Faunce for a lot at Jonses River I do yield up all my interest in the said lot & half of land to Thomas Faunce"; "the rest of my estate I leave in the hands of my son Joseph Howland and my daughter his wife & my brother Constant Southworth to be disposed of as they shall see reason for the supply of my wife in her poor condition" [MD 18:185, citing PCPR 3:1].

The undated inventory of the estate of Thomas Southworth was untotalled; no real estate was included, and many debts against the estate were listed [PCPR 3:1-2].

BIRTH: About 1617 (based on age at death), son of Edward and Alice (Carpenter) Southworth.
DEATH: Plymouth 8 December 1669 in his 53rd year [PCR 8:32].
MARRIAGE: Plymouth 1 September 1641 Elizabeth Reynor [PCR 2:23]. She died after 3 June 1679 [PCR 6:14].
CHILD:
    i   ELIZABETH SOUTHWORTH, b. say 1644; m. Plymouth 7 December 1664 Joseph Howland [PCR 8:25], son of JOHN HOWLAND [PM 279].
ASSOCIATIONS: Thomas Southworth was brother to CONSTANT SOUTHWORTH, and both were sons of the second wife of WILLIAM BRADFORD [PM 62].

COMMENTS: On 20 June 1654, "Lieut. Thomas Southworth, now residing at Cushenage [Cushenoc on the Kennebeck]," was entrusted to be the assistant in that part of the jurisdiction of New Plymouth [PCR 3:58]. On 1 May 1660, he informed on his Quaker neighbors [PCR 3:185]. On 3 December 1660, Mr. Thomas Southworth told how Ephraim Hicks of Plymouth died a violent death 12 December 1649 and how the night before his death he made a nuncupative will [PCR 3:202].

On 3 June 1679, the court contracted with "Mistress Elizabeth Southworth" to
> make provision for the magistrates' table in all respects as formerly, and for the use of bedding and household stuff improved thereabouts, for the full year following, viz:, for four courts, for and in consideration of £42 current silver money of New England, and at the expiration of the year, at the making up of her accounts in this behalf, if she doth not find herself a sufficient gainer, that then the court will consider thereof with some additional satisfaction according to equity and righteousness [PCR 6:14].

This record would seem to apply to the widow of Thomas Southworth, as the provision for the courts would have taken place in Plymouth, and the widow of Constant Southworth, also Elizabeth, resided in Duxbury.

RICHARD SPARROW

ORIGIN: Unknown.
MIGRATION: 1632.

FIRST RESIDENCE: Plymouth.
REMOVES: Eastham by 1653.

OCCUPATION: Yeoman.
FREEMAN: In 1633 Plymouth list of freemen, in close proximity to others admitted on 1 January 1632/3 [PCR 1:4]. In 7 March 1636/7 Plymouth list of freemen [PCR 1:52]. In Plymouth section of 1639 list of freemen, and in Eastham section of 1658 list [PCR 8:174, 202].
EDUCATION: He signed his name to an agreement regarding the Kennebec trade, 6 October 1659 [PCR 3:171]. His inventory included "a Bible [and] 2 small books" valued at 10s. [PCPR 2:2:67].
OFFICES: Deputy for Eastham to Plymouth General Court, 6 April 1653, 8 June 1655, 3 June 1656 [PCR 3:24, 79, 99].

Plymouth grand jury, 4 June 1639, 6 June 1643, 7 June 1653, 7 June 1659 [PCR 1:126, 2:56, 3:32, 162]. Petit jury, 3 March 1639/40, 1 September 1640, 1 February 1640/1, 1 June 1641, 6 July 1641, 6 September 1641, 7 December 1641, 7 June 1642, 7 November 1643, 3 March 1644/5, 28 October 1645, 7 July 1646, 2 March 1646/7, 1 June 1647, 7 June 1648, 3 October 1648, 4 October 1648, 6 March 1648/9, 29 October 1649, 6 March 1649/50, 6 June 1650, 2 October 1650, 4 March 1650/1, 7 June 1651, 4 June 1652, 4 June 1657 [PCR 2:7, 112, 117, 126, 134, 7:16, 18, 20, 22-23, 25, 28, 31, 36, 40-43, 45-47, 49, 52-54, 60, 83]. Coroner's jury, 5 June 1638, 1 August 1648 [PCR 1:88, 2:132].

Committee to survey land, 5 May 1640 [PCR 1:152]. Committee on Kennebec trade, 3 October 1659 [PCR 3:170-71].

Plymouth constable, 3 March 1639/40, 2 June 1640, 7 March 1642/3 [PCR 1:141, 155, 2:53]. Surveyor of highways, 3 March 1639/40, 2 June 1640, 4 June 1645, 1 June 1647, 7 June 1648 [PCR 1:141, 155, 2:84, 116, 124]. Tax collector, 4 June 1650 [PCR 2:155].

Eastham surveyor of highways, 1 June 1658 [PCR 3:136].

In Plymouth section of 1643 Plymouth Colony list of men able to bear arms [PCR 8:188]. His inventory included "1 musket, a sword, an old pair of bandoliers" valued at £1 4s. and "powder and shot" valued at 5s. [PCPR 2:2:67].
ESTATE: Assessed 9s. in the Plymouth tax lists of 25 March 1633 and 27 March 1634 [PCR 1:11, 28].

On 7 November 1636, granted six acres at Plymouth "to belong to their dwelling houses there, & not to be sold from their houses" [PCR 1:46]. On 5 March 1637/8, granted forty acres "at the north end of Fresh Lake, and a parcel of marsh for meadow lying on the south side of Fresh Lake" [PCR 1:78]. On 1 June 1640, granted five acres of meadow [PCR

1:154]. On 2 November 1640, granted five acres at Lakenham [PCR 1:166].

On 12 January 1639/40, John Barnes of Plymouth sold to Richard Sparrow of the same four two-year-old steers and one three-year-old bull, for £83 [PCR 1:138]; Richard Sparrow immediately sold the bull and two of the steers to Josias Winslow of Plymouth, for £50 [PCR 1:139]. On 16 September 1641, Richard Sparrow was granted two acres of meadow ground at Wood Island "which was Mrs. Fullers" [PCR 2:25]. On 7 December 1641, he was granted a parcel of upland [PCR 2:29]. On 17 October 1642, he was granted four acres of upland at the head of Mr. Hicks's field [PCR 2:48].

In 1653 (day and month not given) Richard Sparrow of Eastham sold to George Bonum of Plymouth "all that his house and garden plot on which the house standeth being scituate in Plymouth aforesaid in the South Street near the mill together with six acres of upland ... in the new field" [MD 3:138-39, citing PCLR 2:1:69]. (This same transaction was entered again under date of 22 November 1656 [MD 10:215, citing PCLR 2:1:183].) On 4 June 1657, "Richard Sparrow of Eastham, planter," sold to Giles Rickard Sr. of Plymouth, weaver, "a parcel of upland meadow in the meadow commonly called Doten's Meadow in the township of Plymouth aforesaid containing five acres" [MD 11:18, citing PCLR 2:1:191].

On 6 October 1657, Richard Sparrow and others were allowed to claim lands about thirteen English miles from Rehoboth [PCR 3:123]. On 1 June 1658, he was granted a portion of land between Bridgewater and Weymouth [PCR 3:142].

On 4 October 1658, Richard Sparrow of Eastham, planter, sold to Abraham Sampson of Duxbury, carpenter, "a parcel of marsh meadow containing three acres and three quarters or thereabouts ... lying on the east side of the great wood island in the township of Marshfield ... whereof two acres of the said three acres and three-quarters was at first granted to Joshua Pratt and by him sold to Josias Cooke, and by him sold to Richard Sparrow; and the other acre and three-quarters granted to Mistress Bridgett Fuller and exchanged with Richard Sparrow for two acres in Dotie's Meadow"; "the wife of the said Richard Sparrow hath given her consent" [MD 13:141-42, citing PCLR 2:2:11].

In his will, dated 19 November 1660 and proved 5 March 1660/1, Richard Sparrow bequeathed to "Pandora my loving wife my dwelling house and housing with my garden plot adjacent in the Township of Eastham during her life and then to belong to Jonathan Sparrow my son" (along with some moveables); "as for my uplands at Poche and my meadow ground ... the one half I have already given to Jonathan my son and the other half ... I give to John Sparrow my grandchild as his proper inheritance only my wife to have the use of my meadow or as much as she shall need during her life"; "whatsoever land shall befall to me from the country as my right it being purchased I give to John Sparrow my grandchild"; "to the church of Eastham one ewe sheep to be disposed of according to the discretion of my overseers"; to "Pressila Sparrow my grandchild one ewe sheep to be improved in a small stock for her, and the rest of my ewe sheep I give to John and Rebecca Sparrow my grandchildren to be improved as a stock for them"; to "Jonathan Sparrow my son my great cloth coat, and for the rest of my wearing apparel, my wife to dispose of them as she see cause"; wife Pandora and son Jonathan to be executors; friends and brethren Mr. Thomas Prence of Eastham, Mr. Thomas Willett of Rehoboth and Lieutenant Thomas Southworth of Plymouth to be overseers; residue of estate to be equally divided between wife and son [MD 12:57-58, citing PCPR 2:2:66].

The inventory of the estate of Richard Sparrow, taken 22 January 1660/1, totalled £85, with no real estate included [MD 12:58, citing PCPR 2:2:67].

BIRTH: By about 1604 (based on estimated date of marriage).
DEATH: Eastham 8 January 1660/1 [MD 6:203; see also MD 8:4].
MARRIAGE: By about 1629 Pandora _____ (assuming she was mother of Jonathan). She survived her husband. (According to some sources, in "1665 the widow [Pandora] and son [Jonathan] sold the Eastham home and removed to what is now East Orleans where Pandora probably died" [Dawes-Gates 2:765, citing Library of Cape Cod History and Genealogy 32:3]; this transaction is not recorded in the Plymouth Colony land records.)
CHILD:

    i   JONATHAN SPARROW, b. say 1629; m. (1) Eastham 26 October 1654 Rebecca Bangs [PCR 8:15], daughter of EDWARD BANGS [PM 23]; m. (2) by 1671 (and probably by 1669) Hannah (Prence) Mayo, daughter of THOMAS PRENCE [PM 374] and widow of Nathaniel Mayo [MD 14:193-203]; m. (3) Barnstable 23 November 1698 Sarah (Lewis) Cobb, daughter of George Lewis and widow of James Cobb (son of HENRY COBB [PM 118]) [MD 14:87; TAG 68:26].

COMMENTS: On 24 June 1639, "Mary Moorecock hath of her own voluntary will, with consent of her father-in-law, Thomas Whitton, put herself apprentice with Richard Sparrow, of Plymouth, and Pandora, his wife," for a term of nine years [PCR 1:128-29].

On 5 November 1638, "Richard Sparrow, of Plymouth, yeoman," was surety for William Burne (i.e., Bourne) of Duxbury [PCR 1:101]. On 7 December 1641, he was one of eight men who brought various actions against James Luxford, primarily for trespass [PCR 7:27]. On 2 October 1650, Richard Sparrow was censured for failing to report the theft of corn from his barn and for "concealing of the aforesaid act of Tho[mas] Shereve, upon an engagement so to do unless called before authority" [PCR 2:162-63]. On 7 March 1653/4, Sparrow won an action against Nathaniel Mayo for defamation [PCR 7:69]. On 5 October 1656, Captain Miles Standish brought suit against Richard Sparrow of Eastham, in behalf of Elizabeth Hopkins, charging that Sparrow had not performed the terms of an agreement concerning Elizabeth [PCR 7:80]. On 6 October 1657, Richard Sparrow won his suit against Ralph Smith for taking away a piece of timber, though having been forbidden, and refusing to give it back [PCR 7:84].

BIBLIOGRAPHIC NOTE: George Ernest Bowman took a special interest in the Sparrow family and published a number of articles on the immigrant and his son [MD 11:231-34, 12:57-60, 14:1-5, 193-203].

In 1931 Mary Walton Ferris published a typically thorough study of Richard Sparrow and his son Jonathan [Dawes-Gates 2:763-68], and in 1960 Donald Lines Jacobus also prepared a briefer account [Ackley-Bosworth 41-42].

FRANCIS SPRAGUE

ORIGIN: Unknown.
MIGRATION: 1623 in *Anne*.
FIRST RESIDENCE: Plymouth.
REMOVES: Duxbury by 1638.

OCCUPATION: Innkeeper (1 October 1638: "Francis Sprague is licensed to keep victualling on Duxborrow side" [PCR 1:99]; 3 March 1639/40: "Francis Sprague, of Duxborrow, for drawing & retailing wine at Duxborrow, contrary to the express order of the Court, is fined by the Bench 20s. sterling" [PCR 1:143]; 5 May 1640: "Francis Sprague, of

Duxborrow, is prohibited by the Court to draw any wine or strong water until the next General [Court], without special license from the Court so to do" [PCR 1:153]; 2 June 1640 and 1 September 1640: Francis Sprague presented for selling & retailing of wine contrary to order [PCR 1:156, 162]). Licensed 7 July 1646 to draw wine and keep an ordinary at Duxbury [PCR 2:104]. On 5 June 1666, his license was revoked [PCR 4:129].

FREEMAN: Admitted 7 June 1637 [PCR 1:60] (and as a result added to the list of freemen compiled on 7 March 1636/7 [PCR 1:53]). In Duxbury sections of 1639, 1658 and 29 May 1670 lists of freemen [PCR 5:275, 8:175, 198].

EDUCATION: Signed his deeds by mark.

OFFICES: Duxbury surveyor of highways, 7 June 1648, 3 June 1657 [PCR 2:124, 3:116]. Constable, 4 June 1653 [PCR 2:153].

In Duxbury section of 1643 Plymouth Colony list of men able to bear arms [PCR 8:190].

ESTATE: In the 1623 Plymouth land division "Francis Spragge" was granted three acres as a passenger on the *Anne* [PCR 12:5]. In the 1627 Plymouth cattle division Francis Sprage, Anna Sprage and Mercye Sprage were the eleventh through thirteenth persons in the sixth company [PCR 12:11].

Assessed 18s. in the Plymouth tax lists of 25 March 1633 and 27 March 1634 [PCR 1:10, 27]. He was one of the purchasers [PCR 2:177].

In 1637 Francis Sprague of Duxbury sold to Mr. Ralph Partridge "all his right and title into so much of the lot of his land lying in Ducksburrow aforesaid as is now enclosed by the said Mr. Partridg" [PCR 12:19]. On 28 March 1642, Francis Sprague sold to Morris Truant "two acres of marsh meadow lying at the Wood Island" [PCR 12:78]. On 1 April 1644, Francis Sprague of Duxbury sold to "Will[ia]m Laurence my son-in-law of the same town ... fifty acres" [PCR 12:138].

On 26 October 1659, Francis Sprague of Duxbury, planter, sold to "his son-in-law Ralph Earle of Road Island in the Jurisdiction of Providence Plantation the one-half of all his share, part or portion of land lying or being at the place or places commonly called by the Indians by the names of Coaksett and Acushena" [MD 14:90-91, citing PCLR 2:2:30a].

On 27 April 1661, "Francis Sprague of Duxburrow ... planter" deeded "unto John Sprague his true and natural son all that his dwelling house and outhouses and buildings scituate in Duxburrow aforesaid, and all and singular the upland and meadow now thereunto belonging, whether obtained by grant or purchased of other persons ... containing in all forty or fifty acres or thereabouts with three acres of meadow" [MD 16:205-7, citing PCLR 2:2:75-76]. On 3 May 1664, "Francis Sprague of Duxburrow ... planter" deeded to "his son John Sprague all that his part, portion and share of land and meadow he hath at or near Namasakett ... which was granted to him and others" on 3 June 1662 [MD 19:107, citing PCLR 3:4; see also PCR 4:19 and MD 34:81, citing PCLR 3:21].

BIRTH: By about 1589 (based on estimated date of marriage).
DEATH: Living 1670 [PCR 5:275] but deceased by 2 March 1679/80 [PCR 7:221].
MARRIAGE: (1) By about 1614 _____ _____. She died in England by 1623.
    (2) By about 1630 _____ _____.
CHILDREN:
  With first wife
    i ANNA SPRAGUE, b. say 1614; m. by 1644 William Lawrence [PCR 12:138].
    ii MERCY SPRAGUE, b. say 1617; m. Plymouth 9 November 1637 William Tubbs [PCR 1:68]; William Tubbs was granted a divorce from his wife Mercy, 7 July 1668, at which time she was living in Rhode Island [PCR 4:192].
  With second wife
    iii JOHN SPRAGUE, b. say 1630; m. by about 1655 Ruth Bassett, daughter of WILLIAM BASSETT [PM 48] (on 8 June 1655, "we present John Sprague and Ruth Bassett, of Duxburrow, for fornication before they were married" [PCR 3:82]). (John Sprague is treated in detail by Maclean W. McLean, who estimates his birth as about 1635, whereas we make him slightly older [TAG 41:178-81].)
    iv DORCAS SPRAGUE, b. say 1632; m. by 1659 Ralph Earle [MD 14:90-91].

COMMENTS: There are few dates for this family and many unanswered questions. The household of Francis Sprague consisted of three persons in 1623 and again in 1627 [PCR 12:5, 11], and we assume here that these three are in both cases Francis, Anna and Mercy. Mercy was clearly the daughter who married in 1637, but opinion is divided as to whether Anna was wife or daughter of Francis.

We know that a daughter of Francis Sprague had married William Lawrence by 1644, but we have no record that gives her Christian name. But to have married by that date, and be born after the cattle division of

1627, she would be seventeen at marriage at most, and perhaps younger. The more likely solution is that the Anna of the cattle division was a second daughter, and Francis did not bring a wife with him to New England.

The other two children of Francis (John and Dorcas) were apparently born in the 1630s, and so fifteen or twenty years younger than Mercy and Anna, with no evidence of any children born in between. This alone suggests that these were children of a second marriage. We postulate, therefore, that Francis Sprague had two wives, the first of whom died in England before 1623, and the second of whom he married in New England about 1630. If our conclusion that Anna Sprague of the 1627 cattle division became wife of William Lawrence is correct, then we do not know the given name of either of the wives of Francis, nor do we have dates of birth, marriage or death for either of them.

On 2 August 1642, Francis Sprague, innholder, of Duxborrow, was accused of selling a fowling piece to an Indian [PCR 2:43].

BIBLIOGRAPHIC NOTE: In 1919 Mary Lovering Holman compiled a concise account of the family of Francis Sprague [Scott Gen 241].

HUGH STACY

"Hugh Statie" appears in the 1623 Plymouth division of land, receiving one acre as a passenger on the *Fortune* in 1621 [PCR 12:5].

In his account of his adventures in early 1623, Phineas Pratt, having just reached the safety of Plymouth, reported that "the next day a young [mutilated] named Hugh Stacye went forth to fell a tree" [MHSC 4:4:484].

COMMENTS: This name does not appear in the 1627 Plymouth division of cattle. A Hugh Stacy appears in Salem in 1639, and soon moves to Dedham; most previous writers have assumed that this man is identical with the Plymouth man, but the long lapse of time without any intervening record makes this highly unlikely.

MILES STANDISH

ORIGIN: Holland.
MIGRATION: 1620 on the *Mayflower.*
FIRST RESIDENCE: Plymouth.
REMOVES: Duxbury.
RETURN TRIPS: Sent to London in late 1625 and returned early 1626.

OCCUPATION: Soldier.
FREEMAN: In the 1633 Plymouth list of freemen "Capt[ain] Myles Standish" is first among the Assistants, immediately after the governor [PCR 1:3]. In 7 March 1636/7 list of freemen [PCR 1:52]. In 1639 list of freemen, among Assistants and in Duxbury section [PCR 8:173, 174].
EDUCATION: He signed several documents sent to the Bay and must have been conversant with figures to be colony treasurer. His inventory included several dozen books, valued at £9 3s., among which there were three Bibles and a number of other theological volumes, as well as such titles as Homer's *Iliad* and Caesar's *Commentaries* [MD 3:155].
OFFICES: Plymouth Acting Governor, 3 May 1653 [PCR 3:27]. Assistant, 1 January 1632/3, 1 January 1634/5, 14 January 1636/7, 6 March 1637/8, 5 March 1638/9, 3 March 1639/40, 2 March 1640/1, 4 June 1645, 2 June 1646, 1 June 1647, 7 June 1648, 6 June 1649, 4 June 1650, 5 June 1651, 3 June 1652, 7 June 1653, 6 June 1654, 8 June 1655, 3 June 1656 [PCR 1:5, 32, 48, 79, 116, 140, 2:8, 83, 100, 115, 123, 139, 153, 166, 3:7, 30, 48, 77, 99]. Treasurer, 20 August 1644, 2 June 1646, 1 June 1647, 7 June 1648, 6 June 1649, 5 June 1651, 3 June 1652, 7 June 1653, 6 June 1654, 8 June 1655 [PCR 2:76, 101, 115, 123, 139, 166, 3:7, 30, 48, 77]. Council of War 27 September 1642, 10 October 1643, 6 April 1653 [PCR 2:47, 64, 100, 3:26, 28].

"Capt. Standish" is in the Duxbury section of the 1643 Plymouth Colony list of men able to bear arms [PCR 8:190].

Captain, 1620-56 [PCR 1:52, 59, 80, 82, 84, 90-92, 98, 100]. Commander of forces [PCR 2:47, 146]. Captain of troops raised for Dutch war [PCR 3:29, 55]. His inventory included "one fowling piece, 3 muskets, 4 carbines, 2 small guns, one old barrel" valued at £8 1s. and "one sword, one cutlass, 3 belts" valued at £2 7s. [MD 3:155].
ESTATE: In the 1623 Plymouth division of land "Captain Myles Standish" received two acres as a passenger on the *Mayflower* [for himself and his first wife, Rose], and "Mrs. Standish" received one acre as a passenger on the *Anne* in 1623 [PCR 12:4, 6]. In the 1627 Plymouth division of cattle Captain Standish, Barbara Standish, Charles Standish,

Alexander Standish and John Standish are the first five persons in the third company [PCR 12:10].

In 1631 "Captain Myles Standish of Plymouth" sold to Edward Winslow of Plymouth "two acres of land lying in the north field" [PCR 12:16].

In the Plymouth tax lists of 25 March 1633 and 27 March 1634 "Capt[ain] Myles Standish" was assessed 18s. [PCR 1:9, 27]. He was one of the purchasers [PCR 2:177].

From 1633 to 1637, Captain Standish was allowed to mow land he had formerly mowed [PCR 1:14, 40, 56]. On 4 December 1637, "Captain Myles Standish" was granted the surplusage of land on "Ducksborrow side" in consideration of the "want of lands he should have had to his proportion" [PCR 1:70]. On 2 July 1638, "Captain Myles Standish" received three hundred acres of uplands [PCR 1:91]. On 1 October 1638, he was granted a garden place at "Duxborrow side," which was formerly laid forth for him [PCR 1:99]. On 4 March 1650/1, "whereas Captain Miles Standish hath been at much trouble and pains, and hath gone sundry journeys into Yarmouth aforesaid in the said town's business, and likely to have more in that behalf, in respect whereunto the Court have granted unto the said Captain Standish" about forty or fifty acres [PCR 2:164].

On 9 May 1654, "Capt. Myles Standish" sold to Capt. Thomas Willett of Plymouth his purchaser's right at Sowamsett, Mattapoisett and places adjacent; "Mrs. Barberye Standish wife of the said Capt. Standish" consented to his deed [MD 6:246-47, citing PCLR 2:1:111].

On 3 June 1656, the General Court granted to "Captain Myles Standish" "three hundred acres of upland ... with a competency of meadow to such a proportion of upland lying and being at Satuckquett Pond, provided it come not within the court's grant of Bridgwater" [PCR 3:101, 107].

In his will, dated 7 March 1655[/6] and proved 4 May 1657, "Myles Standish Senior of Duxburrow" asked that "if I die at Duxburrow my body to be laid as near as conveniently may be to my two daughters Lora Standish my daughter and Mary Standish my daughter-in-law" and bequeathed to "my dear and loving wife Barbara Standish" one-third of his estate after all debts are paid; to "my son Josias Standish upon his marriage" cattle to the value of £40 (if possible); "that every one of my four sons viz: Allexander Standish, Myles Standish, Josias Standish and Charles Standish may have forty pounds apiece"; to "my eldest son Allexander ... a double share in land," and "so long as they live single that the whole be in partnership betwixt them"; "my dearly beloved wife

Barbara Standish, Allexander Standish, Myles Standish and Josias Standish" to be joint executors; "my loving friends Mr. Timothy Hatherley and Capt. James Cudworth" to be supervisors; to "Marcye Robinson whom I tenderly love for her grandfather's sake" £3; to "my servant John Irish Jr." 40s. beyond what is due him by covenant; and to "my son & heir apparent Allexander Standish all my lands as heir apparent by lawful descent in Ormistick, Borsconge, Wrightington, Maudsley, Newburrow, Crawston and the Isle of Man and given to me as right heir by lawful descent but surruptuously [sic] detained from me my great-grandfather being a second or younger brother from the house of Standish of Standish" [MD 3:153-55, citing PCPR 2:1:37-38].

The inventory of the estate of "Captain Miles Standish gent.," taken 2 December 1656, totalled £358 7s., of which £140 was real estate: "one dwelling house and outhouses with the land thereunto belonging," £140 [MD 3:155-56, citing PCPR 2:1:39-40].

On 4 May 1657, "Mr. Allexander Standish and Mr. Josias Standish do accept of being executors with Mrs. Barbery Standish, their mother, on the estate of Captain Myles Standish, deceased" [PCR 3:114].

On 5 October 1658, confirmation was made of a sale by "Capt. Myles Standish" (with consent of his wife Barbara) to Mr. Thomas Howes of Yarmouth of "a certain farm lying in the liberties of Yarmouth," which had been granted to Standish by the court on 4 March 1650 [MD 13:142-43, citing PCLR 2:2:11].

BIRTH: By about 1593 (based on date of marriage).
DEATH: Duxbury 3 October 1656 [MD 1:12-13 (and especially footnote on page 12); NEHGR 87:152].
MARRIAGE: (1) By about 1618 Rose _____. She died Plymouth 29 January 1620/1 ("January 29 [1620/1]. Dies Rose, the wife of Captain Standish" [Prince 184]).

(2) By 1624 Barbara _____. She died after 6 October 1659 [MD 4:119].
CHILDREN:
  With second wife
    i   CHARLES STANDISH, b. say 1624; living 1627; d. by about 1635.
    ii ALEXANDER STANDISH, b. say 1626 (died 6 July 1702 "being about 76 years of age" [NEHGR 87:153]); m. (1) by about 1660 Sarah Alden, daughter of JOHN ALDEN [PM 4]; m. (2) by 1689 Desire (Doty) (Sherman) Holmes, daughter of EDWARD DOTY [PM 177].

iii JOHN STANDISH, b. say 1627; no further record.
iv MILES STANDISH, b. say 1629; m. Boston 19 July 1660 Sarah Winslow, daughter of JOHN WINSLOW [PM 511; BVR 76].
v LORA STANDISH, b. say 1631; d. by 7 March 1655[/6], unm. (from father's will).
vi JOSIAS STANDISH, b. say 1633; m. (1) Marshfield 19 December 1654 Mary Dingley [MarVR 1]; m. (2) after 1655 Sarah Allen, daughter of Samuel Allen (in his will of 2 August 1669 Samuel Allen bequeathed to "my son-in-law Josiah Standish" [SPR 6:27]).
vii CHARLES STANDISH, b. say 1635; living 7 March 1655[/6] (named in father's will); no further record.

COMMENTS: Bradford listed "Captain Myles Standish and Rose his wife" as passengers on the *Mayflower* [Bradford 442]. In 1651 Bradford stated that "Captain Standish his wife died in the first sickness and he married again and hath four sons living and some are dead" [Bradford 445].

Standish was a leader of the first and third discovery expeditions on Cape Cod in November and December 1620 [Mourt 19-24, 32-37]. On 22 March 1620/1, Captain Standish and Master Williamson [William Brewster] met Massassoit at the brook and began negotiations, soon joined by the governor [Mourt 55-57].

Although we have been left with THOMAS MORTON's description of Standish as "Captain Shrimp," Bradford described him in gentler terms during the first great sickness:

> so as there died sometimes two or three of a day ... that of one hundred & odd persons, scarce fifty remained. And of these in the time of most distress, there was but six or seven sound persons, who, to their great commendations be it spoken, spared no pains, night nor day, but with abundance of toil and hazard of their own health ... did all the homely & necessary offices for them, which dainty & queazy stomachs cannot endure to hear named; and all this willingly & cheerfully, without any grudging in the least, showing herein their true love unto their friends & brethren. A rare example & worthy to be remembered. Two of these seven were Mr. William Brewster, their Reverend Elder, & Myles Standish, their Captain & military commander, unto whom myself & many

others, were much beholden in our low & sick condition [Bradford 77].

In the winter of 1622, Captain Standish was to go to the Bay, but was twice driven back by high winds, the latter time being sick with a "violent fever" [Good News 299-300]. The Governor took his place and the meeting occurred as intended; Standish recovered within the month [Good News 304].

Lyford and Oldham, in their derogatory letters to England about the early settlement at Plymouth, said "Captain Standish looks like a silly boy, and is in utter contempt" [Bradford 156]. Standish had a facility with language, but one editor remarked that "Standish, though 'the best linguist among them,' in the Indian dialects, was more expert with the sword than the pen" [Young's Pilgrim Fathers 115].

In early 1623, Captain Standish went to trade with the Indians. On meeting some of greater number than his little band, he soon missed some beads, and taking his men "set them on their guard about the sachem's house ... threatening to fall upon them without further delay if they would not forthwith restore them, signifying ... that as he would not offer the least injury, so he would not receive any at their hands, which should escape without punishment or due satisfaction" [Good News 309]. This bold stance won respect as well as the return of the beads.

In a 1623 trip to the area near what would be Boston, Captain Standish warned the men there of the Indians' violent intentions. When a number arrived to trade, Standish boldly faced them down and averted a skirmish, but not without suffering some personal slights:

> Also Pecksuot, being a man of greater stature than the Captain, told him, though he were a great captain, yet he was but a little man; and, said he, though I be no sachem, yet I am a man of great strength and courage. These things the Captain observed, yet bare with patience for the present [Good News 338].

In a running conflict in spring of 1623, Standish and a small troop took the high ground and as one assailant drew his bow to fire at Standish, Standish and one other fired at him and broke his arm, "whereupon they fled into a swampe. When they were in the thicket, they parleyed, but to small purpose, getting nothing but foul language. So our Captain dared the sachem to come out and fight like a man, showing how base and woman-like he was in tonguing it as he did, but he refused, and fled" [Good News 341].

In late 1625 Captain Standish was sent to England with letters and instructions both to their friends of the company ... and also the Honorable Council of New England to the company to desire that seeing that they meant only to let them have goods upon sale, that they might have them upon easier terms, for they should never be able to bear such high interest ... But he came in a very bad time, for the State was full of trouble, and the plague very hot in London, so as no business could be done, yet he spake with some of the Honored Council, who promised all helpfulness to the plantation which lay in them ... yet with much ado he took up £150 (& spent a good deal of it in expences) at 50 per cent, which he bestowed in trading goods & such other most needful commodities as he knew requisite for their use, and so returned passenger in a fishing ship [Bradford 177-79].

In 1628, Captain Standish was sent to capture Thomas Morton by force. Coming upon Morton's dwelling, Standish found him to be well armed and locked within. Fortunately, they were "over armed with drink" and, coming out of the house

they were so steeled with drink as their pieces were too heavy for them, [Morton] ... with a carbine ... had thought to have shot Captain Standish; but he [Standish] stepped to him, & put by his piece, & took him. Neither was there any hurt done to any of either side, save that one was so drunk that he ran his own nose upon the point of a sword that one held before him as he entered the house; but he lost but a little of his hot blood [Bradford 209-10].

In 1634 when Mr. Alden was imprisoned in Massachusetts Bay, Captain Standish was sent to free him [Bradford 264-65].

BIBLIOGRAPHIC NOTE: The last clause of the will of Miles Standish, in which he complains of being "surruptuously detained" from his rightful inheritance, and then lists a number of estates, has spawned a great amount of research into the origin of this immigrant.

In 1914 Thomas Cruddas Porteus published "Some Recent Investigations Concerning the Ancestry of Capt. Myles Standish" [NEHGR 68:339-69]. He transcribed many estate documents and came to the tentative conclusion that Miles Standish descended from a certain Huan Standish of the Isle of Man.

In 1933 Merton Taylor Goodrich prepared a study of "The Children and Grandchildren of Capt. Myles Standish" [NEHGR 87:149-60]. Goodrich touches only briefly on the matter of the Standish ancestry; the most important part of his article is a careful study of both wives and each of the children of Miles Standish, dealing in detail with a number of matters of chronology and proof. This article is the bedrock on which all later work is based.

More recently G.V.C. Young has tackled the problem of the ancestry of Miles Standish and has advanced our knowledge greatly. In 1984 he presented an extended argument that Miles Standish was born on the Isle of Man, and that he was the son of a John Standish of Ellanbane on the Isle of Man [*Myles Standish: First Manx American* (Isle of Man 1984)]. This John Standish was son of another John Standish, who was son of a Huan Standish of Ellanbane, the very man proposed by Porteus in 1914. Although this conclusion is well argued, the proof is not yet complete, although Young's identification is highly probable.

Young has published two brief supplements to this work: *More About Pilgrim Myles Standish* (Isle of Man 1987) and *Ellanbane Was the Birthplace of Myles Standish* (Isle of Man 1988).

JAMES STEWARD

In the 1623 Plymouth land division James Steward received one acre as a passenger on the *Fortune* in 1621 [PCR 12:5]. He does not appear in the 1627 cattle division, or in any later record.

ELIAS STORY

Elias Story came to Plymouth in 1620 on the *Mayflower* as a servant of Edward Winslow and died soon after arrival [Bradford 441, 444].

THOMAS SYMONS

In his will of 30 July 1633 Samuel Fuller desired "my two servants Thomas Symons & Rob[er]t Cowles for the remainder of their several terms to be employed for the good of my children" [MD 1:26, citing PCPR 1:1].

On 1 February 1641/2, Thomas Symons and Edward Doty were in court over a disagreement about keeping cows [PCR 2:33].

"Thomas Symons" appears in the Scituate section of the 1643 Plymouth Colony list of men able to bear arms [PCR 8:191].

On 26 January 1649, "Thomas Simmons of Scituate ..., planter," sold to Gilbert Brooks of Scituate, planter, nine acres of upland with the buildings thereon, along with another ten acres of upland [PCR 12:217-18].

COMMENTS: Various authors have tried to make Thomas Symons a son or brother of MOSES SIMONSON [PM 419], but there is no evidence for this. Raymon Meyers Tingley went so far as to fabricate a deposition by Symons making him brother-in-law of SAMUEL NASH [PM 341] and father-in-law of Gilbert Brooks [Tingley-Meters 371-72], but this alleged document is impeached by its own internal chronological impossibilities.

T

WILLIAM TENCH

Arrived in Plymouth in 1623 on the *Fortune*, and received with John Cannon two acres in the 1623 land division [PCR 12:5]. He was not in the 1627 cattle division, but in a deed of 14 September 1638 was said to have earlier sold the land to JOHN BILLINGTON [PCR 12:37].

COMMENTS: See JOHN CANNON for comments, which apply equally to both men [PM 93].

EDWARD THOMSON

Edward Thompson came to Plymouth in 1620 on the *Mayflower* as a servant to WILLIAM WHITE [PM 495], and Thompson and White "died soon after their landing" [Bradford 442, 445].

On 4 December 1620 "[d]ies Edward Thomson, servant of Mr. White, the first that dies since their arrival" [Prince 165].

JOHN THORPE

ORIGIN: Unknown.
MIGRATION: 1632.
FIRST RESIDENCE: Duxbury.

OCCUPATION: Carpenter.
EDUCATION: His inventory included a "psalm book" valued at 1s. and "a Bible" valued at 6s. [MD 1:160].
OFFICES: His inventory included "1 fowling piece" valued at £1 15s. and "one powder horn" valued at 4d. [MD 1:159].
ESTATE: Assessed 18s. in the Plymouth tax list of 25 March 1633 [PCR 1:11].

On 28 October 1633, "Alice, the late wife of John Thorp, [was] appointed to bring in an inventory of the goods & chattels of her deceased husband on Monday, the 11th of November next ensuing" [PCR 1:18].

The inventory of the estate of "Joh: Thorp, carpenter, late of Plymouth deceased," taken 15 November 1633, was untotalled and included no real estate [MD 1:158-61, citing PCPR 1:15-16].

On 25 November 1633, "whereas John Thorp, carpenter, late of Duxburrow, in the liberties of Plymouth aforesaid, deceased, died indebted far more than the estate of the said John would make good, insomuch as Alice, his wife, durst not administer, it was ordered, that Captain Myles Standish, Gent., & Stephen Hopkins should enter upon his estate, according to an inventory presented upon oath by the said Alice, his wife, in behalf of the Court, that so the creditors might be satisfied, so far as the estate will make good, and the widow be freed from & acquitted of all & all manner of claim or claims or demands by all & every his creditors whatsoever" [PCR 1:20].

BIRTH: By about 1608 (based on estimated date of marriage).
DEATH: Between 1 April 1633 and 15 August 1633 [PCR 1:12, 16].
MARRIAGE: By 1633 Alice _____, who survived him; she was presumably still quite young, and may well have married someone else in Plymouth; the fate of their child is unknown.
CHILD:
  i   Child THORPE, b. 1633; no further record. (On 1 April 1633, "John Thorp & Alice his wife likewise adjudged to sit in the stocks & amerced in forty shillings fine, because his wife conceived with child before marriage, but in regard of their present poverty, twelve months time given for payment" [PCR 1:12].)

COMMENTS: On 20 January 1632/3, "Robert Barker, servant of John Thorp, complained of his master for want of clothes. The complaint being found to be just, it was ordered, that Thorp should either forthwith apparel him, or else make over his time to some other that was able to provide for him" [PCR 1:7].

On 15 August 1633, "[w]hereas Robert Barker had bound himself an apprentice to John Thorpe, in the trade of carpentry, the said Thorp being dead, Alice, his wife, hath turned over his time" to William Palmer, nailer, of Plymouth [PCR 1:16].

In 1910 George H. Williams wrote to Samuel Forbes Rockwell, suggesting that John Thorpe's widow Alice married second William Davis [Samuel Forbes Rockwell, *Davis Families of Early Roxbury and Boston* (North Andover, Massachusetts, 1932), p. 15], but this results from confusion with an event that took place in Roxbury a generation later. On 21 October 1658, William Davis and Alice Thorpe were married in Roxbury. The identity of this Alice is unknown, but as she had children baptized in 1663, it would be biologically impossible for her to be identical with the widow of John Thorp.

THOMAS TILDEN

In the 1623 Plymouth land division Thomas Tilden received three acres as a passenger on the *Anne* in 1623 [PCR 12:6]. He is not seen in the 1627 division of cattle or in any later record.

COMMENTS: The grant of three acres indicates that Thomas Tilden was the head of a household of three, perhaps a wife and child [MQ 40:60]. He could be brother of NATHANIEL TILDEN {1635, Scituate} [Joseph Neal Anc 53-55], although this is far from proven. (Stratton notes that in Torrey the wife is named Ann. This may be another instance in which the name of the ship has been transferred to one of its passengers; see also THOMAS FLAVELL [PM 203].)

EDWARD TILLEY

ORIGIN: Leiden, Holland [NEHGR 143:208].
MIGRATION: 1620 on the *Mayflower*.
FIRST RESIDENCE: Plymouth.

BIRTH: Baptized Henlow, Bedfordshire, 27 May 1588 (as "Edmond"), son of Robert and Elizabeth (_____) Tilley [TAG 52:203].
DEATH: Late 1620 or early 1621 [Bradford 446].
MARRIAGE: Henlow 20 June 1614 Agnes Cooper. She died at Plymouth about the same time as her husband [Bradford 446].
CHILDREN: None recorded.
ASSOCIATIONS: JOHN TILLEY of the *Mayflower* was Edward's brother [PM 462].

COMMENTS: Bradford named "Edward Tilley and Ann his wife, and two children that were their cousins, Henry Sampson and Humility Cooper" in his list of *Mayflower* passengers [Bradford 442]. "Edward Tilley and his wife both died soon after their arrival, and the girl Humility, their cousin, was sent for into England and died there. But the youth Henry Sampson is still living and is married and hath seven children" [Bradford 446].

On their first landing in November 1620, sixteen men were equipped with musket, sword and corslet, under the command of Capt. Miles Standish "unto whom was adjoined, for counsel and advice, William Bradford, Stephen Hopkins, and Edward Tilley" [Mourt 19]. On 6 December, when another group of discoverers went out, both John Tilley and Edward Tilley were among the ten [Mourt 32]. The voyage along the coast was bitterly cold and "Edward Tilley had like to have sounded [swooned] with cold" [Mourt 32]. He survived the seven-day trip, although the exposure probably did not help him when the little group was visited by sickness.

BIBLIOGRAPHIC NOTE: In 1976 Robert Leigh Ward explored the English origin of the Tilley family at Henlow, Bedfordshire, and the close connections with HUMILITY COOPER [PM 156] and HENRY SAMSON [TAG 52:198-208; PM 401]. In 1985 he further extended the ancestry of this group of immigrants [TG 6:166-86].

JOHN TILLEY

ORIGIN: Leiden, Holland.
MIGRATION: 1620 on the *Mayflower*.
FIRST RESIDENCE: Plymouth.

BIRTH: Baptized Henlow, Bedfordshire, 19 December 1571, son of Robert and Elizabeth (____) Tilley [TAG 52:203].
DEATH: Late 1620 or early 1621 [Bradford 446].
MARRIAGE: Henlow 20 September 1596 Joan (Hurst) Rogers. She had married (1) Thomas Rogers. She died in late 1620 or early 1621 [Bradford 446].
CHILDREN:
    i ROSE TILLEY, bp. Henlow 23 October 1597; no further record.

ii   JOHN TILLEY, bp. Henlow 26 August 1599; no further record.
iii ROSE TILLEY, bp. Henlow 28 February 1601/2; no further record.
iv   ROBERT TILLEY, bp. Henlow 25 November 1604; no further record.
v   ELIZABETH TILLEY, bp. Henlow 30 August 1607; m. about 1625 JOHN HOWLAND [PM 279].

ASSOCIATIONS: John Tilley was the elder brother of EDWARD TILLEY [PM 461], who also died in the first sickness.

COMMENTS: "John Tilley and his wife, and Elizabeth their daughter," were passengers on the *Mayflower* [Bradford 442]. "John Tilley and his wife both died a little after they came ashore. And their daughter Elizabeth married with John Howland and hath issue as is before noted" [Bradford 446].

John Tilley joined the expedition of 6 December 1620 along the coast with nine others, under the leadership of Miles Standish [Young's Pilgrim Fathers 149].

BIBLIOGRAPHIC NOTE: In addition to the items noted in the sketch of EDWARD TILLEY, Robert Leigh Ward in 1985 published some additional biographical information on John Tilley [TAG 60:171-73].

THOMAS TINKER

"Thomas Tinker and his wife and a son" came to Plymouth in 1620 on the *Mayflower* and "all died in the first sickness" [Bradford 442, 446]. Thomas Tinker signed the Mayflower Compact.

COMMENTS: Banks suggested two quite different origins for Thomas Tinker, without any basis other than identity of name [English Homes 89]. Dexter thought he was the Thomas Tinker admitted an inhabitant of Leiden in 1617 [Dexter 636].

STEPHEN TRACY

ORIGIN: Leiden, Holland.
MIGRATION: 1623 on the *Anne*.

FIRST RESIDENCE: Plymouth.
REMOVES: Duxbury.
RETURN TRIPS: Returned to England permanently, perhaps as early as 1643, and certainly by 1654.

OCCUPATION: Sayworker (in Leiden).
FREEMAN: In 1633 Plymouth list of freemen, before those admitted on 1 January 1632/3 [PCR 1:3]. In list of freemen of 7 March 1636/7 [PCR 1:52]. In Duxbury section of 1639 Plymouth Colony list of freemen (with his name lined through) [PCR 8:174].
OFFICES: Plymouth coroner's jury, 2 March 1635/6 [PCR 1:39]. Grand jury, 7 March 1636/7, 2 June 1640, 7 June 1642 [PCR 1:54, 155, 2:41].

Duxbury representative on committee to lay out highways, 1 October 1634 [PCR 1:31]. Plymouth colony committee to assess taxes, 3 March 1634/5, 1 March 1635/6 [PCR 1:33, 38]. Duxbury representative to committee on the "nearer uniting of Plymouth & those on Duxburrough side," 14 March 1635/6 [PCR 1:41]. Committee to apportion hay grounds, 20 March 1636/7 [PCR 1:55].

Duxbury constable, 5 March 1638/9, 4 June 1639 [PCR 1:116, 125]. Arbiter, 7 September 1642 [PCR 2:44].

ESTATE: In 1623 Plymouth land division, granted three acres as passenger on *Anne* [PCR 12:6]. In 1627 Plymouth cattle division, "Stephen Tracie, Triphosa Tracie, Sarah Tracie, Rebecka Tracie" were the fifth through eighth names in the tenth company [PCR 12:12].

Assessed 18s. in Plymouth tax lists of 25 March 1633 and 27 March 1634 [PCR 1:10, 27]. He appears on the list of purchasers [PCR 2:177].

Permitted to mow "within his own ground," 1 July 1633 [PCR 1:14]. Assigned mowing ground, 14 March 1635/6, 20 March 1636/7 [PCR 1:40, 56]. Granted eighty acres with some meadow additional, at the North River, 2 November 1640 [PCR 1:165].

On 20 March 1654/5, while in London, Stephen Tracy "at present of Great Yarmouth in old England" made his will, in the form of a power of attorney to John Winslow, disposing to son John "what land and houses I have there in Duxburrow" (along with some cattle), to "my daughter Ruth Tracy one cow and one two year old mare," and "what cattle I have more (Marye's two cows being cast in amongst them) to be equally divided among my five children living in New England," noting that some of his children are married with children, and others are unmarried [PLR 2:179, transcribed in full in MD 10:143-44].

Stephen Tracy

BIRTH: Probably the "Stephen Trace" baptized 28 December 1596 at Great Yarmouth, Norfolk, son of Stephen and Agnes/Anne (Erdley) Tracy [TAG 51:73; Tracy Gen 19-20].

DEATH: After 20 March 1654/5 (date of will).

MARRIAGE: Leiden, Holland, 3 January 1621 [NS] Tryphosa Lee [Plooij XLII; Leiden Pilgrims 264]. She was born about 1597 (aged 27 on 1 May 1624 [TAG 51:242]) and presumably predeceased her husband.

CHILDREN:
  i   SARAH TRACY, b. Leiden about January 1623 [TAG 51:242]; m. Plymouth [blank] November 1638 George Partridge [PCR 1:103].
  ii REBECCA TRACY, b. Plymouth say 1625; m. say 1645 William Merrick [Dawes-Gates 2:801-2].
  iii RUTH TRACY, b. say 1628; living unm. 1655.
  iv MARY TRACY, b. say 1630; living perhaps unm. 1655.
  v   JOHN TRACY, b. say 1632; m. by about 1661 Mary Prence, daughter of THOMAS PRENCE [PM 374; Tracy Gen 26].

ASSOCIATIONS: WILLIAM PALMER the elder of Duxbury, nailer, left a legacy to Stephen Tracy in his will of 4 December 1637 [PM 349]. How he might have been associated or related to Tracy is unknown.

COMMENTS: Robert S. Wakefield discusses some important records relating to the Tracy family at Leiden, and to the date of arrival of Stephen's wife Tryphosa, and eldest daughter Sarah, and concludes that they came in 1625 on the *Jacob* [TAG 51:71-73, 242].

On 7 July 1638, the Plymouth court noted that Tracy "had hired John Price for four months; his time was to begin the first week in June" [PCR 1:92].

Stephen Tracy is not included in the 1643 list of men able to bear arms, and is not seen in any later Plymouth Colony record, so he may have returned to England late in 1642 or early in 1643.

BIBLIOGRAPHIC NOTE: In 1936 Sherman Weld Tracy published a genealogy of some of the descendants of Stephen Tracy [*The Tracy Genealogy* (Rutland, Vermont, 1936)]. Mary Walton Ferris treated Stephen Tracy in 1931 [Dawes-Gates 2:799-802], and Donald Lines Jacobus twice prepared accounts of this immigrant [Waterman Gen 1:688-90; Ackley-Bosworth 37-38].

WILLIAM TREVOR

"There were also other two seamen hired to stay a year here in the country, William Trevor, and one Ely. But when their time was out they both returned" [Bradford 443].

COMMENTS: The above note is from Bradford's account of the passengers on the *Mayflower*. Trevor may also have been in New England in 1619 and in 1650 [see NEHGR 9:248, and DAVID THOMSON [GMB 3:1807-9].

HUMPHREY TURNER

ORIGIN: Little Baddow, Essex.
MIGRATION: 1632.
FIRST RESIDENCE: Plymouth.
REMOVES: Scituate 1633.

OCCUPATION: Tanner [PCLR 3:175, 218, 282, 5:208; PCPR 3:1:71].
CHURCH MEMBERSHIP: Founding member of Scituate church, 8 January 1634/5 [NEHGR 9:279]. "Goody Turner," presumably his wife, joined the same church 10 January [1635/6] [NEHGR 9:280].
FREEMAN: In the 1633 Plymouth list of freemen, in close proximity to men made free on 1 January 1632/3 [PCR 1:4]. In 7 March 1636/7 Plymouth list of freemen [PCR 1:52]. In Scituate sections of 1639, 1658 and 29 May 1670 lists of Plymouth Colony freemen [PCR 5:275, 8:175, 198].
EDUCATION: He signed his deeds until 1 November 1672, when he made his mark.
OFFICES: Deputy for Scituate to Plymouth General Court, 2 June 1640, 1 June 1641, 7 June 1642, 5 June 1644, 20 August 1644, 28 October 1645, 3 March 1645/6, 7 July 1646, 1 June 1647, 4 June 1650, 5 June 1651, 3 June 1652, 7 June 1653 [PCR 1:155, 2:16, 40, 72, 74, 94, 95, 104, 117, 154, 167, 3:8, 32].

Plymouth petit jury, 6 March 1637/8, 4 September 1638, 3 March 1639/40, 2 March 1640/1, 1 March 1641/2, 7 March 1642/3, 4 June 1645 [PCR 1:96, 7:8, 16, 19, 28, 34, 41]. Grand jury, 7 June 1642, 7 March 1642/3, 6 June 1643 [PCR 2:41, 53, 56]. Coroner's jury, 5 June 1666 [PCR 4:130].

Scituate constable, 5 January 1635/6, 5 March 1638/9, 4 June 1639 [PCR 1:36, 116, 125]. Committee to divide lands in Scituate, 30 November 1640 [PCR 1:168]. Supervisor of highways, 1 June 1647, 7 June 1648 [PCR 2:115, 124].].

In Scituate section of 1643 Plymouth Colony list of men able to bear arms [PCR 8:191].

ESTATE: Assessed 9s. in the Plymouth tax lists of 25 March 1633 and 27 March 1634 [PCR 1:10, 28].

On 18 May 1633, "Humphrey Turner, having obtained leave to make use of a piece of ground by the pond on the western side of the fort, near the town, & having enclosed the same with a firm palisado, hath sold his right & title to the same, as also the palisado itself, together with a small randevow, to Josias Winslow, the elder, for & in consideration of eight pounds sterling" [PCR 1:13].

On 14 October 1633, the town of Scituate granted to "Humpherey Turner the fourth lot on the south side of the Stony Brook containing four acres" [ScitTR 1:234]. Additional grants followed: 20 February 1634[/5?], "twenty-six acres of upland ... upon the southwest corner of the third cliff"; 7 February 1636[/7?], "a portion of meadow lying against the southwest side of his forementioned lot"; 7 February 1636[/7?], "fourscore acres of upland"; 7 February 1636[/7?], "a proportionable quantity of marsh land according to the quantity of his lot of uplands"; 6 February 1643[/4], "ten acres of upland" [ScitTR 1:234-35]. On 10 January 1645[/6?], there was "made over unto Jn. Turner Senior per his father Humphery Turner" the fourscore acres of upland and the associated marsh land [ScitTR 1:251].

Humphrey Turner had built a house at Scituate by September 1634 [NEHGR 10:42]; by 1636 he had built a second house "on his lot," and at some point his first house had passed to Goodman Jackson [NEHGR 10:42, 43].

On 1 January 1637/8, "Humfrey Turner" was one of a number of freemen of Scituate who complained that their proportions of land were so small that they could not subsist upon them, and the Court of Assistants granted them a portion of upland and neck between the North & South rivers and all the meadow between the rivers from North River to Beaver Pond "always provided and upon condition that they make a township there & inhabit upon the said lands" [PCR 1:72].

On 7 March 1639[/40?], Thomas Roberts of Plymouth sold to "Humfrey Turner of Scituate" one acre and three-quarters of swamp in Scituate "lately purchased of George Lewis of Scituate" [PCR 12:55].

On 27 May 1648, "Humphery Turner" of Scituate, tanner, sold to Henry Ewell of Scituate, joiner, "all that my ten acres of upland lying and being by the water mill in Scittuate" [PCLR 5:208].

On 1 October 1668, "Humphery Turner" of Scituate, tanner, deeded to "my sons Joseph Turner and Nathaniell Turner ... all that my lot of upland lying and being on the easterly side of Taunton River"; on 23 July 1669, wife Lydia consented [PCLR 3:175]. On 21 February 1669, "Humphery Turner" of Scituate, tanner, deeded to "my son Nathaniell Turner" of Scituate twenty-seven acres of upland at the Third Cliff, with housing, and thirty acres of marsh meadow adjoining [PCLR 3:282]. On 24 February 1669, "Humphery Turner" of Scituate, tanner, deeded to "my son Thomas Turner" of Scituate twenty acres of upland at the Third Cliff, which "sometimes was John Whetcomb's," along with nine acres of marsh meadow adjoining [PCLR 3:218]. On 1 November 1672, "Humphery Turner" of Scituate deeded to "my loving son Joseph Turner" of Scituate all right to undivided land in Scituate "or any way appertaining to the right of a purchasing freeman of the patent of Plymouth"; acknowledged 29 May 1673 by the witnesses, the grantor being deceased [PCLR 3:321].

In his will, dated 28 February 1669[/70] and proved 5 June 1673, Humphrey Turner of Scituate, tanner, "being weak in body" bequeathed "to my eldest son John Turner" his farm; to "my son Joseph Turner," £40, also £12; to "my son John Turner," £5; to "my son Daniel Turner," £12; to "my son Nathaniel Turner," £50; to "my daughter Mary [illegible]," £10; to "my daughter Lydia Doughtey," £12; "unto my grandchild Humphrey Turner," £5; to "my grandchild Mary Doughtey," £10; to "my grandchildren Jonathan Turner, Josiah Turner and Elizabeth Turner, being the fruits of my eldest son," 10s. a year; to "son Nathaniel Turner all my livestock both cattles, horses, sheep, etc."; to "my son Thomas Turner all my wearing clothes, one wood bed and blankets" [Briggs Gen 313-14; MD 24:42-43, citing PCPR 3:1:71].

BIRTH: About 1593 (based on date of marriage).
DEATH: After 1 November 1672 and before 29 May 1673 [PCLR 3:321]. (A tombstone gives his age in 1673 as 78, and says he was born in 1594, but this stone was erected in 1869 [Briggs Gen 312].)
MARRIAGE: Sandon, Essex, 24 October 1618 Lydia Gaymer, baptized Terling, Essex, 18 May 1602, daughter of Richard and Margaret (Mason) Gaymer [NEHGR 151:286-90]. She was living on 23 July 1669 when she consented to her husband's deed of 1 October 1668, but had died by 28 February 1669[/70] when she was not named in her husband's will.

CHILDREN:
    i   JOHN TURNER, bp. Terling, Essex, 24 March 1621 [NEHGR 151:287]; m. 10 or 12 November 1645 Mary Brewster [PCR 2:94; MD 1:8 (from "Brewster Book")], daughter of Jonathan Brewster and granddaughter of WILLIAM BREWSTER [PM 66].

    ii   JOHN TURNER, b. say 1624 (in Scituate section of 1643 Plymouth Colony list of men able to bear arms [PCR 8:191]); m. Scituate 25 April 1649 Ann James [MD 2:33].

    iii   THOMAS TURNER, b. say 1627; m. Scituate 6 January 1651[/2] Sarah Hiland [PCR 8:21].

    iv   LYDIA TURNER, bp. Little Baddow, Essex, 17 February 1629[/30] [NEHGR 151:287]; m. Scituate 15 August 1649 James Doughty [MD 2:33].

    v   MARY TURNER, bp. Scituate 25 January 1634/5 [NEHGR 9:281]; m. Scituate 13 November 1651 William Parker [PCR 8:19].

    vi   JOSEPH TURNER, bp. Scituate 1 January 1636/7 [NEHGR 9:281]; d. unm. after 1681 [Briggs Gen 314].

    vii   NATHANIEL TURNER, bp. Scituate 10 March 1638/9 [NEHGR 9:281]; m. (1) Scituate 29 March 1664/5 [*sic*] Mehitable Rigby, daughter of John Rigby of Dorchester (see *COMMENTS* below); m. (2) by 1691 Abigail (Eames?) Stockbridge, widow of Charles Stockbridge [NEHGR 133:191-92; TAG 38:186].

    viii   DANIEL TURNER, b. say 1641; m. Scituate 20 June "1665 or 1666" [*sic*] Hannah Randall, daughter of William Randall.

ASSOCIATIONS: WILLIAM VASSALL {1630, Boston} [GMB 3:1871-75], who also came to Scituate to reside, also had two children baptized at Little Baddow.

COMMENTS: Deane says that Turner "arrived with his family, in Plymouth 1628. He had a house lot assigned him 1629" [p. 360]. This date of arrival is not supported by any contemporary records and is contradicted by the baptism of daughter Lydia in Little Baddow, Essex, on 17 February 1629[/30].

The two eldest surviving children of Humphrey Turner were both named John. In England at the time of birth of these sons, they could be by the same mother, as was the case with this family, but in New England this practice was discontinued, and two siblings of the same name would always be half-siblings.

On 4 December 1638, Humphrey Turner was fined twice, 3s. each time, for non-appearance [PCR 1:104]. On 7 June 1649, "Humfry Turner" and others deposed that William Gilson had requested land on behalf of two of his sister's children, whom he had brought from England [PCR 2:143].

In the printed Scituate vital records the first wife of Nathaniel Turner is given as "Mehetabell Bigbee," but in the Dorchester church records is the baptism on 23 April 1643 of "Mehitabell Rigby," with the annotation "(to Mr. Turner of Scittuate)" [DChR 156].

BIBLIOGRAPHIC NOTE: In 1938 L. Vernon Briggs published a substantial treatment of Humphrey Turner, unfortunately perpetuating several of the nineteenth-century myths about the man [*History and Genalogy of the Briggs Family, 1254-1937* (Boston 1938), pp. 309-15].

In 1997 Vernon Dow Turner published the records identifying the wife of Humphrey Turner [NEHGR 151:286-90].

JOHN TURNER

ORIGIN: Leiden, Holland.
MIGRATION: 1620 on the *Mayflower*.
FIRST RESIDENCE: Plymouth.

BIRTH: By about 1590 (based on estimated date of marriage).
DEATH: Late 1620 or early 1621 in the first sickness [Bradford 446].
MARRIAGE: By about 1615 _____ _____. She did not come over.
CHILDREN:
    i   Son, b. say 1615; d. Plymouth 1620-21 [Bradford 446].
    ii   Son, b. say 1617; d. Plymouth 1620-21 [Bradford 446].
    iii (probably) ELIZABETH, b. say 1619; m. and living in Salem in 1650 (see *COMMENTS* below).

COMMENTS: Robert Cushman sent his letters to those intending to sail on the *Mayflower* by way of John Turner [Bradford 365-66].

Bradford describes the *Mayflower* passengers, including "John Turner, and two sons; he had a daughter came some years after to Salem, where she is now living" [Bradford 443]. In 1651 Bradford reported that "John Turner and his two sons all died in the first sickness. But he hath a daughter still living at Salem, well married, and approved of" [Bradford 446].

Robert S. Wakefield in "Mayflower Passengers Turner and Rogers: Probable Identification of Additional Children" (TAG 52:110-13) presents evidence indicating that the daughter of John Turner who came to New England after 1620 (probably in 1629 or 1630) was "Lysbet Turner" who appears in the 1622 Poll Tax list for Leiden. Wakefield argues convincingly that she was the Elizabeth Turner who witnessed a deed in Salem on 8 October 1635, and joined the church there on 28 December 1637. These dates would indicate that she was born no later than 1621; if this is in fact her date of birth, then she would have been born after her father sailed for New England, and posthumously; she could also have been born a few years earlier. In order to complete this identification, a search should be undertaken for a Salem man with wife named Elizabeth, the marriage taking place between 1637 and 1650, and probably closer to the earlier date.

CHRISTOPHER WADSWORTH

ORIGIN: Unknown.
MIGRATION: 1632.
FIRST RESIDENCE: Plymouth.
REMOVES: Duxbury.
RETURN TRIPS: Possibly returned to England in 1636 "to fetch Mr. [Ralph] Partridge," who would become minister at Duxbury [Sewall 432].

FREEMAN: In 1633 Plymouth list of freemen prior to those admitted 1 January 1632/3 [PCR 1:4]. In list of 7 March 1636/7 [PCR 1:52]. In Duxbury sections of lists of 1639, 1658 and 29 May 1670 [PCR 5:274, 8:174, 198].
EDUCATION: Signed his will. His inventory included "books" valued at £3.
OFFICES: Deputy for Duxbury to Plymouth Colony General Court, 2 June 1640, 27 September 1642, 1 August 1654, 5 June 1666, 5 June 1667 [PCR 1:154, 2:46, 3:63, 4:122, 148].

Duxbury delegate to Plymouth Colony committee to revise laws, 4 October 1636 [PCR 1:44]. Committee to divide lands, 3 June 1656 [PCR 3:102].

Plymouth petit jury, 4 October 1636, 2 March 1640/1, 7 December 1641, 1 March 1642/3, 7 November 1643, 5 November 1644, 7 June 1648, 2 October 1650, 4 March 1650/1, 7 June 1651, 4 October 1653, 7 March 1653/4, 3 October 1654, 5 June 1656, 6 October 1657, 3 May 1659, 3 October 1659, 2 October 1662, 6 March 1665/6 [PCR 1:44, 2:126, 4:115, 7:19, 25, 28, 36, 38, 52, 53, 54, 67, 70, 72, 79, 85, 93, 94, 105]. Grand jury, 7 March 1636/7, 4 June 1639, 7 June 1642, 7 June 1652, 3 June 1656, 6 June 1660 [PCR 1:54, 126, 2:41, 3:9, 100, 188]. Coroner's jury, 7 May 1662 [PCR 4:12].

Constable for the ward between Jones River and Green's Harbor [Duxbury], 1 January 1633/4 [PCR 1:21]. Duxbury constable, 6 March 1637/8, 5 June 1638 [PCR 1:80, 86].

Duxbury surveyor of highways, 3 June 1662 [PCR 4:15]. Selectman, 5 June 1666, 2 June 1667, 3 June 1668, 1 June 1669, 7 June 1670, 6 June 1671 [PCR 4:124, 149, 182, 5:19, 35, 56].

In Duxbury section of 1643 Plymouth Colony list of men able to bear arms [PCR 8:190].

ESTATE: Assessed 12s. in Plymouth tax list of 25 March 1633 [PCR 1:10]. Not included in list of 27 March 1634.

On 1 July 1633, granted mowing land where he "mowed last year" [PCR 1:15]. Granted mowing land at Morton's Hole, 14 March 1635/6 [PCR 1:39]. Granted mowing land he had the year before, 20 March 1636/7 [PCR 1:55].

On 2 October 1637, the "two lots of land on Ducksborrow side, formerly granted to Christopher Wadsworth, containing forty acres and upwards," were reconfirmed to Wadsworth, with some minor adjustments in the boundaries [PCR 1:66].

On 2 July 1638, Christopher Wadsworth "requested a parcel of land in the woods at the head of the Great Marsh, near Mr. Collyer's wolf trap" [PCR 1:90]. On 4 February 1638/9, granted fifty acres of upland about the head of South River [PCR 1:112-13].

On 20 September 1643, Christopher Wadsworth sold to "Mr. Raph Partrich" his uplands and meadow in Duxbury [PCR 12:96]. On 13 August 1651, Job Cole of Eastham sold Christopher Wadsworth of Duxbury a house and land lying against a place called Morton's Hole [PCR 12:216].

On 20 October 1655, John Starr of Duxbury sold to Christopher Wadsworth of Duxbury "all that my mansion and dwelling house" in Scituate, with eighty acres of upland, along with some marsh or meadow; also another parcel of upland [PCLR 4:253-55]. On 10 May 1664, John Bradford of Marshfield sold to Christopher Wadsworth of Duxbury "all my houses, orchards, uplands and meadows" in Duxbury [PCLR 3:1:66-67].

In his will, dated 31 July 1677 and proved 27 October 1680, Christopher Wadsworth bequeathed to "my eldest son Joseph" "one-half of those lands which I bought of Mr. John Bradford," upland and meadow, in Duxbury, he paying to "my daughter Mary Andrews two cows with calf not exceeding the age of five years old each of them" (and also confirmed to son John two shares of land in Bridgewater previously given to him); to "Grace my wife the one-half of my dwelling house during her natural life and half the lands thereunto belonging"; to "my son John" all remaining lands; to "Grace my wife" all household goods and some cattle [PCPR 4:1:68-70].

The inventory of the estate of Christopher Wadsworth, exhibited 7 June 1681, was untotalled and included no real estate [PCPR 4:1:71].

In her will, dated 13 January 1687/8 and proved 13 June 1688, Grace Wadsworth, widow, "by reason of old age and the many infirmities usually attending the same," bequeathed to "my son Joseph Wadsworth, a Dutch kettle, and to his wife my red petticoat, beside the pewter dishes & Bible which they have heretofore received"; to "the children of my son Samuel Wadsworth, deceased, the sum of £5 to be equally divided among them"; to "my daughter Mary Andrews, widow, a brass kettle"; to "my grandson John Wadsworth" 5s.; to "my granddaughters Mary and Abigaile Wadsworth to each of them a pair of my finest sheets, moreover to Abigaile I bequeath my bed bolster, red rug and blankets"; "to my son John Wadsworth" residue after the payment of legacies and debts; "my son John Wadsworth" executor [PPR 1:17-19; Gen Adv 1:20].

BIRTH: About 1609 (based on estimated date of marriage).
DEATH: After 31 July 1677 (date of will) and before 27 October 1680 (date of probate). (Pope and some other sources assign to the immigrant the death date of 18 April 1676, but this was the death of his son Samuel [Sewall 15; NEHGR 7:221-24].)
MARRIAGE: By about 1634 Grace _____. She died between 13 January 1687/8 (date of will) and 13 June 1688 (date of probate). (Many sources state that she was Grace Cole, but there is no evidence for this identity.)
CHILDREN:
    i   JOSEPH WADSWORTH, b. say 1634; m. by an unknown date Mary _____ (his widow, named in his will of 22 March 1689[/90], was Mary [Gen Adv 1:115-16, citing PPR 1:68-69]). (See *COMMENTS* below.)
    ii   SAMUEL WADSWORTH, b. say 1636; m. by about 1660 Abigail Lindall, daughter of James Lindall (so stated in 1853 by John A. Vinton, with no evidence supplied [NEHGR 7:17]).
    iii   JOHN WADSWORTH, b. say 1638 (d. Duxbury 15 May 1700 aged "about sixty-two years"); m. Duxbury 25 July 1667 Abigail Andrews, daughter of Henry Andrews of Taunton [NEHGR 52:16-23].
    iv   MARY WADSWORTH, b. say 1640; m. say 1659 Henry Andrews, son of Henry Andrews of Taunton [NEHGR 52:16-23].
ASSOCIATIONS: Some secondary sources claim that Christopher Wadsworth came to New England in 1632 on the *Lyon*. This is based on

a supposed relationship with WILLIAM WADSWORTH, who did come on that ship in 1632. Christopher Wadsworth is not on the passenger list for the *Lyon* in 1632, and there is no evidence that he was brother or any other relation of William, and, although he must have been in New England by 1632, he could have come earlier, so there is no basis for this claim.

COMMENTS: Christopher Wadsworth led a long, blameless and uneventful life. He held a number of offices, but was never before the court as a defendant in either a civil or criminal case. He carefully amassed land for his sons, never sold any, and apparently was never in debt.

The family of his son Joseph Wadsworth needs careful examination. All secondary sources state that he had first wife Abigail Waite, whom he married about 1655. No contemporary record of a wife named Abigail has been found, and there was no Waite family in Duxbury or vicinity from which Abigail could have come. According to his will Joseph had six children, three sons (Elisha, Joseph and Samuel) and three daughters (unnamed). Elisha married in 1694 and Samuel about 1700, indicating births in the early 1670s, and so no need for a marriage as early as 1655. Since Elisha named a son Wait, and this name was carried down in the family, some later historian of the family may have thought this indicated the surname of Elisha's mother, rather than a popular Puritan virture.

RALPH WALLEN

ORIGIN: Unknown.
MIGRATION: 1623 on *Anne*.
FIRST RESIDENCE: Plymouth.

FREEMAN: In 1633 Plymouth list of freemen, among those made free before 1 January 1632/3 [PCR 1:3]. In list of 7 March 1636/7 [PCR 1:53]. In Plymouth section of list of 1639, with later annotation "dead" [PCR 8:174].
ESTATE: In 1623 Plymouth land division "Ralfe Walen" granted an unknown number of acres as a passenger on the *Anne* [PCR 12:6]. In 1627 Plymouth land division Ralph Wallen and Joyce Wallen were the ninth and tenth persons in the company of Francis Eaton [PCR 12:12].

Assessed 9s. in Plymouth tax list of 25 March 1633 [PCR 1:10], but not included in list of 27 March 1634. He was one of the purchasers [PCR 2:177].

On 24 February 1633/4, "Raph Wallen" sold to Thomas Clark, for twenty bushels of corn and 40s. in money, "so much land next adjoining to the said Thomas, on the south side of his dwelling, as maketh up a former moiety the said Thomas bought of the said Raph twenty acres," and also "one share of meadow ground belonging to the said lot when division shall be made thereof" [PCR 1:25]. On 5 February 1637/8, "Raph Wallen acknowledgeth to have received of Thomas Clark £18, in full payment for the lands he bought of him" [PCR 1:76].

On 20 March 1636/7, allotted mowing ground "where he had the last year" [PCR 1:57].

BIRTH: By about 1595 (based on estimated date of marriage).
DEATH: By 1644 when his wife remarried.
MARRIAGE: By 1623 Joyce _____. She married (2) by 1644 THOMAS LOMBARD {1630, Dorchester} [GMB 2:1194-98; TAG 67:47-53].
CHILDREN:
  i (probably) MARY WALLEN, b. say 1628; m. (1) say 1648 John Ewer [TAG 67:52], son of THOMAS EWER {1635, Charlestown} [GM 2:2:479-83]; m. (2) Barnstable 2 February 1652[/3] John Jenkins [PCR 8:45].
  ii (possibly) THOMAS WALLEN, b. say 1630; living 1650 (and perhaps later) [TAG 67:52-53].

COMMENTS: The evidence for identifying the widow Joyce Wallen as the third wife of Thomas Lumbard is presented by Eleanor Cooley Rue in "Widow Joyce Wallen of Plymouth (1645) and Widow Joyce Lombard of Barnstable (1664): One and the Same?" [TAG 67:47-53]. This article includes a detailed and comprehensive discussion of Ralph Wallen's land holdings and transactions.

RICHARD WARREN

ORIGIN: London [Mourt 32].
MIGRATION: 1620 on the *Mayflower.*
FIRST RESIDENCE: Plymouth.

ESTATE: In the 1623 Plymouth division of land Richard Warren received an uncertain number of acres (perhaps two) as a passenger on the *Mayflower*, and five acres as a passenger on the *Anne* (presumably for his wife and children) [PCR 12:4-6]. In the 1627 Plymouth division of cattle Richard Warren, his wife Elizabeth Warren, Nathaniel Warren, Joseph Warren, Mary Warren, Anna Warren, Sarah Warren, Elizabeth Warren and Abigail Warren were the first nine persons in the ninth company [PCR 12:12]. He was one of the purchasers [PCR 2:177].

In the 25 March 1633 Plymouth tax list Widow Warren was assessed 12s., and in the list of 27 March 1634, 9s. [PCR 1:10, 27].

On 1 July 1633 "Mrs. Warren and Rob[er]t Bartlet" were allowed to mow where they did the previous year, and again 14 March 1635/6 [PCR 1:15, 41].

On 28 October 1633, "a misted that was granted formerly to Richard Warren, deceased, & forfeited by a late order, for want of building, the said misted was granted to Mr. Raph Fog & his heirs forever, provided the said Raph within twelve months build a dwelling house upon the same, & allow widow Warren so much for her fence remaining thereon as Rob[er]t Heeks & Christopher Wadsworth shall think it may be serviceable to the said Raph" [PCR 1:18].

On 7 March 1636/7, "it is agreed upon, by the consent of the whole Court, that Elizabeth Warren, widow, the relict of Mr. Richard Warren, deceased, shall be entered, and stand, and be purchaser instead of her said husband, as well because that (he dying before he had performed the said bargain) the said Elizabeth performed the same after his decease, as also for the establishing of the lots of lands given formerly by her unto her sons-in-law Richard Church, Robert Bartlett and Thomas Little, in marriage with their wives, her daughters" [PCR 1:54, 2:177].

On 5 May 1640, "Richard Church, Rob[er]te Bartlett, Thomas Little, & Mrs. Elizabeth Warren are granted enlargements at the heads of their lots to the foot of the Pyne Hills, leaving a way betwixt them and the Pyne Hills, for cattle and carts to pass" [PCR 1:152].

On 11 June 1653, as the result of a disagreement between Mrs. Elizabeth Warren and her son, Nathaniel, and a petition offered in court by Mrs. Jane Collier on behalf of her grandchild, Sarah, wife of Nathaniel Warren, the court chose four indifferent men to settle the matter of access to lands [MD 2:64, citing PCLR 2:73].

On 4 March 1673/4, Mary Bartlett, wife of Robert Bartlett, came into this court and owned "that she hath received full satisfaction for whatsoever she might claim as due from the estate of Mistress Elizabeth Warren, deceased, and John Cooke, in the behalf of all her sisters, testified the same before the court; and the court doth hereby settle the remainder of the said estate on Joseph Warren" [PCR 5:139-40].

BIRTH: By about 1578 (based on estimated date of marriage).
DEATH: Plymouth 1628. ("This year died Mr. Richard Warren, who hath been mentioned before in this book, and was an useful instrument; and during his life bore a deep share in the difficulties and troubles of the first settlement of the plantation of New-Plymouth" [Morton 85].)
MARRIAGE: Great Amwell, Hertfordshire, 14 April 1610 Elizabeth Walker, daughter of Augustine Walker [TAG 78:81-86]. She died at Plymouth on 2 October 1673, aged about 90 (probably an exaggeration) [PCR 8:35].
CHILDREN:
    i   MARY WARREN, b. about 1610 (d. Plymouth 27 March 1683 "in her 73d year" [PChR 1:250]); m. say 1629 ROBERT BARTLETT [PM 42] (date based on estimated age of children at their marriages).
    ii   ANN WARREN, b. about 1612 (deposed 6 June 1672 "aged sixty years or thereabouts" [MD 2:178, citing PCPR 3:1:40]); m. Plymouth 19 April 1633 THOMAS LITTLE [PCR 1:13; PM 305].
    iii   SARAH WARREN, b. by 1613 (named in grandfather's will of 19 April 1613 [TAG 78:83, citing Commissary Court of London, Essex and Herts, D/ABW 41/186]); m. Plymouth 28 March 1634 John Cooke Junior [PCR 1:29], son of FRANCIS COOKE [PM 144].
    iv   ELIZABETH WARREN, b. say 1615; m. by 7 March 1636/7 [PCR 1:54; TAG 60:129-30] (and probably by 14 March 1635/6 [PCR 1:41, 56, 152]) RICHARD CHURCH [PM 105] (he shared mowing land with Mrs. Warren 14 March 1635/6 [PCR 1:41]).
    v   ABIGAIL WARREN, b. say 1619; m. Plymouth 8 (or 9) November 1639 Anthony Snow [PCR 1:134].
    vi   NATHANIEL WARREN, b. about 1624 (deposed 15 October 1661 "aged thirty-seven years or thereabouts" [MD 2:178-79, citing PCLR 2:2:56]); m. Plymouth 19 November 1645 Sarah Walker [PCR 2:94]. (See WILLIAM COLLIER for discussion of her possible ancestry [PM 128].)
    vii   JOSEPH WARREN, b. Plymouth by 1627; m. by 1653 Priscilla Faunce (eldest child b. Plymouth 23 September 1653 [PCR 8:33]), daughter of JOHN FAUNCE [PM 201].

COMMENTS: In his accounting of the passengers on the *Mayflower* Bradford included "Mr. Richard Warren, but his wife and children were left behind and came afterwards" [Bradford 442]. As of 1651, Bradford reported that "Mr. Richard Warren lived some four or five years and had his wife come over to him, by whom he had two sons before [he] died, and one of them is married and hath two children. So his increase is four. But he had five daughters more came over with his wife, who are all married and living, and have many children" [Bradford 445-46].

Richard Warren was in the party that explored the outer cape in early December 1620; he was described as being of London [Mourt 32].

On 5 July 1635, Thomas Williams, servant of widow Warren, confessed that "there being some dissention between him and his dame, she, after other things, exhorted him to fear God & do his duty, he answered, he neither feared God, nor the devil" [PCR 1:35]. He was reproved and released [PCR 1:35]. On 5 January 1635/6, widow Warren paid 30s. to Thomas Clarke for borrowing his boat, and although returning it to a place of usual safety, an extraordinary storm wrecked it [PCR 1:36]. On 3 June 1639, "Mr. Andrew Hellot" was ordered to pay Mrs. Warren 10s. to settle an account between them [PCR 7:12].

BIBLIOGRAPHIC NOTE: In 1938 L. Effingham deForest published a thorough study of Richard Warren [Moore Anc 561-70]. In 1999 the Five Generations Project of the General Society of Mayflower Descendants published the first of three volumes of the descendants of Richard Warren, covering the first four generations, compiled by Robert S. Wakefield. The second and third volumes, covering the fifth-generation descendants, were published in 1999 and 2001. In 2003 Edward J. Davies published two articles that present the evidence for the marriage of Richard Warren and for some of his wife's family [TAG 78:81-86, 274-75].

JOHN WASHBURN

ORIGIN: Bengeworth, Worcestershire.
MIGRATION: 1632.
FIRST RESIDENCE: Plymouth.
REMOVES: Duxbury.
RETURN TRIPS: Possibly to England and back in 1634.

OCCUPATION: Tailor [PCR 1:85].

FREEMAN: "John Washburne, Senior," was in the 1639 list of those who had taken the oath of fidelity at Duxbury [PCR 8:182]. Admitted to freemanship on 2 June 1646 [PCR 2:101] (and as a result added to the Duxbury section of the 1639 list of freemen [PCR 8:175]). In the Duxbury sections of the 1658 and 29 May 1670 (as "John Washburne, Senior") lists of freemen [PCR 5:275, 8:198].

EDUCATION: He signed his name to a coroner's inquest.

OFFICES: Plymouth petit jury, 7 September 1642, 5 November 1644, 7 June 1648, 5 June 1666, 25 October 1668 [PCR 2:126, 4:125, 7:32, 38, 150]. Grand jury, 4 June 1645 [PCR 2:84]. Coroner's jury, 18 November 1669 [PCR 5:29].

Committee on property boundaries, 1 June 1647, 2 May 1648, 10 June 1650 [PCR 2:117, 122, 160]. Committee to lay out highways, 10 June 1650 [PCR 2:160].

Duxbury surveyor of highways, 5 March 1638/9, 6 June 1649 [PCR 1:117, 2:139]. Fined 4 March 1650/1 for failing to mend the highways [PCR 2:165].

In the Duxbury section of the 1643 Plymouth Colony list of men able to bear arms [PCR 8:190]. (The son of the immigrant was probably the John Washburn who was one of six men from Duxbury sent forth as soldiers in the "late expedition against the Narrohiggansets and their confederates," 28 October 1645 [PCR 2:90].)

ESTATE: Assessed 9s. in Plymouth tax list of 25 March 1633 [PCR 1:10]. He was not included in the tax list of 27 March 1634.

In early 1635, "Edward Bompass" sold to "John Washborne" "his house & palisado" [PCR 1:33].

On 14 March 1635/6 and on 20 March 1636/7, John Washburn had rights for one cow on Captain Standish's hay ground [PCR 1:40, 56].

On 6 April 1640, William Sherman and "John Washborne" were "to have such accommodations of land as may be spared in the place where they desire" [PCR 1:145]. On 5 April 1641, it was ordered that John Washbourne might have forty acres in Duxbury "if it be there to be had" [PCR 2:12]. On 3 May 1642 and on 7 March 1642/3, efforts were made to establish the boundary between the lands of John Washburn and Thomas Besbeech [PCR 2:39, 52].

On 4 March 1647[/8], Morris Truant of Duxbury and his wife Jane sold to "John Washburne" of Duxbury twenty acres of planting land, eight acres of planting land and two parcels of meadow [PCR 12:153-54].

On 3 June 1662, "John W[ashburn] Senior as an ancient freeman and as a servant" was granted land [PCR 4:18].

On 26 May 1666, "John Washburne Senior of Duxburrow," planter, deeded to "Phillip Washborne his true and natural son all that his dwelling house, outhouses and buildings situate in Duxburrow aforesaid, and all and singular the upland and meadow now thereunto belonging" [MD 16:249-50, citing PCLR 3:61].

BIRTH: Baptized at Bengeworth, Worcestershire, 2 July 1597, son of John and Martha (Timbrell) (Stephens) Washburn [Washbourne Gen 47].
DEATH: Early in 1671 (apparently living on 17 March 1670/1 and 22 May 1671 when his son was called Jr., but died soon after, as the document was altered to call the son Sr. [MD 16:248, 250, citing PCLR 3:209]).
MARRIAGE: Bengeworth, Worcestershire, [23 November?] 1618 Margery Moore [Washbourne Gen 48]. She sailed for New England in 1635 with her two sons [Hotten 57], but is not seen in any New England record.
CHILDREN:
  i   JOHN WASHBURN, bp. Bengeworth 26 November 1620 [Washbourne Gen 48]; m. Plymouth 6 December 1645 Elizabeth Mitchell [PCR 2:94], daughter of EXPERIENCE MITCHELL [PM 324].
  ii PHILIP WASHBURN, bp. Bengeworth 2 June 1622 [Washbourne Gen 48, 49]; bur. there 7 June 1622 [Washbourne Gen 48].
  iii PHILIP WASHBURN, b. about 1624 (aged eleven in 1635 [Hotten 57]); m. by about 1664 Elizabeth Irish, daughter of JOHN IRISH [PM 287].

COMMENTS: "Margerie Washborn," aged 49, and her two sons, "Jo[hn] Washborne," aged 14, and "Phillipp Washborne," aged 11, were passengers on the *Elizabeth & Ann* to New England in 1635 [Hotten 57].

Washburn was taxed in 1633 but not in 1634, and then in March of 1635 he purchased some land, and soon after his wife and children arrived in New England. This sequence of events suggests that John Washburn returned to England late in 1633 to arrange for the passage of his family, and that he returned late in 1634, some months before the rest of his family sailed in the spring of 1635.

On 2 January 1632/3, John Washburn failed to win his suit against Edward Dowty over a stolen pig [PCR 1:6]. On 4 June 1638, "John Washburne" posted a bond of £40 as surety for "Will[ia]m Corvannell" [PCR 1:85].

BIBLIOGRAPHIC NOTE: In 1907 James Davenport published a study of a Washburn family in England, and included a section on the immigrant to New England [*The Washbourne Family of Little Washbourne and Wichenford in the County of Worcester* (London 1907), cited above as Washbourne Gen, pp. 35-58]. In 1913 and 1914 George E. Bowman published a series of "Washburn Notes," the third installment having direct relevance to the immigrant [MD 15:247-53, 16:47-53, 248-53]. Stratton's treatment of John Washburn and his two sons is especially useful [Stratton 368-70].

GEORGE WATSON

ORIGIN: Unknown.
MIGRATION: 1631.
FIRST RESIDENCE: Penobscot.
REMOVES: Plymouth by 1634.

OCCUPATION: Mariner. On 3 May 1653, "the barque in which G[e]orge Watson sails, together with him the master thereof," was impressed for the campaign against the Dutch [PCR 3:29].
FREEMAN: In 1633 Plymouth list of freemen (between those admitted 1 January 1633/4 and those admitted 1 January 1634/5) [PCR 1:4]. In the 7 March 1636/7 list of freemen [PCR 1:52]. In the Plymouth sections of the 1639, 1658, 29 May 1670 and 1 [blank] 1683/4 Plymouth Colony lists of freemen [PCR 5:274, 8:174, 197, 202].
EDUCATION: He signed the coroner's inquest into the death of James Glasse [PCR 3:16] and other documents. His inventory included "books" valued at 13s. [PPR 1:37].
OFFICES: Plymouth petit jury, 2 January 1637/8, 1 September 1640, 2 March 1646/7, 8 June 1654, 6 March 1654/5, 5 March 1655/6, 7 March 1659/60, 5 March 1661/2, 2 October 1662, 3 March 1662/3, 5 March 1666/7, 1 March 1669/70, 7 June 1670, 7 March 1670/1, 29 October 1673 [PCR 2:111-12, 3:75, 5:42, 7:7, 17, 18, 70, 77, 95-6, 102, 105, 108, 136, 159, 163, 186]. Grand jury, 4 June 1639 [PCR 1:126]. Coroner's jury, 26 July 1652, 5 June 1678, 8 March 1678/9, 28 October 1684 [PCR 3:16, 5:263, 6:8, 148].

Committee to lay out land, 7 January 1638/9 [PCR 1:109]. Committee to lay out highways, 1 February 1640/1 [PCR 2:7]. Arbiter, 5 March 1643/4, 6 October 1659, 29 October 1667 [PCR 2:69, 3:174, 7:139-40,

142]. Delegated by town of Plymouth to meet with colony committee on lands at Sepecan, 10 January 1661/2 [PTR 1:45].

Plymouth constable, 6 June 1660, 5 June 1666, 5 June 1672 [PCR 3:187, 4:124, 5:90]. Selectman, 5 February 1665[/6], 13 October 1667 [PTR 1:82, 91]. Committee on exchange of Plymouth land, 21 February 1663[/4] [PTR 1:60].

In Plymouth section of 1643 Plymouth Colony list of men able to bear arms [PCR 8:188]. His inventory included "arms & ammunition" valued at £2 2s. [PPR 1:37].

ESTATE: On 14 March 1635/6 and 20 March 1636/7, George Watson was granted mowing rights at Plymouth [PCR 1:40, 56]. On 5 February 1637/8, he was granted "a parcel of land containing about four acres ... lying next to Mr. Thomas Hill" [PCR 1:76]. On 30 November 1640, he was granted "six acres of marsh meadow in Greens Harbor Marsh" [PCR 1:167].

In 1635 "Mr. John Jeney" sold to "Georg[e] Watson the dwelling house & garden with all the appurtenances thereunto belonging, which was sometimes Richard Maisterson's" [PCR 12:51]. In 1639 William Bradford sold to "Georg[e] Watson a parcel of land estimated to be about 3 acres ... lying beyond a small creek or slough to the eastward of that street where his now dwelling house is, being part of the acres that were allotted to the said William Bradford, and part of what he bought of Francis Cooke" [PCR 12:51].

On [blank] March 1651, George Watson was one of those with interest in the town's land at Punckateesett over against Rhode Island [PTR 1:37]. On 17 March 1654, Goodman Watson was granted "a little slip of meadow above the bridge ... at the South meadows" [PTR 1:208]. On 24 May 1662, George Watson's request for land at Mannomett Ponds caused Plymouth to select men to take charge of disposing of lands [PTR 1:47]. On 27 October 1662, he was on a list of men requesting meadow at the lower south meadow [PTR 1:49]. On the same day, he was granted fifty acres of upland at Mannomett Ponds [PTR 1:51]. On 22 March 1663, George Watson shared lot twenty-two at Puncateesett Neck with John Shaw Sr. [PTR 1:67]. On 14 April 1664, the six acres belonging to George Watson, which he bought of George Bonum, was acknowledged to him and an exchange of three acres for two acres was ordered [PTR 1:75].

On 14 March 1663, "Gyles Gilbert of Taunton," yeoman, sold to George Watson of Plymouth, yeoman, the land that had been bequeathed to him by his father Mr. John Gilbert [MD 34:23, citing PCLR 3:1:19]. James Davis, sometimes of Plymouth, seaman, sold to George Watson of

Plymouth, seaman, "five acres of upland ground lying on the south side of the town of Plymouth"; Mr. Nathaniel Souther, yeoman, sometimes of Plymouth, sold to George Watson of Plymouth, seaman, half an acre of marsh meadow in Plymouth; these two undated instruments were recorded on 18 November 1664 [MD 34:22, citing PCPR 3:1:18].

On 26 October 1670, "Nathaniell Masterson living at York in New England" resigned to "G[e]orge Watson living at Plymouth ... a house and garden which was my father's at Plymouth" [PCLR 3:181].

On 22 August 1681, George Watson of Plymouth, seaman, sold to Joseph Bartlett Sr. of Plymouth, yeoman, a parcel of land at Mannomett Ponds in Plymouth being one-third of a tract granted by the town to George Watson, William Harlow Sr. and Nathaniel Morton Sr. [PCLR 5:158]. On 9 December 1681, George Watson of Plymouth, mariner, deeded to "Elkanah Watson my dear and natural son" the seventh lot in the Freeman's Land [PCLR 5:108].

On 28 October 1681, George Watson of Plymouth acknowledged that he had exchanged land with Mr. Edward Gray [PCR 6:76].

The inventory of the estate of "Georg[e] Watson of Plimouth deceased," taken 2 February 1688[/9], was untotalled and included no real estate [PPR 1:37; Gen Adv 1:43].

BIRTH: About 1602 (based on age at death, but this is probably exaggerated by about five years).
DEATH: Plymouth 31 January 1688/9, "being 87 years of age" [PChR 1:262].
MARRIAGE: By about 1636 Phoebe Hicks, baptized St. Mary Magdalen, Bermondsey, Surrey, 15 March 1614/5, daughter of ROBERT HICKS [PM 243]. She died at Plymouth on 22 May 1663 [PCR 8:23].
CHILDREN:
    i   JOHN WATSON, b. say 1636; living in 1660 [PCR 3:186]; no further record.
    ii   PHOEBE WATSON, b. say 1638; m. Plymouth 22 January 1657[/8?] Jonathan Shaw [PCR 8:17], son of JOHN SHAW [PM 413].
    iii MARY WATSON, b. say 1642; m. Plymouth 21 August 1662 Thomas Leonard [PCR 8:23].
    iv SAMUEL WATSON (twin), b. Plymouth 18 January 1648[/9] [PCR 8:5]; d. 20 August 1649 [PCR 8:8].
    v   ELIZABETH WATSON (twin), b. Plymouth 18 January 1648[/9] [PCR 8:5]; m. Plymouth 28 November 1667 Joseph Williams [PCR 8:31].

vi JONATHAN WATSON, b. Plymouth 9 March 1652 [PCR 8:13]; no further record.

vii ELKANAH WATSON, b. Plymouth 25 February 1656 [PCR 8:16]; perhaps m. Mercy Hedges, daughter of WILLIAM HEDGES {1633, Lynn} [GMB 2:904-8].

ASSOCIATIONS: George Watson was not son of Robert Watson of Plymouth and Windsor, since there was no such person (see ROBERT WATSON in Phantom File).

COMMENTS: On 19 July 1631, George Watson testified regarding the activities of EDWARD ASHLEY at Penobscot [MHSP 45:495; PM 20].

George Watson appears in the list of freemen immediately preceding the court of 1 January 1632/3, but it is likely that he was actually admitted freeman in early 1634. The names immediately preceding his were admitted at the court of 1 January 1633/4. There then begins a column of names headed by "The rest admitted afterwards," which starts off with five men for whom there is no record of admission, and then seven who were admitted on 1 January 1634/5 (James Cudworth through Henry Rowley). Since in both Plymouth and Massachusetts colonies men were made freemen at or immediately before a meeting of the court, we can assume that George Watson and his four cohorts were admitted at some court between 1 January 1633/4 and 1 January 1634/5. The only courts recorded during this interval were held in late March of 1634, and this is likely the time when George Watson was admitted. The other four men surrounding him on the list of freemen, and probably admitted at the same time, are all known to have been in Plymouth in 1633 or earlier. Since George Watson was not in either of the tax lists of 1633 or 1634, and married about 1635, it may be that he had just finished a term of servitude in the winter of 1633/4 and did not yet have any property. This would further suggest that he may have come to Plymouth as a servant of one of the families that arrived in 1629.

On 6 February 1636/7, George Watson and others were fined for trading with the Indians for corn [PCR 1:50].

On returning home with a load of wood, George Watson and his servant John Bond went to unload the wood, but Bond bumped the mare and she ran away with him on the cart, and he leapt from the cart in front of the wheel and was crushed, as the coroner's jury ruled on 23 July 1661 [PCR 3:223].

On 3 May 1664, George Watson and others complained that the whole town of Taunton suffered as a result of James Walker neglecting to leave a sufficient passage for the herrings to go up river [PCR 4:57].

On 1 May 1660, George Watson petitioned the court in behalf of "his son John Watson and his nephew John Banges" that Samuel Hickes was entered in error as the purchaser of their land, when Mr. Robert Hickes should have been entered [PCR 3:186].

Phoebe and Mary are included as daughters of George Watson because there was no other Watson family in Plymouth at this time, the chronology is right, and Phoebe would have been named for her mother.

On 6 March 1665/6, George Watson was granted administration on the estate of Mrs. Margarett Hickes, deceased [PCR 4:117].

FRANCIS WESTON

ORIGIN: Unknown.
MIGRATION: 1632.
FIRST RESIDENCE: Plymouth.
REMOVES: Salem 1633, Providence 1638, Warwick 1642.

CHURCH MEMBERSHIP: Admission to Salem church prior to 5 November 1633 implied by freemanship.
FREEMAN: In 1633 Plymouth list of freemen, ahead of those admitted 1 January 1632/3 [PCR 1:3]. "Frauncis Weston" made freeman of Massachusetts Bay, 5 November 1633 [MBCR 1:368].
OFFICES: Deputy to Massachusetts Bay General Court for Salem, 14 May 1634 [MBCR 1:117]. Salem representative on "committee to consider of the act of Mr. Endicott, in defacing the colors," 6 May 1635 [MBCR 1:145].

Essex petit jury, 3 October 1637 [EQC 1:6].
ESTATE: Assessed 15s. in Plymouth tax list of 25 March 1633 [PCR 1:9]. Not in list of 27 March 1634.

In the 1 July 1633 allocation of mowing land at Plymouth, "Mr. Fogg & Mr. Weston" were granted "the watering place & thereabout ... together with that Mr. Weston ... had last year" [PCR 1:14].

Received 120 acres in the 1636 Salem land grant (in the section of "freemen") [STR 1:20, 27, 37]; on 17 April 1637, "Mr. Francis Weston" had ten acres added to this grant [STR 1:47]. In the 25 December 1637 grant of marsh and meadow, "Mr. Weston" received one acre for a household of six(?) [STR 1:103]; on the same day, he and Mr. Stileman shared six acres of meadow [STR 1:61].

In the second year of the Providence plantation Francis Weston and others were to pay 1s. 6d. each if they did not improve their ground granted to them by preparing to fence, break ground and build [RICR 1:15]. His grant of grass and meadow was confirmed on 10 June 1637 [RICR 1:17]. In 1638 he was a proprietor of Providence and jointly owned the meadow ground at Pawtuxet [RICR 1:20].

On "5 (4) 1645" [5 June 1645], Massachusetts Bay General Court sent a warrant "to the executors of Francis Weston ... to take notice of an attachment against the lands of Francis Weston" [Chapin 1:257]. (This action grew out of Weston's Gortonist activities.)

On 4 November 1646, "Richard Harcourt sells Thomas Angel his house lot or home share & housing, which formerly belonged unto his uncle Francis Weston and lately he bought the rest of it of his aunt Margaret Weston which she had her life in" [Chapin 1:242]. On 24 June 1652, Ralph Earle of Portsmouth sold to William Arnold land that he had bought of Nathaniel Dickens, "which premises the said Dickens formerly bought of one Richard Harcutt the heir or assign of Fraunces Weston and Margarett his wife" [PrTR 1:106]. On 5 May 1656, "Richard Harcarte of Warwick" confirmed that he had five or six years earlier sold to Nicholas Power of Providence "commonage [which] was once my uncle Francis Weston's" [PrTR 4:231].

BIRTH: By 1611 (based on Plymouth freemanship).
DEATH: By 5 June 1645 [Chapin 1:257].
MARRIAGE: By an unknown date Margaret _____.

There are two competing versions of her later history, each of which has its problems. We prefer the first of these two stories. On 3 November 1635, it was ordered "that John Pease shall be whipped, & bound to his good behavior, for striking his mother, Mrs. Weston, & deriding of her, & for diverse other misdemeanors, & other evil carriages" [MBCR 1:155]. On 1 September 1644, "Margit Pease" of Salem made a will in which the principal beneficiaries were the children of her son Robert Pease; this will was proved on 1 January 1644/5 [EPR 1:40-41]. For this to be the widow of Francis Weston, we would have to assume that he had died before 1 September 1644 (and there is nothing to contradict this), and that after his death she had returned to Salem and reassumed the name of an earlier husband. Richard Harcourt, who later held some of the land of Francis Weston, noted that Margaret had held a life interest in these lands, so there should not have been a competing claim from her Pease heirs.

The second story is that she married (2) by early 1651 Adam Goodwin, was supported by the town because of her distracted condition, and died on 2 May 1651 [Bradford F. Swan, "Roger Williams and the

Insane," *Rhode Island History* 5:65-68; RWCorr 329-31; PrTR 2:55, 104]. This later history for Margaret is dependent on a letter of Roger Williams in which in early 1651 he mistakenly called her "Mrs. Weston" when she was already married to Adam Goodwin.

CHILDREN: None recorded.

ASSOCIATIONS: The conclusion that Francis Weston of Plymouth went to Salem in 1633 is based on the disappearance of the man of that name from the Plymouth records after 1 July 1633, and the appearance of a man of that name in Massachusetts Bay records by 5 November 1633 (with later records placing him in Salem), and the departure of other Plymouth residents for Salem about the same time, presumably with ROGER WILLIAMS [PM 503] (RALPH FOGG [PM 206], WILLIAM BENNETT [PM 52]). As a corollary to this, we conclude that the Francis Weston (or West) who appeared in Duxbury by 1639 [PCR 1:139, 164] was a different man, not known to be related to the Francis who went to Salem.

COMMENTS: On 4 March 1633/4, "Josuah Harris is bound as an apprentice with Frauncis Weston, for 5 years from this day, his said master finding him meat, drink, & clothes" [MBCR 1:113].

On 12 March 1637/8, Francis Weston was included in a list of eight men (four, including Weston, from Salem) who were licensed to leave Massachusetts Bay [MBCR 1:223]; all of the Salem men joined Roger Williams at Providence.

At a Quarter Court held at Cambridge on 5 June 1638, "Francis Weston's wife was censured to be set 2 hours in the bilboes here, & 2 hours at Salem, upon a lecture day" [MBCR 1:233].

The curious entry in court 26 December 1637 is not further explained: "Margret Weston challenged three of the jurymen of Salem, Jeffrey Massie, Edm[und] Batter and Anth[ony] Dike" [EQC 7]. On 26 June 1638, Marmeduke Barton "servant of Franc[i]s Weston" was ordered whipped and a lock put on his foot for "running away from his master and filing off his lock" [EQC 1:8]. On 12 July 1642, Michael Shaflen deposed that Francis Weston had at some earlier date removed a boundary stake [EQC 1:43].

On 17 October 1643, Francis Weston and several other men were confined to various towns (Dorchester in Weston's case) "to be set on work, & to wear such bolts or irons as may hinder his escape" and not to "either by speech or writing, publish, declare, or maintain any of the blasphemous or abominable heresies wherewith he hath been charged by the General Court contained in either of the two books sent unto us" by

Samuel Gorton or Randall Holden [MBCR 2:52]. (Francis Weston had associated himself with Gorton as early as 1641 [RWCorr 214; Perley 1:273-75].)

THOMAS WESTON

ORIGIN: London.
MIGRATION: 1623.
FIRST RESIDENCE: Weymouth.
RETURN TRIPS: Sailed soon for Virginia, not to return.

OCCUPATION: Merchant.
EDUCATION: Admitted to Ironmongers' Company of London in 1609, after having completed apprenticeship with Rowland Heylyn [NGSQ 62:164].
ESTATE: The deposition of RICHARD MORE (see *COMMENTS* below) indicated that Thomas Weston owned two plantations, one in York River in Virginia at a place called Cheesecake, the other in Maryland at West St. Mary's by Story's Island [NEHGR 50:203].

The will of Thomas Weston was exhibited by John Hansford and approved. Administration was granted to John Hansford and he was ordered to bring in an inventory by 1 March 1647[/8] [*Archives of Maryland* 10 (1891):102].

BIRTH: Baptized Rugeley, Staffordshire, 21 December 1584, son of Ralph Weston [NGSQ 62:170].
DEATH: Bristol after 1 May 1646 (when Weston was presumably still alive and William Barwick of Bristol deposed that Weston had come to London in June 1645 on the *Trewlove*) and before 23 November 1647 (when Christopher Weaver allowed a generous bequest to his daughter, the widow Elizabeth Weston, for "her better advancement in marriage" [NGSQ 62:168]). Bradford says of him "So Mr. Weston came hither again, and afterward shaped his course for Virginia, and so for present I shall leave him. He died afterwards at Bristol, in the time of the wars, of the sickness in that place" [Bradford 138].
MARRIAGE: By 17 October 1623 Elizabeth Weaver, daughter of Christopher and Anne (Green) Weaver [NGSQ 62:167].

CHILD:
    i   ELIZABETH WESTON, b. say 1630; m. before 22 January 1661[/2] Roger Conant, son of ROGER CONANT [SChR 93; PM 134].

ASSOCIATIONS: His brother Andrew and brother Richard were involved in Thomas's affairs in England [NGSQ 62:163-72].

COMMENTS: Bradford described "one Mr. Thomas Weston, a merchant of London, came to Leyden about the same time (who was well acquainted with some of them and a furtherer of them in their former proceedings), having much conference with Mr. Robinson and others of the chief of them, persuaded them to go on (as it seems) and not to meddle with the Dutch or too much to depend on the Virginia Company. For if that failed, if they came to resolution, he and such merchants as were his friends, together with their own means, would set them forth; and they should make ready and neither fear want of shipping nor money; for what they wanted should be provided" [Bradford 37]. It is clear from his subsequent remarks that Bradford thought Weston's involvement with the group at Leiden was crassly opportunistic [Bradford 37-49]. "Mr. Weston makes himself merry with our endeavors about buying a ship" [Bradford 43]. Robert Cushman shared the thought and wrote on 17 August 1620 that "as for Mr. Weston, except grace do greatly sway him, he will hate us ten times more than ever he loved us, for not confirming the conditions" of the purchase of the ship [Bradford 56]. Finally, Bradford revealed that though Weston had "made that large promise in his letter ... that if all the rest should fall off, yet he would never quit the business ... all proved but wind, for he was the first and only man that forsook them" [Bradford 94].

The disenchanted Weston attempted to establish another settlement at Wessagusset, but as John Peirce described the settlers as "in all appearance not fit for an honest man's company" and in great want, the attempt failed [Bradford 109].

> Shortly after, Mr. Weston came over with some of the fishermen, under another name, and the disguise of a blacksmith, where he heard of the ruin and dissolution of his colony. He got a boat and with a man or two came to see how things were. But by the way, for want of skill, in a storm he cast away his shallop in the bottom of the bay between Merrimac River and Piscataqua, and hardly escaped with life. And afterwards fell into the hands of the Indians, who pillaged him of all he saved from the sea, and stripped him out of all his

clothes to his shirt. At last he got to Piscataqua and borrowed a suit of clothes, and got means to come to Plymouth. A strange alteration there was in him, to such as had seen and known him in his former flourishing condition; so uncertain are the mutable things of this unstable world [Bradford 119].

Weston was soon in difficulty with Sir Ferdinando Gorges and was forced to ask Governor Bradford to intervene for his safety, which Bradford did, but with little thanks, Weston insulting them by saying "that though they were but young justices, yet they were good beggars" [Bradford 136].

A deposition of Richard Norman of Marblehead, aged fifty years or thereabouts

> That John Connant now resident in New England & bound for Virginia the said John Connant I knew him of a child & was a near neighbor to his father Roger Connant and his wife Elizabeth the daughter and the only daughter of Thomas Weston by common repute ... the said Elizabeth's father was that Thomas Weston that used formerly to trade in Virginia and so to New England and afterwards went home for Bristol and there died as by credible and common report and further that I have been in Maryland in Virginia in West St. Mary's and likewise in some part of York River in both which places there was land commonly said to be and called by the name the said Thomas Weston his land or plantation and understood to be the same Thomas Weston aforesaid and further that I never heard of any other child the said Thomas Weston had but only the said Elizabeth but have often heard the said Elizabeth say her father had no other child but her [NEHGR 50:203].

On 27 September 1684, the following deposition was taken before Simon Bradstreet, Governor:

> The deposition of Richard Moore Senr. aged seventy years or thereabouts. Sworn saith that being in London at the house of Mr. Thomas Weston, ironmonger, in the year 1620 he was from thence transported to New Plymouth in New England and about two years and a half after the said deponent's arrival at Plymouth aforesaid the above mentioned Thomas Weston sent over a ship upon his proper account with passengers to settle in the Massachusetts Bay now called Braintree but soon after they deserted the same by reason of Indians and sickness and within a short space of time after the above said Weston personally came over from London to Plymouth in New England and

made his abode there sometime and traded from thence to Virginia and Maryland and at that time the said deponent knew that the said Thomas Weston had and was possessed of two plantations the one in York River in Virginia at a place called Cheesecake, the other in Maryland at West St. Mary's by Story's Island and heretofore were commonly known to be in the tenure & occupation of these persons here under expressed, viz: Mr. Wilkinson, Mr. Dent, merchant, &c. and they all acknowledged the said Weston to be the true proprietor and lawful owner of the said plantations and further that the said deponent knew Elizabeth Weston now Elizabeth Conant of Marblehead to be the reputed and only child of the said Thomas Weston [NEHGR 50:203].

BIBLIOGRAPHIC NOTE: In 1896 Christopher Johnston compiled records related to the estate of Thomas Weston in Maryland [NEHGR 50:201-6]. In 1974 Peter Wilson Coldham added English records of Weston, particularly his difficulties with customs laws [NGSQ 62:163-72].

JOHN WHISTON

ORIGIN: Unknown.
MIGRATION: 1632 on the *William & Francis* [Hotten 149].
FIRST RESIDENCE: Scituate.

FREEMAN: Oath of fidelity at Scituate, 1657 [PCR 8:180].
OFFICES: Plymouth grand jury, 3 June 1657 [PCR 3:115].
   In the Scituate section of the 1643 Plymouth Colony list of men able to bear arms [PCR 8:191].
ESTATE: On 3 October 1662, John Whiston was added to the list of men to be considered in an accommodation of land on the north bounds of Rehoboth [PCR 4:27].
   On 4 October 1664, the court noted that John Whiston had died intestate, and so the land of the said Whiston "falls by right of law unto Joseph Wheston, the heir apparent unto the said John Wheston; and that it doth likewise appear to the Court that the estate of the said John Wheston is but little, the lands excepted, and that there are divers small children to be brought up out of the said estate, therefore, upon the free will and condescendency of the said Joseph Wheston, he is content and

hath by these presents taken the house and land that his father lived on and died in, in the town of Scituate, for his full and entire portion ... freely allowing that the profit and benefit of the said house and land shall redound unto his mother, Susanna Wheston, for the full term of six years from the date herefore, for and towards the bringing up of the other children of the said John Wheston." As for the residue of the lands, Joseph released them to the rest of his brothers and sisters, with first option to buy if they should choose to sell [PCR 4:75-76]. On 6 March 1665/6, the court reasoned that the land at Conihassett set aside for the benefit of the small children was not likely to do them much good in its present state, and empowered Joseph Whiston "with the help of his father-in-law William Brookes, and his uncle, Edward Jenkens," to sell the land on behalf of the children [PCR 4:114].

On 30 April 1672, the Suffolk County Court ordered that "the estate that is left of Joseph Whetstone shall be divided amongst the children, the eldest son to have a double portion & Edw[ard] Jenkins to be discharged" [SCC 108]. This probably did not refer to the children of Joseph, but rather to his siblings.

BIRTH: By about 1616 (based on estimated date of marriage).
DEATH: By 4 October 1664 [PCR 4:75-76].
MARRIAGE: By about 1641 Susanna Hanford, daughter of Jeffrey and Eglin (Hatherly) (Downe) Hanford (and niece of TIMOTHY HATHERLY) [GM 2:3:205-7; PM 234; Stevens-Miller Anc 1:485-86]. She married (2) by 1665 William Brookes.
CHILDREN:

    i   JOSEPH WHISTON, b. say 1641 (adult 1664); d. Boston by 31 October 1666 [PCR 4:139], unm.

    ii   SARAH WHISTON, b. say 1643; m. Scituate 25 May 1663 Thomas Nichols.

    iii   JOHN WHISTON, b. about 1648 ("aged eighteen years or thereabouts, being the next eldest brother to Joseph Whiston, late deceased at Boston," on 4 January 1666[/7], chose "his uncle, Edward Jenkens, of Scittuate," to be his guardian [PCR 4:139]); m. by 1678 Abigail Lombard, daughter of Joshua Lombard (eldest known child bp. Scituate 26 May 1678 [NEHGR 57:182]; in his will of 22 January 1689/90, Joshua Lombard bequeathed to "Abigail Whitstone my grandchild" [MD 12:88, citing BarnPR 1:43]).

    iv   SUSANNA WHISTON, b. say 1650; m. Scituate 2 May 1671 Thomas Perry [TAG 70:43-44].

        v   INCREASE WHISTON, bp. Scituate 10 August 1656 [NEHGR 57:85]; no further record.
      vi   BATHSHEBA WHISTON, bp. Scituate 1 July 1660 [NEHGR 57:86]; m. about 1682 Eleazer Dunham [TAG 30:154, 173, citing PCPR 4:2:21].

COMMENTS: On 7 March 1631[/2], "John Whetston" appears on the passenger list of *William & Francis*, the same ship on which TIMOTHY HATHERLY sailed for New England that year [Hotten 149].

On 7 December 1641, a warrant was issued for John Whetston of Scituate and others "to answer at the next General Court for goods they took, which were found by shipwreck" [PCR 2:29]. On 4 January 1641/2, "John Whetston confesseth that he had (of the goods taken up in the bottom of the bay about Satuckquet) a pair of drawers, a waistcoat & a shirt" [PCR 2:31].

WILLIAM WHITE

ORIGIN: Leiden, Holland (but see MF 13:2).
MIGRATION: 1620 on the *Mayflower*.
FIRST RESIDENCE: Plymouth.

ESTATE: In the 1623 Plymouth division of land William White received five acres as a passenger on the *Mayflower* (even though he had been dead for two years) [PCR 12:4]. In the 1627 Plymouth division of cattle Resolved White and Peregrine White were the tenth and eleventh persons in the third company [PCR 12:10].

BIRTH: By about 1590 (based on estimated date of marriage).
DEATH: Plymouth 21 February 1620[/1] [Prince 184].
MARRIAGE: About 1615 Susanna ____. She married (2) Plymouth 12 May 1621 EDWARD WINSLOW [Bradford 86].
CHILDREN:
       i   RESOLVED WHITE, b. say 1615; m. (1) Scituate 8 April 1640 Judith Vassall [PCR 8:19], daughter of WILLIAM VASSALL {1630, Boston} [GMB 3:1871-75]; m. (2) Salem 5 October 1674 Abigail (____) Lord, widow of WILLIAM LORD {1635, Salem}.
      ii   PEREGRINE WHITE, b. 4 December 1620 ("Whilst some were employed in this discovery [of a good harbor], it

pleased God that Mistress White was brought abed of a son, which was called Peregrine" [Mourt 31]); m. by 6 March 1648/9 Sarah Bassett, daughter of WILLIAM BASSETT [PCR 2:183; PM 48].

COMMENTS: In his list of those who came in the *Mayflower,* Bradford includes "Mr. William White and Susanna his wife and one son called Resolved, and one born a-shipboard called Peregrine, and two servants named William Holbeck and Edward Thompson" [Bradford 442]. In his accounting of 1651 Bradford tells us that "Mr. White and his two servants died soon after their landing. His wife married with Mr. Winslow, as is before noted. His two sons are married and Resolved hath five children, Peregrine two, all living. So their increase are seven" [Bradford 445].

Most Mayflower researchers argue that Susanna (____) (White) Winslow was not, as often claimed, sister of SAMUEL and EDWARD FULLER [MF 5:7, 13:2, 5:7; NEHGR 110:182-83; MD 53:67-69; PM 215, 217]. Jeremy Dupertuis Bangs has, however, recently dissented from this view, arguing that William White of the *Mayflower* did marry in Leiden a sister of the Fuller brothers [NEHGR 154:109-18].

On 30 October 1623, EDWARD WINSLOW wrote from London to "his much respected Uncle Mr. Robert Jackson" who was clerk of the sewers at Spalding, Lincolnshire. In his letter he wrote that "almost two years since I wrote to my father-in-law declaring the death of his son White & the continued health of his daughter and her two children; also how that by God's providence she was become my wife.... My wife hath had one child by me, but it pleased him that gave it to take it again unto himself; I left her with child at my departure (whom God preserve) but hope to be with her before her delivery" [NEHGR 1955:242-43]. This remains the best clue to the identity of the wife of William White.

BIBLIOGRAPHIC NOTE: In 1975 Robert M. and Ruth W. Sherman published an account of William White and his descendants as part of the first volume of the Five Generations Project of the General Society of Mayflower Descendants [MF 1:95-187]. Robert S. Wakefield revised and republished this material in 1997 [MF 13].

ROGER WILDER

Roger Wilder came to Plymouth in 1620 on the *Mayflower* as a servant to JOHN CARVER [PM 95], and died before Carver did (which was in the spring of 1620/1) "of the common infection" [Bradford 441, 443].

THOMAS WILLETT

ORIGIN: Leiden, Holland.
MIGRATION: 1630.
FIRST RESIDENCE: Penobscot.
REMOVES: Plymouth, Rehoboth, New York 1665, Swansea 1668.

OCCUPATION: Merchant, magistrate and soldier.
FREEMAN: Admitted freeman of Plymouth 1 January 1633/4 (and appended to the 1633 list of freemen) [PCR 1:4, 21]. In the list of 7 March 1636/7 [PCR 1:52]. In the Plymouth sections of the Plymouth Colony lists of 1639 and 1658 (first in list, as "Capt. Thomas Willett") [PCR 8:174, 197]. In the Swansea section of the Plymouth Colony list of 29 May 1670 [PCR 5:279].
EDUCATION: On 19 February 1660/1, "Capt. Willet" was one of five men "chosen by the town to transcribe the land records out of the town book" [Early Rehoboth 4:13, citing Rehoboth TR 1:136]. His inventory included more than a hundred books, on theology, history, law, navigation and other subjects [MD 33:35-37].
OFFICES: Plymouth Assistant, 5 June 1651, 3 June 1652, 7 June 1653, 6 June 1654, 8 June 1655, 3 June 1656, 3 June 1657, 1 June 1658, 7 June 1659, 6 June 1660, 4 June 1661, 3 June 1662, 1 June 1663, 8 June 1664 [PCR 2:166, 3:7, 30, 48, 77, 99, 114, 134, 162, 187, 214, 4:13, 36, 60].

Deputy for Plymouth to Plymouth Colony General Court, 7 July 1646 [PCR 2:104].

Plymouth selectman, 18 February 1649[/50] [PTR 1:30]. Committee to distribute the poor's cattle, 16 July 1638, 7 July 1642, 22 July 1644 [PTR 1:4, 8, 18]. Assessor, 17 December 1640, 26 November 1641 [PTR 1:6, 8]. Surveyor, 17 May 1649 [PTR 1:28]. Supplier of coats to pay Indians for killing wolves, 4 November 1650 [PTR 1:31]. Agent to rent land at Punckateesett to Captain Cooke, 26 September 1657 [PTR 1:35].

In Plymouth section of 1643 Plymouth Colony list of men able to bear arms [PCR 8:188]. On 7 March 1647/8, he succeeded Capt. Miles Standish as captain of the military company at Plymouth [PCR 2:121].

His inventory included "1 French dagger" valued at 1s. 6d., "3 small fowling pieces" valued at £2 14s., "4 large ditto" valued at £4 8s., "a blunderbuss" valued at £1, "a large musket" valued at 16s., "10 firelock muskets" valued at £7 10s. and "5 matchlock ditto" valued at £3 [MD 33:37].

Mayor of New York, 1665, 1667 [Berthold Fernow, ed., *The Records of New Amsterdam from 1653 to 1674 Anno Domini* (New York 1897; rpt., Baltimore 1976) 5:250-52].

ESTATE: On 4 February 1638/9, Plymouth Court granted to "John Done and Thomas Willett one hundred acres apiece of upland and meadow" at Jones River [PCR 1:112]. On 1 June 1640, he was granted ten acres of meadow at Jones River [PCR 1:154]. On 3 August 1640, "Thomas Willett is granted six acres of upland for his houselot at the little swamp on the north side Mr. Done's field towards Fresh Lake" [PCR 1:159]. On 2 November 1640, he received twelve acres in the North Meadow by Jones River [PCR 1:166].

On 3 February 1648, Edmond Freeman Sr. of Sandwich sold to "Mr. Thomas Willit and Mr. William Paddy" of Plymouth, merchants, "an house and land at Joanese's River sometimes appertaining unto Mr. Isaack Allerton" [PCR 12:133]. On 18 February 1649[/50], Thomas Willett surrendered back to the town his right in Clark's Island granted by the town of Plymouth [PTR 1:29]. On 22 March 1663[/4], Thomas Willett received lot 32 in Punkateesett Neck and shared it with "Mr. Paddy" [PTR 1:69].

In his will, dated 26 April 1671 and proved 25 November 1674, "Thomas Willett of Swansey ... being going on in the sixty-fourth year of my age," having named "my loving sons James, Hezekiah, Andrew and Samuell" as joint executors and having appointed as overseers "my well beloved son-in-law Mr. John Saffin and my loving friend Mr. Robert Holmes and my dear brother-in-law Mr. James Browne and my dear son-in-law Mr. Samuell Hooker and the Reverend Mr. John Myles," bequeathed to "my four sons my said executors, namely James Willett, Hezekiah Willett, Andrew Willett and Samuell Willett all my now dwelling house, warehouse, outhouses, barns and all other edifices, gardens, orchards and pasture fields whatsoever, thereunto belonging ... to be equally divided amongst them" (land described in detail, with an attempt at entail); to "my said four sons ... all my study or library of books" to be divided equally; to "my said four sons ... all my estate of commonage, either in the township of Rehoboth or Swansey except what I shall give unto my grandson Samuell Hooker"; to "my grandson Samuell Hooker ... eighty acres of upland ..., together with fifty pounds estate of commonage" in Rehoboth; to "my grandchildren hereafter mentioned all my lands ... in the Narragansett Country"; to "my grandson Thomas Saffin a double portion of all my said lands in the Narragansett Country"; to "my son Hooker's six sons aleady born and to all and every such son, as shall be born to him by his wife my daughter Mary ... and to my son Saffin's four sons not already mentioned ... and to all and every such son as shall be born to him by his wife my daughter Martha ... and to all such sons as shall be borne by my daughter Ester," a share in the Narragansett Country; to "my eldest son James Willett fifty pounds ... in land remote from my dwelling house"; to "my dear daughter Ester Willett fifty pounds ... in land remote from my said dwelling house"; to "my said four sons James, Hezekiah, Andrew and Samuell" all other lands not disposed of; to "my three sons Hezekiah, Andrew and Samuell fifty pounds apiece in money, towards their maintenance in schools and other ways and means for attainment of learning"; to "my grandson Samuell Hooker" £25; to "my granddaughter Sarah Elliott" £50; to "my old servant John Padducke" £10; to my overseers forty shillings apiece; to the church of Plymouth ten pounds and to the church of Swansea ten pounds and to the church at Rehoboth five pounds; to "the Reverend Mr. John Myles ten pounds"; residue equally to "my said four sons ... James Willett, Hezekiah Willett, Andrew Willett and Samuell Willett ... and also to my three beloved daughters namely Mary Hooker, Martha Saffin and Ester Willett" [MD 26:80-84, citing PCPR 3:1:114-16].

The inventory of the estate of "Capt. Thomas Willett," taken 21 August 1674, totalled £2798 14s. 7d., of which £1289 was real estate: "the dwelling house, outhouses, warehouse and barn and all other edifices, gardens or orchards and all the land given by Mr. John Browne Senior whereon the before specified houses now stand and two 80 acre lots thereunto adjoining whereof by estimation there is 100 and 50 acres improved, 20 acres of meadow at Broad Cove and 20 acres at Cooper's Meadow, and twenty acres at Papasquash," £720; "ten acres at Poquanamsquot and ten acres at Kekamuett and 5 acres at Musquashcocke," £255; "450 acres of upland in several allotments," £225; "35 acres of upland at Torrey's Creek," £10; "80 acres of upland at Cooper's Meadow," £25; "300 pound commonage in Rehoboth," £15; "400 acres of upland and 40 acres of fresh meadow on the north side of the town of Rehoboth," £10; "1 whole share of upland and meadow on the north side of Rehoboth," £15; and "1 lot at Wachamauquatt containing 48 acres," £14; to which was appended the "land at Narragansett not appraised, as also land at Pocasset one whole share not appraised" [MD 33:35-39, citing PCPR 3:1:117-28].

BIRTH: About 1608 (from will). (He was possibly son of Thomas and Alice (_____) Willett of Norwich and Leiden [NEHGR 61:157-60].)

DEATH: Swansea 3 August 1674 [SwVR 408] (according to Burgess, his gravestone says he died at Swansea on "August 4, 1674, in the 64th year of his age" [NEHGR 61:159]).

MARRIAGE: (1) Plymouth 6 July 1636 Mary Brown [PVR 652], daughter of JOHN BROWN {1635, Plymouth} [GM 2:1:420-29]. She died on 8 January 1669[/70] [NEHGR 2:376].

(2) Milford 19 September 1671 Joanna (Boyse) Prudden, widow of Rev. Peter Prudden [TAG 19:139-40]. (Savage says her gravestone of 1699 calls her his only wife and finds the error peculiar, but Burgess reads the stone to say 1669 and attributes it more correctly to the first wife [NEHGR 61:159].)

CHILDREN (see *COMMENTS* below):

  i MARY WILLETT, b. 10 November 1637; m. Plymouth 22 September 1658 Samuel Hooker [PCR 8:21; PVR 662], son of THOMAS HOOKER {1633, Cambridge} [GMB 2:982-85]; m. (2) Farmington 10 August 1703 Rev. Thomas Buckingham [Farm VR Barbour 24, citing Farmington LR 1:4].

  ii MARTHA WILLETT, b. 6 August 1639; m. Plymouth 2 December 1658 John Saffin [PCR 8:22; PVR 662].

  iii JOHN WILLETT, b. 21 August 1641; m. in 1663 Abigail Collins, daughter of EDWARD COLLINS {1636, Cambridge} [NEHGR 89:151; MHSP 2:7:150; Goodwin Anc 1:393].

  iv SARAH WILLETT, b. 4 May 1643; m. by 1662 John Eliot, son of JOHN ELIOT {1631, Boston} [GMB 1:630-32].

  v REBECCA WILLETT, b. 2 December 1644; d. Plymouth 2 April 1652 [PCR 8:14; PVR 660]. (The death record does not give her age.)

  vi THOMAS WILLETT, b. 1 October 1646; no further record.

  vii HESTER WILLETT, b. Plymouth 6 July 1648 [MD 15:27; PCR 8:4, 291]; m. 24 January 1671/2 Rev. Josiah Flint of Dorchester [Sibley 2:153 (the marriage is said to have taken place in Swansea, but the event does not appear in the published vital records of that town or of Dorchester)], son of HENRY FLINT {1635, Boston} [GM 2:2:534-37].

  viii JAMES WILLETT, b. Plymouth 24 November 1649 [PCR 8:8; PVR 657]; m. (1) Rehoboth 17 April 1673 Elizabeth Hunt

[PCR 8:52], daughter of Peter Hunt; m (2) Swansea 2 August 1677 Grace Frinck [SwVR 23].

ix   HEZEKIAH WILLETT, b. Plymouth 20 July 1651 [PCR 8:12; PVR 659]; d. 26 July 1651 [PCR 8:13].

x   HEZEKIAH WILLETT, b. Plymouth "16 November or thereabouts" 1653 [PCR 8:15]; m. Swansea 7 January 1675[/6] Anna Brown, daughter of John Brown [SwVR 23; PCR 8:61].

xi   DAVID WILLETT, b. 1 November 1654; no further record.

xii   ANDREW WILLETT, b. 5 October 1655; m. Braintree 6 March 1693/4 Susannah Holbrook [BrVR 721; NEHGR 59:145 (defective entry)].

xiii   SAMUEL WILLETT, b. 27 October 1658; said to have married and had a large family at Flushing, Long Island, but there is much confusion with the descendants of another Thomas Willet who did settle in Flushing [NYGBR 10:181; Austin 430].

ASSOCIATIONS: William Paddy remembered Willett's wife with a small bequest and was often closely paired with Willett in town duties and land grants. Willett was an executor of Paddy's estate [RCA 3:185].

COMMENTS: On 30 July 1631, Thomas Willett was one of those who deposed about the activities of EDWARD ASHLEY [PM 20] at Penobscot [MHSP 45:496-97]. Willett managed the Plymouth fur trading interests in Maine at various later dates.

In his journal kept in the summer of 1635 when he came to New England on the *James*, Richard Mather mentioned stopping at Richmond Island and

> one Mr. Willett, of New Plymouth, and other three men with him, having been turned out of all their havings at Penobscot [by the French] about a fortnight before, and coming along with us in our ship from Richmond's Island, with his boat and goods in it made fast at the stern of our ship, lost his boat [in the terrible storm] with all that was therein, the violence of the waves breaking the boat in pieces, and sinking the bottom of it into the bottom of the sea [Young's First Planters 475].

Bradford's version was that

> This year they sustained another great loss from the French. Monsier de Aulnay coming into the harbor of Penobscote, and having before got some of the chief that belonged to the house aboard his vessel, by subtly coming upon them in their shallop,

he got them to pilot him in, and after getting the rest into his power, he took possession of the house in the name of the king of France; and partly by threatening, & otherwise, made Mr. Willett (their agent there) to approve of the sale of the goods there unto him, of which he set the price himself, in effect, and made an inventory thereof (yet leaving out sundry things), but made no payment for them, but told them in convenient time he would do it if they came for it. For the house & fortification, &c. he would not allow, nor account anything, saying that they which build on another man's ground do forfeit the same. So thus turning them out of all, (with a great deal of compliment and many fine words), he let them have their shallop and some victuals to bring them home. Coming home and relating all the passages, they here were much troubled at it, & having had this house robbed by the French once before, and lost then above £500 (as is before remembered), and now to lose house & all, did much move them [Bradford 275-76].

Despite these troubles, Thomas Willett had a facility for dealing with the Dutch and he proceeded from unfavorable dealings with the French to positive dealings with the Dutch. In a letter dated 22 May 1637, Edward Winslow wrote to John Winthrop that "Thomas Willet is come in from the Dutch" [WP 3:419]. On 4 April 1650, Thomas Broughton of Watertown, merchant, gave Capt. Thomas Willett of Plymouth power to request the sum of £47 3s. 6d. from "Mijn Heere Peter Stuijvesant, Governor of the New Netherlands" [Aspinwall 277].

Capt. William Davis and Capt. Thomas Willett were joint executors of the estate of Mr. William Paddy and were sued by Capt. Thomas Clarke at the General Court on 21 October 1666 and 31 May 1670, with a neutral result [MBCR 4:2:447, 455].

On 5 March 1667/8, Plymouth Court did "allow and approve that the township granted unto Captain Willet and others, his neighbors, at Wannamoisett and places adjacent, shall henceforth be called and known by the name of Swansey" [PCR 4:175-76].

On 11 November 1673, Thomas Willett petitioned the Court of Assistants for permission to detain the goods of some Dutchman in New England, as security against his goods that had been detained by the Dutch when they retook New York [RCA 3:257].

Full dates of birth for all thirteen of the children of Thomas Willett have been published in various secondary sources [NEHGR 2:376; Austin 426-30], but contemporary records for only four [vii-x] have been found. If the remaining nine birthdates are correct, they presumably derive from a private record that has vanished from sight.

BIBLIOGRAPHIC NOTE: The items offerred above depict only a few of the many aspects of the life of Thomas Willett. In 1907 George Canning Burgess published an excellent summary of the career of Thomas Willett [NEHGR 61:157-164]. Willet deserves attention from a modern biographer.

ROGER WILLIAMS

ORIGIN: High Laver, Essex.
MIGRATION: 1631 on the *Lyon* [WJ 1:49-50].
FIRST RESIDENCE: Salem.
REMOVES: Plymouth 1631, Salem 1633, Providence 1636.
RETURN TRIPS: To England in 1643-44 (to obtain a charter for Rhode Island [RWCorr xciii, 217]), and to England in 1651-54 [RWCorr xciv, 355-90].

OCCUPATION: Minister.
CHURCH MEMBERSHIP: On 12 April 1631, at "a court holden at Boston, (upon information to the governor, that they of Salem had called Mr. Williams to the office of a teacher,) a letter was written from the court to Mr. Endecott to this effect: That whereas Mr. Williams had refused to join with the congregation at Boston, because they would not make a public declaration of their repentance for having communion with the churches of England, while they lived there; and, besides, had declared his opinion, that the magistrate might not punish the breach of the Sabbath, nor any other offense, as it was a breach of the first table; therefore, they marvelled they would choose him without advising with the council; and withal desiring him, that they would forbear to proceed till they had conferred about it" [WJ 1:63].

In his account of the year 1632 William Bradford spoke of "Mr. Roger Williams, a man godly and zealous, having many precious parts but very unsettled in judgment, came over first to the Massachusetts; but upon some discontent left that place and came hither, where he was friendly entertained according to their poor ability, and exercised his gifts amongst them and after some time was admitted a member of the church.... He this year began to fall into some strange opinions, and from opinion to practice, which caused some controversy between the church and him. And in the end some discontent on his part, by occasion whereof he left them something abruptly. Yet afterwards sued for his dismission to the church of Salem, which was granted, with some caution to them concerning him and what care they ought to have of him" [Bradford 257; see also WJ 1:109].

Williams was back in Salem by 1633, but was not chosen teacher again until 1635, and then, after the death of Rev. SAMUEL SKELTON {1629, Salem} [GMB 3:1684-87], was chosen pastor [WJ 1:117, 122, 151, 162, 164, 166].

In March 1638/9 Winthrop lamented that at "Providence things grew still worse; for a sister of Mrs. Hutchinson, the wife of one Scott, being infected with Anabaptistry, and going last year to live at Providence, Mr. Williams was taken (or rather emboldened) by her to make open profession thereof, and accordingly was rebaptized by one Holyman, a poor man late of Salem. Then Mr. Williams rebaptized him and some ten more. They also denied the baptizing of infants, and would have no magistrate" [WJ 1:352-53].

(The passages extracted here do not cover all of the church activities of Roger Williams during these early years in New England, and do not touch at all on his expulsion from Massachusetts. The intent is to demonstrate his beginnings and his offices at Salem, at Plymouth, at Salem again, and finally at the establishment of the Baptist Church at Providence.)

FREEMAN: In Providence section of 1655 Rhode Island lists of freemen [RICR 1:299].

EDUCATION: Matriculated at Cambridge from Pembroke College, 29 June 1623; B.A. 1626-27 [Venn 4:417; Morison 407].

OFFICES: President of Rhode Island and Providence Plantations, 12 September 1654, 22 May 1655, 11 March 1655/6, 20 May 1656 [RICR 1:282, 303, 325, 336]. Assistant, 19 May 1647, 16 May 1648, 1 March 1663/4, 4 May 1664, 4 May 1670, 3 May 1671 [RICR 1:148, 209, 2:22, 37, 374, 302]. Deputy for Providence to Rhode Island Court, 22 May 1655, 28 June 1655, 11 March 1655/6, 17 March 1655/6, 21 May 1656, 10 October 1656, 2 November 1658, 23 August 1659, 27 August 1661 [RICR 1:304, 316, 326, 327, 337, 345, 394, 419, 447]. (Williams held many other lesser colony and town offices.)

ESTATE: Roger Williams purchased from the local sachems the land that became Providence, and he then transferred this land to those who settled Providence with him [RICR 1:12-27].

The early records of Providence contain many land transactions involving Roger Williams. Neither Roger Williams nor his wife left a will.

BIRTH: About 1606, son of James and Alice (Pemberton) Williams [TAG 28:197-200].
DEATH: Providence after 27 January 1682/3 and before 15 March 1682/3 [TAG 28:207].
MARRIAGE: High Laver, Essex, 15 December 1629 Mary Bernard, daughter of Rev. Richard Bernard [NEHGR 113:189-92]. She died after August 1676 (in late August 1676 "it seasonable came to pass that Providence Williams brought up his mother from Newport in his sloop & cleared the town of all the Indians to the great peace and content of all the inhabitants" [PrTR 8:14]).
CHILDREN:
 i MARY WILLIAMS, b. Plymouth "the first week in August 1633" [PrTR 1:7]; m. by 1652 John Sayles [TAG 15:228-30]. (Recent research by Gwenn F. Epperson has shown that this man was not related to John Sales of Charlestown and New Netherland [NYGBR 123:72-73].)
 ii FREEBORN WILLIAMS, b. Salem "in the latter end of October 1635" [PrTR 1:7]; m. (1) by about 1661 Thomas Hart; m. (2) Newport 6 March 1683 Walter Clarke [RIVR 7:10, 20].
 iii PROVIDENCE WILLIAMS, b. Providence "in the latter end of ... September 1638" [PrTR 1:7]; on 22 July 1686, Providence Town Council received a report that "Providence Williams is dead at Newport" and, on 14 September 1686, Daniel Williams "exhibited an inventory of his deceased brother Providence Williams" and the Town Council appointed Daniel administrator "as he is next of the kin" [PrTR 6:154-56].
 iv MERCY WILLIAMS, b. Providence "about the 15th of July 1640" [PrTR 1:7]; m. (1) Resolved Waterman; m. (2) Providence 2 January 1676/7 Samuel Winsor [PrTR 15:153, 156-57].
 v DANIEL WILLIAMS, b. Providence "about the 15 of February 1641 (so called) counting year to begin about the 25 of March so that he was born above a year & a half after Mercy" [PrTR 1:7]; m. Providence 2 December 1676 Rebecca (Rhodes) Power [PrTR 15:153], daughter of

   Zachariah Rhodes and widow of Nicholas Power [Austin 356, 364].
vi JOSEPH WILLIAMS, b. Providence "about the beginning of the 10th month [December] 1643" [PrTR 1:7]; m. 17 December 1669 Lydia Olney [PrTR 5:329; RIVR 2:Providence:201].

ASSOCIATIONS: Brother of Robert Williams who came to New England by 1644 [TAG 28:199]. The wife of Roger Williams was sister of MUSACHIELL BERNARD {1635, Weymouth} [GM 2:1:261-63].

COMMENTS: For two of the daughters of Roger Williams, evidence was not found for the marriage to the first husband (Freeborn to Thomas Hart and Mercy to Resolved Waterman), although both unions are confidently asserted in any number of modern publications. The rarity of the name Freeborn speaks in favor of the marriage to Thomas Hart, but additional information would be welcome in both instances. Assuming these first marriages, the evidence is more than adequate in each case for the marriage to the second husband.

BIBLIOGRAPHIC NOTE: Given the many facets of the well-documented career of Roger Williams, and the many books and articles that have been written about his life, no attempt will be made here to cover all of his actions or all of the most important writings about him. In 1988 Glenn W. LaFantasie prepared a new edition of the correspondence of Roger Williams [*The Correspondence of Roger Williams*, two volumes (Providence 1988)]. The editorial material in this set includes an extensive bibliography, both of Williams's own writings and of later biographical material [lxxvi-lxxxviii]. One important item not included there is an article by Winifred Lovering Holman published in 1952 [TAG 28:197-209].

THOMAS WILLIAMS

Thomas Williams came to Plymouth in 1620 on the *Mayflower* and signed the Mayflower Compact. He died soon after arrival in the general sickness [Bradford 443, 447].

EDWARD WINSLOW

ORIGIN: Leiden, Holland.
MIGRATION: 1620 on the *Mayflower*.
FIRST RESIDENCE: Plymouth.
REMOVES: Marshfield by 1643.
RETURN TRIPS: Made many trips on personal and colony business. Returned to England in 1646 and never returned to New England.

OCCUPATION: Merchant.
FREEMAN: As governor, appears at head of 1633 list of Plymouth freemen [PCR 1:3]. In list of Plymouth Colony freemen of 7 March 1636/7 [PCR 1:52]. In Plymouth section of 1639 Plymouth Colony list of freemen [PCR 8:173], then erased and entered in Marshfield section of same list [PCR 8:177, 195].
EDUCATION: Attended the King's School of Worcester Cathedral from April 1606 until April 1611 [Edward Winslow 2]. Apprenticed to "John Beale, citizen and stationer, for the term of eight years," on 19 August 1613, but left his master in 1617 [Edward Winslow 3-4].

He had a hand in writing *Mourt's Relation* and also authored three other important pamphlets: *Good Newes from New England, or A Relation of Things Remarkable in That Plantation* (1624), *Hypocrisie Unmasked* (1646) and *New England's Salamander* (1647).

OFFICES: Plymouth Colony governor, 1 January 1632/3, 5 January 1635/6, 5 June 1644 [PCR 1:5, 36, 2:71]. Assistant, 1 January 1633/4, 1 January 1634/5, 3 January 1636/7, 6 March 1637/8, 2 March 1640/1, 1 March 1641/2, 7 March 1642/3, 4 June 1645, 1 June 1647, 7 June 1648, 4 June 1650 [PCR 1:21, 32, 48, 79, 2:8, 15, 33, 40, 52, 56, 83, 115, 123, 153].

In Marshfield section of 1643 Plymouth Colony list of men able to bear arms [PCR 8:196].

ESTATE: In the 1623 Plymouth division of land Edward Winslow was granted four acres as a passenger on the *Mayflower* [PCR 12:4]. In the 1627 Plymouth division of cattle Edward Winslow, Susanna Winslow, Edward Winslow and John Winslow were the sixth through the ninth persons in the third company [PCR 12:10].

In the 25 March 1633 Plymouth tax list "Edward Wynslow, Gov[erno]r," was assessed £2 5s., and the same amount in the list of 27 March 1634 [PCR 1:9, 27].

In his will, dated 18 December 1654 and proved 16 October 1655, "Edward Winslowe of London, Esquire, being now bound in a voyage to sea in the service of the commonwealth," bequeathed to "Josia my only son" the entire estate "he allowing to my wife a full third part thereof for her life"; to "the poor of the Church of Plymouth in New England £10 and to the poor of Marshfield where the chiefest of my estate lies £10"; "my linen which I carry with me to sea to my daughter Elizabeth"; residue to "my son Josias, he giving to each of my brothers a suit of apparel"; "son Josias my executor"; "my four friends Dr. Edmond Wilson, Mr. John Arthur, Mr. James Shirley & Mr. Richard Floyd" overseers "for the rest of my personal estate in England" [MD 4:1-2; Waters 179, citing PCC 377 Aylett].

BIRTH: Baptized Droitwich, Worcestershire, 20 October 1595, son of Edward and Magdalen (Oliver) Winslow [NEHGR 4:297, 21:210; TAG 42:52].
DEATH: At sea near Hispaniola 8 May 1655 "aged 59 years, 6 months, and 18 days" [NEHGR 4:297].
MARRIAGE: (1) Leiden, Holland, 12 May 1618 [NS] Elizabeth Barker [Plooij XXXV; Leiden Pilgrims 290; MD 22:66-67]. She died at Plymouth on 24 March 1620/1 [Prince 189].

(2) Plymouth 12 May 1621 Susannah (____) White, widow of WILLIAM WHITE ("The first marriage in this place, is of Mr. Edward Winslow to Mrs. Susanna White, widow of Mr. William White" [Prince 190]). (For the argument that Susannah's maiden surname was not Fuller, see the sketch of WILLIAM WHITE [PM 495].) She died between 1654 and 1675 [MF 5:6].
CHILDREN:
With second wife
- i Child WINSLOW, b. and d. 1622 or 1623 (in a letter dated 30 October 1623, Edward Winslow wrote that "[m]y wife hath had one child by me, but it pleased him that gave it to take it again unto himself; I left her with child at my departure ... but hope to be with her before her delivery" [NEHGR 109:243]).
- ii EDWARD WINSLOW, b. say 1624; living in 1627; no further record.
- iii JOHN WINSLOW, b. say 1626; living in 1627; no further record.
- iv JOSIAH WINSLOW, b. after 22 May 1627 (not in cattle division); m. by 1658 Penelope Pelham, daughter of Herbert Pelham (eldest known child b. Marshfield 13 March 1658 [MarVR 5]; in his will of 1 January 1672/3, Herbert Pelham

makes bequests to "my daughter Penelope Winslow" and "my son Josias Winslow" [NEHGR 33:291, 293; TAG 18:144]).

v ELIZABETH WINSLOW, b. say 1631; m. (1) by about 1656 Robert Brooks [MD 1:238-40]; m. (2) Salem 22 September 1669 GEORGE CURWEN {1638, Salem} (called "loving sister Corwin" in brother Josiah's will [MD 1:238-40, 5:82-85; NEHGR 150:193]).

ASSOCIATIONS: Brother of GILBERT WINSLOW, JOHN WINSLOW, JOSIAH WINSLOW and KENELM WINSLOW.

COMMENTS: Bradford describes his fellow *Mayflower* passenger as "Mr. Edward Winslow, Elizabeth his wife and two men-servants called George Soule and Elias Story; also a little girl was put to him, called Ellen, the sister of Richard More" [Bradford 441]. In 1651 Bradford reported that "Mr. Edward Winslow his wife died the first winter, and he married with the widow of Mr. White, and hath two children living by her marriageable, besides sundry that are dead" [Bradford 444].

Edward Winslow was a valued agent for Plymouth Colony, as is evident from the pages of Bradford's history, and for Massachusetts Bay Colony as well. Winslow left Plymouth for London in 1646 and never returned. He rose rapidly in the service of Cromwell's Commonwealth and was part of Cromwells' expedition to the West Indies when he died in 1655. All these aspects of Edward Winslow's life are portrayed in great detail in Jeremy Bangs's biography of the man.

BIBLIOGRAPHIC NOTE: In 1850 Lemuel Shattuck published a "Genealogical Memoir of the Descendants of Edward Winslow, Governor of Plymouth Colony," which included in a footnote a list of birth and baptismal dates for Edward and his siblings [NEHGR 4:297-303]. Savage objected to this list of dates [Savage 4:598-99], but in 1866 William S. Appleton examined the original parish registers of Droitwich and in 1867 published the results of his research, which were in agreement with the 1850 article [NEHGR 21:209-11].

From 1965 through 1970 John G. Hunt published seven short, intriguing articles on the Winslow family, examining the ancestry of the five brothers, both on the paternal and maternal sides [TAG 41:168-75, 42:52-55, 186-87, 43:239-41; NEHGR 121:25-29, 122:175-78, 124:182-83].

The standard genealogy of the Winslows, now considerably out of date, was published in 1887 and 1888 by David P. and Frances K. Holton

[*The Winslow Memorial*, 2 volumes (New York 1877, 1888)]. The bulk of these two volumes is devoted to the descendants of Kenelm Winslow, who had far more posterity in the male line than his four brothers combined.

Edward Winslow has been treated by Ruth C. McGuyre and Robert S. Wakefield in the fifth volume of the Five Generations series of the General Society of Mayflower Descendants [MF 5:3-27].

In 2004 Jeremy Dupertuis Bangs published *Pilgrim Edward Winslow: New England's First International Diplomat, A Documentary Biography* [Boston 2004], replete with complete transcriptions of many of Winslow's writings. Nearly half of this volume covers the last decade of Winslow's life, after he left Plymouth.

GILBERT WINSLOW

ORIGIN: Droitwich, Worcestershire.
MIGRATION: 1620 on the *Mayflower*.
FIRST RESIDENCE: Plymouth.
RETURN TRIPS: Returned to England by 1627.

ESTATE: In the 1623 Plymouth division of lands "Gilbard Winslow" received one acre as a passenger on the *Mayflower* [PCR 12:4]. His name does not appear in the 1627 Plymouth division of cattle.

The inventory of the estate of his brother KENELM WINSLOW included "one-half of the portion of land granted by the Court to him [Kenelm Winslow] and his brother Josias Winslow upon the account of their brother Gilbert Winslow as he was a first comer" [MD 24:42, citing PCPR 3:1:56].

On 1 June 1663, Plymouth Court acknowledged "Gilbert Winslow, deceased, who was one of the first comers, to have a right of land, and do allow his heirs to look out and propose to the Court some parcel of land that the Court may think meet to accommodate them in" [PCR 4:40].

BIRTH: Baptized Droitwich, Worcestershire, 29 October 1600, son of Edward and Magdalen (Oliver) Winslow [NEHGR 4:297, 21:120].
DEATH: In England by 1650 [Bradford 447].
MARRIAGE: None recorded.
CHILDREN: None recorded.
ASSOCIATIONS: Brother of EDWARD WINSLOW, KENELM WINSLOW, JOHN WINSLOW and JOSIAH WINSLOW.

COMMENTS: In his list of those on the *Mayflower,* Bradford included Gilbert Winslow, and reported of him in 1651 that "after diverse years here, [he] returned into England and died there" [Bradford 443, 447].

Writing in 1994 about *Mayflower* passengers who returned to England, Doris Jones-Baker was unable to find anything about Gilbert Winslow in English records [*Genealogists' Magazine* 24:490-91].

JOHN WINSLOW

ORIGIN: Droitwich, Worcestershire.
MIGRATION: 1621 on the *Fortune.*
FIRST RESIDENCE: Plymouth.
REMOVES: Boston 1655.

OCCUPATION: Merchant.
FREEMAN: In the 1633 Plymouth list of freemen "John Wynslow" appears early in the list, ahead of those admitted on 1 January 1632/3 [PCR 1:3]. In list of Plymouth Colony freemen of 7 March 1636/7 [PCR 1:52]. In Plymouth section of 1639 Plymouth Colony list of freemen [PCR 8:173].
EDUCATION: Presumably educated as well as his siblings, and certainly well enough to be successful in trade.
OFFICES: Deputy for Plymouth to Plymouth General Court, 3 June 1652, 7 March 1653/4, 6 June 1654, 1 August 1654 [PCR 3:8, 44, 49, 63]. Council of War, 6 April 1653 [PCR 3:26].

In Plymouth section of 1643 Plymouth Colony list of men able to bear arms [PCR 8:187].
ESTATE: In the 1623 Plymouth land division John Winslow received one acre as a passenger on the *Fortune* [PCR 12:5]. In the 1627 Plymouth division of cattle John Winslow and Mary Winslow were the fifth and sixth persons in the sixth company [PCR 12:11].

In the Plymouth tax list of 25 March 1633 "John Wynslow" was assessed 18s. and in the list of 27 March 1634 the same amount [PCR 1:9, 27].

In his will, dated 12 March 1673/4 and proved 21 May 1674, "John Winslow Senior of Boston ... merchant" bequeathed to "my dear and well beloved wife Mary Winslow the use of my now dwelling house with the gardens and yards thereunto belonging for and during the term of her natural life," along with "all my household goods" and £400; to "my son John Winslow" the house and land after wife's decease, he paying £50 apiece to "William Payne the son of my daughter Sarah Meddlecott and also to Parnell Winslow daughter to my son Isack Winslow"; "my ketch *Speedwell* ... and the net produce thereof [to] be equally divided amongst my children my son John only excepted"; to "my son Benjamin" £100 at age twenty-one; "if my son Edward Winslow shall see cause to relinquish his said part and interest in the said ketch *Speedwell* and her proceeds, then my will is that he shall have one-quarter part of my ketch *John's Adventure* unto his own proper use, and then the said ketch and cargo to be equally divided among my other children my son John excepted as aforesaid together with my son Edward"; to "my grandchild Susanna Latham the sum of thirty pounds in money to be paid her at the day of her marriage and to the rest of my daughter Latham's children ... five pounds" apiece when they come of age or marry; to "my son Edward Winslow's children" £5 apiece when they come of age or marry; to "my son Edward Grey his children that he had by my daughter Mary Grey" £20 apiece when the come of age or marry; to "my son Joseph Winslow's two children" £5 apiece as aforesaid; to "my grandchild Mercy Harris her two children" £5 apiece as aforesaid; to "my kinsman Josiah Winslow now governor of New Plimoth" £20; to "my brother Josiah Winslow" £20; to "my kinswoman Eleanor Baker the daughter of my brother Kenelm Winslow" £5; residue to be divided after wife's decease "among my seven children in equal proportions"; to "Mr. Paddye's widow five pounds as a token of my love"; "my negro girl Jane (after she hath served twenty years from the date hereof) shall be free"; "my son John Winslow" to be sole executor; "my loving friends Mr. Thomas Brattle, Mr. William Tailer and Mr. John Winsley" to be overseers, they to have £5 apiece [MD 3:129-33, citing SPR Case #688].

The inventory of the estate of John Winslow, taken 27 October 1674, totalled £2946 14s. 10d., of which £450 was real estate: "the dwelling house, garden & land adjoining to it," valued at £450; most of the value was in shares in vessels, hard currency, debts due and trade goods [MD 3:133-34, citing SPR 5:211-12].

In her will, dated 31 July 1676 and proved 11 July 1679, "Mary Winslow of Boston in New England" bequeathed to "my son John Winslow my great square table"; to "my daughter Sarah Middlecott" moveables "and to each of her children a silver cup with a handle"; to "my grandchild William Paine my great silver tankard"; to "my daughter Susanna Latham" moveables; to "my grandchild Ann Gray" moveables and £10; "my executor shall pay four pounds in money per annum for three years unto Mrs. Tappin ... towards the maintenance of the said Ann Gray"; to "Mary Winslow daughter of my son Edward Winslow my largest silver cup with two handles and unto Sarah daughter of the said Edward my lesser silver cup with two handles, also I give unto my said son Edward's children six silver spoons to be divided between them"; to "my grandchild Parnell Winslow" £5; to "my grandchild Chilton Latham" £5; "the rest of my spoons be divided amongst my grandchildren according to the discretion of my daughter Middlecott"; to "my grandchild Mercy Harris my white rug"; to "my grandchild Mary Pollard forty shillings"; to "my grandchild Susanna Latham my petticoat with silk lace"; to "Mary Winslow daughter of my son Joseph Winslow" £20; residue to be equally divided among "my children John Winslow, Edward Winslow, Joseph Winslow, Samuel Winslow, Susanna Latham and Sarah Middlecott"; "my trusty friend Mr. William Tailer of Boston aforesaid merchant" to be sole executor; to "Mr. Thomas Thacher pastor of the third church in Boston" £5 [MD 1:65-69, citing SPR 6:300-1].

The inventory of the estate of "Mrs. Mary Winslow," taken 29 July 1679, totalled £212 11s. 9d., of which £67 was real estate: "one-half of the house which was formerly Mr. Joseph Winslow's" valued at £67 [MD 1:69-71, citing SPR 12:314-15].

BIRTH: Born Droitwich, Worcestershire, 16 April 1597 and baptized there 18 April 1597, son of Edward and Magdalen (Oliver) Winslow [NEHGR 4:297, 21:120].
DEATH: Between 12 March 1673/4 (date of will) and 21 May 1674 (probate of will).
MARRIAGE: Plymouth by 22 May 1627 Mary Chilton, daughter of JAMES CHILTON [PCR 12:11; MF 15:5-7; PM 103]. She died between 31 July 1676 (date of will) and 1 May 1679 (renunciation of executorship).
CHILDREN:
    i   JOHN WINSLOW, b. say 1628; m. (1) by 1664 Elizabeth _____ (eldest known child b. Boston 18 April 1664 [BVR 94]); m. (2) by an unknown date Judith _____ (in his will of 3 October 1683, John Winslow bequeathed to "my beloved wife Judith Winslow" [MD 10:54, citing SPR 6:435]).
   ii   SUSANNA WINSLOW, b. say 1630; m. by 1650 Robert Latham (eldest known child b. Plymouth 2 June 1650 [PCR 8:11]).
  iii   MARY WINSLOW, b. say 1632; m. Plymouth 16 January 1650/1 Edward Gray [PCR 8:11].
  iv   EDWARD WINSLOW, b. about 1635 (d. 19 November 1682 "in the 48th year of his age" [MD 12:129]); m. (1) by 1661

Sarah Hilton, daughter of William and Sarah (Greenleaf) Hilton (eldest known child b. Boston 18 June 1661 [BVR 80]); m. (2) 8 February 1668 Elizabeth Hutchinson, daughter of Edward and Catherine (Hamby) Hutchinson [MD 12:129; NEHGR 145:261].

v SARAH WINSLOW, b. about 1638 (d. 9 April 1726 "age 88" [NEHGR 15:308]); m. (1) Boston 19 July 1660 Miles Standish [BVR 76], son of MILES STANDISH [PM 451]; m. (2) by 1668 Tobias Payne (only known child b. Boston 21 January 1668[/9] [BVR 108]); m. (3) by 1674 Richard Middlecott (eldest known child b. Boston 1 July 1674 [BVR 133]) [MD 12:1-10].

vi SAMUEL WINSLOW, b. about 1641 (d. 14 October 1680 "aged 39 years" [Copp's Hill W 50]); m. by 1675 Hannah Briggs, daughter of Walter Briggs (on 22 June 1675, "Walter Briggs of Sittuate ... yeoman" and "Samuell Winslow of Boston merchant" drafted an agreement covering "part of his the said Samuell Winslow's wife['s] portion" [SLR 9:212-13]).

vii ISAAC WINSLOW, b. say 1643; m. Charlestown 14 August 1666 Mary Nowell [ChVR 1:24], daughter of INCREASE NOWELL {1630, Charlestown} [GMB 2:1342-46].

viii JOSEPH WINSLOW, b. say 1645; m. by 1668 Sarah Lawrence, daughter of Thomas Lawrence of Newtown, Long Island [TAG 17:76].

ix Child WINSLOW, b. by 1651 [Bradford 446]; no further record.

x BENJAMIN WINSLOW, b. Plymouth 12 August 1653 [PCR 8:15; PVR 660]; d. between 12 March 1673/4 (date of father's will) and 31 July 1676 (date of mother's will); unm.

ASSOCIATIONS: Brother of EDWARD WINSLOW, KENELM WINSLOW, GILBERT WINSLOW and JOSIAH WINSLOW.

COMMENTS: The varied abilities of this group of five siblings are interesting to observe. Gilbert left too slight a mark on the records to judge. Edward, the eldest, was also the ablest. The second brother, John, was also quite talented, but was not inclined to public service; he died as one of the wealthiest merchants in Boston in the mid-1650s. The two younger siblings, Kenelm and Josiah, remained in Plymouth Colony, were publicly visible so long as their two elder brothers were still present, and then faded slowly from sight.

BIBLIOGRAPHIC NOTE: John Winslow and his family are treated in the fifteenth volume of the Five Generations series of the General Society of Mayflower Descendants, in the section on JAMES CHILTON [MF 15:5-7, 10-19].

JOSIAH WINSLOW

ORIGIN: Droitwich, Worcestershire.
MIGRATION: 1631.
FIRST RESIDENCE: Plymouth.
REMOVES: Marshfield by 1643.

OCCUPATION: Bookkeeper [Stratton 375].
FREEMAN: Admitted 1 January 1633/4 (and appended to list of 1633) [PCR 1:4, 5]. In list of Plymouth Colony freemen of 7 March 1636/7 [PCR 1:52]. In Plymouth section of 1639 Plymouth Colony list of freemen [PCR 8:173], then erased and entered in Marshfield section of same list [PCR 8:177, 195]. In Marshfield sections of 1658 and 29 May 1670 lists of Plymouth Colony freemen [PCR 5:277, 8:201].
EDUCATION: The inventory of his estate included "1 Great Bible & psalm book" valued at 8s., "1 book of Ursinus on Christian Religion" valued at 9s., "2 books of Mr. Burrowghes" valued at 6s., "1 book of Mr. Weemes" valued at 2s. 6d., "1 book called Bloody Tenett" valued at 2s. and "26 old books" valued at 6s. [PCPR 3:1:135].
OFFICES: Deputy for Marshfield to Plymouth General Court, 6 June 1643, 10 October 1643, 5 March 1643/4, 3 March 1645/6, 1 June 1647, 5 June 1651 [PCR 2:57, 63, 68, 95, 117, 168]. Council of War, 5 June 1671 [PCR 5:64, 73].

Marshfield selectman, 3 June 1674 [PCR 5:144].

In Marshfield section of 1643 Plymouth Colony list of men able to bear arms [PCR 8:196]. His inventory included "1 fowling piece" valued at 16s., "1 old matchlock musket" valued at 6s. and "2 swords, one rest and bandoliers" valued at 16s. [PCPR 3:1:135].
ESTATE: Granted one hundred acres at Teticutt, 4 March 1673/4 (pursuant to an order of June 1662) [PCR 5:141].

In his will, dated 12 April 1673 and proved 4 March 1674/5, "Josiah Winslow of the town of Marshfield Senior" appointed "Margarett my dear and loving wife my sole executrix" and bequeathed to her for life "one half of my dwelling house ... and one half of the orchard and outhousing and also the one half of the land thereunto belonging, both meadow and upland, ... in the town of Marshfield ... and the one half of all the lands belonging to me, by any grant granted to me formerly or to be granted"; "for the other part of my lands, house and housing I do give unto my natural son Jonathan Winslow ... with that half given to my wife after her decease ... but in case the said Jonathan shall die without heirs ... the whole and every part of the said lands and housing shall be disposed of [after the decease of Jonathan's wife] unto my four daughters and their heirs"; to "Hannah Miller my grandchild now living with me, if she continue with her grandmother during her life, or day of the said Hannah her marriage," moveables; "for my Indian apprentice I leave him and his time to my wife"; to "my grandchildren" ten shillings apiece; to "my faithful and truly loving friend Mr. Samuell Arnold our Reverend teacher my black cloak"; to "my son Jonathan my best suit and what bedding he now makes use of and the Bible that is mine"; "my loving nephew Major Josiah Winslow and Captain William Bradford" to be overseers [MD 34:33-34, citing PCPR 3:1:131-32].

The inventory of the estate of "Mr. Josiah Winslow deceased," taken 17 December 1674, totalled £107 16s. 1[illegible]d.; the real estate, not valued, was "one dwelling house and one hundred acres of upland without housing thereon and a considerable parcel or parcels of meadow belonging thereunto the quantity unknown to us" in Marshfield, also "1 hundred acres of upland lying in the town of Middleberry or Bridgwater near Teticutt River" [MD 34:34-35, citing PCPR 3:1:135, 136, 138].

On 1 March 1674/5, "[w]hereas the last will and testament of Mr. Josiah Winslow, Senior, deceased, the 12th day of the 2cond month, 1673, was presented unto the Court to be proved: Before probate of which caution was presented, grounded on sundry testimonies upon oath, whereby it did appear unto this Court that Mr. Josias Winslow, Senior, aforesaid, his house, and all his lands lying and being in Marshfeild, were given by him the said Josias Winslow unto his son and heir, Jonathan Winslow, in frank marriage unto Ruth, the daughter of Mr. Will[i]am Serjeant, which said house and lands in Marshfeild are again devised by his last will and testament unto his son, Jonathan Winslow, in tail; the Court apprehending that a man cannot by his last will and testament defeat and make void a gift of lands made unto his son and heir in frank marriage, but that such gift is extinct, and made void by a former gift in frank marriage, and therefore do declare that part of the will, so far as the disposal of the said house and land, to be a void gift, and do order that the abovesaid testimonies upon oath to be herewith recorded, and the rest of the said will abovesaid to stand valid, and do grant letters of administration unto Mistress Margarett Winslow, executrix to the said will, and do request the honored Governor to take her oath to the inventory of the estate" [PCR 5:159-60].

BIRTH: Born Droitwich, Worcestershire, 11 February 1605/6 and baptized there 16 February 1605/6, son of Edward and Magdalen (Oliver) Winslow [NEHGR 4:297, 21:210].
DEATH: Buried Marshfield 1 December 1674 in his sixty-ninth year [MarVR 9].
MARRIAGE: By 1637 Margaret Bourne, daughter of Thomas and Elizabeth (____) Bourne [Waterman Gen 1:615-16, 619]. She died 28 September 1683, aged seventy-five years [PChR 1:250], and was buried at Marshfield on 2 October 1683 [MarVR 14].
CHILDREN:
- i ELIZABETH WINSLOW, b. Marshfield 24 September 1637 [MarVR 2]; apparently killed accidentally by her brother Jonathan in late 1646 [WJ 2:368; Edward Winslow 235].
- ii JONATHAN WINSLOW, b. Marshfield 8 August 1639 [MarVR 2]; m. by 1664 Ruth Sargent (eldest known child b. Marshfield 1 March 1664 [MarVR 7]; Josiah Winslow gave his Marshfield land "unto his son and heir, Jonathan Winslow, in frank marriage unto Ruth, the daughter of Mr. Will[i]am Serjeant" [PCR 5:159]).
- iii MARGARET WINSLOW, b. Marshfield 15 (or 16) July 1640 [MarVR 2; NEHGR 51:33]; m. Marshfield 24 December 1659 John Miller [NEHGR 51:33-34].
- iv REBECCA WINSLOW, b. Marshfield 15 July 1643 [MarVR 2]; m. by 1665 John Thatcher (eldest known child b. Yarmouth 20 May 1665 [MD 13:221]). (Savage gives the date of this marriage as 6 November 1661, at Marshfield, but this event does not appear in the Marshfield records.)
- v HANNAH WINSLOW, b. Marshfield 30 November 1644 [MarVR 2]; m. (1) Plymouth 5 April 1664 William Crow [MD 17:185]; m. (2) by 1687 John Sturtevant (eldest known child b. Plymouth 10 April 1687 [MD 1:145, 17:185]).
- vi MARY WINSLOW, b. say 1646; m. Marshfield 10 June 1670 John Tracy [MarVR 427].

ASSOCIATIONS: Brother of EDWARD WINSLOW, JOHN WINSLOW, GILBERT WINSLOW and KENELM WINSLOW.

KENELM WINSLOW

ORIGIN: Droitwich, Worcestershire.
MIGRATION: 1631.
FIRST RESIDENCE: Plymouth.
REMOVES: Marshfield by 1643.

OCCUPATION: Joiner. On 6 January 1633/4, "Sam[uel] Jenny, the son of John Jenny, hath bound himself apprentice to Kanelm Winslow, of Plymouth, joiner" [PCR 1:24].
FREEMAN: Admitted 1 January 1632/3 [PCR 1:4, 5]. In list of Plymouth Colony freemen of 7 March 1636/7 [PCR 1:52]. In Plymouth section of 1639 Plymouth Colony list of freemen [PCR 8:173], then erased and entered in Marshfield section of same list [PCR 8:177, 195]. In Marshfield sections of 1658 and 29 May 1670 lists of Plymouth Colony freemen [PCR 5:277, 8:201].
EDUCATION: He signed his will. His inventory included "1 Bible and 7 other books" valued at 12s. [PCPR 3:1:57].
OFFICES: Deputy for Marshfield to Plymouth General Court, 7 June 1642, 27 September 1642, 29 August 1643, 10 October 1643, 5 June 1644, 20 August 1644, 6 June 1649, 4 June 1650, 5 June 1651, 7 June 1652, 7 June 1653 [PCR 2:40, 46, 60, 63, 72, 75, 144, 154, 168, 3:9, 32].

Plymouth petit jury, 7 June 1636, 4 October 1636, 4 June 1639, 3 September 1639 [PCR 1:42, 44, 7:12, 13]. Grand jury, 7 March 1636/7, 5 June 1638, 6 June 1654 [PCR 1:54, 87, 3:49]. Coroner's jury, 3 May 1653, 14 February 1654/5 [PCR 3:28, 70].

Plymouth Colony assessor, 27 March 1634 [PCR 1:26]. Committee on laborers' wages, 5 January 1635/6 [PCR 1:36]. Plymouth member of colony committee on highways, 5 March 1638/9 [PCR 1:117]. Committee on provisions for the governor and magistrates, 3 June 1657 [PCR 3:120].

On 1 December 1640, "Kenelme Winslow, being elected surveyor of the highways for the town of Plymouth, and neglecting the same, is fined 10s." [PCR 2:4].

Marshfield constable, 1 June 1647 [PCR 2:115].

In Marshfield section of 1643 Plymouth Colony list of men able to bear arms [PCR 8:196].

ESTATE: Assessed 12s. in Plymouth tax list of 25 March 1633 and 18s. in list of 27 March 1634 [PCR 1:11, 28].

On 8 January 1632/3, "Francis Eaton acknowledgeth that he hath sold to Kanelm & Josias Wynslow the now dwelling house of the said

Francis" [PCR 1:8]. Granted mowing ground, 14 March 1635/6, 20 March 1636/7 [PCR 1:40, 55]. Granted "threescore acres of land lying upon the south side of the Eele River, above the great swamp.... This grant was made void upon a grant made to him at Green's Harbor," 6 January 1636/7 [PCR 1:47]. On 5 February 1637/8, "Kenelme Winslow requesteth a grant of lands at Green's Harbor" [PCR 1:76], and, on 5 March 1637/8, he received, in partnership with Love Brewster, "all that parcel of land remaining of that neck of land lying on the east side of the lands lately granted to Josias Winslow, at Greene's Harbor" [PCR 1:78, 111].

On 26 October 1647, "Mr. Hatherley here in Court acknowledgeth that Helene, the wife of Kanelme Winslow, acknowledgeth her free assent and consent to the sale of all such lands as her husband had sold unto Samuell Sturdevant. Captain Miles Standish" deposed the same regarding her consent to sales to Henry Sampson [PCR 2:118-19].

Granted one hundred acres at Teticutt, 4 March 1673/4 (pursuant to an order of June 1662) [PCR 5:141].

In his will, dated 8 August 1672 and proved 5 June 1673, "Kanelme Winslow Senior" ordered that "what estate I have formerly settled on my eldest son Kanelme ... shall remain unaltered" and bequeathed to "my son Nathaniel ... the half of my farm that I last lived upon ... as I gave him by a former deed of gift"; "and the other half of the farm to my wife, for the term of her natural life" and "after the decease of my wife Ellinor Winslow the said half of the farm shall return unto my son Nathaniel"; to "my son Job ... half of my land at Namassakett which is about fifty acres ... and the other fifty acres or thereabouts unto Kanelme Baker my grandchild"; to "my daughter Ellinor" £5; "my wife shall at her decease give unto Mary Addams an equal portion of the goods and moveables as to the rest of my grandchildren"; wife to be sole executrix and "Major Josias Winslow and my son Kanelme Winslow" to be overseers [MD 24:41-42, citing PCPR 3:1:56].

The inventory of the estate of "Mr. Kenelme Winslow deceased the 12 of September 1672," taken 25 September 1672, totalled £87 15s. 4d.; the real estate, unvalued, followed: "one half of the dwelling house and housings and meadow lands and uplands belonging to the said farm he had lived on and now died possessed of in the town of Marshfield"; "one half of all the lands granted him by the Court with the ancient freemen which lieth on the west side of Taunton River either divided or to be divided hereafter"; and "one half of the portion of land granted by the court to him and his brother Josias Winslow upon the account of their brother Gilbert Winslow as he was a first comer" [MD 24:42, citing PCPR 3:1:57].

BIRTH: Baptized Droitwich, Worcestershire, 3 May 1599, son of Edward and Magdalen (Oliver) Winslow [NEHGR 4:297, 21:210].
DEATH: Buried at Salem 13 September 1672 [MarVR 427].
MARRIAGE: Plymouth in June 1634 "Elen Adames" [PCR 1:30]. She was ELLEN NEWTON [PM 344], widow of JOHN ADAMS [TAG 55:212-13; PM 1]. She was buried at Marshfield 5 December 1681, aged 83 [MD 2:250; MarVR 13].
CHILDREN:

    i KENELM WINSLOW, b. say 1635; m. (1) by 1668 Mercy Worden (eldest known child b. Scituate 9 August 1668, father stated to be of Yarmouth; in her will of 6 March 1686[/7], Mary Worden, widow, of Yarmouth bequeathed to daughter Mercy Winslow [MD 3:201-2, citing BarnPR 1:12]); m. (2) by 1693 Damaris Eames, daughter of Mark Eames (in his will of 12 July 1693, Mark Eames of Marshfield bequeathed to "daughter Damaris Winslow" [Gen Adv 3:93-94, citing PPR 1:172]).

    ii ELLEN WINSLOW, b. say 1636; m. Marshfield 20 [December 1656 Samuel Baker] (the marriage record as published is missing all but the name of the bride and the day of the event; the month and the year are suggested by the preceding marriage record, which was for November 1656, and the date of birth of the first child, on 23 March 1657/8 [MarVR 2, 4]). On 7 March 1653/4, "Kanelme Winslow complained against John Soule for speaking falsely of and scandalizing his daughter in carrying diverse false reports betwixt Josias Standish and her; the which complaint, at the request of G[e]orge Soule, father of the said John Soule, was referred until another Court, to be tried by a jury of twelve of his equals" [PCR 3:46-47].

    iii NATHANIEL WINSLOW, b. say 1639; m. Marshfield 3 August 1664 Faith Miller [MarVR 5].

    iv JOB WINSLOW, b. say 1641; m. by 1674 Ruth _____ (eldest known child b. Swansea 16 November 1674 [SwVR 21]). (In 1914 Richard Henry Greene rejected the claim that Ruth was daughter of Daniel Cole; he examined several other possibilities, including a placement in the family of

STEPHEN HOPKINS, but came to no firm conclusion [NYGBR 45:2-8; see also MF 6:7, 11].)

ASSOCIATIONS: Brother of EDWARD WINSLOW, GILBERT WINSLOW, JOHN WINSLOW and JOSIAH WINSLOW.

COMMENTS: Although Kenelm Winslow first appears of record in Plymouth in the tax list of 25 March 1633, and was therefore certainly in New England by 1632, he is paired in the early years with his brother Josiah Winslow, who is known to have arrived in 1631, and so we assume that Kenelm came at the same time.

On 4 June 1645, "Kenelme Winslow complained that he had injustice, in that he could not be heard in the suit betwixt John Mynard and himself"; after investigation by the court, he "was committed to prison and fined £10," whereupon he reversed himself and was released from prison and the fine was eventually remitted [PCR 2:85].

On 5 May 1645/6, "upon hearing of the cause betwixt Roger Chaundler and Kenelme Winslow, for his daughter's clothes, which the said Kenelme detaineth, upon pretense of some further service which he required of her, whereunto the said Roger utterly refused to consent, it is ordered by the Court, that the said Kenelme Winslow shall deliver the maid her clothes without any further delay" [PCR 2:98].

On the same day, "Kenelme Winslow, for opprobrious words against the church of Marshfeild, saying they were all liars, &c., was ordered by the Court to find sureties for his good behavior, which he refusing to do, was committed to prison, where he remained until the General Court following" [PCR 2:98].

Despite this bad year, Kenelm Winslow continued to hold important town and colony offices for another decade. His last year as deputy was 1653, and he virtually disappears from public view at that time, although he lived for another two decades. By this time his two elder and more prominent brothers, Edward and John, had left Plymouth Colony; perhaps Kenelm owed his limited success to the presence of these brothers, and once they were gone his own abilities, or his own inclinations, were not sufficient to maintain this level of public service.

WALTER WOODWORTH

ORIGIN: Unknown.
MIGRATION: 1633.
FIRST RESIDENCE: Plymouth.

522   *The Pilgrim Migration*

REMOVES: Scituate.

FREEMAN: Propounded as a freeman on 1 December 1640 and admitted 2 March 1640/1 [PCR 2:3, 8]. "Walter Woodward" in Scituate sections of 1639 (added after his admission on 2 March 1640/1), 1658, 29 May 1670 and early 1684 lists of Plymouth Colony freemen [PCR 5:275, 8:175, 198, 204].

EDUCATION: Signed his will by mark. His inventory included his "purse & apparel & books" valued at £5 10s.

OFFICES: Scituate surveyor of highways, 4 June 1645, 2 June 1646, 3 June 1656 [PCR 2:84, 102, 3:100]. Arbiter, 4 June 1645, 3 June 1662/3, 9 June 1665 [PCR 2:85, 4:31, 100]. Coroner's jury, 1 July 1680 [PCR 6:45].

"Walter Woodworth" was in the Scituate section of 1643 Plymouth list of men able to bear arms [PCR 8:191].

ESTATE: "Walter Woodart" assessed 9s. in Plymouth tax list of 27 March 1634 [PCR 1:29].

He is on the 3 June 1662 list of servants and ancient freemen granted land [PCR 4:18] and as a consequence on 4 October 1664 was granted sixty acres [PCR 4:75].

In his will, dated 26 November 1685 and proved 2 March 1685/6, "Walter Woodward of Sittuate" bequeathed to "Thomas Woodward my eldest son a parcel of upland containing five acres" in Scituate; to "my two sons Thomas & Joseph Woodward ten acres of marshland" in Scituate to be equally divided; to "the said Thomas my son one-third part of all my lands at Seconet which is purchased, & the other two-thirds I give unto my son two sons Beniamin & Isaak Woodward" to be equally divided, "excepting twenty & five acres which I do give unto my son Joseph ... & ten acres the which I do give unto my daughter Martha"; "all the rest of my land at Seconett which is yet to be purchased I give unto my two sons Thomas & Joseph Woodward" to be equally divided; to "Beniamin my son aforesaid my dwelling house with my barn & other outhousing with all my land both upland and marshland thereunto belonging, that is to say twenty acres of upland ... & six acres of marshland ... upon condition that my son Beniamin aforesaid do pay & allow the sum of seventy pounds unto my son Joseph & my six daughters Sarah, Elyzabeth, Mary, Martha, Mehetabel & Abigaile," £10 apiece, and permit "my two daughters Mehetable & Abigaile" to live in the house as long as they are unmarried; to "my said two daughters Mehetable & Abigaile my feather bed with the furniture thereunto belonging & all the rest of my household goods I give unto my six daughters Sarah, Elyzabeth, Mary, Martha, Mehetabel & Abigaile" to be divided equally; residue of estate to "all my children"; "my son Beniamin" to be sole executor and "my two sons Thomas & Joseph" to be overseers [PCLR 5:382-83].

The inventory of the estate of "Walter Woodworth of Situate late deceased," taken 25 February 1685/6, totalled £355 10s., of which £310 was real estate: "one dwelling house & barn & upland & meadow land adjoining thereto with common privileges," £140; "ten acres of salt meadow land," £50; "five acres of upland," £20; and "one whole share of land at Saconet," £100 [PCLR 5:383-84].

BIRTH: By about 1612 (based on taxation in 1633).
DEATH: Scituate between 26 November 1685 (date of will) and 25 February 1685/6 (date of inventory).
MARRIAGE: By about 1641 _____ _____. She died after about 1664.
CHILDREN:
- i THOMAS WOODWORTH, b. say 1641; m. Scituate 8 February 1666[/7] Deborah Daman, daughter of John Daman.
- ii SARAH WOODWORTH, b. say 1643; apparently married by 26 November 1685 (father's will).
- iii JOSEPH WOODWORTH, b. say 1645; m. Scituate 6 January 1669[/70] Sarah Stockbridge [NEHGR 133:100-1].
- iv ELIZABETH WOODWORTH, b. say 1648; in court 27 October 1675, 7 March 1675/6 and 22 July 1676 [PCR 5:181-82, 188, 208] about a child she had with Robert Stetson Junior, which Stetson acknowledged; apparently married by 26 November 1685 (father's will implies that four eldest daughters were all married), but not to Robert Stetson, who had probably married Deborah Brooks, daughter of WILLIAM BROOKS {1635, Scituate} [GM 2:1:414].
- v MARY WOODWORTH, b. Scituate 10 March 1650/1; m. Scituate 24 December 1677 Aaron Simmons (or Simonson), son of MOSES SIMONSON [PM 419].
- vi BENJAMIN WOODWORTH, b. say 1656; m. (1) by about 1680 Deborah _____ ("Deborah the wife [and] Elizabeth [and] Deborah the children of Beniamin Woddward" were bp. at Scituate on 16 July 1682 [NEHGR 57:319]); m. (2) by 1691 Hannah _____ (on 24 June 1691, "Benjamin Woodworth and Hannah Woodworth his wife" acknowledged a

deed in which Benjamin sold the land he had inherited from his father [PLR 3:11]).
vii ISAAC WOODWORTH, b. say 1658; m. by an unknown date Lydia Standlake, daughter of Richard Standlake [PLR 8:172-74, 207-8; NEHGR 87:84].
viii MARTHA WOODWORTH, b. say 1660; m. Scituate June 1679 Zachary Daman, son of John Daman.
ix MEHETABEL WOODWORTH, b. Scituate 15 August 1662; "Mehittable Woodworth," daughter of "Walter Woodworth" of Scituate, was a victim of witchcraft, "almost bereaved of her senses," 6 March 1676/7 [PCR 5:223]; unmarried on 26 November 1685 (father's will).
x ABIGAIL WOODWORTH, b. say 1664; unmarried on 26 November 1685 (father's will).

COMMENTS: Savage, following Deane, says that the immigrant had a son Walter Woodworth who had children "Mary, b. 1658; Mehitable, 1662; and Ebenezer, 1664" [Savage 4:648]. There is only evidence of one Walter Woodworth in early New England, as no record refers to Walter Sr. or Jr. The immigrant had daughters named Mary and Mehitable. Ebenezer was probably a grandson.

Paul W. Prindle and Robert S. Wakefield have commented briefly on some errors in secondary sources regarding marriages in this family [TAG 32:203, 61:140].

In arranging the children of Walter Woodworth, the assumption has been made that in his will he named his sons in birth order and his daughters in birth order. This permits a birth sequence for the children which is consistent with other known dates.

On 7 July 1681, "Walter Woodworth of Scittuate" sued Japhett Turner for tearing down some of his fencing, and was awarded "five shillings damage and the cost of the suit"; the "Bill of Cost," apparently prepared by Woodworth himself, totalled £3 16s. [PCR 7:238-39].

WILLIAM WRIGHT

ORIGIN: Unknown.
MIGRATION: 1621 on the *Fortune.*
FIRST RESIDENCE: Plymouth.

OCCUPATION: In the inventory, listed in the loft over the bedchamber, were many carpentry tools: one broad ax, two felling axes, two hand saws, one thwart saw, three augers, one chisel, one gouge, one drawing knife, one "prser" [piercer], one gimlet, two hammers, one pair of old hinges, two chest locks, one padlock, one splitting knife [MD 1:205]. These may point to his occupation. On the other hand, the average husbandman may have needed many such tools during the early years of settlement, when everyone had to have a newly built house.

CHURCH MEMBERSHIP: List of books in inventory and gift to Plymouth church make it very likely that he was a member of the church.

FREEMAN: In 1633 Plymouth list of freemen, in early part of list, before those admitted 1 January 1632/3 [PCR 1:3].

EDUCATION: Signed his will. His inventory included, in the bedchamber, "one great Bible & a little Bible. 1 Greenham's works. 1 psalm book with 17 other small books," valued at £1 3s. [MD 1:205].

OFFICES: His inventory included "one fowling piece" valued at £2 10s. [MD 1:204].

ESTATE: In the 1623 Plymouth land division William Wright and William Pitt were paired in the receipt of two acres of land [PCR 12:5]. In the 1627 Plymouth cattle division William Wright was the fifth person in the company of John Howland [PCR 12:10].

On 1 July 1633, Christopher Wadsworth and William Wright were allowed to mow where they had mowed the year before [PCR 1:15]; a reference to "widow Wright" in this same allocation of mowing ground is probably a later alteration of the record [PCR 1:14].

In his will, dated 16 September 1633 and proved 2 January 1633/4, "Will[iam] Wright of New Plymouth" bequeathed to "Prisilla Wright my loving & lawful wife all that my mansion or dwelling house situate ... in New Plymouth ... together with all that parcel of ground or garden or garden plot that adjoineth ... with all barns, stables, beast houses with all their several appurtenances, privileges & immunities"; also to "Prisilla my loving wife" any lands that might be granted in the future and all moveables and all debts owing to the estate, she to give to the church at Plymouth "one ewe lamb" and to "my reverend & respected friend Mr. Will[iam] Brewster of Plymouth elder that cloth suit of apparel which were given me by my brother Fuller"; "my trusty & beloved friend & brother William Bradford" to be overseer and "Prisilla my wife" to be sole executrix [MD 1:200-3].

The inventory of the estate of "Will[iam] Wright late of Plym[outh] deceased," taken 6 November 1633, totalled £99 12s., of which £10 was real estate: "the house and garden," £10 [MD 1:203-5, citing PCPR 1:19-21].

BIRTH: About 1600 (based on estimated age of wife).
DEATH: Plymouth between 16 September 1633 (date of will) and 6 November 1633 (date of inventory).
MARRIAGE: Plymouth between 1629 and 1633 PRISCILLA CARPENTER [PM 93]. She m. (2) Plymouth 27 November 1634 JOHN COOPER {1634, Scituate} [PCR 1:32; GM 2:2:200-2].
CHILDREN: None recorded.
ASSOCIATIONS: In his will of 30 July 1633, Samuel Fuller makes several references to "my brother William Wright," including a bequest of "one cloth suit not yet fully finished lying in my trunk at town" [MD 1:24-27]. Fuller and Wright had married sisters [see PRISCILLA CARPENTER].

COMMENTS: William Wright appears alone in both the 1623 land division and the 1627 cattle division. This indicates that Priscilla Carpenter did not come to Plymouth until the remnant of the Leiden congregation arrived in 1629 and 1630. William and Priscilla were no doubt married sometime not long after her arrival, and certainly before 30 July 1633.

PHANTOM FILE

The families and individuals briefly noted in this section have been claimed as immigrants to Plymouth Colony by the end of 1633, but are not here accepted as such. Either they came at a later date or they never existed at all.

JOHN ALLEN

Deane says that John Allen of Scituate "possibly had lands in Plymouth in 1633" [Scituate Hist 212], which is probably the reason that Savage assigns him the same date. The earliest record for this John Allen is 5 March 1637/8 [PCR 1:78]; someone has apparently misread a John Alden entry as being for Allen.

EDWARD BANCROFT

Pope includes an Edward Bancroft who was taxed at Plymouth in 1632 (apparently meaning 1633) and was in the 1643 list of men able to bear arms [Pope 30]. No such name appears in the Plymouth records on these dates, but EDWARD BANGS does, and these records belong to him [PM 23].

JOHN BARKER

Otis and Deane claim that John Barker married in 1632 Ann Williams, daughter of John Williams of Scituate, also claiming that the latter came in 1632 with Timothy Hatherly. There are a number of problems with this. First, the earliest record of John Williams is on 5 March 1638/9, when he was propounded for a freeman of Plymouth Colony [PCR

1:116], and the first record of John Barker is as a proprietor of Marshfield on 5 November 1638 [Pope 32]. Second, the other known children of John Williams marry or first appear in the records in the late 1640s and early 1650s. Third, John Barker's children were three daughters who married between 1660 and 1668, indicating births in the 1640s. The likely time of arrival for both John Barker and John Williams is late in the 1630s.

JOHN DAMON

John Damon of Scituate and his sister Hannah were nephew and niece of WILLIAM GILSON, who came to New England by 1632, and probably a little earlier [PM 223]. Some sources say that Damon came to New England with his uncle, and this may well be correct, but there is no evidence directly supporting this, and there are many cases of members of the same family coming to New England many years apart.

MANASSEH FAUNCE

In the 1623 Plymouth Colony land division is a grant of two acres to "Manasseh & John Fance" [PCR 12:5]. This is a defective entry, being a joint grant of land to MANASSEH KEMPTON [PM 297] and JOHN FAUNCE [PM 201].

ROBERT WATSON

Various secondary sources claim a Robert Watson, immigrant of 1632 to Plymouth, as brother of JOHN WATSON of Roxbury and father of GEORGE WATSON of Plymouth [PM 483] and of several other later immigrants [Windsor Hist 2:776; Bassett-Preston 311; Snow-Estes 1:162]. This family construct should be rejected totally, as there is no evidence in Plymouth or elsewhere in New England for such a Robert, or for any connection between John Watson and George Watson. An assignment of a servant by "Elizabeth Watson, widow, ... unto Thomas Watson," on 8 November 1638 [PCR 1:102], is cited in partial support of this claim, but this record says nothing about a Robert, nor does it connect to records of the other Watson immigrants.

JOHN WILLIAMS

John Williams is claimed by Deane as an arrival in 1632 with Timothy Hatherly [Scituate Hist 385]. He more likely arrived toward the end of the decade. See John Barker above.

INDEX SECTION

This final section contains four indices, three of a familiar variety and one that is experimental. The three familiar ones are of surnames, places and ships. The unusual index is a rearrangement of the surname index, by first name, instead of last.

INDEX OF SURNAMES

This index lists all persons in this volume who resided in New England in the seventeenth century. Modern authors, historians and genealogists are not indexed. Some of the more prominent inhabitants of New England, most notably John Winthrop and William Bradford, were indexed only if directly involved in the material cited; if they appeared merely because evidence from their writings was cited, their names were generally not indexed.

INDEX OF FIRST NAMES

While the Index of First Names is derived from the Index of Surnames, there are a number of differences that should be noted. In the first place, this index is intended not for assistance in finding one's place in the text, but for providing clues to further research. As a result this index has been simplified, with each entry including only one of the surnames used by a married woman during her life. All of the surnames are included, but in a different form than in the Index of Surnames. For example, a woman who was married twice will appear in the Index of Surnames three times, as "Smith, Mary," as "Jones, Mary (Smith)" and as "Brown, Mary (Smith) (Jones)." In the Index of First Names she will also appear three times, but now as "Smith, Mary," as "Jones, Mary" and as "Brown, Mary."

George Ernest Bowman conceived the idea of an Index of First Names nearly a century ago, but he never implemented it in print. There are many ways in which such an index might be useful, some of them unexpected. When the first version of this index was printed, it became obvious that such an arrangement of names would be a useful proofreading tool; all occurrences of "Willaim" instead of "William" would be grouped together and could be corrected at the same time.

Beyond this aid to index production, the Index of First Names should be helpful to researchers in a number of ways. Anyone searching for an unidentified wife with an unusual first name might want to look at all the entries for "Prudence," for example. Or an onomastic argument for identity, dependent on name usage within a family and on the relative frequency of use of a name, should be assisted by this index. Resourceful genealogists will undoubtedly find more uses for this listing.

This index of first names has already borne fruit. In the second volume of the second Great Migratiis series, Melinde Lutz Sanborn was writing the sketch of PENELOPE DARLOE [GM 2:2:285-86] and used the list of Penelopes in the index to *The Great Migration Begins* to identify her as the wife of ROBERT TURNER {1633, Boston} [GMB 3:1851-55].

INDEX OF PLACES

The index to places includes, but is not limited to, the residences of the early settlers of Plymouth Colony, both in England and New England.

Three features of this index should be noted. First, localities within towns, such as field names and neighborhoods, are generally not indexed. Second, when a town is referred to on the same page by both its native and its English names, the index will usually include only the reference to the English name. Third, many English places are entered in this index under the spelling inflicted upon them in the early New England records; these spellings may in some cases be so bizarre as to be unrecognizable.

INDEX OF SHIPS

Most of the entries in this index are for the ships that brought passengers to Plymouth Colony in the years between 1620 and 1633.

INDEX OF SURNAMES

ADAMS
  Elizabeth (____) 2
  Ellen (Newton) 1, 2, 520
  Frances (Vassall) 2
  James 1, 2
  Jane (James) 2
  John 1, 2, 344, 520
  Mary 519
  Susan 1, 2
ADEY
  Webb 2-4, 293
  William 4
ALDEN
  Abigail (Hallett) 8
  Anne 9
  David 6-8, 10, 440
  Elizabeth 5, 7, 9
  Elizabeth (Phillips) (Everill) 7
  Henry 9, 10
  John 4-10, 113, 167, 245, 268,
    308, 328, 340, 417, 421, 439,
    440, 442, 453, 456, 527
  Jonathan 6-10
  Joseph 6-9, 420, 421
  Mary 7-9
  Mary (Simonson) 8, 420, 421
  Mary (Southworth) 8, 438,
    440
  Priscilla 7-9
  Priscilla (Mullins) 5, 7, 9, 340
  Rebecca 8, 9, 167
  Ruth 8, 9
  Sarah 8, 453
  Zachariah 9
ALFORD
  Charity (Dike) 169, 170
  John 169, 170

ALLARD
  Arnold 248
ALLCOCK
  Samuel 260
ALLDRIDGE
  William 116
ALLEN/ALEN/ALLYN
  Elizabeth (Howland) 277, 278
  Hannah 34
  Jedediah 278
  Joan 78, 79
  John 195, 527
  Mehitable 19
  Priscilla (Brown) 84
  Samuel 40, 454
  Sarah 454
  Walter 171
  William 80, 84
  ____ Mr. 270
ALLERTON
  Bartholomew 11, 13, 14
  Elizabeth 12
  Elizabeth (____) 13
  Elizabeth (Willoughby)
    (Overzee) (Colclough) 13
  Fear (Brewster) 11, 13, 68
  Isaac 10-16, 67, 68, 70, 116-
    118, 132, 145, 154, 155, 159,
    227, 228, 271, 292, 382, 395,
    498
  Joanna (Swinnerton) 12, 13
  John 16, 199
  Margaret (____) 13
  Mary 11, 13-15, 159
  Mary (Norris) 12, 14
  Remember 11, 13-15

Allerton continued
  Sarah 11, 13, 14, 227, 372, 382
  Sarah (Fairfax) 13
ALMY/ALMEY
  John 44, 124, 125, 264
  Mary (Cole) 125
ALTHAM
  Edward 295
  Emmanuel 88, 223, 295
ANDREWS
  Abgiail 475
  Henry 475
  Joan 260
  Mary (Wadsworth) 474, 475
  Richard 235
ANGEL
  Thomas 488
ANNABLE
  Ann (Elcock/Clark) 17-19
  Anthony 16-20, 61, 386, 400
  Deborah 19
  Desire 18, 19
  Elizabeth 19
  Esek 19
  Hannah 17, 18, 61
  Jane (Moumford) 17, 18
  Mehitable (Allyn) 19
  Samuel 17-19
  Sarah 17, 18
  Susanna 19
APPLEGATE
  Thomas 118
ARCHER
  Samuel 206, 207
ARMSTRONG
  Elinor (_____) (Billington) 57
  George 57
ARNOLD
  John 132
  Oliver 33
  Phebe (Cook) 33
  Samuel 516
  William 488
ARTHUR
  John 508
ASHLEY
  Edward 20, 161, 352, 486, 501
ATKINSON
  Thomas 270
ATWOOD see also WOOD
  John 128, 173, 176, 233
  _____ Mr. 429
AUGER
  William 207
AULNAY
  _____ Monsier de 501
BAKER
  Alice (Pierce) 357, 358
  Eleanor (Winslow) 512
  Ellen (Winslow) 520
  Fear (Robinson) 237, 394
  Francis 357
  Hannah 357
  Joan (_____) 23
  John 22, 358
  Kenelm 519
  Mary (_____) 23
  Mary (Eddington) 23
  Mary (Pierce) 357, 358
  Nathaniel 22, 191, 358
  Pilgrim (Eddy) 23, 191, 192
  Samuel 237, 358, 394, 520
  William 21-23, 36, 37, 106, 192, 270
BALCH
  Benjamin 135, 143
  John 138, 143
  Mary (Conant) 138, 143
BALDEN
  John 132

Index of Surnames 535

BALLIOU
  Abigail 185
  Thomas 185
BANCROFT
  Edward 527
BANGS
  Apphia 27
  Bethia 27
  Edward 23-29, 151, 175, 247, 251, 299, 424, 446, 527
  Hannah 27, 175
  Hannah (Scudder) 27
  Hannah (Smalley) 26, 423, 424
  John 24-26, 28, 245, 246, 300, 424, 487
  Jonathan 25-27
  Joshua 25-27
  Lydia 27, 251
  Lydia (Hicks) 26, 28, 247
  Mary (Mayo) 27
  Mercy 27
  Rebecca 26, 446
  Rebecca (_____) 25, 26, 299
  Ruth (Cole) (Young) 27
  Sarah 26
  Sarah (_____) 27
BANKS
  Catherine 209
  Elizabeth 87
  John 209
  Richard 87
  Susanna 209
BARKER
  Abigail 33
  Alice (Snow) 32-34
  Ann 372
  Ann (_____) 304
  Ann (Williams) 32, 527
  Deborah 32
  Desire (Annable) 19

  Elizabeth 508
  Francis 31, 32
  Hannah (Allen) (Wanton) 34
  Hannah (Wanton) 34
  Isaac 31, 32, 34, 378-380
  Jabez 31
  James 34
  John 19, 30, 32, 33, 155, 304, 372, 417, 527-529
  Judith 31
  Judith (Prence) 32, 377, 379, 380
  Luce/Lucy (_____) 30, 32
  Luceanna 32
  Lydia 31, 34
  Martha 31
  Mary 31, 155, 372
  Mary (Lincoln) 32
  Phebe (Cook) (Arnold) (Marsh) 33
  Rebecca 31, 32, 34, 308
  Robert 29-34, 308, 351, 380, 460
  Samuel 31
BARLOW
  Elizabeth (_____) 155
  George 114
  Thomas 155
BARNAART
  Casper 205
  Elizabeth (Fletcher) 205
BARNABY
  James 44-46
  Lydia (Bartlett) 44, 46
BARNARD
  _____ Widow 191
BARNARDISTON
  Catherine (Banks) 209
BARNES
  Elizabeth (Hedges) 39
  Hannah 37, 39

Barnes continued
  Hester 40
  Joan (_____) 38, 39
  John 1, 22, 35-42, 47, 97, 114, 125, 126, 154, 235, 244, 249, 263, 264, 359, 376, 426, 433, 445
  Jonathan 37-39
  Lydia 37-39
  Mary 37, 39
  Mary (Plumer) 39, 359
  Thomas 40, 41
BARSTOW
  Patience 421
  Sarah 108
  William 29, 421
BARTHOLOMEW
  Eliza (_____) 331
  Henry 331
BARTLETT
  Benjamin 38, 46, 47, 130, 294, 295, 403
  Elizabeth 46, 47
  Hannah (Pope) 46, 364
  Joseph 45-47, 326, 327, 364, 485
  Lydia 46, 47
  Mary 46, 47
  Mary (Warren) 43, 45, 46, 478, 479
  Mercy 47
  Rebecca 46, 47, 403
  Robert 35, 41-48, 106, 109, 205, 295, 364, 412, 413, 478, 479
  Sarah 46
  Sarah (Brewster) 46
  Sissilla (_____) 46
  Susanna (Jenny) 46, 295
BARTON
  Marmeduke 489

BARWICK
  William 490
BASS
  John 7-9
  Ruth (Alden) 7-9
  Samuel 8
BASSETT
  Cecily 51
  Dorcas (Joyce) 51
  Elizabeth 49-51
  Elizabeth (_____) 49-51
  Jane 51
  Joseph 50, 51
  Martha (Hobart) 51
  Mary (Lapham?) 51
  Mary (Rainsford) 50
  Mary (Tilden) (Lapham) 49, 50
  Nathaniel 49, 51
  Ruth 51, 449
  Sarah 50, 51, 496
  William 48-52, 157, 237, 320, 449, 496
BATES
  James 311
  Ruth (Lyford) 311
  _____ Elder 77, 370
BATTER
  Edmund 169, 489
BAXTER
  George 116
BAYLEY
  Guydo 287
  Henry 135
BEALE/BEALS
  Agnes (Hilton) 257
  Arthur 257
  John 185, 507
  Martha 185
  William 52, 159

Index of Surnames 537

BEAUCHAMP
  John 20, 235
BEAVEN
  John 52
BEDE
  James 137
  _____ (____) Ellot 137
BEEDLE
  Joseph 308
BEESON
  Thomas 323
BELL
  Ann (____) 340
  Thomas 340
BELLINGHAM
  Richard 255
BEMIS
  Joseph 22
BENJAMIN
  Abigail (Eddy) 193, 197
  John 193, 197
BENNETT/BENNET
  Aaron 53-55
  Ann (____) 55
  Deliverance 55
  Elizabeth (____) 55
  James 55
  Jane 55
  Jane (Knowles) 53-55, 138
  John 56
  Mary 54, 55
  Moses 53, 55
  William 52-56, 108, 138, 187, 412, 413, 489
BENNISTER
  Gertrude 286
BERNARD
  Mary 505
  Musachiell 506
  Richard 505

BESBEECH
  Thomas 98, 481
BIDLE
  Joseph 97
BIGBEE
  Mehitable 470
BIGELOW
  John 71
BIGFORD
  Mary 431
BILLING
  _____ Widow 322
BILLINGTON
  Christian (Penn) (Eaton) 57, 188, 352
  Elinor (____) 56, 57, 176
  Francis 56, 57, 187, 188, 352, 370
  John 56-58, 93, 188, 344, 352, 459
  Joseph 126
  Josiah 187
  Martha 188
  _____ (____) 154
BIRCHER see BURCHER
BISHOP
  James 31
  Nathaniel 426
  Thomas 356
  Townsend 208
BLADEN
  William 313
BLAGUE
  Henry 33
  Joseph 440
  Martha (Kirtland) 440
BLAKEWAY
  Jacob 329
BLAKEWOOD
  Christopher 236

BLISH see BLUSH
BLOSSOM
  Annabel (____) 58
  Anne (Elsdon) 58, 60, 399
  Elizabeth 59
  Peter 58, 59
  Sarah (Bodfish) 59
  Sarah (Ewer) 59
  Thomas 58-60, 318, 390, 399
BLUNDEN
  Sarah (Mullins) 339, 340
BLUSH
  Abraham 19, 331
  ____ Goodman 17
BOARDMAN
  Luce (____) 61
  Thomas 60, 61
BOARE
  George 272
BODFISH
  Sarah 59
BOND
  John 486
BONHAM
  George 151, 202, 337, 363, 445, 484
  Patience 267
  Sarah (Morton) 337
BONNEY
  Dorcas (Samson) 402, 403
  Mary 327
  Sarah 307
  Thomas 327, 402, 403
BOREMAN
  Hannah (Annable) 18, 61
  Thomas 18, 60, 61
BOSSEROTT
  ____ Mr. 117
BOSWORTH
  Hannah (Howland) 280-282
  Jonathan 282

BOURNE
  Elizabeth (____) 517
  Margaret 517
  Martha 65
  Thomas 65, 517
  William 447
BOWEN
  Elizabeth (Nichols) 220
  Thomas 220
BOWER
  John 3
BOWES
  Cordelia 65
BOWMAN
  John 62
  Nathaniel 62, 97
BOYSE
  Joanna 500
BRABROOK
  John 71
BRADFORD
  Alice 327
  Alice (Carpenter) (Southworth) 63, 64, 94, 174, 219, 376, 410
  Alice (Hanson) 64
  Alice (Richards) 65
  Dorothy (May) 64, 65
  Jael (Hobart) 65
  John 63, 65, 474
  Joseph 63-65
  Martha (Bourne) 65
  Mary (Wood) (Holmes) 65
  Mercy 63, 65
  Rebecca (Bartlett) 403
  Samuel 288
  Sarah (____) (Griswold) 65
  William 11, 43, 57-59, 62-66, 70, 94, 105, 108, 110, 117, 140, 145, 157, 158, 161, 162, 173, 174, 193, 217, 219, 220,

Index of Surnames

Bradford continued
  223, 227, 236, 244, 254, 298,
  300, 336, 337, 349, 351, 376,
  377, 395, 404, 410, 428, 438,
  440, 442, 443, 462, 484, 491,
  492, 503, 516, 525

BRADSTREET
  Simon 492

BRADWICK
  Joyce 324

BRATTLE
  Thomas 512

BRETT
  William 244

BREWSTER
  Edward 69
  Fear 13, 67, 68, 309
  Francis 69
  Jonathan 30, 43, 67, 68, 70,
    320, 346, 469
  Love 46, 67, 68, 130, 132, 519
  Lucretia (Oldham) 68, 346
  Mary 469
  Mary (_____) 68, 69
  Nathaniel 69
  Patience 67, 68, 309, 379
  Sarah 46
  Sarah (Collier) 68, 130
  William 13, 14, 66-70, 83,
    130, 159, 187, 219, 304, 309,
    317, 329, 331, 333, 344, 379,
    454, 469, 525
  Wrestling 67, 68

BRIAN see BRYAN
BRIANT see BRYANT

BRIDGER
  Joan 339

BRIDGES/BRIDGE
  Christian (Stoddard) (Pierce)
    72
  Hannah (_____) 72

  John 88, 89
  Mary 72
  Persis 72
  Persis (Pierce) 71, 72, 74, 75
  Rebecca 72, 75
  Robert 73
  Samuel 72
  William 70, 71, 73-75, 345,
    346

BRIGGS
  Ann (_____) 78
  Clement 76-79, 244, 248, 254,
    370, 388
  David 77, 78
  Edmund 77
  Elizabeth (_____) 77-79
  Experience (_____) 78
  Hannah 514
  Hannah (Packard) 78
  Joan (Allen) 78, 79
  John 77-79
  Jonathan 76-78
  Mary (_____) 74, 78
  Peter 74, 75
  Remember 77, 78
  Thomas 76-78
  Walter 514
  William 74

BRITTERIDGE
  Richard 80

BROOKS/BROOKE
  Deborah 523
  Elizabeth (Winslow) 509
  Gilbert 458
  Robert 509
  Susanna (Hanford) (Whiston)
    237, 238, 494
  William 237, 238, 269, 494,
    523
  _____ Lord 261, 262

BROUGHTON
  Thomas 502
BROWN/BROWNE
  Anna 501
  Benjamin 332
  Dorothy 282
  Jabez 282
  James 281, 282, 498
  John 76, 80-82, 84, 85, 98,
    147, 176, 197, 198, 226, 233,
    282, 376, 499-501
  Lydia (Howland) 280-282
  Martha (____) (Ford) 82, 83,
    211
  Mary 82, 84, 176, 500
  Mary (____) 83
  Persis (Bridges) 72
  Peter 80-85, 98, 176, 211, 226,
    228, 402
  Phebe (Harding) 80, 81, 233
  Priscilla 83, 84, 226
  Rebecca 84
  Remember 81, 82
  William 72, 81, 83, 263, 331,
    332
BRUFF
  Edmund 102
  Mary (Chandler) 102
BRYAN/BRYANT
  Abigail (Shaw) 415
  Stephen 29, 37, 178, 196, 408,
    413, 415
  Thomas 70, 197
BUCK
  Elizabeth 99
  John 99, 202
  Sarah (Faunce) (Doty) 202
BUCKETT
  Mary 85, 435
BUCKINGHAM
  Mary (Willett) (Hooker) 500

Thomas 500
BUCKLEY
  Edward 376
BULL
  Dixey 170
BULLOCK
  Elizabeth 197
BUMPAS
  Edward 85-88, 98, 168, 481
  Elizabeth 86
  Elizabeth (Banks) (Whitmer)
    87
  Hannah 87
  Hannah (____) 86, 98
  Isaac 87
  Jacob 87
  John 86
  Joseph 87
  Mary 87
  Phebe (Lovel) 87
  Philip 87, 168
  Samuel 87, 168
  Sarah 86
  Sarah (____) 86
  Sarah (Eaton) 87
  Thomas 87, 168
  Wybra (Glass) 87
BUNDY
  John 102
  Martha (Chandler) 102
BUNKER
  George 370
BUNTING
  Thomas 373
BURCHAM
  Edward 89
BURCHER
  Edward 88, 89, 218
BURGE
  Thomas 44

Index of Surnames

BURGESS
 Elizabeth (Bassett) 50
 Thomas 50
BURMAN see BOREMAN
BURNES
 ____ Mr. 375
BURROUGHS
 James 108
 Sarah (Church) 108
BURSELL
 Anna 411
 Emett (____) 411
 James 411
BURSLEY
 Elizabeth 91, 281
 Elizabeth (Howland) 91
 Jemima 91
 Joanna 90, 91
 Joanna (Hull) 90
 John 89-92
 Mary 90
 Temperance 91
 Thomas 90
BUTHO
 Mary 69
BUTTERWORTH
 Samuel 241
BUTTLES
 Leonard 269
BUTTON
 William 92, 221
BYRAM
 Nicholas 165, 420
BYRD
 Thomas 98

CAMPION
 Clement 259
CANEDY see KENNEDY
CANNON
 John 93, 459

CAREW
 John 320
CARMAN
 John 93
CARPENTER
 Agnes 94, 220
 Alexander 64, 93, 94, 220, 336
 Alice 64, 94, 439, 443
 Juliana 94, 301, 336-338
 Mary 94, 95
 Priscilla 64, 93-95, 220, 301, 337, 526
 Susannah (England) 180
CARTER
 Robert 95, 339, 340
CARVER
 Catherine (White) (Leggatt) 95, 96
 Elizabeth (Doty) (Rowse) 179
 John 11, 95-97, 158, 159, 188, 283, 304, 315, 318, 324, 329, 330, 339, 395, 497
 Robert 96
 William 179
CARY
 Sarah 295
CHANDLER
 Anna 98, 99, 101
 Benjamin 98, 99, 101
 Edmund 36, 86, 97-102, 250, 252, 298
 Elizabeth (Buck) 99
 Isabella (Chilton) 102, 104
 John 99, 101
 Joseph 98, 99, 101
 Lydia 99-101, 250
 Martha 102, 103
 Mary 98, 99, 101-103
 Mercy (____) 99
 Nathaniel 102
 Roger 100-104, 521

Chandler continued
  Ruth 98-101
  Samuel 98-102, 252, 296
  Sarah 98, 99, 101, 102
CHAPMAN
  Ralph 30
CHARD
  William 241
CHASE
  William 272
CHAULKLY
  Robert 75
CHAUNCY/CHANCEY
  Charles 234, 236, 245, 246, 293
  Elnathan 246
CHESS
  Mary (Hall) 27
CHEW
  John 219
CHICHESTER
  Mary (_____) 331
  William 331
CHILLINGSWORTH
  Thomas 127
CHILTON see also GILTEN
  Christian 104
  Elizabeth 104
  Ingle 104
  Isabella 102, 104
  James 102-105, 513, 515
  Jane 104
  Joel 104
  Lionel 104
  Mary 104, 105, 513
CHIPMAN
  Hope 122
  Hope (Howland) 280, 282
  John 122, 282
  Samuel 122
  Sarah (Cobb) 122

CHURCH
  Abigail 108
  Alice (Southworth) 107, 438, 439
  Benjamin 107, 439
  Caleb 107, 108
  Charles 108
  Deborah 108
  Deborah (_____) 108
  Elizabeth 107
  Elizabeth (Warren) 107, 479
  Joanna (Sprague) 108
  Joseph 107
  Mary 108
  Mary (Tucker) 107
  Nathaniel 108, 436
  Rebecca (_____) (Scottow) 108
  Richard 21, 43-45, 105-109, 299, 306, 319, 351, 376, 439, 478, 479
  Sarah 108
  Sarah (Barstow) 108
CHURCHILL
  Hannah (Pontus) 360, 361
  Henry 179
  John 165, 167, 179, 360, 361
  Mary 179
  Mary (Churchill) (Doty) 179
  Rebecca (Delano) 167
  William 442
CHURCHMAN
  Anna 396
CHURCHWELL
  John 250
CLAPP/CLAP
  Elizabeth (Bursley) (Goodspeed) 91
  Increase 91
  Roger 136, 170
  Thomas 236

Index of Surnames

CLARK/CLARKE
 Abiah (Wilder) 112
 Abigail (Lathrop) 112
 Agnes 133, 137
 Alice (Hallett) (Nichols) 112
 Andrew 111, 112
 Ann 18
 Dorothy (Lettice) (Gray) 112
 Faith 178
 Freeborn (Williams) (Hart) 505
 George 181
 Hannah (Griswold) 112
 Henry 113
 James 111, 112, 123
 Jane 130
 Jane (_____) 131
 John 111, 112
 Martha (Nash) 342, 343
 Mehitable (Scotto) 112
 Nathaniel 111, 112
 Richard 109
 Sarah (_____) 112
 Sarah (Wolcott) 112
 Scotto 112
 Susanna 112
 Susanna (Ring) 111, 389-391
 Thomas 109-115, 130, 264, 294, 305, 320, 356, 378, 391, 412, 413, 477, 480, 502
 Thurston 178
 Tristram 154
 Walter 505
 William 29, 111, 112, 129, 132, 342, 343
 _____ Goodwife 294
CLOUGH
 Richard 112-118, 125, 194, 293, 412
COBB
 Eliezer 120, 121, 285
 Elizabeth (Taylor) 122
 Experience 122
 Gershom 120, 121, 285
 Hannah 120, 121, 285
 Henry 118-122, 185, 224, 286, 298, 398, 446
 Hope (Chipman) (Huckins) 122
 James 120, 121, 285, 446
 John 120, 121, 285
 Jonathan 120, 122
 Lois (Hallet) 122
 Martha (Nelson) 121
 Mary 120, 121, 185
 Mehitable 122
 Patience 120, 121, 285
 Patience (Hurst) 121, 286
 Samuel 120, 122
 Sarah 120, 122
 Sarah (Hinckley) 120, 121
 Sarah (Lewis) 121, 446
COGGEN/COGAN/COGGAN
 Henry 301, 395
 John 395
 Mary 264
COGSWELL
 Elizabeth 317
 John 317
COIT
 Priscilla (Fletcher) 204
 Thomas 204
COLCLOUGH
 Elizabeth (Willoughby) (Overzee) 13
 George 14
COLE
 Abigail (_____) 125
 Daniel 25-27, 127-131, 176, 520
 Esther (_____) 125
 Frances (_____) 128, 131

Cole continued
  Grace 475
  Hepzibah 176
  Hugh 38, 124, 125, 263
  James 44, 113, 122-126, 171
  Job 25, 126-128, 130, 131, 474
  John 125, 127, 128, 131, 431
  Mary 125
  Mary (Foxwell) 125
  Mary (Tibbes) 123, 124
  Mary (Tilson) 125
  Mercy (Fuller) 127
  Nathaniel 128, 131
  Rebecca 127, 131
  Rebecca (Collier) 127, 130
  Ruth 27, 520
  Ruth (Collier) 128, 131
  Ruth (Snow) 431
  Samuel 127
  Zaccheus 128, 131
COLEMAN
  Joseph 241-243, 420
  Thomas 241
COLLARD
  Alice 237
COLLICOTT
  Richard 90
COLLIER
  Catheren 131
  Elizabeth 127, 131, 439
  Hannah 130
  James 131
  Jane (____) (Clark) 131
  Jane (Clark) 130, 133, 478
  John 130, 131
  Lydia 131
  Martha 131
  Mary 130, 379
  Rebecca 127, 130
  Ruth 128, 131
  Sarah 68, 130
  William 68, 114, 127-133, 379, 439, 474, 479
COLLINS/COLLEN
  Abigail 500
  Edward 500
  George 118
  Karen (____) 353
CONANT
  Agnes (Clarke) 133, 137
  Anne (Wilton) 133
  Caleb 137
  Christian (More) 333
  Christopher 133, 134, 138
  Elizabeth 136-138
  Elizabeth (Walton) 138
  Elizabeth (Weston) 138, 491-493
  Exercise 136-138
  Jane 55
  Joanna 138
  John 134, 136, 137, 492
  Joshua 136, 138, 333
  Lot 135-138
  Mary 138
  Rebecca 137
  Richard 133, 137
  Roger 55, 133-143, 170, 208, 491, 492
  Sarah 136-138
  Sarah (____) 138
  Sarah (Horton) 135, 137
  Seeth (Gardner) 138
  Sicily (Croxon) 133
CONNER
  William 143, 144
CONVERSE
  Sarah 218
COOK/COOKE
  Anna 152, 431
  Bethiah 152, 233

Index of Surnames

Cook continued
  Damaris (Hopkins) 147, 274
  Deborah (Hopkins) 152
  Elizabeth 147, 179
  Elizabeth (Lettice) (Shurtleff) 147
  Elizabeth (Ring) (Deane) 151, 152, 163, 391
  Francis 144-149, 152, 179, 201, 274, 325, 326, 369, 419, 479, 484
  Hester 145, 147
  Hester (Mahieu) 145, 146
  Jacob 145-147, 179, 274, 376
  Jane 145, 146, 326, 328
  John 43, 145-149, 188, 358, 370, 373, 374, 376, 404, 478, 479
  Josiah 152, 430
  Josias 116, 149-153, 163, 174, 181, 233, 272, 367, 391, 431, 445
  Mary 145, 147
  Phebe 33
  Richard 151
  Roger 304
  Sarah (Warren) 43, 146, 479
  Thomas 33
  Thomasin (_____) 33
  _____ Capt. 497
  _____ Goodman 285
COOMBS/COMBE/COMBS/ COOMB/COOMBE
  Deborah (Morton) 155
  Elizabeth (_____) (Barlow) 155
  Francis 155, 372
  Jane (Pope) 155
  John 11, 36, 153-156, 173, 227, 369, 370, 372, 375, 382
  Mary (Barker) (Pratt) 155, 372
  Sarah (Priest) 154, 155, 375, 382
COOPER
  Agnes 156, 461
  Ann 337
  Humility 156, 157, 404, 462
  John 95, 241, 432, 526
  Lydia 336
  Martha 403
  Priscilla (Carpenter) (Wright) 95, 526
  Robert 156
CORVANNEL/CORRANNEL L/CORNELLY
  William 412, 482
COSFORD
  Alice 396
  George 396
COTTLE
  Anne 394
COUCHMAN see CUSHMAN
COWLES
  Elizabeth 218
  Robert 218, 457
CRACKSTONE
  Anna 157, 158
  John 157, 158
CRADDOCK
  Matthew 345, 346
  Rebecca (_____) 346
CRISP
  George 25, 176
  Hepzibah (Cole) 176
CROCKER
  Daniel 87
  John 90
  Joseph 91
  Mary (Bumpas) 87
  Mary (Bursley) 90
  Patience (Cobb) (Parker) 121
  Temperance (Bursley) 91

Crocker continued
 William 121
CROCKETT
 Thomas 320, 323
CROMWELL
 Oliver 509
 Philip 332, 334
CROSBY
 Symond 334
CROW/CROWELL
 Aaron 54
 Abigail 54
 Christopher 55
 Deliverance (Bennett) 55
 Elizabeth 115
 Hannah (Winslow) 517
 John 54, 56
 William 517
CROXON
 Sicily 133
CRUMP
 Willem 118
CRUMPTON
 Jane (_____) 332
 Samuel 332, 333
CUDWORTH
 James 214, 278, 453, 486
 Mary (Howland) 277, 278
CUGLEY
 Hannah 248
CUMMINGS
 Abraham 373
 Sarah (Wright) 373
CURWEN
 Elizabeth (Winslow) (Brooks) 509
 George 509
CUSHMAN
 Desire 282
 Elinor (Hubbard) 158

Mary (_____) (Shingelton) 158
Mary (Allerton) 13, 15, 159
Robert 13, 96, 140, 142, 158-160, 330, 470, 491
Ruth (Howland) 280, 283
Sara 159
Sara (Reder) 158
Thomas 11, 13, 15, 46, 52, 154, 155, 158-160, 184, 245, 283, 285, 294

DALE
 Thomas 274
DAMON/DAMAN/DAMMAN
 Deborah 523
 Hannah 224, 225, 395, 528
 John 224, 225, 395, 523, 524, 528
 Martha (Woodworth) 524
 Zachary 524
DANFORTH
 Jonathan 136
DAVENPORT
 Humphrey 306
 Rachel (_____) 306
 Richard 386, 387
DAVIS
 Alice (Thorp) 461
 Dolor 90
 James 417, 484
 Joanna (Hull) (Bursley) 90
 John 323
 Joseph 260
 Nicholas 59
 Phillip 404
 Sarah (Ewer) (Blossom) 59
 William 461, 502
DAVISON
 Nicholas 345, 346

Index of Surnames

DEACON see also FRANCIS *alias* DEACON
  John 161, 162, 352
DEAN/DEANE
  Elizabeth 163
  Elizabeth (Ring) 152, 163, 390, 391
  Miriam 151, 163
  Stephen 150-152, 162, 163, 165, 227, 244, 389-391, 431
  Susanna 163, 431
DELANO/DE LANNOY
  Elizabeth (Sampson) 167, 342
  Elizabeth (Standish) 167
  Esther 167, 168, 435
  Hester (Dewsbery) 166
  Jan 166
  Jane 166-168
  John 165-168
  Jonathan 167, 168
  Marie (Mahieu) 166
  Mary 167, 168, 185
  Mary (Pontus) (Glass) 165, 166, 361
  Mary (Weston) 167
  Mercy (Warren) 167
  Philip 6, 8, 87, 162, 164-168, 185, 244, 293, 328, 361, 419, 421, 435
  Rebecca 166-168
  Rebecca (Alden) 8, 167
  Samuel 166-168
  Thomas 7, 8, 165-168, 342
DENBY
  Sarah (_____) 204
  William 204
DENGAYNE
  Henry 71
DENNIS
  Edward 388
  Robert 278
  Sarah 388
  Sarah (_____) 388
  Sarah (Howland) 277, 278
DENT
  _____ Mr. 493
DENTON
  Richard 214
  Ruth (Tileston) 214
DERBY
  Richard 41, 155, 177, 180, 181
DEWSBERY
  Hester 166
DEXTER
  Thomas 115
DICKENS
  Nathaniel 488
DICKENSON/DICKERSON
  Elizabeth (Howland) (Hicks) 247, 280-282
  John 247, 282
DIKE
  Anthony 143, 169-171, 489
  Charity 170
  Jonathan 171
  Margery (_____) 170, 171
  Tabitha (_____) 170, 171
DIMMOCK
  Joanna (Bursley) 90
  Shubael 90
DIMOND
  Grace (_____) 323
  John 323
DINGLEY
  John 107
  Mary 454
DIX see DIKE
DOANE
  Abigail 174, 175
  Ann (_____) 175
  Daniel 174, 176
  Ephraim 174, 176

Doane continued
  Hannah (Bangs) 26, 27, 175
  Hepzibah (Cole) (Crispe) 176
  John 25, 27, 70, 83, 150, 154,
    171-177, 188, 227, 232, 233,
    247, 263, 366, 426, 498
  Lydia 175, 247
  Lydia (_____) 174, 175
  Martha 176, 233
  Mary (Smalley) (Snow) 176
  Mercy (Knowles) 176
  Rebecca (Pette) 175
  _____ Mr. 123
DODGE
  Mary (Conant) 136
  Mary (Conant) (Balch) 138,
    143
  Richard 135
  William 135, 137, 138, 143
DOGGETT
  Amy 192, 193
  Bathsheba (_____) (Pratt) 367
  Hepzibah 196
  John 194, 196, 367
  Sarah 418
  Susan 193
  Thomas 328, 418
DOTTERICH
  Phillip 123
DOTY
  Deborah (Ellis) 180
  Desire 178, 179, 182, 418, 453
  Edward 24, 55, 56, 152, 177-
    182, 187, 202, 267, 275, 305,
    367, 412, 418, 425, 453, 457,
    482
  Elizabeth 178, 179, 182
  Elizabeth (Cooke) 179
  Elizabeth (England) 179, 180
  Faith 182
  Faith (Clarke) 178
  Isaac 179, 182
  Jeane (Harman) 179
  John 178, 179, 182
  Joseph 180, 182
  Mary 178, 180, 182
  Mary (Churchill) 179
  Samuel 179, 182
  Sarah (_____) Edwards 180
  Sarah (Faunce) 179, 202
  Sarah (Jones) 179
  Thomas 179, 182
  William 182
DOUGHTY
  James 469
  Lydia (Turner) 468, 469
  Mary 468
DOWNE
  Eglin (Hatherly) 214, 238,
    393, 494
DOWNING
  Emanuel 210
DOWSE
  John 214
  Lawrence 75
  Relief (Holland) 214
DOXSEY
  Thomas 118
DRAPER
  Edward 209
  Mary 209
  Susanna 209
  Susanna (Banks) 209
DUDENY
  _____ Mr. 137
DUNFORD
  John 41
DUNHAM
  Abigail 185
  Abigail (Balliou) 184, 185
  Bathsheba (Whiston) 495
  Benajah 184, 186, 368

Index of Surnames

Dunham continued
  Daniel 184-186
  Eleazer 495
  Elizabeth (Tilson) 186
  Esther (Wormall) 185
  Hannah 186
  Hannah (_____) 186
  Humility 185, 186
  John 121, 167, 182-186, 194, 360-362, 367, 368, 416
  Jonathan 121, 167, 184-186, 369
  Joseph 185
  Martha (Beals) (Falloway) 185
  Mary (_____) 185
  Mary (Cobb) 121, 185, 285
  Mary (Delano) 167, 185
  Mercy (Morton) 185
  Persis 186, 367, 369, 416
  Richard 185
  Samuel 124, 183-185, 301, 360
  Susan (Kaino) 185
  Thomas 184-186
DURRAM
  Sarah (Bumpas) 86
  Thomas 86
DURRANT/DURANTE
  Mary 111, 391
DUTCH
  Samuel 332, 333
  Susanna (More) 332, 333
DWELLEY/DWELLY
  Elizabeth (Simonson) 420, 421
  Richard 123, 420, 421

EAMES
  Abigail 469
  Dararis 520
  Mark 520

EARLE
  Dorcas (Sprague) 449
  Ralph 448, 449, 488
  William 165
EATON
  Benjamin 189, 406
  Christian (Penn) 57, 187, 188, 352
  Dorothy (_____) 188
  Dorothy (Smith) 188
  Elizabeth (_____) 188
  Francis 4, 57, 187-189, 304, 336, 352, 476, 518, 519
  John 188
  Martha (Billington) 188
  Rachel 187, 188
  Samuel 98, 187-189
  Sarah 87
  Sarah (_____) 188, 189
  Sarah (Hoskins) 189
EDDENDEN
  Edmond 213
EDDINGTON
  Mary 23
EDDY
  Abigail 193, 197
  Abigail (_____) (Smith) 197
  Alice (Padduck) 197
  Amy (Doggett) 192, 193
  Anna 197
  Anne 193
  Benjamin 193
  Bennet (Ellis) 197
  Caleb 196-198
  Elizabeth (_____) 196-198
  Elizabeth (Bullock) 197
  Hannah 197
  Hepzibah (Doggett) 196
  Joanna (_____) (Meade) 192
  John 23, 189-194, 196, 197, 254, 388

Eddy continued
  Mary 192
  Mary (Fosten) 191, 196
  Obadiah 195-197
  Pilgrim 23, 192
  Ruth 193
  Samuel 70, 191-198, 245, 293, 325, 406-408, 429
  Sarah 192
  Sarah (Meade) 192, 193
  Sarah (Woodward) 193
  Susanna (Padduck) 197
  William 191, 196
  Zachariah 195-197, 406
EDWARDS
  Edward 36
  John 101
  Sarah (_____) 180
EIRE/EYRE/EYER
  Christian 72
  Elizabeth (Allerton) 12
  Simon 12, 71
ELCOCK
  Ann 18
ELIOT/ELIOTT
  John 500
  Sarah 499
  Sarah (Willett) 500
ELITHORPE
  Abigail 355
  Thomas 355
ELLIS
  Bennet 197
  Deborah 180
  Elizabeth (Freeman) 197
  John 197
ELLOT
  _____ 137
ELSDON
  Anne 58, 399

ELY
  _____ 198, 466
ENDICOTT
  John 73, 142, 217, 219, 345, 425, 487, 503
ENGLAND
  Elizabeth 179, 180
  Elizabeth (_____) 180
  Susannah 180
  Thomas 199
  William 180
ENGLISH
  Thomas 199
ENSIGN
  Thomas 236
ERDLEY
  Agnes/Anne 465
EVANS
  Mary 204
  Thomas 128
EVELETH
  Pilgrim (Eddy) (Baker) (Steadman) 191, 192
  Sylvester 192
EVERILL
  Abiel 7
  Elizabeth (Phillips) 7
  James 7, 8
EWELL
  Henry 18, 468
  Sarah (Annable) 18
EWER
  John 477
  Mary (Wallen) 477
  Sarah 59
  Thomas 59, 113, 477

FAIRFAX
  Benjamin 13
  Elizabeth 13
  Sarah 13

Index of Surnames

FALLOWAY
  Martha (Beals) 185
  William 185
FALLOWELL
  Anne 364
  Catherine (Finney) 364
  Gabriel 293, 364
  William 426
FARREL
  Thomas 117
FAUNCE
  Elizabeth 203
  Jane (Nelson) 202
  John 179, 201-203, 245, 267, 298, 337, 442, 479, 528
  Joseph 203
  Judith (Rickard) 203
  Manasseh 528
  Mary 202
  Mercy 203, 267
  Patience 202, 267
  Patience (Morton) 202, 337
  Priscilla 202, 479
  Sarah 179, 202
  Thomas 202, 442
FAY
  Bathsheba 369
FETCHER
  Antoine 94
  Jenneken (Richeman) 94
FINNEY
  Catherine 364
FISHER
  Elizabeth 273
  John 313
FISK
  John 190
FITZ RANDOLPH
  Edward 59
  Elizabeth (Blossom) 59
  Isaac 252
  Ruth (Higgins) 252
FLAVELL
  Anne (_____) 204
  Elizabeth (_____) 204
  Thomas 203, 204, 461
  _____ Goodwife 203
FLETCHER
  Catherine 204
  Elizabeth 205
  Jane 205
  John 204
  Josina (Sachariasdaughter) 204
  Judith 205
  Mary 204
  Mary (Evans) 204
  Moses 204, 205
  Priscilla 204
  Richard 204
  Sarah (_____) (Denby) 204
FLINT
  Henry 500
  Hester (Willett) 500
  Josiah 500
  William 331
FLOOD
  Edmond 205
FLOYD
  John 236
  Richard 508
FOGG
  Ann (_____) 209, 210
  David 208-210
  Ezekiel 208-210
  Grace (_____) 210
  John 208-210
  Ralph 56, 206-210, 478, 487, 489
  Susanna (Draper) 209
FOLGER
  Dorcas 373

Folger continued
  Peter 373
FORD
  John 211
  Martha 211
  Martha (_____) 83, 211, 212
  Michael 34
  William 212
  _____ 211, 212
FOSTEN
  Mary 191, 196
FOSTER
  Benjamin 44
  Christopher 215
  Edward 212-214, 224, 238, 302
  Elizabeth 214, 237
  George 215, 218
  Lettice 214
  Lettice (Hanford) 213, 214, 238
  Mary (_____) 44
  Mary (Bartlett) 46
  Relief (Holland) (Dowse) 214
  Richard 44, 46, 306
  Ruth (Tileston) (Denton) 214
  Timothy 213, 214, 237
FOXWELL
  Mary 125
FRANCIS alias DEACON
  Richard 161, 162
FREEMAN
  Alice 365
  Apphia (Quick) 379, 381
  Constant 439
  Edmund 365, 380, 498
  Elizabeth 197
  John 114, 151, 376-380
  Margaret (Perry) 365
  Mercy (Prence) 377, 378, 380
  Mercy (Southworth) 376, 438, 439
  Rebecca (Prence) 380
  Samuel 376, 379, 439
  _____ Lt. 174
FRIEND
  Samuel 356
FRINCK
  Grace 501
FULLER
  Agnes (Carpenter) 94, 220
  Alice (Glascock) 220
  Bridget 189, 220
  Bridget (_____) 181, 366, 445
  Bridget (Lee) 217, 218, 220
  Edward 215-218, 220, 496
  Elizabeth 399
  Elizabeth (Nichols) (Bowen) 220
  Frances (_____) 215
  Jane (Lothrop) 216
  Matthew 89, 109, 113, 215, 216, 399
  Mercy 127, 218-220
  Robert 215, 216, 220
  Samuel 59, 60, 89, 92, 94, 127, 150, 215-221, 337, 338, 390, 392, 457, 496, 525, 526
  Susanna 496, 508
  _____ Mrs. 292
FURNER
  Susanne 104

GALLUP
  Elizabeth (Southworth) 440
  Samuel 440
GARDNER/GARDINER
  Ezekiel 191, 193
  Richard 223
  Ruth (Eddy) 191, 193
  Samuel 191

Gardner continued
  Seeth 138
  Thomas 138
GARRETT
  Lydia (Tilden) 237
GAYMER
  Lydia 468
  Margaret (Mason) 468
  Richard 468
GENTLEMAN
  Susan 332
GERAERDI
  Philip 118
GILBERT
  Gyles 484
  Jane (Rossiter) 51
  John 484
  Thomas 51
GILSON
  Frances (____) 224, 225
  William 1, 70, 83, 223-226, 395, 416, 470, 528
GILTEN see also CHILTON
  Engeltgen 104
GLASCOCK
  Alice 220
GLASS
  Amy 264
  Hannah 357
  James 87, 165, 166, 264, 301, 360, 361, 483
  Mary (Cogan) 264
  Mary (Pontus) 87, 166, 361
  Wybra 87
GLOVER
  Rebecca (____) (Craddock) 346
GLYN
  James 14
GODBERTSON
  Elizabeth (Kendall) 227

Godbert 14, 36, 154, 155, 162, 163, 176, 226-228, 252, 369, 370, 372, 382
  Samuel 226, 228, 249, 252, 370, 422, 424
  Sarah (____) 176
  Sarah (Allerton) (Vincent) (Priest) 14, 226, 227, 372, 382
GODFREY
  Edward 323
  Francis 102, 438, 442
GOODALL
  Mary 317, 427
GOODHUE
  Bethia (Ray) (Lothrop) (Grafton) 387
  William 387
GOODMAN
  John 67, 82, 228, 229
GOODSPEED
  Elizabeth (Bursley) 91
  Nathaniel 91
GOODWIN
  Adam 488, 489
  Christopher 72
  Margaret (____) 488, 489
GOODYEAR
  Hugh 60, 317
GOOLE
  Francis 125
GORGES
  Ferdinando 229, 260, 347, 492
  Robert 91, 229, 230, 335
GORHAM
  Desire (Howland) 280, 282
  John 282
  Ralph 4, 428
GORTON
  Samuel 113, 490

GOTT
  Sarah 388
  Sarah (Dennis) 388
GOULDER
  Francis 197
  Katherne (_____) 197
GRAFTON
  Bethia (Ray) (Lothrop) 387
  Joseph 387
GRAY
  Ann 512
  Desire 440
  Dorothy (Lettice) 112
  Edward 112, 286, 308, 402, 485, 512, 513
  Lydia (Irish) 289
  Mary (Winslow) 512, 513
  Sarah 308
  Thomas 128, 355
GREEMES
  John 362
GREEN/GREENE
  Anne 490
  Richard 230
GREENLEAF
  Edmund 256
  Sarah 256, 514
GRISWOLD
  Anna (Wolcott) 372
  Elizabeth 372
  Francis 65
  Hannah 112
  Matthew 372
  Sarah (_____) 65
GROMES
  _____ Mr. 113
GROVE
  Edward 331
GUNN
  Jean 328

GUNNISON
  Hugh 321, 323
  Sarah (Tilley) (Lynn) 260
  _____ Mrs. 323
GUPPIE
  Ruben 388
GUTCH
  Lydia 138
  _____ Mr. 206
GYLES
  _____ Goodman 390

HAGGAT
  Henry 136
HALL
  Bethia (Bangs) 26, 27
  Edward 6
  Elizabeth (White) 368
  Gershom 27
  John 27
  Jonathan 27
  Mary 27
  Samuel 27, 368
  Thomas 116, 117
HALLETT/HALLET
  Abigail 8
  Alice 112
  Andrew 8, 480
  Josias 37
  Lois 122
  Mary (_____) 37
  Richard 112
  William 118
HAMBY
  Catherine 514
HAMPDEN
  John 231, 232, 373
HANBURY
  William 125, 174, 358, 416

HANFORD
Eglin (Hatherly) (Downe) 214, 236, 238, 393, 494
Elizabeth 214, 238
Hannah (Newberry) 238
Jeffrey 214, 238, 494
Lettice 214, 238
Margaret 214, 238, 393
Mary (Miles) (Ince) 238
Susanna 214, 238, 494
Thomas 214, 237, 238

HANMORE
John 402, 403
_____ (Samson) 403

HANSCOME/HANSCOM
Thomas 259, 323

HANSFORD
John 490

HANSON
Alice 64
Wybra 361

HARCOURT
Richard 488

HARDING
Bethiah (Cooke) 151, 152, 233
Joseph 151, 152, 233, 300, 301
Josiah 151
Maaziah 151
Martha (_____) 152, 232, 233
Martha (Doane?) 176
Phebe 81, 233
Winifred 233

HARLOW
Mary (Faunce) 202
Rebecca (Bartlett) 46
Thomas 79, 248
William 46, 202, 299, 485

HARMON/HARMAN
Jeane 179
John 3, 147

HARRINGTON
Edward 75
Richard 75

HARRIS
Joshua 489
Mercy 512, 513
Walter 176, 233, 234

HARRISON
John 71, 72
Persis (Pierce) (Bridges) 72

HART
Freeborn (Williams) 505, 506
Thomas 505, 506

HASKELL/HASKALL
John 434, 436
Patience (Soule) 434, 436

HATCH
Abigail (Hewes) 241, 242
Jane 418
Jeremiah 241, 242
Jonathan 398, 399
Lydia 237
Mary (Doty) 180
Mary (Hewes) 242
Phebe 241, 242
Samuel 180
Sarah (Rowley) 399
Susanna (Annable) 19
Thomas 19, 357
Walter 418
William 19, 224, 237, 241, 242

HATHAWAY
Joanna (Pope) 365
John 365

HATHERLY
Alice (Collard) 237
Eglin 214, 238, 393, 494
Ellinor (_____) 237
Lydia (Huckstep) (Tilden) 237, 238

Hatherly continued
  Nathaniel 238
  Robert 237
  Susan (____) 236, 238
  Timothy 50, 81, 115, 213, 214, 224, 234-240, 264, 289, 337, 393, 394, 453, 494, 495, 519, 527, 529
HATHORNE
  John 386, 387
  William 208, 210, 355, 386
HAWKINS
  Job 269
HAYWARD/HAWARD
  Hannah (Mitchell) 326, 327
  John 37, 327
  Joseph 327
  Mary 327
  Sarah (Mitchell) 326, 327
  Thomas 327
HEARD
  William 240
HEATH
  Thomas 248
  William 255
HEDGE/HEDGES
  Elisha 42
  Elizabeth 39
  Mercy 486
  William 486
HELLOT see HALLETT
HEWES
  Abigail 242
  Joan 243
  Joan (____) 241, 242
  John 240-242
  Mary 242
  Ruth (Sawtell) 242
  ____ Mr. 142
HEWETT
  Elizabeth (Foster) 214
  Ephraim 214
HEYLYN
  Rowland 490
HICKS
  Daniel 248
  Elizabeth 248
  Elizabeth (Howland) 247, 282
  Ephraim 244-248, 282, 443
  John 247
  Lydia 26, 28, 244, 247
  Lydia (Doane) 175, 246, 247
  Margaret 175
  Margaret (____) 28, 244-248, 487
  Mary 247
  Phoebe 244, 247, 485
  Rebecca (____) 28
  Richard 247
  Robert 26, 28, 36, 76, 79, 85, 97, 175, 243-248, 282, 419, 433, 445, 478, 485, 487
  Samuel 25, 28, 44, 175, 244-247, 487
  Sara 247
  Thomas 247
  ____ Mr. 218
  ____ Mrs. 219
HIGGINS/HIGGENS
  Alice (Newbould) 251
  Benjamin 27, 250, 251
  Eliakim 251, 252
  Elizabeth (Hull) 251
  Elizabeth (Oliver) 251
  Elizabeth (Rogers) 251
  Hannah (Rogers) 251
  Jadiah 251
  Jonathan 251
  Lydia 251
  Lydia (Bangs) 26, 27, 251
  Lydia (Chandler) 99, 100, 250
  Mary 251

Index of Surnames 557

Higgins continued
  Mary (_____) (Yates) 250, 253
  Mary (Newbold) 251
  Rebecca 251, 252
  Richard 27, 36, 99, 100, 150, 174, 228, 249-253, 300, 422-424
  Ruth 252, 253
  Sarah 252, 253
  Thomas 251, 253, 254, 296
  William 252
  Zera 251
HIGGINSON
  John 332
HILAND
  Sarah 469
HILL
  John 254, 388
  Prudence 417
  Thomas 36, 484
HILLER/HILLIER
  William 117, 132, 153, 287, 320, 322, 438
HILTON
  Agnes 257
  Ann (_____) 257
  Edward 257, 258
  Elizabeth 256
  Frances (_____) 256, 259, 260
  Joane 260
  John 257, 260, 261
  Magdalene 257, 259
  Mainwaring 257
  Mary 256, 258, 259
  Mary (Moulton) 257
  Mehitable (Nowell) 256
  Richard 257
  Sarah 514
  Sarah (Greenleaf) 256, 514
  William 142, 254-261, 323, 514
HILTON *alias* DOWNER
  Mary 259
HINCKLEY
  Samuel 121, 236, 365
  Sarah 121
  Sarah (Pope) 365
  Thomas 120
HINDES
  James 331
HIX
  Robert 162
HOAR
  Elizabeth 143
  Mary 143
  William 143
HOBART
  Caleb 107
  Edmund 28, 65, 310, 312, 313
  Elizabeth (Church) 107
  Jael 65
  Martha 51
  Peter 65
  Sarah (_____) (Lyford) (Oakley?) 310, 312, 313
HOCKING
  John 261, 262, 283, 289, 408, 428
HODGES
  Nicholas 265
HODGKINS
  Elizabeth 351
  Sara (Cushman) 159
  William 159
HOLBECK
  William 262, 263, 496
HOLBROOK
  Susannah 501
HOLDEN
  Randall 490

HOLLAND
 John 214
 Relief 214
HOLLINGSWORTH
 Richard 334
HOLLWAY
 Joseph 153
HOLMAN
 Amy (Glass) (Willis) 263-265
 Edward 36, 235, 249, 263-265, 296
 Jeremiah 373
 Mercy (Pratt) 373
 William 373
HOLMAR
 Edward 265
HOLMES
 Bathsheba 268, 269
 Desire (Doty) (Sherman) 179, 182, 453
 George 118
 Hannah (Samson) 402, 403
 Isaac 182
 Israel 179
 John 65, 156, 181, 202, 203, 265-267, 275, 325, 436
 Josiah 402, 403
 Margaret 268, 269
 Mary 268, 269
 Mary (Wood) 65
 Mercy (Faunce) 203, 267
 Nathaniel 203, 267
 Patience (Bonham) (Willis) 267
 Patience (Faunce) 202, 267
 Rachel 268, 269
 Robert 498
 Sarah (____) 267
 Thomas 268
 William 179, 267-270, 306, 309

HOLT
 John 12
 William 12
HONYWELL
 Wiliam 270, 271
HOOKE
 John 14, 271
HOOKER
 Mary (Willett) 499, 500
 Samuel 498-500
 Thomas 500
HOPKINS
 Caleb 271-273
 Catherine (Whelden) 273
 Constance 273-275, 431, 432
 Damaris 147, 271-274
 Deborah 152, 271-273, 391
 Eliezer 274
 Elizabeth 272-274, 447
 Elizabeth (Fisher) 271, 273, 274
 Giles 152, 271-275
 Mary (____) 273
 Oceanus 273, 274
 Ruth 272, 274
 Stephen 42, 70, 125, 147, 150, 152, 176, 180, 227, 267, 271-275, 305, 351, 391, 429, 431, 432, 460, 462, 521
HORNE
 John 331
HORTON
 Catherine (Satchfield) 137
 Sarah 137
 Thomas 137
HOSKINS
 Sarah 189
 William 189
HOWELL
 Thomas 30

Index of Surnames

HOWES
  Jeremiah 378, 379, 381
  Mary (____) 380
  Sarah (Bangs) 26
  Sarah (Prence) 377, 379, 381
  Thomas 26, 380, 453
HOWLAND
  Abigail 277, 279
  Abigail (____) 277
  Arthur 278, 283, 320, 328, 378-380
  Bethiah (Thatcher) 282
  Desire 280, 282
  Elizabeth 91, 247, 277, 278, 280, 282
  Elizabeth (Prence) 377-380
  Elizabeth (Southworth) 64, 282, 442, 443
  Elizabeth (Tilley) 280-283, 463
  Elizabeth (Vaughn) 283
  Hannah 282
  Henry 176, 233, 275-279, 282, 283, 402
  Hope 282
  Isaac 280, 281, 283
  Jabez 280-282
  James 64
  John 5, 10, 49, 76, 91, 96, 161, 245, 247, 261, 277-284, 293, 338, 358, 443, 463, 525
  Joseph 276-278, 280-282, 442, 443
  Lydia 282
  Margaret (____) 282
  Mary 277, 278
  Mary (____) 277, 279
  Mary (Lee) 282
  Mary (Sampson) 277, 342
  Mary (Walker) 278
  Nathaniel 281
  Rebecca (Hussey) 278
  Ruth 283
  Samuel 277, 278
  Sarah 276, 278
  Zoeth 276, 277, 279
HUBBARD
  Elinor 158
  William 255
HUCKINS
  Hope (Chipman) 122
  John 122
  Sarah (Pope) (Hinckley) 365
  Thomas 253, 365
HUCKSTEP
  Lydia 238
HUDSON
  William 193
HULEN
  Luys 117
HULL
  Elizabeth 251
  Isaac 135, 136
  Joanna 90
  Joseph 90, 91
HUMPHREY
  John 134, 141
HUNT
  Elizabeth 500
  Enoch 343
  Peter 501
HUNTER
  Christian 332
  Susan (Gentleman) 332
  Thomas 332
HURDMAN
  William 132
HURST
  Gertrude (Bennister) 285, 286
  James 121, 266, 268, 284-286
  Joan 462
  Patience 121, 286

HUSE
  Abel 259
  Mary (Hilton *alias* Downer)
    (Sears) 259
HUSSEY
  Rebecca 278
HUTCHESON
  Richard 386, 387
HUTCHINSON
  Ann (Marbury) 504
  Catherine (Hamby) 514
  Edward 514
  Elizabeth 514
HUTTON
  Richard 333
  Susanna (More) (Dutch) 333

INCE
  Mary (Miles) 238
IRISH
  Dorothy (Witherill) 288
  Elias 288
  Elizabeth 288, 482
  Elizabeth (_____) 287, 288
  John 261, 287-289, 439, 453, 482
  Lydia 289
  Priscilla (Southworth) (Talbot) 288, 439

JACKSON
  Abraham 300
  Robert 496
  _____ Goodman 467
JACOB
  Henry 297
JAMES
  Ann 469
  Jane 2
JEFFREYS
  William 91

JENKINS
  Edward 214, 237, 238, 494
  John 25, 393, 477
  Lettice (Hanford) (Foster) 214, 238
  Mary (Wallen) (Ewer) 477
JENNY/JENNEY
  Abigail 292, 293, 295
  Anne (Lettice) 295
  John 1, 3, 46, 89, 100, 219, 253, 264, 265, 291-296, 327, 364, 424, 484, 518
  Mary (Mitchell) (Shaw) 327
  Samuel 114, 292-295, 300, 518
  Sarah 114, 292-295, 364
  Sarah (_____) 46, 114
  Sarah (Cary) 291-295
  Susanna 46, 293-295
  Susanna (Wood) 295
JOHNSON
  Francis 143, 170
  Humphrey 241
JONES
  Agnes (_____) 411
  Bethia 387
  Dorothy 411
  Elizabeth 411
  George 411
  John 306, 307
  Joseph 179, 307, 308
  Morgan 113
  Patience (Little) 307-309
  Rice 260
  Richard 411
  Sarah 179
JOURDAINE
  John 37, 265
JOY
  Joan (_____) 107
  John 47

Index of Surnames

Joy continued
  Mercy (Bartlett) 47
  Thomas 107
JOYCE
  Dorcas 51
  John 51

KAINO
  Susan 185
  Thomas 185
KEENE
  Abigail (Little) 307
  Hezekiah 307
  Josiah 306, 307
KEMP/KEMPE
  William 414
  _____ Mr. 98, 245
KEMPTON
  Ephraim 299, 301
  George 301
  Jane (_____) 202
  Juliana (Carpenter) (Morton) 94, 298, 301, 336
  Manasseh 25, 94, 106, 120, 201, 202, 245, 297-301, 336, 338, 528
  _____ Goodman 44
KENDALL
  Elizabeth 227
KENNEDY/CANEDY
  Alexander 19
  Annable 19
  Elizabeth (Annable?) 19
KENNING
  Henry 257
  Magdalene (Hilton) (Wiggin) 257
KERMAN
  John 123
KERSLEY
  William 400

KEYSER
  Thomas 304
KIDBY
  Lewis 193
  Susan (Doggett) 193
KILLAM
  Anna (Pickworth) 354
  Anne 354
  Austin 354
  John 354
KING
  Abigail (Hewes) (Hatch) 242
  John 242
  Thomas 357
KIRBY
  Francis 239
KIRMAN
  John 93
KIRTLAND
  Martha 440
KNIGHT
  John 72
  Mary (Bridges) 72
  Persis 72
KNOP
  William 190
KNOWLES
  Apphia (Bangs) 27
  James 113
  Jane 55, 138
  Jane (Conant) 55
  John 27
  Mercy 176
  Samuel 113
  Thomas 55
KNOWLTON
  John 333
  Susanna (More) (Dutch) (Hutton) 333

LAKE
　David 363
LANE
　Thomas 92
LANGMORE
　John 302, 316
LANKFORD
　Richard 128, 302
LAPHAM
　Lydia 237
　Mary 51
　Mary (Tilden) 50
　Thomas 50, 51, 237
LASLE
　Francis 117
LATHAM
　Chilton 513
　Robert 513
　Samuel 78, 79, 248
　Susanna 512
　Susanna (Winslow) 512, 513
　William 86, 96, 304
LATHROP/LATHRUP
　John 16
　Mary 327
LATTIMORE
　Christopher 333
LAUNDER
　William 156
LAWRENCE/LORANCE
　Anna (Sprague) 449, 450
　Georg 190
　Sarah 514
　Thomas 514
　William 448-450
LEACH
　John 137, 138
　Mary 137
　Robert 54, 353
　Samuel 54
　Sarah (Conant) 137, 138

LEE
　Bridget 220
　Josephine (＿＿＿) 220
　Mary 282
　Tryphosa 465
LEGGATT
　Catherine (White) 95, 96
　Marie 96
LEISTER
　Edward 180, 275, 304, 305
LENDALL/LENDAL
　James 98, 440
　Mary (＿＿＿) 440
LEONARD/LEONARDSON
　Mary (Watson) 485
　Sarah (Chandler) 102
　Solomon 86, 102
　Thomas 485
LETTICE
　Anne 295
　Dorothy 112
　Elizabeth 147
　Thomas 112, 147, 148, 295, 362, 365, 408
LEVERETT
　Thomas 20
LEVERICH
　William 49
LEVETT
　Christopher 229
LEWIS
　Edward 121
　George 121, 446, 467
　Hannah (Cobb) 121
　Sarah 121, 446
LIGHT
　Cecily 51
LINCOLN
　Martha (Lyford) 311
　Mary 32
　Samuel 311

Index of Surnames 563

Lincoln continued
  Thomas 32
LINDALL
  Abigail 475
  James 475
LITTLE
  Abigail 307
  Ann (Warren) 306, 307, 479
  Bethia (Thomas) 308
  Ephraim 306-308
  Hannah 307, 308
  Isaac 306-308
  Mary (Sturtevant) 308
  Mercy 307, 308
  Patience 307, 308
  Ruth 307, 308
  Samuel 306-308
  Sarah (Gray) 308
  Thomas 43, 45, 111, 249, 298, 305-309, 478, 479
LOMBARD
  Abigail 494
  Joshua 494
  Joyce (_____) (Wallen) 477
  Thomas 477
LONG
  Robert 309
LOOKER
  Mary (Higgins) 251
  William 251
LORD
  Abigail (_____) 495
  William 208, 495
LOTHROP
  Abigail 112
  Abigail (Doane) 175
  Barnabas 112
  Bethia (Ray) 387
  Bethiah (Ray) (Lothrop) 388
  Jane 216

  John 112, 119, 175, 213, 214, 216, 224, 234-236, 238, 393, 398
  Samuel 175
  Susanna (Clark) 112
  Thomas 333, 386-388
LOVELL/LOVEL
  James 370
  Phebe 87
LOWLE
  John 208
LUCAS
  Thomas 126, 408, 409
LUDLOW
  George 261
LUNT
  Enoch 343
LUVET
  John 388
LUXFORD
  James 125, 270, 447
  John 181
LYFORD
  John 58, 66, 93, 139, 140, 255, 258, 309-313, 345-347, 395, 455
  Martha 311
  Mordecai 310, 311, 313
  Obadiah 310, 313
  Ruth 310, 311
  Sarah (_____) 310

MAGOONE
  John 30
MAHIEU
  Hester 146
  Marie 166
MANSFIELD
  Andrew 138
  Elizabeth (Walton) (Conant) 138

MANTER
  John 394
  Mary 394
MARGESSON
  Edmund 315
MARION
  John 191, 192
  Sarah (Eddy) 191, 192
MARSH
  Jonathan 33
  Phebe (Cook) (Arnold) 33
MARSHALL
  John 38
  Mary (Barnes) 39
  Robert 38, 39
MARSTON
  Sarah 355
MARTIN/MARTEN
  Christopher 302, 315, 316, 383
  Lydia 424
  Mary (____) (Prowe/Prower) 315
  Nathaniel 315
  Rebecca (Higgins) 251
  Richard 321
  Solomon 316
  Thomas 251
MASON
  Ann 260
  Jane (____) (Steevens) 137
  John 347
  Margaret 468
MASSIE
  Jeffrey 169, 489
MASTERS
  John 354
  Nathaniel 354, 355
  Ruth (Pickworth) 353, 354
MASTERSON
  Elizabeth (Cogswell) 317
  Mary (Goodall) 317, 427
  Nathaniel 317, 426, 427, 485
  Richard 59, 60, 292, 316-318, 427, 484
  Sarah 317, 318
MATHER
  Richard 501
MATHEWS
  James 25
MAVERICK
  John 13
  Moses 11, 13, 15
  Remember (Allerton) 13, 15
MAY
  Cordelia (Bowes) 65
  Dorothy 64, 65
  John 65
MAYHEW
  Thomas 346
MAYO
  Hannah (Prence) 380, 446
  Mary 27
  Nathaniel 380, 446, 447
  Theophilus 377, 378
MEADE
  David 192
  Gabriel 192, 193
  Israel 192
  Joanna (____) 192
  Sarah 192, 193
MENDUM/MANLOVE/
    MENDALL/MENDLOVE
  David 321, 323, 324
  Jonathan 321-324
  Judith (____) (____) 321
  Mark 36, 37, 109, 319, 322, 412, 413
  Mary (____) 321-323
  Mary (Raynes) 322, 324
  Robert 113, 259, 319-324
  Sarah 322

Index of Surnames 565

Mendum continued
  William 106, 318, 319, 322, 351
MERRICK
  Henry 30, 32
  Mercy (Bangs) 26, 27
  Rebecca (Tracy) 465
  Steven 27
  William 357, 465
MIDDLECOTT
  Richard 514
  Sarah (Winslow) (Standish) (Payne) 512-514
MILES/MYLES
  John 498, 499
  Mary 238
MILLER
  Alexander 191
  Faith 520
  Hannah 516
  John 517
  Margaret (Winslow) 517
MINTER
  Desire 96, 324
MITCHELL
  Alice (Bradford) 327
  Edward 326, 327
  Elizabeth 327, 328, 482
  Experience 146, 194, 195, 266, 276, 306, 324-329, 336, 364, 410, 415, 482
  Hannah 327, 328
  Jacob 306, 327, 363, 364
  Jane (Cooke) 146, 326, 328
  John 326, 327
  Mary 326, 327, 415
  Mary (____) 326, 328
  Mary (Bonney) 327
  Mary (Hayward) 327
  Mary (Lathrup) 327
  Mary (Prior) 327

  Sarah 327
  Susanna (Pope) 327, 364
  Thomas 146, 326-328
MONGER
  ____ Mr. 132
MONK
  George 259
MOORE/MORE
  Caleb 332, 333
  Catherine 329, 332
  Catherine (Moore) 329, 330, 332, 333
  Christian 332, 333
  Christian (Hunter) 331, 332
  Ellen/Ellinor/Helen 329, 330, 509
  Jane (____) (Crumpton) 332
  Jasper 96, 329, 330
  Joshua 333
  Margery 482
  Mary 329, 330
  Richard 329-335, 490, 492, 509
  Samuel 250, 252, 329, 330, 332, 333
  Sarah (____) 333
  Sarah (Higgins) 252
  Susanna 332, 333
  Thomas 333
  William 257, 260
MOORECOCK/MORECOCK
  Bennett 425
  Mary 447
MOREY
  Jonathan 46, 306
  Mary (Bartlett) (Foster) 46
MORGAN
  Bennett 335
  Elizabeth 247
  Robert 353

MORRELL
  William 229, 335, 336
MORRIS
  William 132
MORTON
  Ann (Cooper) 337
  Deborah 155, 442
  Ephraim 45, 299, 301, 336, 337
  George 94, 202, 203, 301, 325, 336-338, 391
  John 37, 155, 300, 336, 337, 391
  Juliana (Carpenter) 94, 301, 336-338
  Lettice (_____) 337, 391
  Lydia (Cooper) 336
  Mercy 185
  Nathaniel 245, 295, 298-300, 336, 337, 429, 485
  Patience 202, 336, 337
  Rose (_____) 338
  Sarah 336, 337
  Thomas 43, 91, 301, 338, 339, 344, 347, 429, 454, 456
MOSES
  John 304
MOSESZ.
  Simon 422
MOULTON
  Mary 257
  Robert 208
  Thomas 257
MOUMFORD
  Jane 18
MUCHMORE
  James 322
  Robert 321, 322
  Sarah (Mendum) 322
MULLINS
  Alice (_____) 339, 340

Ann (_____) (Bell) 340
Joan (Bridger) 339
John 339
Joseph 339, 340
Priscilla 7, 9, 339, 340
Sarah 340
William 7-9, 95, 339, 340
MYNARD
  John 125, 521

NASH
  Elizabeth 343
  James 343, 420, 421
  Martha 343
  Samuel 5, 341-343, 458
  Sarah (Simonson) 420, 421
NEAL
  Walter 20
NELSON
  Engletgen (Gilten) 104
  Jane 202
  John 46
  Lydia (Bartlett) (Barnaby) 46
  Martha 121
  Martha (Ford) 211, 212
  Robert 104
  William 211
NEWBERRY
  Hannah 238
NEWBOLD/NEWBOULD
  Alice 251
  Mary 251
NEWCOMEN
  John 57, 344
NEWLAND
  Mary 277
  William 41
NEWTON
  Ellen 2, 344, 520
NICHOLAS
  Austen 344

Index of Surnames

NICHOLS/NICOLLS
  Alice (Hallett) 112
  Elizabeth 220
  John 111, 220
  Mordecai 112
  Sarah (Whiston) 494
  Thomas 494
NICKERSON
  Rebecca (Cole) 127
  Robert 127
  William 153, 412
NORMAN
  John 355, 356
  Richard 492
  William 323
NORRIS
  Mary 12
NORTON
  John 428
NOWELL
  Increase 256, 310, 514
  Mary 514
  Mehitable 256
NUTTER
  Hatevell 259

OAKLEY
  Sarah (____) (Lyford) 310
OGHDEN
  Jan 117
OLDHAM
  John 58, 68, 71-75, 140, 141, 258, 310-312, 345-348, 455
  Lucretia 68, 345, 346
  Thomas 346, 348
  William 346
  ____ (____) (Bridges) 75, 346
OLIVER
  Elizabeth 251
  Magdalen 508, 510, 513, 517, 520
OLNEY
  Lydia 506
ORDWAY
  Abner 388
  Sarah (____) (Dennis) 388
ORTON
  Mary (Eddy) 191, 192
  Thomas 191, 192
OSGOOD
  Peter 332
OVERZEE
  Eizabeth (Willoughby) 13
  Simon 13

PABODIE/PAYBODY
  Elizabeth (Alden) 7, 10
  Mary 439
  Mercy 421
  Rebecca 440
  William 7, 325, 421, 439, 440
PACKARD
  Hannah 78
  Samuel 78
PADDOCK/PADDUCK
  Alice 197
  Deborah (Sears) 410, 411
  Ichabod 410, 411
  John 499
  Mary (____) (Palmer) 350
  Robert 350
  Susanna 197
  Zachariah 410, 411
PADDY
  William 2, 52, 299, 358, 498, 501, 502, 512
PAINE see also PAYNE
  Mary (Snow) 431
  Thomas 377, 430, 431

PALFREY
  Peter 143, 170
PALMER
  Bridget 350, 400
  Elizabeth (Hodgkins) 351
  Frances (_____) 349, 350
  Henry 350, 400
  Mary (_____) 350
  Rebecca 350
  Susanna (_____) 351
  William 33, 37, 86, 266, 318, 319, 349-352, 399, 460, 465
PARKER
  Mary (Turner) 468, 469
  Patience (Cobb) 121
  Robert 121
  William 469
PARSONS
  Elizabeth (_____) (England) 180
  Hugh 179
PARTRIDGE/PATRICH
  George 26, 245, 465
  Ralph 49, 164, 304, 350, 448, 473, 474
  Sarah (Tracy) 465
PAYBODY see PABODIE
PAYNE see also PAINE
  Sarah (Winslow) (Standish) 514
  Tobias 514
  William 512
PEARCE/PEIRCE see PIERCE
PEASE
  John 488
  Margaret (_____) 488
  Robert 488
PELHAM
  Herbert 508
  Penelope 508

PEMBERTON
  Alice 505
PENN
  Christian 57, 188, 352
  James 269
PERRY
  Deborah 364
  Ezra 364
  Margaret 365
  Susanna (Whiston) 494
  Thomas 494
PETERSON
  John 435
  Mary (Soule) 435
PETTEE
  Rebecca 175
PHILLIPS
  Elizabeth 7
  Faith (Clarke) (Doty) 178
  George 194, 379
  John 30, 178, 304, 320
  William 7
PHIPS
  William 352, 353
PICKMAN
  Nathaniel 169-171
  Tabitha (_____) (Dike) 170
PICKWORTH
  Abigail 353, 355
  Abigail (Elithorpe) 355
  Anna 354
  Anne (_____) 353-355
  Benjamin 353, 355
  Elizabeth (_____) 355
  John 353-356
  Jonathan 355
  Joseph 353-356
  Rachel 355
  Ruth 354
  Samuel 353-356
  Sarah 355

Index of Surnames

Pickworth continued
  Sarah (Marston) 355
PIERCE/PEARCE/PEIRCE
  Abraham 110, 167, 356-359, 367
  Alice 357, 358
  Caleb 358
  Christian (Stoddard) 72
  Elizabeth (_____) 72
  Hannah (Baker) 357
  Hannah (Glass?) 357
  Isaac 357, 358
  James 359
  John 356, 358, 491
  Mary 358
  Mary (Orton) 191
  Michael 436
  Nathaniel 72
  Persis 72, 74
  Rebecca 358
  Rebecca (_____) 357
  Samuel 191
  Thomas 71, 72, 358
  _____ Mr. 142
PIKE
  Elizabeth (Blossom) (FitzRandolph) 59
  John 59
PITFORD
  Edward 355
PITMAN/PITTMAN
  Nathaniel 170
  Tabitha (_____) (Dike) 170
  Thomas 331
PITT
  William 359, 525
PITTS
  _____ Mrs. 136
PLEYDOEN
  Edman 117

PLUMMER/PLUMER
  Anne 39, 359, 403
  Mary 39, 359
POCOCKE
  John 125
  Mary (Cole) (Almy) 125
POLIN
  John 170
  Margery (_____) (Dike) 170
POLLARD
  George 132, 438
  Mary 513
PONTUS
  Hannah 361
  Mary 87, 166, 360, 361
  William 87, 165, 166, 245, 360-362
  Wybra (Hanson) 361
POPE
  Alice (Freeman) 365
  Anne (Fallowell) 364
  Deborah 363
  Deborah (Perry) 364
  Hannah 46, 364
  Isaac 363-365
  Jane 155
  Joanna 365
  John 365
  Rebecca (_____) 364
  Sarah 365
  Sarah (Jenny) 294, 295, 364, 365
  Seth 363, 364, 402
  Susanna 294, 327, 364, 365
  Thomas 46, 144, 294, 295, 327, 362-365
POWELL
  Michael 260
POWER
  Nicholas 488, 506
  Rebecca (Rhodes) 505

PRATT
Aaron 371, 373
Abigail (Wood) 368
Ann (Barker) 372
Anna (_____) 372
Bathsheba 368
Bathsheba (_____) 367, 368
Bathsheba (Fay) 369
Benajah 186, 367, 368, 416
Bennaniah 165
Daniel 371, 372
Dorcas (Folger) 373
Elizabeth (Griswold) (Rogers) 372
Elizabeth (White) (Hall) 368
Hannah 368
John 369, 371, 372
Jonathan 363, 368, 369
Joseph 371, 373
Joshua 56, 148, 150, 154, 177, 245, 302, 356, 365-369, 372, 373, 405, 406, 417, 445
Mary 371, 372
Mary (Barker) 155, 372
Mary (Priest) 370-372, 382
Mercy 371, 373
Persis (Dunham) 186, 367, 416
Peter 371, 372
Phineas 36, 77, 154, 177, 227, 231, 365, 366, 368-374, 382, 450
Samuel 155, 371, 372
Sarah 373
Sarah (Pratt) 373
Sarah (Wright) (Cummings) 373
_____ Goodman 3

PREBLE
Judith (Tilden) 237

PRENCE
Apphia (Quick) (Freeman) 379, 381
Elizabeth 380, 381
Hannah 380, 446
Jane 380, 431
Judith 32, 380
Mary 380, 465
Mary (_____) (Howes) 130, 377, 378, 380, 381
Mary (Collier) 379
Mercy 380
Patience (Brewster) 68, 70, 375, 379
Rebecca 219, 375, 380
Sarah 381
Susanna 377, 378
Thomas 3, 32, 41, 63, 64, 67, 68, 106, 130, 145, 153, 154, 188, 218, 219, 261, 265, 270, 349, 351, 370, 374-381, 390, 431, 446, 465

PRESCOTT
John 331

PRESLAND
Nicholas 111

PRICE
John 465
Margaret 407

PRIEST
Degory 14, 155, 226-228, 372, 374, 382, 383
Mary 226, 372, 382
Sarah 155, 226, 382
Sarah (Allerton) (Vincent) 14, 227, 372, 382
William 190

PRIOR
Joseph 132
Mary 327

Index of Surnames 571

PROWER
  Mary (_____) 315
  Solomon 316, 383
PRUDDEN
  Joanna (Boyse) 500
  Peter 500
PRUST see also PRIEST
  Digorius 382
PUTNAM
  John 386, 387
PYNCHON
  William 171

QUICK
  Apphia 379
  William 379

RAINSFORD
  Edward 50
  Mary 50
RAMSDEN/RANSDELL
  Joseph 126, 189, 296, 405
  Rachel (Eaton) 189
RAND
  James 385
RANDALL
  Hannah 469
  William 241, 469
RANSOM
  Robert 115, 363
RATTLIFE
  Robert 385
RAWLINS
  Thomas 17
RAY
  Bethia 387
  Bethiah (_____) 387
  Daniel 17, 254, 385-388
  Elizabeth (Foster) (Hewett) 214
  James 214

  Joshua 386, 387
  Rebecca 386, 388
  Sarah 386, 388
  Sarah (Walters) 387
RAYMENT
  John 135
RAYNES
  Mary 322, 324
REDER
  Sara 158
REES
  John 76
RENOLDS
  William 261, 276
REYNER/RENER
  John 3, 98, 294
REYNOR
  Elizabeth 443
  John 172, 245, 375
RHODES/ROADS
  Henry 334
  Rebecca 505
  Zachariah 506
RICH
  Nathaniel 262
RICHARDS
  Alice 65
  Thomas 65
  William 388, 389
RICHEMAN
  Jenneken 94
RICKARD/RICKET/RICKETT
  Esther 38, 39
  Giles/Gyles 150, 184, 186, 250, 264, 285, 361, 365, 367, 395, 445
  Hannah (Dunham) 186
  Hannah (Pontus) (Churchill) 361
  Hannah (Snow) 432
  Hester (Barnes) 40

Rickard continued
  John 40, 151, 300
  Judith 203
  Rebecca (Snow) 432
RICKDALL
  Alice 389
RIDER/RYDER
  Mary 123
  Samuel 46, 196
  Sarah (Bartlett) 46
RIGBY
  John 469
  Mehitable 469, 470
RIGSDALE
  Alice (____) 389
  John 389
RING
  Andrew 3, 219, 263, 273, 325, 337, 389-391
  Deborah (Hopkins) 273, 391
  Elizabeth 163, 391
  Lettice (____) (Morton) 337, 391
  Mary (____) 389-391
  Mary (Durrant) 111, 152, 163, 219, 273, 337, 391
  Susanna 111, 391
  William 111, 163, 391
RISLEY
  Elizabeth 288
ROBERTS
  Mary (____) (Palmer) (Paddock) 350
  Thomas 350, 467
ROBINSON
  Anne (____) 394
  Anne (Cottle) 394
  Bridget (White) 96, 393
  Elizabeth (Weeks) 394
  Experience (____) 394
  Experience (Rogers) 394
  Fear 237, 394
  Isaac 96, 97, 213, 214, 225, 237, 238, 391-395
  Israel 394
  Jacob 394
  John 96, 237, 262, 317, 393, 394, 491
  Margaret (Hanford) 214, 238, 393
  Mary (____) 393, 394
  Mary (Manter) 394
  Mercy 237, 394, 453
  Peter 394
  Susanna 394
  Thomas 395
ROES
  Bartholomew 334
ROGERS
  ____ Mr. 395, 396
  Abigail (Barker) 31, 33
  Alice (Cosford) 396
  Anna (Churchman) 396
  Eleanor (____) 396
  Elizabeth 251, 397
  Elizabeth (Griswold) 372
  Elizabeth (Snow) 431
  Experience 394
  Hannah 251
  Hannah (____) 396
  Joan (Hurst) 462
  John 33, 36, 77, 97, 246, 372, 396, 397
  Joseph 33, 85, 163, 300, 357, 396, 397, 431
  Margaret 397
  Richard 396
  Susanna (Deane) 163, 431
  Thomas 163, 396, 397, 431, 462
  William 396

Index of Surnames 573

ROICE
  Bathsheba (Pratt) 368
  Joshua 368
  Robert 368
ROPES
  George 208
ROSE
  Elizabeth (Bumpas) 86
  Joseph 86
ROSSITER
  Jane 51
ROUSE/ROWSE
  Elizabeth (Doty) 179
  John 41, 98, 178, 179, 287
ROWDEN
  John 388
ROWE
  John 320
ROWLAND
  _____ 397, 398
  John 397
  William 397
ROWLEY
  Anne (Elsdon) (Blossom) 58, 399
  Elizabeth (Fuller) 399
  Henry 58, 350, 398-400, 486
  Joseph 400
  Moses 350, 399, 400
  Sarah 399
  _____ Goodman 119
  _____ (Palmer) 350, 399
RUMBALL/RUMBLE
  Daniel 224, 225, 388
RUSSELL
  George 213
  John 165
  Joseph 402
  William 132

SACHARIASDAUGHTER
  Josina 204
SAFFIN
  John 498, 500
  Martha (Willett) 499, 500
  Thomas 499
  _____ Mrs. 198
SALMON
  Daniel 161, 162
  John 162
  Joseph 162
SALTONSTALL
  Robert 117
SAMPSON/SAMSON
  Abraham 167, 277, 343, 445
  Anne (Plumer) 39, 359, 403
  Benjamin 403
  Caleb 402-404
  Dorcas 403
  Elizabeth 167, 403, 404
  Elizabeth (_____) 403
  Esther (_____) 343
  Esther (Delano) 167, 435
  Hannah 403, 404
  Hannah (_____) (Wait) 403
  Henry 38, 39, 156, 306, 359, 401-404, 462, 519
  Ichabod 342
  James 402, 403
  John 402, 403
  Martha (Cooper) 403
  Mary 277, 403
  Mercy (Standish) 403
  Rebecca (Bartlett) (Bradford) (Stanford) 403
  Samuel 167, 342, 343, 435
  Stephen 402, 403
  _____ (Nash) 167, 343
SARGENT
  Ruth 516, 517
  William 516, 517

SATCHFIELD
  Catherine 137
SAUNDERS
  Henry 126
SAVORY
  Aaron 406-409
  Ann/Annis (_____) 406-408, 414
  Anthony 405, 407-409
  Benjamin 407, 408, 414
  Elizabeth 288
  Jonathan 407
  Joseph 409
  Margaret (Price) 407
  Mary 407
  Mary (Shepperd) 405
  Moses 407
  Samuel 407, 408
  Thomas 195, 196, 261, 367, 405-409, 414
  _____ Goodman 3
SAWTELL
  Ruth 242
SAWYER
  John 32, 307
  Mercy (Little) 307
  Rebecca (Barker) (Snow) 32, 308
SAYE AND SELE
  _____ Lord 261, 262
SAYLES
  John 505
  Mary (Williams) 505
SCOTT
  Katherine (Marbury) 504
  Richard 504
  Robert 118, 269
SCOTTOW/SCOTTO
  John 108
  Mehitable 112
  Rebecca (_____) 108

SCUDDER
  Hannah 27
  Hannah (_____) 357
  John 27, 357
SEARS
  Anna (_____) 411
  Deborah 411
  Deborah (_____) 411
  Dorothy (Jones) 410, 411
  Knyvett 412
  Mary (Hilton *alias* Downer) 259
  Paul 410, 411
  Richard 409-412
  Silas 410, 411
  Thomas 259
SEWALL
  Samuel 393
SHAFLEN/SHAFFLYN
  Michael 208, 489
SHAKKERLEY
  William 334
SHAPLEIGH
  Nicholas 322
  _____ Miss 323
  _____ Mr. 254, 323
SHAW
  Abigail 415
  Alice (_____) 408, 414, 415
  Edward 112, 113, 412, 413
  James 125, 327, 413, 415
  John 37, 113, 177, 178, 181, 225, 327, 370, 408, 413-416, 484, 485
  Jonathan 186, 247, 408, 414, 415, 485
  Mary (Mitchell) 326, 327, 415
  Persis (Dunham) (Pratt) 186, 416
  Phoebe (Watson) 247, 415485
  Thomas 18

Index of Surnames

Shaw continued
　____ Goodman 145
SHEIRES
　Jeremy 259
SHEPPERD
　Mary 405
SHERIVE/SHEREVE/SHRIVE
　/SHREIVE
　Martha (____) 265
　Thomas 3, 41, 47, 151, 265, 447
SHERMAN
　Desire (Doty) 179, 182, 418, 453
　Hannah (____) 418
　Jane (Hatch) 418
　John 417, 418
　Prudence (Hill) 417
　Samuel 417, 418
　Sarah (Doggett) 418
　William 179, 182, 416-419, 481
SHETLE
　William 114
SHINGELTON
　Mary (____) 158
　Thomas 158
SHIRLEY/SHERLEY
　James 88, 223, 235, 508
　____ Mr. 132
SHREIVE/SHRIVE see SHERIVE
SHRIMPTON
　Henry 331
　Samuel 331
SHURTLEFF/SHIRTLEY/
　SHIRTLIFF/SHURTLIFF
　Elizabeth (Lettice) 147
　William 114, 125, 144, 147, 308

SIBLEY
　Anne 354
　John 355
　Rachel (Pickworth) 354, 355
SILLIS
　Eglin (Hatherly) (Downe) (Hanford) 214
　Richard 213, 214
SIMMONS/SIMONSON
　Aaron 420, 421, 523
　Elizabeth 421
　Elizabeth (Nash) 343
　John 420, 421
　Mary 8, 421
　Mary (Woodworth) 421, 523
　Mercy (Pabodie) 421
　Moses 8, 85, 97, 98, 165, 167, 419-422, 435, 458, 523
　Patience (Barstow) 420, 421
　Rebecca 421, 435
　Sarah 421
　Sarah (____) 420, 421
　Thomas 181, 218, 343, 421, 457, 458
SIMPKINS
　Isabel 269
　Nicholas 269
SIRKMAN
　Bridget (Fuller) 220
　Henry 220
SKEFF
　Stephen 34
SKELTON
　Samuel 504
SMALL
　Edward 147, 148
SMALLEY
　Ann (Walden) 423, 424
　Esther (Wood) 424
　Hannah 26, 424
　Isaac 423, 424

Smalley continued
  John 26, 176, 228, 233, 250, 252, 300, 422-424, 431
  Jonathan 423
  Lydia (Marten) 424
  Mary 176, 424, 431
  Mary (White) 424
SMEDLEY
  Mary (____) 328
SMITH/SMYTH
  Abigail (____) 197
  Anna (Crackstone) 157, 158
  Bennett (Morecock) 425
  Dermot 197
  Dorothy 188
  James 77
  Jeremiah 197
  John 28, 153, 155, 181, 244, 257, 296, 370, 424, 425
  Mary 64
  Mary (Goodall) (Masterson) 317, 426, 427
  Ralph 25, 60, 172, 266, 268, 292, 317, 425-428, 447
  Samuel 114, 127
  Thomas 157, 158, 330
SNELL
  Anne (Alden) 9
  Josiah 9
SNOW
  Abigail (Warren) 33, 479
  Alice 32-34
  Anna 151
  Anna (Cooke) 152, 431
  Anthony 33, 34, 106, 376, 479
  Constance (Hopkins) 272, 273, 429-432
  Elizabeth 431
  Elizabeth (____) 431
  Hannah 432
  Jabez 430, 431
  Jane (Prence) 377-380, 431
  John 176, 424, 430, 431
  Joseph 430, 431
  Josiah 32, 34, 308
  Mark 152, 377-380, 430, 431
  Mary 431
  Mary (____) 431
  Mary (Bigford) 431
  Mary (Smalley) 176, 423, 424, 431
  Nicholas 151, 152, 163, 194, 195, 272, 273, 380, 424, 428-432
  Rebecca 432
  Rebecca (Barker) 31, 32, 34, 308
  Rebecca (Brown) 84
  Ruth 431
  Sarah 431
  Stephen 163, 430-432
  Susanna (Deane) (Rogers) 163, 431
  William 80, 84, 181
SOULE
  Benjamin 436
  Deborah (____) 435
  Elizabeth 436
  Esther (Delano) (Samson) 167, 343, 435
  George 85, 244, 298, 421, 432-436, 438, 442, 509, 520
  John 167, 342, 343, 420, 421, 434-436, 520
  Margaret (____) 435
  Mary 434, 435
  Mary (Buckett) 85, 433-435
  Nathaniel 434-436
  Patience 436
  Rebecca (Simonson) 420, 421, 435
  Rose (____) 435

Soule continued
 Susanna 434, 435
 Zachariah 433, 435
SOUTHER/SOWTHER
 Nathaniel 389, 485
SOUTHWORTH
 Alice 107, 439
 Alice (Carpenter) 64, 94, 439, 443
 Constant 8, 64, 65, 94, 108, 114, 130, 131, 298, 337, 379, 437-440, 442, 443
 Desire (Gray) 440
 Edward 64, 94, 158, 288, 337, 438-440, 443
 Elizabeth 282, 438-440, 443
 Elizabeth (Collier) 131, 438, 439, 443
 Elizabeth (Reynor) 443
 Martha (Kirtland) (Blague) 440
 Mary 8, 440
 Mary (Pabodie) 439
 Mercy 439
 Nathaniel 438-440
 Priscilla 288, 439
 Rebecca (Pabodie) 440
 Thomas 63, 64, 94, 184, 248, 281, 282, 294, 300, 438, 440-443, 446
 William 439, 440
 _____ Capt. 246
SPARROW
 Hannah (Prence) (Mayo) 377, 379, 380, 446
 John 446
 Jonathan 26, 378-380, 445-447
 Pandora (_____) 445-447
 Priscilla 446
 Rebecca 446

Rebecca (Bangs) 26, 446
 Richard 26, 150, 380, 443-447
 Sarah (Lewis) (Cobb) 446
SPOONER
 Hannah (Pratt) 368
 William 155, 156, 267, 368
SPRAGUE
 Anna 448-450
 Anthony 46
 Dorcas 449, 450
 Elizabeth (Bartlett) 46
 Francis 51, 181, 447-450
 Joanna 108
 John 49, 51, 123, 448-450
 Mercy 448-450
 Ruth (Bassett) 51, 449
 William 46, 108
SPROUT
 Elizabeth (Samson) 403
 Robert 402, 403
STACY
 Hugh 450
 John 334
STANDISH
 Alexander 7, 8, 167, 179, 182, 403, 452, 453
 Barbara (_____) 451-453
 Charles 451-454
 Desire (Doty) (Sherman) (Holmes) 179, 182, 453
 Elizabeth 167
 Huan 456, 457
 John 452, 454, 457
 Josias 452-454, 520
 Lora 452, 454
 Mary (Dingley) 452, 454
 Mercy 403
 Miles 5, 8, 67, 86, 110, 142, 158, 179, 214, 219, 268, 272, 294, 328, 356, 373, 417, 447, 451-457, 460, 462, 463, 481,

Standish continued
    497, 514, 519
  Rose (____) 451, 453, 454
  Sarah (Alden) 7, 8, 453
  Sarah (Allen) 454
  Sarah (Winslow) 454, 514
STANDLAKE
  Lydia 524
  Richard 524
STANFORD
  Rebecca (Bartlett) (Bradford) 403
  Robert 404
STARESMORE
  Sabin 318
STARR
  John 474
  Richard 334
  Robert 334
  Susanna 334
STEADMAN
  Isaac 192
  Pilgrim (Eddy) (Baker) 191, 192
STEPHENS/STEEVENS
  Edward 418
  Love 137
  Martha (Timbrell) 482
  William 418
  ____ (Sherman) 418
STERNES
  Isaac 190
STETSON
  Deborah (Brooks) 523
  John 31
  Robert 523
STEWARD
  James 457
STILEMAN
  Elias 487

STILLWELL
  Nicholas 116, 118
STINNINGS
  Richard 47
STOCKBRIDGE
  Abigail (Eames?) 469
  Charles 363, 469
  Sarah 523
STODDARD
  Anthony 72
  Christian 72
  Christian (Eire) 72
STORY
  Elias 457, 509
STOUGHTON
  Thomas 78, 79
STRATTON
  John 210
STRENGWITS
  William 118
STUIJVESANT
  Peter 502
STURTEVANT
  Hannah (Winslow) (Crow) 517
  John 517
  Lydia 378
  Mary 308
  Samuel 286, 308, 519
SUMMERS
  John 402, 403
  Mary (Samson) 402, 403
SUTTON
  George 237
  Richard 421
SWAN
  John 372
  Mary (Pratt) 372
SWINNERTON
  Joanna 13

Index of Surnames

TALBOT
  Moses 261, 262, 283, 284, 408, 428
  Priscilla (Southworth) 288, 439
  Samuel 288, 439
TAPPIN
  _____ Mrs. 512
TAYLOR/TAILER
  Elizabeth 122
  Richard 122
  Tobias 113
  William 512, 513
TEMPLE
  Dorothy 267, 275
  Richard 71
TENCH
  William 93, 459
TERRY
  Help 204
  Priscilla (Fletcher) (Coit) 204
  Samuel 147
  Solomon 204
THATCHER/THACHER
  Anthony 282, 411
  Bethiah 282
  Elizabeth (Jones) 411
  John 410, 411, 517
  Rebecca (Winslow) 517
  Thomas 513
THAXTER
  Abigail (Church) 108
  Samuel 108
THOMAS
  Bethia 308
  James 388
  John 51
  Mary (_____) 308
  Nathaniel 308, 436
  Ruth (Bassett) (Sprague) 51
  William 156

THOMPSON/THOMSON
  David 258, 466
  Edward 459, 496
  John 145-147, 195
  Mary (Cooke) 146, 147
THORPE/THORP
  Alice 461
  Alice (_____) 33, 460, 461
  John 33, 60, 252, 351, 361, 459-461
TIBBES
  Mary 124
TILDEN
  Hannah (Little) 307
  Joseph 88, 237, 298, 393
  Lydia (Huckstep) 238
  Mary 50
  Nathaniel 50, 238, 307, 461
  Stephen 237, 307
  Thomas 306, 461
TILESTON
  Ruth 214
  Thomas 214
TILLEY
  Agnes (Cooper) 156, 404, 461, 462
  Edmond 461
  Edward 156, 404, 461-463
  Elizabeth 282, 283, 463
  Elizabeth (_____) 461, 462
  Hugh 253
  Joan (Hurst) (Rogers) 462
  John 156, 282, 283, 404, 461-463
  Robert 461-463
  Rose 462, 463
TILSON
  Edmond 423
  Elizabeth 186
  Joan (_____) 37
  Mary 125

TIMBRELL
  Martha 482
TINKER
  Thomas 463
TINKHAM
  Ephraim 80, 84, 238, 239, 289, 402
  Mary (_____) 402
  Mary (Brown) 80, 84
TISDALE
  John 275
TOMPKINS
  Lettis (Foster) 214
  Samuel 214
TRACY
  Agnes/Anne (Erdley) 465
  John 378-380, 464, 465, 517
  Mary 464, 465
  Mary (Prence) 377, 379, 380, 465
  Mary (Winslow) 517
  Rebecca 464, 465
  Ruth 464, 465
  Sarah 464, 465
  Stephen 298, 350, 358, 463-465
  Tryphosa (Lee) 464, 465
TRASK
  William 334
  _____ Capt. 209
TREADWAY
  Nathaniel 190
TREVOR/TREVORE
  William 198, 466
  _____ Mr. 239
TREWORGYE
  John 322
TROTT
  Symon 114
TRUANT/TREWANT
  Jane (_____) 481
  Morris 86, 306, 448, 481
TUBBS
  Judith (Prence) (Barker) 380
  Mercy (Sprague) 449
  William 380, 449
TUCK
  Thomas 334
TUCKER
  Mary 107
  Robert 77
TUFTS
  Elizabeth 72
  Peter 71, 72
  _____ (Pierce) 71
TURNER
  Abigail (Eames?) (Stockbridge) 469
  Ann (James) 469
  Daniel 468, 469
  Elizabeth 468, 470, 471
  Hannah (Randall) 469
  Humphrey 466-470
  Japhett 524
  John 467-471
  Jonathan 468
  Joseph 468, 469
  Josiah 468
  Lydia 469
  Lydia (Gaymer) 466, 468
  Lysbet 471
  Mary 469
  Mary (Brewster) 469
  Mehitable (Rigby) 469, 470
  Nathaniel 468-470
  Sarah (Hiland) 469
  Thomas 468, 469
TUTTLE
  Ruth (Higgins) (FitzRandolph) 252
  Stephen 252

Index of Surnames

TWINING
  Elizabeth (Deane) 163
  Steven 151
  William 163
TWISDEN
  _____ Goodman 393

UPHAM
  John 89
USHER
  Hezekiah 426

VANE
  Henry 171
VASSALL
  Frances 2
  Judith 495
  William 2, 234, 469, 495
VAUGHN
  Elizabeth 283
  George 283
VENNER
  Thomas 208
VEREN
  Adoniron 136
  Hannah 136
  Hillier 137
  Mary (_____) 137
VERMAYES
  Benjamin 65
  Mercy (Bradford) 65
VERMOUT
  Jan Jans 205
  Priscilla (Fletcher) (Coit) (Terry) 205
VINALL
  _____ Goodman 119
VINCENT
  Jan 382
  John 14, 227

  Sarah (Allerton) 14, 227, 372, 382
VOBBES
  William 439
VOORCHOREN
  Elizabeth (Fletcher) (Barnaart) 205
  Michiel 205

WADE
  Elizabeth (Hanford) 214, 238
  John 264
  Nicholas 214, 237, 238
WADSWORTH
  Abigail 475
  Abigail (Andrews) 475
  Abigail (Lindall) 475
  Abigail (Waite) 476
  Christopher 127, 473-476, 478, 525
  Elisha 476
  Grace (_____) 474, 475
  John 474, 475
  Joseph 474-476
  Mary 475
  Mary (_____) 475
  Samuel 475, 476
  Wait 476
  William 476
WAITE/WAIT/WAYTE
  Abigail 476
  Hannah (_____) 403
  John 75
  Samuel 403
WALDEN
  Ann 424
WALDRON
  William 323
WALKER
  Augustine 479
  Elizabeth 479

Walker continued
  Elizabeth (Soule) 434, 436
  Francis 434, 436
  James 486
  Mary 278
  Sarah 131, 479
  Sarah (Snow) 431
  William 113, 131, 431
WALLEN
  Joyce (_____) 25, 476, 477
  Mary 477
  Ralph 110, 153, 476, 477
  Thomas 477
  _____ Goodwife 218
WALLIS
  Henry 287
WALTERS
  Sarah 387
WALTON
  Elizabeth 138
  Nathaniel 138
  William 138
WAMPATUCKE
  Josias 281
WANTON
  Edward 34
  Hannah 34
  Hannah (Allen) 34
  Stephen 34
WARD
  Lawrence 11
WARDEN
  Peter 163
WARNER
  Augustine 334
WARREN
  Abigail 33, 478, 479
  Ann 307, 478, 479
  Arthur 78
  Elizabeth 107, 180, 478, 479
  Elizabeth (Walker) 43, 45, 110, 113, 272, 390, 478-480
  Jane (_____) (Clark) (Collier) 131
  Joseph 202, 267, 294, 363, 478, 479
  Mary 45, 478, 479
  Mercy 167
  Nathaniel 35, 131, 167, 478, 479
  Priscilla (Faunce) 202, 479
  Richard 33, 45, 47, 48, 107, 131, 146, 167, 179, 202, 207, 307, 477-480
  Sarah 146, 478, 479
  Sarah (Walker) 131, 478, 479
WASHBURN
  Elizabeth (Irish) 288, 482
  Elizabeth (Mitchell) 327, 482
  John 86, 288, 327, 417, 480-483
  Margery (Moore) 482
  Martha (Timbrell) (Stephens) 482
  Philip 288, 482
WATERMAN
  Joseph 34
  Mercy (Williams) 505, 506
  Resolved 505, 506
  Robert 263
WATSON
  Elizabeth 485
  Elizabeth (_____) 528
  Elkanah 485, 486
  George 28, 39, 246, 247, 292, 376, 415, 416, 483-487, 528
  John 28, 245, 246, 485, 487, 528
  Jonathan 486
  Mary 485, 487
  Mercy (Hedges) 486

Index of Surnames

Watson continued
  Phoebe 247, 415, 485, 487
  Phoebe (Hicks) 246, 247, 485
  Robert 486, 528
  Samuel 485
  Thomas 528
  _____ (Hicks) 28
WAY
  Thomas 260
WEAVER
  Anne (Green) 490
  Christopher 490
  Elizabeth 490
WEBB
  Ady 4, 367 see also ADEY, Webb
  _____ Mr. 108
WEBB *alias* HOLMES
  Margaret 268, 269
WEEKS
  Elizabeth 394
  John 417
  Judith (_____) 321
  Mercy (Robinson) 394
  Nicholas 321, 322
  William 394
WENTWORTH
  Mary 69, 344
  Thomas 69
WEST
  Francis 229, 435, 489
  Susanna (Soule) 435
  Twiford 432
WESTER
  Margaret 169
WESTON
  Andrew 491
  Edmund 167
  Elizabeth 138, 491-493
  Elizabeth (Weaver) 490
  Francis 56, 487-490

  Margaret (_____) 488, 489
  Mary 167
  Ralph 490
  Richard 491
  Thomas 138, 229, 230, 368, 373, 490-493
WETHERELL/WITHERILL
  Dorothy 288
  William 234, 288
WEYT
  Philip 117
WHELDEN
  Catherine 273
WHETCOMB
  John 468
WHISTON
  Abigail 494
  Abigail (Lombard) 494
  Bathsheba 495
  Increase 495
  John 214, 238, 493-495
  Joseph 493, 494
  Sarah 494
  Susanna 494
  Susanna (Hanford) 214, 238, 494
WHITE
  Abigail (_____) (Lord) 495
  Alexander 95, 96
  Bridget 95, 96, 393
  Catherine 95
  Edward 75
  Eleanor (_____) 95
  Elizabeth 368
  Emanuel 125, 190
  Frances 95, 96
  Frances (_____) (Hilton) 256, 257, 260
  Jane 95, 96
  John 141, 321
  Judith (Vassall) 495

White continued
 Mary 424
 Nicholas 368
 Peregrine 49, 50, 299, 495, 496
 Resolved 495, 496
 Richard 255-257, 260
 Sarah (Bassett) 50, 496
 Susanna (_____) 495, 496, 508
 William 50, 262, 280, 340, 459, 495, 496, 508, 509
WHITEHEAD
 Isaac 250
 Mary (_____) (Yates) (Higgins) 250
WHITMER
 Elizabeth (Banks) 87
 William 87
WHITNEY
 Patience (Morton) (Faunce) 202
 Thomas 36, 202
 Winifred 40
WHITTON/WHITON
 Thomas 233, 447
 Winifred (Haring) 233
WHITT
 Paul 323
WHITYARE
 Abraham 353
WIGGIN
 Jame 260
 James 257
 Magdalene (Hilton) 257, 260
WILDER
 Abiah 112
 Roger 96, 497
WILKINSON
 _____ Mr. 493

WILLARD
 Deborah 411
 George 411
WILLETT/WILLET
 Abigail (Collins) 500
 Alice (_____) 500
 Andrew 498, 499, 501
 Anna (Brown) 501
 David 501
 Elizabeth (Hunt) 500
 Grace (Frinck) 501
 Hester 499, 500
 Hezekiah 498, 499, 501
 James 498-500
 Joanna (Boyse) (Prudden) 500
 John 500
 Martha 500
 Mary 500
 Mary (Brown) 500
 Rebecca 500
 Samuel 498, 499, 501
 Sarah 500
 Susannah (Holbrook) 501
 Thomas 39, 63, 116, 118, 173, 248, 324, 352, 446, 452, 497-503
WILLIAMS
 Alice (Pemberton) 505
 Ann 527
 Anna 32
 Anna (_____) 32
 Daniel 505
 Elizabeth (Watson) 485
 Freeborn 505, 506
 George 355
 James 505
 John 32, 115, 241, 527-529
 Joseph 485, 506
 Lydia (Olney) 506
 Mary 505
 Mary (Bernard) 505

Index of Surnames

Williams continued
  Mercy 505, 506
  Providence 505
  Rebecca (Rhodes) (Power) 505
  Robert 506
  Roger 21, 22, 56, 171, 188, 218, 219, 270, 428, 489, 503-506
  Thomas 480, 506
WILLIAMSON see BREWSTER
WILLIS
  Amy (Glass) 264
  Elizabeth (Hodgkins) (Palmer) 351
  John 351
  Patience (Bonham) 267
  Richard 41, 264, 267, 409
  Robert 125
WILLOUGHBY
  Elizabeth 13
  Thomas 13
WILLS
  Rebecca (Pierce) 357, 358
  Samuel 358
WILSON
  Edmond 508
  John 393
WILTON
  Anne 133
WINES
  Anne (Eddy) 193, 197
  Barnabas 193, 197
WING
  Daniel 113
  John 163
  Miriam (Deane) 163
WINSLEY
  John 512

WINSLOW
  Benjamin 512, 514
  Damaris (Eames) 520
  Edmund 233
  Edward 67, 111, 132, 144, 145, 187, 219, 230, 231, 259, 270, 275, 299, 302, 329, 349-351, 432, 436, 452, 457, 495, 496, 502, 507-510, 512-514, 517, 520, 521
  Elizabeth 508, 509, 517
  Elizabeth (_____) 513
  Elizabeth (Barker) 508, 509
  Elizabeth (Hutchinson) 514
  Ellen 519, 520
  Ellen (Newton) (Adams) 2, 519, 520
  Faith (Miller) 520
  Gilbert 258, 259, 509-511, 514, 517, 520, 521
  Hannah 517
  Hannah (Briggs) 514
  Isaac 512, 514
  Job 519, 520
  John 1, 36, 52, 105, 189, 219, 239, 244, 259, 292, 413, 414, 454, 464, 507-515, 517, 521
  Jonathan 516, 517
  Joseph 512-514
  Josiah 352, 353, 378, 379, 508-510, 512, 514-519, 521
  Josias 36, 378, 445, 467
  Judith (_____) 513
  Kenelm 1, 2, 102, 103, 187, 344, 402, 416, 426, 509, 510, 512, 514, 517-521
  Magdalen (Oliver) 508, 510, 513, 517, 520
  Margaret 247, 517
  Margaret (Bourne) 516, 517
  Mary 513, 517

Winslow continued
  Mary (Chilton) 104, 105, 511-513
  Mary (Nowell) 514
  Mercy (Worden) 520
  Nathaniel 309, 519, 520
  Parnell 512, 513
  Penelope (Pelham) 508, 509
  Rebecca 517
  Ruth (_____) 520
  Ruth (Sargent) 517
  Samuel 513, 514
  Sarah 454, 513, 514
  Sarah (Hilton) 514
  Sarah (Lawrence) 514
  Susanna 513
  Susanna (_____) (White) 495, 496, 507, 508
WINSOR
  Mercy (Williams) (Waterman) 505
  Samuel 505
WINTHROP
  John 21, 53, 132, 193, 194, 219, 239, 262, 269, 270, 344, 347, 379, 381, 428, 502, 504
WISWALL
  _____ Mr. 403
WOLCOTT
  Anna 372
  Sarah 112
WOOD/ATWOOD
  Abigail 368
  Abigail (Dunham) 185
  Abigail (Jenny) 293-295
  Apphia (Bangs) (Knowles) 26, 27
  Esther 424
  Henry 219, 293, 295
  John 65, 317, 318
  Mary 65
  Sarah 294
  Sarah (Masterson) 317, 318
  Stephen 27, 184, 185
  Susanna 295
  _____ Goodman 339
WOODBURY
  John 208
  Peter 135
WOODMAN
  John 322
  Mary (Raynes) (Mendum) 321, 322
WOODWARD
  Sarah 193
WOODWORTH
  Abigail 522-524
  Benjamin 522-524
  Deborah (_____) 523
  Deborah (Daman) 523
  Ebenezer 524
  Elizabeth 522, 523
  Hannah (_____) 523
  Isaac 522, 524
  Joseph 522, 523
  Lydia (Standlake) 524
  Martha 522-524
  Mary 421, 522-524
  Mehetabel 522-524
  Sarah 522, 523
  Sarah (Stockbridge) 523
  Thomas 522, 523
  Walter 421, 521-524
WOOTON
  Jane (Conant) (Knowles) 55
  Philip 55
WORDEN
  Mary (_____) 520
  Mercy 520
WORMALL
  Esther 123, 186
  John 80

Index of Surnames

Wormall continued
  Joseph 186
  Josiah 80-82
  Lydia 81
  Miriam (_____) 186
  Phebe 81
  Remember (Brown) 80-82
WRIGHT
  George 109
  Hester (Cooke) 146, 147
  Joseph 373
  Priscilla (Carpenter) 93, 95,
    218, 219, 525, 526
  Richard 145-147
  Sarah 373
  William 93, 95, 218-220, 337,
    359, 524-526
WYATT
  John 426
WYRRALL
  Mary 69

YATES
  John 250
  Mary (_____) 250
YOUNG
  Abigail (Howland) 277
  John 27, 277
  Ruth (Cole) 27

NO SURNAME
  Canonicus 348
  Conbatant 231
  Hobbamock 231
  Jane 512
  Massasoit 231, 275, 454
  Pecksuot 455
  Penwatechet 318, 351
  Peter 113
  Pompino 151
  Simon 151

Tahanto 255
Tinsin 322

INDEX OF FIRST NAMES

AARON
  Bennett 53-55
  Crow 54
  Pratt 371, 373
  Savory 406-409
  Simonson 420, 421, 523
ABEL
  Huse 259
ABIAH
  Clark 112
  Wilder 112
ABIEL
  Everill 7
ABIGAIL
  Alden 8
  Andrews 475
  Balliou 185
  Barker 33
  Benjamin 193, 197
  Bryant 415
  Church 108
  Clark 112
  Cole 125
  Collins 500
  Crow 54
  Doane 174, 175
  Dunham 184, 185
  Eames 469
  Eddy 193, 197
  Elithorpe 355
  Hallett 8
  Hatch 241, 242
  Hewes 242
  Howland 277, 279
  Jenny 292, 293, 295
  Keene 307
  King 242
  Lindall 475
  Little 307
  Lombard 494
  Lord 495
  Lothrop 112, 175
  Pickworth 353, 355
  Pratt 368
  Rogers 31, 33
  Shaw 415
  Smith 197
  Snow 33, 479
  Stockbridge 469
  Thaxter 108
  Turner 469
  Wadsworth 475, 476
  Waite 476
  Warren 33, 478, 479
  Whiston 494
  White 495
  Willett 500
  Wood 293-295, 368
  Wood/Atwood 185
  Woodworth 522-524
  Young 277
  _____ 125, 197, 277, 495
ABNER
  Ordway 388
ABRAHAM
  Blish 19
  Blush 19, 331
  Cummings 373
  Jackson 300
  Pierce 110, 167, 356-359, 367
  Samson 167, 277, 343, 445
  Whityare 353
ADAM
  Goodwin 488, 489

ADDY
  Webb 4, 367
ADONIRON
  Veren 136
AGNES/ANNIS
  Beale 257
  Carpenter 94, 220
  Clarke 133, 137
  Conant 133, 137
  Cooper 156, 461
  Erdley 465
  Fuller 94, 220
  Hilton 257
  Jones 411
  Savory 406-408, 414
  Tilley 156, 404, 461, 462
  Tracy 465
  _____ 407
ALEXANDER
  Carpenter 64, 93, 94, 220, 336
  Kennedy/Canedy 19
  Miller 191
  Standish 7, 8, 167, 179, 182, 403, 452, 453
  White 95, 96
ALICE
  Baker 357, 358
  Barker 32-34
  Bradford 63-65, 94, 174, 219, 327, 376, 410
  Carpenter 64, 94, 439, 443
  Church 107, 438, 439
  Clark 112
  Collard 237
  Cosford 396
  Davis 461
  Eddy 197
  Freeman 365
  Fuller 220
  Glascock 220
  Hallett 112

Hanson 64
Hatherly 237
Higgins 251
Mitchell 327
Mullins 339, 340
Newbold/Newbould 251
Nichols 112
Padduck 197
Pemberton 505
Pierce 357, 358
Pope 365
Richards 65
Rickdall 389
Rigsdale 389
Rogers 396
Shaw 408, 414, 415
Snow 32-34
Southworth 64, 94, 107, 439, 443
Thorpe 33, 460, 461
Willett 500
Williams 505
_____ 33, 340, 389, 408, 415, 460, 500
AMY
  Doggett 192, 193
  Eddy 192, 193
  Glass 264
  Holman 263-265
  Willis 264
ANDREW
  Clark 111, 112
  Hallett 8, 480
  Mansfield 138
  Ring 3, 219, 263, 273, 325, 337, 389-391
  Weston 491
  Willett 498, 499, 501
ANN/ANNA/ANNE
  Alden 9
  Annable 17-19

Ann continued
 Barker 32, 304, 372, 527
 Bell 340
 Bennett 55
 Blossom 58, 60, 399
 Briggs 78
 Brown 501
 Bursell 411
 Chandler 98, 99, 101
 Churchman 396
 Clark 18
 Conant 133
 Cooke 152, 431
 Cooper 337
 Cottle 394
 Crackstone 157, 158
 Doane 175
 Eddy 193, 197
 Elcock 18
 Elsdon 58, 399
 Erdley 465
 Fallowell 364
 Flavell 204
 Fogg 209, 210
 Gray 512
 Green 490
 Griswold 372
 Hilton 257
 Hutchinson 504
 James 469
 Jenny 295
 Killam 354
 Lawrence 449, 450
 Lettice 295
 Little 306, 307, 479
 Mason 260
 Morton 337
 Mullins 340
 Pickworth 353-355
 Plummer 39, 359, 403
 Pope 364
 Pratt 372
 Robinson 394
 Rogers 396
 Rowley 58, 399
 Samson 39, 359, 403
 Savory 406-408, 414
 Sears 411
 Sibley 354
 Smalley 423, 424
 Smith 157, 158
 Snell 9
 Snow 151, 152, 431
 Sprague 448-450
 Tracy 465
 Turner 469
 Walden 424
 Warren 307, 478, 479
 Weaver 490
 Willett 501
 Williams 32, 527
 Wilton 133
 Wines 193, 197
 Wolcott 372
 _____ 32, 55, 78, 175, 204, 210, 257, 304, 340, 354, 372, 394, 407
ANNABEL
 Blossom 58
 _____ 58
ANNABLE
 Kennedy/Canedy 19
ANNIS see AGNES
ANTHONY
 Annable 16-20, 61, 386, 400
 Dike 143, 169-171, 489
 Dix 171
 Savory 405, 407-409
 Snow 33, 34, 106, 376, 479
 Sprague 46
 Stoddard 72
 Thatcher 282, 411

ANTOINE
  Fetcher 94
APPHIA
  Bangs 27
  Freeman 379, 381
  Knowles 27
  Prence 379, 381
  Quick 379
  Wood 26, 27
ARNOLD
  Allard 248
ARTHUR
  Beale 257
  Howland 278, 283, 320, 328, 378-380
  Warren 78
AUGUSTINE
  Walker 479
  Warner 334
AUSTIN/AUSTEN
  Killam 354
  Nicholas 344

BARBARA
  Standish 451-453

BARNABAS
  Lothrop 112
  Wines 193, 197
BARTHOLOMEW
  Allerton 11, 13, 14
  Roes 334
BATHSHEBA
  Doggett 367
  Dunham 495
  Fay 369
  Holmes 268, 269
  Pratt 367-369
  Roice 368
  Whiston 495
  _____ 367

BENAJAH
  Dunham 184, 186, 368
  Pratt 186, 367, 368, 416
BENJAMIN
  Balch 135, 143
  Bartlett 38, 46, 47, 130, 294, 295, 403
  Browne 332
  Chandler 98, 99, 101
  Church 107, 439
  Eaton 189, 406
  Eddy 193
  Fairfax 13
  Foster 44
  Higgins 27, 250, 251
  Pickworth 353, 355
  Samson 403
  Savory 407, 408, 414
  Soule 436
  Vermayes 65
  Winslow 512, 514
  Woodworth 522-524
BENNANIAH
  Pratt 165
BENNET/BENNETT
  Eddy 197
  Ellis 197
  Morecock 425
  Morgan 335
  Smith 425
BETHIA/BETHIAH
  Bangs 27
  Cooke 152, 233
  Goodhue 387
  Grafton 387
  Hall 26, 27
  Harding 151, 152, 233
  Howland 282
  Jones 387
  Little 308
  Lothrop 387, 388

Bethia continued
  Ray 387
  Thatcher 282
  Thomas 308
  _____ 387
BRIDGET
  Fuller 181, 189, 217, 218, 220
  Lee 220
  Palmer 350, 400
  Robinson 96, 393
  Sirkman 220
  White 95, 96, 393
  _____ 181

CALEB
  Church 107, 108
  Conant 137
  Eddy 196-198
  Hobart 107
  Hopkins 271-273
  More 332, 333
  Pierce 358
  Samson 402-404
CASPER
  Barnaart 205
CATHERINE/KATHERINE
  Banks 209
  Barnardiston 209
  Carver 95, 96
  Collier 131
  Fallowell 364
  Finney 364
  Fletcher 204
  Goulder 197
  Hamby 514
  Hopkins 273
  Horton 137
  Hutchinson 514
  Leggatt 95, 96
  Marbury 504
  More 329, 330, 332, 333

  Satchfield 137
  Scott 504
  Whelden 273
  White 95
  _____ 197
CECILY
  Bassett 51
  Light 51
CHARITY
  Alford 169, 170
  Dike 170
CHARLES
  Chancey/Chauncy 234, 236, 245, 246, 293
  Church 108
  Standish 451-454
  Stockbridge 363, 469
CHILTON
  Latham 513
CHRISTIAN
  Billington 57, 188, 352
  Bridges 72
  Chilton 104
  Conant 333
  Eaton 57, 187, 188, 352
  Eire 72
  Hunter 332
  More 331-333
  Penn 57, 188, 352
  Pierce 72
  Stoddard 72
CHRISTOPHER
  Blakewood 236
  Conant 133, 134, 138
  Crow 55
  Foster 215
  Goodwin 72
  Lattimore 333
  Levett 229
  Martin 302, 315, 316, 383

Christopher continued
  Wadsworth 127, 473-476, 478, 525
  Weaver 490
CLEMENT
  Briggs 76-79, 244, 248, 254, 370, 388
  Campion 259
CONSTANCE
  Hopkins 273-275, 431, 432
  Snow 272, 273, 429-432
CONSTANT
  Freeman 439
  Southworth 8, 64, 65, 94, 108, 114, 130, 131, 298, 337, 379, 437-440, 442, 443
CORDELIA
  Bowes 65
  May 65
CUDBERT see GODBERT

DAMARIS
  Cooke 147, 274
  Eames 520
  Hopkins 147, 271-274
  Winslow 520
DANIEL
  Cole 25-27, 127-131, 176, 520
  Crocker 87
  Doane 174, 176
  Dunham 184-186
  Hicks 248
  Pratt 371, 372
  Ray 17, 254, 385-388
  Rumble 224, 225, 388
  Salmon 161, 162
  Turner 468, 469
  Williams 505
  Wing 113
DAVID
  Alden 6-8, 10, 440
  Briggs 77, 78
  Fogg 208-210
  Lake 363
  Meade 192
  Mendum 321, 323, 324
  Thomson 258, 466
  Willett 501
DEBORAH
  Annable 19
  Barker 32
  Brooks 523
  Church 108
  Cooke 152
  Coombs 155
  Daman 523
  Doty 180
  Ellis 180
  Hopkins 152, 271-273, 391
  Morton 155, 442
  Paddock 410, 411
  Perry 364
  Pope 363, 364
  Ring 273, 391
  Sears 411
  Soule 435
  Stetson 523
  Willard 411
  Woodworth 523
  _____ 108, 435, 523
DEGORY
  Priest 14, 155, 226-228, 372, 374, 382, 383
DELIVERANCE
  Bennett 55
  Crow 55
DERMOT
  Smith 197
DESIRE
  Annable 18, 19
  Barker 19
  Cushman 282

Index of First Names 595

Desire continued
  Doty 178, 179, 182, 418, 453
  Gorham 280, 282
  Gray 440
  Holmes 179, 182, 453
  Howland 280, 282
  Minter 96, 324
  Sherman 179, 182, 418, 453
  Southworth 440
  Standish 179, 182, 453
DIGORIUS see also DEGORY
  Prust 382
DIXEY
  Bull 170
DOLOR
  Davis 90
DORCAS
  Bassett 51
  Bonney 402, 403
  Earle 449
  Folger 373
  Joyce 51
  Pratt 373
  Samson 403
  Sprague 449, 450
DOROTHY
  Bradford 64, 65
  Browne 282
  Clark 112
  Eaton 188
  Gray 112
  Irish 288
  Jones 411
  Lettice 112
  May 64, 65
  Sears 410, 411
  Smith 188
  Temple 267, 275
  Witherill 288
  _____ 188

EBENEZER
  Woodworth 524
EDMOND/EDMUND/EDMAN
  Batter 169, 489
  Briggs 77
  Bruff 102
  Chandler 36, 86, 97-102, 250, 252, 298
  Eaton 188
  Eddenden 213
  Flood 205
  Freeman 365, 380, 498
  Greenleaf 256
  Hobart 28, 65, 310, 312, 313
  Margesson 315
  Tilley 461
  Tilson 423
  Weston 167
  Wilson 508
  Winslow 233
EDWARD
  Altham 295
  Ashley 20, 161, 352, 486, 501
  Bancroft 527
  Bangs 23-29, 151, 175, 247, 251, 299, 424, 446, 527
  Brewster 69
  Buckley 376
  Bumpas 85-88, 98, 168, 481
  Burcham 89
  Burcher 88, 89, 218
  Collins 500
  Dennis 388
  Doty 24, 55, 56, 152, 177-182, 187, 202, 267, 275, 305, 367, 412, 418, 425, 453, 457, 482
  Draper 209
  Edwards 36
  Fitz Randolph 59
  Foster 212-214, 224, 238, 302
  Fuller 215-218, 220, 496

Edward continued
  Godfrey 323
  Gray 112, 286, 308, 402, 485, 512, 513
  Grove 331
  Hall 6
  Harrington 75
  Hilton 257, 258
  Holman 36, 235, 249, 263-265, 296
  Holmar 265
  Hutchinson 514
  Jenkins 214, 237, 238, 494
  Leister 180, 304, 305
  Lester 275
  Lewis 121
  Mitchell 326, 327
  Pitford 355
  Rainsford 50
  Shaw 112, 113, 412, 413
  Small 147, 148
  Southworth 64, 94, 158, 288, 337, 438-440, 443
  Stephens 418
  Thompson 459, 496
  Tilley 156, 404, 461-463
  Wanton 34
  White 75
  Winslow 67, 111, 132, 144, 145, 187, 219, 230, 231, 259, 270, 275, 299, 302, 329, 349-351, 432, 436, 452, 457, 495, 496, 502, 507-510, 512-514, 517, 520, 521
EGLIN
  Downe 214, 238, 393, 494
  Hanford 214, 236, 238, 494
  Hatherly 214, 238, 393, 494
  Sillis 214
ELEANOR/ELINOR
  Armstrong 57
  Baker 512
  Billington 56, 57, 176
  Cushman 158
  Hubbard 158
  Rogers 396
  White 95
  _____ 57, 95, 396
ELEAZER/ELIEZER
  Cobb 120, 121, 285
  Dunham 495
  Hopkins 274
ELIAKIM
  Higgins 251, 252
ELIAS
  Irish 288
  Stileman 487
  Story 457, 509
ELISHA
  Hedge 42
  Wadsworth 476
ELIZABETH
  Adams 2
  Alden 5, 7, 9
  Allen 277, 278
  Allerton 12, 13
  Annable 19
  Banks 87
  Barker 508
  Barlow 155
  Barnaart 205
  Barnes 39
  Bartholomew 331
  Bartlett 46, 47, 49-51
  Bennett 55
  Blossom 59
  Bourne 517
  Bowen 220
  Briggs 77-79
  Brooks 509
  Buck 99
  Bullock 197

Elizabeth continued
  Bumpas 86, 87
  Burgess 50
  Bursley 91, 281
  Carver 179
  Chandler 99
  Chilton 104, 107
  Church 107, 479
  Clap 91
  Cobb 122
  Cogswell 317
  Colclough 13
  Collier 127, 131, 439
  Conant 136-138, 491-493
  Cooke 147, 151, 152, 163, 179, 391
  Coombs 155
  Cowles 218
  Crow 115
  Curwen 509
  Deane 152, 163, 390, 391
  Delano 167, 342
  Dickenson/Dickerson 247, 280-282
  Doty 178-180, 182
  Dunham 186
  Dwelly 420, 421
  Eaton 188
  Eddy 196-198
  Ellis 197
  England 179, 180
  Everill 7
  Eyre/Eyer 12
  Fairfax 13
  Faunce 203
  Fisher 273
  Fitz Randolph 59
  Flavell 204
  Fletcher 205
  Foster 214, 237
  Freeman 197
  Fuller 220, 399
  Gallup 440
  Godbertson 227
  Goodspeed 91
  Griswold 372
  Hall 368
  Hanford 214, 238
  Hedges 39
  Hewett 214
  Hicks 247, 248, 282
  Higgins 251
  Hilton 256
  Hoar 143
  Hobart 107
  Hodgkins 351
  Hopkins 271-274, 447
  Howland 64, 91, 247, 277, 278, 280-283, 377-380, 442, 443, 463
  Hull 251
  Hunt 500
  Hutchinson 514
  Irish 287, 288, 482
  Jones 411
  Kendall 227
  Kennedy/Canedy 19
  Lettice 147
  Mansfield 138
  Masterson 317
  Mitchell 327, 328, 482
  Morgan 247
  Nash 343
  Nichols 220
  Oliver 251
  Overzee 13
  Pabodie/Paybody 7, 10
  Palmer 351
  Parsons 180
  Phillips 7
  Pickworth 355
  Pierce 72

Elizabeth continued
  Pike 59
  Pratt 368, 372
  Prence 380, 381
  Ray 214
  Reynor 443
  Ring 163, 391
  Risley 288
  Robinson 394
  Rogers 251, 372, 397, 431
  Rose 86
  Rowley 399
  Rowse 179
  Samson 167, 403, 404
  Savory 288
  Shurtleff 147
  Simonson 421
  Snow 431
  Soule 436
  Southworth 131, 282, 438-440, 443
  Sprague 46
  Sprout 403
  Standish 167
  Symons 343
  Taylor 122
  Thatcher 411
  Tilley 282, 283, 461-463
  Tilson 186
  Tufts 72
  Turner 468, 470, 471
  Twining 163
  Vaughn 283
  Voorchoren 205
  Wade 214, 238
  Walker 434, 436, 479
  Walton 138
  Warren 43, 45, 107, 110, 113, 180, 478-480
  Washburn 288, 327, 482
  Watson 485, 528
  Weaver 490
  Weeks 394
  Weston 138, 491-493
  White 368
  Whitmer 87
  Willett 500
  Williams 485
  Willis 351
  Willoughby 13
  Winslow 508, 509, 513, 514, 517
  Woodworth 522, 523
  _____ 2, 50, 55, 72, 78, 155, 180, 188, 196, 204, 288, 331, 355, 403, 431, 461, 462, 513, 528
ELKANAH
  Watson 485, 486
ELLEN
  Adams 1, 2, 520
  Baker 520
  Hatherly 237
  More 509
  Newton 2, 344, 520
  Winslow 2, 519, 520
  _____ 237
ELNATHAN
  Chancey 246
EMANUEL/EMMANUEL
  Altham 88, 223, 295
  Downing 210
  White 125, 190
EMETT
  Bursell 411
  _____ 411
ENGELTGEN
  Gilten 104
  Nelson 104
ENOCH
  Hunt 343
  Lunt 343

EPHRAIM
  Doane 174, 176
  Hewett 214
  Hicks 244-248, 282, 443
  Kempton 299, 301
  Little 306-308
  Morton 45, 299, 301, 336, 337
  Tinkham 80, 84, 238, 239, 289, 402
ESEK
  Annable 19
ESTHER
  Barnes 40
  Cole 125
  Cooke 145-147
  Delano 166-168, 435
  Dewsbery 166
  Dunham 185
  Flint 500
  Mahieu 146
  Rickard/Ricket/Rickett 38-40
  Samson 167, 343, 435
  Smalley 424
  Soule 167, 343, 435
  Willett 499, 500
  Wood 424
  Wormall 123, 186
  Wright 146, 147
  _____ 125, 343
EXERCISE
  Conant 136-138
EXPERIENCE
  Briggs 78
  Cobb 122
  Mitchell 146, 194, 195, 266, 276, 306, 324-329, 336, 364, 410, 415, 482
  Robinson 394
  Rogers 394
  _____ 78, 394

EZEKIEL
  Fogg 208-210
  Gardner 191, 193
EZRA
  Perry 364

FAITH
  Clarke 178
  Doty 178, 182
  Miller 520
  Phillips 178
  Winslow 520
FEAR
  Allerton 11, 13, 68
  Baker 237, 394
  Brewster 13, 67, 68, 309
  Robinson 237, 394
FERDINANDO
  Gorges 229, 260, 347, 492
FRANCES
  Adams 2
  Cole 128, 131
  Fuller 215
  Gilson 224, 225
  Hilton 256, 259, 260
  Palmer 349, 350
  Vassall 2
  White 95, 96, 256, 257, 260
  _____ 128, 131, 215, 225, 256, 350
FRANCIS
  Baker 357
  Barker 31, 32
  Billington 56, 57, 187, 188, 352, 370
  Brewster 69
  Cooke 144-149, 152, 179, 201, 274, 325, 326, 369, 419, 479, 484
  Coombs 155, 372

Francis continued
  Eaton 4, 57, 187-189, 304, 336, 352, 476, 518, 519
  Godfrey 102, 438, 442
  Goole 125
  Goulder 197
  Griswold 65
  Johnson 143, 170
  Kirby 239
  Lasle 117
  Sprague 51, 181, 447-450
  Walker 434, 436
  West 229, 435, 489
  Weston 56, 487-490
FREEBORN
  Clarke 505
  Hart 505, 506
  Williams 505, 506

GABRIEL
  Fallowell 293, 364
  Meade 192, 193
GEORGE
  Armstrong 57
  Barlow 114
  Baxter 116
  Boare 272
  Bonham 151, 202, 337, 363, 445, 484
  Bunker 370
  Clarke 181
  Colclough 14
  Collen 118
  Cosford 396
  Crisp 25, 176
  Curwen 509
  Foster 215, 218
  Holmes 118
  Jones 411
  Kempton 301
  Lewis 121, 446, 467
  Lorance 190
  Ludlow 261
  Monk 259
  Morton 94, 202, 203, 301, 325, 336-338, 391
  Partridge 26, 465
  Patrich 245
  Phillips 194, 379
  Pollard 132, 438
  Ropes 208
  Russell 213
  Soule 85, 244, 298, 421, 432-436, 438, 442, 509, 520
  Sutton 237
  Vaughn 283
  Watson 28, 39, 246, 247, 292, 376, 415, 416, 483-487, 528
  Willard 411
  Williams 355
  Wright 109
GERSHOM
  Cobb 120, 121, 285
  Hall 27
GERTRUDE
  Bennister 286
  Hurst 285, 286
GILBERT
  Brooks 458
  Winslow 258, 259, 509-511, 514, 517, 520, 521
GILES/GYLES
  Gilbert 484
  Hopkins 152, 271-275
  Rickard/Ricket/Rickett 150, 184, 186, 250, 264, 285, 361, 365, 367, 395, 445
GODBERT
  Godbertson 14, 36, 154, 155, 162, 163, 176, 226-228, 252, 369, 370, 372, 382

Index of First Names 601

GRACE
  Cole 475
  Dimond 323
  Fogg 210
  Frinck 501
  Wadsworth 474, 475
  Willett 501
  ____ 210, 475
GUYDO
  Bayley 287

HANNAH
  Allen 34
  Annable 17, 18, 61
  Baker 357
  Bangs 26, 27, 175, 423, 424
  Barker 34
  Barnes 37, 39
  Bartlett 46, 364
  Boreman 61
  Bosworth 280-282
  Bridges 72
  Briggs 78, 514
  Bumpas 86, 87, 98
  Burman 18
  Churchill 360, 361
  Clark 112
  Cobb 120, 121, 285
  Collier 130
  Crow 517
  Cugley 248
  Damman 395
  Damon 224, 225, 528
  Doane 26, 27, 175
  Dunham 186
  Eddy 197
  Glass 357
  Griswold 112
  Hanford 238
  Hayward 326, 327
  Higgins 251

  Holmes 402, 403
  Howland 282
  Lewis 121
  Little 307, 308
  Mayo 380, 446
  Miller 516
  Mitchell 327, 328
  Newberry 238
  Packard 78
  Pierce 357
  Pontus 361
  Pope 46, 364
  Pratt 368
  Prence 380, 446
  Randall 469
  Rickard/Ricket/Rickett 186, 361, 432
  Rogers 251, 396
  Samson 403, 404
  Scudder 27, 357
  Sherman 418
  Smalley 26, 424
  Snow 432
  Sparrow 377, 379, 380, 446
  Spooner 368
  Sturtevant 517
  Tilden 307
  Turner 469
  Veren 136
  Wait 403
  Wanton 34
  Winslow 514, 517
  Woodworth 523
  ____ 72, 86, 98, 186, 357, 396, 403, 418, 523
HATEVELL
  Nutter 259
HELP
  Terry 204
HENRY
  Alden 9, 10

Henry continued
  Andrews 475
  Bartholomew 331
  Bayley 135
  Blague 33
  Churchill 179
  Clarke 113
  Cobb 118-122, 185, 224, 286,
    298, 398, 446
  Coggan 301, 395
  Dengayne 71
  Ewell 18, 468
  Flint 500
  Haggat 136
  Howland 176, 233, 275-279,
    282, 283, 402
  Jacob 297
  Kenning 257
  Merrick 30, 32
  Palmer 350, 400
  Roads 334
  Rowley 58, 350, 398-400, 486
  Samson 38, 39, 156, 306, 359,
    401-404, 462, 519
  Saunders 126
  Shrimpton 331
  Sirkman 220
  Vane 171
  Wallis 287
  Wood 219, 293, 295
HEPZIBAH
  Cole 176
  Crisp 176
  Doane 176
  Doggett 196
  Eddy 196
HERBERT
  Pelham 508
HESTER see ESTHER
HEZEKIAH
  Keene 307

  Usher 426
  Willett 498, 499, 501
HILLIER
  Veren 137
HOPE
  Chipman 122, 280, 282
  Cobb 122
  Howland 282
  Huckins 122
HUAN
  Standish 456, 457
HUGH
  Cole 38, 124, 125, 263
  Goodyear 60, 317
  Gunnison 321, 323
  Parsons 179
  Stacy 450
  Tilley 253
HUMILITY
  Cooper 156, 157, 404, 462
  Dunham 185, 186
HUMPHREY
  Davenport 306
  Johnson 241
  Turner 466-470

ICHABOD
  Paddock 410, 411
  Samson 342
INCREASE
  Clap 91
  Nowell 256, 310, 514
  Whiston 495
INGLE
  Chilton 104
ISAAC
  Allerton 10-16, 67, 68, 70,
    116-118, 132, 145, 154, 155,
    159, 227, 228, 271, 292, 382,
    395, 498
  Barker 31, 32, 34, 378-380

Isaac continued
  Bumpas 87
  Doty 179, 182
  Fitz Randolph 252
  Holmes 182
  Howland 280, 281, 283
  Hull 135, 136
  Little 306-308
  Pierce 357, 358
  Pope 363-365
  Robinson 96, 97, 213, 214, 225, 237, 238, 391-395
  Smalley 423, 424
  Steadman 192
  Sternes 190
  Whitehead 250
  Winslow 512, 514
  Woodworth 522, 524

ISABEL/ISABELLA
  Chandler 102, 104
  Chilton 102, 104
  Simpkins 269

ISRAEL
  Holmes 179
  Meade 192
  Robinson 394

JABEZ
  Barker 31
  Browne 282
  Howland 280-282
  Snow 430, 431

JACOB
  Blakeway 329
  Bumpas 87
  Cooke 145-147, 179, 274, 376
  Mitchell 306, 327, 363, 364
  Robinson 394

JADIAH
  Higgins 251

JAEL
  Bradford 65
  Hobart 65

JAMES
  Adams 1, 2
  Barker 34
  Barnaby 44-46
  Bates 311
  Bede 137
  Bennett 55
  Bishop 31
  Brown 281
  Browne 282, 498
  Burroughs 108
  Bursell 411
  Chilton 102-105, 513, 515
  Clark 111, 112, 123
  Cobb 120, 121, 285, 446
  Cole 44, 113, 122-126, 171
  Collier 131
  Cudworth 214, 278, 453, 486
  Davis 417, 484
  Doughty 469
  Everill 7, 8
  Glass 87, 165, 166, 264, 301, 360, 361, 483
  Glyn 14
  Hindes 331
  Howland 64
  Hurst 121, 266, 268, 284-286
  Knowles 113
  Lendall 98, 440, 475
  Lovell 370
  Luxford 125, 270, 447
  Mathews 25
  Muchmore 322
  Nash 343, 420, 421
  Penn 269
  Pierce 359
  Rand 385
  Ray 214
  Samson 402, 403

James continued
  Shaw 125, 327, 413, 415
  Sherley 88, 223, 235, 508
  Smith 77
  Steward 457
  Thomas 388
  Walker 486
  Wiggin 257, 260
  Willett 498-500
  Williams 505

JAN
  Delano 166
  Oghden 117
  Vincent 382

JAN JANS
  Vermout 205

JANE
  Adams 2
  Annable 17, 18
  Bassett 51
  Bennett 53-55, 138
  Chilton 104
  Clark 130, 131
  Collier 130, 131, 133, 478
  Conant 55
  Cooke 145, 146, 326, 328
  Coombs 155
  Crumpton 332
  Delano 166-168
  Faunce 202
  Fletcher 205
  Fuller 216
  Gilbert 51
  Hatch 418
  James 2
  Kempton 202
  Knowles 55, 138
  Lothrop 216
  Mason 137
  Mitchell 146, 326, 328
  More 332
  Moumford 18
  Nelson 202
  Pope 155
  Prence 380, 431
  Rossiter 51
  Sherman 418
  Snow 377-380, 431
  Truant/Trewant 481
  Warren 131
  White 95, 96
  Wooton 55
  _____ 131, 202, 332, 481, 512

JAPHETT
  Turner 524

JASPER
  More 96, 329, 330

JEAN/JEANE
  Gunn 328
  Harman 179
  Doty 179

JEDEDIAH
  Allen 278

JEFFREY
  Hanford 214, 238, 494
  Massie 169, 489

JEMIMA
  Bursley 91

JENNEKEN
  Fetcher 94
  Richeman 94

JEREMIAH
  Hatch 241, 242
  Holman 373
  Howes 378, 379, 381
  Smith 197

JEREMY
  Sheires 259

JOAN
  Allen 78, 79
  Allerton 12, 13
  Andrews 260

Index of First Names

Joan continued
  Baker 23
  Barnes 38, 39
  Boyse 500
  Bridger 339
  Briggs 78, 79
  Bursley 90, 91
  Church 108
  Conant 138
  Davis 90
  Dimmock 90
  Eddy 192
  Hathaway 365
  Hewes 241-243
  Hilton 260
  Hull 90
  Hurst 462
  Joy 107
  Meade 192
  Mullins 339
  Pope 365
  Prudden 500
  Rogers 462
  Sprague 108
  Swinnerton 13
  Tilley 462
  Tilson 37
  Willett 500
  ____ 23, 37, 39, 192, 242
JOB
  Cole 25, 126-128, 130, 131, 474
  Hawkins 269
  Winslow 519, 520
JOEL
  Chilton 104
JOHN
  Adams 1, 2, 344, 520
  Alden 4-10, 113, 167, 245, 268, 308, 328, 340, 417, 421, 439, 440, 442, 453, 456, 527
  Alford 169, 170
  Allen 195, 527
  Allerton 16, 199
  Almy 44, 124, 125, 264
  Arnold 132
  Arthur 508
  Atwood 128, 173, 176, 233
  Baker 22, 358
  Balch 138, 143
  Balden 132
  Bangs 24-26, 28, 245, 246, 300, 424, 487
  Banks 209
  Barker 19, 30, 32, 33, 155, 304, 372, 417, 527-529
  Barnes 1, 22, 35-42, 47, 97, 114, 125, 126, 154, 235, 244, 249, 263, 264, 359, 376, 426, 433, 445
  Bass 7-9
  Beale 507
  Beals 185
  Beauchamp 20, 235
  Beaven 52
  Benjamin 193, 197
  Bennett 56
  Bigelow 71
  Billington 56-58, 93, 188, 344, 352, 459
  Bond 486
  Bower 3
  Bowman 62
  Brabrook 71
  Bradford 63, 65, 474
  Bridge 88, 89
  Briggs 77-79
  Brown 76, 80-82, 84, 85, 98, 147, 176, 197, 198, 226, 233, 499-501
  Buck 99, 202
  Bumpas 86

John continued
  Bundy 102
  Bursley 89-92
  Cannon 93, 459
  Carew 320
  Carman 93
  Carver 11, 95-97, 158, 159, 188, 283, 304, 315, 318, 324, 329, 330, 339, 395, 497
  Chandler 99, 101
  Chew 219
  Chipman 122, 282
  Churchill 165, 167, 179, 360, 361
  Churchwell 250
  Clark 111, 112
  Cobb 120, 121, 285
  Coggen 395
  Cogswell 317
  Cole 125, 127, 128, 131, 431
  Collier 130, 131
  Combe 36, 227, 369, 370
  Conant 134, 136, 137, 492
  Cooke 43, 145-149, 188, 358, 370, 373, 374, 376, 404, 478, 479
  Coomb 11, 153-156, 173, 372, 375, 382
  Cooper 95, 241, 432, 526
  Crackstone 157, 158
  Crocker 90
  Crow 54, 56
  Damon 224, 225, 395, 523, 524, 528
  Davis 323
  Deacon 161, 162, 352
  Delano 165-168
  Dickenson/Dickerson 247, 282
  Dimond 323
  Dingley 107

Doane 25, 27, 70, 83, 150, 154, 171-177, 188, 227, 232, 233, 247, 263, 366, 426, 498
Doggett 194, 196, 367
Doty 178, 179, 182
Dowse 214
Dunford 41
Dunham 121, 167, 182-186, 194, 360-362, 367, 368, 416
Eaton 188
Eddy 23, 189-194, 196, 197, 254, 388
Edwards 101
Eliot 500
Ellis 197
Endicott 73, 142, 217, 219, 345, 425, 487, 503
Ewer 477
Faunce 179, 201-203, 245, 267, 298, 337, 442, 479, 528
Fisher 313
Fisk 190
Fletcher 204
Floyd 236
Fogg 208-210
Ford 211
Freeman 114, 151, 376-380
Gilbert 484
Goodman 67, 82, 228, 229
Gorham 282
Greemes 362
Hall 27
Hampden 231, 232, 373
Hanmore 402, 403
Hansford 490
Harmon 3, 147
Harrison 71, 72
Haskall 434, 436
Hathaway 365
Hathorne 386, 387
Haward 37

John continued
  Hayward 327
  Hewes 240-242
  Hicks 247
  Higginson 332
  Hill 254, 388
  Hilton 257, 260, 261
  Hocking 261, 262, 283, 289, 408, 428
  Holland 214
  Holmes 65, 156, 181, 202, 203, 265-267, 275, 325, 436
  Holt 12
  Hooke 14, 271
  Horne 331
  Howland 5, 10, 49, 76, 91, 96, 161, 245, 247, 261, 277-284, 293, 338, 358, 443, 463, 525
  Huckins 122
  Humphrey 134, 141
  Irish 261, 287-289, 439, 453, 482
  Jenkins 25, 393, 477
  Jenny 1, 3, 46, 89, 100, 219, 253, 264, 265, 291-296, 327, 364, 424, 484, 518
  Jones 306, 307
  Jourdaine 37, 265
  Joy 47
  Joyce 51
  Kerman 123
  Killam 354
  King 242
  Kirman 93
  Knight 72
  Knowles 27
  Knowlton 333
  Langmore 302, 316
  Leach 137, 138
  Lothrop 16, 112, 119, 175, 213, 214, 216, 224, 234-236, 238, 393, 398
  Lowle 208
  Luvet 388
  Luxford 181
  Lyford 58, 66, 93, 139, 140, 255, 258, 309-313, 345-347, 395, 455
  Magoone 30
  Manter 394
  Marion 191, 192
  Marshall 38
  Mason 347
  Masters 354
  Maverick 13
  May 65
  Miller 517
  Mitchell 326, 327
  Morton 37, 155, 300, 336, 337, 391
  Moses 304
  Mullins 339
  Myles 498, 499
  Mynard 125, 521
  Nelson 46
  Newcomen 57, 344
  Nichols 220
  Nicolls 111
  Norman 355, 356
  Norton 428
  Oldham 58, 68, 71-75, 140, 141, 258, 310-312, 345-348, 455
  Paddock 499
  Pease 488
  Peterson 435
  Phillips 30, 178, 304, 320
  Pickworth 353-356
  Pierce 356, 358, 491
  Pike 59

John continued
  Pococke 125
  Polin 170
  Pope 365
  Pratt 369, 371, 372
  Prescott 331
  Price 465
  Putnam 386, 387
  Rayment 135
  Rees 76
  Reyner/Rener 3, 98, 172, 245, 294, 375
  Rickard/Ricket/Rickett 40, 151, 300
  Rigby 469
  Rigsdale 389
  Robinson 96, 237, 262, 317, 393, 394, 491
  Rogers 33, 36, 77, 97, 246, 372, 396, 397
  Rouse 41, 98, 178
  Rowden 388
  Rowe 320
  Rowland 397
  Rowse 179, 287
  Russell 165
  Saffin 498, 500
  Salmon 162
  Samson 402, 403
  Sawyer 32, 307
  Sayles 505
  Scottow 108
  Scudder 27, 357
  Shaw 37, 113, 177, 178, 181, 225, 327, 370, 408, 413-416, 484, 485
  Sherman 417, 418
  Sibley 355
  Simonson 420, 421
  Smalley 26, 176, 228, 233, 250, 252, 300, 422-424, 431
  Smith 28, 153, 155, 181, 244, 257, 296, 370, 424, 425
  Snow 176, 424, 430, 431
  Soule 167, 342, 343, 420, 421, 434-436, 520
  Sparrow 446
  Sprague 49, 51, 123, 448-450
  Stacy 334
  Standish 452, 454, 457
  Starr 474
  Stetson 31
  Stratton 210
  Sturtevant 517
  Summers 402, 403
  Swan 372
  Thatcher 410, 411, 517
  Thomas 51
  Thorp 33, 60, 252, 351, 361, 459-461
  Tilley 156, 282, 283, 404, 461-463
  Tisdale 275
  Tompson 145-147, 195
  Tracy 378-380, 464, 465, 517
  Treworgye 322
  Turner 467-471
  Upham 89
  Vincent 14, 227
  Wade 264
  Wadsworth 474, 475
  Washburn 86, 288, 327, 417, 480-483
  Watson 28, 245, 246, 485, 487, 528
  Wayte 75
  Weeks 417
  Whetcomb 468
  Whiston 214, 238, 493-495
  White 141, 321
  Willett 500

John continued
　Williams 32, 115, 241, 527-529
　Willis 351
　Wilson 393
　Wing 163
　Winsley 512
　Winslow 1, 36, 52, 105, 189, 219, 239, 244, 259, 292, 413, 414, 454, 464, 507-515, 517, 521
　Winthrop 21, 53, 132, 193, 194, 219, 239, 262, 269, 270, 344, 347, 379, 381, 428, 502, 504
　Wood 65
　Wood/Atwood 317, 318
　Woodbury 208
　Woodman 322
　Wormall 80
　Wyatt 426
　Yates 250
　Young 27, 277
JONATHAN
　_____ 328
　Alden 6-10
　Bangs 25-27
　Barnes 37-39
　Bosworth 282
　Brewster 30, 43, 67, 68, 70, 320, 346, 469
　Briggs 76-78
　Cobb 120, 122
　Danforth 136
　Delano 167, 168
　Dike 171
　Dunham 121, 167, 184-186, 369
　Hall 27
　Hatch 398, 399
　Higgins 251

Marsh 33
Mendum 321-324
Morey 46, 306
Pickworth 355
Pratt 363, 368, 369
Savory 407
Shaw 186, 247, 408, 414, 415, 485
Smalley 423
Sparrow 26, 378-380, 445-447
Turner 468
Watson 486
Winslow 516, 517
JOSEPH
　Alden 6-9, 420, 421
　Bartlett 45-47, 326, 327, 364, 485
　Bassett 50, 51
　Beedle 308
　Bemis 22
　Bidle 97
　Billington 126
　Blague 440
　Bradford 63-65
　Bumpas 87
　Chandler 98, 99, 101
　Church 107
　Coleman 241-243, 420
　Crocker 91
　Davis 260
　Doty 180, 182
　Dunham 185
　Faunce 203
　Grafton 387
　Harding 151, 152, 233, 300, 301
　Hayward 327
　Hollway 153
　Howland 276-278, 280-282, 442, 443
　Hull 90, 91

Joseph continued
  Jones 179, 307, 308
  Mullins 339, 340
  Pickworth 353-356
  Pratt 371, 373
  Prior 132
  Ramsden/Ransdell 126, 189, 296, 405
  Rogers 33, 85, 163, 300, 357, 396, 397, 431
  Rose 86
  Rowley 400
  Russell 402
  Salmon 162
  Savory 409
  Snow 430, 431
  Tilden 88, 237, 298, 393
  Turner 468, 469
  Wadsworth 474-476
  Warren 202, 267, 294, 363, 478, 479
  Waterman 34
  Whiston 493, 494
  Williams 485, 506
  Winslow 512-514
  Woodworth 522, 523
  Wormall 186
  Wright 373

JOSEPHINE
  _____ 220
  Lee 220

JOSHUA
  Bangs 25-27
  Conant 136, 138, 333
  Harris 489
  Lombard 494
  More 333
  Pratt 56, 148, 150, 154, 177, 245, 302, 356, 365-369, 372, 373, 405, 406, 417, 445
  Ray 386, 387
  Roice 368

JOSIAH
  Billington 187
  Flint 500
  Harding 151
  Holmes 402, 403
  Keene 306, 307
  Snell 9
  Snow 32, 34, 308
  Turner 468
  Winslow 352, 353, 378, 379, 508-510, 512, 514-519, 521
  Wormall 80-82

JOSIAS
  Cooke 116, 149-153, 163, 174, 181, 233, 272, 367, 391, 430, 431, 445
  Hallott 37
  Standish 452-454, 520
  Wampatucke 281
  Winslow 36, 378, 445, 467

JOSINA
  Fletcher 204
  Sachariasdaughter 204

JOYCE
  Bradwick 324
  Lombard 477
  Wallen 25, 476, 477
  _____ 25, 477

JUDITH
  Barker 31, 32, 377, 379, 380
  Faunce 203
  Fletcher 205
  Mendum 321
  Preble 237
  Prence 32, 380
  Rickard/Ricket/Rickett 203
  Tubbs 380
  Vassall 495
  Weeks 321
  White 495

Judith continued
  Winslow 513
  _____ 321, 513
JULIANA/JULIANN
  Carpenter 94, 301, 336-338
  Kempton 94, 298, 301, 336
  Morton 94, 301, 336-338

KATHERINE see
  CATHERINE
KENELM
  Baker 519
  Winslow 1, 2, 102, 103, 187,
    344, 402, 416, 426, 509, 510,
    512, 514, 517-521
KNYVETT
  Sears 412

LAWRENCE
  Dowse 75
  Ward 11
LEONARD
  Buttles 269
LETTICE
  Foster 213, 214, 238
  Hanford 214, 238
  Jenkins 214, 238
  Morton 337, 391
  Ring 337, 391
  Tompkins 214
  _____ 337, 391
LEWIS
  Kidby 193
LIONEL
  Chilton 104
LOIS
  Cobb 122
  Hallet 122
LORA
  Standish 452, 454

LOT
  Conant 135-138
LOVE
  Brewster 46, 67, 68, 130, 132,
    519
  Steevens 137
LUCE/LUCY
  Barker 30, 32
  Boardman 61
  _____ 32, 61
LUCEANNA
  Barker 32
LUCRETIA
  Brewster 68, 346
  Oldham 68, 345, 346
LUYS
  Hulen 117
LYDIA
  Bangs 26-28, 247, 251
  Barker 31, 34
  Barnaby 44, 46
  Barnes 37-39
  Bartlett 46, 47
  Brown 280-282
  Chandler 99-101, 250
  Collier 131
  Cooper 336
  Doane 174, 175, 247
  Doughty 468, 469
  Garrett 237
  Gaymer 468
  Gray 289
  Gutch 138
  Hatch 237
  Hatherly 237, 238
  Hicks 26, 28, 175, 244, 246,
    247
  Higgins 26, 27, 99, 100, 250,
    251
  Howland 282
  Huckstep 238

Lydia continued
 Irish 289
 Lapham 237
 Marten 424
 Morton 336
 Nelson 46
 Olney 506
 Smalley 424
 Standlake 524
 Sturtivant 378
 Tilden 238
 Turner 466, 468, 469
 Williams 506
 Woodworth 524
 Wormall 81
 _____ 175
LYSBET
 Turner 471

MAAZIAH
 Harding 151
MAGDALEN
 Hilton 257, 259
 Kenning 257
 Oliver 508, 510, 513, 517, 520
 Wiggin 257, 260
 Winslow 508, 510, 513, 517, 520
MAINWARING
 Hilton 257
MANASSEH
 Faunce 528
 Kempton 25, 94, 106, 120, 201, 202, 245, 297-301, 336, 338, 528
MARGARET
 Allerton 13
 Bourne 517
 Freeman 365
 Gaymer 468
 Goodwin 488, 489
 Hanford 214, 238, 393
 Hicks 28, 175, 244-248, 487
 Holmes 268, 269
 Howland 282
 Mason 468
 Miller 517
 Pease 488
 Perry 365
 Price 407
 Robinson 214, 238, 393
 Rogers 397
 Savory 407
 Soule 435
 Webb *alias* Holmes 268, 269
 Wester 169
 Weston 488, 489
 Winslow 247, 516, 517
 _____ 13, 28, 247, 282, 435, 487, 488
MARGERY
 Dike 170, 171
 Moore 482
 Polin 170
 Washburn 482
 _____ 170
MARIE see MARY
MARK
 Eames 520
 Mendall/Mendlove 109
 Mendlove 36, 37, 319, 412, 413
 Mendlove/Manlove 322
 Snow 152, 377-380, 430, 431
MARMEDUKE
 Barton 489
MARTHA
 _____ 83, 152, 211, 233, 265
 Barker 31
 Bassett 51
 Beals 185
 Billington 188

Index of First Names 613

Martha continued
  Blague 440
  Bourne 65
  Bradford 65
  Brown 82, 83, 211
  Bundy 102
  Chandler 102, 103
  Clark 342, 343
  Cobb 121
  Collier 131
  Cooper 403
  Daman 524
  Doane 176, 233
  Dunham 185
  Eaton 188
  Falloway 185
  Ford 83, 211, 212
  Harding 152, 176, 232, 233
  Hobart 51
  Kirtland 440
  Lincoln 311
  Lyford 311
  Nash 343
  Nelson 121, 211, 212
  Saffin 499, 500
  Samson 403
  Sherive 265
  Southworth 440
  Stephens 482
  Timbrell 482
  Washburn 482
  Willett 500
  Woodworth 522-524
MARY
  Adams 519
  Alden 7-9, 420, 421, 438, 440
  Allerton 11-15, 159
  Almy 125
  Andrews 474, 475
  Baker 23, 357, 358
  Balch 138, 143
  Bangs 27
  Barker 31, 32, 155, 372
  Barnes 37, 39, 359
  Bartlett 43, 45-47, 478, 479
  Bassett 49-51
  Bennett 54, 55
  Bernard 505
  Bigford 431
  Bonney 327
  Bradford 65
  Brewster 68, 69, 469
  Bridges 72
  Briggs 74, 78
  Brown 82-84, 176, 500
  Bruff 102
  Buckett 85, 435
  Buckingham 500
  Bumpas 87
  Bursley 90
  Butho 69
  Carpenter 94, 95
  Chandler 98, 99, 101-103
  Chess 27
  Chichester 331
  Chilton 104, 105, 513
  Church 107, 108
  Churchill 179
  Cobb 120, 121, 185
  Cogan 264
  Cole 123- 125
  Collier 130, 379
  Conant 138
  Cooke 145, 147
  Coombs 155, 372
  Crocker 87, 90
  Cudworth 277, 278
  Cushman 13, 15, 158, 159
  Delano 166-168, 185, 361
  Dingley 454
  Doane 176
  Dodge 136, 138, 143

Mary continued
  Doty 178-180, 182
  Doughty 468
  Draper 209
  Dunham 121, 167, 185, 285
  Durrant/Durante 111, 391
  Eddington 23
  Eddy 191, 192, 196
  Evans 204
  Ewer 477
  Faunce 202
  Fletcher 204
  Fosten 191, 196
  Foster 44, 46
  Foxwell 125
  Glass 87, 166, 264, 361
  Goodall 317, 427
  Gray 512, 513
  Hall 27
  Hallett 37
  Hanford 238
  Harlow 202
  Hatch 180, 242
  Hayward 327
  Hewes 242
  Hicks 247
  Higgins 250, 251, 253
  Hilton 256-259
  Hilton *alias* Downer 259
  Hoar 143
  Holmes 65, 268, 269
  Hooker 499, 500
  Hopkins 273
  Howes 380
  Howland 277-279, 282, 342
  Huse 259
  Ince 238
  Jenkins 477
  Jenny 327
  Knight 72
  Lapham 50, 51
  Leach 137
  Lee 282
  Leggatt 96
  Lendall 440
  Leonard 485
  Lincoln 32
  Little 308
  Looker 251
  Lothrop 327
  Mahieu 166
  Manter 394
  Marshall 39
  Martin 315
  Masterson 317, 427
  Mayo 27
  Mendum 321-324
  Miles 238
  Mitchell 326-328, 415
  Moorecock 447
  More 329, 330
  Morey 46
  Moulton 257
  Newbold/Newbould 251
  Newland 277
  Norris 12
  Nowell 514
  Orton 191, 192
  Pabodie/Paybody 439
  Paddock 350
  Paine 431
  Palmer 350
  Parker 468, 469
  Peterson 435
  Pierce 191, 358
  Plumer 359
  Plummer 39
  Pococke 125
  Pollard 513
  Pontus 87, 166, 360, 361
  Pratt 155, 370-372, 382
  Prence 130, 377-381, 465

Mary continued
  Priest 226, 372, 382
  Prior 327
  Prower 315
  Rainsford 50
  Raynes 322, 324
  Ring 111, 152, 163, 219, 273, 337, 389-391
  Roberts 350
  Robinson 393, 394
  Ryder 123
  Samson 277, 403
  Savory 405, 407
  Sayles 505
  Sears 259
  Shaw 326, 327, 415
  Shepperd 405
  Shingelton 158
  Simonson 8, 421, 523
  Smalley 176, 424, 431
  Smedley 328
  Smith 64, 317, 426, 427
  Snow 176, 423, 424, 431
  Soule 85, 433-435
  Southworth 8, 439, 440
  Standish 452, 454
  Sturtevant 308
  Summers 402, 403
  Swan 372
  Thomas 308
  Tibbes 124
  Tilden 50
  Tilson 125
  Tinkham 80, 84, 402
  Tompson 146, 147
  Tracy 377, 379, 380, 464, 465, 517
  Tucker 107, 469
  Veren 137
  Wadsworth 475
  Walker 278
  Wallen 477
  Warren 45, 478, 479
  Watson 485, 487
  Wentworth 69, 344
  Weston 167
  White 424
  Whitehead 250
  Willett 500
  Williams 505
  Winslow 104, 105, 511-514, 517
  Wood 65
  Woodman 321, 322
  Woodworth 421, 522-524
  Worden 520
  Wyrrall 69
  Yates 250
  ____ 23, 37, 44, 68, 74, 78, 83, 137, 152, 158, 163, 185, 250, 273, 277, 308, 315, 321, 326, 331, 350, 380, 391, 394, 402, 431, 475, 520

MATTHEW
  Craddock 345, 346
  Fuller 89, 109, 113, 215, 216, 399
  Griswold 372

MEHITABLE/MEHETABEL
  Allyn 19
  Annable 19
  Bigbee 470
  Clark 112
  Cobb 122
  Hilton 256
  Nowell 256
  Rigby 469, 470
  Scotto 112
  Turner 469
  Woodworth 522-524

MERCY
  Bangs 27

Mercy continued
  Bartlett 47
  Bradford 63, 65
  Chandler 99
  Cole 127
  Delano 167
  Doane 176
  Dunham 185
  Faunce 203, 267
  Freeman 376-378, 380. 438, 439
  Fuller 127, 218-220
  Harris 512, 513
  Hedges 486
  Holman 373
  Holmes 203, 267
  Joy 47
  Knowles 176
  Little 307, 308
  Merrick 26, 27
  Morton 185
  Pabodie/Paybody 421
  Pratt 371, 373
  Prence 380
  Robinson 237, 394, 453
  Samson 403
  Sawyer 307
  Simonson 421
  Southworth 439
  Sprague 448-450
  Standish 403
  Tubbs 449
  Vermayes 65
  Warren 167
  Waterman 505, 506
  Watson 486
  Weeks 394
  Williams 505, 506
  Winslow 520
  Winsor 505
  Worden 520

_____ 99

MICHAEL
  Ford 34
  Pierce 436
  Powell 260
  Shafflyn 208
  Shaflen 489

MICHIEL
  Voorchoren 205

MILES
  Standish 5, 8, 67, 86, 110, 142, 158, 179, 214, 219, 268, 272, 294, 328, 356, 373, 417, 447, 451-457, 460, 462, 463, 481, 497, 514, 519

MIRIAM
  Deane 151, 163
  Wormall 186
  _____ 186

MORDECAI
  Lyford 310, 311, 313
  Nichols 112

MORGAN
  Jones 113

MORRIS
  Truant/Trewant 86, 306, 448, 481

MOSES/MOYSES
  Bennett 53, 55
  Fletcher 204, 205
  Maverick 11, 13, 15
  Rowley 399, 400
  Savory 407
  Simonson 8, 85, 167, 419-422, 435, 458, 523
  Talbot 261, 262, 283, 284, 408, 428
  Rowley 350
  Simonson 165
  Symons 98
  Symonson 97

MUSACHIELL
　Bernard 506

NATHANIEL
　Baker 22, 191, 358
　Bassett 49, 51
　Bishop 426
　Bowman 62
　Brewster 69
　Chandler 102
　Church 108, 436
　Clark 111, 112
　Cole 128, 131
　Dickens 488
　Goodspeed 91
　Hatherly 238
　Holmes 203, 267
　Howland 281
　Martin 315
　Masters 354, 355
　Masterson 317, 426, 427, 485
　Mayo 380, 446, 447
　Morton 245, 295, 298-300, 336, 337, 429, 485
　Pickman 169-171
　Pierce 72
　Pittman 170
　Rich 262
　Soule 434-436
　Souther 389, 485
　Southworth 438-440
　Thomas 308, 436
　Tilden 50, 238, 307, 461
　Treadway 190
　Turner 468-470
　Walton 138
　Warren 35, 131, 167, 478, 479
　Winslow 309, 519, 520
NICHOLAS
　Byram 165, 420
　Davis 59
　Davison 345, 346
　Hodges 265
　Power 488, 506
　Presland 111
　Shapleigh 322
　Simpkins 269
　Snow 151, 152, 163, 194, 195, 272, 273, 380, 424, 428-432
　Stillwell 116, 118
　Wade 214, 237, 238
　Weeks 321, 322
　White 368

OBADIAH
　Eddy 195-197
　Lyford 310, 313
OCEANUS
　Hopkins 273, 274
OLIVER
　Arnold 33
　Cromwell 509

PANDORA
　Sparrow 445-447
　_____ 446
PARNELL
　Winslow 512, 513
PATIENCE
　Barstow 421
　Bonham 267
　Brewster 67, 68, 309, 379
　Cobb 120, 121, 285, 286
　Crocker 121
　Faunce 202, 267, 337
　Haskall 434, 436
　Holmes 202, 267
　Hurst 121, 286
　Jones 307-309
　Little 307, 308
　Morton 202, 336, 337
　Parker 121

Patience continued
  Prence 68, 70, 375, 379
  Simonson 420, 421
  Soule 436
  Whitney 202
  Willis 267
PAUL
  Sears 410, 411
  Whitt 323
PENELOPE
  Pelham 508
  Winslow 508, 509
PEREGRINE
  White 49, 50, 299, 495, 496
PERSIS
  Bridges 71, 72, 74, 75
  Brown 72
  Dunham 186, 367, 369, 416
  Harrison 72
  Knight 72
  Pierce 72, 74
  Pratt 186, 367, 416
  Shaw 186, 416
PETER
  Blossom 58, 59
  Briggs 74, 75
  Brown 80-85, 98, 176, 211, 226, 228
  Browne 402
  Folger 373
  Hobart 65
  Hunt 501
  Osgood 332
  Palfrey 143, 170
  Pratt 371, 372
  Prudden 500
  Robinson 394
  Stuijvesant 502
  Tufts 71, 72
  Warden 163
  Woodbury 135

_____ 113
PHEBE
  Arnold 33
  Barker 33
  Brown 80, 81, 233
  Bumpas 87
  Cook 33
  Harding 81, 233
  Hatch 241, 242
  Hicks 244, 247, 485
  Lovel 87
  Marsh 33
  Shaw 247, 415, 485
  Watson 246, 247, 415, 485, 487
  Wormall 81
PHILIP
  Bumpas 87, 168
  Cromwell 332, 334
  Davis 404
  Delano 6, 8, 87, 162, 164-168, 185, 244, 293, 328, 361, 419, 421, 435
  Dotterich 123
  Geraerdi 118
  Washburn 288, 482
  Weyt 117
  Wooton 55
PHINEAS
  Pratt 36, 77, 154, 177, 227, 231, 365, 366, 368-374, 382, 450
PHOEBE see PHEBE
PILGRIM
  Baker 23, 191, 192
  Eddy 23, 192
  Eveleth 191, 192
  Steadman 191, 192
PRISCILLA
  Alden 5, 7-9, 340
  Allen 84

Priscilla continued
  Brown 83, 84, 226
  Carpenter 64, 93-95, 220, 301, 337, 526
  Coit 204
  Cooper 95, 526
  Faunce 202, 479
  Fletcher 204
  Irish 288, 439
  Mullins 7, 9, 339, 340
  Southworth 288, 439
  Sparrow 446
  Talbot 288, 439
  Terry 204
  Vermout 205
  Warren 202, 479
  Wright 93, 95, 218, 219, 525, 526
PROVIDENCE
  Williams 505
PRUDENCE
  Hill 417
  Sherman 417

RACHEL
  Davenport 306
  Eaton 187, 188
  Holmes 268, 269
  Pickworth 355
  Ramsden/Ransdell 189
  Sibley 354, 355
  _____ 306
RALPH
  Chapman 30
  Earle 448, 449, 488
  Fogg 56, 206-210, 478, 487, 489
  Gorham 4, 428
  Partridge 49, 164, 304, 350, 448, 473, 474

  Smith 25, 60, 172, 266, 268, 292, 317, 425-428, 447
  Wallen 110, 153, 476, 477
  Weston 490
RANDALL
  Holden 490
REBECCA
  Alden 8, 9, 167
  Bangs 25, 26, 299, 446
  Barker 31, 32, 34, 308
  Bartlett 46, 47, 403
  Bradford 403
  Bridges 72, 75
  Brown 84
  Church 108
  Churchill 167
  Cole 127, 130, 131
  Collier 127, 130
  Conant 137
  Craddock 346
  Delano 8, 166-168
  Doane 175
  Freeman 380
  Glover 346
  Harlow 46
  Hicks 28
  Higgins 251, 252
  Howland 278
  Hussey 278
  Martin 251
  Merrick 465
  Nickerson 127
  Pabodie/Paybody 440
  Palmer 350
  Pettee 175
  Pierce 357, 358
  Pope 364
  Power 505
  Prence 219, 375, 380
  Ray 386, 388
  Rhodes 505

Rebecca continued
  Rickard/Ricket/Rickett 432
  Samson 403
  Sawyer 32, 308
  Scottow 108
  Simonson 421, 435
  Snow 31, 32, 34, 84, 308, 432
  Soule 420, 421, 435
  Southworth 440
  Sparrow 26, 446
  Stanford 403
  Thatcher 517
  Tracy 464, 465
  Willett 500
  Williams 505
  Wills 357, 358
  Winslow 517
  ____ 26, 108, 346, 357, 364
RELIEF
  Dowse 214
  Foster 214
  Holland 214
REMEMBER
  Allerton 11, 13-15
  Briggs 77, 78
  Brown 81, 82
  Maverick 13, 15
  Wormall 80-82
RESOLVED
  Waterman 505, 506
  White 495, 496
RICE
  Jones 260
RICHARD
  Andrews 235
  Banks 87
  Bellingham 255
  Bernard 505
  Britteridge 80
  Church 21, 43-45, 105-109, 299, 306, 319, 351, 376, 439, 478, 479
  Clark 109
  Clough 112-118, 125, 194, 293, 412
  Collicott 90
  Conant 133, 137
  Cooke 151
  Davenport 386, 387
  Denton 214
  Derby 41, 155, 177, 180, 181
  Dodge 135
  Dunham 185
  Dwelley 123, 420, 421
  Fletcher 204
  Floyd 508
  Foster 44, 46, 306
  Francis *alias* Deacon 161, 162
  Gardiner 223
  Gaymer 468
  Greene 230
  Hallett 112
  Harcourt 488
  Harrington 75
  Hicks 247
  Higgins 27, 36, 99, 100, 150, 228, 249-253, 257, 300, 422-424
  Hilton 257
  Hollingsworth 334
  Hutcheson 386, 387
  Hutton 333
  Jones 411
  Lanckford 128, 302
  Martin 321
  Masterson 59, 60, 292, 316-318, 427, 484
  Mather 501
  Middlecott 514
  More 329-335, 490, 492, 509

Index of First Names 621

Richard continued
  Norman 492
  Rogers 396
  Scott 504
  Sears 409-412
  Sillis 213, 214
  Sparrow 26, 150, 380, 443-447
  Standlake 524
  Starr 334
  Stinnings 47
  Sutton 421
  Taylor 122
  Temple 71
  Warren 33, 45, 47, 48, 107, 131, 146, 167, 179, 202, 207, 307, 477-480
  Weston 491
  White 255-257, 260
  Willis 41, 264, 267, 409
  Wright 145-147
ROBERT
  Barker 29-34, 308, 351, 380, 460
  Bartlett 35, 41-48, 106, 109, 205, 295, 364, 412, 413, 478, 479
  Bridges 73
  Brooks 509
  Carter 95, 339, 340
  Carver 96
  Chaulkly 75
  Cooper 156
  Cowles 218, 457
  Cushman 13, 96, 140, 142, 158-160, 330, 470, 491
  Dennis 278
  Fuller 215, 216, 220
  Gorges 91, 229, 230, 335
  Hatherly 237
  Hicks 26, 28, 36, 76, 79, 85, 97, 175, 243-248, 282, 419, 433, 445, 478, 485, 487
  Hix 162
  Holmes 498
  Jackson 496
  Latham 513
  Leach 54, 353
  Long 309
  Marshall 38, 39
  Mendlove/Manlove 320, 322
  Mendum 113, 259, 319-324
  Morgan 353
  Moulton 208
  Muchmore 321, 322
  Nelson 104
  Nickerson 127
  Paddock 350
  Parker 121
  Pease 488
  Ransom 115, 363
  Rattlife 385
  Roice 368
  Saltonstall 117
  Scott 118, 269
  Sprout 402, 403
  Stanford 404
  Starr 334
  Stetson 523
  Tilley 461-463
  Tucker 77
  Waterman 263
  Watson 486, 528
  Williams 506
  Willis 125
ROGER
  Chandler 100-104, 521
  Clap 136, 170
  Conant 55, 133-143, 170, 208, 491, 492
  Cooke 304

Roger continued
  Wilder 96, 497
  Williams 21, 22, 56, 171, 188,
    218, 219, 270, 428, 489,
    503-506
ROSE
  Morton 338
  Soule 435
  Standish 451, 453, 454
  Tilley 462, 463
  _____ 338, 435, 453
ROWLAND
  Heylyn 490
RUBEN
  Guppie 388
RUTH
  Alden 8, 9
  Bangs 27
  Bass 7-9
  Bassett 51, 449
  Bates 311
  Chandler 98-101
  Cole 27, 128, 131, 431, 520
  Collier 128, 131
  Cushman 280, 283
  Denton 214
  Eddy 193
  Fitz Randolph 252
  Foster 214
  Gardner 191, 193
  Hewes 242
  Higgins 252, 253
  Hopkins 272, 274
  Howland 283
  Little 307, 308
  Lyford 310, 311
  Masters 353, 354
  Pickworth 354
  Sargent 516, 517
  Sawtell 242
  Snow 431

Sprague 51, 449
Thomas 51
Tileston 214
Tracy 464, 465
Tuttle 252
Winslow 517, 520
Young 27
_____ 520

SABIN
  Staresmore 318
SAMUEL
  Allcock 260
  Allen 40, 454
  Annable 17-19
  Archer 206, 207
  Arnold 516
  Baker 237, 358, 394, 520
  Barker 31
  Bass 8
  Bradford 288
  Bridges 72
  Bumpas 87, 168
  Butterworth 241
  Chandler 98-102, 252, 296
  Chipman 122
  Cobb 120, 122
  Cole 127
  Crumpton 332, 333
  Delano 166-168
  Doty 179, 182
  Dunham 124, 183-185, 301,
    360
  Dutch 332, 333
  Eaton 98, 187-189
  Eddy 70, 191-198, 245, 293,
    325, 406-408, 429
  Freeman 376, 379, 439
  Friend 356

Samuel continued
  Fuller 59, 60, 89, 92, 94, 127, 150, 215-221, 337, 338, 390, 392, 457, 496, 525, 526
  Gallup 440
  Gardner 191
  Godbertson 226, 228, 249, 252, 370, 422, 424
  Gorton 113, 490
  Hall 27, 368
  Hatch 180
  Hicks 25, 28, 44, 175, 244-247, 487
  Hinckley 121, 236, 365
  Hooker 498-500
  Howland 277, 278
  Jenny 114, 292-295, 300, 518
  Knowles 113
  Latham 78, 79, 248
  Leach 54
  Lincoln 311
  Little 306-308
  Lothrop 175
  Moore 250, 252
  More 329, 330, 332, 333
  Nash 5, 341-343, 458
  Packard 78
  Pickworth 353-356
  Pierce 191
  Pratt 155, 371, 372
  Rider 46, 196
  Samson 167, 342, 343, 435
  Savory 407, 408
  Sewall 393
  Sherman 417, 418
  Shrimpton 331
  Skelton 504
  Smith 114, 127
  Sturtevant 286, 308, 519
  Talbot 288, 439
  Terry 147
  Thaxter 108
  Tompkins 214
  Wadsworth 475, 476
  Wait 403
  Watson 485
  Willett 498, 499, 501
  Wills 358
  Winslow 513, 514
  Winsor 505
SARAH/SARA
  Alden 8, 453
  Allen 454
  Allerton 11, 13, 14, 227, 372, 382
  Annable 17, 18
  Bangs 26, 27
  Barstow 108
  Bartlett 46
  Bassett 50, 51, 496
  Blossom 59
  Blunden 339, 340
  Bodfish 59
  Bonham 337
  Bonney 307
  Bradford 65
  Brewster 46, 68, 130
  Buck 202
  Bumpas 86, 87
  Burroughs 108
  Cary 295
  Chandler 98, 99, 101, 102
  Chipman 122
  Church 108
  Clark 112
  Cobb 120-122, 446
  Collier 68, 130
  Conant 135-138
  Converse 218
  Cooke 43, 146, 479
  Coombs 154, 155, 375, 382
  Cummings 373

Sarah continued
  Cushman 158, 159
  Davis 59
  Denby 204
  Dennis 277, 278, 388
  Doggett 418
  Doty 179, 180, 202
  Durram 86
  Eaton 87, 188, 189
  Eddy 192, 193
  Edwards 180
  Eliott 499, 500
  Ewell 18
  Ewer 59
  Fairfax 13
  Faunce 179, 202
  Fletcher 204
  Godbertson 14, 176, 226, 227, 372, 382
  Gott 388
  Gray 308
  Greenleaf 256, 514
  Griswold 65
  Gunnison 260
  Hatch 399
  Hayward 326, 327
  Hicks 247
  Higgins 252, 253
  Hiland 469
  Hilton 256, 514
  Hinckley 121, 365
  Hobart 310, 312, 313
  Hodgkins 159
  Holmes 267
  Horton 137
  Hoskins 189
  Howes 26, 377, 379, 381
  Howland 276, 278
  Huckins 365
  Jenny 46, 114, 292-295, 364
  Jones 179
  Lawrence 514
  Leach 137, 138
  Leonard/Leonardson 102
  Lewis 121, 446
  Little 308
  Lyford 310
  Marion 191, 192
  Marston 355
  Masterson 317, 318
  Meade 192, 193
  Mendum 322
  Middlecott 512-514
  Mitchell 327
  Moore 252
  More 333
  Morton 336, 337
  Muchmore 322
  Mullins 340
  Nash 420, 421
  Nichols 494
  Oakley 310
  Ordway 388
  Partridge 465
  Payne 514
  Pickworth 355
  Pope 294, 295, 364, 365
  Pratt 373
  Prence 381
  Priest 14, 155, 226, 227, 372, 382
  Ray 386-388
  Reder 158
  Rider 46
  Rowley 399
  Sherman 418
  Simonson 420, 421
  Snow 431
  Sparrow 446
  Standish 7, 8, 453, 454, 514
  Stockbridge 523
  Tracy 464, 465

Index of First Names

Sarah continued
  Turner 469
  Vincent 14, 227, 372, 382
  Walker 131, 431, 479
  Walters 387
  Warren 131, 146, 478, 479
  Whiston 494
  White 50, 496
  Willett 500
  Winslow 454, 513, 514
  Wolcott 112
  Wood 294
  Wood/Atwood 317, 318
  Woodworth 193, 522, 523
  Wright 373
  ____ 27, 46, 65, 86, 112, 138, 180, 188, 204, 267, 310, 333, 388, 420
SCOTTO
  Clark 112
SEETH
  Conant 138
  Gardner 138
SETH
  Pope 363, 364, 402
SHUBAEL
  Dimmock 90
SICILY
  Conant 133
  Croxon 133
SILAS
  Sears 410, 411
SIMON
  Bradstreet 492
  Eire 71
  Eyre/Eyer 12
  Mosesz. 422
  Overzee 13
  Zzno surname 151
SISSILLA
  Bartlett 46

  ____ 46
SOLOMON
  Lenner 86
  Leonard/Leonardson 102
  Martin 316
  Prower 316, 383
  Terry 204
STEPHEN
  Bryan 178
  Bryant 29, 37, 196, 408, 413, 415
  Deane 150-152, 162, 163, 165, 227, 244, 389-391, 431
  Hopkins 42, 70, 125, 147, 150, 152, 176, 180, 227, 267, 271-275, 305, 351, 391, 429, 431, 432, 460, 462, 521
  Merrick 27
  Samson 402, 403
  Skeff 34
  Snow 163, 430-432
  Tilden 237, 307
  Tracy 298, 350, 358, 463-465
  Tuttle 252
  Twining 151
  Wanton 34
  Wood 27, 184
  Wood/Atwood 185
SUSAN/SUSANNAH
  Adams 1, 2
  Annable 19
  Banks 209
  Bartlett 46, 295
  Brooks 237, 238, 494
  Carpenter 180
  Clark 111, 112, 389-391
  Deane 163, 431
  Doggett 193
  Draper 209
  Dunham 185
  Dutch 332, 333

Susan continued
  Eddy 197
  England 180
  Fogg 209
  Fuller 496, 508
  Furner 104
  Gentleman 332
  Hanford 214, 238, 494
  Hatch 19
  Hatherly 236, 238
  Holbrook 501
  Hunter 332
  Hutton 333
  Jenny 46, 293-295
  Kaino 185
  Kidby 193
  Knowlton 333
  Latham 512, 513
  Lothrop 112
  Mitchell 327, 364
  More 332, 333
  Padduck 197
  Palmer 351
  Perry 494
  Pope 294, 327, 364, 365
  Prence 377, 378
  Ring 111, 391
  Robinson 394
  Rogers 163, 431
  Snow 163, 431
  Soule 434, 435
  Starr 334
  West 435
  Whiston 214, 238, 494
  White 495, 496, 508
  Willett 501
  Winslow 495, 496, 507, 508, 513
  Wood 295
  _____ 238, 351, 495, 508

SYLVESTER
  Eveleth 192
SYMON
  Trott 114
SYMOND
  Crosby 334

TABITHA
  Dike 170, 171
  Pickman 170
  Pittman 170
  _____ 170
TEMPERANCE
  Bursley 91
  Crocker 91
THEOPHILUS
  Mayo 377, 378
THOMAS
  Angel 488
  Applegate 118
  Atkinson 270
  Balliou 185
  Barlow 155
  Barnes 40, 41
  Beeson 323
  Bell 340
  Besbeech 98, 481
  Bishop 356
  Blossom 58-60, 318, 390, 399
  Boardman 60, 61
  Bonney 327, 402, 403
  Boreman 60, 61
  Bourne 65, 517
  Bowen 220
  Brattle 512
  Brian 70, 197
  Briggs 76-78
  Broughton 502
  Buckingham 500
  Bumpas 87, 168
  Bunting 373

Index of First Names

Thomas continued
  Burge 44
  Burgess 50
  Burman 18
  Bursley 90
  Byrd 98
  Chillingsworth 127
  Clapp 236
  Clark 109-115, 130, 264, 294,
    305, 320, 356, 378, 391, 412,
    413, 477, 480, 502
  Coit 204
  Coleman 241
  Cook 33
  Crockett 320, 323
  Cushman 11, 13, 15, 46, 52,
    154, 155, 158-160, 184, 245,
    283, 285, 294
  Dale 274
  Delano 7, 8, 165-168, 342
  Dexter 115
  Doggett 328, 418
  Doty 179, 182
  Doxsey 118
  Dunham 184-186
  Durram 86
  Elithorpe 355
  England 199
  English 199
  Ensign 236
  Evans 128
  Ewer 59, 113, 477
  Farrel 117
  Faunce 202, 442
  Flavell 203, 204, 461
  Gardner 138
  Gilbert 51
  Gray 128, 355
  Hall 116, 117
  Hanford 214, 237, 238
  Hanscom 259
  Hanscome 323
  Harlow 79, 248
  Hart 505, 506
  Hatch 19, 357
  Hayward 327
  Heath 248
  Hicks 247
  Higgins 251, 253, 254, 296
  Hill 36, 484
  Hinckley 120
  Holmes 268
  Hooker 500
  Horton 137
  Howell 30
  Howes 26, 380, 453
  Huckins 253, 365
  Hunter 332
  Joy 107
  Kaino 185
  Keyser 304
  King 357
  Knowles 55
  Lane 92
  Lapham 50, 51, 237
  Lawrence 514
  Leonard 485
  Lettice 112, 147, 148, 295,
    362, 365, 408
  Leverett 20
  Lincoln 32
  Little 43, 45, 111, 249, 298,
    305-309, 478, 479
  Lombard 477
  Lothrop 333, 386-388
  Lucas 126, 408, 409
  Martin 251
  Mayhew 346
  Michell 146
  Mitchell 326-328
  More 333

Thomas continued
  Morton 43, 91, 301, 338, 339, 344, 347, 429, 454, 456
  Moulton 257
  Nichols 494
  Oldham 346, 348
  Orton 191, 192
  Paine 377, 430, 431
  Perry 494
  Pierce 71, 72, 358
  Pitman 331
  Pope 46, 144, 294, 295, 327, 362-365
  Prence 3, 32, 41, 63, 64, 67, 68, 106, 130, 145, 153, 154, 188, 218, 219, 261, 265, 270, 349, 351, 370, 374-381, 390, 431, 446, 465
  Rawlins 17
  Richards 65
  Roberts 350, 467
  Robinson 395
  Rogers 163, 396, 397, 431, 462
  Saffin 499
  Savory 195, 196, 261, 367, 405-409, 414
  Sears 259
  Shaw 18
  Sherive/Sherive/Shreive 3, 41, 47, 151, 265, 447
  Shingelton 158
  Smith 157, 158, 330
  Southworth 63, 64, 94, 184, 248, 281, 282, 294, 300, 438, 440-443, 446
  Stoughton 78, 79
  Symons 181, 218, 343, 421, 457, 458
  Thacher 513
  Tilden 306, 461
  Tileston 214
  Tinker 463
  Tuck 334
  Turner 468, 469
  Venner 208
  Wallen 477
  Watson 528
  Way 260
  Wentworth 69
  Weston 138, 229, 230, 368, 373, 490-493
  Whitney 36, 202
  Whiton 233, 447
  Willett 39, 63, 116, 118, 173, 248, 324, 352, 446, 452, 497-503
  Williams 480, 506
  Willoughby 13
  Woodworth 522, 523

THOMASINE
  Cook 33
  _____ 33

THURSTON
  Clarke 178

TIMOTHY
  Foster 213, 214, 237
  Hatherly 50, 81, 115, 213, 214, 224, 234-240, 264, 289, 337, 393, 394, 453, 494, 495, 519, 527, 529
  _____ 33

TOBIAS
  Payne 514
  Taylor 113

TOWNSEND
  Bishop 208

TRISTRAM
  Clark 154

TRYPHOSA
  Lee 465
  Tracy 464, 465

Index of First Names

TWIFORD
  West 432

WAIT
  Wadsworth 476
WALTER
  Allen 171
  Briggs 514
  Clarke 505
  Harris 176, 233-234
  Hatch 418
  Neal 20
  Woodworth 421, 521-524
WEBB
  Adey 2-4, 293, 367
WILLEM
  Crump 118
WILLIAM
  Adey 4
  Alldridge 116
  Allen 80, 84
  Arnold 488
  Auger 207
  Baker 21-23, 36, 37, 106, 192, 270
  Barstow 29, 421
  Barwick 490
  Bassett 48-52, 157, 237, 320, 449, 496
  Beale 52, 159
  Bennett 52-56, 108, 138, 187, 412, 413, 489
  Bladen 313
  Bourne 447
  Bradford 11, 43, 57-59, 62-66, 70, 94, 105, 108, 110, 117, 140, 145, 157, 158, 161, 162, 173, 174, 193, 217, 219, 220, 223, 227, 236, 244, 254, 298, 300, 336, 337, 349, 351, 376, 377, 395, 404, 410, 428, 438, 440, 442, 443, 462, 484, 491, 492, 503, 516, 525
  Brett 244
  Brewster 13, 14, 66-70, 83, 130, 159, 187, 219, 304, 309, 317, 329, 331, 333, 339, 344, 379, 454, 469, 525
  Bridges 70, 71, 73-75, 345, 346
  Briggs 74
  Brooks 237, 238, 269, 494, 523
  Brown 72, 81, 83, 263, 331, 332
  Button 92, 221
  Carver 179
  Chard 241
  Chase 272
  Chichester 331
  Churchill 442
  Clark 29, 111, 112, 129, 132, 342, 343
  Collier 68, 114, 127-133, 379, 439, 474, 479
  Conner 143, 144
  Corvannel/Corrannell 412, 482
  Crocker 121
  Crow 517
  Davis 461, 502
  Denby 204
  Dodge 135, 137, 138, 143
  Doty 182
  Earle 165
  Eddy 191, 196
  England 180
  Falloway 185
  Fallowell 426
  Flint 331
  Ford 212

William continued
- Gilson 1, 70, 83, 223-226, 395, 416, 470, 528
- Goodhue 387
- Hallett 118
- Hanbury 125, 174, 358, 416
- Harlow 46, 202, 299, 485
- Hatch 19, 224, 237, 241, 242
- Hathorne 208, 210, 355, 386
- Heard 240
- Heath 255
- Hedges 486
- Higgins 252
- Hiller 117, 132, 153, 287, 320, 322
- Hillier 438
- Hilton 142, 254-261, 323, 514
- Hoar 143
- Hodgkins 159
- Holbeck 262, 263, 496
- Holman 373
- Holmes 179, 267-270, 306, 309
- Holt 12
- Honywell 270, 271
- Hoskins 189
- Hubbard 255
- Hudson 193
- Hurdman 132
- Jeffreys 91
- Kemp 414
- Kersley 400
- Knop 190
- Latham 86, 96, 304
- Launder 156
- Laurence 448
- Lawrence 449, 450
- Leverich 49
- Looker 251
- Lord 208, 495
- Mendlove 106, 318, 319, 322, 351
- Merrick 357, 465
- Moore 257, 260
- Morrell 229, 335, 336
- Morris 132
- Mullins 7-9, 95, 339, 340
- Nelson 211
- Newland 41
- Nickerson 153, 412
- Norman 323
- Oldham 346
- Pabodie/Paybody 7, 325, 421, 439, 440
- Paddy 2, 52, 299, 358, 498, 501, 502, 512
- Palmer 33, 37, 86, 266, 318, 319, 349-352, 399, 460, 465
- Parker 469
- Payne 512
- Phillips 7
- Phips 352, 353
- Pitt 359, 525
- Pontus 87, 165, 166, 245, 360-362
- Priest 190
- Pynchon 171
- Quick 379
- Randall 241, 469
- Renolds 261, 276
- Richards 388, 389
- Ring 111, 163, 391
- Rogers 396
- Rowland 397
- Russell 132
- Sargent 516, 517
- Shakkerley 334
- Sherman 179, 182, 416-419, 481
- Shetle 114

William continued
  Shurtleff 114, 125, 144, 147, 308
  Snow 80, 84, 181
  Southworth 439, 440
  Spooner 155, 156, 267, 368
  Sprague 46, 108
  Stephens 418
  Strengwits 118
  Tailer 512, 513
  Tench 93, 459
  Thomas 156
  Trask 334
  Trevor 198, 466
  Tubbs 380, 449
  Twining 163
  Vassall 2, 234, 469, 495
  Vobbes 439
  Wadsworth 476
  Waldron 323
  Walker 113, 131, 431
  Walton 138
  Weeks 394
  Wetherell 234
  White 50, 262, 280, 340, 459, 495, 496, 508, 509
  Whitmer 87
  Witherill 288
  Wright 93, 95, 218-220, 337, 359, 524-526

WINIFRED
  Harding 233
  Whitney 40
  Whiton 233

WRESTLING
  Brewster 67, 68

WYBRA
  Bumpas 87
  Glass 87
  Hanson 361
  Pontus 361

ZACCHEUS
  Cole 128, 131

ZACHARIAH
  Alden 9
  Eddy 195-197, 406
  Paddock 410, 411
  Rhodes 506
  Soule 433, 435

ZACHARY
  Daman 524

ZERA
  Higgins 251

ZOETH
  Howland 276, 277, 279

INDEX OF PLACES

Agamenticus see York
Agawam 298
Alverdiscott (Devon) 214, 238
Amsterdam (Holland) 64, 94, 284-286, 328, 389
Antigua 268
Austerfield (Yorkshire) 64
Bahama Islands 304
Bamfield (Suffolk) 13
Barbados 15, 98, 99, 101, 273, 275, 358, 400
Barlston (Leicester) 161
Barnstable 16-19, 27, 28, 37, 59-61, 87, 89-91, 96, 109, 112, 113, 119-122, 127, 213, 214, 236, 249, 253, 301, 357, 358, 365, 391-394, 398-400, 441, 446, 477
Barnstaple (Devon) 122, 124, 125, 209, 210, 238, 239
Bath (Somerset) 94
Bengeworth (Worcester) 480, 482
Bermondsey (Surrey)
  St. Mary Magdalen 26, 131, 247, 485
Bermuda 274
Berwick-upon-Tweed (Northumberland) 301
Beverly 134-139
Billerica 9, 22, 23
Block Island 327, 346, 348
Boston 2, 6-8, 10, 23, 27, 47, 50, 64, 72, 74, 75, 107-109, 111-115, 118, 155, 191-193, 198, 208, 209, 234, 238, 239, 268, 269, 331, 340, 345, 359, 368, 387, 393, 418, 425, 427, 428, 454, 455, 494, 495, 500, 503, 511-514
Boxted (Essex) 189, 193, 194
Braintree 8, 492
Bramfield (Suffolk) 13
Bridgewater 6, 48-50, 64, 80, 165, 168, 174, 287, 288, 324-327, 420, 423, 445, 452, 474, 516
Bristol 439, 440
Bristol (Gloucester) 187, 490, 492
  St. Thomas 188
Budleigh (Devon) 139
Cambridge 78, 90, 193, 197, 282, 308, 327, 372, 373, 426, 489, 500
Cambridge (Cambridge) 16, 58, 67, 310, 335, 504
  All Saints 18
  St. Clement 58
Canterbury (Kent) 104, 158
  St. Alphege 158
  St. Andrew 159
  St. Martin 104
  St. Paul 104
Cape Ann 134, 138-143, 169, 170, 347
Cape Cod 104, 114, 130, 170
Cape Porpoise 210
Castine 20
Charlestown 7, 22, 23, 46, 59, 65, 70-75, 106, 107, 171, 192, 218, 256, 258, 310, 313,

327, 346, 347, 368-372, 477, 505, 514
Cheesecake (Maryland) 490, 493
Chelmsford (Essex) 316
Clerkenwell (Midd)
   St. James 229
Cliddesden (Hants) 289
Clisdon (Somerset) 287, 289
Clophill (Beds) 185
Cohasset 373
Colchester (Essex) 102, 158, 267, 297
Concord 103, 418
Cork (Ireland) 138
Cranbrook (Kent) 191, 194, 196
Culleton (Devon) 136
Curaçao 15
Danzig (Poland) 228
Dartmouth 28, 37, 44, 45, 165, 167, 263, 264, 285, 292, 299, 336, 362-365, 367, 402, 403, 420, 434, 435
Dedham 9, 77, 107, 450
Derby (Derby) 345
   All Saints 346, 411
Dinder (Somerset) 411
Doncaster (Yorkshire) 96
Dorchester 8, 13, 65, 78, 79, 90, 92, 99, 193, 214, 234, 254, 389, 411, 469, 470, 477, 489, 500
Dorchester (Dorset) 136
Dorking (Surrey) 80-83, 85, 339
Dover 10, 254, 255, 257, 258
Dover (Kent) 361
Droitwich (Worcester) 508, 510, 511, 513, 515, 517, 518, 520
Dublin (Ireland) 310, 313
Dunstable 136, 137

Duxbury 4-8, 10, 24, 29-34, 43, 48, 49, 66, 68, 80-82, 85-88, 97-103, 108, 113, 114, 126-130, 132, 150, 164-168, 176, 195, 233, 245, 246, 264, 266, 268, 270, 276-278, 281, 287, 288, 292, 297, 299, 300, 304, 319, 320, 322, 324-327, 331, 340-343, 349-351, 356-358, 374, 380, 381, 401-403, 412-414, 416, 417, 419-421, 432-434, 436-440, 442, 443, 445, 447-453, 459, 460, 464, 465, 473-476, 480-482, 489
East Budleigh (Devon) 55, 133, 137
East Orleans 446
Eastham 23-27, 64, 106, 114, 126-129, 131, 149-153, 163, 171-176, 233, 249-253, 299-301, 358, 374, 376-378, 380, 381, 422, 424, 428-431, 439, 444-447, 474
Elizabethtown (New Jersey) 251
Ellanbane (Isle of Man) 457
Essex (England) 265
Exeter 91
Falmouth 391, 394
Farmington 500
Fenstanton (Hunts) 275, 277, 279, 282
Fisher's Island 348
Flushing 501
France 289
Freetown 278
Gravesend 115, 116, 118
Great Amwell (Herts) 479
Great Burstead (Essex) 315
   Billericay 315, 316
Great Shelford (Cambridge) 58

Index of Places

Great Yarmouth (Norfolk) 464, 465
Groton (Suffolk) 194
Guilford 395
Hamburg 194
Hampton 91, 192, 278
Hartford 21, 270
Hartland (Devon) 382
Hemel Hempstead (Herts) 155
Henlow (Beds) 185, 282, 401, 403, 461-463
High Laver (Essex) 503, 505
Hingham 28, 30, 32, 51, 65, 106-108, 138, 213, 214, 307, 310, 312, 313, 397
Hispaniola 508
Holland 156, 451
Hull 134, 140, 141, 143, 309, 345, 347, 425, 427
Hursley (Hants) 273, 274
Ipswich 135, 317, 387, 425, 426
Ipswich (Suffolk) 14
Ireland 310
  County Tyrone 313
Isle of Man 453, 456, 457
Jamestown 33
Kecoughtan (Virginia) 117
Kennebec 5, 10, 63, 110, 183, 235, 249, 261, 279, 283, 289, 407, 408, 428, 437, 441, 443, 444
Kingston 403
Kingstown (Rhode Island) 372
Kittery 91, 254, 319-322
Langford (Beds) 185
Larden (Salop) 329, 332
Lechlade (Gloucester) 379
Leiden (Holland) 10, 12, 51, 58-60, 62, 66, 87, 94-97, 100-105, 144, 146-148, 157-159, 164, 166-168, 182, 185, 186, 199, 204, 205, 215-217, 219, 220, 226-228, 263, 286, 291, 295, 316-318, 324, 336, 338, 360, 361, 368, 382, 389, 391, 393, 396, 397, 419, 421, 422, 462-465, 470, 471, 491, 495-497, 500, 507, 508, 526
  Pieterskerk 13, 58, 99, 158, 159
  St. Pancras 68, 96
Levalleglish (County Armagh)
  Loughgall Parish 309, 313
Lexington 242
Little Baddow (Essex) 466, 469
Little Compton 7, 288, 440
London 2, 14, 20, 61, 96, 128, 131-134, 136, 158, 159, 173, 176, 199, 206, 208, 209, 220, 231, 233, 235, 238, 239, 243, 248, 254, 260, 268, 271, 291, 297, 335, 358, 378-380, 382, 451, 456, 464, 477, 480, 490-492, 507, 509
  All Saints Barking 374
  Holy Trinity Minories 156
  St. Ann Blackfriars 133, 137
  St. Lawrence Jewry 133, 137
  St. Mary Matfellon 273 Whitechapel
Long Island 116, 180, 348
Lyme 372
Lynn 89, 138, 161, 162, 215, 218, 331, 380, 386, 486
Manchester 53-56, 353-356, 425, 428
Manchester (Lancashire) 115, 116, 118
Manhattan 118
Marblehead 10, 11, 15, 134, 138, 331, 409, 410, 412, 492, 493

Marlborough 369
Marshfield 2, 18, 29, 30, 32, 33, 49, 51, 85-88, 96, 98, 106, 107, 127, 178, 179, 212, 269, 270, 280, 299, 305-308, 341, 376, 380, 416-418, 438, 439, 445, 454, 474, 507, 508, 515-521, 528
Martha's Vineyard 367, 392
Maryland 330, 334, 493
Medford 345
Merrymount 91
Middleborough 6, 155, 165, 168, 228, 280, 281, 326, 377, 378, 434, 436, 440, 516
Middlesex
   St. Leonard Shoreditch 431
Milford 500
Monk's Soham (Suffolk) 295
Mount Wollaston 345
Namasket 326, 357, 377, 402, 406, 415, 430, 434, 438, 442, 449, 519
Nantasket see Hull
Nantucket 392
Narragansett Bay 348
Naumkeag 134
Nayland (Suffolk) 192, 194
New Amsterdam 10, 11, 115
New Haven 10-15, 69, 115
New London 234
New Netherland 15, 116, 117, 502, 505
New Sweden 15
New York 497, 502
Newbury 114, 256-258, 411
Newbury (Berks) 12
Newfoundland 15, 334
Newport 44, 505
Newtown (New York) 352, 514
Northwich (Cheshire) 256, 261

Norwalk 214
Norwich 175
Norwich (Norfolk) 144, 263, 294, 500
   St. Andrew 262
Oxford (Oxon) 310
Panfield (Essex) 27
Pawtucket 87, 308, 407
Pawtuxet 488
Pembroke 34, 278, 358
Penobscot 20, 161, 216, 483, 486, 497, 501
Pequot 21, 118
Peterborough (Northants) 335
Pettistree (Suffolk) 391
Piscataqua 10, 254, 257-259, 261, 262, 320, 491, 492
Piscataway (New Jersey) 59, 179, 249-253, 422-424
Plymouth 1-8, 10-18, 20-25, 27-29, 32, 33, 35-53, 56-70, 72, 76, 77, 79-90, 93-95, 97, 99-104, 106-112, 114-116, 118-134, 139, 140, 142-154, 156-159, 161-167, 169-189, 193-198, 201-220, 223-235, 239, 240, 243-252, 254-259, 261-268, 271-277, 279, 280, 282-287, 289, 291-293, 295, 297-301, 303-309, 312, 315-319, 324, 325, 327, 330-332, 335-342, 344-347, 349-353, 356, 357, 359-370, 373-383, 385, 388, 389, 391, 392, 396-399, 401, 402, 405-410, 412-419, 421, 422, 424-429, 431-433, 435, 437-453, 455, 457, 459-470, 473, 474, 476-489, 492, 495, 497-504, 506-508, 510, 511, 513-515, 517, 518, 520-522, 524-528

Index of Places

Plymouth (Devon) 208, 209, 219
Port Royal (Nova Scotia) 334
Portsmouth 488
Portsmouth (Rhode Island) 22, 23, 44, 124, 125, 179, 264, 278
Providence 487-489, 503-506
Prudence Island 348
Puddletown (Dorset) 47
Punckateesett 195, 285, 299, 367, 406, 484, 497
Purleigh (Essex) 203
Ratcliffe (Middlesex) 111
Reading 373
Redenhall (Norfolk) 215, 216, 220
Rehoboth 81, 149, 150, 174, 197, 235, 376, 415, 445, 446, 493, 497-500
Retford (Notts) 286
Rochester 180, 186
Rolveden (Kent) 158
Rowley 82
Roxbury 8, 9, 75, 421, 461, 528
Royston (Hertford) 132
Rugeley (Stafford) 490
Saco 125, 413
Saconeesett 357
Sagadahoc 209
Salem 11, 14, 20, 53, 55, 56, 133-139, 141-143, 169-171, 206-210, 217, 225, 254, 278, 309, 310, 330-334, 353-355, 385-387, 410, 419, 426, 450, 470, 471, 487-489, 495, 503-505, 509, 520
Salisbury (Wilts) 405
Sandon (Essex) 468
Sandwich 50, 51, 60, 61, 80, 84, 90, 113, 278, 438, 498

Sandwich (Kent) 51, 158, 317, 318
St. Peter 104, 105, 204, 205
Satuckett 440
Saugus see also Lynn 134, 161
Saybrook 112, 171, 440
Scituate 2, 13, 16-19, 30, 32, 34, 36, 41, 59, 82, 86, 87, 96, 98, 99, 108, 112, 119-121, 129, 179, 212-214, 216, 223-225, 234-236, 238-243, 249, 270, 272, 278, 293, 298, 307, 357, 389, 391-394, 398, 403, 420, 421, 458, 461, 466-470, 474, 493-495, 514, 520, 522-524, 526-528
Scrooby (Notts) 62, 66, 68, 69
Seaton (Devon) 138
Shipton (Salop) 329, 330, 332
Shobrooke (Devon) 133
Siberia 20
South Carolina
  Charleston 334
Southampton 79
Southampton (Hants) 4, 8, 9
Southwark (Surrey) 76, 79, 128, 132, 248
  St. Olave 127, 128, 130, 131, 234, 237, 238, 289
Spalding (Lincolnshire) 56, 57
Stepney (Middlesex)
  St. Dunstan 111, 333
Stokeclere (____) 132
Story's Island (Maryland) 490, 493
Stow Maries (Essex) 203
Suffolk [England] 15
Swansea 121, 124, 194, 196, 197, 281, 282, 331, 497-502, 520

Taunton 38, 51, 77, 81, 102, 197, 288, 325, 368, 423, 437-439, 442, 475, 484, 486
Terling (Essex) 468, 469
Tisbury 391, 393
Ufford (Suffolk) 163, 391
Virginia 13, 15, 117, 118, 139, 170, 229, 274, 304, 305, 309, 310, 316, 330, 334, 339, 347, 490-493
  Shirley Hundred 310
Warwick 149, 487, 488
Watertown 22, 23, 70-72, 74, 75, 82, 108, 189-194, 196, 197, 241-243, 254, 345-347, 354, 367, 379, 421, 439, 502
Watford (Northants) 396
Wenham 136, 333, 354
Wessaguscus see Weymouth
Wessagusset 335, 491
West Indies 509
West St. Mary's (Maryland) 490, 492, 493

Wethersfield 346, 350
Weymouth 76-79, 89-92, 105, 165, 174, 234, 241, 242, 248, 254, 307, 308, 343, 369, 370, 373, 389, 420, 421, 423, 445, 490, 506
Windsor 84, 486
Winkleigh (Devon) 237, 238
Wisbech (Cambridge) 64, 65
Woodbridge (New Jersey) 250, 252
Wooten Underedge (Gloucester) Wortley 274
Wrington (Somerset) 93, 94, 220
Yarmouth 25, 26, 37, 42, 60, 61, 126, 128, 182, 249, 272, 273, 358, 366, 381, 409-411, 441, 452, 453, 517, 520
York 90, 91, 254, 255, 257, 259, 260, 320, 485
York (England) 336

INDEX OF SHIPS

Anne 16, 23, 24, 42, 43, 63, 67, 70, 75, 85, 88, 89, 109, 110, 133, 138, 140, 145, 169, 188, 201, 203, 205, 217, 226, 240, 244, 255, 256, 263, 297, 298, 309, 324, 336, 338, 344, 345, 349, 350, 352, 356, 365, 366, 368, 369, 382, 385, 428, 429, 447, 448, 451, 461, 463, 464, 476, 478
Blessing 330, 332
Charity 309
Charles 238, 239
Elizabeth & Ann 346, 348, 482
Fortune 1, 2, 48-52, 76, 85, 93, 143, 158, 159, 162, 164, 165, 203, 211, 212, 243, 244, 254, 255, 335, 338, 344, 349, 359, 374, 375, 419, 450, 457, 459, 511, 524
Friendship 210, 239, 330
Handmaid 189, 193, 194, 197
Hopewell 334
Jacob 465
James 501
John's Adventure 512
Little James 88, 89, 291, 295
Lyon 20, 82, 265, 475, 476, 503
Mayflower 4, 5, 7, 8, 10, 13, 14, 16, 56, 57, 62, 63, 65-68, 80, 82, 84, 91, 92, 95, 96, 103-105, 109, 111, 144, 145, 147, 156, 157, 159, 177, 180, 187-189, 198, 199, 204, 205, 215-217, 221, 223, 228, 262, 271, 273-275, 279, 280, 283, 303, 304, 315, 316, 324, 328-330, 333, 339, 340, 382, 383, 389, 396, 397, 401, 404, 432, 433, 436, 451, 454, 457, 459, 461-463, 466, 470, 477, 478, 480, 495-497, 506, 507, 509-511
Planter 238
Sea Venture 274
Sparrow 369, 373
Speedwell 59, 159, 234, 316, 512
Swan 334
Talbot 252
Truelove 176, 490
White Angel 210
William 239
William & Francis 422, 493, 495